This book is given
In honor of
Meredith Osborne
By
Her parents
May 2001

Rediscovering Antiquity: Karl Weber and the Excavation of Herculaneum, Pompeii, and Stabiae examines the early history of the excavations at three important sites of Classical antiquity that first came to light in 1738 through the life and work of Karl Jakob Weber, a Swiss military engineer who supervised these investigations from 1750 to 1764. Whereas many of his contemporaries sought only the recovery of precious antiquities to the exclusion of the architectural remains, Weber sought to retrieve evidence of the ancient urban fabric and to relate his discoveries to their archaeological context, thereby establishing the first systematic approach for these excavations. He also proposed a revolutionary manner of publishing his findings, in which all of the works of art from an individual site would appear together with detailed plans, drawings, and commentary drawn from Classical and modern sources. His more scientific methodology had a profound impact not only on subsequent excavation at these sites but on the history of archaeology in general. This study is based on original excavation documents and plans, contemporary correspondence, and the extant archaeological remains.

Rediscovering Antiquity

Rediscovering Antiquity

Karl Weber and the Excavation of Herculaneum, Pompeii, and Stabiae

Christopher Charles Parslow

Wesleyan University

CAMBRIDGE
UNIVERSITY PRESS

PUBLISHED BY THE PRESS SYNDICATE OF THE UNIVERSITY OF CAMBRIDGE
The Pitt Building, Trumpington Street, Cambridge CB2 1RP

CAMBRIDGE UNIVERSITY PRESS
The Edinburgh Building, Cambridge CB2 2RU, United Kingdom
40 West 20th Street, New York, NY 10011-4211, USA
10 Stamford Road, Oakleigh, Melbourne 3166, Australia

First published 1995
First paperback edition 1998

Printed in the United States of America

Library of Congress Cataloging-in-Publication Data is available.

A catalog record for this book is available from the British Library.

ISBN 0-521-47150-8 hardback
ISBN 0-521-64664-2 paperback

For Lawrence Richardson, jr.,
and
Roger A. Hornsby

Magistris Optimis

Contents

Illustrations

Preface

The idea for this study of the life and work of Karl Jakob Weber came to me during my research into his documentation of the Bourbon excavations in the Praedia Iuliae Felicis in Pompeii. In particular, I became interested in determining the kinds of influences – historical, cultural and personal – that led him to draw his axonometric plan of the Praedia, with its commentary blending his own experiences in the field with references to Classical authorities. Shortly after I began my inquiry, I stumbled upon a fascicle of correspondence in the Archivio di Stato in Naples concerning an inquest into the disappearance of a number of Weber's excavation documents after his death. The effort the Bourbon court expended on this struck me as remarkable, considering its repudiation of his work during his life and its failure to publish any of his architectural plans. I also found several petitions Weber wrote to the court in the weeks and days leading up to his death. These documents presented a truly pathetic image of Weber, disconsolate and destitute, pleading desperately for money to pay his medical bills and sustain his life. Ironically, they breathed life into this character in a manner that all of his perfunctory excavation reports and all the comments of his contemporaries could not. This archival material led me to conclude he would be the ideal subject on which to base a study of the early history of the excavations in the Vesuvian landscape.

Though I was frustrated in my attempts to locate Weber's final resting place, I had the great good fortune of spending several days in Schwyz, Switzerland, with Dr. Werner Alois von Weber, a direct descendant of Weber's brother Franz Dominik and the present keeper of the family tree. Dr. von Weber and his wife graciously showed me the home in Arth where Karl was born and shared with me their knowledge not only of the history of the Weber family but also of Switzerland and the canton of Schwyz. I am profoundly grateful to them for their hospitality and assistance. My portrait of Weber is more complete as a result and I hope it does justice to their ancestor.

I began this study while a Samuel H. Kress Fellow in Classical Archaeology at the American Academy in Rome. This fellowship afforded me the time and resources to complete much of my initial research in the archives in Naples. Then, and in the years following, I benefited enormously from the assistance of the directors and staff of the Academy and its excellent library. An Andrew W. Mellon Fellowship and a travel grant from Duke University allowed me to participate in a conference, held at Ravello, Italy, in 1988, on the history of the excavations at Herculaneum, where I presented some preliminary thoughts on Weber. In 1990 I returned to the Neapolitan archives with the help of an NEH Summer Stipend. Since 1991 generous grants from Wesleyan University have helped support my research. I wish to acknowledge in particular my fellow members of the Wesleyan Archaeology Group as stewards of the Smith Fund for Archaeological Research. I could not ask for better institutional and collegial support.

My research would have been impossible without the patient assistance of the directors and staffs of the Archivio di Stato, the Società Napoletana di Storia Patria, and the Biblioteca Nazionale, all in Naples. In Pompeii, Baldassare Conticello, superintendent of the Soprintendenza Archeologica di Pompeii, granted me access to a number of important sites. The most memorable of these was an exhilarating tour of the Villa dei Papiri guided by the director of the excavations, Umberto Cioffi, in the summer of 1992. There is no better way to appreciate the Herculean task Weber confronted on a daily basis than to crawl through these tunnels, twenty-seven meters below ground in a volcanic region. I also would like to extend special gratitude to Enrica Pozzi-Paolina and Stefano De Caro, respectively former and current superintendents of the Soprintendenza Archeologica di Napoli e Caserta; Guiseppe Magi, Renata Cantilena, Valeria Sampaolo and Eva Nardella of the Museo Nazionale in Naples; Marcello Gigante and the Officina dei Papiri; Antonio Varrone, Antonio D'Ambrosio, and Ernesto De Carolis of the Soprintendenza Archeologica di Pompeii; and Franz Auf der Maur of the Staatsarchiv Schwyz, Switzerland. I benefited as well from the resources of the rare book rooms in Olin Library at Wesleyan University, the Department of Fine Arts at the University of Pennsylvania, the University of Toronto, and the Beinecke Rare Book and Manuscript Library at Yale University, as well as from the print collections in Wesleyan's Davison Art Center, and the Metropolitan Museum of Art in New York.

Friends and colleagues have contributed to this study in numerous ways. I especially would like to thank Russell T. Scott, Mary T. Boatwright, Jim Packer, Alden Gorden, Claire Lyons, Ingrid Rowland, John Pinto, Nancy Ramage, Bernie Frischer, Agnes Allroggen-Bedel, Mario Pagano, Luciana Jacobelli, Cecilia Miller, Antonio Gonzalez, and Kathryn Gleason. Drs. Tristram Parslow, Carolyn Katzen, and Martha Warnock provided the advice I needed to render my medical diagnosis. John Wareham worked wonders with my photographs, some taken under very difficult conditions. My father, Morris Parslow, meticulously proofread a draft of the manuscript, and Amy Barrett helped check references. I am obliged as well to my editor, Beatrice Rehl, and her excellent production staff at Cambridge University Press.

Finally, I owe an enormous debt of gratitude to my mentors, Lawrence Richardson, jr., and Roger A. Hornsby. Without their encouragement, sage advice, and support throughout the years, I never would have been in a position to write this book.

Abbreviations

Abbreviations for titles of journals follow those of the *American Journal of Archaeology* 95 (1991) 1–16, with the exception of the titles given below. References to Classical authorities follow the standard abbreviations for authors and books in the *Oxford Classical Dictionary* (Oxford 1970), ix–xxii.

ASN *CRA*	Archivio di Stato, Naples. Fondo: Casa Reale Antica
BdE	*Le Antichità di Ercolano esposte con qualche spiegazione: Bronzi di Ercolano.* 2 vols. Naples 1767–1771.
CIL	*Corpus Inscriptionum Latinarum*, C. Zangemeister, ed. Vol. 4. Berlin 1871. T. Mommsen, ed. Vol. 10. Berlin 1883.
CollMN	*Le Collezioni del Museo Nazionale di Napoli.* Vol. 1.1. Naples 1986. Vol. 1.2. Naples 1989.
CTP	*Corpus Topographicum Pompeianum.* Vol. 4. Rome 1977. Vol. 5. Rome 1981. Vol. 3a. Rome 1987.
Giornale	U. Pannuti. "Il 'Giornale degli scavi' di Ercolano (1738–1756) (SNSP Ms. 20.B.19bis)." *MemLinc* Ser. 8, 26.3 (1983) 163–410.
La Vega	"Giornale di ciò che mi occorre di rimarchevole," and "Notizie appartenti all' excavazioni d'Ercolano secondo le relazioni avute da varie persone," 110–20 and 281–320. In G. Fiorelli. *Giornale degli scavi di Pompei.* Nos. 1–4 and 8–10. Naples 1861–65.
MN	Museo Archeologico Nazionale, Naples.
MN. ADS	Archivio Disegno, Soprintendenza Archeologica di Napoli e Caserta.

"Museo"   A. Allroggen-Bedel and H. Kammerer-Grothaus, "Il
                   Museo ercolanese di Portici," 83–127. In *La Villa dei
                   Papiri. CronErc* 13 Suppl. 2. Naples 1983.

PAH   *Pompeianarum Antiquitatum Historia quam ex cod. mss. et a
                   schedis diurnisque R. Alcubierre, C. Weber, M. Cixia, I.
                   Corcoles, et al.* G. Fiorelli, ed. 3 vols. Naples 1860–64.

PAH I.ii.Addenda iv   A. Ribau. "Epitome Diurnorum," 134–87. In *PAH.* Vol.
                   1, Pars 2. Naples 1860.

PdE   Reale Accademia Ercolanese di Archeologica. *Le An-
                   tichità di Ercolano Esposte: Le pitture antiche d'Ercolano e
                   contorni incise con qualche spiegazione.* Vol. 5. Naples
                   1757–79.

PhilTrans   *Philosophical Transactions of the Royal Society of London.*

SNSP   Società Napoletana di Storia Patria, Naples.

StErc   M. Ruggiero. *Storia degli scavi di Ercolano ricomposta su'
                   documenti superstiti.* Naples 1885.

Stabiae   M. Ruggiero. *Degli scavi di Stabia dal 1749–1782.* Na-
                   ples 1881.

Introduction: Karl Weber and the Rediscovery of Herculaneum, Pompeii, and Stabiae

Scholars have condemned the archaeological methods employed by the Bourbon excavators in the Vesuvian cities since virtually the onset of the investigations in 1738. Their concerns often have centered on the fear that much was lost through the haphazard manner of digging and the ineptitude of those directing the work. Among the earliest to express this concern openly was Cardinal Angiolo Maria Quirini, who wrote in 1748:

> Everyone would be happy if we could explain to foreigners what place this was where we are finding these superb and precious remains. But how can we tell for certain, since the mining is done in such a confused manner, and they leave none of the excavated portions empty but fill them in again as they go on?[1]

For more than two centuries, such comments have depicted Charles of Bourbon, king of the Two Sicilies, as little more than a common treasure hunter and have classed those responsible for supervising his excavations as indifferent plunderers completely lacking in culture. Rocque Joaquin de Alcubierre, chief director of the royal excavations for more than forty years, has been roundly accused of incompetency. Johann Joachim Winckelmann, whose pointed criticism helped focus international attention on the excavations in the eighteenth century, observed that Alcubierre was "as familiar with antiquity as the moon is with crabs," a phrase now frequently repeated and used emblematically to characterize this early period.[2] Giovanni Castaldi, the nineteenth-century chronicler of the Reale Accademia Ercolanese di Archeologia, observed that the directors of the excavations were "well versed in military architecture but with little or no knowledge of ancient monuments."[3] Michele Ruggiero reflected that Alcubierre and his assistants were "so utterly devoid of the most basic knowledge of art and things antique as naively to report an opinion [that was] not only peculiar but laughable."[4] Soon thereafter Ethel Barker remarked, "Yet one is disposed to think that the ignorance of the men engaged on the excavations was something quite phenomenal. . . . Someone else describes the workmen as 'galley slaves toiling under an ignorant superintendent.' "[5] More recently, Marcel Brion concluded that

> Alcubierre's technique was bungling, disastrous for the ruins themselves and void of all scientific method. . . . Tunnels were bored in a happy-go-lucky way, frescoes were torn from the walls that they adorned, weapons, vases, coins were swept up, and all removed without any question of the state or place in which they had been found.[6]

There can be little doubt that much was lost and destroyed in these early years, but much more was retained than these sources would lead one to think. The lot had fallen to Alcubierre to direct this work because military engineers like him were trained in the mining techniques required to bore tunnels through the solidified pyroclastic flow covering Herculaneum, where the first ten years of the excavations were spent. Alcubierre was determined to recover antiquities worthy of his king and did whatever was necessary to find them quickly and in quantity, abandoning unfruitful locations rapidly and moving elsewhere. He showed little interest in the architectural remains themselves and initially received no indications from the court that he should. Architecture, especially non-Greek temple architecture, could not have been viewed as more inconsequential in this period, during which the ruins were viewed as mere repositories of the works of art whose recovery would enrich the king's collection.

Alcubierre's progress was monitored by scholars in Naples, but the conditions of preservation were unique and could not have been more challenging. The science of archaeology had yet to be discovered, and the concept of an applied methodology, even a simple one, was completely foreign. Since this was the first concerted effort at the systematic excavation of an entire city, there were no rules or precedents for how to proceed or how to publish the results. It was largely a matter of trial and error and adapting technique to widely varying circumstances.

The documentation was maintained in a manner believed adequate for the court's purposes. It consisted of detailed inventories of the finds and schematic plans of the sites. The quantity and quality of these documents varied over the years but gradually improved with experience and can be of much greater value for reconstructing the course of these excavations than is generally believed. Yet such documents were produced only for the benefit of the king and prime minister, not for publication. The artifacts themselves were displayed in the royal museum but were guarded jealously, as were the ruins. A royal edict prohibited visitors from taking notes both at the sites and in the museum. The court was excruciatingly slow in publishing the finest of the antiquities, despite the bitter protests of foreign scholars. Most of these records remained unpublished for more than a century, others were lost in the turbulent events in the interim, while still others have resurfaced only in the past quarter century. All these circumstances, along with the failure of scholars and writers to look to primary rather than secondary sources, have helped sustain a badly distorted tradition about the ineptitude of these early investigations and allowed it to become ever more firmly fixed in the popular mind.

One figure often singled out for particular recognition is Alcubierre's principal assistant, Karl Jakob Weber, a Swiss military engineer of the Royal Guard. Weber might have been condemned to obscurity had Winckelmann not drawn attention to him by observing that "to this intelligent man are owed all the sensible arrangements" in the excavations and had he not praised the detailed plans Weber drew of the ancient sites under his care. Sources generally credit Weber as a key figure in the history of the excavations, although none has explored his contributions in depth and some have even been reluctant to acknowledge his ability. Amedeo Maiuri, the great excavator of the Vesuvian cities who followed in Weber's footsteps in more ways than one, remarked that Weber's inventories "revealed more diligence than knowledge and discernment of the excavated material," while Cosenza attributed certain of Weber's errors to "his lack of culture in history and archaeology."[7] A close study of his life and work in the excavations, however, reveals that such characterizations are not only arbitrary but grossly unfair.

Weber established the first truly systematic approach to the excavations, anticipating, in the process, the scientific methodologies of modern archaeology. Through experience and careful observation, he learned what to expect and calculated how and where best to direct his efforts. The method he adopted was anything but haphazard and was founded on the simple principle of following the lines of streets and entering buildings encountered along them through their doors. Yet he instituted this approach only in the face of persistent opposition from his superiors.

He experimented with new ways of excavating and new ways of presenting the results to the public. He advocated the abandonment of the practice of reburying the ruins, in order to allow visitors to experience the impressiveness of the remains *in situ*. He actively pursued investigation of the urban fabric as a whole, features such as streets and fountains, in order to gain a better understanding of the form of these ancient cities. His interests extended to both public and private architecture, and he demonstrated a concern for the context of his discoveries, in exploring where objects were displayed and how they were meant to be viewed in antiquity, how individual spaces functioned, and what architectural clues could be read to determine that function.

Weber's plans are the most complete and accurate produced during this early phase of the excavations. Without his plans and documents for the Villa dei Papiri, for example, virtually nothing would be known about the original context of its ancient library. He recognized the value of relating the works of art to their archaeological context and devised a system for cataloging the finds and illustrating their precise provenance directly on the plans he produced for each site. He also realized the potential of these archaeological remains for illustrating aspects of ancient art and society known previously only through literature and sought to combine the by-products of archaeology with the evidence from Classical literature. Finally, he further anticipated later methodology by advocating publication of descriptions of these ancient sites in a monographic format in which all the works of art from an individual site would appear together, along with detailed plans, drawings, and commentary drawn from Classical and modern sources.

Weber was not, however, the greatest archaeologist of the age nor even a great architectural draftsman. He did not lead the most interesting of lives. Nor is it clear to what extent he was an independent thinker and to what degree he was influenced or even used by other members of the court to advance their own interests. Several of his approaches were not new when compared to the methods employed in contemporary excavations elsewhere in northern Italy and Europe, but they had never been tried in the Vesuvian cities. Part of his attraction, and the reason for focusing on his character for a history of these early excavations, is that he is an essentially tragic figure, a victim of circumstances: a military engineer with a vision of producing the first true archaeological monographs, who sought appointment to the most distinguished learned society in Naples over the objections and opposition of Alcubierre, and who some believed died as a result of the relentless persecution he endured for this and other alleged gestures of insubordination.

This study examines Weber's life and work against the background of the Bourbon court and the vicissitudes of the excavations, while attempting to explain his contributions to the development of archaeological method and theory. Although Weber is the principal figure in the narrative, which is arranged more or less chronologically, this book is not meant to be a biography. It is rather a history of the excavations in these earliest years, woven around the story of one man's attempts to alter and improve their course at this pivotal point in the history of archaeology.

As far as possible, this account is based on original documents: the correspondence of Weber and his associates among themselves and with the court; the excavation reports; the few surviving architectural plans; the archaeological and artistic remains; and the writings of figures not involved in the excavations. No previous study has explored in detail the kind of information this rich and varied documentation holds. These documents speak volumes about the day-to-day operations of the excavations, the interaction between individual personalities, and the effect of these discoveries on the contemporary world in Naples and abroad. Many of the documents used in this study have suffered indignities and damage over time: some disappeared into private collections, many were dispersed in wars, while others were published but the originals have since been lost. Given the history of archaeology, especially that of the Vesuvian region, only publication can ensure they will not suffer further in the future. Most of the archival material included here has never been published, and little has been used for studies of this nature. Many are quoted here at length because they offer firsthand accounts of the period, others because the original publications in which they appeared are difficult to obtain today. The translations offered here attempt to prescrve the phraseology and idiomatic expressions of the original wherever possible, although some liberties have been taken, in the interest of clarity.

This book is divided into three parts, beginning, in Part I, with the historical background. Chapter 1 provides a biographical sketch of Weber and a chronicle of the excavations up to the time he assumed his duties. It also introduces the leading figures of the drama, the principal controversies and the main discoveries, and describes the excavating conditions and techniques during this early period. Chapter 2 outlines the tradition of documentation that Weber inherited: who had drawn what plans of which monuments, what aspects these plans highlighted and why, which plans are now extant and which are missing. The purpose of this historical background is to set Weber's later methodology and contributions in sharper relief.

Part II is concerned with the first decade of Weber's tenure, focusing on the technical aspects of the work and the principal buildings Weber excavated for which there is sufficient documentation. The detailed descriptions of the art and architecture of the individual monuments provided in Part II and throughout this book are meant only to illustrate the progress of the excavations and to highlight the principal discoveries, in particular those that figured in Weber's later documentation: what was found where, when, and under what circumstances. They are not intended to serve as complete studies in their own right but should provide useful background information for any future research on these buildings.

Chapter 3 is a survey of Weber's important investigations in the Villa dei Papiri at Herculaneum, along with the circumstances that led to the founding of the Reale Accademia Ercolanese di Archeologia in 1755 and the ensuing decline in Weber's own enthusiasm about the villa. In contrast to his work at Herculaneum are the investigations in the Praedia Iuliae Felicis at Pompeii, where the excellent conditions of preservation, ease of excavation, and richness of the finds afforded him the opportunity to develop his revolutionary approach to documentation. At Herculaneum, his excavations in what he believed were the first verifiable temples allowed him to experiment with his more systematic methodology. Despite long months of intense investigation, however, the site yielded more in the way of architecture than art. Yet he continued to excavate here, over the objections of his superiors, who viewed his methods as squandering precious resources.

Part III describes in greater detail Weber's efforts to document and publish descriptions and plans of the sites excavated under his superintendence. His work at the Praedia and in the villas in the Ager Stabianus led him to recommend that the discoveries be published in a form similar to a modern archaeological monograph, in which all the finds from a single monument are published together. A brief sketch of the history of archaeological documentation, which, given this topic's complexity, is intended to provide only the broadest of backgrounds to Weber's own work, illustrates how innovative his proposal was for its time. Yet the Bourbon court was committed to the publication of the works of art alone, gathered together by genre, and refused to adopt this new approach. He had sought admission to the Accademia Ercolanese so that he might pursue this work with greater freedom, but his request was never taken seriously. Weber's attempt to secure greater recognition for his contributions further split those responsible for the excavations into factions, aggravating the impression of chaos which had concerned outside scholars from the beginning and which Winckelmann now witnessed and even advertised to the world. Yet Weber's work greatly influenced Winckelmann's own understanding of, and appreciation for, the excavations. This is especially clear in his discussion of the theater at Herculaneum, Weber's last project. In excavating the theater, the first monument discovered in 1738 and one repeatedly excavated and drawn over the years, Weber came closest to realizing his professional ambition, that of playing the scholar-archaeologist for his king, but death carried him off before he could complete his studies.

During Weber's tenure, the Bourbon excavations reached their broadest extent geographically and garnered the richest return in the variety, quantity, and quality of the finds. This was the period of the greatest discoveries, not only at the Villa dei Papiri but all around the Bay of Naples, from the so-called Temple of Serapis at Pozzuoli to the rich private houses of Pompeii and the luxury villas in the Ager Stabianus. None of his work was published during his lifetime, and most of his plans fell into private hands in the years after his death and went unpublished. Consequently his contributions were eclipsed by the work of his successors and received only passing recognition in the historical record. The rapidity with which his work lapsed into obscurity is demonstrated by a remark of Goethe's, in a letter written at Naples after he had visited Herculaneum in March 1787, only twenty years after Weber's death. "It is a great pity," he observed, "that the site was not excavated systematically by German miners, since it is certain that many noble antiquities were destroyed through random digging."[8] When Weber's plans finally resurfaced in the late nineteenth century, they were immediately recognized for their remarkable accuracy and enormous value for illustrating the ruins, many of which remained buried at that time. Ruggiero observed that despite Weber's deficient knowledge of antiquity the quality of his plans revealed the "diligence and serious toil he endured in this arduous work, and therefore the injustice of the complaints with which the writings of Alcubierre are filled and of the persecution which afflicted him [Weber] right up to his death."[9] Charles Waldstein, reflecting on this irony of Weber's life and work, calls him "the most pathetic figure in the history of the excavations."[10]

This early period of the excavations has become increasingly the focus of modern scholarship for the light the discoveries shed on eighteenth-century trends in collecting and connoisseurship, and for their role in the Neoclassical movement and the Grand Tour. But because of the common perception that this work was tantamount to plundering, along with a persistent tendency for more popular studies to romanticize this period and the individual personalities involved, few studies have seriously explored the contemporary background and the excavation methods.

All research on this period is heavily dependent on the excavation reports from the Bourbon era published by Giuseppe Fiorelli and Michele Ruggiero. From 1860 to 1864, Fiorelli, who directed the excavations from 1863 to 1875, collected and collated the reports relating to Pompeii alone.[11] He included only a handful of original plans and did not provide inventory numbers for the works of art nor offer any historical overview. These drawbacks, when compounded with the difficulty of ascertaining precisely where the various excavations were located during the earliest years and hence of determining the provenance for many of the finds, render Fiorelli's volumes difficult to understand without reference to other sources.

Fiorelli's successor, Michele Ruggiero, director of the excavations from 1875 to 1893, also was instrumental in making the early documents widely available through the publication of two separate volumes on the excavations at Stabiae and Herculaneum.[12] His introductions to these books include a wealth of factual detail on the history of the excavations, the state of the archival records and the works of art in his day, and, to the extent he could ascertain them, descriptions of the physical remains of the ancient monuments themselves. Ruggiero included personal correspondence between members of the court along with plans, sketches, and finished engravings from the period. Many of these documents are no longer extant, and so Ruggiero's volumes remain the sole source for much of this information. Wherever possible, Ruggiero provided inventory numbers for the works of art recovered from the sites and housed in his day in the museum and storerooms at Naples. Subsequent scholarship has relied heavily on Ruggiero's work to identify the provenance of other objects recovered during this period or to reconstitute the decorative program of an individual private house or public monument, but no one has used it to reconstruct systematically the course and methods of the excavations in detail.

In the period between the publications of Fiorelli and Ruggiero, Felice Barnabei published a short article in 1877 entitled "Gli scavi di Ercolano" that demonstrated the potential importance of these documents from the Bourbon era for illustrating aspects of the excavations. Barnabei drew upon a number of original manuscripts covering the period from the rediscovery of Herculaneum through the years of Weber's tenure. He was interested especially in the practical aspects of the project, such as methodology, costs, and the division of labor and supervision. He showed a particular fascination with Weber's contribution, including what could be ascertained about the contents and completeness of his notebooks and plans. Barnabei's was therefore the earliest attempt to examine in any depth Weber's contribution to the history of the excavations.[13]

Soon thereafter, in 1879, followed the work of Domenico Comparetti and Giulio de Petra on the remarkable discoveries from the Villa dei Papiri at Herculaneum. Their respective researches into the excavation documents, the library and its papyri, and the sculptural program of the villa evolved into what might be considered the first archaeological monograph about these excavations, although produced more than a century after the excavation tunnels were sealed and even though neither had ever set foot in the remains.[14]

In the following half century, research making use of primary sources for the early excavations gradually tapered off. It was during this period that the synopses of the events and discoveries from the early years that appeared in guide-books and histories became increasingly conventionalized. For example, in 1940 Egon Cäsar Conte Corti published the first edition of his *Untergang und Aufer-stehung von Pompeji und Herculaneum*, roughly half of which he devoted to a detailed and reasonably accurate account of the ancient history of these cities and the modern excavations, with the description of the Bourbon era enriched in part by documents from the state archives in Vienna. The clarity and liveli-ness of Conte Corti's account quickly helped make this a standard text, referred to by both popular and scholarly writers.[15]

Also in 1940, Carlo Gallavotti published excerpts from a Bourbon-era docu-ment that described work in the Villa dei Papiri from 1750 to 1752, a period for which Ruggiero and Comparetti and de Petra had lamented the loss of virtually all the original documents.[16] This document is in fact a diary prepared by Alcubierre for the king, in 1757, to catalog the discoveries from all the ancient sites under his direction. It therefore serves both as a check on the inventories in the publications of Fiorelli and Ruggiero and as a supplement for the other inadequatedly documented years, 1740 and 1744 to 1749. Yet despite the impor-tance of this document, discovered among the manuscripts in the library of the Società Napoletana di Storia Patria (Ms. 20.B.19bis), it remained unedited until 1983, when Ulrico Pannuti published the entire contents.[17]

The years following Gallavotti's publication saw only sporadic interest in the early excavations. In 1954 Reinhard Herbig's *Don Carlos de Borbón, Excavador de Herculano y Pompeya* appeared, a short study of the royal family's role in initiat-ing the excavations.[18] This was followed in 1962 by Felix Fernandez Murga's brief thesis entitled "Roque Joaquin de Alcubierre, descubridor de Herculano, Pompeya y Estabia."[19] Through the use of unpublished archival documents in Naples and Spain, Fernandez Murga championed this Spanish military engi-neer's claim that he had been responsible for rediscovering ancient Hercula-neum. In 1989, Fernandez Murga produced a more detailed history of the excavations under Charles III. This relied essentially on the documents pub-lished by Ruggiero and focused on many of the same methodological, techno-logical, and personal problems that are the subject here; he did for Alcubierre what this book attempts to do for Weber.[20]

In 1967, Maria Pia Rossignani published an article exploring the methods employed by the Bourbon excavators in removing, restoring, and displaying the ancient paintings discovered in the archaeological sites. The article included a catalog of all the paintings and fragments mentioned in the excavation reports along with inventory numbers for those that could be identified in the collections and storerooms of the Museo Archeologico Nazionale in Naples.[21] Important research along these same lines was pursued in the early 1970s by Agnes

Allroggen-Bedel. In a series of articles, Allroggen-Bedel drew extensively upon an assortment of published and unpublished documents and plans to reconstruct the course of the Bourbon excavations and ascertain the provenance of ancient paintings and sculptures both in the Naples museum and on the sites themselves.[22] Of particular value for this book were her studies of the plans by Pierre Bardet de Villeneuve of his excavations in the area of the so-called Basilica and Palestra of Herculaneum, and a fascinating history, compiled with Helga Kammerer-Grothaus, of the establishment of the Museum Herculanense in the royal villa at Portici.[23] The latter work effectively demonstrated how these documents could be used to examine aspects of the excavations other than the recovery of the finds and the monuments themselves.

Much of Allroggen-Bedel's early work appeared during the halcyon years for the documents housed in the Neapolitan archives. This was due in large part to a project undertaken by local archivists to locate and inventory all the material in the Archivio di Stato relating to the excavations. The fruit of their labors appeared in 1979: a detailed catalog of all the extant documents and plans from the period 1739 to 1861.[24] This catalog opened a rich lode of information on every conceivable aspect of the excavations and made accessible a number of documents of crucial importance for this study.

The last two decades have witnessed a blossoming of interest in the history of the Bourbon excavations, fostered in part by the marking of the anniversary, in 1979, of the eruption of Vesuvius in A.D. 79 and in part by the celebration, in 1988, of the two hundred fiftieth anniversary of the commencement of the excavations. Exhibitions, conferences, and papers have focused not only on the excavations themselves but on the individual personalities involved in the work and the contributions of the discoveries to the cultural climate and artistic taste of the eighteenth century.[25] A number of recent works have contributed in substantial ways to the present study: Chantal Grell, on the experiences of eighteenth-century French travelers to these ancient sites;[26] Fausto Zevi and Francesco Bologna, on the impact of the early discoveries on European culture;[27] Francesco Strazzullo, on the lives of Alcubierre and Marcello Venuti;[28] Giuseppe Guadagno, on the inscriptions and the archival documents;[29] Marcello Gigante, on Charles III and the papyri;[30] and Marietta De Vos, on Camillo Paderni,[31] to name only the most outstanding examples. An indispensable research tool for this study was I. C. McIlwaine's exhaustive bibliography of writings on Herculaneum, published in 1988.[32] Many previous studies have dealt with specific aspects of the excavations in greater depth than this book or are set in a broader chronological context than that dealt with here, which is essentially the period of Weber's tenure at the excavations.

PART I

The Historical Background

I

Weber, Alcubierre, and the First Years of the Excavations

Arth lies nestled in a narrow Alpine valley at the southern tip of the Zugersee in the canton of Schwyz in Switzerland (Fig. 1). The canton derived its name from the larger, historically far more important city at the opposite end of the valley. The city of Schwyz, the traditional seat of cantonal government and the representative council headed by a *landammann*, is known today primarily for its manufacturing of fine cutlery. As one of the three original cantons of Switzerland, Schwyz had given both its name and its flag – a white cross on a red field – to the new Swiss confederacy founded after the Austrian defeat at the battle of Morgarten in 1315. The symbols and legends surrounding this celebrated victory and bold expression of independence pervade the public and private art of the canton, often juxtaposed with the crests of the ancient families who helped found the confederacy and build its churches and council houses. Among these crests is that of the Weber family of Arth, a white band bearing three clovers placed diagonally across a blue escutcheon.

Already upon his birth in Arth on August 1, 1712, Karl Jakob Weber was linked through blood and marriage to most of the great cantonal families. A pedigree painted for him by a nephew vividly illustrates this fact (Fig. 2).[1] He could, for example, claim among his maternal forebears the great Rudolf Reding von Biberegg (1539–1609), who had fought in France in the war against the Huguenots and been ennobled along with his descendants by Henry III and Henry IV of France, as well as by Pope Clement VIII (1592–1605). Reding served the Bourbon house in Spain and France and appeared as well among the Swiss mercenaries serving Charles of Bourbon in Naples.[2]

The Weber family was equally distinguished and noble, its members having ministered to both the sword and the cross: Webers had served the Hapsburgs at Arth, produced eight *landammanns* for Schwyz, and many others were enno-

Figure 1. View of Arth, Switzerland, on the Zugersee at the foot of the Rigi. From a 1755 engraving by Daniel Düringer (1720–1786).

bled through their service as officers at home and abroad. Karl Jakob's great-grandfather, Jakob Weber (died 1665), had been one of the chief promoters of the construction of the Capuchin convent at Arth. The convent stands only a few meters away from the Weber family house, built in 1632 and still standing today, where Karl Jakob was born.[3]

Such noble tradition imparted a certain degree of importance in Schwyz to his family, though probably they were not particularly wealthy. His father, Beat Jakob Weber (1678–1723), was the prefect of a chapel in Arth, perhaps the one dedicated to Saint George which stands adjacent to a tract of land he is believed to have owned as well. His mother was Anna Flora Zay (1686–1737), the daughter of Johann Karl Zay (1654–1734), a *landammann* from one of the leading families in Arth. His maternal grandmother, Maria Barbara Büeler, came from one of the oldest families in Schwyz.

Weber's two younger brothers devoted their lives to the same religious and military pursuits as their forebears. The youngest, Peter Anton (1720–1748), entered the Benedictine monastery at Einsiedln, where he served as a professor of rhetoric (1744), philosophy (1745), and theology before his death at a young age. The other brother, Franz Dominik (1717–1793), followed his elder sibling to Italy, where he climbed through the ranks of the Swiss Guard to the kings of Naples to become a brigadier general, earning noble titles for himself and,

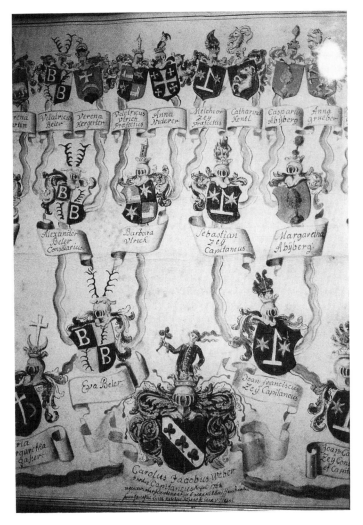

Figure 2. Pedigree painted for Karl Jakob Weber by his nephew sometime prior to 1764, bearing the crest of the Weber family of Arth: a white band with three clovers placed diagonally across a blue escutcheon. (Courtesy of the Familienschriften von Weber, Sedlern, Schwyz.)

posthumously, Karl Jakob (Fig. 3). He maintained close ties with Switzerland but remained stationed in Italy until his death in 1793 in Messina.[4] Little is known of his two sisters, Maria Anna Katharina (1708–1724) and Anna Maria (1710–1761).

In 1728, Karl Jakob entered the prestigious Jesuit College in Lucerne, where his name – Carolus Jacobus Weber Suitensis – appears in 1730 in the rolls of the highest class in the Gymnasium, "Logics." He advanced to the class of

Figure 3. Portrait of Weber's younger brother, Franz Dominik von Weber (1717–1793), a brigadier general in the Tschudi regiment of the Swiss Guard to the Bourbon kings of Naples. There are no known portraits of Karl Jakob Weber. (Courtesy of the Familienschriften von Weber, Sedlern, Schwyz.)

"Metaphysics" in the Lycaeum in the following year. His record shows that he earned above average marks for "overall improvement and character."[5]

In 1731, Karl Jakob left Switzerland and spent the next four years studying mathematics at the Collegio Ghislieri in Pavia, Italy. Pope Pius V (Michele Ghislieri) had established the Collegio in 1569 in order to permit young unmarried men of legitimate birth, high scholastic aptitude, and strong moral fiber, but otherwise lacking adequate financial means, to attend the Università di Pavia.

Presumably Weber had been recommended to the Collegio by the Jesuit priests in Lucerne, and his family's ecclesiastical connections may have played an important part in his admission as well. Here, as was the Collegio's intent, Weber could pursue his own studies, free from the corrupting influences of the university, while building his spiritual and moral character within the austere environment of the Collegio, with its regimen of devotions and strict code of conduct.[6]

With his studies at the Collegio completed in 1735, Karl Jakob enlisted as a career officer in the infantry regiment of Colonel Leonhard-Ludwig Tschudi. The Tschudi family, of the canton of Glaron, adjacent to Schwyz, had made their first historical appearance in 1289 and thereafter had a long history of commanding battalions of Swiss mercenaries for foreign leaders. During the Reformation the family had split along Catholic and Protestant lines. The Catholic line was headed by Ludwig Tschudi, who had established the original regiment of Swiss Guards for the Vatican before his death in 1534. In 1734, Josef-Anton Tschudi (1703–1770) had contracted with Charles of Bourbon, king of Naples, for a battalion of guards of which he was colonel, along with a regiment of infantry commanded by his brother Leonhard-Ludwig (1701–1779).[7] Weber held the rank of first lieutenant and lieutenant captain in the infantry and served as a voluntary adjutant major before receiving his commission on January 9, 1737.[8]

The prerogatives of ties to such noble blood played a decisive role in the next episode of Weber's life and rescued him from certain infamy and humiliation. Sometime after his arrival in Italy with the infantry, Weber had fallen in love with an Italian woman, Maria Luisa Salzano de Luna. They married in early 1739 at Ortona a Mare, near Pescara. It is not known whether Weber was stationed with the Bourbon infantry at the fortress in Pescara at the time or whether they had originally met in Naples and been married in Ortona a Mare, where the bride's family probably had ties. The Luna family, members of the Neapolitan nobility, demanded and received a nuptial settlement of 1,500 ducats, a sum that would have far exceeded the compensation for an officer of Weber's rank.[9] That Franz Dominik guaranteed to pay this sum jointly with his older brother confirms that Karl Jakob had married well beyond his means.[10] As a nobleman from Arth, however, he may have felt that to have done otherwise would be viewed as marrying below his proper station.

Yet the burden of so sizable a settlement did not weigh as heavily as the consequences of the marriage itself, for Weber had violated a standing order that required soldiers to receive the consent of their commanding officer before marrying a foreigner. A letter dated November 6, 1739, from Colonel Leonhard-

Ludwig Tschudi to the *landammann* and Council of Schwyz, outlined the charges
and the penalties imposed on Weber: six months' detention and demotion in rank.
Weber's distraught family appealed to the members of the council to intercede on
their behalf. The council appealed to the Bourbon prime minister, José Joaquin
Montealegre, duca di Salas, through the court's ambassador in Lucerne, on the
grounds that imprisonment was contrary to their doctrine of independence for all
Swiss nationals.[11] The prime minister relented, and Weber was freed. In announcing this fact in a letter to the Council of Schwyz, Colonel Tschudi underscored
the merits of the regulation, saying experience had shown that marriages between
Swiss officers and Italian women, though infrequent, rarely endured.

Although Weber was free, his demotion remained in effect, so the council
was forced to make additional entreaties for reinstatement of his original rank,
which the prime minister agreed to in late January of 1740. Yet Weber's reputation was irreparably tarnished, and the affair was to haunt him for the rest of his
career, in more ways than one. He was ordered by royal decree to hand over a
portion of his wages to his wife toward payment of the nuptial settlement, but he
evidently ignored this order, and she never received a single ducat from him.
Perhaps as a consequence, their marriage does not appear to have been particularly successful. She is referred to nowhere else in the records until after his
death, and although this in itself is not extraordinary for the time, it appears that
she remained in Naples even after he was posted elsewhere. Their marriage was
childless.[12]

Despite these difficulties with his superior officers, Weber's military record
was clean in 1742 and makes no mention of his previous misfortunes. On
December 30 of that year he was rated "good" in the categories of conduct,
valor, application to duty, and health and habits; he had not been absent from
duty and was still married.[13]

He next determined to put his education to good use and in 1743 successfully
completed the examinations for admission to the corps of military engineers of
the Royal Guard, under the command at that time of Giovanni Battista
Bigotti.[14] Weber must have spent the next six years engaged in various engineering projects, perhaps in the neighborhood of Pescara and L'Aquila, but this
period is not well documented. His duties must have included drafting plans of
military fortifications, for a small plan of the Castello Sant' Elmo in Naples was
found among his papers following his death.[15] In the course of this period
Weber came to the attention of Rocque Joaquin de Alcubierre, a Spanish-born
military engineer in charge of conducting the royal excavations at Herculaneum.
In late 1749, Alcubierre requested that Weber be made his assistant to oversee
the daily operations of the excavations.[16]

ALCUBIERRE'S "DISCOVERY" OF HERCULANEUM

Alcubierre had come to Naples with Charles VII of Bourbon in 1734. Born in 1702 in Zaragoza, Spain, he began service in the Spanish corps of military engineers to King Philip V in 1711 at the tender age of nine. Although he did not receive his commission in the corps until 1733, he was supported in his quest for it by Andrés de los Cobos, the man who later became Charles of Bourbon's field marshal. De los Cobos's task as Alcubierre's advocate had been complicated by certain unspecified charges and accusations against Alcubierre, termed false and unjust by him, but evidently taken seriously enough by the court to stall his promotion for some time. In 1736, Alcubierre was stationed at the fortress of Pescara and the Castello dell' Aquila as an engineer; it may have been here that he encountered Weber for the first time. By 1738, Alcubierre was an engineer and artillery captain stationed at Portici under the command of the chief royal engineer at that time, Giovanni Antonio Medrano.

On August 3, 1738, Medrano ordered Alcubierre to begin surveying a site and preparing the plans for a new summer palace and pleasure gardens to be built for the king at Portici (Fig. 4).[17] The plans eventually called for the additional construction of a small fortress to guard the coast at Granatello, and Alcubierre must have been responsible for surveying the site for this as well.[18] In the course of this work, he undertook the exploration of ancient ruins buried beneath nearby Resina at a site where he had learned that ancient statues and marbles had been recovered in the past.

The true extent of the court's prior knowledge of the existence of these antiquities, its interest in pursuing them, and the precise sequence of events that finally led to the official commencement of the excavations at Herculaneum has been obscure since the day Alcubierre first set off to conduct his survey. The historical record has been confused through the loss of important documents and the improper dating of others, through the contradictory statements made by the chief parties involved, and through the deliberate distortion or suppression of facts by individuals hoping to claim a portion of the glory of having discovered this famous site. Alcubierre was a chief offender in regard to the latter, for he gradually came to recognize that the excavations were among the greatest treasures of the Bourbon kings. Over the course of the forty-two years he served as director of the excavations, this military engineer attempted to claim most of the credit for the discovery of the ruins for himself, above the claims of, among others, the eminent antiquarian Marchese Marcello Venuti, keeper of antiquities to Charles of Bourbon until 1740, and he did so despite

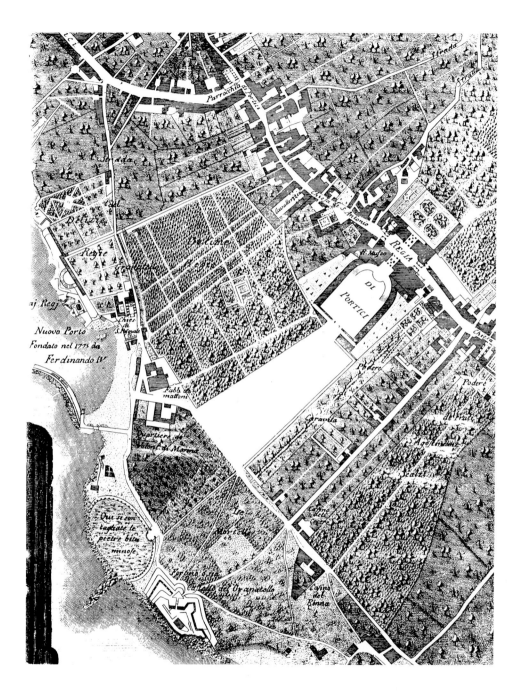

Figure 4. Topographical map from the eighteenth century showing the relationship of the Palazzo Reale (the "Regia") at Portici (*center left*) to the town of Resina (*center right*), with the fortress at Granatello (*lower left*) and the Chiesa di S.M. a Pugliano (*upper right*). The Royal Road from Naples to Salerno cuts diagonally across the map from the upper left to the lower right. From Giovanni Carafa, duca di Noja, *Mappa topografica della città di Napoli e de' suoi contorni* (1775).

the fact that other contemporary scholars were cognizant of, and even ordinary residents knew about, the presence of these ancient cities.[19]

Because throughout this area local residents got their water by drilling artesian wells, they had long been aware of the ancient ruins that lay below them. Reports of chance discoveries of antiquities had appeared in literature from the Renaissance to the eighteenth century and had long been familiar to Neapolitan scholars.[20] One particularly visible testament to this phenomenon in Alcubierre's day were four acephalous, marble togate torsos that stood in the Piazza dei Colli Mozzi (modern Piazza Fontana) behind the church of S. Caterina in Resina. The exact circumstances of their discovery are unclear, but it was believed that they had been recovered, with their heads intact, from a well on private property during the reign of Charles V (1516–1556). In 1715, after the heads had become separated, the torsos were mounted on an arch erected by the community, where Alcubierre still could see them in his day.[21]

Shortly after Alcubierre arrived in Resina and had begun to hear rumors of the existence of antiquities in the area, he was shown a manuscript prepared by Andrea Simone Imperato, rector of S. Maria di Pugliano in Resina from 1684 to 1727. Imperato's primary intention in writing this had been to catalog the eruptions of Vesuvius from the earliest times down to the last major eruption in 1730 and to describe the effect of these catastrophes on the landscape and inhabitants of Resina and the surrounding countryside.[22] In the process, he reported the location of a number of wells where antiquities had been recovered, including one behind the church of S. Caterina, in which could be seen "Many marbles and evidence of habitations. Above the water table is a great grotto, supported by large timbers which are all joined together and seem to form a spacious granary, but these timbers, when touched, quickly turn to dust, since they have been there many, many centuries. This is said to be near the site of ancient Herculaneum."[23] Imperato described as well the remarkable cache of statues, column capitals, numerous colored marbles, and even ancient inscriptions recovered only a quarter century earlier by a prince serving under Charles VI. A statue of Hercules was described as "so lifelike that whoever sees it is left perplexed and at the same time in admiration." Completely ignorant of local history, yet enchanted by these tales of buried treasure, Alcubierre must have believed he had stumbled upon a novel find when he first reported the existence of these ruins to his superiors.

The first public notice of the recent discoveries mentioned by Imperato had already appeared in 1711 in the *Giornale de' Letterati d'Italia*, which reported that antiquities had been recovered from the ruins of what was believed to be a temple at the site of ancient Herculaneum. The discovery, as Imperato had noted, was attributed to a general in the Austrian army serving in Naples under Charles VI: Emmanuel-Maurice de Lorraine, later Duc d'Elbeuf.[24] Like Weber, d'Elbeuf had fallen in love with and married an Italian, the Neapolitan Principessa Salsa. According to one source, his failure to receive permission for this marriage from his commanding officer may have jeopardized his command as well, but this cannot be confirmed. Like Charles of Bourbon, d'Elbeuf also had come to Portici in 1709 to construct a seaside villa.[25] When he expressed an interest in acquiring marbles for its interior decor, he inevitably learned of some recent discoveries made in a well by a landowner in nearby Resina. This well was located near the chapel of S. Giacomo Apostolo in Resina, on the property of one Cola Aniello Nocerino, called "Enzecchetta," which passed into the hands of her son, Giovanni Batista Nocerino.[26] Enzechetta had come upon colored marbles while deepening her well during a drought. She later sold some of these to a marble worker, who had used them to decorate several chapels in Naples and who in turn had alerted d'Elbeuf to the existence of this well.[27]

D'Elbeuf soon purchased the property and began excavations directed by Tommaso la Monica with the assistance of Minico Imperato and as many as seven workmen.[28] Although they believed they had come upon the ruins of an ancient temple, the shaft of their well in fact had dropped some 25 meters directly onto the scaena of an ancient theater decorated with polychrome marble revetments, columns, and statuary, including the statue of Hercules mentioned in Padre Imperato's manuscript. D'Elbeuf's workmen investigated the surrounding areas most intensively over the course of some nine months. Their tunnels were narrow, barely large enough for a man to get through, and at times could be negotiated only by crawling on all fours. Their torches quickly turned them black, and the sole source of air was Enzechetta's original well.[29]

By the time d'Elbeuf had been ordered back to Austria in 1716, thus bringing to an end, once and for all, his depredations at this site, his excavators had not only successfully extricated a vast assortment of decorative marbles and portrait heads to adorn his villa but had also retrieved as many as eighteen life-size marble portrait statues, nine in a good state of preservation. The subsequent owner of d'Elbeuf's villa at Granatello, Duca Giacinto Falletti di Cannalonga, is said to have found 177 additional busts there in 1716, which then devolved to Charles of Bourbon when he acquired the villa in 1746.[30]

At some point, d'Elbeuf had successfully smuggled three complete female statues out of Italy to his cousin in Vienna, Prince Eugene of Savoy, in consideration of his having subsidized d'Elbeuf's extravagent lifestyle; other statues may have gone to France. D'Elbeuf had attempted in vain to conceal his discoveries from the court in Naples, even to the point of transporting the finds from the

excavation site to his villa wrapped in sheets, but officials in Naples, alerted by
the report in the *Giornale de' Letterati*, claimed that such antiquities rightfully
belonged to the royal treasury. Evidently a deal was struck, stipulating that they
would look the other way as long as d'Elbeuf recovered only marbles but that he
was to turn over any real treasures to the king.

Imperato's manuscript and the fact that d'Elbeuf had employed local laborers
make it clear that the people of Resina knew precisely where all these antiquities
had been found and could easily have pointed out the important wells to any
interested party. As early as 1731, a letter read before the Royal Society of
London reported that visitors to Resina could be lowered into a well and crawl
through underground tunnels, observing the foundations of houses and streets.
No doubt these were d'Elbeuf's old tunnels, but the ruins were not positively
identified yet as those of Herculaneum.[31] Giacomo Martorelli, professor of
Greek in Naples, specifically stated that "the excavations began . . . because it
was known that forty years earlier statues of noble workmanship were removed
and sent out of Italy."[32] As late as 1765, La Vega was still able to conduct a
detailed inquiry into the circumstances leading up to d'Elbeuf's discoveries,
including questioning one of the original excavators, Nicola Imperato.[33] It therefore is virtually impossible that, as the Frenchman Moussinot d'Arthenay and
others professed, all memory of d'Elbeuf's work had vanished within only
twenty years. That this was not the case is confirmed as well by Alcubierre's
reports of his own research, in which he says that he learned about the antiquities almost immediately after undertaking his inquiry.[34]

The decision in 1738 to build a summer palace at Portici had been Charles of
Bourbon's, but his motivation has long been in question (Fig. 5). The attraction
of the area in terms of its opportunities for hunting and fishing certainly played
a crucial role, since the king was an avid sportsman. Tradition said that Charles
of Bourbon's initial enchantment with the area had come upon him while
passing through on his way to Naples following a rained-out fishing expedition
in May of 1738, but in fact the site already had been under consideration for
some time. On June 18, 1737, a study into the area's suitability for a royal villa
had been undertaken after some concern had been expressed about the potential danger posed by the site's proximity to Vesuvius and the possibility of
noxious odors rising in the vicinity. In the end the king's physician assured him
the air here was salubrious, and his advisers confirmed that the fishing was
excellent as well.[35]

In July 1738, Charles married Maria Amalia Christina, daughter of Augustus
III of Poland, the former Frederick Augustus II of Saxony. Maria Amalia, a
mere thirteen and a half years old, had arrived in Naples from Dresden in June

Figure 5. Portrait of Charles of Bourbon, king of Naples (1734–59) and, as Charles III,
king of Spain (1759–88). Engraved by Filippe Morghen from a drawing by Camillo
Paderni for the first volume of *Le antichità di Ercolano esposte* (Naples 1757).

1738, and fresh in her mind were the three ancient statues her father had
recently acquired from the estate of Prince Eugene of Vienna, who had died
intestate in 1736. The king had placed these statues on public display in the
Antikensammlung in Dresden. The provenance of the statues was well known,
so it is likely that Maria Amalia was aware of the existence of the ruins at Resina
even before her arrival in Italy. If she championed Portici as the best site for the
new villa, she may have been thinking not only of the king's fondness for the site

Figure 6. Seaward façade of the Palazzo Reale at Portici. (Author's photograph.)

but its proximity to these ancient ruins and the treasures they might yield. Yet her support would have come after the fact, since the site had been under consideration for a year before the king's wedding. More likely Maria Amalia was instrumental in urging the king to continue the excavations.[36]

The evidence weighs heavily in favor of the conclusion that the site for the summer palace of Charles of Bourbon at Portici had been chosen for its attractive qualities, independent of the existence of the ancient ruins (Fig. 6). The original plans for the palace, for example, had not called for the museum of antiquities later installed here. More likely is that, despite the knowledge of d'Elbeuf's success, the king's advisers had never conceived of the possibility that the area would yield more than what average citizens reported finding in their wells: colored marbles, column fragments, and building materials, all of which could be used to decorate the royal garden and palace. The effect of this preconception can be seen in the reluctant manner in which the excavations got under way.

A serious obstacle to reconstructing the events leading up to the start of the excavations is that Alcubierre attempted to claim sole responsibility for the discovery of Herculaneum. In a series of documents written over a span of thirty-one years, Alcubierre gradually refined and expanded his role, as his memories grew dim and he saw that others were attempting to piece the story together without giving him due credit. His earliest account appears in a digest of the discoveries made between October 23, 1738, and May 31, 1741, prepared specifically for the prime minister. In his prefatory remarks, he states that the king had ordered him to "make some grottoes and see what might be discovered," without claiming any important role in persuading the king.[37] His second account appears in the prefatory remarks to a second digest, of the weekly reports for the period October 22, 1738, through October 22, 1756, the day on which the digest was completed. This is a relatively modest recounting of the circumstances, in which Alcubierre again is careful not to emphasize his own role too much.[38] Chronologically, the latest document is a letter Alcubierre wrote in 1769 to Prime Minister Tanucci. This letter, along with details provided in La Vega's own roughly contemporary notes, helps fill out the picture, and it becomes clear that in 1769, with all the principal figures of the early years dead or otherwise absent, Alcubierre took the liberty of elevating himself into the role of chief instigator of the excavations. He depicts himself as a key figure, who had the ear not only of his prime minister but also of Charles of Bourbon.[39]

In Alcubierre's own words, his original orders concerning the palace were to draw up a plan of the area that would illustrate the location of all the existing estates, groves, and roadways and be accompanied by a verbal description of the site. While questioning the local populace to learn as much about the area as he could, Alcubierre was told by a surgeon named Giovanni De Angelis of the well where d'Elbeuf had excavated some twenty years before. Judging that the water table would have stood below the level of the ancient ruins, Alcubierre reasoned that he could gain access to these by means of the local wells.

On his own initiative, Alcubierre had tools, rope, and torches brought from Portici one morning and lowered a man 20 meters down to the bottom of the well, where he encountered a wall covered with red stucco, samples of which were taken as proof of its existence. A cage was brought from Naples so that Alcubierre himself could descend more comfortably into the well. Although occupied with work on the royal villa, Alcubierre later mentioned these discoveries while dining with Prime Minister Montealegre, who, after some initial misgivings, granted him permission to conduct further inquiries. Despite the recovery of fragments of metal and colored marble, these first investigations lasted only six days before, according to Alcubierre, Montealegre ordered him to stop, since the excavations had been made an object of derision by certain members of the court. Alcubierre singled out in particular Giovanni de Guevara, duca di Bovino and the king's chief huntsman. A month later, for reasons not specified, the king approved Alcubierre's renewed request to resume the investigations. Alcubierre claimed that on the first day he recovered a marble statue, which the king awoke to find triumphantly erected in his courtyard at Portici after an all-night effort to extract it from the underground tunnels. This discovery alone, according to Alcubierre, proved remarkable enough to convince the king to continue the work.[40]

Nothing in Alcubierre's accounts explicitly precludes the certainty that members of the court knew of the ruins' existence beforehand; Alcubierre himself remarks that his own curiosity had been piqued in part by the statues at Colli Mozzi, although he studiously avoids mentioning Padre Imperato's manuscript.[41] Montealegre's reluctance to pursue the investigations must have derived in part from a commonly held belief that the site would not yield any more treasures or that even if it did the effort to recover them would not be worthwhile. It is clear from the records that both Montealegre and Medrano maintained a careful watch on the progress of the excavations, at first approving just a minimal crew of workmen and allowing the investigations to continue only as more significant finds were made. For Alcubierre, luck had played a greater role in winning the court's approval for undertaking full-scale excavations than had his own powers of persuasion.

Alcubierre stated that his first investigations had been stopped after six days, evidently because the finds had been inconsiderable and not judged worthy of the king. No date is given, but this first phase must have occurred in late August and September 1738, since on August 31, 1738, Medrano, Alcubierre's direct superior, named Josef de Corcoles to serve as supervisor of the work.[42] One later source suggested that after Medrano ordered the work stopped Alcubierre had continued clandestine investigations in the belief that other wells in the city held the potential for better finds. Again according to Alcubierre, it was only sometime later, when he found himself alone with the king himself, that he dared ask for permission to take several men from the seven hundred members of the Royal Guard stationed at Portici to assist him in searching for additional antiquities. Indeed, there must have been something of substance to encourage the king to change his mind. On October 19, 1738, Montealegre gave Medrano the order to resume the work. Alcubierre received his instructions to begin excavating an "ancient temple" on October 20, worded as follows:

To excavate by following the walls; in order to prevent his health from deteriorating in the grottoes, he should order the voluntary engineer Don Pietro Sbarbi to conduct the excavations with the same foreman [Minico Imperato?] as in the excavations of Prince d'Elbeuf, and that when struc-

tures are found to give him two or three laborers who should take care not
to break the marbles which they find.[43]

The fact that the court relied on one of d'Elbeuf's workmen also indicates that
some local people had come forward to serve as guides to the known locations of
antiquities. Work began in earnest on October 22, 1738.

In claiming, in his letter of 1769, that the first finds had included a marble
statue, Alcubierre conflated events somewhat to make this success reflect well
on himself. The daybooks reveal that it was in fact November before this
statue – a marble "Hercules" – was recovered.[44] Moreover, by 1769 the only
individuals who could dispute Alcubierre's account were out of the picture:
Medrano had been disgraced in 1745; Maria Amalia had seen to it that
Montealegre was pushed aside in 1746;[45] Marcello Venuti, Alcubierre's chief
rival to claiming credit for the discovery of Herculaneum, had died in 1755; and
Charles of Bourbon had assumed the throne of Spain and left Naples in 1759.
It thus becomes clear from Alcubierre's accounts that his jealous protection of
these sites throughout his career and his perceived position of influence with
the court were directly related to his conviction that he was personally responsible for the discovery of Herculaneum.

Several other documents that have been cited frequently in both the scholarly
and the popular literature have also contributed to the distortion of the historical record. The first of these is a letter by Alcubierre to Montealegre, dated
January 14, 1738, printed by Ruggiero in his edition of the daybooks from
Herculaneum. In this, Alcubierre claims that he was ordered to oversee the
restoration of certain fragmentary marble statues said to have come from "the
ancient theater at Resina." Ruggiero believed that this was clear proof that the
court was fully aware of the provenance of these antiquities even before
Alcubierre began his survey of the area in May 1738. Yet none of the early
reports refers to the first site under investigation as anything but a "temple," as
the *Giornale de' Letterati* had called it in 1711. It was only after the discovery on
January 12, 1739, of an inscription of L. Annius Mammianus Rufus (*CIL*
10.1443), which contained the word "theater," that the structure was defini-
tively identified. Thus, the date on this letter of January 1738 is a full year
before Alcubierre could have referred to the site as a theater.[46]

Additional problems are posed by Venuti's correspondence. His writings
make it clear that he believed he had been the first to recognize d'Elbeuf's site
as a theater rather than a temple and that he had positively identified the area
itself as that of ancient Herculaneum. He had determined that the site was a
theater partly as a result of reading a letter written by Giuseppe Stendardo, who

asserted that he had been d'Elbeuf's chief excavator. Stendardo recalled how in 1711 he had recovered a variety of colored marble revetments, two marble statues identified as a Hercules and a Cleopatra, and a marble plaque inscribed "Appius Pulcher Caii Filius." He concluded that they had landed upon a circular temple with an exterior colonnade of twenty-four alabaster columns and twenty-four columns of giallo antico on the interior. In the intercolumniations would have stood twelve marble statues, seven of which in fact were eventually recovered, including those sent by d'Elbeuf to Vienna. Stendardo explicitly stated, moreover, that he had arrived at his conclusions about the physical appearance of the monument only after long discussions with Neapolitan scholars.[47]

The original date of Stendardo's letter – and therefore the date after which Venuti could have read it – is not known, since the letter only came to light when it was communicated to Anton Francesco Gori in Florence by Bindo Simone Peruzzi on April 24, 1741.[48] Venuti later claimed that Stendardo had died in 1735, thereby establishing for this letter a *terminus ante quem* which was both convenient and crucial for Venuti's objective of advancing his own role in the discovery of the site and the history of the excavations.[49]

On that same date in 1741, Peruzzi also gave Gori a letter written by Venuti in which the latter explained how he had identified the ruins as a theater after observing the architectural remains themselves and recalling that the literary tradition had described the town's population as seated in the theater at the moment of the eruption (Cassius Dio 66.23). Gori incorrectly printed the date on this letter as January 17, 1738, months before Alcubierre was ordered to conduct his survey. Moreover, by his own account, Venuti had not arrived on the scene until November 12, 1738, and all the antiquities he describes in his letter – fragments of two bronze equestrian statues, three marble togate statues, and the inscription of L. Annius Mammianus Rufus – were found only between December 1738 and January 1739.[50]

As one of the founding members of the Accademia Etrusca di Cortona, Venuti would have viewed himself as a leading antiquarian in the Bourbon court. He clearly longed to be acknowledged as the one responsible for first identifying the site as Herculaneum and as being a key player in the early excavations. His efforts, however, had brought him into direct conflict with the court, for later it was generally believed that he had been relieved of his duties in part for having broadcast these discoveries to the outside world at a time when the king was highly sensitive and guarded about such matters, and in part because Ottavio Antonio Bayardi, the man designated by the court to be its sole spokesman about the antiquities, already was well along with his work. On the other hand, Venuti successfully convinced the outside world that it was through his recognition of the site as Herculaneum that he had been able to persuade the king to excavate there, since this is often what the literature reports. This role was advanced first by Gori, who had written to Venuti in early 1748 for permission to "attribute to you the glory of being the first to recognize, describe and observe these superb remains of Herculaneum about which the whole world is now talking."[51] Gori then acknowledged Venuti's importance in the preface to his own published collection of correspondence on the discoveries, the *Notizie del memorabile scoprimento dell' antica città di Ercolano* . . . (Florence 1748), which appeared shortly before Venuti's *Descrizione*.[52] In fact, there can be little doubt that it was the wide acceptance of Venuti's role, despite its author's disgrace, that was the real reason for Alcubierre's attempts to revise the history of this period and claim the credit for himself.[53]

EARLY SUCCESSES AND CRITICS

Alcubierre's renewed excavations in the theater at Herculaneum soon began to yield a remarkable variety of finds, despite the extreme difficulty of the work. Montealegre had approved Alcubierre's initial request that up to ten men be assigned to the tasks of digging and removing the fill. A net attached by a rope to a winch was used to lower and raise both men and artifacts from the shafts that provided access to the excavations; Alcubierre would boast of the danger to life and limb of being lowered more than two hundred times at the end of a rope into the wells.[54] From there the explorations were conducted by means of underground tunnels that tended to follow the lines of the ancient masonry walls but were diverted often in the search for antiquities. These tunnels averaged only about 2 meters high and 1 meter wide, with niches carved intermittently to allow workmen to pass each other and with columns of the volcanic matrix left standing to support the roof of the tunnels.[55] Initially, the fill was allowed to pile up along the Royal Road in Resina, and some of it was used for landscaping the gardens of the new royal palace (Fig. 7). But as the pile grew in size and became an eyesore and a nuisance to traffic, the decision was made to backfill the old tunnels. This approach limited the amount of fill that had to be lifted out of the site but prevented areas from being reexamined at a later time.[56] Alcubierre and his immediate assistants supervised the work as a whole, and production grew over the years as forced laborers, housed in the nearby fortress at Granatello, were brought in in increasing numbers to do the heavy digging.[57]

Alcubierre saved time and expense by relying on existing wells to gain access to the ruins and determine whether an area looked promising enough to justify

Figure 7. The Royal Road as it passes through the piazza of Colli Mozzi in Resina, with
one of the equestrian statues of M. Nonius Balbus imaginatively reerected. Mount Vesuvius looms in the background. From the frontispiece of the first volume of *Le antichità di
Ercolano esposte* (Naples 1757).

cutting lateral tunnels. In this way he was able to begin work as early as May
1739 at a site along the Royal Road and the Vico di Mare about 156 meters to
the east of the theater. Within a month the excavators had recovered, along with
numerous inscriptions, the marble statues attributed to the M. Nonii Balbi
(MN. 6167 and 6246) and Vicaria Archade (MN. 6168), as well as several
smaller bronze figures and a wheel pertaining to a quadriga group that may have
once decorated a triumphal quadrifrons arch.[58] By the end of 1740 the excavators had moved another 100 meters to the south in the direction of the sea,
where several weeks and a great deal of effort were expended in extracting a
large mosaic fountain niche from the nymphaeum of a private house and hoisting it up some 10 meters.[59] Montealegre enthusiastically ordered the exploration of all the wells where finds were likely to be made, but Alcubierre feared
this would only lead to chaos, so he limited himself to seventeen workmen and
three sites. This quickly expanded to five sites.[60]

Although visitors were enormously impressed by the tantalizing glimpses of
ancient structures offered by the dimly lit galleries, their correspondence and

other writings often virulently attacked Alcubierre's method of excavating. One
early critic was Camillo Paderni, an artist working in Rome, who, ironically, later
became a leading figure in the excavations, replacing Venuti as keeper of the royal
antiquities and eventually becoming curator of the Museum Herculanense.
Paderni had received early reports on the work from his friend Joseph Canart, a
sculptor also from Rome, and then responsible for extracting the bronze and
marble antiquities, as well as the paintings, from the excavations and restoring
them in his workshop in the royal villa. Canart had shown Paderni the first ancient
paintings found at Herculaneum and taken him on his first tour of the ruins in
February 1740.[61] Paderni offered the members of the Royal Society of London
one of the earliest descriptions of the remains:

> I went down into the pit. The part where they are at work must have been
> a stupendous building; conjectured to have been an amphitheater [i.e., the
> theater] by the circumference of the walls and the large steps which are
> still preserved. But it is impossible to see the symmetry of the whole,
> because one must travel through strait passages like our catacombs in
> Rome . . .
>
> The first mistake those men they call intendents [i.e., the engineers]
> have committed is their having dug out the pictures without drawing the
> situation of the place, that is, the niches where they stood: for they were all
> adorned with grotesques composed of most elegant masques, figures and
> animals; which, not being copied, are gone to destruction, and the like will
> happen to the rest. Then, if they meet with any pieces of painting not so
> well preserved as the rest, they leave them where they are found. Besides,
> there are pillars of stucco extremely curious, consisting of many sides, all
> variously painted, of which they do not preserve the memory.[62]

Paderni's criticism of the methods used probably arose from the fact that he was
caught making drawings of some paintings in the museum and was asked to
leave; this incident later was cited as the cause of the prohibition against taking
notes in the museum.[63] Another scholar, Scipio Maffei of Verona, wrote a
scathing attack on the method of excavation in a letter to Bernardo De Rubeis of
Venice in November 1747:

> Uncovering one part and then another in this manner, who can say how
> many precious objects, how many desirable monuments, perhaps could be
> found in the rooms and the cabinets? Proceeding blindly through tunnels
> and through narrow passages, much will be broken, much will be de-
> stroyed, nor will it ever be possible to see the noble buildings in their

entirety, nor their facades, nor to know where and how were arranged the great number of statues and other ornaments, because with only a small space ever being open (and moreover it being necessary to fill it back in bit by bit) one returns to rebury and conceal all the walls as they were. It will also be necessary to break up many things into pieces to remove them from their site and transport them. Such has happened with the painted walls, many pieces of which have been sawed and carried off with much industry.[64]

Another disgruntled visitor could still criticize the unscientific techniques as late as 1750:

The method of digging is this: whenever they find a wall, they clear a passage along the side of it. When they come to an angle, they turn with it, and when they come to a door or a window, they make their way into it. But when they have so done, they are far from finding themselves in a spacious room or open area, for all the rooms and places they have yet found are so filled with lava that it sticks on the sides of the walls; and they can advance no further than they can make their way by digging, which is such a labour that, when they cease to find anything worth their search, they fill up the place again and begin to dig elsewhere. By which means no place is quite cleared.[65]

Given Alcubierre's reliance on existing wells and the speed with which this allowed him to move about the area, there can be little doubt that in these early years the excavations were conducted in a haphazard and reckless manner. The disorganization to which the early documents refer was not lost on visitors, whose acute sense of disorientation among the ruins is evident in their correspondence. The Englishman John Russell (ca. 1720–63) wrote of his concern that the haphazard layout of the tunnels must have rendered it difficult to record the discoveries accurately but added somewhat naively, "I was assured, however, that whenever any apartment or room is discovered, a plan and draft of the whole is taken exactly as everything is found standing, which in time will be made public."[66] Another visitor remarked, after his candle-lit guided tour,

The appearance of this city would greatly disappoint such as should have raised their expectations to see in it spacious streets and fronts of houses. For they would find nothing but long narrow passages, just high enough to walk upright in, with a basket on the head, and wide enough for the workmen who carry them to pass each other with the dirt they dig out.

There is a vast number of these passages, cut one out of another, so that one might perhaps walk the space of two miles [3.2 km], by going up every turning.[67]

Also in 1750, one Englishman expressed a sentiment supported by many others when he observed,

They have satisfied themselves with cleaning [the city] out like a mine, by leaving a number of pillars to support the roof, which otherwise would be in danger of falling. In most cases they have filled up the houses, which they had already gutted of whatever was curious with the rubbish they took from adjacent ones. And after wandering some hours with torches, I cannot say I was able to form a distinct notion of the situation of the houses, streets, or anything, except of the theater, which was not again filled up. Such was the confusion that reigned everywhere![68]

The question of whether it would not be better to excavate out the sites fully, rather than merely investigate them by tunnels, was debated by many scholars and visitors during these early years. Martorelli complained that the finds came out of the tunnels all mixed together, which rendered it impossible to determine whether they had been found in public or private contexts.[69] Yet these critics failed to recognize that Alcubierre, and presumably his superiors as well, were interested only in recovering antiquities and took little notice of the architecture, except as a means of identifying in the broadest terms the provenance of these treasures for the king's benefit.

Conditions inside the tunnels themselves were appallingly insalubrious. After a visit to the ruins in November 1739, the Frenchman Charles de Brosses later described how he had been lowered down a deep shaft on a rope as in a mine; how the tunnels had been poorly dug and in a haphazard fashion; and how the torches that lit the way, day and night, had so filled the tunnels with smoke he had had to return to the entrance shaft – the only source of fresh air – to catch his breath (Fig. 8).[70] Russell reported that the tunnels were so narrow and threatening that "one cannot think oneself entirely secure from some fatal accident," yet conceded that the peril itself was exhilarating.[71] In addition to the blinding, choking dust and the poor air circulation, the ground water that percolated down through the earth made the tunnels damp at all times, and the rainwater that often flooded in during downpours only compounded this problem.[72] In addition to these minor inconveniences, the entire region was particularly liable to earthquakes as well as volcanic eruptions.[73] Despite numerous precautions, the threat of collapse was a constant danger, made real on more

Figure 8. View of a torch-lit tour of the buried theater at Herculaneum in the eighteenth century, including the inscription of Appius Claudius Pulcher (*CIL* 10.1424) from the right tribunal. From Niceto de Zamacois, *La destruccion de Pompeya* (Mexico 1871).

than one occasion, though not often mentioned in Alcubierre's reports. Nor is there ever any mention of the acute trauma such working conditions inflicted, either directly or passively over time, on the forced laborers, who were kept chained together and under close guard, because they were prone to escape and constantly under suspicion of pilfering small finds (Fig. 9).[74]

Ironically, the documents reveal that Alcubierre himself was the first excavator afflicted by his frequent exposure to the damp air and volcanic dust of the tunnels. Apparently he had ignored the orders he had been given to guard his own health by avoiding excessive time in the tunnels. His problems began in late November 1739, when he became ill and his brother Felippe was obliged to replace him for one month.[75] In this instance, simple exhaustion finally may have taken its toll. He was being lowered into the tunnels almost daily to supervise work in the Basilica, where the large paintings of Theseus and the Minotaur, Hercules in Arcadia, and Achilles and Chiron were in the course of being revealed.[76] Moreover, as part of his continued work at landscaping the gardens of the palace at Portici, Alcubierre had been ordered, as a member of

Figure 9. Forced laborers quarrying lava stone along the Bay of Naples near Resina. In the background are Mount Vesuvius and the Palazzo Reale at Portici and, at the far right, a portion of the fortress at Granatello. From Raffaele Morghen [*84 vedute di Napoli*] (1777), pl. 17.

the corps of royal military engineers, to conduct waters from Pugliano, which lies northeast of Resina, to the royal grove.[77]

The following year Alcubierre came under intense pressure from his superiors. An inquiry was conducted to determine why one of the tunnels had collapsed, damaging the foundations and walls of modern houses above, and to decide what precautions should be taken to prevent future mishaps. Prior to this, Alcubierre appears to have been given a relatively free hand, but now the manner in which the excavations were to proceed was examined by his superiors. As a result, a number of direct orders were issued, and the prime minister scrutinized each of Alcubierre's actions more carefully. In essence these orders prescribed a more systematic approach to excavation, based exclusively on following the lines of the walls of ancient buildings, along with the adoption of more careful techniques of documentation, which included drawing up detailed plans and elevations of the underground ruins, which would illustrate their relation to the stratigraphy of the soil and the modern structures on the surface.[78]

Alcubierre's response to these new orders was to request to have his brother Felippe officially named his assistant, but apparently this request was denied, for Felippe nowhere appears in the excavation records as actively involved in the

work.[79] The final blow came in 1741, when, at the age of thirty-seven,
Alcubierre was forced to request a more extended leave of absence to seek relief
in Naples from a variety of disorders attributed to his daily descents into the
tunnels. His ailments included extreme exhaustion, blurred vision, and a serious case of scurvy which had caused sores on his gums and loosening of his
teeth.[80]

As his substitute during this absence, Alcubierre again proposed his brother
Felippe, but Prime Minister Montealegre appointed instead Pierre Bardet de
Villeneuve, a French engineer whose appointment had been negotiated by the
French ambassador to Naples, the marquis de l'Hôpital.[81] Like Alcubierre,
Bardet had been a member of the corps of engineers for some time and had
military duties as well: since at least 1737 he had been a second engineer
stationed at Portici, in charge of the infantrymen who had been put to work on
the palace.[82]

When Bardet was unable to assume his new duties immediately and Alcubierre
requested release earlier than anticipated, Franceso Rorro, a second engineer at
Naples, served as director of the excavations for a period of fifty-one days, from
June 1 to July 21, 1741. Little is known about Rorro, since his term was so brief,
but it is known that at that time he was stationed at the fortress of Granatello, near
Resina. Apparently he had been opposed to working in the excavations from the
start and considered even the discovery of a bronze statue of Augustus insignificant. He sought and received quick release from these duties.[83]

EXCAVATIONS AT HERCULANEUM UNDER BARDET
(1741–1745)

Bardet took over from Rorro on July 24, 1741, and managed to investigate a
remarkably broad area of the ancient city during his four years as director.[84] He
accomplished this by following the lines of the city's streets and tunneling back
into the buildings that opened onto them.[85] Areas not deemed worthy of extensive investigation were abandoned in short order. Teams of workmen tunneled
in different areas, so that the general excavations could push on while buildings
meriting a more detailed inspection could be picked through more carefully.
The main civic buildings explored in this manner were the theater; the Basilica;
the "Collegium of the Augustales" (Augustalium); the "Galleria Balba," the
structure with an apsidal niche adjacent to the Augustalium; and much of the
enormous building along the eastern edge of the city now commonly identified
as the Palestra.[86] He also made extensive excavations in areas along the north-
eastern extremities of the known city that primarily featured private architec-

ture, such as shops and atrium-plan houses.[87] In addition to baskets full of small finds, Bardet's success was both immediate and remarkable, with the recovery of several major works of art in the Basilica. These included the marble portrait statues of the emperors Augustus, Claudius, and Titus, found in the central rectangular niche of the building, along with three more bronze statues, of Tiberius, Claudius, and Agrippina Minor, evidently displayed in niches along the walls.[88] From shallow, apsidal niches in this same building Alcubierre already had removed the now-famous paintings of Achilles and Chiron, Theseus and the Minotaur, and Hercules and Telephus in Arcadia.

Bardet's excavations greatly expanded the network of tunnels accessible to visitors, although not all left with a clear understanding of what they had seen. Beyond the theater, which remained the most readily comprehensible feature, visitors were left with an impression of disorder and ruin. The most detailed description of a tour during this period could speak only in vague terms of the visible ruins:

> You sometimes see plainly the outsides of walls, that have apparently fallen inward; sometimes the insides of such as have apparently fallen outwards; and sometimes the insides of buildings which stand directly upright. . . . You have all the way such a confusion of brick and tiles, of mortar and marble, in cornices and friezes, and other ornaments and members of buildings, together with stucco, beams, and rafters, and even what seems to have been the trees which stood in the town, and blocks and billets for fuel, and earth and matter, which appears to have overwhelmed the whole place; all so blended, crushed, and as it were mixed together, that it is far easier to conceive than describe. The ruin in general is not to be expressed.[89]

The description continues with a catalog of individual sites, including chambers painted bright red and upper-story rooms in private dwellings, some accessible only by creeping through narrow holes. The author thought he had seen street corners and the façades of houses and public buildings but could not be sure.

Despite his remarkable success in recovering antiquities, Bardet's abrasive and headstrong personality earned him the enmity of both his colleagues and the community of Resina. He was reprimanded by Montealegre for cutting down paintings from the ruins and seeking to collect the wages normally paid to Canart, the man responsible for removing the paintings and mounting them for display in the museum. Bardet then attempted to prevent Canart from entering the excavation tunnels without his consent, which led to a fierce altercation and ultimately to permanent hostility between the two.[90]

The citizens of Resina had grown increasingly hostile toward the excavations because the tunnels had undermined their homes and caused cracks in their walls. Bardet succeeded in intensifying their hostility by his response to their complaints that buildings were collapsing and fields subsiding into tunnels he had failed to buttress properly. The women feared for the health and safety of their husbands and sons who worked as hired hands and daily surrendered themselves to the vagaries of work in the underground tunnels. In 1740, Knapton reported that the local citizenry allowed only an unmarried man to serve as their guide in the tunnels and that his entourage was almost mobbed when it was feared the young man had perished in making the initial descent.[91]

After protesting to a furious Montealegre that he had been wrongly accused of negligence, Bardet invited his chief accuser, a merchant named Sportullo, to tour the tunnels and see for himself how many buttresses had been constructed. When Sportullo refused, Bardet sent armed Swiss Guards from the excavations, who ferreted the man out of his hiding place with their bayonets fixed. The sight of one of their citizens being paraded down the street under guard attracted the attention of the mayor, priests, and curate of Resina, who rallied to Sportullo's defense. Although subsequently persuaded of his error, Sportullo, already famous for his fondness for litigation, complained to Montealegre of mistreatment at Bardet's hands. In retaliation, Bardet had Sportullo's well investigated for possible antiquities and threatened to excavate under his own home. Bardet was spared from incarceration only by the chance discovery of a marble head in Sportullo's well, which Sportullo protested had been planted but enabled Bardet to regain some of his lost esteem at court.[92]

Bardet refers to these difficulties with the court in a letter dated October 19, 1743, in which he assures the prime minister that he would be delighted to be released from this assignment, for which he feels particularly ill suited anyway as a military engineer. Nor could he, like Rorro, appreciate the value of what he believed were the paltry finds being made at that time. Then, in late February 1744, having barely escaped a tunnel collapse, he appealed again for transfer. Shortly thereafter his request was granted, at least temporarily, since the excavating was halted during the war against Austria that ended at Velletri on August 11 of that year.[93] He then returned to the excavations and, when he later complained that the commute from Naples was too arduous, was advised to move to Resina.[94]

After his recovery Alcubierre had been transferred to Gaeta, a post both he and his wife evidently found agreeable enough. Yet already in early 1743 Alcubierre had written from here to request permission from the prime minister to return to his post in the excavations. Even though Bardet had lost the support of Charles of Bourbon, his dismissal on grounds of insubordination could have soured the court's relationship with the French ambassador. As Alcubierre himself later recounted the affair, Bardet refused to vacate his post to someone of lower rank, despite the fact that he had been seeking a transfer for some time.

To circumvent this delicate situation, Montealegre first made Alcubierre a second engineer, a rank equivalent to Bardet's. Coincidentally, on February 8, 1745, Alcubierre was admitted into the "Real Archicofradia y Monte del Santisimo Sacramento de los Nobles Españoles," a distinquished confraternity whose members served as "elder brothers" of the king. Shortly thereafter, Giovanni Medrano, the chief royal engineer in Naples, was demoted and condemned to five years in prison for his involvement in a scandal. Bigotti, Alcubierre's direct military superior, moved into Medrano's position, vacating the post of chief of the corps of engineers at Portici. Both Alcubierre and Bardet competed for Bigotti's former position, and Alcubierre was favored. Once this promotion had been granted, Bardet's hands were tied. He finally ceded the directorship to Alcubierre on August 28, 1745, but he retaliated by being very slow to turn over the daybooks and the plans he had drawn during his tenure.[95]

ALCUBIERRE'S RETURN (1745)

Alcubierre set to work again immediately, distributing his crews of workmen throughout the excavations with a view to extending Bardet's tunnels in three directions.[96] The inventory of paintings, mosaics, statues, and small finds recovered during the following years is extraordinarily rich. Although Alcubierre made almost daily reports to the prime minister, these amount to little more than inventories of the finds – lists describing the material, dimensions, and some indication of subject matter – with only vague references to provenance. When Alcubierre learned from Canart that the wall paintings would be much appreciated by connoisseurs in Rome and England, he arranged for Canart and his assistants to oversee the removal of these from the site.[97] Entire panels and even individual decorative motifs were chiseled out of the wall paintings, with the result that a single wall could produce a great number and variety of small paintings, all of which Alcubierre described in the daybooks in a very cursory fashion.

Complicating matters further is the very nature of these underground excavations that makes it difficult or impossible to follow the course of the work in the daybooks, for no overall plans of the underground tunnels themselves were produced to serve as a guide. The provenance of even the most famous of finds from this period is disputed, since tunnels began to crisscross the site and were being dug at a rapid pace. Moreover, Alcubierre had been given explicit instructions from the prime minister that he was to record the discovery of only the minor finds, since the king would see for himself the most significant antiquities on his frequent visits to Portici: part of his evening ritual included formal presentations and discussions of the day's key discoveries.[98] The most telling example of the resulting confusion is the marble equestrian statues of the Nonii Balbi, long thought to have stood originally in the Basilica but which are now believed to have been found in what the excavators called the Forum of Herculaneum, a building in the vicinity of the theater whose precise location and architectural form have yet to be identified.[99]

These enormous statues, each 2.60 meters high, were both found in a relatively complete state of preservation, within two months of each other, in mid-1746 (Fig. 10). Their colossal size and fragility required a number of alterations in the techniques employed in the tunnels. Extricating the first statue from the volcanic matrix required the labor of all the workmen for ten days: they had to dig the statue out, open up the old tunnels, link these with new ones in order to allow the statue to pass through, and widen the access shaft through which men and artifacts were lifted. A special crate had to be constructed as well, to protect the statue as it was hoisted up the shaft and transported to Portici. Some time later the huge cavity left by the statue was in danger of collapsing and required special bracing.[100]

Removing the second statue proved even more arduous, for its location was poorly ventilated, and the lack of sufficient oxygen to burn the torches was compounded by the thick dust and the sweat of the workmen. Alcubierre first attempted to solve the problem by cutting a ventilation shaft, evidently the first of its kind. He then equipped this with a type of manual air pump, fashioned from a large bellows fitted with a length of tin tubing, that expelled the stale air and introduced fresh air into the tunnels. This new instrument, one with which Alcubierre was clearly pleased, given his respiratory problems, and which must have been equally popular with the laborers, was portable enough for two men to handle and could be transported to trouble spots throughout the excavations as needed.[101]

A colossal marble female portrait statue came to light soon after the equestrian ones, and special measures were adopted for its removal as well. The labor of hoisting such enormous objects out of the shafts was apparently excessive, so Alcubierre decided to cut a ramp to allow easier access to the tunnels, a process which took a month. A sheath of volcanic material was left on the statue to protect it during transport. Then it was secured to a base with plaster and maneuvered through newly widened tunnels to the ramp, where it could be wheeled out.[102]

Figure 10. Marble equestrian statue of Marcus Nonius Balbus, *filius* (MN. 6104), from Herculaneum (1746); the statue of Marcus Nonius Balbus, *pater* (MN. 6211), is visible in the background. Museo Archeologico Nazionale, Naples. (Author's photograph.)

Over the course of the next few years, the excavators managed to probe through much of what is known of ancient Herculaneum today. In addition to ongoing investigations in the areas around the theater and the Basilica, Alcubierre explored several funerary monuments to the northeast of the Palestra that probably mark the outer limits of the city in that direction.[103] Tunnels also began to crisscross their way through the elegant houses to the south, overlooking the Bay of Naples. This work would have exposed the layout of the city's narrow streets and the orthogonal grid of the city blocks in this area, but such features probably went unnoticed, since the excavators ignored Bardet's system of following the lines of streets and instead cut through common house walls, filling in their old tunnels behind them as they proceeded.

The precise location of part of this work can be identified, thanks to a few poorly preserved paintings left behind on the walls of a house that match a series of paintings listed in the daybooks as having been removed and taken to Portici. This is the case with a bakery, located at Ins.Occ 2.1–3 in the modern numbering scheme used at Herculaneum, where fragments of painting indicate that Alcubierre had passed through here in April 1746.[104] By August 1748, the excavators had hit upon the remains of the Casa dell' Atrio a Mosaico (Ins. 4.2). Moving to the east, they broke through a wall into the adjacent Casa dei Cervi (Ins. 4.21) and tunneled around its enclosed cryptoporticus in a counterclockwise direction, selecting for removal the choicest ancient paintings and opus sectile pavements from here and the surrounding rooms. Finds were still being removed from rooms to the north of the central garden of the Casa dei Cervi through mid-1749.[105]

Despite these efforts, the domestic buildings of Herculaneum failed to yield up another gold mine of bronze and marble statues to match those found around the theater and Basilica, and, after 1746, the number of finds began to dwindle. Even if Alcubierre was not under direct orders to ensure that a steady stream of treasures worthy of the king were being brought to light, he evidently felt he had such a mandate or feared that continued failure would reflect poorly on his own position, and so he soon began to scout out new sites for excavation.

INVESTIGATIONS AT "LA CIVITÀ" AND STABIAE

The town of Torre Annunziata, some 18 kilometers southeast of Naples, had long been of great strategic value to the kingdom because of the gunpowder factories established there in 1654. These factories relied on water originally channeled from the town of Sarno through a canal, laid out in part by Domenico Fontana from 1592 to 1600 on behalf of Conte Muzio Tuttavilla of Sarno. The water had been used initially to operate grain mills at Torre Annunziata. After Charles of Bourbon determined in 1753 to construct an important new arms factory here, the area increased in importance, thanks to a number of critical military and state-run industrial works, all dependent upon this water's power.[106]

Throughout this period of the early excavations Alcubierre had continued to perform his duties as a military engineer, which included overseeing the maintenance and repair of military installations. In late March 1748, while surveying the channel of the old Sarno canal, he learned that local inhabitants had been turning up antiquities in their fields at a site near Torre Annunziata called "la Cività", a mound through which the canal had to pass underground. Alcubierre believed this was the site of ancient Stabiae, but it was in fact ancient Pompeii;

other antiquities had already been found at nearby Gragnano and Castellamare di Stabia, which later was recognized as the true site of Stabiae.

Beyond the assurance that they would yield additional precious antiquities, Alcubierre acknowledged that these sites offered one significant advantage over Herculaneum: the volcanic lapilli which covered them could be quarried with relative ease by means of open trenches worked by a small corps of men. He immediately proposed to the prime minister that he be allowed to transfer a few of the workmen to Torre Annunziata to make trial excavations. The forced laborers were to be left to work in the tunnels at Herculaneum, since there were no barracks in which to house them near these new sites. Private homes housed the twelve-man civilian crew initially assigned to Torre Annunziata. Alcubierre laid out his first two trenches on the basis of reports about finds from local inhabitants of the area, and excavations began by April 6, 1748.[107]

Although the excavations could now be conducted in the full light of day, certain perils remained for the excavators themselves. Documents from this period reveal the extent and variety of these hazards and include several workmen's requests for paid sick leave because of injuries caused by accidents such as falling into the trenches or being swallowed up by mounds of the loose lapilli.[108] A more frequently encountered danger was the *mofeta*, in this case not fumaroles but pockets of odorless, lethal carbon dioxide trapped in the pyroclastic debris from the eruption of Mount Vesuvius. Such gaseous pockets could also contain carbon monoxide, if decaying organic material was present, as well as trace quantities of hydrogen sulfide, in which case the excavators would be tipped off to its presence by the distinctive odor of rotten eggs. The slightest suspicion of the *mofeta* could send the workmen scurrying. On several occasions at Pompeii, a moist, choking mass of hot air in the form of a southeasterly sirocco afflicted the excavators and brought work to a halt. A combination of the *mofeta* and the sirocco was the culprit when, on July 6, 1748, the work at Pompeii had to be suspended for some three months, until the air had cleared.[109] On the other hand, one visitor would remark some years later how much more pleasant it was to stroll with a parasol at Pompeii than to negotiate the tunnels at Herculaneum.[110]

In late October 1748, Alcubierre returned with his twelve workmen to the site he continued to believe was ancient Stabiae. Still determined to discover a public building comparable to the theater at Herculaneum, he chose to open his new trenches at the site of Pompeii's amphitheater, whose elliptical shape and the central depression caused by the settling of the volcanic material were clearly discernible in the modern landscape. The realization that this would not yield the desired treasures came quickly, and in less than two months Alcubierre dutifully noted the amphitheater's dimensions and architectural features and speculated about its seating capacity in his final report to the prime minister. The excavations then shifted to the opposite side of the ancient city, where structures just beyond the city walls were investigated and a number of small paintings removed. On April 19, 1749, the *mofeta* again caused a halt. Work resumed in July 1750, but in September, less than eighteen months after he had begun, Alcubierre conceded that nothing substantial had been encountered for some time at la Città and so transferred his workmen elsewhere.[111]

Excavations had been undertaken at a number of sites during these years, including a brief period at Polena, where the main take consisted only of some eighteen thousand bricks.[112] Once Polena had proved inadequate, the excavators opened trenches, on June 7, 1749, in an area around the bridge of San Marco, between Gragnano and Castellamare di Stabia. These excavations at ancient Stabiae were to continue, off and on, until 1762.

In 1749, Alcubierre was promoted to lieutenant colonel, in addition to retaining his position as second-in-command of the royal corps of military engineers.[113] These increased responsibilities required that he be present more frequently in Naples, leaving him less time to devote to the excavations. He therefore requested a subordinate who could oversee the day-to-day operations at each site and recommended Karl Jakob Weber for the post.

Weber's skills as an architect and military engineer apparently had already won him a certain degree of recognition. He must have been among the most educated officers in the corps and was also a polyglot, capable of communicating in the dialects of Spanish and Italian necessary for dealing both with the court and with the workmen. In June 1750, shortly before Weber was to report for duty in Portici, Bigotti wrote to Prime Minister Fogliani regarding the latter's request for three engineers to help in the production and reduction of plans of the ruins at Herculaneum. Bigotti expressed concern, since he needed additional engineers just then to construct military barracks at Aversa and S. Maria di Capua Vetere. Moreover, he specifically asked that Weber, because of his experience and skill in working on fortifications, not be assigned to the excavations and that the post be given to another engineer, Emanuel de Montemayor.[114] If this request ever was granted, Montemayor's tenure was of short duration. More likely Alcubierre used his new position to force through his request, for Weber presented himself to Alcubierre on June 28 and assumed his post in Portici on July 2, 1750. Two days later, Alcubierre took him for the first time to Torre Annunziata.[115]

2

The Earliest Plans of the Vesuvian Monuments

When Weber assumed control of the excavations, he inherited the traditions and methodologies of a twelve-year-old operation. Yet Alcubierre and Bardet each had used different approaches to excavating the ruins, and each left forms of documentation that, philosophically, were diametrically opposed. The recovery of antiquities was the only guiding principle. Neither had been able to devote his undivided attention to the excavations in some years, leaving the daily operations more or less in the hands of civilian site foremen. The situation afforded Weber a golden opportunity to step in and alter significantly the course of the excavations, to fashion them according to his own vision. But Alcubierre was not prepared to yield full control to Weber, and in only a year the two had split over what Weber's role should be and what direction the excavations should take.

On July 20, 1750, Alcubierre had handed Weber a long and detailed list of responsibilities, which included maintaining an inventory of all the tools, equipment, and instruments belonging to the excavations. Topping the list was a wooden box containing the air pump, with its bellows and thirty-six sections of tin tubing that could extend 169 palms (42.5 m.).[1] For lifting earth, artifacts, and workmen from the tunnels they had three winches, each consisting of an iron wheel supported by a wooden superstructure. Weber also had at his disposal four small wagons for use inside the tunnels and one large cart for transporting the finds to Portici. There was also a wooden hut with four benches inside, which, Alcubierre noted, could be transported to work sites and used for writing daily reports.

Weber was to maintain a careful watch over the laborers, ensuring that none concealed the smallest artifact, under penalty of flogging and imprisonment. He was to supply a weekly summary of all the finds encountered in the excavations to

Alcubierre, who would in turn report them to the prime minister.[2] He was to keep
a record of the monthly earnings of all the hired laborers and all the excavation's
expenses, operating within a budget of 200 ducats per month.[3] Also under Weber's control were the guards who watched over the forced laborers at Resina and
served as sentinels at Gragnano, protecting the excavation sites from thieves at
night and on holidays.[4] He was to ensure that these guards were vigilant in
performing their duties and did not while away the hours playing cards. Finally,
Alcubierre gave explicit orders concerning cartographic documentation:

> One must continue the plan he has been consigned, on which is delin-
> eated all the buildings discovered at Gragnano since that site was under-
> taken one year ago. And of any other place where buildings are found,
> whether it be in Resina, Torre Annunziata, or changing sites at Gragnano,
> one must likewise draw up a plan at the same scale, and upon all one must
> write with equal clarity (as one observes on this one) that which is encoun-
> tered in each place.[5]

For his own part, Alcubierre had not been particularly diligent about producing plans yet was quite proud and protective of those he had undertaken or
completed, as his concern for the plan of Gragnano illustrates.[6] As early as
February 1740 his superiors had pointed out the need for accurate plans,[7] but
when he was asked to turn over all his papers to Bardet in August 1741,
Alcubierre had been forced to admit that he had been unable to produce a
general plan of the excavations.[8] Francesco La Vega, Weber's successor, learned
in 1765 that, despite intense pressure from Medrano, Alcubierre had even
failed to complete the original topographical plan of the area of Portici where
the summer palace was to be built and how, on the king's first visit to the site,
Alcubierre had been obliged to show him the plan still literally on the drawing
board.[9]

Part of the difficulty of making plans of the underground excavations,
Alcubierre was to note elsewhere, was the method of filling in the old tunnels
with the material removed in cutting new ones. This made it impossible to
double-check measurements or maintain a clear sense of orientation within the
tunnels. Alcubierre also complained that the tunnels were so narrow it was
impossible to operate the circumferentor, a surveying instrument.[10] The circumferentor operated much like a theodolite, except that the entire instrument
was rotated and the angles measured with a compass. Such an instrument would
have been extremely difficult to negotiate in the tunnels, where even a plane
table may have been deemed too unwieldy; it would have been more useful for
taking simple elevations. Orientation, inclination, and length of the tunnels

probably were recorded by a simple device developed in the seventeenth century that employed a gimbal compass and clinometer suspended from a cord stretched between two uprights.[11] The relative crudeness of the early plans, however, suggests that a chain had been used for taking most dimensions and for measuring the angles of rooms and that this task had been delegated to the unskilled laborers. La Vega was told later that Alcubierre rarely entered the tunnels himself because he easily became disoriented and that a workman named Giuseppe ("Peppe") Palumbo had taken all the measurements for both Alcubierre and Bardet.[12]

Shortly after Weber assumed his post, Alcubierre handed over seven plans of ancient buildings, including one of the theater at Herculaneum, that needed to be reduced in size so that engravings of them might be made. Eleven other plans still remained in an incomplete state.[13] The excavation records themselves specifically document fourteen plans drawn between the years 1739 and 1750, but these records are probably incomplete.[14]

Six plans are now known to be extant from this early period, but only four of these could have been among the original seven finished plans Alcubierre had provided Weber. Missing are a plan that illustrated what Alcubierre referred to as the forum of Herculaneum, where he stated that the marble equestrian statues had been found, along with all the other buildings investigated during the year 1746.[15] Among the eleven unfinished plans may have been a sketch plan of a tomb at Herculaneum and one of the so-called Villa of Cicero at Pompeii. Other documents may have been illustrations of curious or interesting finds rather than plans per se, such as the drawing of a stone grinding mill found in Gragnano.[16]

BARDET'S EARLY PLANS OF HERCULANEUM

The earliest extant plan is of the Basilica at Herculaneum. Two nearly identical versions of this plan, one with its title and legend in French and the other in Spanish, are now in the Archivio di Stato in Naples (Fig. 11). Bardet apparently drew both plans but signed only the French version. He failed to provide either with a date. Much of the sheet is filled by the ground plan of the Basilica, with no indication that this is a ruin still buried some 16 meters belowground or that narrow tunnels had been used in recovering the essential features of its plan. Instead it shows in careful detail all the niches in the side walls, the interior colonnade, the bases for the honorary statues removed from here, and even the lines of the marble paving blocks inside the building, where the excavators had barely ventured. Bardet's most serious inaccuracy was in showing a series of five

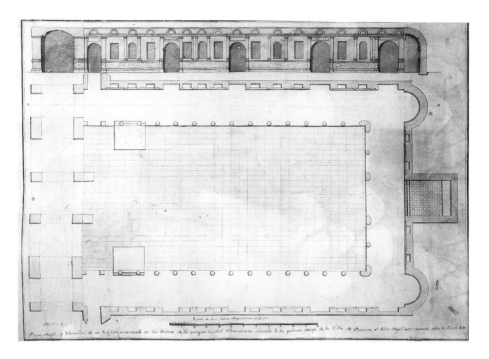

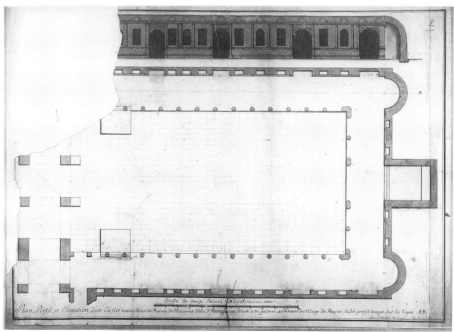

Figure 11. The two versions of the plan and cross section of the Basilica at Herculaneum drawn by Pierre Bardet de Villeneuve, one with its title in Spanish (*top*) and the other in French (*bottom*). The paintings of Hercules and Telephus in Arcadia (MN. 9008) and Theseus and the Minotaur (MN. 9049) were removed from the large semicircular niches on the right; the colossal statues of the emperors Augustus (MN. 6040), Claudius (MN. 6056), and Titus (MN. 6095) were found in the central rectangular niche on the right. (Courtesy of the Archivio di Stato, Napoli [Raccolta Piante e Disegni, Cart. xxiv.1 and xxiv.2; 0.50 m. H × 0.70 m. W].)

cross vaults carried on a portico across the front of the building; recent excavations have revealed that the façade in fact was flanked by only two quadrifrontal arches at either end. On the other hand, this is the earliest plan to comply with the directive originally issued to Alcubierre that plans be provided with a detailed elevation. Along the top of the page is an elevation of the west wall of the Basilica, with its alternating rectangular and semicircular niches framed by engaged Tuscan columns. Bardet illustrated only the architectural remains on his plan: he made no indication directly on the plan of the important finds he had made here.[17] The sole exception to this is the illustration of a marble plaque engraved with the word "Augustales," shown above one of the lateral niches. Bardet had recovered an inscription reading "AVGVSTALES.S.P." (CIL 10.977) on September 11, 1741, from somewhere in this area, although perhaps not in the Basilica itself.[18]

There are also two extant versions of a second plan, both drawn by Bardet and dated July 7, 1743 (Figs. 12 and 13). The annotations to both of these plans are in French. Only slight discrepancies in the overall format of each are evident; one sheet is somewhat wider than the other. This plan is the most detailed of those which have survived for these early years, for it shows the full extent of the excavations through 1743, including a number of structures only investigated in part by Bardet. In so doing, it was the first plan known to depict a series of buildings and their relation to one another and the known city streets rather than merely showing an individual monument in isolation. Bardet drew this plan in response to a direct order from the prime minister to produce a plan that showed "the architecture, symmetry, and layout of the city." This was to be shown to the king, who had expressed an interest in seeing the course of the ancient road from Neapolis to Stabiae, which coincidentally ran parallel to, and almost directly below, his own Royal Road from Naples to Salerno.[19]

In the upper left-hand corner of Bardet's plan is the design of the theater as it was understood at that time. The alignment of the scaena, and thus the entire theater, has been rotated in an odd fashion some ninety degrees from its true nearly north-south axis, so that it runs parallel to the top of the sheet. But, in keeping with the king's request, the main focus of the plan is on the buildings along the "Decumanus Maximus," moving east from the Basilica to the structures surrounding the Palestra on the north. Prior to the rediscovery of this plan in the Archivio di Stato in Naples during the 1970s, it was not clear that Bardet's investigations had extended as far as the Palestra.[20] This is also the first plan to illustrate the fact that the excavations had been conducted at a variety of levels, for the buildings making up the Palestra at street level were illustrated on a separate sheet of vellum that was hinged and could be folded back to reveal

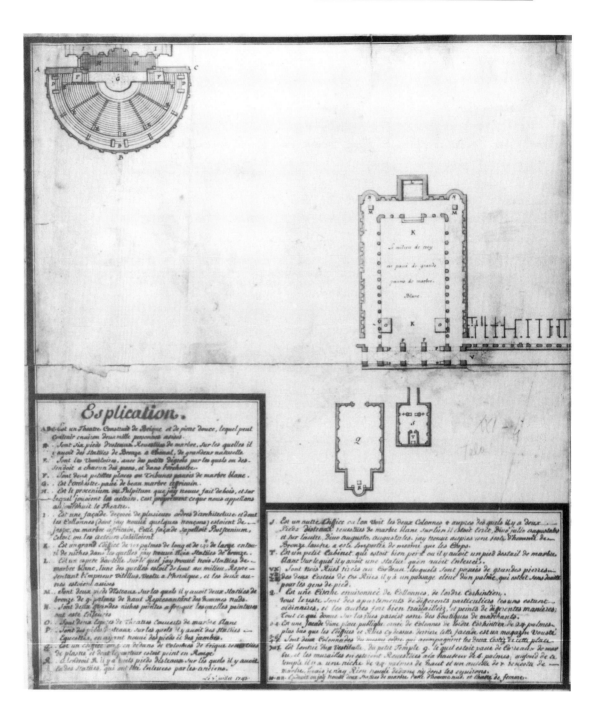

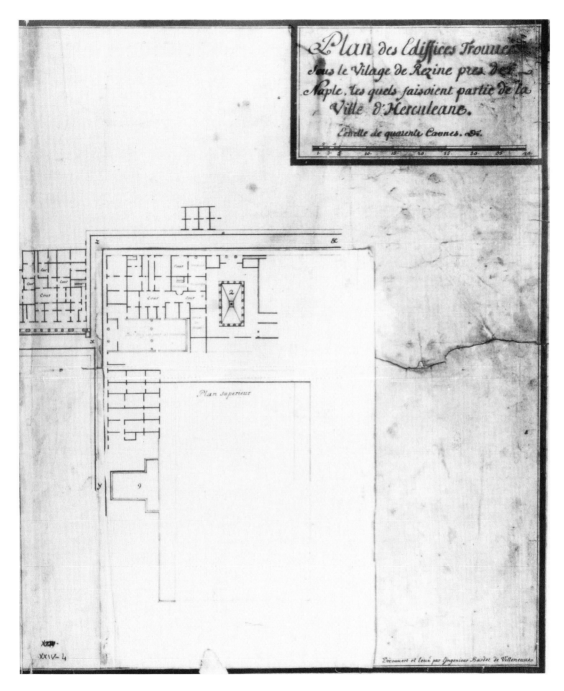

Figure 12. Plan, with annotations in French, drawn by Pierre Bardet de Villeneuve in 1743 showing the extent of the Bourbon excavations along the "Decumanus Maximus" in Herculaneum. The principal buildings illustrated are the improperly oriented theater (*upper left*), the Basilica with the Galleria Balba and the Augustalium (*center*), and the Palestra (*lower right*) with the Corinthian atrium (*upper right*). Courtesy of the Archivio di Stato, Naples [Raccolta Piante e Disegni, Cart. xxiv.4; 0.59 m. H × 1.02 m. W].)

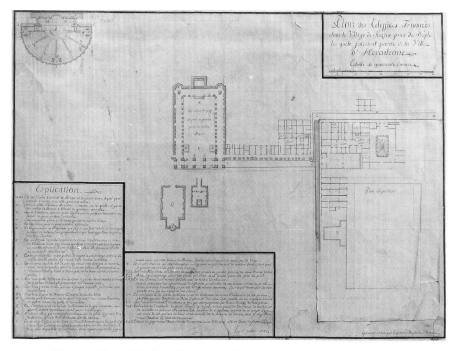

Figure 13. Copy of Bardet's "Decumanus Maximus" plan. (Courtesy of the Archivio di
Stato, Naples [Raccolta Piante e Disegni, Cart. xxiv.3; 0.62 m. H × 0.85 m. W].)

the structures, a technique referred to as a *retomb* (Fig. 14). As a result, Bardet
was able to depict the relationship of the structures at street level with the
porticoes and cryptoporticus situated at a lower level.

In these plans Bardet again placed greater emphasis on the architectural
elements than on the artifacts recovered from these buildings. This is evident in
both his title to the plan and in the brief legend provided in the lower left-hand
corner. For example, he describes the Basilica as simply "a large building 208
palms long and 142 wide surrounded by niches in which I found three bronze
statues." The apses in the Basilica that contained the extraordinary paintings of
Hercules in Arcadia and of Achilles and Chiron are passed over with a note
stating simply: "S: These are two big niches painted with stucco, whose paintings have been removed." The paintings, however, had been removed almost
two years earlier, under Alcubierre, and Bardet may not have been aware precisely which ones they were. He copied his earlier plan of the Basilica directly
onto this one and also took some care in rendering the Augustalium and the
Galleria Balba, even though these buildings are not linked together on the plan
and so tend to float in isolation.[21]

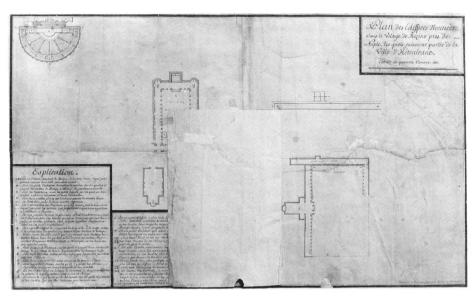

Figure 14. Bardet's "Decumanus Maximus" plan, showing the *retomb* folded back to reveal the plan of those features of the Palestra that stood at a lower level. (Courtesy of the Archivio di Stato, Naples [Raccolta Piante e Disegni, Cart. xxiv.4; 0.59 m. H × 1.02 m. W].)

On the other hand, the minor structures to the east are suspiciously regular in form, especially the outlines of what must be several shops lining the street. The most distinctive feature here is a large peristyle courtyard with a central fountain, resembling a Corinthian-style atrium in a private house. Like the two entrances into the Palestra, however, this peristyle is approached through an entrance flanked with twin columns, facing the street, suggesting that this building too had a public nature. The rooms to the west may make up a bath complex, since at least one of the small rooms appears to have a schola labri, an apsidal niche for a fountain like those found in the caldaria of baths, and what may be an alveus, or bath basin, opposite this.

Only the simplest features are noted throughout this area, such as several spaces labeled courtyards and five rooms said to have been paved in mosaic. All the walls run parallel to one another or at strict right angles, taking no account, for example, of the thirty-degree angle at which the Palestra actually sits in relation to the regular grid of the streets. This may have been a consequence of the inability to survey the underground buildings accurately, although the modern reexcavation of the Augustalium confirmed the accuracy of Bardet's plan of this building in many details.[22] More likely Bardet concluded that these areas did not warrant a more careful survey because of the insignificant finds recovered here and so had settled for the crude surveying skills of one of his assistants, perhaps "Peppe" Palumbo himself.

A somewhat earlier plan by Bardet is known only from copies of its legend, one in French, written by Bardet himself, and the second a later translation into Italian; neither copy bears a date.[23] The plan, which is no longer extant, included a ground plan and elevation of the theater of Herculaneum. This must be the same plan referred to in the excavation records between April and July 1742 and is no doubt the same one Bardet used as a model for the small illustration of the theater in his later plan of the "Decumanus Maximus." No dimensions are given in the legends, nor is it known at what scale the plan was drawn. Finds are described in the same cursory manner seen on the other plans, with Bardet claiming to have found only a small bronze "table" with bronze feet attached by means of lead to the marble pavement. Although it is difficult to know the precise findspot, this may be one of the sellae curules known to have been in the tribunalia overlooking the orchestra.[24] He attempted some interpretation of the ruins as well, explaining that Greek actors performed in the orchestra, whereas Roman actors remained on the proscenium, since in a Roman theater the senators occupied the orchestra. He postulated a seating capacity of fifteen hundred spectators. In July 1742, Bardet's plan was given to Matteo Egizio for comment, and Egizio systematically attacked it as full of inaccuracies and errors and not worthy of publication.[25] This explains why the plan was never engraved and perhaps as well why no copy was preserved in the archives of the prime minister.

None of Bardet's plans were among those that Alcubierre handed over to Weber, however, since Bardet retained possession of his own plans of the excavations at Herculaneum through 1766, when he offered four of them to Tanucci in exchange for copies of *Le antichità di Ercolano*.[26] In all likelihood both Alcubierre and Weber were completely unaware of the existence of these plans. In fact, ignorance of the extent of Bardet's tunneling was to cause Weber much difficulty and embarrassment in the years to come.

On the other hand, it is precisely the work accomplished during Bardet's tenure that was the first to be published widely abroad, although some years after the fact. Bardet's own role in this may have been crucial, for it was his compatriots, such as the Frenchman Moussinot d'Arthenay, who first described the ruins of the Basilica and gave measurements of this building as well as of the theater. It can hardly be coincidental that d'Arthenay had been secretary to the marquis de l'Hôpital, the French ambassador to Naples and the man responsible for securing for Bardet his post in the excavations.[27]

Some years later, in 1750, Charles-Nicolas Cochin *fils* and Jérôme-Charles
Bellicard traveled through Naples on the Grand Tour in the company of the
future director of royal works to Louis XV, Abel-François Poisson de Vandières,
later (1754) marquis de Marigny et de Menars. Bellicard's original notebook
from this tour has survived and includes all of the original sketches he drew of
the ruins and of works of art that he later engraved for his *Observations sur les
antiquités de la ville d'Herculanum*, published in 1754 with Cochin.[28] His book
included a brief description and a schematic plan of the Basilica and the two
buildings directly across from it, as well as a plan and profile of the theater.

Bellicard's plan of the Basilica, the first widely published plan from Herculaneum, closely mirrors the portion of Bardet's plan that illustrates these buildings; he even duplicated Bardet's error of drawing the portico with five cross
vaults across the entire facade of the Basilica, a feature that Bellicard identified
with the chalcidicum described by Vitruvius (Vitr. 5.1.4). Included as well are a
few details and several variations not found on Bardet's plans, such as two
entrances from the street into the Galleria Balba, shops flanking the entrance of
the Augustalium, and, directly behind these latter two structures, interior walls
and street entrances to several other buildings. The tunnels in these areas and
along the main street in front of the Basilica may still have been accessible at the
time of Cochin and Bellicard's tour and so were appended to this plan. By
extending the lines of the city streets and the colonnaded walkways flanking the
main street, Bellicard helped tie these buildings together better, creating a
greater architectural unity than on Bardet's plan.[29]

Despite the inclusion of details that could have been drawn only from personal observation of the ruins, it seems likely from the original sketch in his
notebook that Bellicard drew most of his plan while consulting copies of
Bardet's plans and on the basis of what others familiar with the site had described to him (Fig. 15). Many of the tunnels in this area would have been
inaccessible in 1750, and indeed Bellicard himself observed that

> Virtually nothing of these buildings remains that can be visited; most have
> been filled back in with the earth taken from other tunnels being dug. I
> only examined a very small part, and the few columns that I found col-
> lapsed and in ruins were of brick covered in stucco, as is done throughout
> Italy today.[30]

Nor would it have been possible for Bellicard to perform the extensive surveying
necessary to draw as accurate a plan as this, because of the royal prohibition

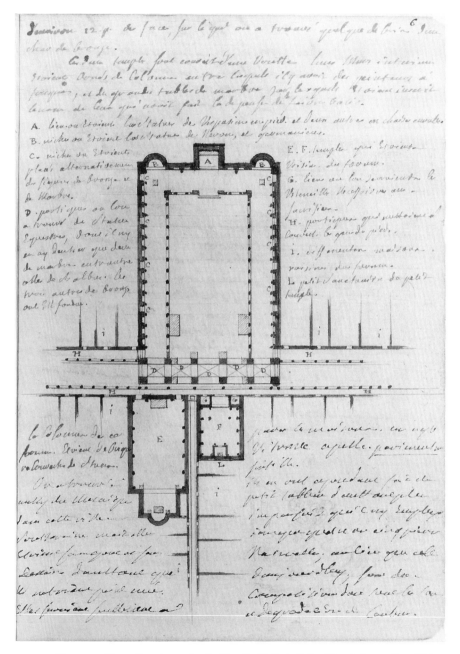

Figure 15. Plan with notes on the Basilica, the Galleria Balba (*E*) and Augustalium (*F*) in
Herculaneum as drawn by Jérôme-Charles Bellicard in his "Italian Notebook" (1750–51).
(Courtesy of the Metropolitan Museum of Art, New York, Harris Brisbane Dick Fund,
1940 [40.59.6].)

against taking notes or measurements of any kind, whether in the excavations or in the museum. This ban was aimed precisely at preventing publications like Cochin and Bellicard's.[31] In fact, Bellicard specifically remarks that he had been supplied with a plan of the theater, and this too must have been Bardet's. To judge from the small plan of the theater on the "Decumanus Maximus" plan, Bellicard appears to have copied Bardet's plan and cross section wholesale into his notebook, with only a few inaccuracies creeping in. For the published version he superimposed a schematic representation of the underground tunnels to illustrate how these had served to reveal the plan of the theater. The resulting plan is similar to one of Alcubierre's plans of the theater, although Bellicard showed fewer tunnels and his more detailed plan of the theater, in particular the scaena, supports the conclusion that he had based his on Bardet's.[32]

Since Bellicard could not have seen the copies housed in the prime minister's archives, he must have been granted access to Bardet's plans either directly by Bardet, who was stationed at Pescara at the time of Bellicard's visit, or through Moussinot d'Arthenay, or perhaps indirectly through the marquis de l'Hôpital, who is known to have kept copies of plans of many of the ancient sites his group visited in Italy. That Bardet had regularly supplied copies of his plans to the French ambassador might explain why he drew two nearly identical versions of his plans, with legends in both French and Spanish: he needed to satisfy the demands of these two different audiences.

Both Bardet's and Bellicard's plans betray a significant difference in attitude between French and Neapolitan scholars toward the value of these excavations, an attitude that was to endure until late in the eighteenth century and figure largely in the history of the Bourbon excavations. From the onset, the French were highly interested in the architectural ruins, taking a scientific attitude toward the study of these sites and the knowledge about antiquity that they could impart. The Neapolitan court, on the other hand, placed greater emphasis on the recovery of artifacts and on how these might be used to increase the glory of their king. This is seen most clearly in the creation of the Museum Herculanense and the later publications of the Accademia Ercolanese. The unique divergence from this attitude was the court's interest in the theater at Herculaneum, but this seems to have been piqued only after several other versions of the theater's plan (albeit largely inaccurate, especially in regard to the scaena) had appeared in French publications, after some twenty years had intervened.

Normally, copies of the finished plans from the excavations were sent first to the prime minister, who eventually passed them along to the king. These plans, or duplicates of them, were then deposited in the archives of the Secretaria di Stato in Naples. In October 1766, La Vega obtained five of Bardet's plans from these archives. He did not state which ruins these documented but praised their close attention to detail and noted how unfortunate it was that they had been unavailable to Weber, whose own excavations had frequently stumbled unwittingly into Bardet's old tunnels.[33]

Bardet's plans were completely unknown again by the early nineteenth century. Andrea de Jorio, for example, had to rely solely on the plan in Cochin and Bellicard's book when discussing the Basilica in his *Notizie degli Scavi di Ercolano*, published in 1827. Evidently La Vega had returned Bardet's plans to the archives of the Secretaria di Stato, where they were filed away and forgotten, only to resurface again in the late 1970s during archival research in the Archivio di Stato.[34]

ARCHITECTURAL DOCUMENTATION UNDER ALCUBIERRE

One plan Alcubierre almost certainly passed along to Weber was that of the theater at Herculaneum (Fig. 16). The legend on the only extant copy of this plan bears the date March 20, 1747, but since none of the finds whose provenance is recorded here was recovered later than May 1739, this plan probably is based either on one Alcubierre had produced in June 1739 or on another he refers to in July of that year.[35] The date of 1747 must be the year in which the plan was engraved. This delay underscores how indifferent Alcubierre was to documenting the architecture; although by this time further investigations in the theater had rendered the earlier plan obsolete, Alcubierre did not bother to update it. Plan and legend were engraved separately, and no dimensions or even a scale was provided on either. The legend is divided into two sections: the first briefly identifies the various parts of the theater, and the second catalogs the finds. Alcubierre was unclear on the architectural and functional difference between a Roman theater and an amphitheater, however, for he identified a set of gates as those through which wild animals for spectacles could enter and exit.[36]

Nevertheless, the plan is invaluable for the early history of the excavations, as it represents a significant departure from the practice of showing only the basic archaeological remains of the ruins. Instead it delineates the architectural elements of the theater as they were revealed by the labyrinth of tunnels used to explore the site: the plan, like Bellicard's own published version of 1755,

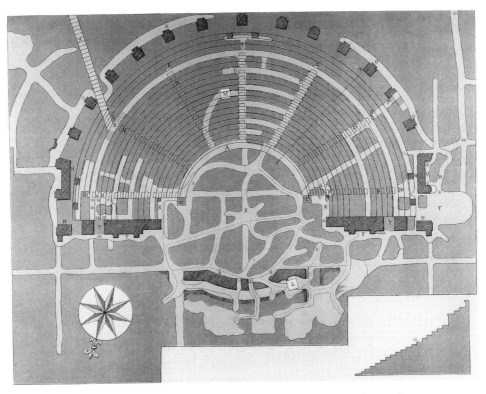

Figure 16. Plan and cross section of the theater at Herculaneum, drawn by Rocque Joaquin de Alcubierre about 1739 but not engraved until March 20, 1747. The numbers and letters were keyed to a legend that was printed separately. *L* marks the shaft used first by d'Elbeuf, while the dotted lines indicate his tunnels; *N* is the later stairway giving access to the site; *Q* the niche in the exterior façade from which Alcubierre removed three togate statues; *20* is the tunnel heading in the direction of the Basilica. From *StErc*, pl. 4.

thereby acknowledges that this was still a buried ruin. It marks the location of the so-called Pozzo di Nocerino, the well that first led to the theater's discovery, and illustrates the paths of d'Elbeuf's original tunnels. Later ramps and auxiliary shafts giving access to the theater itself and adjacent sites are depicted as well. Although no indication is provided of the relation between the level of these tunnels and the theater building, one annotation in the legend does break down the stratigraphy of the 84 palms (21.00 m.) of earth covering the theater, albeit in a cursory and unreliable manner: first, 7 palms (1.75 m.) of soft, friable topsoil; then 54 palms (13.50 m.) of pappamonte tufa, the general term used at that time for the volcanic matrix covering Herculaneum; and finally 23 more palms (5.75 m.) of soft earth.[37] A simple section taken through the theater gives some approximation of its appearance in elevation. Numbers indicate the findspots of the various marble fragments, bronze statues, statue bases, and inscriptions. The annotations are relatively vague, however; for example, "T: Various fragments of a horse and of two metal statues," and "9: The greater part of the fragments of two metal horses and four medallions." It is difficult or impossible to identify more than a few of these finds, since the list consists more of the building materials than of statuary; even a bronze "Vestal" referred to repeatedly in later documents has not been accurately identified.

This plan was found among the papers of de Jorio, who had obtained it between 1827 and 1831 from his friend Andrea Serao, who in turn claimed to have found it among the papers of a client. In publishing this plan in 1861 for the first time, Giuseppe Minervini concluded, as de Jorio himself had previously, that it was the work of Weber. Ruggiero, correctly noting that the date on the plan preceded the beginning of Weber's tenure at the excavations by three years, suggested the plan was by Bardet or, even more likely in his opinion, by Alcubierre, since he would have been in the best position to distinguish d'Elbeuf's original tunnels from his own.[38] Bardet is an unlikely candidate, however, since he left the excavations in 1745, two years before the date of this plan. Alcubierre is the most likely author, even though the legend is in Italian rather than his normal Spanish; this may be a later translation.

A fourth plan, finished on March 24, 1749, shows the remains of buildings constituting some four blocks from the western extremities of the then-known city of Herculaneum (Fig. 17).[39] The original plan is apparently no longer extant, but again the engraving published by Ruggiero in the nineteenth century shows that it was drafted originally in much the same fashion as Bardet's 1743 plan of the buildings along the "Decumanus Maximus." Simple parallel and perpendicular lines show the walls along with the streets and sidewalks bordering these blocks. Large areas are left blank or filled with hatch marks to indicate open courtyards. Additional buildings surrounded these structures in all directions but were "so ruined it was impossible to discern the form," as is noted on the plan.

The overall impression this plan leaves is of excavations conducted in a very cursory manner that had yielded few noteworthy finds. The annotations were kept to a minimum, with only a few pieces of marble listed as finds. All these aspects suggest that Alcubierre had abandoned the site quickly and felt it did not merit a more detailed plan. In fact, only five months later the excavators had already traversed the length of the city from east to west and had begun to recover paintings in the Casa del Atrio a Mosaico and the Casa dei Cervi.[40]

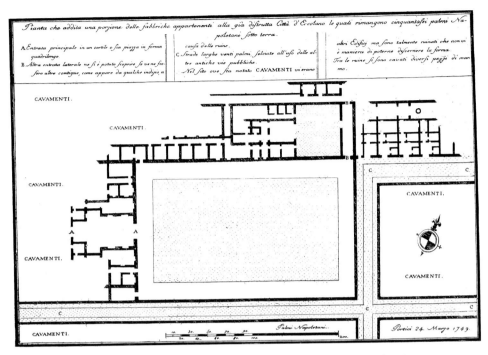

Figure 17. Plan of four *insulae* located along the western extremities of the area of ancient
Herculaneum investigated by the Bourbons. It bears the date of March 24, 1749, and,
though unsigned, is probably the work of the engineers Emanuel de Montemayer and
Joseph-Anton Dorgemont. From *StErc*, pl. 7.

In the meantime another plan was completed and passed on to the prime
minister only two months later, on May 19, 1749. Alcubierre's reports note that
the site illustrated on this plan stood 54 palms (13.5 m.) belowground, differing
by only 2 palms from the depth given on the plan of March 24, 1749.[41] Since
the scarp of the volcanic flow slopes rapidly from north to south above the
ruins,[42] the investigations must have been proceeding due east in areas buried
as deep as those shown on the earlier plan. This plan, which is no longer extant,
is likely to have shown some of the buildings that stood between the four
western blocks of the 1749 plan and the Casa del Atrio a Mosaico to the east,
that is, in the area of the so-called Casa d'Argo and the Casa dell' Albergo (Ins.
2 and 3).

The earliest plan from Stabiae was completed on January 20, 1750, and
illustrated the remains of a building excavated near the Capella di S. Marco,
northeast of the present Castellamare di Stabia, now referred to as the Villa of

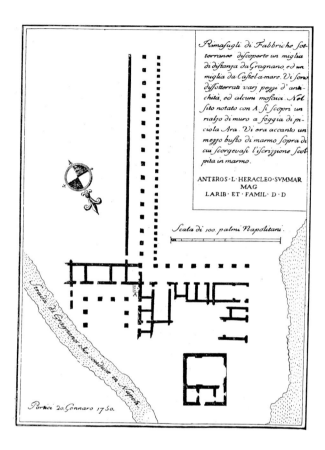

Antèros and Heracleo. The original plan of this site also survives only in an engraving (Fig. 18, *left*).[43] Its rectilinear form closely follows the drafting techniques found on the earlier plans from Herculaneum, although here some attempt has been made to show the ruins in relation to the surrounding landscape: it depicts a modern road to Gragnano from Naples that had cut off a portion of the building to the southwest, as well as damage from erosion on the southeast side. The few excavated portions included a series of rooms decorated with mosaics and opening onto two peristyles, the larger of these bordered by a covered ambulatio, suggesting that these were the remains of a villa. A brief legend in the upper right-hand corner notes that a lararium found in the

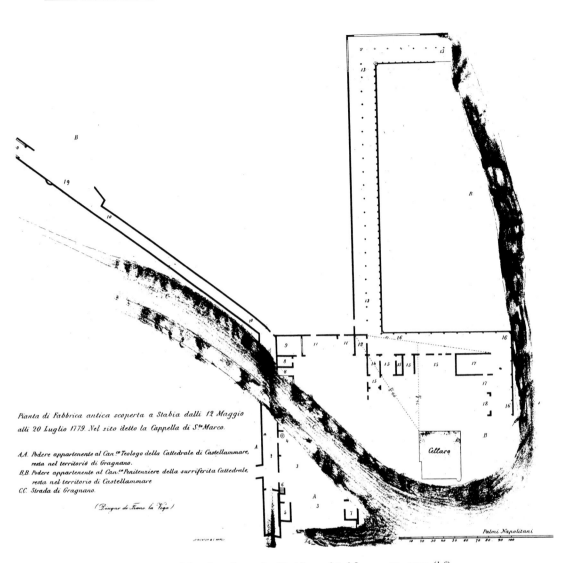

Pianta di Fabbrica antica scoperta a Stabia dalli 12 Maggio
alli 20 Luglio 1779. Nel sito detto la Cappella di S.ta Marco.

A.A. Podere appartenente al Can.co Teologo della Cattedrale di Castellammare,
resta nel territorio di Gragnano.
B.B. Podere appartenente al Can.co Penitenziere della surriferita Cattedrale,
resta nel territorio di Castellammare.
C.C. Strada di Gragnano.

(Disegno di Franco la Vega)

Palmi Napolitani

Figure 18. Comparison of the plans drawn, by Alcubierre, dated January 20, 1750 (*left*),
and by Francesco La Vega, dated July 20, 1779 (*right*), of the Villa of Antèros and
Heracleo, the first site investigated by the Bourbons at ancient Stabiae. From Ruggiero,
Terraferma, 56 (*left*) and *Stabiae*, pl. 11 (*right*).

northeast corner of the smaller peristyle contained a marble bust, now thought to be "Livia Minor," along with a dedicatory inscription: ANTEROS L HERACLEO SUMMAR / MAG LARIB ET FAMIL D D (*CIL* 10.773). The statue and inscription piqued the interest of many scholars, but no other finds are recorded.[44]

This site was one of only a handful to be fully reexcavated under the Bourbons some thirty years later. La Vega drew up a new, enlarged plan of these second excavations that had revealed significantly more of the larger peristyle (Fig. 18, *right*). Although the colonnade of the smaller peristyle and several walls are missing from La Vega's plan, the public road and the lines of erosion to the east are retained.[45]

The draftsmen responsible for the three extant plans of the theater and the four city blocks of Herculaneum and of the villa at Stabiae are not credited in the engraved versions. Although the titles and annotations were written in Italian, these plans were probably the work of Emanuel de Montemayor and of another French engineer, Josef-Anton Dorgemont. The similarity in drafting technique and overall appearance of the plans suggests that these two men had become involved in the excavations during Bardet's tenure as director and further support the notion that the Frenchmen associated with the excavations were more concerned about documenting the architectural remains. Montemayor was the one who had been recommended for the position Weber assumed in 1750 and no doubt had been working in the excavations for some time prior to that. Dorgemont is found in contemporary documents working on engineering problems at royal ports and fortresses, but otherwise his role in the excavations is suggested in only a single document, a notice, dated July 18, 1750, naming Montemayor and Dorgemont as the engineers in charge of drawing plans from Herculaneum, Gragnano, and Cività.[46]

Alcubierre speaks directly of only two plans drawn by his own hand, although he probably took credit for all the plans drawn during his tenure. Even though the excavation records ascribe to him a total of seven plans during the years when he was in direct charge (1738–41 and 1745–50), only four can be identified with any certainty. This leaves it unclear whether the others were actually drawn by him or were unfinished plans or ones that had been finished but never engraved.[47]

The earliest plans known to have been drawn for the excavations were two of the theater, produced within two months of each other in 1739. At this early stage of the excavations, it is entirely likely that Alcubierre had drawn them himself, but he never speaks of them as his own, and they are no longer extant.

They should probably be counted among the plans he later handed over to Weber, however.[48]

The first plan Alcubierre admitted drawing himself was one completed in December 1749 of the excavations carried out in and around the so-called Villa of Cicero at Pompeii, on which was noted, according to Alcubierre, "everything encountered there." This plan too is no longer extant and may never have been finished. In 1759, Alcubierre wrote to the prime minister stating that the original plan of the site where he had found "pictures of some centaurs and others of dancing women" was missing but that he had located a sketch copy of it among his notes.[49] The design of the building is known only from a plan drawn sometime after 1771 by La Vega, who had reexcavated the site. La Vega produced his own plan with a descriptive inventory of the finds, indicating precisely which rooms Alcubierre had investigated. These apparently amounted to only two large rooms, so presumably Alcubierre's plan was relatively unambitious and probably quite crude.[50]

Alcubierre's month-long investigation of the site of Pompeii's amphitheater in 1748 had revealed little more than its basic outline.[51] The result is the earliest extant plan from the excavations at Pompeii (Fig. 19). This too should have been among the seven plans that Alcubierre gave to Weber in 1750. Drawn in ink and watercolor on vellum, it is almost certainly the work of Alcubierre himself, since the title and annotations are in Spanish and the site is said to be Stabiae rather than Pompeii, a misidentification maintained by Alcubierre and few others at that time. One interesting new feature is the cross section through the site, given along the bottom of the page. It shows the buried amphitheater in relation to the ancient ground level as well as to the modern topography, indicated by ground cover and trees. Some brief remarks about the amphitheater's location, dimensions, number of seats, and the access routes are noted in legends flanking the plan.[52]

Although this plan gives some idea of the overall form of the amphitheater, it is clear that Alcubierre had extrapolated many of the details based on inadequate soundings, no doubt out of frustration over not having found a suitably rich site. In his weekly reports he mentions that he had managed "to conceive an idea of the amphitheater" from the few existing bits he had excavated and believed that his plan would be well received by "modern academics."[53] Complete excavations, carried out from 1813 through 1816, however, revealed paintings and inscriptions and a remarkably more complex design that betrayed Alcubierre's plan as hopelessly inadequate.[54]

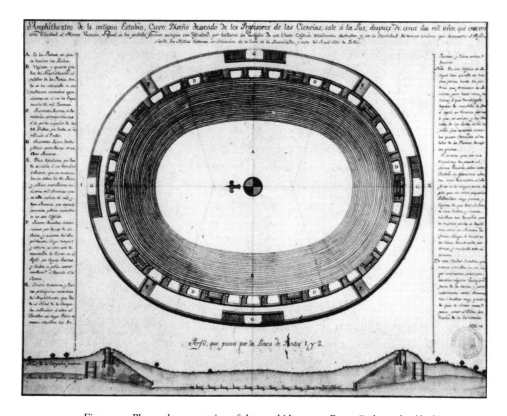

Figure 19. Plan and cross section of the amphitheater at Pompeii, drawn by Alcubierre in December 1748. The title begins "Amphitheater of ancient Stabiae, whose plan has been desired by the Professors of Knowledge, brought to light almost two thousand years after Mount Vesuvius buried this city." (Courtesy of the Soprintendenza Archeologica di Napoli e Caserta [Archivio Disegno, #78].)

THE "CRATERE MARITIMO" PROJECT AND THE FIRST RIFT

Among the unfinished projects that Alcubierre handed over to Weber was the completion of the so-called Cratere Maritimo map. This was to be a detailed map showing all the modern towns, roads, property lines, and topographical features around the Bay of Naples, the area still referred to today, as in antiquity, as the "Crater."[55] The primary purpose of the map was to illustrate the location of all the sites where ancient ruins had been found or were known to exist. The project had been undertaken in 1742, but by June of 1750 Alcubierre had completed only the area from Posillipo to Castellamare.[56]

Weber was given the task of completing this map, for it was slated for publication in Bayardi's *Prodromo delle antichità d'Ercolano*, the long-awaited (albeit long-winded) preface to a catalog of the finds from the ancient sites making up the Bourbon collection.[57] Weber first acknowledged that Bayardi had requested the Cratere Maritimo map for publication in a note dated February 13, 1751, yet in 1752 the first five volumes of the *Prodromo* were published in Naples without the benefit of Weber's map.[58]

The official correspondence during this period reveals that Weber's relationship with Alcubierre cooled within the first year, at least in part because of Weber's sluggish progress on the Cratere Maritimo map. In a lengthy letter to Prime Minister Fogliani dated July 24, 1751, only a year after Weber had assumed his post, Alcubierre already had a number of criticisms of Weber's performance:

> I should explain to his Excellency how, at the time when I had to name an engineer to oversee the excavations under my direction, I inclined toward Don Carlos Wever [*sic*], having believed with certainty on that occasion that he would have the [appropriate] knowledge through his engineering work in Naples and that he would be the best for such a duty. My experience since then, however, has shown me that his presence has served me little in those tasks, and more recently he has altered on several occasions the manner in which matters have been carried out in the past. . . .
>
> Concerning the general geographical map of the "Cratere" of Naples which I am in charge of surveying, I gave him this to reduce, as well as to add from the Punta di Posillipo to as far as the reef of Orlando, 2 miles beyond Castellamare, and to include on it all the frontage of Naples, the marina, and the buildings one encounters there. I gave Wever this task in mid-April past [1751], providing him what was necessary for fulfilling it, along with three men from the excavations to help him. But up to now, although in Naples much of the time under this pretext, he has accomplished nothing in three months, although able in this time to conclude all that needed to be added to this map, which was made in December 1742 and part of January 1743.[59]

Apart from the map of the Cratere Maritimo, the circumstance behind Alcubierre's outpouring of dissatisfaction appears to have been requests by Weber for a substantial increase in his monthly expenses and benefits. The substance of his petition is contained in two letters that Weber wrote near the end of March 1751, one addressed directly to Charles of Bourbon and the other to Prime Minister Fogliani. Both cast light upon the burdens of Weber's respon-

sibilities and show that he was growing increasingly aware of his importance to
the court:

> Captain Engineer Don Carlos Weber, placing himself with the greatest
> veneration at the Royal Feet of Your Majesty, reverently explains to Your
> Majesty how his continual travels from Portici to Gragnano, and Portici to
> Pozzuoli, as well as his drafting of the maps from Torre del Fusaro and the
> Dead Sea of Baiae and Misenum up to Sorrento, have compelled him to
> go into debt and have depleted his resources. He maintains dwellings at
> Portici, Gragnano, and Naples, is in continual movement and for the
> greater part of the time out of his house (the reason he is losing both his
> health and his money), without mentioning the rounds he makes of the
> numerous grottoes with the obvious danger to his life of being lowered on
> a rope 102 palms [27 meters] into the Pozzo dei Ciceri [at the Villa dei
> Papiri] (a thing he does solely out of love for Your Majesty), where he has
> encountered the four very graceful bronze fountain statues for Your Maj-
> esty as well as the two so beautiful and noble pavements, and yesterday a
> beautiful marble statue of a youth.[60]

> The clemency of Your Majesty has deigned to grant him another ration,
> which together with the other makes two. This suffices for one horse
> alone, however, which is in frequent travel, and what remains is spent on
> equipment. Do not doubt that these travels cost a great deal, and they are
> unending and consume all sustenance; nor is the recompense commensu-
> rable. His lodgings, the wear and tear on his carriage,[61] his clothing, must
> all be quadrupled: already he has worn out a uniform in less than one year
> that should have lasted another two or more; already he has spent 10
> ducats to shelter his carriage, which he uses every day. For his daily
> expenses the money does not suffice: his landlords are now asking to be
> paid in Portici and Gragnano, and in Naples he pays every time he passes
> through there.

> This supplicant has never come with a petition of personal concern, yet
> the present urgency forces him to interrupt this period in which he always
> has tried to apply himself in matters of discovery useful for Your Royal
> Service – when his slight powers have permitted – and to pay the expenses
> of his assignments without begging for anything. All the other employees in
> service to Your Royal House enjoy free houses and other assistance, such as
> the draftsmen, engravers, and others who are of less character yet receive a
> greater salary than the supplicant. Nor are their chores less scientific and
> burdensome than his own, and they are comfortable and can subsist and

attend to their duties. The supplicant, however, not only has to copy drawings and be in his house, but he must survey the plans and maps of all kinds,
organize work in three distant locales, acting practically like a courier, mine
the tunnels, respond to the concerns of Your Royal Treasury, and inconveniences of every sort that can happen . . .

Therefore he humbly supplicates the Clemency of Your Majesty to
deign in his regard and in that of Your Royal Munificence to grant him
some 15 ducats a month in aid, as well as a house in Portici or Resina.[62]

In another letter to Fogliani which he must have dispatched at roughly the same
time, he repeated that his rations did not suffice for feeding and maintaining his
horse and that his frequent travels wore out his uniforms (in particular the
buttons) three times more quickly than usual. He pointed out how expensive it
was to live and eat out constantly, especially when he had to support at the same
time his servant and the assistants that helped him in the surveying and recon-
naissance of sites throughout the bay in preparation of his cartographic map. He
noted in particular that his weekly trips to Gragnano alone took two days and
that in addition he used six days out of each month at Pozzuoli, which meant
that he spent at least fourteen days each month on the road. To facilitate these
frequent, often hurried travels, he now stipulated that the court should pay to
upgrade his conveyance from a single-horse to a two-horse carriage, estimating
the cost at 150 ducats for the new carriage and a second horse; that his rations
be raised accordingly; and that he receive an additional 14 ducats for his
expenses for the days he had to travel. Alcubierre, he pointed out, drew monthly
pay of 70 ducats, four rations, and 6 ducats per month travel expenses, plus a
bonus of 30 ducats a year, whereas Weber drew only 28 ducats of monthly pay
and 7 ducats per month expenses yet traveled at least as much as Alcubierre.[63]

When a copy of Weber's petition was forwarded to Alcubierre for his comment, he evidently became incensed, and this must have precipitated the outpouring of disgust over Weber's behavior communicated to Fogliani in his letter
quoted earlier. In addition to those remarks, he complained in particular that
the overall site plans that he had wanted of Pompeii, Stabiae, and Herculaneum,
as well as the map of the Cratere Maritimo, had yet to be finished:

Concerning the other buildings discovered in Pompeii (or perhaps another of the cities [previously] cited) at Torre Annunziata, plans were also
made of its amphitheater. As for those relating to Stabiae in Gragnano,
when Weber entered into service I handed him the design of all the
buildings, roads, and districts which had appeared up until that time [i.e.,
his "general plan"], and since little more needed to be done there to

continue the survey, little was in fact done. Considering how little has been accomplished of this order for topographic charts, or rather the plans of these cities, since it is not possible to draw any design of them except for [one showing] a few disparate fragments of buildings disinterred in various places, it is impossible to make a plan of the whole (which would be very good) of each one of these cities. Virtually nothing has been done in a year in carrying out the order to make a plan of the subterranean excavations at Resina, or rather "ichnographics," in the two grottoes of Ciceri and Moscardillo [properties at Herculaneum], where work has gone on for some time . . .

And concerning the matter expressed in this same petition of his inability to subsist on his salary and rations, of the destruction of his uniforms, the wear and tear on his carriage, and the debts he has contracted: all is the result of his lack of conduct, the salary being ample for an engineer and his rations [being] enough to pay his expenses and maintain his horse without having to incur the many debts he has, about which he appeals to me constantly in Resina and even to the workmen in the excavations . . .

Don Carlos Weber has performed poorly . . . and I am little satisfied. Nor do I fail to rebuke him continually, in particular that he not alter the manner in which matters have proceeded in the past, with better progress than at the present.[64]

Even the excavation foreman at Resina, Josef de Corcoles, later complained to Alcubierre, in late August 1751, that Weber rarely visited the excavations but nevertheless regularly vetoed Corcoles's plans for expanding the tunnels. It may have been such open criticism that induced Weber to attempt to placate Alcubierre by announcing a few days later that he was returning to work on the Cratere Maritimo map and that measurements had been taken for several other plans at Herculaneum.[65]

Alcubierre had clearly begun to recognize Weber as a growing threat to his own authority and control of the excavations. A two-horse carriage alone would have imparted a certain prestige to Weber's position that Alcubierre could not have tolerated. But just as Alcubierre could boast of his "discovery" of Herculaneum, Weber saw that he was now the one responsible for the continued recovery of these buried treasures, whereas Alcubierre was residing in Naples to attend to his military duties. Weber's perception of his own worth and the need for such symbols of prestige as a larger carriage, an ample expense account, and free lodgings are further indications, along with the enormous burden of his nuptial settlement, that he longed to maintain a style of living in keeping with his noble ancestry yet well beyond the means of a military engineer. Alcubierre's grip on the excavations was firm, however, and he successfully persuaded his superiors to deny Weber's requests both on this occasion and again in November 1751, when Alcubierre reiterated his belief that Weber was performing his duties poorly.[66]

PART 2

Excavations and Methodology

3

The Discovery of the Villa dei Papiri

During 1750 and 1751 excavations were taking place at a wide range of sites, so it is hardly surprising that in these first years Weber found himself overwhelmed by his responsibilities. The sites under his care stretched from Baiae and Pozzuoli, along the northwest coast of the Bay of Naples, to the Villa of San Marco at Stabiae and the "Villa of Pollio" at Sorrento, at the southwest end of the bay.[1] A number of tunnels were still in use at Herculaneum, where Weber was completing a large air shaft into the theater and reorienting the ramp that gave access to the underground tunnels.[2] He had begun work on a plan of the theater as well. Several tombs had been uncovered on the Moscardillo property in Resina, but the high water table was causing water to seep into the tunnels beneath the Bisogno property along the Vico di Mare, causing numerous difficulties.[3]

The most rewarding site had been opened on May 2, 1750, along the "Calle de Ciceri" (Via Cecere, the modern Via Roma) and beneath the Bosco di Sant' Agostino between Portici and Resina, just two months before Weber assumed his duties. As in the case of the theater, the initial discovery had been made when a landowner drilling a well had turned up a number of colored marble fragments. Alcubierre brought in one of the winches, and work began some 25 meters below ground level in conditions described in the early reports as "very narrow and difficult," owing to the density of the volcanic matrix and the constant seepage of water into the tunnels. By the end of the month neither workmen nor torches could function within the tunnels, and the work ceased temporarily, so that a second shaft could be sunk to accommodate the air pump and the bucket and cables for a second winch.[4]

The remarkable discoveries made here were to far offset these inconveniences. After some initial problems with orienting the tunnels to the architectural remains, the site foreman, Miguel de Çiria, with his five excavators work-

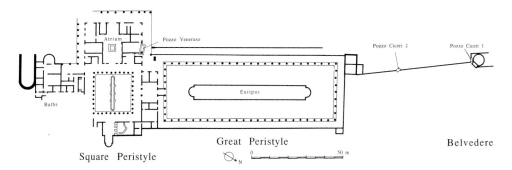

Figure 20. Schematic plan showing the principal architectural features of the Villa dei
Papiri at Herculaneum. The alignment of the belvedere and the terrace wall with the rest
of the villa has been corrected in accordance with the discoveries made in the recent
excavations (1986–93). The Pozzo Ciceri 1 and Pozzo Ciceri 2 are the original Bourbon-
era shafts; the Pozzo Veneruso is the access shaft employed at present. (Author's plan.)

ing below and two forced laborers operating the winch, finally hit upon a
circular pavilion buried some 30 meters below the surface.[5] This elegant structure later proved to be connected, by means of a terraced footpath lined with
grapevines, to a great villa suburbana that stands roughly 100 meters west of the
theater (Fig. 20). The most striking feature of this villa's plan is its large
rectangular peristyle, measuring about 94.4 meters by 31.7 meters. The
peristyle encloses a green space, or viridarium, with an enormous central
euripus, or pool, itself measuring about 66.7 meters long, 7.1 meters wide, and
1.8 meters deep. Linked to this is a canonical atrium house, with alae and a
tablinum looking onto the bay and the atrium backing onto a smaller, square
peristyle of 100 Roman feet (29.6 m.), its thirty-six columns enclosing a fountain garden traversed by a long narrow pool. Since Vitruvius (Vitr. 6.5.3) states
that suburban villas were entered through their peristyles, the principal entrance should lie somewhere in the direction of the Royal Road, the modern
Corso Resina. Beyond the atrium, in the direction of ancient Herculaneum,
stands another set of rooms that includes a small bath complex and a library. In
all, the villa sprawls over some 250 meters of prime bayfront property.[6] Over the
course of the next eleven years, excavations in this villa yielded a spectacular
array of bronze statues, which quickly became the center of the king's collection
of antiquities, along with the charred remains of the library's papyrus scrolls,
which sparked the curiosity of eighteenth-century intellectuals and gave the villa
its popular modern name, the "Villa dei Papiri" at Herculaneum.

The pavilion's opus sectile pavement, made of giallo antico, africano, and other
precious marbles, cut into triangles and intricately arranged in concentric circles,

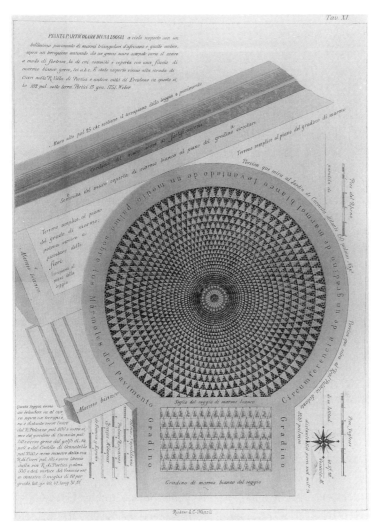

Figure 21. Engraving of Weber's plan of the belvedere, with its circular mosaic, from the
Villa dei Papiri, Herculaneum, dated January 13, 1751. From *StErc*, pl. 11.

served as the subject of what must have been Weber's first completed illustration
(Fig. 21). The discovery of this pavement appears in the report for August 1,
1750, just shortly after Weber arrived in Portici, and already by the middle of that
month he had begun this drawing, of which only an engraving now remains. The
original drawing may have been intended primarily for archival purposes, since
the mosaic was too large to remove intact and so had to be cut into segments and
reassembled later at the museum.[7] On the engraved version, Weber worked out
the scales in Neapolitan, Spanish, German, English, Milanese, and French feet,

but he gave most of the measurements in Neapolitan palms alone. As in the plans of Montemayor and Dorgemont, the primary annotations are written in Italian, although certain remarks do appear in Spanish, the language used at that time by Weber and the Bourbon court for all official correspondence.[8] The annotations describe the design and content of the pavement in detail and its relation to the terrace wall and to the adjacent architectural elements such as the stairs leading up to the pavement. Weber called the pavilion a "belvedere" overlooking the sea, the first indication that he was attempting to place the archaeological ruins within their original landscape. Moreover, he triangulated the site into several important topographical features, stating the precise distances from the site to the gardens in the nearby palace of Caravita and to the fortress of Granatello and even to as far away as the summit of Mount Vesuvius, providing as well its longitudinal and latitudinal coordinates.

The demands of the excavations clearly took time away from the extensive surveying required for completing the Cratere Maritimo project, and, as a consequence, Weber did not finish this map until late in 1752. In November of that year, however, Bayardi wrote to the prime minister complaining that Weber's completed map had been drawn on so large a scale that it would not fit even the large folio pages of his publications. Moreover, he complained that Vesuvius appeared flat, that several details were superfluous or confused, and that sites had been inaccurately identified.[9]

BAYARDI, TANUCCI, AND THE ACCADEMIA ERCOLANESE

Ottavio Bayardi, whose ties to the Farnese family and the court of Pope Clement XII had earned him something of a reputation in Parma and Rome, was a cousin of Prime Minister Fogliani. He was a member of numerous Italian academies, including the Accademia Etrusca di Cortona,[10] as well as English ones, such as the Royal Society of London and the Society of Antiquarians. After serving as an advocate of Charles of Bourbon at the Vatican, he had come to Naples in June 1746, and by 1747 his cousin had arranged for him to have sole responsibility for publishing Charles's rapidly expanding collection of antiquities. His annual compensation was some 4,000 Neapolitan ducats, more than ten times what Weber earned. He had been favored for this position over the distinquished Neapolitan scholars Alessio Simmaco Mazzocchi[11] and Giacomo Martorelli and thus immediately became subject to bitter resentment from this faction, especially since, despite his impeccable credentials, he had no background in field archaeology. Bayardi undertook this project with enthusiasm, making frequent visits to the excavations, as he later stated in the preface to his first publication: "I entered the excavations and observed the structures at my leisure; I considered the antiquities removed from the ruins."[12] But like Alcubierre before him, he fell victim to the noxious conditions inside the tunnels, and by 1750 severe asthma prevented him from further visits to the ruins and slowed his work considerably.[13]

Bayardi finally managed to publish his *Prodromo delle antichità d'Ercolano* in 1752, but it was quickly ridiculed as completely inadequate: in the five initial volumes, totaling 2,678 pages, Bayardi chronicled the life and labors of Hercules, including digressions on the genealogy of the kings of Crete and the different forms of measurement used in the ancient world. Only in the first volume did he deal in any manner with the antiquities of Herculaneum, specifically mentioning the statues and inscriptions of the Balbi. His primary object was to prove unequivocably to the skeptics that this city was in fact the ancient Herculaneum founded by Hercules and known from classical literature.

Criticism of his *Prodromo* was swift and unrelenting, appearing even before the work was complete. As Sir James Gray wryly remarked, "A more exact account of these discoveries will some time or other be given by Monsignor Bayardi, who, in three large quarto volumes already printed, has not finished his introduction."[14] Yet none of these criticisms affected Bayardi, who, at the conclusion of his fifth volume, proclaimed his intention of continuing to at least a ninth.[15]

The indictments of Bayardi's work, both by his contemporaries and by modern scholars,[16] are primarily leveled against his tedious prose style – although Martorelli's later excursus on ancient writing and writing instruments carried on for a full two volumes[17] – and against his dilatoriness in finishing this project while preventing others from pursuing their own research on these fascinating antiquities. Yet by his own account Bayardi envisaged the *Prodromo* as the indispensable foundation of a much greater work that would encompass all aspects of the excavations:

> I will open the way to a much greater undertaking, that of placing before the eyes of each man in many volumes the explanation of the structures, both public and private, of the pictures, statues, vases, inscriptions, and of every antiquity that has been found within the circuit of the discovered city. I will follow the method of the noted Father Montfaucon; I will have each illustration displayed scrupulously. Then I will add a succinct but pithy explanation, sending the reader from time to time to the *Prodromo*, in which he will find the foundations of all I will assert bit by bit regarding the chronology, geography, distances, and other principles pertaining to antiquity.[18]

Bayardi responded to the harsh criticism with which his *Prodromo* had been received by quickly publishing, in 1754, a catalog of all the major finds from the Vesuvian cities. This *Catalogo degli antichi monumenti dissotterrati dalla discoperta città di Ercolano* amounts to little more than a listing and brief description of the artifacts, similar in many ways to the contents of Alcubierre's own weekly reports to the king, although Bayardi at times provides even less information about provenance.[19] He apparently perceived this work as merely a stopgap measure to assuage his critics in the court, who had become increasingly frustrated by his blocking of their own research and embarrassed by the continual censure from the international community for the Bourbons' long delay in adequately publishing the finds. Bayardi still maintained that the unfinished *Prodromo* would represent the real fruit of his labors, for he planned to produce at least two additional volumes. He reiterated in the preface of his *Catalogo* the goals laid out in his *Prodromo* of publishing the ruins of Herculaneum in a form approaching an archaeological monograph:

> In the *Prodromo* I will deal in a short time with the origins, the progress, and the ruins of Herculaneum; I will point out its precise location and describe the history of its discovery since Prince d'Elbeuf resided in that region down to today, and I will deal with all the adventures of that same discovery. I will add plans of the excavations and of the ruins, and I will give an account of the precise spots where this or that piece was unearthed, and moreover I will make known the site of Herculaneum as well as its remains. I will place before the eyes of all the coast of this maritime crater, formed and verified with minute, meticulous exactitude.[20]

These later volumes were never published, for Bayardi's claims on this material were supplanted by the foundation of the Accademia Ercolanese in 1755, of which he became a reluctant and inactive member.

Bayardi's fortunes had begun to wane when Marchese Bernardo Tanucci assumed many of Prime Minister Fogliani's duties on June 9, 1755. Tanucci, who had served as minister of justice since 1734, had long been opposed to Bayardi's appointment and now quickly sought to isolate him from the court's inner circle. On December 14, 1755, Tannuci acted upon his own displeasure and the complaints of Neapolitan scholars about the direction of the excavations by creating the Reale Accademia Ercolanese di Archeologia, a committee of scholars that was to oversee the publication of the antiquities uncovered at sites throughout the Vesuvian region. He appointed as its first members fifteen of Naples's most preeminent scholars in the fields of philology, philosophy, jurisprudence, literature, history, geology and archaeology. Several of them had already written short treatises on various aspects of the excavations, especially on matters that did not require direct consultation of the ruins or the artifacts themselves, such as inscriptions.

Tanucci's creation of the Accademia underscored that the exclusive right of publishing the finds from the Vesuvian cities was to be a purely Neapolitan concern. The members were to convene twice a month to debate how to frame the commentaries for each artifact, whether it be a painting, statue, or other small find, for final publication. Written elucidations were exchanged among members so that each could make the appropriate emendations, but the final distillation was left to the Accademia's secretary to ensure a homogeneous style. The final publications were arranged typologically, and each artifact was dealt with in isolation, stating the general provenance for each (e.g., "Resina," "Civitá") but with no information provided on the specific building, whether public or private, in which it had been found. The discussions were based largely on visual analysis and description of the particular subject depicted in each piece, supported by profuse reference to Classical and Renaissance texts as well as more contemporary writings.[21]

With the creation of the Accademia Ercolanese, the manner of publishing the antiquities from these ancient sites was radically altered. Although Bayardi's control of his material had been somewhat tyrannical, his approach had at its core a single guiding vision that sought to present a complete picture of the antiquities. On the other hand, the Accademia's approach was rooted in scholarly, interdisciplinary debate that dealt with the antiquities in a piecemeal and compartmentalized, albeit erudite, manner.[22] Nor did the Accademia necessarily speed up the process of publishing the finds: the first volume of paintings appeared in 1757 and the last in 1779, whereas the first volume of bronzes was published only twelve years after the Accademia's foundation, in 1767. As one anxious scholar observed in 1756, "according to their method of discussing things in their assemblies, [the Accademia Ercolanese] will not explain two dozen antiquities a year."[23] Following the completion of only the first two volumes of paintings and then the departure to Spain of Charles of Bourbon in 1759, the Accademia ceased its regular meetings and was held together only through the strength of its secretary, Pasquale Carcani. Already in May 1756, Bayardi, whose grand vision had fallen victim to his pedantic, sluggish manner and the fact that it was perhaps too great a task for a single man, had been granted leave by Tannuci to return to Rome, ostensibly for reasons of health.[24]

Weber's map of the Cratere Maritimo therefore had formed an integral part of Bayardi's original concept of the best means for illustrating the ancient ruins of Herculaneum. When the map failed to meet Bayardi's requirements, however, Alcubierre was ordered to correct its errors and reduce the size.[25] These corrections and the reduction were made by Giuseppe Liberati with the advice of Bayardi, and the whole was engraved by Pierre Jacques Gaultier in 1754, the same year as the publication of Bayardi's *Catalogo*, though Bayardi had apparently already rejected the notion of including it in that work.[26] The final version of Weber's map was published only three years later, in 1757, immediately following the title page of the first volume of the Accademia Ercolanese's *Le antichità di Ercolano esposte*.[27]

The centerpiece of the map is the collapsed cone of Mount Vesuvius with the peak of Monte Somma (Fig. 22). Spread out around the foot of Vesuvius and along the inner shore of the Bay of Naples are inscribed the names of all the towns, with separate symbols used to differentiate large towns from small. The area included on the map begins at Foce di Licola on the Tyrrhenian coast and winds down to Punta della Campanella on the Sorrentine Peninsula, covering inland sites as far as Mataloni to the northeast and Lettere to the southeast. These towns and all the churches, church properties, and fortresses are set against a physiographic background, with schematic representations of fields and trees sketched in. The different symbols marking the locations of these features were varied to indicate whether a building was still standing or in ruins. Particular attention was paid to all the known ancient sites, labeled with the popular toponyms of the time, such as "Città," "Schola di Virgilio," "Tempio di Circe." More important, a separate symbol indicated which sites were under excavation at that time. The preface to the volume in which it was published notes that the map thus "places under the eyes of foreigners our whole shoreline and those places where excavations are being made." Weber's map was therefore intended to serve more as a record of the current state of the royal excavations than as a simple topographical reference map. So accurate and detailed a map probably would have illustrated Bayardi's projected opus more successfully than it did the *Antichità*, where it appears to have been inserted almost as an afterthought and is referred to only a single time.

The fact that it documents current excavations sets Weber's Cratere Maritimo map apart conceptually from contemporary plans such as G.B. Nolli's *Nuova pianta di Roma* of 1748, which showed all the known ancient ruins in relation to the topography of the modern city. Even the *Mappa topografica della città di Napoli e de' suoi contorni*, conceived by Giovanni Carafa, duca di Noja, in 1750 but completed only in 1775, recorded only the existence of ancient sites and ruined buildings within the modern topography, not whether a site was under excavation. Moreover, both plans were executed at a scale considerably larger than Weber's published version.[28]

EXCAVATING THE VILLA DEI PAPIRI

Some of the results of Weber's surveying work for the Cratere Maritimo map had already been applied to his illustration of the Villa dei Papiri's belvedere, where the accurate measurements he provided helped orient this underground struc-ture to visible features aboveground. These dimensions proved crucial to modern researchers in locating the "Pozzo Ciceri 1," the well that originally led the Bourbon excavators to the discovery of the belvedere and then served as a primary access shaft to the excavation tunnels, in both the eighteenth- and the twentieth-century investigations. The entrance to the shaft stands 5.10 meters beneath the cortile of the Villa Vittozzi, at Via Roma 31 in modern Ercolano, and is striking testimony to the extremely claustrophobic and difficult conditions under which the excavators had to work. The arched entrance, quoined in square masonry, is itself only 0.85 meters wide and 1.26 meters high in the center. Above this is a secondary window, 0.40 meters wide and 0.60 meters high, through which it is believed the lifting cables were operated. Inside, the mouth of the shaft measures a mere 1.22 meters by 1.16 meters, barely large enough for an individual to pass through, especially if laden down with equipment or finds, and its sheer vertical walls narrow to only 1.05 meters by 1.07 meters as the shaft makes its 27-meter descent to the excavation tunnels below.[29]

Although the techniques that Weber employed in excavating the villa were largely the same as Alcubierre's and differed little from those used in general mining, from the outset Weber initiated a more methodical approach. The tunnel connecting the two shafts sunk in alignment with one another in May 1750 had established an axis along which the excavations could be aligned. This axis was extended to the east as the primary excavation tunnel, the *gruta derecha*, or straight tunnel, referred to frequently in the excavation documents. Although its orientation had been set solely by pursuing the line of the terrace wall connecting the main body of the villa with the belvedere, this artery eventually would cut fortuitously almost straight through the entire length of the villa, running virtually parallel to the outer walls of the great peristyle. Alcubierre or Bardet would have diverted this tunnel immediately to follow the walls of the peristyle, since experience had shown that the greatest number of antiquities was usually concentrated along walls. But Weber maintained the tunnel's straight alignment for the first three years of the excavations, even though almost a full year passed between the time the excavators entered the peristyle and the discovery of the first major statue inside the viridarium.[30] This suggests that Weber recognized that he was excavating a large, open structure like a peristyle and that one of his first goals had been to establish its dimensions.

Figure 22. Weber's *Cratere Maritimo, o parte del Golfo di Napoli,* as engraved by Pierre Jacques Gaultier in 1754. The cone of Mount Vesuvius occupies the upper portion of the center, with the sites of "Cività" and "Lapillo" (Pompeii) indicated to the right of it and the ruins of the "Teatro di Ercolano" drawn cursorily directly below it. From the first volume of *Le antichità di Ercolano* (Naples 1757).

Alternatively, he may have been attempting to link this tunnel with Alcubierre's earlier ramp and tunnels along the Vico di Mare, which he may have reckoned stood closer to the villa than they did.

Apart from serving as the main corridor down which workmen could pass and antiquities could be transported for removal from the site, the *gruta derecha* acted as a baseline with which the excavators could align their secondary perpendicular and parallel tunnels. It was particularly useful in the excavation of the peristyle, where artifacts might be encountered at any point and there were few architectural elements to which to orient the excavations and to tie the finds. When the excavators reached the rooms clustered around the atrium of the villa and the tunnels could trace the lines of architectural features once again, the importance of maintaining the *gruta derecha* as a means of orientation diminished considerably. Nevertheless, because of its importance, great care was taken in the construction and maintenance of this tunnel. It is some 2.50 meters wide and 2.00 meters high, with a vaulted roof and walls finished off with a thin coat of stucco. This last gesture presumably was added for the benefit of dignitaries and other visitors who were ushered down this tunnel to points of interest throughout the site, some of whom scrawled graffiti in its surface (Fig. 23).[31]

The auxiliary tunnels used to investigate the rest of the villa were similar to the ones Cochin and Bellicard encountered in the theater. They were hardly wider than the access shafts, and two workmen could have passed only with great difficulty, since the tunnels averaged between 1.70 meters and 1.80 meters high and 0.80 meter and 1.00 meter wide, only rarely expanding to 2.50 meters wide. These were enlarged, or entire rooms cleared out, only when fragments or groups of statues needed to be pursued or when mosaic pavements had to be extricated. Given such cramped conditions, it is remarkable that the excavators were able to remove marble statues taller than 2.00 meters in sound condition, although the daybooks often mention that large mosaics had to be broken up to allow them to be hoisted up the shafts.[32]

Much of the structure of the villa had been distorted during the eruption as the force of the mud knocked walls off their foundations, buckled mosaic pavements, and leveled colonnades. Just as visitors elsewhere in the city had remarked, the pattern of destruction was uniform yet random, as in the case of the square peristyle, where the mud had come crashing over the roofs into the open courtyard, making the columns collapse inward. Because so many of the architectural elements had been dislocated, Weber had to modify the manner in which he oriented his tunnels. Most of the living spaces here were paved with mosaics. The design was a simple white ground with patterns picked out in

Figure 23. View of the *gruta derecha* in the process of being cleared during the recent excavations (1993). This originally served as the main access tunnel for the Bourbon excavators in the Villa dei Papiri at Herculaneum but was later filled back in to prevent the ground above from subsiding. (Courtesy of Dr. Umberto Cioffi, Director of the Excavations.)

black or polychrome tesserae, though some had more elaborate geometric patterns. Weber soon realized that variations in the mosaic designs could guide him from room to room and help him to reconstruct the villa's plan. In order to recover the design of the square peristyle, for example, he first isolated several of the collapsed columns from the western and southern colonnades, ascertaining their intercolumniations in the process. He then followed a black border that marked the inner line of the colonnade, rather than pursuing the columns themselves, relying only on small cuttings at regular intervals along his tunnels to verify the location of each column. In this way he quickly ascertained the dimensions of the peristyle, since as soon as the black border made a ninety-degree angle, he knew the colonnade had ended and that he need not pursue additional columns. Elsewhere, mosaic patterns or emblemata signaled the thresholds of doorways where the walls themselves had been destroyed or marked the beginning of corridors, and these too he pursued, in an effort to locate other rooms and isolate additional antiquities.

As the number and quality of ancient bronze and marble statues recovered increased, Weber realized that the discovery of this richly decorated villa was a bonanza not only for the Bourbon court but for his own career. In late April 1752, he addressed a letter directly to Prime Minister Fogliani, again requesting monthly compensation of 10 ducats to help cover his expenses and also request-ing a promotion to lieutenant colonel, which would have made him virtually Alcubierre's peer.[33] As justification he pointed to the great perils he endured in extracting these priceless treasures for the king from their underground tombs, which, he claimed, had resulted in illness requiring medical attention and a period of convalescence:

> With the greatest respect and veneration I place myself before the feet of Your Eminence, supplicating you submissively that you deign to keep me in the highest protection and benevolence that I have always had the honor and fortune to enjoy. However, at the present and fitting time, I must be inopportune in imploring with as effective and humble obsequi-ousness as possible His powerful aid and magnanimity. So that it be possible through the generous influence of His Highest Person, as one of His humble servants, to obtain through the Royal Clemency of His Maj-esty the favor which I am soliciting in the present petition to Your Emi-nence concerning extraordinary service to the court, since with evident and inevitable peril to my life I have shunned no fatigue or labor in order to procure numerous finds, singular and indeed rare, and, on reflection, things for which the academics of Europe would pay a fortune. The two pavements alone, to buy similar ones and to buy the African marbles and others, would cost 1,500 ducats each.[34] The great bronze statue of the Roman woman found in the theater, how much would it cost?[35] The statue with its bronze raven[36] and the other four bronzes from the Pozzo di Ciceri transported on the same day by Royal Order to the Royal Palace in Naples;[37] the marble vase [see Fig. 51];[38] the [lacuna] four statues of the same; the candelabra, all of bronze;[39] all the paintings, of which [lacuna] there are very many quite good and rare. Just to make these objects anew would cost a small treasure! But since they are antiquities, nearly 2,000 years old or more, for their verification and restitution to the historical sciences they are worth a great fortune. So grand, laudable, magnificent and glorious a work for His Most Wise Royal Highness!

The greater part of the aforementioned precious objects I have been seeking to procure for the space of two years, with clear danger to my life, not only on a single occasion but daily, and even twice a day, as a result not only of the burden – dangerous and abhorrent, if not despicable – of my being attached to a rope and lowered into a well 102 palms [27 m.] deep, where I have been exposed, and am exposed, to many unfortunate accidents and events of a different kind, but, so as not to tire Your Eminence with but a single example, that the sleeve of thick iron on the wheel [of the winch] broke – what no one could foresee since there were invisible and intrinsic cracks – and by a miracle I had enough time to be lifted from the well, and the supervisor and others congratulated me for having been reborn then; and Pacifico repaired the sleeve.[40] One is exposed to similar accidents in the support for the wheel, the axle, the ropes, the net, and the forced laborers who run it, to whom one commits his life. This activity should obviously be considered dangerous, although it should not be condemned and criticized too much as inconvenient for a person of status, and so I suffer in silence . . .

Therefore I humbly supplicate the benignity of Your Eminence that he deign to reflect upon this matter and this petition and to obtain for me from the Royal Piety the rank and salary for extraordinary services so costly and dangerous to my life, so that with the one I might liquidate my debts, and, with the other, render honor to a duty scorned by all and recompense the danger to my life which for two years I have suffered, and am suffering, with the happy success of discoveries and glory to His Majesty.[41]

Bigotti wrote favorably on Weber's behalf to the prime minister, noting his zeal for royal service, his punctuality and incessant labor, and the competence with which he performed his duties. Acknowledging Weber's "continual and extraordinary debts of which he has informed me," by which he may be referring not only to the burden of Weber's nuptial settlement but also to his penchant for maintaining a style of life well beyond his means, Bigotti recommended Weber be granted this monthly compensation of 10 ducats, but he deferred to the prime minister's authority regarding the promotion. Weber immediately requested that this raise be made retroactive to the date when he was first posted to Portici (Fig. 24).[42] It is doubtful that this was granted, and apparently Fogliani also denied the promotion. Alcubierre's position on the matter is clear from the fact that a few months later he called for Weber's dismissal.[43]

For the first two years of excavation, the sole source of natural light and air

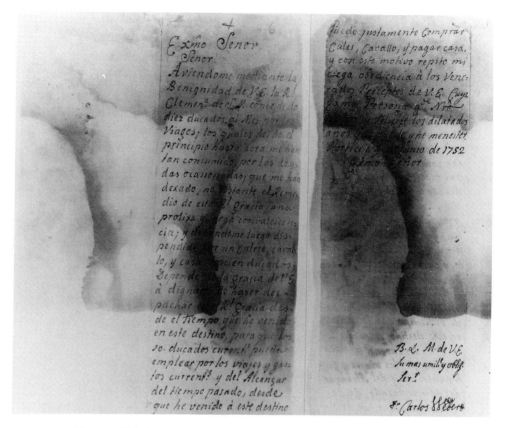

Figure 24. Weber's second request to Prime Minister Fogliani for an increase in compensation for the personal expenses he incurred while performing his duties for the excavations, dated June 4, 1752. (Courtesy of the Archivio di Stato, Naples [Casa Reale Antica 1539, Inc. 44].)

inside the tunnels came from the two Pozzi Ciceri, at the far western extremity of the excavations. It was only in July 1752 that an access ramp was begun, to facilitate the removal of the finds, which had gradually begun to increase in size and number.[44] The entrance to this barrel-vault ramp, 3 meters wide, was not oriented to the *gruta derecha* but began roughly above what eventually would be identified as the euripus of the square peristyle, some 190 meters to the east of the Pozzo Ciceri 1. The ramp sloped down toward the west to intersect with the tunnels that had already begun to pierce the northeast corner of the great peristyle. A third airshaft was added sometime before 1756 near the east end of the *gruta derecha*.[45] This new air shaft became increasingly necessary as the excavators gradually began to fill the *gruta derecha* back in with material excavated from elsewhere. To ensure the stability of this and other abandoned tunnels should later tunneling venture too closely to them, the excavators used rams to compact the backfill as tightly as possible. By July 1756, the *gruta derecha* had been completely resealed from roughly the center of the great peristyle's euripus back to the Pozzi Ciceri.[46]

Because the perception of night and day was lost in these dark, airless tunnels 27 meters belowground, work could continue at all hours by lamplight, if necessary; on several occasions the daybooks report a find made late at night.[47] To light their way, the workmen carved niches to hold small terracotta lamps in the walls of the tunnels, roughly 1 meter from the ground and 3 meters to 6 meters apart.[48] As was the case throughout this area, the excavators also had to contend with the seepage of groundwater, although the problems here seem to have been less severe than at other locations. Weber reported that the water table stood 5 palms (1.25 m.) below one of the wells in the square peristyle, and the euripus in the great peristyle could not be fully excavated until the water table finally dropped during a dry year.[49]

Not long after work began at the villa, the excavators had encountered a number of preexisting tunnels which they believed had been dug by the "ancients" in search of buried works of art and building material. These were not unique to the Villa dei Papiri, for, as already noted, similar tunnels could be found throughout the area of Portici and Resina and even had facilitated the rediscovery of Herculaneum. Piaggio noted, "It frequently happens that during excavation they encounter similar tunnels which were made by the ancients, but so low and narrow that one cannot understand how a man could walk. Upon finding one of these, they can be certain that some precious statues already have been carried off."[50] Piaggio believed that because the tunnels were dug in a systematic fashion, the ancient excavators must have known precisely where to dig. Alcubierre observed in a letter to the prime minister that he believed the tunnels were the work of Romans sent from Rome to recover artifacts from the buried cities and cited an inscription found in the area in support of his theory.[51] D'Arthenay concluded that Domitianic coins found by the excavators of Herculaneum must have been dropped by these ancient plunderers.[52] D'Elbeuf's experience at the theater demonstrates, however, that without conclusive evidence associating such tunnels with specific parties, it is virtually impossible to determine if they had been dug by someone in antiquity or by a landowner sinking a well sometime in the intervening sixteen hundred years.

Evidence of the activities of these earlier plunderers was found in the southwest and northwest corners of the great peristyle and along the north portico of the square peristyle. The signs took the form of abandoned tunnels and large caverns left where mosaic pavements or statues had been removed. Apart from the absence of these pavements and the discovery of an occasional head or arm from a broken statue, it is not clear how extensive their depredations had been. But the presence of these tunnels made arduous working conditions even more complicated and perilous. In August 1755, for example, a fire had broken out when a workman's pick, and then a lamp, ignited some sulfur trapped inside an abandoned tunnel.[53] More common was the need to brace the disintegrating walls of the new tunnels or to fill in portions of the old ones to avoid creating a large void that might collapse when the Bourbon excavators stumbled onto them.[54]

Maintaining the integrity of the tunnels and the earth above was a constant struggle, in which the objectives of the excavations had to be weighed against the concerns of local property owners. Shortly after work began in earnest at the Villa dei Papiri, excavations began at "Epitaffio" in Portici, apparently the site of a moderate-size ancient bath complex.[55] At both sites, Weber experimented with new techniques of excavation intended to help resolve many of the difficulties of surveying and enhance the ability to perceive the architectural unity of the ancient remains. Rather than backfilling old tunnels with the fill from the new, he removed it completely from the site, leaving many of the tunnels accessible. This not only made surveying the site easier but prevented the workmen from following their rather embarrassing habit of tunneling into areas they had already excavated.

Weber's new system was, however, much more labor-intensive than the old system. It meant having shafts located near enough to the digging so that the fill did not need to be hauled an excessive distance to an access shaft; having enough men available to operate the winch for lifting the fill from below; and, ultimately, having to drop the fill down the shaft again and carry it back to refill the tunnels which were no longer of use.[56] Moreover, leaving tunnels accessible meant constructing a greater number of braces, which not only took laborers away from the business of recovering antiquities but increased the costs. Wooden beams were the most common means of support, and although these were relatively cheap and easy to install, elaborate trestlework became necessary as more extensive areas were opened up. These trestles had the unfortunate tendency to collapse, bringing down the roofs of the tunnels with them and also undermining the foundations of the modern houses above.[57] Weber therefore sought permission from Alcubierre to build masonry pillars, whose greater durability and relative ease of construction he believed would, over the long run, offset the initial expense. Many of these pillars were made simply of stones, carried each day from Granatello by the forced laborers, which were mortared together and left rough. Elsewhere, especially in the larger cavities, Weber

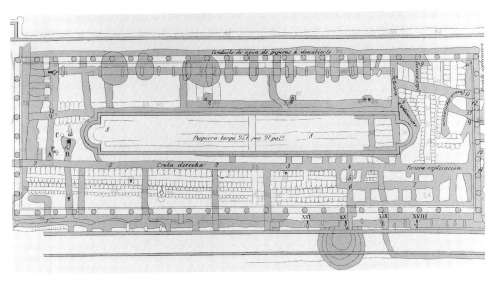

Figure 25. Portion of plan illustrating *los hurnillos*, the technique employed in excavating the great peristyle of the Villa dei Papiri at Herculaneum that created a honeycomb effect. From Comparetti and De Petra, *La villa ercolanese dei Pisoni*, pl. 24; based on Weber's plan of the villa (see Fig. 27 in the present volume), though the orientation has been inverted from Weber's original.

constructed more expensive buttresses made from cut stone blocks finished with stucco, into which both workmen and visitors scratched graffiti.[58]

Nothing could replace the effectiveness of backfilling for ensuring that the land above remained solid, however, and ultimately Weber was forced to return to the old method of excavating, especially as excavations became more intense in the great peristyle, where Weber, goaded on by Alcubierre, was determined to investigate every square meter in the pursuit of more antiquities. By 1757, most of the finds had been recovered fortuitously through a simple grid of tunnels that crisscrossed the area of the viridarium and the borders of the euripus. Secondary tunnels were opened off of these as needed, such as when a statue group or several fragments of a statue were encountered. To complete his search Weber adopted a technique he called *los hurnillos*. This involved carving out a great number of small semicircular niches along either side of a tunnel and refilling each with the material removed from the next one.[59] The resulting honeycomb of tunnels could not have withstood the pressure of the earth above had they been left open or simply been propped up by masonry pillars, so all of these, along with many of the secondary tunnels giving access to them, were backfilled as needed (Fig. 25).

Weber justified the use of these various new techniques by arguing that they

were necessary for drawing up the excavation plans he was under orders to
produce. But to Alcubierre all these new methodologies were tantamont to
"altering the manner in which matters had proceeded in the past," a charge he
had leveled against Weber before. In a letter to Prime Minister Fogliani,
Alcubierre cited the various hazards resulting from the use of the masonry
pillars and the greater expense of removing all of the fill, claiming that in the
past plans had been drawn to reflect the work of each day but that since the new
methods had been used no plans had been produced for some time.[60]

WEBER'S DOCUMENTATION OF THE VILLA

Despite Alcubierre's criticism, the excavation of the Villa dei Papiri resulted in
Weber's most important and enduring work. His detailed notes, sketched plans,
and illustrations are the best, and in some cases the only, documentation of the
ruins of this important villa, which remains buried to this day. In addition to his
drawing of the mosaic in the belvedere, the surviving corpus of Weber's illustrations for the villa includes three small drawings of the patterns of opus sectile
pavements, along with a larger colored illustration of the pavement taken from a
small room opening onto the great peristyle of the villa (Fig. 26). This pavement
has a central emblema of diamond-shaped colored marbles, enclosed in a
complicated meander border, with swastikas marking the center. Smaller pat-
terned panels mark the thresholds of doors, and the entire pavement is shown in
relation to the walls and doors of the room. A caption in Spanish not only
provides the dimensions and coloration of the central emblema but relates it to
the excavations as a whole, stating that it was found along the *gruta derecha*, 700
palms (185.15 m.) from the Pozzo Ciceri 1, in a room adjacent to one from
which were removed statues of "Minerva" and a "Vestal," some bronze herms,
and some papyrus scrolls.[61] The drawing is dated July 19, 1753, and specifically
notes that the excavations of this "Palacio" were ongoing; Weber obviously
realized that his audience included Charles of Bourbon. The trail of Weber's
drawings also leads to Bayardi. It is clear from his reference to the statue of
Minerva and from the dimensions he quotes that he composed the description
of these mosaics that he gives in the last pages of the *Catalogo* not from an
examination *in situ* but by looking at the drawings and their detailed caption.[62]

    Thus, although there is a hiatus of two years between the illustration of the
belvedere and of these mosaics, Weber evidently was drawing at least some of
the antiquities as he was uncovering them and was submitting the drawings to
his superiors. Yet, justifiably, Alcubierre still did not think that the architectural
plans he needed were being drawn. The problem may have been that Weber

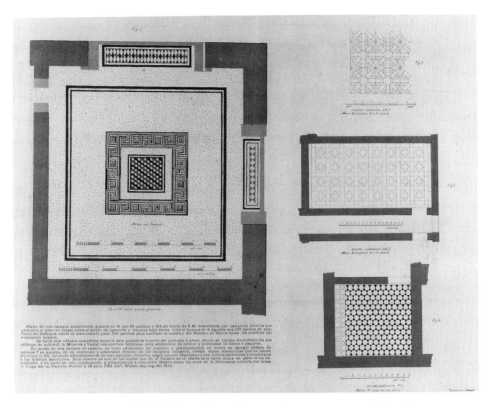

Figure 26. Engraving of Weber's illustrations of four mosaic pavements removed from the
Villa dei Papiri, Herculaneum. The annotations to the largest of these, dated July 19, 1753,
explain precisely where it was found in relation to other finds in the villa, such as the statue
of "Minerva" (i.e., the archaistic Athena Promachos, MN. 6007; see Fig. 63) and the
papyrus scrolls. The three smaller illustrations originally were drawn separately, but
Ruggiero combined all four here for publication. From *StErc*, pl. 10.

saw no reason to produce a plan until he had completed the excavations,
whereas Alcubierre felt that he was in constant need of presentation copies to
impress the prime minister and the king with their accomplishments. In February 1753, Alcubierre wrote again to Fogliani, complaining of certain "obstacles
that I continue to experience in these excavations on account of Don Carlos
Weber and which I have not put in writing, along with problems of his
obediency, which I have alluded to discretely on several occasions." Lamenting
that Weber had not lived up to Alcubierre's initial expectations and that plans
had been few and far between, Alcubierre asked that he be allowed to appoint a
new assistant, more to his liking – his brother Felippe, who was stationed at
Gaeta but was not, he said, being effectively employed there.[63]

That there was an absolute necessity for an overall site plan to permit a fuller comprehension of the architectural forms under investigation is made clear in the correspondence of Camillo Paderni. Despite his earlier criticism of the excavations and the court's concern about his presence at Portici, where as early as 1740 he was copying the ancient paintings without the court's approval, Paderni eventually became one of the handful of royal draftsmen assigned to draw the paintings and other antiquities to illustrate Bayardi's volumes. He later became curator of the royal antiquities and, ultimately, director of the Museum Herculanense, the museum established in 1758 in several rooms of the royal villa at Portici to display the chief finds from the excavations around Vesuvius.[64]

Paderni's responsibilities took him around the various excavation sites, where he made sketches of the wall paintings and mosaics *in situ* and selected the ones suitable for accession. He was, however, an artist rather than an architect, and his apparent indifference to ancient architecture was typical of the mentality of many members of the court at that time.[65] In correspondence written as late as 1754, Paderni failed to recognize that a single large villa was being excavated here, remarking in one letter read before the Royal Society of London that

> All the buildings discovered in this site [under the Bosco di Sant' Agostino] are noble. . . . In one of these buildings there has been found an entire library. . . . A little distant from the preceding site has been discovered another noble building, with a square court belonging to it, the inside of which has been hitherto examined. This square is formed with fluted columns of brick, stuccoed.[66]

In a second letter, written several months later, he was still hopelessly confused about the villa's layout, realizing that there was a garden next to a "palace" but believing that alongside this was "a long square, which formed a kind of forum . . . adorned throughout with columns of stucco; in the middle of which was a bath," evidently a reference to the euripus in the great peristyle. "Our greatest hopes," Paderni concluded, "are from the palace itself, which is of a very large extent. As yet we have only entered into one room, the floor of which is formed of mosaic work, not inelegant."[67]

Weber held firm and did not begin to produce a plan of the villa until 1754, four years after work had begun there. His large plan, drawn at a scale of about 1:230, makes it abundantly clear that the building was a single structure (Fig. 27). Much as in the 1747 plan of the theater, he acknowledged that it was still a buried ruin and gave precedence to the Bourbon-era and "ancient" tunnels used to investigate the site, superimposing the remains of the ancient masonry walls and mosaic pavements onto the maze of tunnels.[68] He drew the courses of the tunnels freehand, outlining them in black ink and giving a kind of mottling in small circles of ink and dabs of black gouache. There is some variation in how the tunnels are drawn, and they frequently overlap, suggesting that Weber wished to show how the excavations had wound their way through the ruins, but this progression is often difficult or impossible to follow. The architectural remains are shown in ruled black lines, and areas believed to have contained water (e.g., pools, water channels, drains) are colored brown. Certain features are drawn with a high degree of detail, such as the pavement of the belvedere and the stepped pyramid of a nearby fountain, whose intricate patterns have been worked out in pencil.[69] Black stippling indicates floors found paved in plain black and white mosaics, whereas crosshatching was used to mark more elaborate pavements of opus sectile or those with decorative patterns. Even so, Weber ensured that his own tunnels would stand out more clearly than most of the ancient architectural features.

Weber refined considerably the technique used on earlier plans of providing annotations by attaching a more detailed inventory of the main finds directly onto the plan and keying this into the ground plan to show the precise findspot of each artifact.[70] The inventory included facts concerning the excavations themselves, such as the location and depth of the access ramp and air shafts, or where additional investigations needed to be made; architectural features, such as the number of doors to a room or suggestions about a room's possible function; and the dimensions and brief descriptions of the works of art encountered in what he, like Paderni, called the "palace." The resulting document therefore combines a visual record of the progress of the excavations with a plan of the site and an inventory of the finds. In many ways it is the only means for following the course of these excavations, since the weekly reports became increasingly perfunctory as work here dragged on.

As essential as this plan is to understanding the archaeological remains, it is not without its faults. Weber rarely bothered to orient his plans to true north, and this one is no exception. Instead, he inverted the directions completely, enhancing the importance of his own work by laying out the plan along the axis of the *gruta derecha*, whose straightness he exaggerated, and labeling it at three points along its course. The top of the plan is therefore oriented toward the bay and closer to southwest than true north. As for errors in drafting, the most obvious is that he drew only nine columns along the west side of the great peristyle, whereas the east side has ten. Moreover, the excavations undertaken since 1986 have proved that the belvedere is on axis with the outer wall of the peristyle toward the bay, rather than with the euripus. Other errors may be revealed only through further excavation; so far, the renewed excavations have

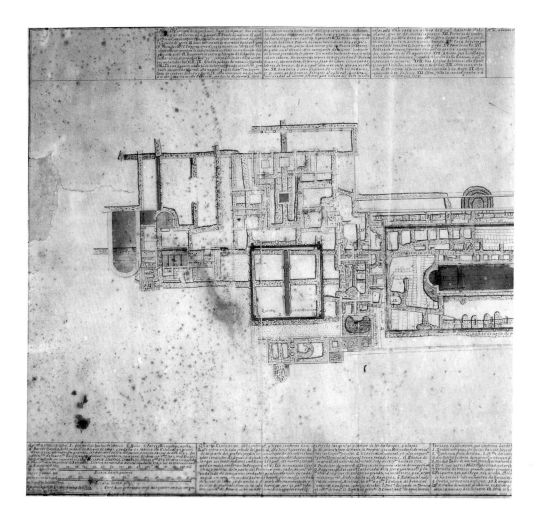

confirmed the accuracy of a number of details on Weber's plan. The plan gives
the impression that all the tunnels were dug on the same plane, although at one
point Weber had tunneled straight up from below to see whether upper stories
might be encountered, and recent investigations have shown that the excavators
also had come upon certain features at a lower level.[71] For the inventory of
finds, inscribed in registers above and below the ground plan, Weber divided
the site into five numbered "Explicaciones," or explanations, covering separate
periods of time, but he did not arrange them from left to right. Instead, the first
"Explicacion," with what appears to be the title of the work, begins in the lower
right-hand corner, and the others follow in a clockwise direction.[72]

Despite this rather awkward organization, Weber's plan appears at first sight to

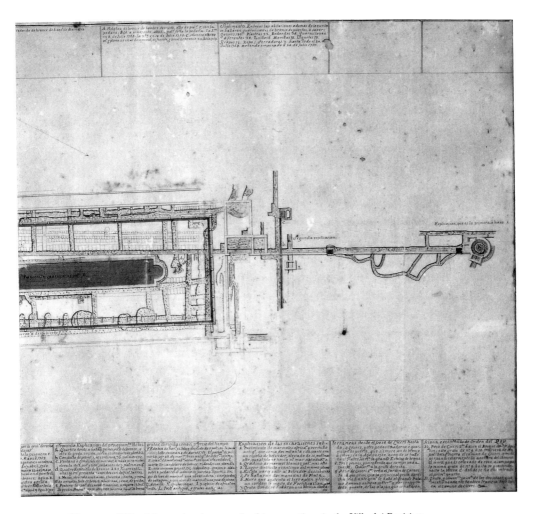

Figure 27. Weber's large plan documenting his excavations in the Villa dei Papiri at Herculaneum. The *gruta derecha* creates the central axis, and the entire structure is oriented with the Bay of Naples toward the top of the plan (cf. Fig. 20). The legend begins in the lower right-hand corner and moves clockwise around the plan. Weber completed this sometime in early 1758. It is now on display in the Museo Archeologico Nazionale, Naples (0.585 m. H × 1.235 m. W). (Courtesy of the Soprintendenza Archeologica di Napoli e Caserta.)

be the product of a single sitting. But in reality the plan shows excavations made some two years later than the dates for the latest finds listed in the inventories, and the whole plan documents the excavations in an incomplete state. The earliest date provided in the first "Explicacion" is August 15, 1750, when some bronze fittings were found near the belvedere at the point labeled "I.7," and although the pavement of the belvedere, found somewhat earlier, is illustrated on the ground plan, it is not described in the legend, presumably because Weber intended his separate drawing of it to accompany this plan. The following four "Explicaciones" encompass discrete blocks of time, arranged chronologically: the second covers the period February 1 through August 13, 1751; the third roughly March 1 through August 19, 1752; the fourth September 18, 1752, through May 21, 1753; and the fifth February 15, 1753, through July 20, 1754. A "Suplimento" at the end of the inventory provides totals for various small finds discovered throughout the site from July 20, 1750, to July 20, 1754, a clear indication that only finds from this four-year period were meant to be included in the inventory. Blank areas left in the upper register to either side of the inventory prove that Weber never intended to make any additions. Thus, Weber must have made the initial preparations for drafting this plan in mid-1754.

Whereas the inventory of finds stops in 1754, the ground plan documents excavations carried out through April 1756, as is clear from other written records, which do not begin to describe investigations in the atrium and the rooms to the east until 1755. In the plan, tunnels opened up after April 1756 are shown in simple black outline but are confined to the area of the great peristyle. These new tunnels, along with *los hurnillos* and small sketches of the major statues recovered during this period, drawn directly onto the plan at their findspots, reflect excavations conducted through October 1758. The outlines of most of these later tunnels were copied from roughly sketched plans Weber made to illustrate his weekly summary of finds for Alcubierre. On the plan, the tunnels illustrating the north portico of the great peristyle appear lighter in color than the others, suggesting that the latter were drawn earlier. Beginning as early as June 11, 1757, Weber made several references to the plan in his correspondence which could be taken as indicating his intention to finish it shortly: "Monday, God willing, I will present Your Eminence with the plan, where he will observe all the galleries as if he saw them from inside."[73]

Because Weber failed to copy a series of tunnels shown on a sketched plan dated February 18, 1758, his serious revisions to the main plan must have stopped prior to that date.[74] He probably terminated his work on it altogether a week earlier, for he intended to send Alcubierre his finished product a fortnight later.[75] It appears that Weber kept the original of this plan, or a copy of it, until his death and never submitted a completed plan of these excavations for presentation to either the prime minister or Charles of Bourbon.

Weber continued full-scale investigations in the Villa dei Papiri until as late as October 4, 1760, with a view to finishing this plan and uniting it with a complete site plan of the excavations at Herculaneum, but the results of this work were never appended to this particular plan.[76] Even after the discovery of several more important statues, Weber made no additions to his plan. Work continued into February 1761, and some minor investigations were conducted in 1763 and 1764.[77]

PADERNI, PIAGGIO, AND THE PAPYRI

Weber's working only by fits and starts on his plan appears to indicate that he had lost interest in the Villa dei Papiri. Several related factors may have induced this apathy. The sensational discovery in October 1752 of the first rolls of papyrus containing texts from an ancient library soon became the topic of discussion for intellectuals throughout Europe and meant that the excavations came under the close scrutiny of Paderni and the members of the Accademia Ercolanese. In particular, it was Mazzocchi who oversaw the transcriptions made from the unrolled papyrus fragments. Paderni, on the other hand, claimed responsibility for recognizing the charred scrolls for what they were in the excavations; for removing – and ultimately destroying – a number of them; and for announcing their discovery to the world in an open letter to the Royal Society of London:

> [One room] appears to have been a library, adorned with presses, inlaid with different sorts of wood, disposed in rows; at the top of which were cornices, as in our own times. I was buried in this spot for more than twelve days, to carry off the volumes found there; many of which were so perished, that it was impossible to remove them.[78]

Paderni's claims, however, were challenged by Padre Antonio Piaggio, the priest brought from Rome in 1753 to unroll and decipher these charred rolls.[79] Piaggio conducted informal interviews with all the parties involved in the initial discovery, in an attempt to ascertain the true number of papyri recovered from the site. He clearly believed that Paderni had greatly exaggerated his own role at Weber's expense and suggested that in fact Weber may have prevented the destruction of more rolls. Piaggio's interpretation of events is colored by the fact that he and Paderni were bitter rivals throughout their tenures at the royal excavations.[80] Nevertheless, the full passage from Piaggio's manuscript describing the initial discovery, though heavily rhetorical and somewhat lengthy, bears quoting in full.

> In the earth that was being carried away to make the initial entry [into the room] and in that which was being taken [away] by necessity, the excavators began to observe a quantity of fragments resembling carbonized wood, and when every trace of this timber was found, and these papyri resembled nothing more than wood . . . they were disregarded and left in the earth without anyone's thinking twice. Such was the lot of the first papyri, which through bad luck came to light. But when later they observed that these fragments had a consistently cylindrical form and the same dimensions, they were moved by curiosity to handle them. It was then that they considered the great delicacy of the sheets, the size and fragility of their mass, part rotted away, part carbonized. This having been established, some believed them rolls of burned cloth, others nets for fishing or hunting, and so, breaking them with their hands or their pick-axes, they threw the fragments back into the earth, where they were mixed together and reburied without any hope of being seen again!
>
> . . . Why were they tossed away, why trampled under foot afterward? To unravel this paradox I cannot omit adding the reasons I heard from someone in the know and in particular from the custodian [Paderni] himself. First: "it was not desirable to embarrass the Museum just then coming into existence and in straitened circumstances with useless things such as those which did not contain intrinsically in themselves some element of noble erudition, which were torn, or which were impossible to repair or reduce into their original form and elegance." Second: "Multiple objects are not as rare as those which are unique. . . ." The implied desecration of the papyri so lamented by me is not owed completely to the ignorance of the excavators but to their obedience and to the capriciousness of he who directs them . . .
>
> Anyone can imagine the mess that was made of the papyri thereafter. The custodian [Paderni] openly attributes to himself the eternal glory of having saved the remaining papyri from this mishap; no one contests him, at present, since Weber is dead. [Paderni] asserts how, having heard secretly after several days the rumor of their function [*In margine*: He boasts of having spent the greater part of his budget to maintain spies in the excavations and in the house of Monsignor Bayardi, at that time the delegate over all the antiquities] and having carried off a few of them himself, at first glance he knew from the characters (what great perspicac-

ity!) that of which the world had had no idea until then, and how all the others that he had labored over [he could now] discern [still buried in the excavations]. He adds how he ran immediately to the palace and introduced himself to Their Majesties, even though it was inconvenient, and having opened one of the rolls (that is, he cut one with a knife) in their presence, made them conceive the value of the hidden treasure he had uncovered. He adds how at his insistence a most stringent order was issued that no one except him could touch them first; how he descended many days on end into the grottoes in the early morning, after dinner, with his pickax in his mouth, in order to dig them out with his own hands, freeing the papyri one by one, with only the benefit of small torches, which were at risk of being extinguished and leaving him in the dark or losing track of the exit, and with the danger of being trapped alive by falling vaults or suffocated in his own sweat. . . . How finally by some miracle he extracted them all and brought them to light a few at a time; and how he accompanied them to the museum in person.[81]

Piaggio refers elsewhere in his manuscript to the fact that Paderni had helped foster the bitter animosity between Weber and Alcubierre, although it should be noted that Piaggio was himself the object of much enmity.[82] More important, Piaggio states explicitly that Weber abandoned the excavations in the villa as Paderni gradually usurped an increasing amount of control over the daily operations:

Out of the aforementioned order, or rather monopoly [over control of the excavations] in favor of [Paderni], there arose disorder, or rather the source of many other disorders and incredible misdeeds that I cannot erase from my mind, but concerning which I am constrained to be quiet out of respect. Concerning the [papyri] I will not be silent about how that same "order" began so to disturb the mind of Weber that during the excavation of the papyri he no longer descended down there [into the villa], where he found himself deprived of the rights attached to his office and where he was more than diligent (all the more so because he was most passionate about the monuments he had found), and so that he should not encounter there the opportunity for some greater disorder, nor the rancor that should have been suppressed lest it carry him to his grave.[83]

The extreme difficulty of working a site that became more and more perilous to excavate as the number of tunnels increased may also have induced Weber to prefer to investigate sites where the work was less dangerous. Weber did not at

this time advocate that the ruins of the Villa dei Papiri be excavated out completely, believing that his method of tunneling could achieve the same results
with less expense in time and money and less risk of finding nothing.[84] He may
well have felt that the effects of his own investigations, combined with the
depredations of earlier explorers and the devastation wrought by Vesuvius, had
left the villa even more literally in ruins and that bringing the whole to light
simply was not worth the effort.

As work in the villa dragged on, the open-air excavations at Pompeii had been
renewed, and several buildings at Stabiae had already been investigated. In the
ruins of Herculaneum itself, Weber believed he had begun to uncover the
remains of ancient temples. He was especially attracted to these sites because
the ruins lay beneath land that could be returned to cultivation once the excavations were completed and the work could proceed unhindered by damage to or
obstruction by crops and modern structures. One of his strongest arguments
against open-air excavations at Herculaneum, which he repeated on several
occasions, was that they would cause the destruction of fruit-bearing trees, not
to mention that of the modern town of Resina.[85] Moreover, he began to recognize features of the ancient urban fabric at these other sites – paved streets,
sidewalks, shops, fountains – features that were completely lacking in the Villa
dei Papiri. It was this interest in the "common architecture of the ancients" that
became a driving force behind much of his remaining work.

4

Pompeii and the Praedia Iuliae Felicis

Alcubierre had ordered the excavations at la Città reopened on March 31, 1755, after a farmer working his field had turned up a white marble pillar.[1] This new site lay immediately north of the ancient amphitheater that Alcubierre had investigated in 1748, and it was crossed by the Sarno canal, whose various hydraulic features remained under his care (Fig. 28). Familiarity with the site therefore must have played as strong a role in exciting Alcubierre's interest as the prospect of recovering more antiquities. Weber began work here on April 2, 1755, and in a matter of days had uncovered a colonnade of sixteen marble pillars. It was an auspicious beginning, and this site was to produce a much richer cache, in a far shorter time, than any other yet investigated by the Bourbon excavators. These marked the start of the excavations at Pompeii that have continued virtually uninterrupted to the present time.

This site differed from those at Herculaneum in that the ruins did not consist of a single building with a single plan and function but rather of a complex of public buildings, which included shops, a set of small baths, and a number of dining rooms and reception halls, several of these built out of an earlier private domus with a traditional atrium (Fig. 29). The marble pillars had created a long colonnade bordering a viridarium with a central euripus, somewhat reminiscent of the great peristyle garden in the Villa dei Papiri. All the living areas had been elegantly appointed with fine wall paintings and statuary, much of it produced in the years just prior to the eruption and found in an excellent state of preservation.[2]

In contrast to the underground excavations in the Villa dei Papiri and elsewhere in Herculaneum, where workmen could tunnel for months without turning up a single find worthy of note, the investigation of this entire site took less than two years, with the bulk of the finds occurring in the first.[3] In fact, this was the first building in Pompeii or Herculaneum to be excavated both completely

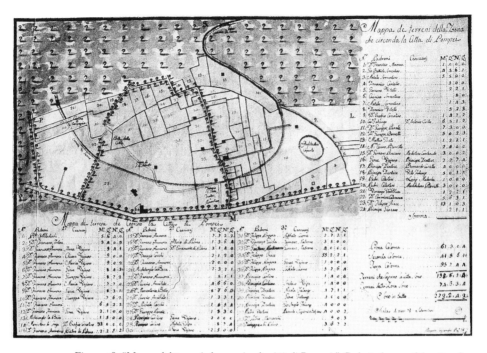

Figure 28. "Mappa de' terreni che coprino la città di Pompei." Cadastral map of the site of
Pompeii, drawn in 1807 by Pietro Scognamillo as part of a project to acquire the necessary
land for extending the open-air excavations. Note the curving S-shape of the Sarno Canal,
the course of the Royal Road across the bottom of the map, and the location of the
reburied amphitheater. (Courtesy of the Soprintendenza Archeologica di Napoli e Caserta
[Archivio Disegno, n.n.; 0.375 m. H × 0.53 m. W].)

and systematically. The corpus of documents relating to this work is remarkably
complete and permits a fairly detailed and accurate reconstruction of the weekly
progress of the excavations. When studied in association with the extant archaeological remains, these documents render it possible not only to determine from
precisely which room the Bourbons had removed wall paintings but also to
reconstitute the original decorative program of the viridarium and other areas of
the building to an extent inconceivable with the remains of the Villa dei Papiri.

The manner in which Pompeii had been buried afforded Weber a great deal
of latitude for applying his more systematic approach to the excavations; he
would later use this site as a model when he came to recommend the manner in
which the Bourbon excavations should proceed. That the volcanic lapilli here
reached an average depth of only 15 palms (ca. 3.96 m.) made it far easier to
estimate the size of the site as a whole: the overall boundaries and total cubic
meters of fill covering an area could be ascertained relatively quickly and the

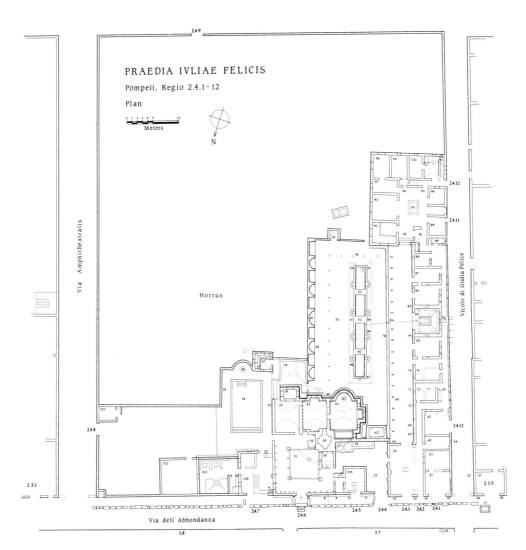

Figure 29. Plan of the Praedia Iuliae Felicis at Pompeii (Regio 2.4.1–12) as it appears today. The principal areas mentioned in the text include the "balneum venerium et nongentum" (26–44), the vestibule of the Forum Frieze (24), the sacrarium of Isis with the ithyphallic Satyr tripod (55), the nymphaeum (83), and the "domus" with painted still-lifes (89–100). (Author's plan.)

approximate time needed for excavation determined. Without the science of stratigraphy to bog them down, the Bourbons considered everything from the surface down to the level of the pavements to be ancient, a mentality that was to persist through much of the history of the excavations at Pompeii. The relative value of the ornamentation of entire rooms or lengths of walls could be ap-

praised at a single glance, rather than piecemeal and by torchlight, and this too
allowed the work of recovering antiquities to proceed more rapidly. Moreover,
the site could be excavated in a more efficient manner, since the workmen could
move on to new areas while leaving previous portions exposed as long as was
necessary for paintings or mosaics to be removed. On the other hand, the
natural elements played a different role here, restricting excavation to the day-
light hours and imposing limits on how long objects could be exposed to the sun
and rain. A corps of guards made up of invalids was posted here to watch over
the ruins at night and on holidays to prevent clandestine diggers from plundering the site for paintings and other antiquities that might end up in the hands of
foreigners. During the day the site foreman even packed a gun to protect the
workmen from armed robbers.[4] Yet just as the underground tunnels were sealed
when they had lost their usefulness, these sites were backfilled as well and
returned to cultivation at the conclusion of the excavations.

The alignment of the colonnade of marble pillars determined the direction in
which Weber pursued his investigation of this site. He first dug out the central
rooms and walls of the portico, removing several terracotta statuettes, small
paintings, and some small marble herm-heads immured in the stucco.[5] From a
barrel-vaulted nymphaeum with a water-stair fountain and a marble-covered
masonry triclinium came several sections of a blue frieze with generic scenes of
pygmies shown among the flora and fauna of the Nile.[6] Moving north into a
vestibule marking the end of the portico, the excavators cut down a number of
fragments of a painted frieze depicting Roman daily life, including market
scenes in the forum (24).[7] They then reversed direction, turning toward the
south end of the viridarium, where they came upon a small barrel-vaulted
sacrarium painted with Egyptian and Roman deities (55).[8] Because of the curious nature of these paintings, Paderni ordered the sacrarium removed whole,
and this was accomplished by chiseling it from its foundations and from the
enclosure wall of the viridarium. On the floor inside the sacrarium stood one of
the great treasures of this site: a bronze tripod decorated with ithyphallic satyrs,
a Hellenistic original that rivaled the finds from the Villa dei Papiri.[9]

The excavators then entered the adjacent domus and moved in a clockwise
direction through its rooms, removing small painted vignettes, one entire wall
with its paintings, and a wide variety of bronze furnishings, such as pots and
candelabra. Following the east enclosure wall of the viridarium brought them to
the bath complex, where work was concentrated for some three months. They
plundered this not only of its wall paintings and mosaics – one from a fountain
decorated with fantastic marine beasts and the other from the center of the
tepidarium, which bore a schematic portrait of the fornacator of the praefurnium,

both of these in black and white – but even stripped it of its building materials, such as the tegulae mammatae of the walls and the brick colonnettes supporting the hypocaustal floor. While the last of the paintings were being removed from the baths, Weber returned to the viridarium, where, in laying bare the central euripus, he came upon seven small marble and terracotta statues adorning its perimeter which stood in their original locations.[10]

The workmen were then transferred back to the north façade of the building, where they dug a wide trench from east to west, exposing the façade of this building and two adjacent ones. In so doing, they found a paved street with a public fountain standing at an intersection with the side street that formed the western boundary of the property. Two more shops fronting the main street were encountered before the excavators turned south again to complete the investigation of the small storage rooms of the portico along the west side of the building. The last months were spent exploring a large hortus that stood between this building and the adjacent amphitheater and in ascertaining the full extent of the property's boundaries.

A constant concern was what to do with the earth removed from the trenches. This must have determined the order in which areas of the site were excavated and why certain portions of the building appear to have been passed over completely or only investigated somewhat cursorily. For example, backfilling probably was carried out in the domus while the baths were being excavated, and the baths were covered over during excavations in the viridarium. On the other hand, an extensive caupona to the east of the baths and a smaller thermopolium to the west went uninvestigated, perhaps because these areas had been buried under mounds of fill or because modern structures that stood over them precluded further investigation. The central portions of rooms often were not excavated fully if it was believed they had only a simple, unadorned mosaic pavement, since experience had shown that few antiquities would be recovered in these areas. The greatest concentration of finds were recovered from small storerooms, and the excavators focused their efforts on these, having unwittingly discovered a characteristic of Roman domestic life by which most household furnishings were kept in storage and brought out only as needed.[11] During the first years of the excavations at Pompeii, land was seized only for the duration of the work, and property owners were compensated for the lost productivity of their land or damage to existing crops. In the case of this site, the owner, Vincenzo Grasso, was reimbursed 39 ducats and 60 carlins after the first year.[12]

The number of wall paintings and mosaics that required removal determined the length of time a portion of any given site remained exposed. Paderni often chose to sketch the designs of these finds first *in situ*, and Weber frequently complained of delays in work or damage to paintings while waiting for Giuseppe Canart of the royal museum, or one of his young assistants, to come to the excavations and remove the objects.[13] Although most of the paintings were small vignettes of subjects such as birds, landscapes, and theatrical masks, one room in the domus yielded several large still-life panels as well as its entire north wall. This wall was the only example in the royal museum to show the overall scheme, from dado to upper frieze, of what came to be identified as Fourth-Style Pompeian wall painting.[14]

Weber was extraordinarily fortunate in having this as his first site in Pompeii, for its prodigious number of wall paintings, mosaics, and statuary satisfied Alcubierre's demands for antiquities suitable for the king's collection. At the same time, the ruins themselves satisfied Weber's curiosity about the domestic architecture and daily life of the Pompeians. Although a small private bath complex had already been excavated in the vast building complex at Stabiae in September 1751, the baths here were the first public baths of moderate scale, with the full complement of rooms prescribed by Vitruvius (Vitr. 5.10.1–5), to be discovered in the Vesuvian cities. At Herculaneum, although the excavators frequently had tunneled through shops, there is little indication in the reports that they recognized them as such or cared much about them. In 1748, in the earliest published account of remains of this type, Venuti had described in some detail the stepped marble shelves for the display of wares found in a thermopolium in Herculaneum.[15] Weber, perhaps influenced by Venuti's account, noted in his reports the masonry counters facing the street and the amphorae found propped up in corners, which served as telltale signs of the function of these areas.

On the façade of the building facing the main street was found Pompeii's first substantial corpus of painted inscriptions (dipinti) announcing the candidacies of local politicians (programmata) and, scratched into the plaster at the entrance to the baths, an early example of the so-called "pater noster" palindrome.[16] One large inscription identified the owner of these properties (praedia) as one Julia Felix, daughter of Spurius, and enumerated the parts of the building available for rent: the baths, shops with lofts, and second-floor apartments (*CIL* 4.1136). Before cutting these inscriptions down for transport to the royal palace, Weber meticulously copied the letters, as well as he could decipher them. Although he was perfectly capable of reading Latin, he was ignorant of the often cryptic Latin abbreviations used in these notices, so several of his transcriptions were largely nonsensical.[17] Observing that their paint was remarkably well preserved, however, he noted that they would be of great interest to historians, an indication he was fully aware that the Bourbon excavations afforded benefits well beyond mere treasure hunting.[18]

As with the ruins of Herculaneum, the excavators recognized signs throughout this site that plunderers had preceded them. Because of the relatively shallow depth of the volcanic ash and lapilli that covered Pompeii, the entire city had been prey to scavengers since only a short time after the eruption; this is clear from a reference in Suetonius (Suet. *Titus* 8) to Titus's appointment of a commission of former consuls to oversee recovery efforts in the region.[19] Just as the forum had been systematically stripped of all its major statuary and salvageable building materials, so too numerous survivors returned to burrow through the ruins of their buried houses to recover portable goods; the same habit of storing furniture and household effects in storerooms that precluded the necessity to excavate the central portions of rooms had simplified the process of recovery for these survivors as well. Pillaging had continued on a much more random basis down to the Bourbon era, with the discovery of skeletons entombed at various levels within the lapilli serving as poignant monuments to the greed of individuals who often can be distinguished from their equally unfortunate ancient predecessors only through the remains of their clothing and jewelry.[20] The same circumstances that led to the discovery of the Praedia – a farmer working his fields – had caused much of the city to be subjected to small, clandestine investigations for centuries, but in the Praedia's case, fear of possible reprisals from the Bourbon court no doubt had induced the property's owner to report his finds to the proper authorities.[21]

The pattern of pillaging seen in the Praedia was much the same as that found elsewhere in the city: polychrome marble revetment stripped from masonry dining couches and walls, holes cut through a succession of walls, and rooms emptied of their contents, in particular several small storerooms along the west side of the building. They observed areas where the earth had been disturbed and believed they had found evidence that these plunderers had cut paintings down from the walls as well. Paderni, who visited the site shortly after the excavations began, remarked, "If the ancients had not dug in this place, we should have discovered many more things, for we find that they have taken away even some of the pictures."[22] But in most instances in the Praedia these cuttings do not indicate where paintings were removed but rather walls that were in the process of receiving the final stages of stucco at the time of the eruption, in particular panels awaiting completion by a master painter.

In one room, however, the excavators uncovered evidence that confirmed a practice described by Vitruvius in which old, valued paintings were salvaged from walls, mounted in wooden frames, and set into new stucco (Vitr. 7.3.10).

In this instance, a small panel painting depicting ritual objects relating to the cult of Dionysus was found on the floor of a room, leaning against a wall. It either had fallen from an iron clamp on which it was hung or it stood here awaiting final incorporation into the stucco on the wall.[23]

Given the number of marble statues and bronze furnishings recovered during these excavations, and their concentration in a few key areas, it is more likely that the signs of plundering were left by individuals from a much later period, since survivors of the eruption would have known precisely where to dig to recover these works of art. Either the survivors could not locate these rooms, because not enough of the buildings projected out of the volcanic debris, or there were no survivors familiar with the layout of this building.

The Bourbon excavators also found evidence of a more macabre nature, both for victims of the eruption and for later plunderers. At Herculaneum, it had long been believed that the infrequent discovery of skeletons among the ruins indicated that the ancient inhabitants had had ample warning of the impending disaster and had managed to escape with most of their valuables. Several visitors who had toured the underground tunnels described a clear impression left in the volcanic cover by the body of an individual carrying a money bag, but this was an exceptional example.[24] The slow manner in which Pompeii had been buried, on the other hand, led many of the ancient inhabitants to delay their escape until it was too late, and they eventually perished on the site. As Fiorelli was to discover in the nineteenth century, the decayed organic material of these victims' bodies often left cavities at levels where the volcanic ash had accumulated, and plaster casts could be taken from these.

The earliest discovery of a skeleton at Pompeii is recorded on April 19, 1748, but no more are mentioned until the work in the Praedia.[25] Near the peristyle courtyard to the baths (*31* and *6*), the excavators uncovered the skeletons of three victims of the eruption, one of whom bore an iron ring on one finger, suggesting servile status. In this same area, near a fountain, were found up to twelve human skulls, which the reports describe as "carelessly reburied." These must be the remains of victims discovered by later scavengers who then reburied this evidence, a practice encountered elsewhere in Pompeii.[26]

The excavation records from this period document a significant increase in the quantity of small finds being recovered, as if it had become an obsession to unearth and record even the smallest artifact. The ability of the underground excavators at Herculaneum to distinguish small gems, jewelry, bronze coins, and household fittings from the volcanic material had been remarkable in itself, but to be able to discern the charred papyrus rolls and even mounds of grain stored in rooms seems almost inconceivable.[27] For some time, however, the royal collection of ancient fruits, nuts, eggs, loaves of bread, and other food-stuffs had been growing, and this eventually made up one of the more popular displays in the museum.[28] The conditions of preservation and excavation at Pompeii and Stabiae made it far easier to recover a variety of artifacts from everyday life, including bone and fragments of glass. Yet surprises still appear in the records. A small mound of what was believed to be flour was identified later by Paderni as papyrus fragments which had not been charred like those from Herculaneum; ironically, the discovery of this mound is followed immediately in the excavation records by a reference to the great depth of the lapilli and the difficulties encountered in their removal.[29] The excavators' skill in recovering artifacts is attested further by the fact that, apart from those few areas that had gone uninvestigated, only a handful of finds was made when the Praedia were rc-excavated by Maiuri in the 1950s.

THE CONTRIBUTIONS OF ANTONIO SCOGNAMILLO

Although Weber oversaw all the excavations in the Vesuvian region, the day-to-day operations at each site were directed by individual foremen. To judge from the excavation documents, the work at the Praedia, along with the sites investi-gated subsequently at Pompeii, appears to have been directed by Miguel de Çiria, with the assistance of Antonio Scognamillo.[30] Few specifics are known about Çiria,[31] but Scognamillo had begun work for the Bourbon excavations as an untrained civilian laborer, with no connection to the corps of military engineers; no doubt he began his career as one of the many young men who spent much of their lives engaged in the hard manual labor at these sites, often even putting their sons to work alongside them.[32] In fact, his uncle was Minico Imperato, who had assisted d'Elbeuf in his earlier plundering of Herculaneum.[33] Scognamillo appar-ently began working for the excavations during Bardet's tenure, but his name appears for the first time in the records only in 1751, during excavations at Pozzuoli and Cumae.[34] Upon being transferred to Portici in December 1752, he requested a raise in pay and quickly fell out of favor with Weber, who refused to initial his reports, claiming Scognamillo was engaged in some other form of work for the king.[35] The precise details of the affair are obscure, but neither Weber nor his successor La Vega respected Scognamillo's work. As a native of the area, Scognamillo was told by other locals of sites where antiquities had been found and drew Weber's ire for shifting the workmen to these sites of his own accord.[36] Evidently he had taught himself how to draw crude plans of the sites to which he had been assigned and managed to accumulate an impressive number of docu-ments illustrating many of the excavations in which he was involved.

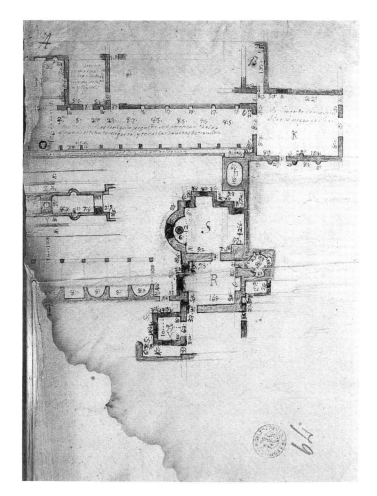

Figure 30. Fragmentary plan of the Praedia Iuliae Felicis in Pompeii, drawn prior to November 1755 by one of the excavation foremen, Antonio Scognamillo. The letters were keyed to a legend which is now lost. The numbers record the dimensions of the architectural features in Neapolitan palms. The annotations describe aspects of the decoration such as mosaics. (Courtesy of the Soprintendenza Archeologica di Napoli e Caserta [Archivio Disegno, n.n.; 0.38 m. H × 0.52 m. W].)

Among the surviving documents that can be attributed to Scognamillo is part of a plan showing the extent of the architectural remains uncovered in the Praedia Iuliae Felicis through November 1755 (Fig. 30).[37] This precise *terminus ante quem* can be determined because the plan fails to show rooms along the front of the building that the excavation reports prove were investigated beginning only in December 1755. The surviving half of the plan covers the northern portion of the Praedia, beginning roughly with the nymphaeum and ending with the vestibule with the Forum Frieze on the Via dell' Abbondanza, both of these among the earliest rooms investigated.

His plan is particularly valuable in being one of the earliest working plans from the excavations rather than a presentation copy for the king: by all appearances this was the draft kept on site and added to as each new wall or feature was uncovered. In support of this conclusion are lines drawn in pencil to indicate the direction it was assumed certain walls would follow, which were not inked in later, since the walls either deviated, ended, or were discovered not to exist. The vellum on which the plan was drawn evidently had been folded in quarters so often that half the sheet eventually tore away and has now been lost, and along with it the plan of the southern half of the viridarium and the rooms of the domus. It seems unlikely that this plan was drawn up to illustrate the state of the excavations at that time and specifically intended to satisfy Alcubierre's demand for plans.

Scognamillo's plan is also unique in that the length of each section of each wall has been written directly onto the plan. This is in contrast to the sketch plans Weber drew to illustrate his weekly reports to Alcubierre or the prime minister, which contain few measurements. Even the completed plans contain only a scale. It is remarkable that the lines of only a few walls are slightly skewed from their true alignment and the rooms are more or less properly proportioned, since there is no indication of what kind of surveying, much less drafting, techniques were employed in drawing up the plan; here again the chain must have been the instrument of choice. A few rooms are labeled with nonconsecutive letters of the alphabet and perhaps were keyed to a legend that may have been given on the lost portion of the plan or else served simply as points of reference to an accompanying report that is likewise no longer extant. Someone – perhaps Scognamillo's son – added several observations in Spanish describing mosaic pavements and the condition in which certain rooms were found.[38]

Although not himself a site supervisor, Scognamillo had kept copious notes on each of the sites he had excavated. By 1764, he had some nine small notebooks in progress in which he had illustrated the architecture, paintings, and artifacts removed from the excavations at Città and Gragnano, "in the manner he knew how," as La Vega remarked later.[39] Weber probably had to rely heavily on the information in these documents, when it came time to complete his own plans, but he hardly mentioned their existence during his years at the excavations.[40] Their suppression probably arose as much from Weber's jealous guarding of his own work as from the poor quality of the plans and the lowly status of their author. In 1767, La Vega received two of Scognamillo's plans illustrating the area of the theater in Pompeii but observed that they were of little value, because "[Scognamillo] does not know the first principles about how to take measurements."[41]

WEBER'S PRELIMINARY PLAN OF THE PRAEDIA

In keeping with his philosophy that it was senseless to draw up plans before a site had been investigated fully, Weber began work on his own plan of the Praedia Iuliae Felicis only as the excavations began to wind down. In concept and design, this plan was modeled closely on that of the Villa dei Papiri, and Weber may well have deliberately intended to highlight the similiarities between these two ancient complexes: both are oriented in roughly the same manner on the page, both have long pools enclosed by porticoes running lengthwise across the center, and both have a core of important rooms arranged around a smaller peristyle with a central fountain toward the viewer's left. But beyond these superficial similarities, the differences become marked.

For example, in terms of its art historical value, it is clear that this type of plan, with the exact findspot of each artifact clearly indicated, works far more effectively here than it had at the Villa dei Papiri. In the latter case, the objects were often found dispersed in fragments or otherwise shifted from their original location by the force of the volcanic mud, while in the Praedia statuary and furnishings alike were found more or less in the precise spot where they had stood in antiquity. Weber's plan therefore allows the original decorative program of the Praedia to be reconstructed with a high degree of accuracy.

The plan of the building is again the central feature on the page (Fig. 31).[42] In drafting it, Weber almost certainly relied on a plan like Scognamillo's, for he would have needed to consult it for its measurements. The plan of the buildings was outlined first in pencil and then ruled in ink before being colored in part with a light wash of watercolor: brown for walls, green for areas containing water, and light hatchmarks for rooms paved in mosaic. There is nothing so detailed as the opus sectile pavement of the pavilion or the water-stair fountain in the Villa dei Papiri, but the difficult curving walls of the caldarium and laconicum in the baths were drafted with a high degree of precision. Indeed, Maiuri's excavations in the 1950s verified the accuracy of much of Weber's plan. The principal errors concern the true appearance of the front of the domus, where Weber had added what appears to be a bench flanking the door, and of the undulating sides of the euripus in the viridarium, where he added a third set of semicircular niches that disrupt its symmetrical design. On the other

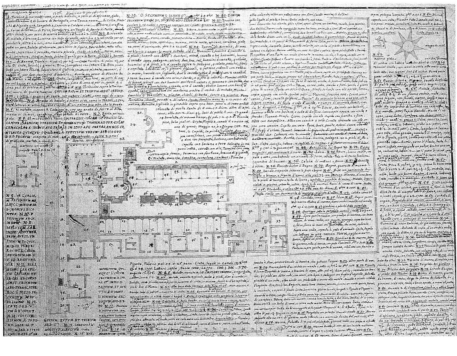

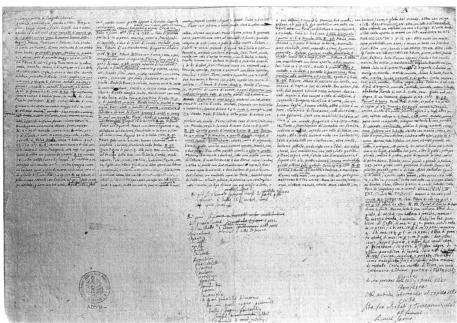

Figure 31. Weber's preliminary draft of his plan of the Praedia Iuliae Felicis in Pompeii, dated May 1, 1757. The obverse (*top*) bears the numbered ground plan, keyed to the annotations that fill the ruled columns surrounding it; the annotations continue onto the reverse (*bottom*), with the title appearing in the lower right-hand corner. (Courtesy of the Soprintendenza Archeologica di Napoli e Caserta [Archivio Disegno, #71; 0.36 m. H × 0.48 m. W].)

hand, Weber's plan also illustrates smaller details that did not survive reburial
and reexcavation and were no longer to be seen in Maiuri's day, such as a
fountain on the central bridge of the euripus.

Each room, along with certain architectural features such as niches, columns,
and the marble-topped counters in the shops, was assigned a number, which
was keyed into an inventory of all the finds recovered from that location. These
numbers, neatly worked out from 1 to 100, are not arranged chronologically
according to the date of their discovery, as in the Villa dei Papiri plan, but weave
their way across the plan in an orderly manner from left to right. The inventories accompanying each number are lengthy, and in many cases the descriptions
of statues, lamps, and paintings are detailed enough to identify those pieces that
still exist in the Bourbon collection and return them to their proper context.[43]
The text was written in Italian, not the Spanish Weber had used in his correspondence with Alcubierre and the court. The information contained here was
probably drawn from Weber's own excavation notes as well as those of
Scognamillo, all of which he must have first organized by date of discovery,
since several numbers combine entries for objects found on different dates.
Emendations and insertions are frequent, but Weber clearly had worked out this
inventory carefully, on a separate sheet, before copying it here. The inventory
entries are arranged in columns of varying width that fill every available free
space, crowding around the plan, a scale in Neapolitan palms near the bottom,
and a compass in the upper right-hand corner, before continuing onto the back
of the sheet. The annotations no longer include references to the excavators'
engineering achievements, such as the depth and location of air shafts and
tunnels, since the relative ease of excavation allowed Weber to concentrate
solely on the archaeological and architectural material.[44] In fact there is no
mention at all of the excavation conditions, only notes recording where evidence
for earlier plunderers had been observed and one area where Weber believed
excavations should be continued. (See Appendix 1, "The Preliminary Plan of
the Praedia Iuliae Felicis".)[45]

Apart from the somewhat monotonous catalog of finds, the annotations reveal
that Weber was interested in recording how this architecture and its ornamentation had functioned in antiquity, for he describes fountains as spouting water,
porticoes and pergolas as creating pleasant walks, and rooms as paved with
figural mosaics or polychrome marbles. Perhaps more important was the variety
of examples this site afforded of what he called the "common architecture" of
the ancients, and he attempted to relate several of these to their modern analogues. He noted that the street in front of the Praedia was paved with blocks of
lava stone (lapis Pompeianus) just as were the streets of Naples, and that a

mixture of crushed terracotta, lime, and pumice (opus signinum) covered the raised sidewalks flanking the street.[46] He carefully drew the two shops fronting onto this street, one of which (4) had a small stepped shelf at one end of its marble counter "for placing dishes, as are used today," while the other (21) had a small hearth as well as another shelf for glassware, both of which Weber labeled separately. Today, after almost six hundred shops and taverns have been brought to light at Pompeii, such shops seem relatively commonplace, but these were among the first to be isolated, described, and illustrated.[47] On the street in front of this second shop stood a public fountain whose lava standard was decorated with a mask wreathed with clusters of grapes (17); the standard was removed and transported to the royal villa at Portici. The baths were given special attention, for in lifting the black and white figural mosaics in these rooms, the excavators had exposed the hypocaustal floor below. This in turn led Weber to the praefurnium, whose opening he identified separately (27).[48] Adjacent to this he found the laconicum (29), with its mosaic pavement and its niches with benches of marble, and called it the "closet of the round bath." One corner of the peristyle courtyard (28) adjoining the laconicum had been furnished with marble benches, and Weber mused that this was where one could withdraw and reflect after a hot bath or walk through the portico. The first clearly identifiable latrines were found here as well (37 and 100). Finally, he recognized a large kitchen in the southwest corner of the building on the basis of its large masonry hearth (100).

Weber probably completed this plan sometime in 1757, to judge from the calligraphy, which more or less matches the hand found in his correspondence from this period. There is no indication that this plan was intended for anyone's use but his own, and it probably served only as a rough draft for the presentation copy he completed sometime later; he did not sign this version. As will be seen, he apparently returned to this plan only in 1759, when he finally settled down to draw up his presentation copy, and many of the insertions, emendations, and underlinings that now appear on the rough draft date from this later period. It was probably only then that he added on the back of this earlier plan, in the more scrawling hand he had developed in the meantime, a general list of small objects found throughout the site and, in the lower right-hand corner, worked out how the title was to appear on the final copy: "Pianta di una porzione della Edificj e Strada della Pompeana Città anticha sottorranea al rapillo della Cività Sita fra Scafati e Torreanunziata al fiume Sarno."[49]

Weber's title rightly recognizes that this was not a villa but an agglomeration of different architectural units with different functions, much like the collection of buildings he had encountered at Stabiae. It also underscores the generic nature of these ruins: "a portion of the buildings and street of Pompeii." Yet it reveals as well that Weber had failed to use the painted inscriptions from the facade to help him identify more accurately the individual spaces and the owner of this building. In fact, it was not until some seventy years later that Bonucci combined the information in the epigraphic material with Weber's plan and inventory and wrongly labeled this site, for the first time, the "Casa di Giulia Felice," the name still attached to this building today.[50]

5

The "Temples" at Herculaneum

During the early years of excavations at the Villa dei Papiri, only sporadic investigations were carried out in the ancient city of Herculaneum itself. This state of affairs changed dramatically during the period between 1756 and 1761, when Weber focused much of his attention on the eastern edges of the known city, in areas surrounding the building identified today as the Palestra (Fig. 32).[1] The work conducted here merits a detailed examination, for it illustrates most vividly the enormous obstacles that had to be overcome in conducting these underground investigations and how months, and even years, could be spent in clearing out substantial sections of the city without a single major discovery being made. On the other hand, these excavations were crucial for Weber's own professional development, for it was here that he began to formulate many of his ideas concerning how best to explicate and illustrate this ancient architecture for his contemporaries and for posterity. The archaeological methodology he developed during this period of trial and error, and the preference he acquired for recovering architectural structures rather than artistic treasures, shaped the approach he took in excavating all the sites under his direction. In turn, despite numerous initial setbacks, he fostered a new outlook upon the importance of these ancient ruins that had a profound impact on the course of the Bourbon excavations.

As early as November 1753, Weber had cut new tunnels through ruins that lay beneath the Bisogno property in Resina. The large tract of cultivated land on the surface roughly corresponded with the open-air excavations visible at Herculaneum today, and indeed it was the rediscovery in 1828 of the Bourbon tunnels that led to renewed interest in the city.[2] These tunnels were reached originally by means of a ramp whose entrance was located along the Vico de Mar (the modern Vico di Mare), the street that runs perpendicular to the Royal

Figure 32. Modern plan of the open-air excavations at Herculaneum. (Courtesy of the
Soprintendenza Archeologica di Pompei.)

Road, toward the sea, and that still serves as the western boundary of the
excavations. The ramp was the same one that Alcubierre had used as early as
1748 to investigate the houses as far east as the Casa dei Cervi as well as the
buildings to the west shown in the plan of 1749. As Weber himself now discovered, and Maiuri's excavations later confirmed, the accessible tunnels in this
area wound their way through the architectural remains in no coherent manner
and made orientation underground extremely difficult.

Despite the paltry number of finds made here, Alcubierre remained confident that more could be found and so even opened a second ramp to the
northeast, along the Royal Road, and began to bore new tunnels. He believed
this latter area had not been excavated well in the past, but this was, in fact,
precisely where Bardet had tunneled extensively in 1743. As a result, the work
here continued for months, encountering little more than building materials,
part of a street, and Bardet's tunnels, before they were broken off in March
1755.[3]

After work resumed here in the spring of 1756, Weber frequently referred in
his reports to the difficulty caused by rainwater flooding the tunnels. This was a
particularly acute problem throughout the ruins of ancient Herculaneum, where
water percolating through the earth already made for damp working conditions
inside the tunnels. In the past, little effort had been made to prevent rain runoff
from entering the openings of the tunnels, resulting in damage to the antiquities
and danger to the workmen.[4] Apparently unable to channel the water away
completely, Alcubierre ordered a dike built at the mouth of the ramp, as well as
at the entrance to the individual tunnels below, to direct the water into the older
tunnels and away from those under active excavation. This approach proved
only moderately successful and failed miserably when the rains were heavy. On
one occasion, work ground to a halt when runoff flooded the lower tunnels,
where the excavators had stored their equipment; on another, the water had the
beneficial effect of uncovering some antiquities.[5] Water evidently was also deliberately channeled into the tunnels occasionally, as a means of carrying off excess
fill through the existing aquifers, a technique Piaggio complained had led to the
destruction of many of the papyrus rolls in the Villa dei Papiri.[6]

The problem with runoff highlights one of Weber's main dilemmas in trying
to map the excavations in this area: not only did the tunnels fail to follow the
lines of walls in an orderly fashion, but they cut through the volcanic matrix at
different levels, depending on the point at which the first walls were encountered or where the tufa could most easily be mined. This practice rendered it
even more difficult to discern individual architectural forms or the course of
streets, for the tunnels could come easily within centimeters of such features
and miss them, without the excavators' realizing it. Over the next three years,
Weber attempted to correct this problem by returning to Bardet's approach of
following streets and by concentrating all his efforts on clearing large portions of
individual buildings, regardless of the quantity of finds, before moving on. In so
doing, he came into direct opposition with Alcubierre, who correctly believed
that Weber's methods inevitably placed greater emphasis on recovering architectural forms than on the recovery of antiquities.

A CONTROVERSIAL METHODOLOGY

Weber began his more systematic approach to the excavations under his care in July 1756. In May, the excavators had come across a tufa gutter in front of a portico of stuccoed brick columns and painted walls, the whole described in the reports as being reminiscent of one of the peristyles in the Villa dei Papiri. For some weeks they investigated this peristyle, cutting down some small paintings and finding several doorways, one of these with a marble threshold, along with a set of stairs. The precise location of this work is difficult to determine, but the peristyle may be that in the Casa del Tramezzo di Legno (Ins. 3.11), since Maiuri later found that tunnels already had cut through here, along with evidence that paintings had been removed from the tablinum, an oecus, and the peristyle.[7] Though initially Weber must have been unsettled by the number of old tunnels his workmen were encountering throughout this area, he eventually began to rely more heavily on such existing tunnels as a means of guiding and even expanding his own work. He reassured Alcubierre that he should expect better results, since "one could not have a better place [to excavate] than habitations that have not been touched."[8]

Having thus distracted Alcubierre's attention, Weber had used another tunnel to follow the line of a city street until it intersected with a second street (Fig. 33). This must have been the intersection of Cardo IV with the Decumanus Inferior (see Fig. 32). Here Weber removed one large and one small lava paving stone for transport to Portici, further evidence that the royal collection was not confined to the finest antiquities but was growing to encompass examples of the more prosaic remains of daily life as well. The provenance of these stones can be confirmed by Weber's description of one of these streets as "a paved street that goes to the right under the town of Resina, where is the Temple with many statues and nearby the bronze horse."[9] For the time being, water prevented Weber from heading toward this "temple," by which he must mean the abandoned caverns of the Basilica, so he continued excavating in the intersection.[10]

Another piece of evidence supports the conclusion that it was this intersection Weber had encountered. In late August he received permission from Alcubierre to begin a new ramp, whose entrance stood in front of the Bellobuono house (also called Belobono and Belonio in the records), just east of the last piazza in Resina and along the Royal Road. There were several important reasons for the selection of this spot. First, its proximity to the Royal Road would facilitate the movement of men and equipment into, and artifacts out of, the excavations. It also was located near the ruins of the Basilica, where Alcubierre maintained the hope of encountering more statuary and which We-

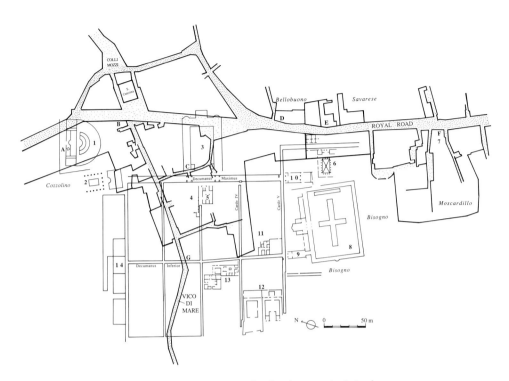

Figure 33. Composite plan of Herculaneum showing the general relation between eighteenth-century properties and the ruins of the ancient city. Ruggiero's plan of Resina in the nineteenth century (*StErc*, pl. 2) served as the base plan, though the Royal Road originally wound its way up through Colli Mozzi; it was straightened only at a later time. The plans and orientations of the theater (*1*) and the "forum" (*2*) have been corrected in accordance with recent discoveries. The plan and scale of the Basilica (*3*) and Corinthian atrium (*6*) were taken from Bardet's "Decumanus Maximus" plan. The insulae (*14*) to the right of the Vico di Mare are based on Francesco La Vega's 1797 plan of the city (see Fig. 76). The approximate locations of the excavation ramps and shafts are as follows: (*A*) Pozzo di Nocerino; (*B*) entrance to stairs into theater; (*C*) Pozzo di Paone; (*D*) Bellobuono ramp; (*E*) Savarese ramp; (*F*) Moscardillo ramp; (*G*) ramp along Vico di Mare. The other monuments include: (*4*) Galleria Balba; (*5*) Augustalium; (*7*) tombs outside the walls; (*8*) Palestra; (*9*) "Templum Matris Deum"; (*10*) second "Temple"; (*11*) Casa di Gran Portale; (*12*) Casa dei Cervi and Casa del' Atrio a Mosaico; (*13*) Casa di Tramezzo a Legno and Casa dello Scheletro. (Author's plan.)

ber was to reinvestigate as well in the near future. Finally, and most important, this ramp was aligned with another ancient street (Cardo V) that the excavators had encountered, and alignment with this too would greatly facilitate access to the excavations, where Weber clearly anticipated he would be spending a good deal of time and would find a wealth of antiquities.[11]

By mid-November 1756, Weber could outline his plans for continuing these excavations. Workmen in one tunnel were investigating somewhere near the

Basilica, where they had found another street, this one somewhat wider than those encountered elsewhere and flanked by colonnaded walks. That this is the road now known as the Decumanus Maximus is clear from the observation in the reports that the street also ran parallel to the Royal Road. Despite his training in surveying, Weber never used the cardinal points or degrees in his reports, no doubt because he recognized that the court could relate more easily to known landmarks, both ancient and modern, and so he used "Portici" to indicate anything to the west, and "Torre del Greco" for the east.[12]

A second tunnel continued to reveal the course of another street (Cardo V) in front of what Weber began to call a "palacio," perhaps because he had discerned the two columns standing at the entrance to this building and was reminded of the columns in the tablinum of the Villa dei Papiri, the other "palacio" he was investigating at that time.[13] This new palace can now be identified as the southern vestibule of the Palestra. The first two years of the excavations here, however, were not spent in the columnar antechamber but in the larger room behind it.

In an early report to Alcubierre describing the situation of these excavations, Weber noted, "One does not want to abandon this principal street, for two reasons: first, the whole plan of the city of Herculaneum is formed by these streets; second, by means of the layout of these streets, all the temples and buildings and everything inside them will be encountered, and one will know where he is going."[14] He therefore had managed to orient the excavations to the grid of the city, as well as to at least one known structure, the Basilica, and was confident that this would greatly simplify the process of drawing up plans of the work. This report also reveals that Weber thought that temples lay along these streets and that it was this belief that drove his relentless pursuit of antiquities here. The next weeks were spent cutting tunnels to link the Bellobuono ramp and Weber's recent tunnels with the network of Bardet's tunnels, such as those around the Basilica and those under the Moscardillo property, where tombs had been found some years earlier.[15] In the course of this consolidation, Weber observed that it might be of interest to historians to know that Herculaneum stood on a 30-palm slope, by which he meant that the area of the "palacio" stood some 8 meters lower than the level at which Bardet had cut his tunnel to investigate these areas east of the Basilica.[16]

It is clear from the investigations carried out here over the next several years that neither Weber nor Alcubierre was aware of Bardet's plans illustrating this part of the city and therefore did not fully comprehend the extent of those earlier investigations; yet Bardet's hand could be seen everywhere, for the site was riddled with his tunnels. As late as 1752, visitors were still able to wander

through them in much of this area, from the Basilica to as far east as the tomb of
the Balbi family. Northall described his descent into the remains of the city (as
opposed to those of the theater) by means of a tunnel in which he could hear the
wheels of the coaches rattling along the Royal Road above.

> In entering this subterranean [city], first there is a steep descent of
> seventy-two paces, straight forward; then, turning to the right, is another
> of seventeen ancient steps; after which is seen the appearance of the
> outside of houses; bases of pillars of brick, some stuccoed and fluted,
> some standing upright, others overset. We went into several rooms, some
> circular like baths, all stuccoed in compartments and painted. We walked
> upon marble floors worked in mosaic, in pretty taste. Here, stamping the
> foot, it sounded hollow; by which we conjectured we were in one of the
> upper rooms of a house. We saw some beams that were burnt to a coal and
> crumbled to pieces when touched; others not burnt, and the wood of
> these so hard and tough that a knife would scarce cut it. The next thing we
> came to was a square monument which belonged to the Balbus family.[17]

Even Weber's foreman, Josef de Corcoles, complained that the area was "very
difficult to excavate, because of the number of ruins."[18] Although it is nowhere
stated to what degree any of Bardet's tunnels still remained accessible, a condition that would have made for somewhat easier going, Weber relied heavily on
their existence to quicken the pace of his own work; Paderni later charged that
Weber had wasted a great deal of time and money excavating areas already
cleared by Bardet.[19] Weber hastily modified his initial identification of the
building to a "ruined palace" and began looking for areas that had not been
previously explored. Under the circumstances, it is not clear what Weber
thought to gain by concentrating his efforts here, unless he hoped to match
Alcubierre's earlier successes in the Galleria Balba.

The search for areas that might contain artifacts soon led the excavators into
rooms on the second story of the "palacio," and a ramp eventually had to be dug
to link the upper tunnels with the lower ones, so that the workmen, only four in
number, could pass more easily from one level to the other. Weber ordered the
tunnels to be widened and began to clear rooms completely and excavate in the
same manner being employed at the Villa dei Papiri. Corcoles evidently had
suggested that it would be better to fully expose these structures to the light of
day, but Weber opposed this approach, noting that twice as much land would
need to be purchased, half for the excavations and half to hold the backfill. He
argued that the value of the land above was too great, concluding that it would
be "almost a sin to destroy so many fruit-bearing trees, which should not be cut

Figure 34. Bronze statuette of Venus binding her sandle (MN. 5133; 0.175 m.). Arm and ankle bracelets of gold. Found on February 22, 1757. (Courtesy of the Soprintendenza Archeologica di Napoli e Caserta.)

down except in great need, even though the damages are reimbursed."[20] He was not averse to boring shafts through which men and matériel could be moved, however, and soon thereafter a small shaft was sunk, so that the enormous amount of excavated fill that had begun to accumulate below could be lifted out of the tunnels.

The finds were few and far between, and almost four months passed before the first major discovery was made. The search had intensified in late February 1757, when the excavators uncovered a small bronze statuette of Venus wearing gold armbands and binding a sandal to her raised foot (MN. 5133) (Fig. 34).[21] Since the great peristyle garden in the Villa dei Papiri was still yielding major bronze statues[22] and the moderately successful excavations at the Praedia Iuliae

Felicis in Pompeii were just winding down, it is little wonder that this isolated find failed to win Alcubierre's enthusiastic support for this site. Nor did it buoy the spirits of the workmen, who remarked to Paderni that in all their years they had not encountered "a worse site than this one."[23]

Weber's real troubles with the building he now referred to as the "Palace of the Venus" began in June 1757, when a dispute with Alcubierre finally erupted concerning the methods Weber was employing to excavate this site. Alcubierre's charges are remarkably similar to those he had leveled against Weber five years earlier, accusing him of "altering the system of excavation employed in the past" and of diverting the excavation tunnels in order to concentrate more on tracing the course of the city's streets than on recovering antiquities. In one lengthy letter Weber concedes that little has been found in the "Palace of the Venus" but says that this was not through lack of effort. He describes the disposition of the tunnels in detail, how they were excavating in second-story rooms whose floors had disintegrated but whose walls were of painted stucco; how they were clearing out the areas near where the Venus had been found, although there was little promise of additional finds; how they were encountering old tunnels and virgin ground.

Weber was particularly indignant with the charges because, only four days earlier, Alcubierre himself had walked these tunnels; he had also seen sketches of the site many times, been briefed on the disposition of the excavations, and had appeared fully satisfied with all of Weber's arrangements. Weber lashed out as well against unspecified foes who were seeking to rob him of the court's favor.

> I have not changed the established method [of the excavations], and if I have changed [the direction of] a tunnel, I have done so out of necessity when it was finished or when there was some need in another area, always, however, according to the established method, silent or expressed, because Your Lordship has ordered that one go from one place to another that promises something. And Your Lordship always has returned from the work completely pleased and congratulatory.[24]

In a second letter, dated June 14, 1757, he reiterated his devotion to Alcubierre and the court:

> I must explain that over the course of seven years that I have held the honor of serving His Majesty in [these] excavations under the orders of Your Lordship I have taken care (despite all desolation and without shunning fatigue) to fulfill my obligation, avoiding neither the dangers nor risks

to my life in order to gain the Royal Good Will and the satisfaction of Your
Lordship by means of many good finds, without specifying in minute
detail the events which have taken place in the excavations and the various
conditions endured during that time. Since it is clear that all have mar-
veled at the benefit of encountering treasures and saving costs to the
Royal Agency, as Your Lordship has seen and approved either expressly or
tacitly, not only would it be a tedious labyrinth to get into these, but also it
would muddle the comprehension of Your Lordship to itemize that which
with such zeal and persistence one has sought to obey.

Thus I content myself to receive the admonitions of Your Lordship with
all resignation, attributing them more to the purpose of some emulation
than to an endeavor to disturb the harmony, subordination, and reverent
effect which through all bonds I declare and will declare inalterably to
Your Lordship.[25]

Despite Weber's good will, even Tanucci sided with Alcubierre and sent him
orders to instruct Weber to "not alter for any reason" Alcubierre's arrangements
in the excavations nor "the good system with which these have been made in the
past; not removing workmen from the principal work at hand in order to make
paths so that plans may be drawn, but rather one should maintain the same
method used by [Alcubierre] for making these [plans]."[26] In response Weber
wrote directly to Tanucci, producing samples of Alcubierre's letters which had
led him to believe his superior was pleased with his arrangements and again
attributing the dispute to some unknown party seeking to discredit him and
"disturb the harmony" between him and his superior.[27]

"BUTCHERS OF ANTIQUITY"

The only individual in a position powerful enough to exercise so great an
influence on the conduct of the excavations was Camillo Paderni, the curator of
the royal collection of antiquities at Portici. For some months, Paderni had been
complaining in his own correspondence with Tanucci that Weber failed to notify
him immediately when an artifact had been uncovered, so that he might supervise its removal, and that Weber was slow in delivering artifacts to the royal
villa.[28] At the heart of the problem was Paderni's perception that both
Alcubierre and Weber were overstepping their bounds and infringing upon his
domain, one for which he felt himself specially trained and uniquely qualified.

The conflict begins to manifest itself in the excavation records most decisively in early December 1757, when Paderni outlined his grievances in a letter

to Tanucci in which he bluntly articulated his feelings about Alcubierre and
Weber. Paderni complained that the crates of artifacts from the excavations
were sent first to the home of the site supervisor (in this case Corcoles), who
emptied them all, noted their contents, and then repacked the crates and sent
them on to Weber, who repeated the process before finally forwarding them to
Paderni.

> Can Your Excellency believe that such objects improve by being handled
> by people who understand nothing? I leave it to Your Eminence to ponder,
> and say nothing more. I only add that Sig. Don Rocque d'Alcubierre said
> that the matter was not handled well, but that one should bring everything
> quickly to me, and that it would have been his responsibility to order Sig.
> Weber to do this. With all of this braggadocio, Alcubierre gave me little
> hope of well being, since both of them are singular minded: the first
> [Alcubierre] suffers from a certain "je ne sais quoi"; the second [Weber]
> suffers in his brain, but in all that regards the primary purpose of his duty,
> I assure Your Excellency that not only is he tireless but he serves the king
> well, yet he diminishes his merit through the obstinacy of his wicked
> brain.[29]

Weber, he concluded, should focus his attention on the operation of the excavations and on drawing up plans of the ruins. In an exercise of the chain of
command that was to become all too familiar, Tanucci sent Alcubierre a letter
ordering Weber not to concern himself with matters pertaining to Paderni.

   This affair also illustrates the interest shown by Charles of Bourbon in the
smooth operation of his excavations, for Tanucci also had asked Paderni, on the
king's behalf, to identify the source of these problems and to offer recommendations on how they might best proceed. Paderni responded somewhat cryptically
in a long letter written at Portici on December 13, 1757, which concluded:

> Finally, Your Excellency advised me that His Majesty commands that I
> should declare who holds the blame for the disorder that has arisen in the
> excavations. I beseech His Majesty to be content for now that I should say
> that the simplicity of a man who, according to his desire, would like to be
> an antiquarian when he is not one, is led to various excesses by such
> delirium, and that many who harbour such delirium become for the most
> part butchers of antiquity.[30]

There are two possible candidates for the object of Paderni's wrath: Corcoles, a
military engineer of lower rank and the foreman of the excavations at Herculaneum; and Weber.

Corcoles had been Alcubierre's original foreman at Herculaneum since work
first began there in 1738 and at the time was considered the most capable
engineer.[31] Weber had long been hostile toward him, considering him too
closely allied to Paderni, Canart, Scognamillo, and Alcubierre.[32] Nevertheless,
Corcoles seems the less likely victim in this case, since he is specifically named
thereafter as the object of a series of corrective measures Paderni believes
should be instituted immediately. These consisted of ensuring that the workmen notify Paderni as soon as they encounter any antiquity, under penalty of
being suspended from work for a week; that the excavators be made aware that
the antiquities were not only precious but fragile and should handle them with
care; that the objects be sent directly to Portici, not to Paderni's house or anyone
else's first; that he receive notification of a find at the same time as Weber, not
after; and, finally, that Weber should obey his orders that extreme diligence be
exercised in retrieving all fragments of any object that Paderni had deemed
worthy of recovery. "These engineers," Paderni lamented, "would like to be
virtuosi in matters they do not comprehend."[33]

As events unfolded over the course of the next few years, it becomes increasingly clear that Paderni viewed Weber, who by now had begun to work closely
with other members of the court and the Accademia Ercolanese, as a growing
threat to his control over the material from the excavations and to him personally. For his part, Weber could only acknowledge that the difficulties presented
by previous excavations in the "palacio" were complicating his work considerably, but he pointed out that they already had spent seven years excavating the
Villa dei Papiri and it could take even longer for the investigation of this building
to become equally fruitful.[34] In terms of antiquities for the museum, this proved
a gross overestimation of the value of this particular site.

THE TEMPLUM MATRIS DEUM

In the period between Weber's initial response to Alcubierre's criticism in June
and Paderni's later accusations in December, Weber's luck with this site had
improved somewhat, since he had undertaken to clear the "palacio" in the same
manner as the Villa dei Papiri and had begun to make new finds. First had been
the discovery, in July 1757, of fragments of a marble plaque with an inscription
commemorating Vespasian's restoration, in A.D. 76, of a temple dedicated to the
Mater Deum that had been damaged by the earthquake of A.D. 62 (Fig. 35).[35]

Inscriptions had always generated a great deal of interest in the excavations,
for they gave names to otherwise anonymous statues and monuments, and their
texts could be readily copied – both openly and by stealth – and transmitted for

Figure 35. Inscription (*CIL* 10.1406) recording the restoration by Vespasian in A.D. 76 of a Templum Matris Deum following the earthquake of A.D. 62. Found in July 1757 in the southern vestibule of the Palestra at Herculaneum; now in the Museo Nazionale (MN. 3708). (Courtesy of the Soprintendenza Archeologica di Napoli e Caserta.)

debate throughout the scholarly community, both in Naples and Europe generally.[36] This inscription proved particularly valuable, since it mentioned both a Roman emperor and a historical event described by the ancient authors. It served as well to positively identify the actual building where Weber was at work, a feature also potentially afforded by the *proscriptio locationis* of the Praedia Iuliae Felicis in Pompeii, but which had eluded Weber as well as others. This was no longer a mere "palace" but a "temple," the first of its kind found anywhere in the Vesuvian landscape. Uncertain of how to weigh the conflicting pieces of evidence he had collected here, Weber now began to refer to this building with the somewhat unwieldy label of "the Temple of the Venus or Vespasian or the Mother of the Gods."[37]

Soon thereafter, the excavators had turned up a small bronze statuette of Mercury carrying his caduceus and money purse (MN. 5227), but the discovery of so small and isolated a find hardly made a stir.[38] This and most of the numerous other small objects recovered nearby had not been found on the floor inside the "temple" itself, however, for Weber later noted in his reports that everything had come to rest 21 palms (5.5 m.) from the ground, along the south side of the room, toward the sea.[39] The vaulted ceiling of this room had collapsed along the entire north side and a single tunnel bored under it had revealed a white stucco ceiling painted with a blue and yellow star pattern; the upper side of the vault still bore traces of a simple black and white mosaic that must have been the floor of a room in the upper story, which explained why, as he had earlier remarked, he had found no floors there. Weber had drawn a sketch of the plan and elevation of this room as it appeared in early August 1757, showing where the vaulted ceiling, the statue of Venus, and the inscription had been found. He also had made a detailed study of the decoration of the vault, counting all 966 extant stars, measuring the average distance between them, and carefully plotting their pattern in a series of sketches. Armed with this information, he had appealed directly to Tanucci, who quickly received the king's permission for Weber to draw a complete plan of the temple in a large scale.[40]

Weber interpreted this as carte blanche for using whatever means he had at his disposal to recover the plan of this "temple" and whatever precious objects it might contain. He had started by sinking a large shaft, 3.25 meters in diameter, directly over the spot where the inscription had been found.[41] The objective of so large a shaft must have been to facilitate the process of clearing out this entire building in the same way that a similar shaft had been bored over the cavea of the theater. A winch was set up to assist in the removal of the fill, and as many as four tunnels now probed the street in front as well as areas farther back inside the building. These latter quickly encountered the first columns of the enormous peristyle courtyard, just east of the "temple," that Bardet had mapped in part years before. Almost five months passed between the discovery of the Mater Deum inscription and the next major find; it was four months since Weber had been ordered to draw up a plan, and still no complete plan of the site existed, although he claimed in late November that one was nearly complete.[42]

Weber's determination with this site finally paid off partially, in December 1757, shortly after Paderni's reproaches. Investigations along the west colonnade of the peristyle had revealed fragments of marble revetment and a small column, perhaps part of a small shrine, and an inscription, broken into four fragments, that read "Ivlia Hygia ex visv" (MN. 3711).[43] The fragments were rushed to Portici, where the text was transcribed by Piaggio, who was at work on the charred papyrus rolls from the Villa dei Papiri and also served as court epigrapher and calligrapher. It was December 24, and Weber had the good fortune of encountering Charles of Bourbon himself, who was at the royal palace in Portici for the holidays. With Paderni and others presumably in attendance, Weber kissed the royal hands and inquired whether His Majesty had seen the inscription. Weber was clearly delighted to learn that he had, for Weber mentioned the king's presence in Portici in two of his subsequent reports.[44]

Only days later, at half past eleven at night on January 3, the excavators located the white marble dedicatory statue of Hygeia to which the inscription referred. In compliance with Tanucci's orders, Paderni was notified immediately, and he assisted in its removal; there is nothing to indicate that the recovery effort was put off until morning. This draped statue, in an excellent state of preservation, stood about 1 meter high. The divinity was described as holding her right hand to her head, clutching a serpent against her breast with her left hand, and standing with her legs crossed.[45]

Despite this auspicious find, the new year did not bring a change in fortune at this site. It does not appear that Weber recognized that this was Hygeia herself, for he later refers to the statue simply as the "Madonna," which leads to confusion with two other female statues he was calling by this designation at this same time, one from the Villa dei Papiri and one found near the Decumanus Maximus.[46] Nevertheless, he became convinced he would find in the vicinity a Temple of Aesculapius, "the father of Hygia, in whose temple the sick must sleep in order to recuperate their health, dreaming of the treatment they need to employ, as the tablet says thus 'Hygia ex visu.' "[47] While he may have overheard this notion about the ritual expressed by Piaggio or other members of the court during a discussion of the inscription's meaning, this is the second instance during the excavation of this site that illustrates that Weber had begun to rely on inscriptional evidence to identify and interpret the function of a building being excavated under his care. By now, another wing of the peristyle had already been discovered, and Weber held out hope of finding more treasures, since the symmetrical design of the portico was beginning to be revealed.

But the euphoria was short-lived, for no other temple, building, or antiquities of any consequence were found in the excavations here for over a year. Finally, in early 1759, they encountered a wall Weber referred to as the "wall of the windows," apparently the north enclosure wall of the peristyle, which takes the form of a cryptoporticus rather than an open colonnade. When the center point of this wall had been determined, Weber ran a perpendicular tunnel back toward the sea (to the southwest), hoping to encounter another prize. Instead his tunnel skirted down one side of the central euripus, an enormous cross-shaped pool which, sometime later, Weber deduced was a fish tank after he discovered terracotta vessels immured in the walls near the floor of the tank and concluded they could only be for fish. He sketched a plan of his findings, but this is no longer extant.[48]

In the meantime, early in 1758, the excavators had returned to the street in front of the "temple" (Cardo V), where a tunnel was extended down the street toward the sea. Weber again remarked that this tunnel was bound to encounter more buildings which could be investigated before returning to the "temple" and expressed the hope of encountering a public fountain as well.[49] In a short time he found an intersection with a small side street heading east. Work in this area was abandoned soon thereafter, but it continued in front of the temple, where the excavators had begun to enter the columnar antechamber and eventually even found the street fountain Weber had sought.[50] Tunneling in this area had become so intensive, creating huge caverns inside the "temple" itself, that segments had to be backfilled with material that stood heaped around the mouth of the air shaft.[51]

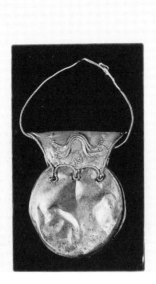

Figure 36. Gold bulla with fili-
gree (MN. 24606) found in
May 1758 during excavations
in the anteroom of the
Templum Matris Deum in
Herculaneum. (Courtesy of
the Soprintendenza
Archeologica di Napoli e
Caserta.)

Figure 37. Bronze statuette of
Hercules with his characteristic
lion's pelt and knotted club (MN.
5270; 0.10 m. H), found in May
1758 during excavations in the Templum Matris Deum in Her-
culaneum. (Courtesy of the
Soprintendenza Archeologica di
Napoli e Caserta.)

To diminish the risks presented by clearing such huge portions of the underground ruins, Weber had been granted permission to bore a second shaft,
measuring 5.1 meters by 4.4 meters, which would drop down directly upon the
two columns of the room at the front of this building, a room he now referred to
as the "atrium" of the temple.[52] This effort finally yielded a small cache of gold
objects, found near a wall on the floor of the room, including a complete gold
bulla (MN. 24606), whose discovery caused something of a sensation and led
Weber to dub this the "Room of the Gold" (Fig. 36). Shortly thereafter,
Corcoles discovered a bronze statuette of Hercules resting a knotted club on his
left shoulder draped with the characteristic lion's pelt (MN. 5270) (Fig. 37).[53]

These last finds had not been made soon enough to be included at first on
Weber's long-promised plan of this site. The plan, which bore the date of April

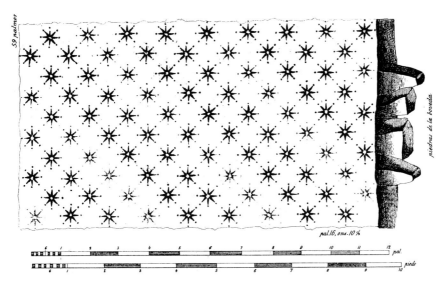

Figure 38. Engraving of Weber's drawing of a portion of the painted decoration from the
barrel-vaulted ceiling of the inner room of the Templum Matris Deum in Herculaneum.
Weber counted 966 stars painted onto the white-stuccoed vault, though here he indicated
only 90. The caption describes as well the black and white mosaic pavement from an
upper-story room found on the opposite side of the vault. From *StErc*, pl. 8.

30, 1758, is no longer extant, but the brief caption that was intended to accompany it survives in a manuscript Weber wrote some two years later. This caption
reveals that he had drawn both a plan and a "profile," or elevation, at a scale of
1:60 palms, by which he must mean that he had drawn the building's entire length
(15.8 m.). He had settled upon the identification of this building as the "Tempio
della Madre de' Dei" and noted that it stood 41 palms (10.4 m.) below the present
ground level. As with the belvedere from the Villa dei Papiri, he tied the building
into local topographical features by providing precise distances from key sites
such as the Palazzo Reale, Vesuvius, Torre del Greco, and the Royal Road.
Moreover, he appended a sketch of the fallen barrel-vaulted ceiling from the
main room, showing its painted stars; explained that the floor of the room above
was paved with black and white mosaic; and illustrated as well several of the
pyramid-shaped stones, such as those used in Roman reticulate masonry, that he
surmised had made up the masonry of the vault. This latter sketch survives in an
engraving, dated May 1, 1758, which may show only a portion of Weber's original
drawing, since only 90 of the 966 stars are illustrated and the dimensions recorded for the sides of the vault (59 palms by 16 palms, 10.5 onzes) do not
conform to the scales provided in Neapolitan palms and Roman feet (Fig. 38).

Weber described some of the steps leading up to the completion of these illustrations in a letter to Alcubierre dated May 17, 1758. This is an especially important document for confirming that the ultimate goal of such plans was not to document the course of the excavations but rather to illustrate for Charles of Bourbon where individual finds had been made. It reveals as well how the king often had to be content with rough drafts. At the same time, the letter betrays Weber's frustration with his superior, whose indifference toward the plans he had long sought cost Weber a key opportunity to show off his work to the king:

> I am remitting to Your Lordship the plan and profile, along with another detailed sketch of the fallen vault with stars painted on its stucco, of the Temple of the Gods, as expressed in the inscription of Vespasian. I completed this plan under your direction as the excavations of this proceeded. After Your Lordship examined and approved this plan on May 9, you told His Majesty of it in the garden [of the Royal Palace of Caramanica at Portici], ordering me in His Royal Presence to copy the plan. However, since my servant had the plan upstairs in the chapel [of the Royal Palace], I could not carry this out, as I had already left it with my servant, because, as Your Lordship knows, at the time I arrived at Caramanica [my servant] told me that Your Lordship, having considered the matter, did not want to present the plan [to the king] until another time. Then, however, as we passed through His Majesty's garden, Your Lordship announced to His Majesty that you had examined and compared this plan at different times and that it should be given to Tanucci for engraving, etc.
>
> As it was late and Your Lordship then had returned to Naples, Paderni presented the gold bulla to His Majesty in my presence, then he took out the draft of the other general plan of the underground excavations, showing His Majesty the place where the bulla had been found at the side of the Temple's atrium. While being shown this, His Majesty had asked after the plan of the temple that Your Lordship had mentioned that morning, and since I did not have it with me and it was then almost nightfall, I was not able to show it to His Majesty, as Your Lordship had ordered me, until the following Sunday. Then, having considered it well, along with the sketch of the stars, you deemed it worthy of passing on to Tanucci for engraving, as Your Lordship had said that morning. Subsequently, I took the measurements and distances of the temple as Your Lordship ordered, including as well the gold bulla, as Your Lordship can observe above my signature, and I submit as well the draft, which can be stored in your

office. . . . P.S. I am remitting as well another copy or draft for preservation in your office.[54]

The fate of Weber's plans, then, rested principally with Alcubierre, who was ambivalent about whether or not to recommend these to Tanucci for engraving. As with paintings removed from the sites, the act of engraving such plans apparently implied official sanction for their ultimate inclusion in the volumes of *Le antichità di Ercolano*, for there could hardly be any other reason for going to such expense, although in the end none were published. Such had been the case with the earlier plans by Montemayor and Dorgement, as well as with Weber's earlier drawings of the mosaics from the Villa dei Papiri, but as a result of the eclipse of Bayardi's control of the publication and the abandonment of his approach to publishing the sites, none of these plans had seen the light of day. Weber's illustration of the vaulted ceiling was engraved; Ruggiero later recovered the copper plate in the excavation's archives and published the engraving in 1885.[55]

The plans of the "Tempio della Madre de' Dei," however, do not appear to have been engraved, and, despite the fact that Weber produced some four copies, not a single one is known today. Even Weber apparently had not kept a copy for himself, since he later became concerned when Alcubierre failed either to acknowledge receipt of the plan and its copy or to return them.[56] Although the plan did not accompany the caption that Weber included in the manuscript he wrote in 1760, at least one copy did exist in that year, when Alcubierre finally acknowledged that he had passed it along to Tanucci for engraving.[57]

Since this was not a terribly complex building, Weber's plan is likely to have been fairly simple, probably a more refined version of the very basic sketches that had accompanied his weekly reports from August 6, 1757, and February 8, 1758 (Fig. 39). The main room of the temple (it is never called the "cella") with its smaller "atrium" and two columns *in antis* would have occupied the central position. This room would have faced onto the two streets forming a T-intersection directly in front, with the public water fountain of stone standing at the southwest corner. The relation of the fallen vault to the walls of the temple could have been shown on both the plan and the elevation, with numbers marking the findspots of the statues of Venus and Mercury and the inscription recording Vespasian's restoration, the text of which would have been provided in the inventory of finds or perhaps reproduced in full to one side of the plan; the bulla's location was apparently appended later. The portico at the rear of the temple could have been illustrated only in part, since work here was still under way, but the location of the statue and inscription of Hygeia almost certainly would have been marked clearly.

Figure 39. Weber's sketch for a plan illustrating the disposition of the excavation shafts and architectural features in and around the Templum Matris Deum in Herculaneum. This sketch appears in his excavation report for February 11, 1758. The annotations read: "(a) Temple; (b) Great airshaft of the [statuette of] Mercury and the [Vespasianic] inscription [naming the Templum Matris Deum]; (c) atrium, or antetemplum; (d) It would be fitting to make a similar air shaft, if Your Highness approves, in order to discover the entire site; (1) street intersection which I am hoping for; (2) where one is excavating at the present time; (3) already-excavated street where one seeks to find the four street corners." Weber completed the final plan, which is no longer extant, on April 30, 1758. (Courtesy of the Società Napoletana di Storia Patria [Ms. 20–5-3, "Rapporti originali di Weber"].)

While work continued in the "Room of the Gold" and along the street in front of the "temple," moving toward the bay, the excavators began to shift their attention back toward the areas below the Royal Road and close to the Basilica.[58] Near the Bellobuono ramp beneath the Bisogno property, another statue also dubbed the "Madonna" had been encountered, along with a road described as paved in brick and heading south, in the direction of Torre del Greco. Near

Figure 40. Weber's sketch of the architectural features, believed to be for an equestrian statue but later identified as a "well," from a building north of the Palestra in Herculaneum. He appended the sketch to an excavation report dated May 6, 1758. The annotations read: "(a) conduit that continues up to 'm' and 'm'; (b) one believes this is a conduit, since it consists of the same pieces of *piperno* [tufa], but not in a channel, though it continues until 'f'; (c) pavement at a lower level that may have held water; (d) structure where the equestrian statue fits, however it rises up like a tomb or a well; its width 'n' is 2.5 palms, its length is not yet known; the structure 'd' of masonry is 8 palms square, but side 'd' is not yet discovered; we have braced the surrounding area." (Courtesy of the Società Napoletana di Storia Patria [Ms. 20–5-3, "Rapporti originali di Weber"].)

this "Madonna," about which nothing further is known, the tunneling had exposed a tufa rain gutter and red columns surrounding what was initially believed to be the base for an equestrian statue but later proved to be a "well," perhaps the impluvium of a private house (Fig. 40). Since this tunnel ran perpendicular to the Bellobuono ramp, in the direction of Torre del Greco, these architectural elements may have been from a private house, or even a

public building, standing opposite the large peristyle courtyard Bardet had
discovered in 1743 directly north of the Palestra.[59]

That Weber had transferred part of his work force to investigate along another ancient street, in the northeast quarter of the city, is confirmed by the
discovery between July 8 and 22, 1758, of a second important inscription, whose
marble plaque was found broken into two fragments. The excavators found the
inscription in the middle of the street, presumably just beyond where they had
found the first "Madonna" but at a height somewhat less than 2 meters above
the paving stones, where evidently it had fallen, along with a portion of the brick
wall to which it had been attached. Both topographically and archaeologically,
the significance of this inscription has not been given adequate attention, since
its precise provenance has long been in question.

The inscription records the construction or restoration of a basilica, city gate,
and walls by M. Nonius Balbus, Herculaneum's greatest benefactor.[60] Such an
inscription would be expected to adorn at least one of the monuments it mentions; at more than 2 meters long, the plaque appears too large to be from an
honorary statue base, as once proposed. Although it is possible that such an
object was carried here by the force of the mud flow, it is less likely that an
inscription secured to a wall could have been knocked loose; less carefully
secured objects like statues and small objects appear to have been most prone to
movement.

One piece of evidence in particular suggests the inscription was found near its
original location. The area under excavation, beneath the Bisogno property and
along the Royal Road, stood relatively near that of the Moscardillo property,
where tombs had been found already in 1750. As seen most clearly at Pompeii
and along the Via Appia Antica in Rome, the Romans were fond of lining the main
thoroughfares leading into their cities with tombs. The largest of those found at
Herculaneum was an aedicula tomb, dedicated to some freedmen of the Balbi.
The tomb may have stood on land decreed for such use by the decuriones in
thanks to Balbus for his work on the adjacent walls and city gates of
Herculaneum. Thus, it seems likely that while investigating this corner of the city,
Weber had unwittingly ventured near one of the main gates of Herculaneum or
even the forum itself, which some scholars have postulated may have been just
northeast of this area.[61]

By late 1758 Alcubierre must have begun to press Weber to return to more
profitable sites, since, apart from the steady stream of ornamental fittings from
doors and furniture, the ones where he was working were not producing returns
in important statuary and painting proportionate to the enormous amount of
time and money expended on them. Under direct orders, Weber began in

December to bore a tunnel toward the "edificio del Teseo," the building where
Alcubierre had recovered the painting of Theseus and the Minotaur (MN.
9049), among others, almost twenty years earlier and where he still hoped to
find more treasures. In anticipation of these finds, Weber cut a new ramp,
starting from underground and working his way up, with a view toward ventilat-
ing his tunnels and allowing easier access to this building. When he finally
reached the site, in mid-May, Weber found it honeycombed with partially filled
or poorly braced tunnels and barely capable of withstanding further tunneling.
He proceeded cautiously, shoring up the old tunnels as best he could with new
fill or by building pillars, and praying for divine succor when Alcubierre ordered
new tunnels dug in areas where Weber was unsure whether, in tunneling back
and forth through the site in an effort to cover every inch, his workmen would
cut into an existing cavity and bring the modern houses of Resina down on their
heads.[62]

    In the seven months spent here, the only finds of note were fragments of two
inscriptions, and these were found in the street rather than inside the building
itself; otherwise, the site refused to yield more than the usual building materials.
Weber, frustrated by the squandering of his efforts here, had begun sealing the
tunnels in early December 1759, hoping that Alcubierre would see the wisdom
of putting off further excavations in this enormous building for a later time.
Much of the backfill for this operation came from investigations that continued
along the Decumanus Maximus in front of the Basilica. Here, in late February
1760, Alcubierre's intuition that the site held more treasures was partially
confirmed when a small equestrian statue and the lower portion of the leg of a
life-size bronze horse, apparently part of an equestrian statue, emerged. But no
other fragments were recovered, and shortly thereafter references to work here
cease for almost a year.[63]

THE SECOND TEMPLE

By maintaining several crews at different parts of the excavations at Herculaneum at one time, Weber was able to minimize the impact of an unprofit-
able site, provided that it was offset by success elsewhere. Investigations in the
Villa dei Papiri continued throughout this period, and although tunnels had by
now almost completely permeated the site, important statues were still turning
up: in August 1758, the seated Hermes (MN. 5625) and the bust of "Sappho"
(MN. 4896), from the great peristyle; in 1759, the busts of Dionysus (MN.
5618), the Landsdowne Hercules-type male (MN. 5594), and the Thespis
(MN. 5598), from the square peristyle.[64] Experience had also begun to en-

lighten Weber that such boustrophedon sweeps through buildings, no matter how systematic and thorough, were precarious exercises at best and could be avoided by reading certain clues provided by the archaeological ruins. This was particularly true of his approach to a structure he identified as another "temple," on the basis of analogues he discerned between the plans and situations of this and the earlier "Temple of the Mater Deum or Vespasian."

This second structure, which is now recognized as the northern vestibule of the Palestra, first appears in a report of September 22, 1759, during continued excavations along Cardo V near the Bellobuono ramp. The plan of 1743 makes it abundantly clear that Bardet had already investigated these ruins, but, as is the case for this entire area, little is known about the extent of his work or what antiquities he had recovered here.[65] Weber had stumbled into Bardet's old tunnels, the same ones Northall had toured in 1752, for Weber later remarked that "this whole site has been perforated by a chaos of tunnels some twenty years old." These permitted him to discern readily many of the basic features of the structure and allowed his investigations to proceed at a relatively rapid pace. He identified this as a small temple first because of the two columns *in antis* he found in the vestibule and second because it fronted onto a public street, with a marble water fountain at one corner. Both of these were features he had encountered in his other temple, whose Vespasianic inscription he believed had supplied irrefutable proof of its function. On the other hand, the absence of these same features confirmed his suspicions that the building with the painting of Theseus could not be a temple, despite Bayardi's having designated it as such.[66] In labeling this new structure a temple, Weber must have felt that the term brought with it a certain cachet that would help legitimatize concentrating his efforts here.

Even more encouragement came from the greater dimensions of this supposed temple, with its four internal columns dividing what he termed the "cella" into two roughly equal chambers, and from the early discovery of several fragments of carbonized wood covered with gold leaf, probably from a piece of furniture decorated with ivory inlay as well. Weber thereupon resolved to excavate this second temple in the same manner as the first: by sinking a shaft 6.25 meters in diameter directly over the door separating what he called the "pronaos" from the "cella," where he hoped to find an inscription that would verify that it was a temple and identify the deity to whom it was dedicated. This failed to have the desired effect, yet Weber felt vindicated in part by the discovery inside the building of a large bronze brazier, or water heater (MN. 72898), that both he and Paderni were convinced had been used as an altar for burnt offerings at sacrifices.[67] In a desperate pursuit of several lost fragments from the brazier, huge cavities were excavated inside this structure and the excess fill hoisted in baskets up through the shaft. But, no doubt due in part to Bardet's earlier depredations, only a mosaic pavement and the usual bronze implements were brought to light, several of the latter found some 1.5 meters above the floor, where the mudflow had propelled them. He had greater success in the street in front of the building, where the excavators found a variety of bronze vases and baking pans; a marble relief plaque showing a figure identified as "Theseus" (MN. 6680) but clearly an athlete; and a badly damaged statue of a youth riding a hippocamp.[68]

Again drawing upon his experiences at the first temple, Weber began driving his tunnels at the level of the second story but was disappointed in his hope of recovering more statuary. As the number of small finds here diminished, the excavators wound their way back south into the private apartments and shops along the western facade of the Palestra; one shaft dropped down into the cryptoporticus that defined the north end of the Palestra's peristyle. Here they encountered a number of rooms on both stories with painted walls and mosaic pavements, among these a black and white mosaic that merited a separate shaft to facilitate its removal.[69]

Some months later, Weber suggested that another mosaic not be removed to Portici, "recognizing that the curiosity of the public and of foreigners will find particular satisfaction in seeing some of those mosaic pavements in their proper places and rooms."[70] This extraordinary proposal must have been intended for the benefit of those who toured the underground tunnels while the excavations were in progress, since there is no indication that the practice of backfilling the tunnels had been halted here, and even the open trenches at Pompeii and Stabiae were still being backfilled at this time. Yet Weber was clearly beginning to advocate that the sites under his care be left accessible and with certain of their furnishings *in situ*. He believed, for example, that allowing visitors to see the great euripus in the Villa dei Papiri would bring glory to the king equal to that he gained from the museum: "foreigners and curiosity seekers get more pleasure and satisfaction from seeing the vestiges of the underground city."[71]

In early July 1760, Weber again tried to whet the appetite of his superiors by announcing the discovery of yet another temple, this one round, whose plan he hoped to recover for comparison with his two quadrilateral ones. It later becomes clear, however, that this structure was not a temple at all but simply the rear of the great apsidal hall of the Palestra or else part of an oven in the adjacent pistrinum. Weber's description of the hollow walls (concamerationes) for allowing the heat to pass through later led Ruggiero and others to believe he was describing the outer walls of the caldarium in the Terme del Foro two blocks away, but the preponderance of the evidence suggests that the excavations remained in the area around the Palestra. Several interesting finds were made here, including the remains of a small wooden wheel and two portable bronze heaters (MN. 73883), the operation of which Weber described in great detail.[72]

Another important find was made in the street near the front of the "Temple of the Mater Deum," where Weber had ordered a workman to excavate precisely because of his earlier luck in recovering antiquities in this area. The find was a square bronze base inscribed with Egyptian hieroglyphics (MN. 1107), whose diminutive size and fragile construction suggest it could not have supported more than the smallest votive statue, perhaps a bronze statuette of Isis.[73] Nevertheless the fervor to recover just such a statue incited an intensive search that lasted several months and produced only a large cache of bronze ornaments and candelabra that had apparently been washed to this point along Cardo V by the pyroclastic flow.

Excavations in the complex of buildings along this street continued well into the new year; the last clear reference to it is made in May 1761. The significant finds had dropped off well before that time, however, since the last discovery of note appears in the reports for February.[74] At that time, Weber's most skilled and trusted workman, Aniello Diacampo, had sunk a shaft from one of the upper-level rooms of the Palestra down into one of the rooms flanking the great apsidal hall. By chance his narrow shaft dropped directly onto a series of small mounted paintings resting on the mosaic floor and leaning up against one wall, where they had amalgamated with the pyroclastic flow (Fig. 41). Paderni, who had himself lowered down to inspect the paintings *in situ*, had to admit to Tanucci that he could offer only some preliminary observations, since he had been overwhelmed by the heat and lack of air in the excavation shaft. It was a scenario Tanucci was evidently beginning to feel was emblematic of the declining fortunes of the royal excavations.[75]

By this time, Weber already had expended almost five years of the royal time and money in excavating the remains of the Palestra. Despite the fact that this remains the largest single building discovered at Herculaneum, it failed to produce nearly the number of antiquities recovered in the Villa dei Papiri, the theater, or the Basilica, much less the modestly scaled Praedia Iuliae Felicis at Pompeii. In fact, it had yielded less than twenty artifacts of high enough quality to become part of the royal collection at Portici and, ultimately, the Museo Nazionale in Naples. It is difficult to comprehend how the Bourbon excavators could have rationalized continuing their work here, except as a direct result of Weber's stubbornness and enthusiasm. He measured success on a different scale, for his interests clearly favored the architectural remains, believing as he

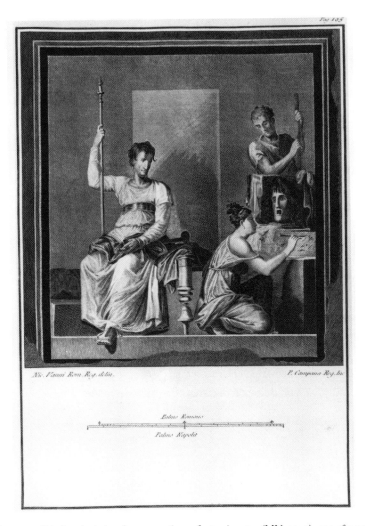

Figure 41. Painting depicting the preparations of a tragic actor (MN. 9019), one of a series
of six small mounted paintings found propped up against a wall in a room near the Palestra
at Herculaneum in May 1761. Drawing by N. Vanni, engraving by P. Campanna.
From *PdE* 4.191–95, pl. 41.

did that this work had uncovered the first ancient temples in Herculaneum
along with the streets and fountains to which they were oriented. He had
predicted already at the start of the investigations here in 1756 that these streets
would lead to "all the temples and buildings and everything inside" and that
only after these elements of the urban fabric had been identified and tracked
completely would it be possible for him to draw the kind of comprehensive plans
Alcubierre had long desired.

During the last months of 1760, Weber noted on several occasions in his reports that he had returned to certain points along these streets to make additional soundings, despite the obstacles he felt Paderni imposed on his efforts:

> One continues the tunnels in such a manner that all the plans can be united and thereby form the entire city. This method has been followed always under the direction of Your Lordship during my tenure with much success, provided that it did not disturb Paderni. And every time something was encountered in the proximity, all the ground around it was searched so that it is not possible for anything to remain buried and not be recovered without Paderni wasting time or suffering the least discomfort or annoyance.[76]

His goal was to link up the plans of all the buildings in this area and finish a plan he had been working on for some time that would show the known extent of the ancient city of Herculaneum.[77]

PART 3

Documentation

6

Weber's Application to the Accademia Ercolanese

Charles of Bourbon succeeded to the throne of Spain, vacated by his brother Ferdinand VI, in September 1759, but the reluctant departure of the new Spanish king and his wife Maria Amalia for Madrid, in early October, had little direct effect on the excavations (Fig. 42). As Charles III of Spain, he remained an enthusiastic and beneficent patron of his beloved "Cratere," celebrated for his refusal to appropriate a single antiquity from the Kingdom of the Two Sicilies for his new realm and intent on being kept apprised of any and all new discoveries in the excavations through regular dispatches, illustrated plans, and even plaster casts taken of the more important sculptural finds.[1]

Prime Minister Bernardo Tanucci, who in effect governed the kingdom during the minority of Charles's successor, the young Ferdinand IV, also came to assume even greater control over the excavations than he had in the past, referring only the most delicate matters to Charles III himself. In his regular correspondence with the king, Tanucci offered frank and perceptive, if not always impartial, observations on the progress of the work, adding a different perspective than can be gleaned from the often dry and repetitive reports of the excavators themselves. Although the Accademia Ercolanese ceased to meet in regular session soon after Charles's departure and the publication of the second volume on the paintings, Tanucci ensured that material continued to be prepared for subsequent volumes and that all aspects of the excavations, in the field and in the museum, proceeded as they had in the past. Paderni, under orders to submit weekly reports on the discoveries to the king, now began to give even greater scrutiny to the operation of the excavations. It was a role he assumed with great gusto, much to the detriment of the antiquities and the spirits of the workmen.[2]

For Weber, on the other hand, these events came during a period of height-

Figure 42. The departure from Naples of Charles III and Queen Maria Amalia to assume
the throne of Spain in September 1759, in a painting by Antonio Joli. Visible in the background are Mount Vesuvius (*left*), the Monti Lattari (*center*), and the island of Capri (*right*).
(Courtesy of the Museo di San Martino, Naples [Inv. #24].)

ened activity in which he found himself juggling the tasks of field supervisor,
surveyor, and military engineer to an unparalleled degree. He used this period
of greater success and productivity in the excavations as a means to improve his
own position by appealing directly to Tanucci for permission to begin work on a
treatise that would focus on the architectural remains of these ancient cities.
Moreover, he suggested that he might best complete this task by working closely
with the members of the Accademia and that such a collaboration would be
greatly facilitated if he himself were enrolled into its august ranks.

Weber outlined his proposal in a letter addressed to Tanucci on October 18,
1759, only twelve days after Charles III's departure and only eight days after
Paderni's role had been expanded. He opened with an autobiographical sketch
that commenced with his education at the Collegio Ghislieri in Pavia and moved
quickly to his rise through the ranks of the Tschoudi regiment of the Royal
Guard to his posting at Portici in 1750. In his decade of work in the excavations,
he claimed to have produced a total of twenty-nine plans, including the map of
the Cratere Maritimo. Although Alcubierre's persistent complaints and the
small number of plans extant today might suggest this was an exaggeration,

Weber must have counted all his unfinished sketches from Herculaneum, Stabiae, Pompeii, and Pozzuoli, and probably also his plans of the various military and royal installations around Portici for whose construction or restoration he had been responsible. He specifically requested from Tanucci the wherewithal to finish his plans of the ancient sites and implied that this would entail additional excavation. Observing that plans alone could not provide a full appreciation for these sites, many of which remained underground or had been reburied, he proposed that his book should include "some explication of their architecture, function, and ancient significance, with the intelligence, intervention, revision, correction, and approval of the Accademia and Colonel de Alcubierre." Finally, he offered to compose a sample of his text so the Accademia could determine whether his own treatise would complement the style and methodology employed in their publications on the ancient paintings. Surprisingly enough, Tanucci was willing to allow the Accademia itself to weigh the merits of Weber's proposal, and so he passed Weber's letter along to Carcani, Mazzocchi, and other unspecified members on January 20, 1760.[3]

Weber may have been contemplating this audacious proposal for some time, in which case the correlation between this and the king's departure was merely coincidental. Alternatively, he may have recognized in Tanucci a strong advocate of his unique skills and believed that the political circumstances had changed to his advantage. It is certain that already in 1758 he had begun to research aspects of antiquity he intended to incorporate in his text and needed only to produce polished versions of his plans, so perhaps the request for admission to the Accademia came only as an afterthought. What he failed to realize was that all fifteen chairs in the Accademia were occupied at the time and Tanucci was not prepared to increase its roll; Giacomo Castelli's death the following month was untimely for Weber, as Giovanni Basso-Bassi was named to fill this opening long before the Accademia could act on Weber's request.[4]

Weber probably resented Camillo Paderni's increasing influence on the direction of the excavations, since Paderni hardly held credentials any more distinguished than his own yet appeared to be being groomed for the Accademia. It is improbable that he would have found Paderni a sympathetic ally. Nor could Weber expect support from Alcubierre, who evidently had received advance warning of Weber's proposal to write a treatise and had long harbored the suspicion that his subaltern might someday challenge him for control of the excavations. Already in August of 1759, Alcubierre had rummaged through his records for the years when he was in direct charge of the excavations, looking for plans of sites he believed Weber had been instructed to finish or that he himself had turned over long ago to Bayardi. Alcubierre had managed to recover only a copy of his own plan of the Villa of Cicero at Pompeii, dating from 1749, and sent this to Tanucci, with the implication that Weber was failing to fulfill his responsibilities by sitting on Alcubierre's unfinished plans.[5] This proved to be only Alcubierre's first salvo in an escalating campaign of propaganda intended to undermine Weber's credibility and subjugate him to his proper station.[6]

It is unlikely that Weber would have advanced his proposal in the first place without some indication it would be received favorably, but whom he could count among his allies is far from certain. There is strong evidence that Weber had begun to spend a good deal of time in Portici with Antonio Piaggio. The fact that he was a Jesuit priest may have appealed to the Jesuit-educated Weber, as he became increasingly isolated. Piaggio's own interest in the excavations suggests that he may have urged Weber to undertake this work. Piaggio was not the wisest choice for an ally, however, since he was not held in high esteem by other members of the court. It may in fact have been a "siege mentality" that brought these two together.

Through his work on the papyri and in transcribing inscriptions, Piaggio frequently came in contact not only with Alessio Simmaco Mazzocchi, who was in charge of editing the transcriptions of the papyri for publication, but with other members of the Accademia as well. Among the latter was Giovanni Maria Della Torre, who directed the Reale Biblioteca, the Reale Tipografia, and the Museo Farnesiano at the Villa Reale di Capodimonte. A physical scientist by training, Della Torre was a vulcanologist who published in 1754 a history and description of the eruptions of Vesuvius.[7] Piaggio also cultivated an interest in the activities of this renowned volcano, which now was one of the key stops on the Grand Tour, and he later kept a journal of its phenomena for Sir William Hamilton.[8] Both Della Torre and Piaggio also had been responsible for entertaining the noted German critic of ancient art, Johann Joachim Winckelmann, during his first visit to the Bay of Naples in 1758. It is clear already in Winckelmann's early letters that the camps of Piaggio and Paderni were polarized and that Winckelmann had sided with Piaggio, who willingly shared his work on the papyri.[9]

Visits from other foreign scholars and dignitaries during these years had transformed the royal villa at Portici into a lively center for intellectual discourse and debate. As a lieutenant colonel of the Royal Guard, Weber would have moved fairly easily within this circle, and it seems almost certain that out of their learned conversations he conceived many of the notions he later put into practice and incorporated in his writings. Not the least important of these was that he might be co-opted into the Accademia; Winckelmann too had been deluded at one time into believing this was a possibility.[10] These scholars must have regularly pressed Weber, as their closest contact with the daily operation of the excavations, for details about such matters as new discoveries, findspots, and the fluctuating density of the volcanic matrix. It would not be surprising if over time Weber came to view himself as uniquely qualified to assist them in their quest to resolve matters of antiquity that continued to vex them.

GALIANI AND THE EVOLUTION OF ARCHAEOLOGICAL DOCUMENTATION

In April 1758, Tanucci had appointed Berardo Galiani to occupy the seat on the Accademia vacated by Bayardi. Galiani had been educated by the great luminaries of eighteenth-century Neapolitan scholarship, including Giovanni Batista Vico, Niccola Capasso, and even his fellow academician Mazzocchi; he had developed a passion for the fine arts, especially architecture, and had been granted the title of marchese in 1754.[11] Tanucci clearly intended Galiani to fill the void in the Accademia in the sphere of architecture created by Bayardi's departure. As if to confirm himself in that role, Galiani published a sumptuous edition of Vitruvius's ten books on architecture in the same year he was appointed to the Accademia (Fig. 43).[12]

Although his book was critically acclaimed, it is remarkable, and not a little ironic, that in it Galiani made only passing reference to the royal excavations, despite the fact that they had been under way for some seventeen years. Although himself a member of the Accademia, Galiani was constrained by the same royal edict that prohibited publication of the antiquities before they appeared in *Le antichità di Ercolano*. In his dedication he stated that his aims were to make Vitruvian canons comprehensible to modern architects and "to understand better and explain the singular monuments of ancient Herculaneum being excavated by His Majesty." This latter statement, in addition to ignoring the work at Pompeii and Stabiae, illustrates what had long been the traditional approach to using Vitruvius as a source: scholars tended to apply the precepts of this text more or less uncritically as a means of interpreting ancient ruins, rather than seeing the ruins themselves as a means of interpreting aspects of Vitruvius or other classical authorities. Galiani failed to utilize the architectural remains from these ancient cities as comparanda, an approach that would have distinguished his book from other commentaries on Vitruvian architectural principles. For example, he completely missed the opportunity to use the archaeological remains of private baths from Stabiae and Pompeii to explain Vitruvius's cryptic instructions on the arrangements for heating baths and bath water. Nor

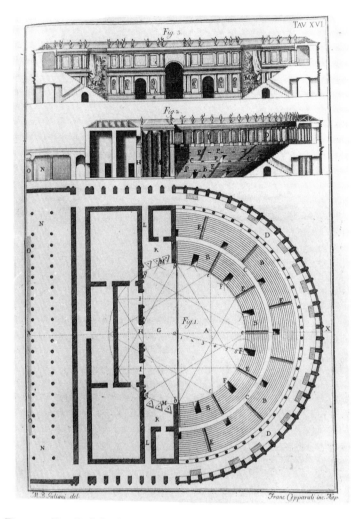

Figure 43. Berardo Galiani's interpretation of the plan and cross section of a Roman theater according to Vitruvius. From B. Galiani, *L'architettura di M. Vitruvio Pollione colla traduzione italiana e comento* (Naples 1758), pl. 16.

did he refer to the sites at Herculaneum and Pompeii, respectively, when contrasting the design of theaters with that of amphitheaters. It was only in his discussion of ancient painting that he submitted as examples two engravings of paintings, both of which had appeared originally in the recently published first volume of *Le antichità*.[13]

In his introduction Galiani elaborated on a section from Vitruvius (1.2.2) dealing with the various modes of expression architects should employ to best communicate their designs: plans, or bird's-eye views (*icnografia*); elevations, both full views of the external facade (*ortografia*) and sections of the internal form (*spaccato*); and perspectives of the entire building (*scenografia*, literally "stage designs"), a technique of rendering both the front and the sides of a structure, which Galiani claimed was no longer used. He also advocated the use of models in paper, wood, or wax, since "only architects and trained individuals understand plans . . . , [whereas] everyone understands models," and because through the process of building a model the architect might resolve problems of construction unanticipated by drawing plans alone.[14] Although Galiani, like Palladio and Serlio before him, was here addressing primarily architects designing modern structures, his methods differed little from those in use for some time by architects in illustrating archaeological discoveries.

Despite the fact that investigations of ancient cultures had been carried out throughout Europe since at least the Renaissance, there were few conventions in the eighteenth century for the illustration and documentation of archaeological remains. Although a detailed excursus on the history of classical archaeology cannot be undertaken here, some basic trends in the recovery and documentation of antiquity may be traced to help set the background to Weber's contributions.[15]

The earliest catalogs of the ruins of Rome were the medieval *Mirabilia*, guidebooks for pilgrims that set forth in simple terms the history and legends surrounding the ruins, arranged according to their regions in the city. The humanists Biondo Flavio's (1392–1463) *Roma instaurata*, of 1447, and Poggio Bracciolini's (1380–1459) *De fortunae varietate*, of 1431–48, were particularly innovative for their critical approach to looking at and describing the ruins themselves and for their reliance on a variety of literary and epigraphic sources for explicating the ruins. But although what they practiced is termed "archaeology," it involved no excavation in the field.[16]

Foreign artists in Rome during the Renaissance, like Martin van Heemskerk (1498–1574) and Etienne Du Pérac (1525?–1604), sketched views that showed the ancient ruins surrounded by modern accretions but that were nevertheless historically accurate records of the remains. The drawings and plans of ruins by such artists as Andrea Palladio (1508–80), Giuliano da Sangallo (1445–1516), and Pirro Ligorio (1514–83) illustrate how architects of the Renaissance had been interested in recovering, through the careful study of these remains, the principles of ancient architecture as prescribed by Vitruvius. They then endeavored to apply these classical canons of proportion and aesthetics to their own designs. In addition to detailed sketches of column capitals, friezes, and entablatures, these architects made measured drawings of the plans of buildings, supplemented by reconstructed elevations and sections. Although on occasion this process of discovery went beyond mere empirical analysis to involve some degree of excavation, their work in fact amounted to little more than clearing and did not constitute a systematic effort to recover the architectural remains of an entire building. Moreover, much of the scientific accuracy these artists gained as a result of clearing was lost in their insistence on restoring or otherwise fabricating elements in their final drawings for which all archaeological evidence was lacking.[17]

In Rome, delegates of the Renaissance popes had overseen nearly all studies of ancient ruins throughout the city, as a means of linking the papacy to the Classical Roman past. Raphael often has been identified as the first representative of the popes to oversee a systematic program of excavation in Rome, after Pope Leo X named him "Commissario delle Antichità" and directed him to draw up a map that would show the location of all the ruins of ancient Rome (1515–20). Although it now appears that Raphael had no such official title, his task of ensuring an adequate supply of stone for the construction of Saint Peter's brought him in contact with ruins both within and outside Rome. In the process, he compared the physical remains with the literary record, applied a more scientific approach to surveying the ruins, and employed plans, elevations, and perspectives to depict the results of his inquiries in accordance with the precepts of Vitruvius. Yet in concentrating his efforts on preventing the loss of the epigraphic material, he failed to safeguard the architectural remains themselves from destruction.[18]

Many excavations in Rome were initiated by private individuals who chanced upon tombs, baths, or other monuments from the Roman era on their own property. The primary goal of many of these haphazard investigations was the recovery of works of art, many of which the papacy claimed for itself, although a portion passed into private collections through sale or theft. Building materials were robbed out for the construction of new churches and palaces. There was little interest in accurately recording, much less in preserving, the architectural remains themselves for posterity, and many monuments were destroyed in the process.[19] Eventually, compilations of such discoveries appeared in the form of descriptive catalogs modeled after the *Mirabilia*. An early example is F. Vacca's *Memorie di varie antichità trovate in diversi luoghi della città di Roma*, from 1594, in which Vacca brought together all the known references to ancient ruins encountered in Rome through chance discovery and plundering.

The following century saw the publication of works that combined description and analysis of the ruins with some illustrations, such as Pietro Santi Bartoli's *Opera anaglyptica* (Rome 1690) and Antoine Desgodetz's *Les édifices antiques de Rome* (Paris 1682), with its carefully measured plans and intricate drawings. This interest in investigating and cataloging the vestiges of Roman civilization could extend beyond the limits of the city as well, as is shown, for example, by Francesco Nardini's *L'antico Veio: Discorso investigativo del sito di quella città*, of 1647.

Beyond Italy, field archaeology rather than excavation figured largest in the earliest published works, such as William Camden's *Britannia* of 1586, the first guide to British antiquities. Among the earliest excavations to be published was that of a Neolithic chamber tomb in northern France. Although the excavation took place in 1685, the results were published only in 1719 by Bernard de Montfaucon in his *L'antiquité expliquée et représentée en figures* (Paris 1719). Montfaucon included a rather crude bird's-eye view showing the physical setting of the site, with a section taken through the tomb to reveal the skeletal remains within. Treatises such as this, on early western European cultures, were not limited to the architectural ruins but included full discussions, and even illustrations, of the anthropological material as well.[20] It was, in fact, precisely upon works such as Montfaucon's that Bayardi had intended to model his multivolume work on Herculaneum.[21]

By the eighteenth century the preoccupation of antiquarians with collecting and connoisseurship led to a spate of catalogs of finds and curiosities drawn from private collections and cabinets, especially statuary, ceramics, gems, coins, and other small objects.[22] With this came a steady decline in interest in the architectural remains. An early attempt to reverse this trend and produce what begins to approach an archaeological monograph, although based on an accidental discovery rather than a systematic inquiry, is Francesco Bianchini's *Camera ed iscrizioni sepulcrali de' liberti, servi ed ufficiali della casa di Augusto scoperte nella Via Appia* (Rome 1727). In 1703, Pope Clement XI had named Bianchini (1662–1729) superintendent of antiquities for Rome, a position which allowed him to become intimately familiar with the ruins of the ancient city. In this volume he had collected and published all the inscriptions and finds from a single site. His engraved view of this Roman columbarium is typical of the contemporary fondness for showing the ruins set in their physical environment, with various fragments and artifacts given prominence in the foreground and minute human figures providing an exaggerated sense of enormous scale to the structures (Fig. 44). Similarly, Antonio Gori's *Monumentum sive columbarium* (Florence 1727) provided views of an ancient tomb, with elevations and placed in its physical setting, but he went farther by including drawings of inscriptions and of the individual sarcophagi along with a plan of the interior where the provenance of each sarcophagus inside the tomb was shown clearly.

These are two rare examples where some attempt was made to maintain a link between the artifacts and their archaeological context; where the excava-

Figure 44. View of excavations in a columbarium on the Via Appia outside Rome. Engraving by Girolamo Rossi, from a drawing by Antonio Buonamici. From Francesco Bianchini's *Camera ed iscrizioni sepulcrali de' liberti, servi ed ufficiali della casa di Augusto scoperte nella Via Appia* (Rome 1727), plate following page 16. (Courtesy of the Beinecke Rare Book and Manuscript Library, Yale University.)

tion, documentation, and illustration of the site occurred at roughly the same time and by roughly the same individuals. Yet even here the purely architectural remains themselves took second billing to inscriptional evidence and artifacts deemed of artistic merit. The historical and archaeological value of numerous other attempts at documenting ancient ruins was severely diminished by the same tendency seen in the work of Renaissance artists to include fanciful reconstructions or otherwise to deviate from presenting a faithful and accurate record of the monument. This is most vividly evident in Bianchini's own *Del Palazzo de' Cesari* (Verona 1738), where the text purports to be based on a critical analysis of the literary and archaeological evidence for the imperial *domus* on the Palatine in Rome but the illustrations are in fact fantastically outrageous constructs having little relation to the architectural remains.[23] This too is the greatest deficiency of the early published engravings of Giovanni Battista Piranesi. Although his "vedute" and plans of Rome are technical and

Figure 45. Giovanni Battista Piranesi's highly imaginative reconstruction of the buildings in the Campus Martius in Rome. From G. B. Piranesi, *Il Campo Marzio dell' antica Roma* (Rome 1762), second frontispiece. (Courtesy of the Davison Art Center, Wesleyan University.)

artistic marvels, they often illustrate the monuments only as they existed in his day and contain wild flights of fancy that had little correlation with the actual remains themselves (Fig. 45).[24] Nor do they represent the product of a systematic program of excavation.

There were, however, some serious efforts to record accurately the few vestiges of ancient architecture to survive the depredations of time. For example, in 1753 Giuseppe Pannini published the results of a survey he had undertaken, on behalf of Cardinal Silvio Valenti, in the small theater in the Accademia of the Villa Adriana in Tivoli.[25] This imperial villa had been of interest to architects and antiquarians since at least 1461, when a description of the ruins was published under Pope Pius II. Later, between 1550 and 1568, Ligorio carefully surveyed and described the site in detail, identifying the individual buildings with the topographical labels of "Canopus" and "Tempe" that the *Historia augusta* (*SHA* 26.5) had ascribed to the villa. If, as seems entirely likely, Ligorio drew up a plan of the entire site based on his preliminary sketches, this is no longer extant. It was not until 1668 that Francesco Contini published a comprehensive plan of the villa. Contini claimed to have cleared the monuments down to their foundations, but his plan was subsequently derided as "made of ideas" and comparable to Bianchini's fantastical reconstructions of the Palatine.[26] Already by 1741, Giovanni Battista Piranesi had undertaken his survey of the ruins, a project that engaged his attention sporadically over the next thirty years.[27] By the 1750s, a number of scholars were at work on different projects in the villa, and Pannini was among these.

Pannini claimed to have dug deep trenches in order to recover the full plan of the scaena of the theater as Ligorio had seen it. He measured all the fragments of columns and capitals still lying about the site, and he attempted to ascertain the provenance of a number of statues he knew had been removed from here under Pope Alexander VI, including a set of the Nine Muses. He illustrated his findings in three engravings, which combine detailed plans and elevations of the existing ruins with discrete reconstructions and a bird's-eye view showing the ruins in their geophysical environment and peopled with small figures (Fig. 46).[28] Because these were presentation plans, intended for general distribution but not for publication in a book, Pannini's plans must stand largely on their own, since the dedication provided in the caption to the first plate describes only in brief the marble elements and sculptures that had once decorated the edifice. The individual captions of the other plates add little more detail. Moreover, Pannini had been unable to show the precise provenance of the works of art, since these had been stripped from their context years before.

Thus, by Galiani's day, few publications had offered the full range of carefully drawn, measured plans he advocated in his text on Vitruvius, and even fewer included plans showing the precise provenance of the finds. Galiani recognized these deficiencies and was clearly addressing architects like Pannini, trained in the Vitruvian and Palladian traditions, when he wrote:

> No one up to today has been able to comprehend of how much greater importance is the study, contemplation, and excavation of the site of a [theater's] scaena, because from any remains of its plan one could acquire the principles [of their general design]. I have seen, however, many plans of excavated theaters, but in all of them either one sees only vestiges of the

Figure 46. The small theater in the Accademia of the Villa Adriana at Tivoli. The top section shows the extant remains of the scaena; the central panel is Pannini's reconstruction of the scaena; and the bottom panel is his reconstruction of the cavea crowned with a small tholos. Engraving from 1753 by Giuseppe Pannini. (Author's photograph; courtesy of the Rare Book Room, Fine Arts Library, University of Pennsylvania, Philadelphia.)

scaena or, what is worse, it is false or added onto by the whim of some imaginative architect.[29]

Galiani may also have been thinking of inadequacies he found in works published by his compatriots. In 1752, Giovanni Maria Pancrazi had produced a two-volume work on Sicily dedicated to Charles of Bourbon and Maria Amalia and entitled *L'antichità siciliane spiegate colle notizie generali di questo regno*.[30] The work was clearly intended to extol the royal family by linking it with the Greek past, just as the popes attempted to link the papacy with Classical Rome and as the excavations in the Vesuvian landscape were intended to do for this same royal family. Pancrazi, however, had been unable to complete a "carta geografica" of Sicily, a map showing the location of all of the ancient ruins there, which sounds much like the Cratere Maritimo map that Weber was working on at precisely the same time. Pancrazi stated in his preface the desirability of "having before one's eyes the plans and elevations of those cities of which remains have been found, [and the] cross sections [*spaccati*] of the temples, theaters, amphitheaters, baths, naumachiae, circi maximi, tombs, and other ancient buildings, in the manner in which they are preserved today."[31] Yet apart from numerous but relatively poorly executed views of the semiburied ruins, especially those around Agrigento, Pancrazi did not concern himself with the artifacts recovered from these sites and offered few accurate plans drawn to scale, all of which he had produced without the benefit of excavation.

THE AXONOMETRIC PLAN OF THE PRAEDIA IULIAE FELICIS

It was against this background of inadequate and even misleading documentation that Weber now pitched his proposal to draft a treatise describing the archaeological remains. Evidently he believed he would be carrying on the work begun by two of his predecessors. One of these was Marcello Venuti, whose book *Descrizione delle prime scoperte dell' antica città di Ercolano* (Rome 1748) was among the first widely available narrative descriptions of the ruins. But Venuti had published this without benefit of plans and had been concerned with only the first two years of the excavations, when he himself had been actively involved. Weber was also seeking to fill the void created by the Accademia's departure from Bayardi's original mission, which had envisaged a fusion of narrative analysis of the discoveries with visual documentation.

Although the absence of firm dates prevents a precise reconstruction of the chronology, Weber evidently followed up his initial letter of inquiry to Tanucci of October 1759 by presenting him with several finished, or nearly finished, copies of his plans. These he had hastened to complete in the last months of 1759 and early 1760 to serve specifically as illustrations of the methodology he proposed to adopt in his treatise.

For his archetype he selected the Praedia Iuliae Felicis at Pompeii, a site now inaccessible to him, since it had been reburied after the completion of the excavations in 1757. Regardless of this inconvenience, a crucial factor in his decision to select this site must have been the quantity and quality of the

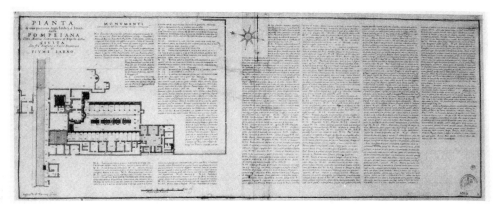

Figure 47. Weber's presentation copy of his plan and inventory of finds from the Praedia
Iuliae Felicis in Pompeii, completed in late 1759. (Courtesy of the Soprintendenza
Archeologica di Napoli e Caserta [Archivio Disegno, #72; 0.348 m. H × 0.865 m. W].)

documentation he had at hand, for he had not only retained copies of his own
correspondence with Alcubierre listing all the discoveries but also had at least
one plan and one notebook drawn up by the site foreman, Antonio Scognamillo.
More importantly, Weber still had his own rough draft of the site from 1757. By
pulling together all this material, he was able to produce two new companion
plans, both extant, that illustrated the site in a fashion radically different from
the kind of archaeological documents published by his predecessors and even
by his contemporaries in both Rome and Naples.

The first of these plans of the Praedia Iuliae Felicis is similar to his rough
draft in that both combine a plan of the site with a complete inventory of the
finds (Fig. 47). Also, the ground plans of the Praedia are virtually identical in
size and in manner of presentation, and the numbers used to label the rooms are
the same, except for several letters drawn on the rough draft which were never
keyed into the inventory and were eliminated in the final product. But the sheet
of vellum for the final version is almost twice as large as that used for the rough
draft, allowing ample space for the title and text on the front of the sheet.[32]
Although in the final version the inventory again surrounds the ground plan and
continues in ruled columns onto the right-hand side of the sheet, it occupies
considerably less space. Weber had apparently gone back over the rough draft,
underlining passages that described architectural or decorative features and lists
of objects he apparently could not confirm had come from a particular spot. He
then eliminated these more colorful and descriptive entries from the new version, leaving only the simple itemization of the finds. His transcriptions of the
programmata are still largely unintelligible, apart from the personal names,

while some words transcribed in the rough draft have dropped out completely, suggesting that he had not taken the time to check these against the originals which had been cut down from the façade of the building and now lay in the storerooms or on display in the royal palace at Portici. Although the hand is neater than that on the rough draft, the dates when finds were made are less precise (e.g., months and years alone, without the days), as are the figures given for the total number of a particular find. The objects themselves are described in an even more cursory manner. Among the more egregious examples of the latter is the public fountain found alongside the Via dell' Abbondanza, whose standard is described on the rough draft as being decorated with a "mask with clusters of grapes for earrings" (*17*), a detail completely left out of this final version. Additions have crept in as well, such as the entry for "twelve heads of dead [persons] beside a fountain" (*31*), a discovery Weber apparently had tracked down in his official reports to Alcubierre. So, although this is a better plan in terms of its aesthetic presentation, the rough draft remains in many ways the more accurate and reliable document, despite the errors of transcription it contains.

Weber used the descriptive elements he had edited out of the rough draft to form the annotations to a second plan of the Praedia Iuliae Felicis. The vellum sheet for the finished plan is slightly wider than that for its companion, but the scale, borders, and compasses are identical; the title again appears in the upper left-hand corner; the same scheme of numbering is followed; and the columns of text also run above and below the ground plan and continue onto the right-hand side of the sheet.[33] These two plans were clearly intended to be consulted in tandem. But Weber employed an innovative approach to the presentation of the building itself and the accompanying critical exegesis, for the ruins of the Praedia are not shown in simple plan but in axonometric projection, and the various constituent elements and their functions are identified and explained in a descriptive commentary drawn in part from ancient literary sources and in part from empirical evidence that Weber had culled from the excavations under his direction (Fig. 48).

Artists and architects had begun to experiment with a form of axonometric projection by at least the early sixteenth century. The *Codex Coner*, a collection of drawings attributed to Andreas Coner and dated around 1515, includes several early attempts to depict architecture (both ancient and modern) graphically through nonorthogonal, perspectival views. These were drawn as sections through the interior but viewed from a particular vantage point, either somewhat above or below the standard perpendicular axis.[34] Baldassare Peruzzi's perspectival view of the interior of a proposed centrally planned Saint Peter's is

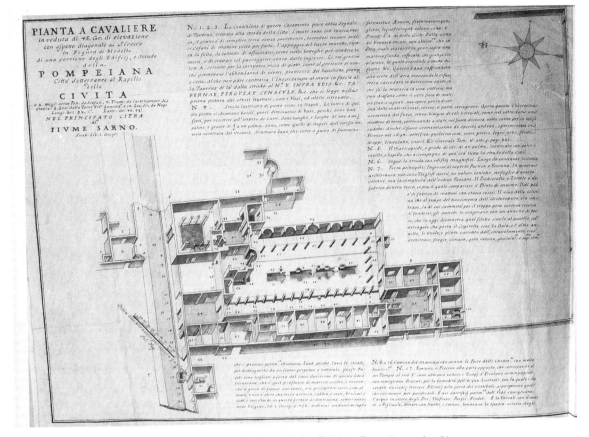

Figure 48. Weber's axonometric plan of the Praedia Iuliae Felicis in Pompeii, completed in late 1759 or early 1760. Only the left-hand portion is illustrated. (Courtesy of the Soprintendenza Archeologica di Napoli e Caserta [Archivio Disegno, #72; 0.348 m. H × 0.865 m. W].)

just one example that illustrates how artists struggled with this graphic technique. In Peruzzi's drawing, the building appears in plan in the foreground, while walls gradually materialize and take form as the view recedes until the apse and part of the vaulting are seen in the background in full perspectival section. The shortcomings of the medium become evident in the inevitable flattening out of the vaulting created by the exaggerated foreshortening and in the way the walls in the foreground block the view of those farther back. Eventually architects abandoned this medium as too unwieldy and unrealistic for representing their buildings.[35]

On the other hand, military engineers were able to employ axonometric projection to good effect for illustrating fortifications and other defensive instal-

lations. The three-dimensional quality lent the requisite sense of solidity, while
the use of the bird's-eye perspective allowed the structure to be viewed as a
single entity within its physical environment and hence best illustrate how the
structure would function.[36] Most likely it was through conventional military
applications that Weber became acquainted with this manner of illustration.

Weber's plan of the Praedia is the earliest known use of axonometric projection in archaeology, though, if the engraving is accurate, he had experimented
with this technique already on his plan of the belvedere from the Villa dei Papiri
(see Fig. 21). His intention here, as his title to the plan indicates, was to
represent the Praedia as if he had built a model and was now drawing the
building from a vantage point above and slightly to the left of it. The angle of
projection is only 45 degrees, so problems with foreshortening have been kept
to a minimum. By projecting all the walls and the colonnades to a uniform
height and leaving off the roofs, he could show virtually all the interior and
exterior spaces at one time. Only a few of the nonstructural interior features are
shown, such as shop counters (2, 21) and a hearth in the kitchen (100). The
public fountain (17), minus its standard, stands out front in the street, which is
shown in section to reveal its lava paving stones and the raised sidewalks that
flank it. Moreover, he effected an accurate sense of volume by cleverly shading
the side of the perpendicular walls facing the viewer to give the impression that
the source of light is from the left. Although only a few of these walls would
have been found standing to the height shown in the plan, this is nevertheless a
remarkably faithful and accurate reconstruction, since Weber added no fanciful
embellishments of any kind nor did he illustrate any feature for which he did not
have solid archaeological evidence.

Drawn in black ink and gray, green, and red gouache, Weber's plan contains a
number of surprising details: water spraying from fountain jets in the peristyle
courtyard of the baths (31) and the central bridge of the euripus in the viridarium
(52); stippling used to illustrate the coarse pumice stone that had been applied to
the east enclosure wall of the viridarium to give it the appearance of a grotto (48);
the stepped display shelves in a shop (24) and the seat supports in a latrine (37);
lines indicating how wooden beams fixed to pillars would have created a *pergola*
around the garden (56); and the engaged pilasters that originally flanked the
entrance to the baths (7). To distinguish between the different types of mosaic
pavings, Weber used a fine crosshatching with a gray (24, 41, 89–94, 97) or red
(31) wash, while uniform scratches of ink indicate rooms once paved in
polychrome marble (42, 80, 83, 86). Another style of crosshatching, worked out
in meticulous detail, illustrates the pavement of the street. As this plan is essentially a projection of his earlier rough draft, all of the errors found there are

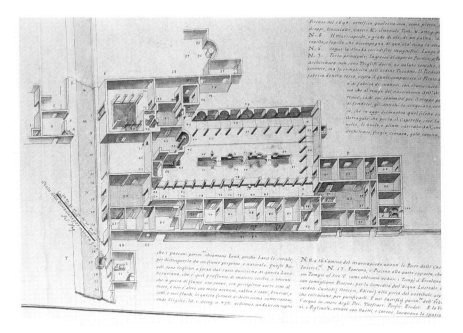

Figure 49. Close-up view of the bath complex and the central viridarium as illustrated on
Weber's axonometric plan. Note the water gushing from the fountains. (Courtesy of the
Soprintendenza Archeologica di Napoli e Caserta [Archivio Disegno, #72; 0.348 m. H ×
0.865 m. W].)

repeated and even enhanced here, in particular the bench across the front of the
domus and the additional semicircular scallops on the euripus. Devoid of all
unnecessary embellishments, however, the plan is extremely effective in illustrating the archaeological remains of the Praedia (Fig. 49).

Although the ground plan itself represents a novel approach to the visual
representation of a site, the true significance of this plan is found in the annotations, for Weber viewed the architecture not merely as a receptacle for works of
art but as a dynamic structure where each space served a specific function. On
the basis of his study of Classical literature and of certain phenomena encountered elsewhere in the excavations, he not only attempted to explain how individual spaces may have been used but also how baths and fountains operated; how
specific areas had been decorated; and even how the architect had designed
rooms to take advantage of the natural light and heat as well as the architectural
and natural vistas. For the first time in the history of the excavations, a descriptive account of the remains was linked to a plan of the site. (For the complete
text of this plan, see Appendix 2 to this volume.)

Along with his personal experience, Weber based his research on three main sources: two annotated texts of Vitruvius dating from the Renaissance; a sixteenth-century lexicon compiled by Guillaume Budé; and, especially for his geological analysis of Pompeii's lava paving stones, the researches and knowledge of Padre Antonio Piaggio.[37] Most striking is the fact that although he quotes from both Philander's and Caporali's commentaries on Vitruvius, he makes no reference whatsoever to Galiani's own recent edition, *L'architettura di M. Vitruvio Pollio* . . . (Naples 1758).[38] This omission might be explained away by concluding that Weber, long familiar with these classic Renaissance commentaries, quotations from which were de rigueur, already had completed much of the text before Galiani's book appeared in October 1758. He managed, however, to incorporate findings from the excavations at Herculaneum dating from at least as late as September 1759. If the omission was deliberate – perhaps to underscore Galiani's own slighting of the merits of the excavations – it was a particularly serious dereliction for someone seeking admission to the Accademia.

In addition to Vitruvius, Weber drew his literary references from eleven other Greek and Latin authors. Although on the surface Weber's reliance upon these authorities may appear scholarly, his selection of sources was indiscriminate and uncritical. This was a trait already discernible in the humanist writings of the early Renaissance, as well as the publications of the Accademia and those of Bayardi, where obscurity frequently was confused with erudition and every imaginable literary reference and gloss was brought into the discussion, often without advocating any particular reading in the end. Digressions were unavoidable; for example, in a rather lengthy discussion of how the lava stones of the street had been formed (*4*), Weber incorporated references from Procopius's *De bello Gothico* (6.4.21–30; 8.25.1–6), where the physical characteristics of eruptions of Vesuvius are set forth, and Vergil's *Georgics* (1.472–73), where an eruption of Mount Aetna is described.[39] Weber's tendency to digress is seen as well in his speculations on the origins of the Doric capital, in a section where he is describing the engaged pilasters on the façade of the baths (*7*).

Many of his remarks seem to indicate that he was trying to address topics he had overheard members of the court debating. Chief among these would have been whether the city where the Praedia stood was indeed the ancient Pompeii known from literature. Ever since Biondo Flavio's *Italia illustrata* of 1453, it had been a popular scholarly exercise to attempt to identify the sites of ancient cities on the basis of literary sources and itineraries. Ambrogio Leone, in his *De Nola* of 1514, for example, had located Herculaneum at Torre del Greco and had been the original source of Alcubierre's own confusion of modern Torre Annunziata with ancient Stabiae. In entitling the axonometric plan of the

Praedia "Pompeiana Città Sotteranea al Rapillo della Civita," Weber referred to
what he considered definitive proof in support of this identification: a passage in
Strabo's *Geography* (5.30) describing Pompeii's location on the Sarno River.[40]

More indicative of how he combined these literary and archaeological
sources is his discussion of the public fountain (*17*) to the west of the Praedia on
the so-called Via dell' Abbondanza. His experiences at Herculaneum had
taught him that such fountains stood in front of structures he believed to be
temples, and so he concluded that a temple would be found across from this
fountain in an area left uninvestigated during the original excavations (marked *T*
on the plan).[41] He explained this temple–fountain association as follows:

> Fountain, or pool, on the opposite side, which is in relation to a temple
> located at position *T*. As we have seen, the temples of Herculaneum were
> provided with similar pools to accommodate lustral water with which the
> priests sprinkled those who entered at the door of the precinct to purify
> them. And likewise in sacrifices with sprays of leaves they sprinkled water
> in honor of the gods.

In support of this argument he named three ancient authorities: Theophrastus,
Porphyrius, and Herodotus. The latter two references are particularly obscure.
The one for Theophrastus evidently refers to his *Characters* (16), where the
superstitious man is described as one who will not start the day before he has
sprinkled himself at the Enneakrounos fountain in Athens and put a bit of bay
leaf from a temple's grove in his mouth. Weber then explained further, "And the
Vestals with young men and girls, decked with fillets and garlands, washed with
water the areas chosen by the Haruspices for the building of the temple," and
also referred to the fourth book of Tacitus's *Historiae* (4.53.10), which describes
the reconsecration, in A.D. 70, of the Temple of Jupiter Optimus Maximus on
the Capitoline in Rome. "And so," Weber deduced, "tanks of water were
necessary near a temple."

As further evidence for the existence of this temple, he described the small
tavern located directly behind the fountain, noting that it contained a counter
with a hearth and stepped shelves for displaying vessels. He had recognized
these same features in another shop across the street, and to confirm his identification of the first building as a tavern, he referred to the painted inscription
from the façade of the Praedia mentioning "tabernae" for rent. He explained
that the Greeks had offered a variety of foods at their sacrifices, while assistants
poured libations of wine. He believed the same practice occurred as well at the
election of Roman priests and the Pontifex Maximus, "a dignity appropriated
first by Julius Caesar; and after his confirmation by the people the ceremony

ended with a festival and banquet."[42] "Taverns near temples, therefore, are not useless," he pronounced.

Weber's most complicated task was to identify the individual rooms in the bath complex and explain how these had functioned. This may be the earliest attempt to describe the archaeological remains of a small private Roman balneum with most of its hydraulic and hypocaustal features intact. Although in several instances his identifications are wrong or he applies several names to the same room, his deductions are remarkably sound given that he had to rely heavily on Philander, who had never confronted ruins of this complexity. It is evident, in fact, that Weber's confusion arose out of his attempts to reconcile these archaeological remains with Philander's incomplete knowledge of the meaning of Vitruvius's remarks. He may also have consulted Montfaucon's *L'antiquité expliquée . . .* , where excavations of a far simpler set of baths in Normandy are described and illustrated by means of a crude plan.[43]

One feature he correctly identified was the praefurnium (*27B*), for he quickly recognized the stoke holes and reasoned that the ample, open space nearby was for the storage of fuel. "One could admire the blackened furnace today, if it were not covered again by lapilli," he observed wryly. The floors of the adjacent rooms were supported on colonnettes (the pilae of the suspensurae, although he does not use these terms), twenty-eight of which had been removed from one room (*41*, the tepidarium) for transport to Portici, while "the rest were left *in situ*," evidently for posterity's sake. Hot air passed beneath the floors to heat the other rooms, the functions of which Weber deduced on the basis of several literary sources and according to their relative distances from the praefurnium. In this way he was able to identify the caldarium (*42*), because of its proximity to the furnace. But he reversed the identifications of the tepidarium (*41*) and laconicum (*29*). The round, domed room "resembling a small tower" and adjacent to the furnace (*29*) he believed to be the tepidarium, not realizing that Vitruvius is here describing a laconicum (Vitr. 5.10.5). So, on the basis of Vitruvius's remark "laconicum sudationesque coniugendae tepidario," Weber had to identify the adjacent room (*41*) as the laconicum. In support of this he also made an obscure reference to Statius's *Silvae*, where the poet describes the amenities of the baths of Claudius Etruscus. In the end Weber called this (*41*) a "vaporatorio," since it stood farthest from the praefurnium.[44]

The cold-water plunge bath of the frigidarium (*39*) created the greatest difficulty for Weber. Vitruvius had described the disposition of three bronze water tanks (miliaria) over the source of heat, designating one the caldarium, one the tepidarium, and the third the frigidarium; the arrangement was intended to allow water from the cooler source to replenish that from the warmer source as hot water was drawn off, thereby ensuring that an ample supply of water at all three temperatures was maintained (Vitr. 5.10.1). Since the Renaissance, scholars like Philander and Caporali had interpreted this passage to mean that the tanks supplied a single bathtub, drained and filled with hot or cold water as needed, not that each tank had served an individual room. Even Galiani had adhered to this interpretation, referring to a painting found in the Thermae Titi in Rome believed to show just such an arrangement.[45] The first-century medical authority Galen offered conflicting evidence by specifying that bathhouses be equipped with three separate rooms with water of different temperatures.[46] Weber conflated Vitruvius and Galen in concluding that this plunge bath, the only one the Bourbon excavators had encountered here, had served all three functions, noting how clever the architect of these baths had been to consolidate into a single room (39) the benefits of three distinct rooms.[47]

The Bourbon excavators had plundered a great amount of lead piping and stopcocks, but by the time Weber began work on this plan he could no longer be certain precisely where any of these plumbing fixtures had been found nor remember the significance of certain details on his and Scognamillo's plans. Along the outer perimeter of the bath complex today runs a wide, open channel of masonry apparently intended to serve as a gutter to carry off the rainwater from the barrel-vaulted roofs, along with the water drained from the baths and the overflow from a nearby reservoir (62). Weber, however, theorized that this channel had carried water from the reservoir to the plunge bath (39) and that the water became heated in transit by its proximity to the hypocaustal floors of the caldarium and tepidarium. He proposed that by operating a stopcock found in the floor directly in front of the plunge bath (in 32), cold water could be made to flow from the fountain in the nearby peristyle courtyard (31), which he had identified as a frigidarium equipped with a cold-water footbath. Although this stopcock was in fact the valve on the bath's drainpipe, nevertheless Weber was attempting to explain on the basis of the archaeological remains themselves how these individual elements of the baths had functioned as a unit.

Another detail illustrated on Scognamillo's plan that Weber evidently was incapable of deciphering was a masonry border framing the central euripus in the viridarium. This border, originally painted bright red and no longer visible in the extant ruins, defined an area along the edges of the euripus in which were displayed a series of marble and terracotta statuettes and where small green shrubs were planted. Weber translated this feature from Scognamillo's plan into parallel dotted lines running the entire length of the east side of the viridarium, suggesting he may have believed this was the drain for runoff from the baths.

Vitruvius had prescribed the proper orientation for dining rooms according to the season of the year in which they would be used (Vitr. 6.4.1–2). On the basis of this, Weber attempted to identify three rooms as triclinia. The first (*67*) he identified as a winter triclinium from its western aspect, although to judge from its decor this room appears to have been used only for storage. Another (*90*), designated the summer triclinium, since he believed it faced north, is actually the vestibule into the atrium of the domus from the west portico. The third room (*83*) was the most luxurious room in the building, a central nymphaeum with a water-stair fountain and masonry triclinium. But, as the first two examples suggest, these special features apparently played little role in leading Weber to conclude that this room had been a spring triclinium: he based his identification on the simple fact that it faced east.

The letters of Pliny also helped Weber read the architectural remains, particularly those of the central viridarium. On the basis of one passage, he concluded that the euripus was a swimming pool, remarking, of "the famous bath or pool in the center of this area, with three bridges where a metal jet sprayed water," that "around are seen ten seats (*a, b, c,* etc.), 6 palms deep [that is, the square and apsidal niches along the sides], all decorated with marble. One could swim under the bridges," and here he quotes from Pliny's description of the pool in his Tuscan villa: "If you wish to swim more extensively or in warmer water, there is a pool in this area; nearby is a well from which you can refresh yourself if you are weary of the heat" (Pliny *Ep.* 5.6.25). Weber then explained that "The fountain in the middle [of the central bridge] was in place of a well, and furnished with cold water; the canal, *# 45*, [supplied] hot water by means of underground lead pipes and stopcocks." In this reading, the square and apsidal niches of the enclosure wall along the eastern side of the viridarium also served as plunge baths, segregated for men and women as Varro had specified in his definition of the term *balneum* (Varro, *LL* 9.41). As proof that these were public baths, Weber again referred to the painted inscription (*CIL* 4.1136) from the façade stating that the baths were for rent.

Weber also made several keen observations concerning the variety of views afforded from different perspectives of this building and its decoration. His comments reveal a great sensitivity to certain aesthetic qualities of the structure and an appreciation for the strong axiality of its Roman design. Thus, he calls the great portico with its marble pilasters a "xystus" that provided an unbroken vista through the entire length of the building, from the street to the rooms of the domus. He saw another axial view across the viridarium that was marked by the round marble table (*84*) standing in front of the nymphaeum to the marble relief of "Socrates" found immurred in the east wall of the viridarium (*49*). Finally, he noted that the hortus could be viewed through the marble-silled window of a room in the domus (*92*), just as Pliny had described a room in his Tuscan villa (Pliny *Ep.* 5.6.23).

EXCAVATIONS AT STABIAE

In addition to these plans of the Praedia Iuliae Felicis at Pompeii, Weber managed to complete, between the end of November 1759 and February 1760, three more plans, in this case of sites at ancient Stabiae, which he used in support of his application to the Accademia. Alcubierre's persistent complaints about Weber's failure to comply with orders to produce plans was certainly true of two of these sites, where work had ended in 1757. Although initially plans of Stabiae were simple, keyed to brief inventories of the finds and lacking any narrative description, Weber eventually used his plan of the largest of these sites, the so-called Villa di San Marco, as the basis of his most ambitious project: a treatise on the archaeological remains of Stabiae.

Work in ancient Stabiae had continued virtually without interruption since its inception in June of 1749. Following the six-month investigation of the "Villa of Antèros and Heracleo," documented in the plan from 1750 described in Chapter 2 of this volume, new trenches had been laid out somewhat to the south, directly in the middle of a vast site that after seven years of excavation came to include some 317 meters by 190 meters of ancient structures buried beneath the property of several modern landowners. The portion of the site that yielded the greatest number and variety of finds coincides with the ruins identified today as the Villa di San Marco, whose painted rooms, baths, and enormous garden peristyle stood beneath property owned at that time by the Sansone family.

Few of the antiquities from this part of the site, investigated primarily between 1751 and 1753, matched the quality of those being found contemporaneously at the Villa dei Papiri, for they consisted primarily of small bronze domestic implements, numerous small paintings, and marble fragments, all shipped by the boatload from Castellamare to the port at Granatello near the palace at Portici.[48] The first trenches had landed near the tablinum of the villa's tetrastyle atrium, where the excavators uncovered an inscribed lead weight; a small bronze statue of Mercury, perhaps from the lararium situated nearby; a candelabrum decorated with silver; and a bronze fountain spout in the shape of a raven.[49] They then moved into a smaller tetrastyle atrium that served as the vestibule of a set of baths whose caldarium was equipped with hypocaustal heating and a deep, marble-lined pool.

The only archaeological illustration extant from this period is a small measured drawing of this small tetrastyle atrium from around 1751 – an even earlier example of this form of documentation than the fragmentary plan of the Praedia Iuliae Felicis. It must have been the work of the foreman in charge of this site, Stefano Caruso or perhaps Miguel de Çiria, since the hand does not appear to match Weber's. Also, like the fragmentary plan of the Praedia, this sketch reveals how crude the surveying methods were at the time, since only the barest sampling of measurements was recorded and no triangulation was used to ensure that the final drawing would be properly squared (see Fig. 52, lower right-hand corner).[50] The existence of such fragmentary plans best illustrates the piecemeal fashion in which portions of these sites were unearthed, investigated, measured, and reburied, with their full plans only reconstructed on paper at a later time.

Over the course of the next year, the excavators explored the limits of the great peristyle courtyard that remains the most outstanding feature of this villa today. The southeast enclosure wall of this formed a shallow hemicycle articulated with apsidal niches that concealed a narrow annular corridor behind but opened in the center to reveal a nymphaeum with a water-stair fountain recessed behind the rear wall. The water from this fountain supplied the garden's central euripus, which, however, the Bourbon excavators failed to uncover, despite its enormous dimensions. The two apsidal niches flanking the water stair were themselves fitted with water pipes and decorated with small wall mosaics, one showing the myth of Phryxis and Helle, and the other the myth of Europa and the bull. The latter of these also retained a small fragment of a still-life scene of a hen and two pomegranates above it.[51] These mosaics eventually were removed and taken to the museum in Portici, as later was a white marble table with lions' paw feet that had stood in the opening between the niches.[52] The other apsidal niches bore stucco reliefs, certain vestiges of which remain visible today, although at the time only one could be salvaged for the museum. This was a figure of a nude gymnast carrying a large hoop (MN. 9578) (Fig. 50).[53] From its place of storage in the annular corridor, the excavators recovered an elegant white marble crater, decorated with an archaistic relief of Pan and eight maenads circling about the vessel in dance (MN. 6779) (Fig. 51).[54] The vase may have been displayed originally on the marble table.

As work here continued into 1754 and the finds dwindled, Alcubierre, who finally had acknowledged that this site, not Cività, was ancient Stabiae, grew

Figure 50. Stucco relief of a gymnast with a hoop. Removed in August 1752 from the portico of the central viridarium of the Villa di San Marco in Stabiae (MN. 9578). (Courtesy of the Soprintendenza Archeologica di Napoli e Caserta.)

impatient and ordered Weber to transfer the Stabiae excavations from the Villa di San Marco to properties owned by the Jesuits and the Irace family. These were some distance away from the villa, also on the hill of Campo Varano but overlooking modern Castellamare di Stabia.[55] Yet Weber, who continued to favor the Sansone and its adjacent properties because the land was not encumbered by modern structures, abruptly halted these new soundings when he discovered they were destroying productive orchards and vineyards. Nor were he and his workmen enthusiastic about digging up church property. Although Alcubierre emphatically renewed his order to investigate these other sites, he eventually had to concede that they were not yielding enough finds and allowed Weber to return with part of the corps of workmen to the area of the Villa di San Marco.[56] The following year, Paderni observed, in a letter to the Royal Philo-

Figure 51. Marble crater decorated with archaistic reliefs of Pan and eight maenads (MN. 6779). Found in April 1752 in the annular corridor of the central viridarium of the Villa di San Marco, Stabiae. (Courtesy of the Soprintendenza Archeologica di Napoli e Caserta.)

sophical Society, that "In the ancient Stabiae they go on digging, but it is long since anything of value has been found there, except that in the beginning of this month two small statues of brass [i.e., bronze] were discovered."[57] The following month, in one of the small shops lining a paved street, the excavators managed to recover from the mounds of lapilli a small red agate cameo decorated with a woman's bust in profile (MN. 26775).[58]

Work at the Villa di San Marco ceased sometime around mid-1757, when Weber returned to work on the Jesuits' and the nearby Irace properties. At the former of these sites, now known as the "Villa del Pastore," the excavators uncovered a structure with an enormous porticoed terrace extending along the crest of the hill of Varano, as well as several small rooms and a modest set of baths.[59]

Just to the west of this, investigations beneath the Irace property, at the site now generally known as the "Villa di Arianna," began in earnest in late 1757 and continued until well into 1762. Here the excavators discovered a complex whose architecture and decoration closely resembled that at the Villa di San Marco, with rooms opening onto a central peristyle, which Weber sketched to illustrate where bronze female portrait busts were found, just as herms had been recovered from the square peristyle of the Villa dei Papiri in 1753. Yet, despite the length of time spent here and the favorable impression that the architectural elements seemed to extend in all directions, this site yielded few noteworthy finds, apart from a curious bronze water heater (MN. 72986), a cache of bronze cooking utensils, and rooms decorated with mosaic pavements and numerous small paintings.[60]

Weber finally finished his plan of the Villa di San Marco on December 24, 1759, after months of apologies to Alcubierre for the delay (Fig. 52). The site illustrated on his plan underlay the properties of the Comparato, Somma, and Sansone families and, much like the earlier plan of the "Villa of Antèros and Heracleo," Weber depicted the ancient ruins in relation to two significant features of the modern topography: the road to Gragnano, which cut through the east side of the site; and the scarp of Varano, whose erosion had destroyed a portion of the northwest side of the villa. The format closely resembles that of his plans of the Praedia Iuliae Felicis, with a combination of ink, gouache in red, green, and blue, and details worked out in pencil. The architecture is a seemingly disparate agglomeration of small square rooms enclosed in larger rectangular spaces, with an occasional colonnade or other small feature added, but all bound together by the streets that run at right angles through the site. It was the presence of these streets, paved with pebbles or lava stones just like those found at Herculaneum and Pompeii, that had convinced the excavators these were the ruins of the ancient city of Stabiae. To distinguish between paths and major streets, Weber stippled the pebbled paths and drafted the paving stones of the streets. The accompanying inventory of finds is neat and concise, with nothing described in any detail, suggesting that this is a polished version of an earlier draft. As was the case with his plan of the Praedia, excavations in the 1950s that uncovered the ruins to the southwest confirmed the remarkable accuracy of Weber's plan; this area corresponds with the portion of the Villa di San Marco still accessible today, while the rest of the site remains buried under modern structures. In June of the following year, Weber submitted copies of his illustrated elevations of the mosaic niches from the southeast wall of the great peristyle.[61]

His second plan showed the ruins of the "Villa del Pastore" (Fig. 53). Even

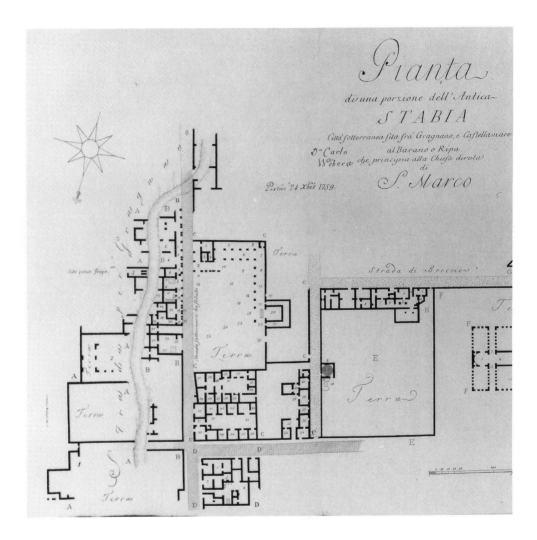

fewer antiquities had been recovered here, so Weber attempted to enliven his
register of the finds by emphasizing certain aesthetic features of the building,
such as the thirty-two shuttered windows with their marble sills that made up a
cryptoporticus overlooking a central pool and, beyond, a colonnade that framed
the vista.

On the other hand, the architectural remains of the third site, the "Villa di
Arianna," were themselves less spectacular than the numerous mosaic pavements and small paintings recovered from here, so the inventory accompanying
the plan of this villa is more lengthy and detailed, if somewhat colorless (Fig.
54). Weber signed and dated both of these plans on February 21, 1760, and

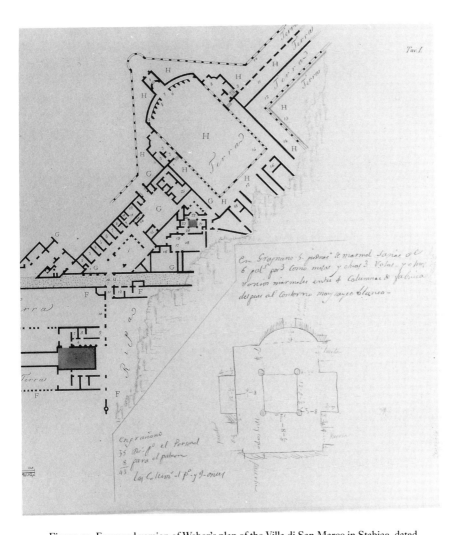

Figure 52. Engraved version of Weber's plan of the Villa di San Marco in Stabiae, dated
December 24, 1759. In the lower right-hand corner is a small measured drawing (by S.
Caruso or M. de Çiria?) from 1751 of the vestibule to the bath complex. From *Stabiae*, pl. 1.

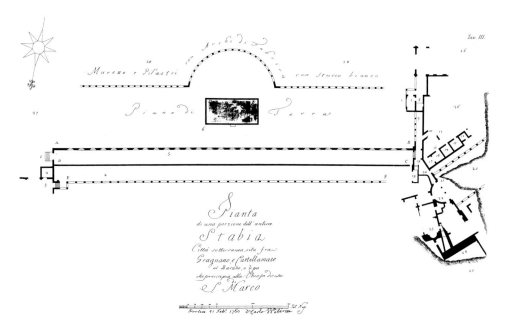

Figure 53. Engraved version of Weber's plan of the Villa del Pastore in Stabiae, dated
February 21, 1760. From *Stabiae*, pl. 3.

submitted all three of his recently completed plans to Alcubierre ten days later,
along with three copies of each for distribution to the court.[62]

THE MONOGRAPH ON STABIAE AND VESUVIUS

Weber probably completed his most significant contribution sometime in early
August 1760, after several months' work.[63] In his original letter to Tanucci
requesting admission to the Accademia, Weber had expressed his desire to
write a treatise on the architectural remains of the ancient sites, and Tanucci
evidently had invited him to submit a sample. The result was a thirty-five-page
manuscript containing one plan of the Villa di San Marco at Stabiae and
illustrations of the two fountains with their wall mosaics from that villa's
peristyle. (For the text of this manuscript, entitled "The Plans of Several Underground Buildings . . . , " see Appendix 3.)

He modeled his format on that used in the first two volumes of *Le antichità di
Ercolano*, so the folios are roughly the same size, and the layout is organized in the
same manner, with the running text at the top of the page and copious notes and
cross-references in twin columns at the bottom. Marginalia serve to highlight

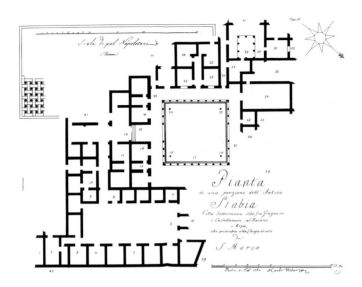

Figure 54. Engraved version of Weber's plan of the Villa di Arianna in Stabiae, dated February 21, 1760. In the upper left-hand corner is a sketch by C. Paderni of a mosaic pavement recovered on the site. From *Stabiae*, pl. 4.

aspects of both the text and the notes.[64] In addition to the three principal illustrations (a plan and two drawings), spaces were left blank for three others, which were prepared but never inserted: his map of the Cratere Maritimo, a drawing of the stucco relief of the gymnast with a hoop from the peristyle of the Villa di San Marco (MN. 9578), and the plan of the "Tempio della Madre de' Dei" from Herculaneum. A total of thirty plates depicting finds such as the marble vase and the paintings was planned to illustrate the text, but there is no indication that these ever were inserted, nor is it known whether illustrations of all these small finds existed. At least two, and perhaps three, different hands are readily discernible in the manuscript, as are penciled drafting lines and some text that was erased after being rewritten in ink. Weber himself penned a good portion of the annotations and many of the marginalia, while Giovanni Furlanetti, a record keeper in the Palazzo Reale at Portici, later claimed to have inscribed most of the annotations. Piaggio, whose work at the Vatican and with the papyri meant that he was also an accomplished calligrapher, wrote all the titles, in capital letters; he also wrote part of the text and drew sketches of the scenes of Europa and Phryxis onto the elevations Weber had drafted of the fountain niches.[65]

The title reflects the ambitious nature of Weber's treatise: "The Plans of

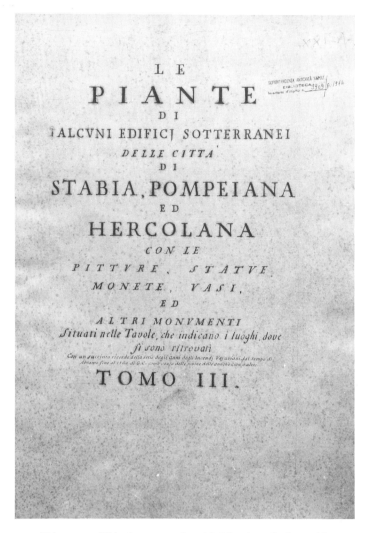

Figure 55. Title page to Weber's monograph entitled *Le piante di alcuni edifici sotterranei delle città di Stabia, Pompeiana ed Hercolana . . .*, completed in August 1760. (Courtesy of the Soprintendenza Archeologica di Napoli e Caserta [Ms. XXI.A.34; 0.475 m. H × 0.375 m. W].)

Several Underground Buildings of the Cities of Stabia, Pompeiana, and Hercolana, with the Paintings, Statues, Coins, Vases, and Other Monuments Situated in Plates which indicate the places where they were found, with a succinct record of the series of years of the eruptions of Vesuvius from the time of Abraham to the year 1760 as the cause of the ruins of the ancient cities and others" (Fig. 55). In fact, however, only a portion of the Villa di San Marco at Stabiae is dealt with

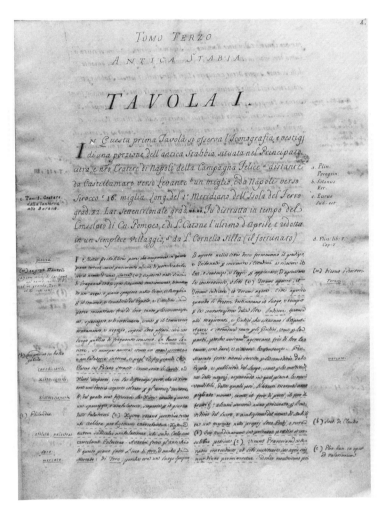

Figure 56. First page of Weber's monograph containing the text and notes intended to accompany his plan of the Villa di San Marco, Stabiae. (Courtesy of the Soprintendenza Archeologica di Napoli e Caserta [Ms. XXI.A.34; 0.475 m. H × 0.375 m. W].)

in any detail, while the ruins at Pompeii are mentioned only in passing and the caption to the plan of the "temple" at Herculaneum appears to have been added as an afterthought. The inclusion of the Cratere Maritimo map, however, makes evident that Weber's intention was to realize Bayardi's vision of a work that would incorporate the history, geography, geology, architecture, and art of these ancient sites in a manner distinctly different from that of *Le antichità*.

The text itself, however, deliberately emulated the critical, antiquarian approach taken by the Accademia in their publications on the paintings. This is evident from the attempt to embrace as wide a body of scholarly material as possible. Weber refers to the works of some thirty ancient authors, from the Latin writings of Varro and Suetonius to the Greek histories of Herodotus and Eusebius, along with an equal number of modern writers, especially classical commentaries like those of Alberti and Palladio on architecture and several histories of the Vesuvian region. There were certain limitations to his erudition, however. He often paraphrased or even misquoted his original sources, changing the order or spelling of words or adding new clauses in passages from Philander's commentary on Vitruvius. Although some problems might be due to scribal error, several passages are attributed entirely to the wrong source. As in his axonometric plan of the Praedia, but to a much greater extent, Weber used his knowledge of the excavations themselves wherever possible, drawing upon the evidence of individual finds, for example, to advance a hypothesis about the original function of a room and then supporting this with literary evidence as well, or illustrating the meaning of a passage from Philander through an archaeological discovery. For the most part he drew on the same limited selection of passages from Vitruvius and Pliny on baths, porticoes, and pools. The main text was used to explain the contents of each illustration and is therefore relatively succinct; the longer digressions were reserved for the footnotes.

The treatise begins with a discussion of the architecture of the Villa di San Marco, here called "vestiges of a portion of the ancient Stabia" (Fig. 56). After providing the essential details of the site's location, Weber relates briefly the history of Stabiae on the basis of what is known from Strabo and Seneca, including references from antiquity to the region's reputation for fine springs and the medicinal value of its milk. In corroboration of Strabo's remark that Stabiae had been destroyed by an earthquake, Weber introduces the inscription from Herculaneum that commemorated the Vespasianic restorations of the Templum Matris Deum. The remainder of the text is devoted to an overview of the peristyle of the Villa di San Marco and the principal finds made there, all intended to be used in consultation with his plan of the site.

The notes to the first plate, the plan of the Villa di San Marco at Stabiae, best illustrate Weber's attempt to imitate the Accademia (Fig. 57). He drew on a variety of literary sources and architectural parallels, proposing several possible functions for the peristyle, among these a forum, a market, and a "civic praetorium" for lawcourts, settling on identifying it as a palestra, or gymnasium, because its architecture compared favorably with Vitruvius's description of one: it had the proper dimensions, and he imagined that the entire ensemble of porticoes, rooms, and greenery would have been ideal for the activities of athletes, philosophers, and rhetoricians. As further support of this reading he

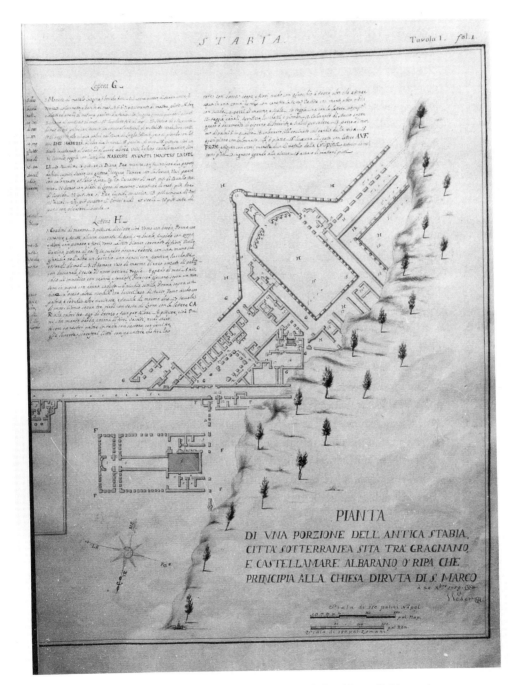

Figure 57. Right-hand portion of Weber's plan of the Villa di San Marco, Stabiae, as it appears in his monograph. Compare with Fig. 52, the engraved version of this same plan. (Courtesy of the Soprintendenza Archeologica di Napoli e Caserta [Ms. XXI.A.34; 0.475 m. H × 0.62 m. W].)

noted the stucco relief of the gymnast; the marble table, and the vase, which he
suggested was a trophy used in victory celebrations held in the peristyle; and the
small rooms behind the porticoes might have served as anointing rooms for the
athletes or perhaps as triclinia, given the subjects of their paintings. On the
other hand, he noted, with all the caution of a member of the Accademia, that if
this was not a gymnasium but a forum, these rooms might have been offices for
the magistrates.

Included in this section are some preliminary observations on the paintings
and mosaics found in the villa and a digression on the architecture of the
porticoes, whose tiled roofs, Weber observed, would have offered protection
from the rain and were disposed in such a way as to offer shade from the
summer heat and warmth in the winter. This is followed by an attempt to
classify the colonnades by type, such as pycnostyle or systyle, based on Vitruvius's specifications for their intercolumniations. The section ends with an
example of how readily Weber could get carried away with detail, for he offers
several speculations on the feminine origins of columns, including the notion
that columnar fluting found its inspiration in the folds of matronly garb while
the capitals represented their heads.

Another footnote is devoted to observations on the atrium and adjacent small
bath complex situated to the northeast of the peristyle. Although Weber interpreted the entrance as a Greek thyroron flanked by porters' rooms, and so
refers to this throughout the treatise as a Greek house, he correctly identified
the Roman atrium itself, referring to Festus's (Fest. Mueller 13) description of
how rainwater entered through an opening in the roof of the atrium and observing that light and air would have been allowed in as well. Yet his inability to
distinquish public from private architecture is evident in his identification of the
baths beyond as public balnea. Although he failed to draw a comparison between these baths and the balneum venerium et nongentum at Pompeii, he
again confused the shallow fountain basin in a peristyle courtyard that served as
the entrance to the baths with a footbath, while the caldarium, whose identifying
features today include a deep pool and extensive hypocaustal heating in the
floors and walls, he inexplicably terms a triclinium.

The last footnote to the plan of the Villa di San Marco treats the structures
beyond the atrium, where the bronze statuettes of Mercury and a raven (MN.
4891) were found. From the plan, these appear to be a series of small rooms
facing a triportico recalling simple servants' quarters seen elsewhere, but to
Weber these become oeci, triclinia, and exedrae for dinner parties and philosophical discussions. At the same time, an inscribed lead weight (*CIL* 10.8067,5)
found in one room suggested to him that some commodity had been weighed

and sold here, which was also a factor in his earlier suggestion that this had been a public market.[66] He traced lead piping across the road to a pool (*F.5*; see Fig. 52), which he called a baptisterium for swimming and supported this with the same passage from the letter by Pliny the Younger (Pliny *Ep.* 5.6.22) he had used to describe the euripus in the Praedia. The rooms flanking this pool would have been separate rooms for men and women, as Varro says was done in such baths, and the discovery here in 1751 of a set of surgical instruments was seen as proof that this particular complex had functioned as a kind of sanatorium. The notes then conclude with the observation that the term "triclinium" came from the Romans' habit of reclining on couches to dine but that such rooms were termed "refectories" once chairs had replaced the couches.

The following sections of the manuscript center on the two fountains from the peristyle decorated with wall mosaics that depict mythological scenes that, appropriately enough, are etymological legends involving bodies of water. The versions of these illustrations published by Ruggiero in 1881 are those submitted by Weber to Tanucci with his report of July 26, 1760, and differ in several ways from those included in this manuscript.[67] Although both provide a plan and elevation of each niche, the manuscript's illustrations of the scenes are more detailed and show that the same background was used for each, with only the central figures altered. While the architecture is drawn in ink and gouache, the scenes themselves were drawn in pencil by Piaggio's more accomplished hand.

Both text and commentary for the second plate of the monograph begin with a physical description of the niche and some remarks on the mosaic technique (Fig. 58). A badly damaged vignette at the top of the fountain shows a rooster pecking at two pomegranates, but this is not described in the treatise. The scene in the main panel shows a woman carried on the back of a bull above water, which Weber could easily identify as the myth of Europa. The text to this plate is quite brief, but the commentary recounts the entire "historical" background to the myth based on references in Herodotus, Eusebius, and Ovid, among other sources, and an attempt is made to explain how the myth of Europa's rape was derived from a version in which Cretan pirates carry her off in a ship whose Phoenician word also means "bull." There is even a summary of recent Cretan history, and the marble vase from the peristyle is introduced as possibly illustrating the annual festivals celebrated on Crete in honor of her arrival and wedding.[68]

The other plate is ostensibly devoted to the mosaic panel from the second fountain depicting the myth of Phryxis and Helle. This shows Phryxis partially submerged in water appealing for help as her sister Helle is carried off on the back of a ram (Fig. 59). After some remarks on the etymology of the word "mosaic," the notes provide an overview of the myth of Phryxis and Helle based

Figure 58. Plan and elevation of a fountain niche showing the myth of the rape of Europa, from the central viridarium of the Villa di San Marco, Stabiae. Plate 2 of Weber's monograph *Le piante di alcuni edifici sotterranei . . .* Dated June 26, 1760. The sketches of the figures may be the work of Antonio Piaggio. (Courtesy of the Soprintendenza Archeologica di Napoli e Caserta [Ms. XXI.A.34; 0.475 m. H × 0.375 m. W].)

on such authorities as Hyginus, Lactantius, and Servius. Nor did Weber miss the opportunity to point out the narrative and visual links between these two mosaic panels, for Europa was the great-aunt of Phryxis and the sister of Cadmus, who was the grandfather of Phryxis and Helle. Moreover, the figures were symmetrically displayed at either side of the central niche at the end of the peristyle (*H.7*), with Europa facing right (on the left side of the mosaic panel [*H.5*]), and Helle facing left (on the right side [*H.6*]).

Figure 59. Plan and elevation of a fountain niche showing the myth of Phryxis and Helle, from the central viridarium of the Villa di San Marco in Stabiae. Plate 3 of Weber's monograph. Dated June 26, 1760. The sketches of the figures may be the work of Antonio Piaggio. (Courtesy of the Soprintendenza Archeologica di Napoli e Caserta [Ms. XXI.A.34; 0.475 m. H × 0.375 m. W].)

The text itself says little more about the myth, but the fact that the niches containing both this mosaic and stucco reliefs such as the nude gymnast were found heavily damaged induced Weber to provide a "succinct record of the series of years of the eruptions of Vesuvius from the time of Abraham to the year 1760." This is by far the longest digression in the manuscript, filling the fourteenth to the thirtieth folio. This is also the most heavily annotated portion of the manuscript, for in addition to cataloging references to eruptions of Vesuvius in Seneca, both Plinys, and Tacitus, among others, Weber relied on later sources such as Fabius Giordano, Giovanni Tarcagnota, Giovanni Domenico Magliocco, Giuseppe Carafa, and the great Neapolitan historian Giulio Cesare Capaccio.[69] The longest passage quoted is the description of the eruption in A.D. 79 that appears in Cassius Dio (Cass. Dio 66.21–23),[70] but Weber felt obligated as well to provide the complete text of the "Epitaffio" at Portici, the inscription erected by Emmanuel Fonseca, viceroy of King Philip IV of Spain, to commemorate the devastations caused by the eruption of 1631. This historical marker would have been familiar to all in the Bourbon court, since it stood in Portici along the Royal Road from Naples at its intersection with the road to the fortress at Granatello.

Throughout this section of the manuscript, Weber is concerned with reporting the geophysical characteristics of the individual eruptions, the lists of towns and areas affected by the rain of ash and the flow of lava, and the human reactions to the ensuing adversities. Weber evidently modeled this portion of his manuscript on the unpublished manuscript of Padre Andrea Simone Imperato, the "Breve descrizzione del Monte Vesuvio . . . " from the 1730s, that had helped Alcubierre locate the ruins of Herculaneum and was by now probably in Weber's possession. Imperato had also given the full text of the "Epitaffio" inscription and had favored relating vignettes of human suffering over scientific data.

As an example of early investigations into Vesuvian phenomena, Weber provided a description of Magliocco's descent into the crater with two Camaldolesian monks in 1619 and the discoveries they made there. Wherever he could, Weber favored sensationalism, in particular recounting in full the miraculous events surrounding the devastating eruption of 1631, which was believed to have caused as much destruction and suffering as the eruption of 79. The miracles included the liquefaction of Saint Gennaro's blood, the parting of a lava flow around the Chiesa di S.M. Pugliano near Resina, the weeping icon of the Madonna in the Chiesa della Madonna del Arco, and similar events witnessed throughout the bay region.[71] Some twenty-five major eruptions are documented here, beginning as early as 2787 B.C. but with the greatest concentration on those of the sixteenth and seventeenth centuries. At the end of this section of his treatise, Weber stated his firm belief in the relevance of this history to the study of the buried cities, especially insofar as it illustrated Vesuvius's destructive influence on the cities and lives of the local populace, but at the same time he acknowledged that a detailed geological study was beyond the scope of the Accademia's publications.

The last section of the treatise was intended to be a commentary on a series of twenty-seven plates that would have illustrated the small finds from the Villa di

San Marco but were never included. Instead the discussion turns more hypothetical, with Weber describing what he would include should the Accademia approve of his publication. Listed here are the stucco relief of the gymnast (MN. 9578) (see Fig. 50), the marble crater (MN. 6779) (see Fig. 51), the inscribed marble table, an inscribed brick stamp, two mosaic pavements, small paintings, a bronze razor with an inscribed lamp and two coins, the statue of Mercury, a candelabrum sheathed in silver, the bronze raven (MN. 4891), the inscribed lead weight (*CIL* 10.8067,5), the surgical instruments, and the red agate cameo (MN. 26775).[72] In order to "satisfy curious foreigners," he also proposed to include a series of sketches illustrating the eruptions of Vesuvius and their effect on the surrounding countryside. With the addition of drawings of all the small finds from the Villa di San Marco, Weber projected that this proposed third volume of *Le antichità di Ercolano* would contain more than 150 plates.

But his proposal did not stop there, for he envisioned another volume of 50 plates illustrating the finds from the other two Stabian villas, on the Jesuit and Irace properties, the latter of which was still under excavation. In fact, Weber proposed an entire series of monographs "in infinitum" devoted to the individual sites and buildings, with at least another two volumes needed for the finds from Cività and another two for Herculaneum. He specifically expressed the need to include the kind of general site plans Alcubierre had been demanding. At Herculaneum, in particular, the haphazard approach to the excavations had fragmented and obscured the layout of the city as a whole, and so Weber proposed systematic excavations to recover it, concluding that "It would be a great satisfaction to have plans of all these ancient cities, with commentaries on the buildings and the antiquities found inside, house by house, with an indication of the place, date [of their discovery], and measurement." As an example of the plans he had of sites at Herculaneum, he chose his 1758 plan of the "Tempio della Madre de' Dei," but although he inscribed the caption, the plan itself never was drawn in the space provided for it in his manuscript.

Although Weber had contributed his knowledge of the archaeological remains, as well as his plans and drawings, there can be little doubt that Piaggio strongly influenced the overall style and content of this treatise. Weber would have been familiar with most of the ancient sources he referred to and even may have known many of the Renaissance authors. He probably also had access, in the royal libraries at Portici and Naples, to more contemporary writings like the works of Cochin and Bellicard, De Brosses, and the volumes of literature relating to the excavations that had been assembled by Gori.

But he must have relied heavily on Piaggio's knowledge of Classical antiquity and especially on the latter's researches into the history of Vesuvius. Piaggio lived on the slopes of Vesuvius, and the fact that he kept a journal of its activities suggests he was more interested in its effect on daily and religious life in the Bay of Naples than in its geological properties.[73] The academician Della Torre's own *Storia e fenomini del Vesuvio* is a scientific study of the volcano and could not have served as a source for the miraculous tales recounted here. This is generally true of the other books on Vesuvius available to Weber. Instead, the style of this portion of the treatise is closer to that found in Piaggio's own "Memorie," the manuscript recounting his work on the papyri, in which he mixed factual material with numerous digressions and pointed attacks on Paderni and Alcubierre.[74] Piaggio also would have been a strong advocate of Weber's project of publishing complete commentaries on the ruins in the manner proposed by Bayardi, and he must have guided and advised Weber at all stages in the writing of this treatise; he later exerted a similar influence on Winckelmann. He may even have been behind Weber's application to the Accademia, in the hopes of gaining a more sympathetic advocate of his own work.

This close alliance with Piaggio probably doomed Weber's proposals more decisively than anything he wrote himself. Tanucci had handed over Weber's treatise and several of his plans to three members of the Accademia for their comments, which they summarized in a letter to Tanucci dated September 10, 1760.[75] The composition of the committee could not have been more inauspicious for Weber, for it consisted of Mazzocchi, with whom Piaggio had quarreled over the handling of the papyri; Nicola Ignarra, a philologist whose antipathy for Piaggio was widely known; and Pasquale Carcani, the secretary of the Accademia, who would have been the only neutral figure except that he was largely responsible for shaping the format of the published volumes of *Le antichità* and would therefore have been opposed to any attempt to alter it.

In their response, the committee focused on two key issues: Weber's own qualifications, and the merits of his proposal to publish an archaeological monograph. They reported on a personal interview they had conducted with him, in which he presented three chief plans, along with several others. The first of these was his unfinished city plan of Herculaneum showing the extent of the excavations from at least 1750, a plan he refers to frequently in his reports throughout 1760 and early 1761 as he endeavored to complete it.[76] The second showed the ruins at Cività, presumably his polished plans of the Praedia. The third was his plan of the Villa di San Marco at Stabiae. Weber responded to the committee's concern about the accuracy of his work by producing his notebooks and rough drafts and assuring them that his site foremen could corroborate everything. The committee praised his systematic approach to excavating each structure room by room and his faithful recording of the findings.

In their judgment it was absolutely necessary to publish Weber's plans. They emphasized how important context was to understanding the antiquities removed from these sites and, echoing the complaints of Galiani, that his plans might help resolve longstanding questions in the interpretation of Vitruvius, particularly in the case of the theater at Herculaneum. Moreover, they hoped that publication of such careful plans would dispel a growing concern in the international community that the excavations were ill managed and poorly documented, referring here to Quirini's and Maffei's scathing comments about the excavators' blind and destructive tunneling. Yet they cautioned that more work was needed, since Weber had arrived relatively late on the scene and his plans would have to be linked with those from earlier years, such as Bardet's. They also recommended that further excavations be undertaken in areas where these plans were incomplete, lest the scholarly world conclude the investigations had been haphazard. To accomplish this, they specifically advised that Weber continue his boustrophedon technique of excavation, that he follow the city streets and enter the principal doors of buildings to get at the antiquities and allow for the systematic plotting of his excavation plans. As Weber's adviser they proposed Marchese Berardo Galiani, since he already had demonstrated in print his sound knowledge of architecture and antiquity.

Though acknowledging the wisdom of Weber's contextual approach to the publication of the archaeological discoveries, the committee concluded that it would be impossible to change the format of their own publications. They maintained that the typological presentation of the antiquities that they already had adopted was "The more natural method . . . to avoid the confusion that would arise from Weber's method of mixing the paintings with the bronzes, marbles, medals, and inscriptions. Such things distinguished by class and published in separate volumes are more successful in conforming to the pleasure and taste of erudite men."[77] With those words the Accademia ensured that the antiquities of the Vesuvian landscape would continue to be published in the more conservative, established manner of the collections of princes and cardinals. As for Weber's application to the Accademia, the committee praised his meritorious service and diligence but deferred this decision to Tanucci, no doubt in full confidence that he was unlikely to augment its enrollment.

Although copies of Weber's plans were provided to Charles III in Spain and continued to be engraved for eventual publication, the Accademia itself did not publish a single plan of the excavations until 1797.[78] Until that time, the architectural remains of these ancient cities continued to be viewed primarily as receptacles of precious antiquities. It was not until well after Carcani's death in 1783, followed by a gradual slackening of Tanucci's and the Accademia's stranglehold on the antiquities, that books of the type envisaged by Weber could be published, where descriptions of the individual monuments were linked to drawings of the finds and accurate site plans.[79] By then, all the individuals who had taken part in the earliest investigations were dead, the excavations at Herculaneum had ceased (in 1780), and, perhaps more importantly, the French had taken over briefly, bringing about a greater appreciation for the architectural remains that recalled the efforts of Bardet and Cochin and Bellicard.[80]

For his efforts, Weber won the greater enmity of Alcubierre and Paderni for seeking to outrank them, but he gained as well the sympathetic ear and enthusiastic counsel of Galiani for his future projects. Despite the denial of his application to the Accademia, Weber felt vindicated by the warm endorsement the committee had given his systematic technique of excavation and his proposed monographs. In the following years he pursued his agenda for the excavations, completing his general site plans and proposing improved methods for the recovery and presentation of these ancient sites. He continued to press for the publication of monographs and undertook to write at least one other exegetical text for the buildings excavated at Herculaneum.[81] If personal politics had been largely responsible for preventing his success in these endeavors, he had at least established precedents that allowed his successor, Francesco La Vega, to begin to realize many of these objectives.

7

Dearth and Discord

In seeking admission to the Accademia and proposing his new approach to the publication of the material remains, Weber had seriously disrupted the hierarchy of command and destroyed the last vestiges of harmony; by driving a wedge between the various factions of the Bourbon court, he had unwittingly opened a Pandora's box. The period from late 1760 through early 1762 was marked by natural catastrophe, bitter disappointment, and dissension on all sides. To complicate matters further, the resulting disarray in the conduct of the excavations was documented in part by the writings of the noted German critic of ancient art, Johann Joachim Winckelmann, in a pair of published letters that subjected what had long been the very private domain of the Bourbon king to the harsh scrutiny of the international community.

The difficulties began with the death of Maria Amalia in Spain on September 27, 1760, from injuries received in a fall from her horse. She had been a principal advocate of the excavations from their inception, and her death made evident Charles III's growing isolation from the project, and, as the correspondence between the king and Tanucci reveals, the latter's increasing control over the direction of the excavations. Less than two months later, on November 24, 1760, Vesuvius erupted again and continued to rumble for some fifty days, interrupting work in the Villa dei Papiri and further underscoring the close connection between the volcano and the buried cities that Weber had sought to portray in his manuscript (Fig. 60). Most notably, this period was marked by an alarming dearth of significant finds, a condition that exacerbated the atmosphere of antagonism between Alcubierre, Paderni, and Weber, as each sought both cause and remedy at the others' expense. Gone were the heady days of the wondrous discoveries at the Villa dei Papiri.

Figure 60. The eruption of Mount Vesuvius in 1760–61 showing lava crossing the Royal
Road between Torre del Greco and Torre Annunziata. From Wm. Hamilton, *Campi
phlegraei* (Naples 1776), pl. 12.

AN ARCHAISTIC DIANA

Although his manuscript had focused on the ruins of Stabiae, Weber had been
promoting Pompeii for some time as the most promising site in the Vesuvian
landscape. After completing investigations in the Praedia Iuliae Felicis in April
1757, Alcubierre had ordered the excavations transferred to the opposite end of
the ancient city, to a site where workmen quarrying pumice stone for construction of the nearby Royal Road already had begun to uncover ancient structures
as early as 1754. The ruins stood beneath a large tract of cultivated land that
belonged to the Irace family. This property lay above the entire southwest
corner of the ancient city, from the theaters on the southeast and the Temple of
Venus on the southwest to the Temple of Fortuna Augusta on the northeast and
the Via delle Terme/Vico del Farmacista on the north.[1]

The extent of the Irace property makes it difficult and at times impossible to
trace the course of the excavations and isolate the exact location of much of the
work carried out here between 1754 and 1759; the excavation reports refer only
in passing to finds made "in the Irace property" (see Fig. 28, #34). One
important guide is a plan of Pompeii compiled and drawn by F. La Vega as early
as 1769 from the excavation notebooks and working plans of Weber and A.
Scognamillo.[2] La Vega's plan shows the partial outlines of a row of houses in the

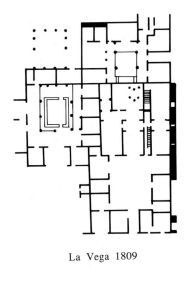
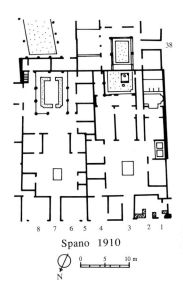

La Vega 1809   Spano 1910

Figure 61. Comparison of the plans of the houses of Regio 7.6.1–8, 36 in Pompeii. (*Left*) Francesco La Vega illustrated these structures on his 1809 plan of Pompeii (MN. 2615), basing his drawing on a now-lost plan of the site that Weber had produced following his excavations here in 1760–61. (*Right*) Giuseppe Spano's plan of the same structures from his reexcavation of the area in 1910 (from *NSc* 1910, 437). (Author's plans.)

modern Regio 8 that the ancient owners had terraced out over the old city walls to exploit the view of the Sarno Valley below. Some nine houses here were excavated in part, all of which bore signs of earlier plundering and so yielded primarily a great number of fixed objects such as paintings and mosaics along with the usual small finds. Among this otherwise indistinct cache of artifacts, with little reference in the reports to architectural elements to assist in orientation, one fixed point of reference is provided by the discovery in August 1758 of an underground vaulted nymphaeum decorated with a painted Nilotic frieze. This corresponds with a subterranean room at Regio 8.2.28, along the southwest edge of the city.[3]

By early 1759, the excavators had moved to the northwest, along this same ridge overlooking the Royal Road, to the property of the Cuomo family, next to the Irace property, where work proceeded simultaneously.[4] Here, too, only a handful of clues remain to indicate which buildings came under investigation in these years. The first clue is a large, late Second Style painting removed intact from a single wall.[5] It features a central tholos flanked by strings of dead birds suspended from hooks and five fountain jets emptying into long basins, all

Figure 62. The archaistic Diana (MN. 6008) found in July 1760 near the atrium of the
Casa di M. Spurius Saturninus e di D. Volcius Modestus (Regio 7.6.1–4) in Pompeii.
This Pentelic-marble statue still bore traces of paint when discovered. (Courtesy of the
Soprintendenza Archeologica di Napoli e Caserta.)

separated by receding colonnades on pedestals (MN. 8594).[6] The provenance
of this painting has been assigned to a house of moderate size (Regio 6.17.41) to
the north of the Villa di M. Fabio Rufo (Regio 7.16.17–22), just beyond the
northernmost boundary of the Irace property.[7] This identification makes sense,
since the house faces a main thoroughfare and a painted political programma
(CIL 4.1167) was removed at the same time. But since the extant reports refer
only in passing to features such as stairways and doors, the provenance of other
finds made during this period is more difficult to ascertain. From this same
house, or one very close by, must have come the eighteen "calendar medal-

Figure 63. The archaistic Athena Promachos (MN. 6007), found in November 1752 in the colonnaded oecus facing the great peristyle of the Villa dei Papiri in Herculaneum. (Courtesy of the Soprintendenza Archeologica di Napoli e Caserta.)

lions," tondi with busts of the gods representing the days of the week, the months, and the seasons, all reportedly removed from a large room with a yellow ground that also stood on the Cuomo property.[8] Yet a third room in this area contained a wall from which a number of features were cut down, including a central panel of Perseus and Andromeda (MN. 8995); two tondi bearing busts of a man (MN. 9085) and a woman – the latter of these the so-called Sappho portrait (MN. 9084); fantastic architecture (MN. 9707, 9710); narrow panels of wild animals in chase along the wall's base (MN. 8804, 8805); and a small panel showing the attributes of Apollo.[9]

It was not until mid-1760, however, when the excavators had passed over the boundary into the Irace property again, that Pompeii began to live up to Weber's expectations and hinted at a treasury of finds comparable to the Praedia Iuliae Felicis or even the Villa dei Papiri (Fig. 61). First came a number of elegant small paintings, including a hermaphrodite being unveiled by an astonished Pan, a portrait of the Three Graces (MN. 9231), and a Phryxis and Helle that could not but remind Weber of the mosaic fountain from the Villa di San Marco at Stabiae that he was in the process of illustrating for his manuscript.[10] In the days thereafter came the discovery of the famous archaistic Diana, a small (1.08 m.) statue in Pentelic marble, found in a near-perfect state of preservation, including traces of features painted in pink, yellow, blue, and black (MN. 6008) (Fig. 62). It was found somewhere in the area of the atrium of the house at Regio 7.6.3 (Casa di M. Spurius Saturninus e di D. Volcius Modestus), a provenance made certain by specific references to architectural features in adjacent buildings in later excavation reports. The similarities in style between this Diana and the archaistic Athena Promachos (MN. 6007) from Herculaneum evidently did not escape Weber either (Fig. 63). The Athena had been among the first marble statues recovered in 1752 in the colonnaded oecus facing the great peristyle of the Villa dei Papiri, and Weber's conclusion on the basis of this evidence is apparent from his report of the following week: the excavators continued to clear the area around three large stucco columns "which promise a great garden, baths, a temple, and a site rich in statuary."[11]

The nature of the excavations at this time, however, prevented Weber from fully pursuing his investigations in this house for some months. In his continuing effort to recover the maximum number of artifacts in as short a time as possible, Alcubierre had split the eight workmen and their young assistants into teams and assigned them to several different sites, both in Pompeii and at Stabiae. The teams remained separate as long as the work was routine, shifting from one site to another, but Tanucci had sanctioned the practice of consolidating their efforts any time a single site showed particular promise. This strategy was as much for the sake of efficiency as in the interest of security: to frustrate clandestine plundering by rapidly clearing the site.

The Diana statue had surfaced during the bleakest years of the excavations: the Palestra at Herculaneum had produced only a handful of small bronze statues and utensils; excavations in the Villa dei Papiri, which ground to a halt with the eruption of Vesuvius and Alcubierre's claims that the *mofeta* was polluting the air, had not yielded a statue since 1759;[12] and Stabiae was offering up only an occasional painting and the usual household fittings while Weber toiled away at plans of the villas there for his manuscript. Yet despite the recovery of the Diana statue and a splendid polychrome marble pavement in a nearby room, Weber encountered great difficulties trying to persuade his superiors of the potential merits of this site.

CAMILLO PADERNI: "DOCTOR OF ANTIQUITIES"

Instead, in August 1760, Tanucci bestowed extraordinary responsibilities on Paderni that included a more direct involvement in the selection of sites and supervision of the excavations' daily operations, a measure intended to ensure that antiquities suitable for the museum continued to be recovered. While good for the Bourbon museum, this new assignment was bad for morale in the excavations; Paderni's meddling in the work at the Villa dei Papiri, for example, was a chief reason Weber had set his sights on Pompeii. Paderni immediately opened trenches in three properties adjacent to the Irace land and became indignant when the foreman, Scognamillo, perhaps under the influence of Weber's more systematic approach, attempted to advise him of a better method of excavating.[13]

Weber behaved diplomatically, since his application to the Accademia Ercolanese remained outstanding at this time, but he was determined that the excavations be concentrated in the area where the Diana had been discovered. As with the "temples" at Herculaneum, he relied on past experience and certain clues which he knew had resulted previously in major discoveries. A second colonnade was isolated here, along with some gold coins, while he described a series of small paintings found at one of the sites opened by Paderni as "not very well preserved, since this spot is a bit pitiful and different from the other in the Irace property where the well-known Diana was found."[14] In a lengthy letter to Tanucci he observed that the ruins beneath the Cuomo/Balzano property promised no statues or pavements, "nor any trace of magnificence," as they consisted solely of "ordinary houses," while near the Diana were "Palaces of some consideration – gardens, other buildings, columns, porticoes, baths, most noble pavements – where one can hope for statues, fountains, and paintings, all well preserved because they are covered in dry lapilli, and because this is a site with a marvelous view of the sea."[15] Weber recognized, therefore, that the area near the Diana was potentially a gold mine, not only because of the favorable conditions for preservation but also because the spectacular views of the bay suggested that it would have been an ideal location for a luxurious villa. The Villa dei Papiri at Herculaneum was on a similar site. Weber was also aware, through the letters of Pliny the Younger, that wealthy Romans built "villae marittimae," luxurious seaside villas, as well as "villae suburbanae," country villas set in the landscape. Weber used this knowledge to guide him in selecting the most promising sites.

Although he complained bitterly of feeling "persecuted rather than re-warded" for his convictions, Weber's confidence paid off, and in six months' time the site produced several more museum-quality finds.[16] First was the discovery of a large marble impluvium with a pedestal fountain, unearthed in an atrium near the Diana. According to Tanucci, Alcubierre was elated by the discovery, while Paderni would eventually reconstruct it in the cortile of the museum.[17] Next came two gold earrings in the shape of chestnuts and a cameo "worth twenty statues," according to Weber, engraved with the helmeted head of Minerva and a hippocamp. Tanucci praised the cameo in a letter to Charles III, remarking ironically,

> Perhaps some four months of expense were worth an agate cameo, very well preserved and flawless, on which is shown a sea monster and a woman who holds a lance – she resembles Diana, or Pallas, from the shield and helmet, but I know interpretations to the contrary. It is not unique, because there are others like it in the museums of sovereigns, but it is most beautiful, and the agate is that very rare type with a red ground which the Latins call *menfite*.[18]

From an adjacent house containing a garden surrounded by four red columns and an oecus fronted by two yellow columns came a large painting from a lararium, complete with Genius, Lares, acolytes, and serpents (MN. 8905) (Fig. 64). Paderni had heralded the initial discovery of this painting to Tanucci, who wrote to Charles III of his eagerness for further news from his excavators.[19]

Tanucci's impatience was a symptom of his anxiety about the current state of the excavations. During March 1761, in particular, he had expressed his concern in almost weekly letters to the king: "The excavations have produced nothing this week, 'not even a nail,' as Paderni says"; "The fruits of the excavations are sparse"; "In the sterility of the excavations there is small consolation in the recovery of a painting of a woman. . . . If God fails to provide more paintings, we will not have enough for a fourth volume [of *Le antichità di Ercolano*], . . . [but] the world will be patient, since we are publishing as we continue to find."[20] Paderni, on the point of utter despair, lamented to Tanucci that "not a single thing, Your Excellency, was found this past week in the royal excavations . . . [at Stabiae], there appears to be little or perhaps nothing to hope for."[21]

Despite these concerns, Paderni, in his role as curator of the Museum Herculanense, had grown increasingly cavalier in his attitude toward the antiqui-

Figure 64. Painting (MN. 8905; 1.28 m. H × 1.83 m. W) removed in April 1761, from a lararium at Regio 7.6.38 (?) in Pompeii. Drawn by G. Morghen and engraved by C. Nolli for *PdE* 4.61–65, pl. 13.

ties. As Piaggio would note later, Paderni had established two criteria for weighing the merits of the finds and their suitability for display: that they be in sound condition, with their "intrinsic value" intact and self-evident, and that they be unique: duplication tended to diminish the significance of objects in the royal collection.[22] Paderni therefore ordered the workmen to destroy many duplicate paintings, along with any paintings damaged through humidity or careless excavation. Those that had already been cut down were smashed, while those that remained on the walls were gouged with pickaxes. No paintings could be destroyed, however, before Paderni had received notice of their discovery and personally inspected and appraised each one. This required that the workmen first take measurements and then provide descriptions of them in their reports. Sketches were often made for Tanucci. The order to destroy did not apply to the major panels of mythological scenes or landscapes, but to decorative vignettes and details, such as theatrical masks, griffins, and wild beasts, with which the storerooms at the royal palace already were bursting. To Paderni, who also kept a vigilant watch to prevent visitors from taking notes in the museum, the rationale behind physical destruction of the paintings was completely logical

and in keeping with royal sentiments about all the material from the excavations:
to prevent them from falling into the hands of foreign collectors.[23]

Alcubierre was in complete accord with this practice, and when he learned
that Paderni's orders to destroy were being countermanded later by foremen in
the field, he ordered the workmen to smash the paintings in front of Paderni.
The foreman at Stabiae, Stefano Caruso, in turn, began to question the need
for taking measurements and describing paintings, or even cutting them from
the walls, before Paderni had passed judgment on them. Since this had disrupted Weber's ability to complete his own reports, he had appealed to Tanucci,
who sanctioned the practice for the same reasons as Paderni.[24]

Foremen like Caruso, Scognamillo, and Çiria, left essentially unsupervised at
these sites, had long been suspected of misbehavior by Alcubierre and others,
who feared they could be easily bribed into selling antiquities to visitors. In
June, Alcubierre dismissed Scognamillo for stealing hay (presumably cut to
clear land for the excavations) from the Irace property and for selling the
ancient roof tiles (evidently normally deemed of no value for royal building
projects and so turned over to the property owner). Scognamillo was reinstated
only after Irace pardoned him.[25] The workmen, on the other hand, were kept
under close surveillance and had caused few problems since 1740, when an
example was made of five citizens of Resina caught stealing several minor finds
from the excavations. They confessed under torture, and the men were sen-
tenced to up to three years in prison, following their public flogging, while the
women were sent into exile for three years. Any workman caught concealing the
smallest object faced immediate imprisonment.[26] When Weber joined the excavations, Alcubierre had advised him of the regulations, and although there had
been no reported incidents in the intervening years, there can be little doubt
that antiquities still managed to find their way into foreign collections.

The poverty of finds in the excavations, the increasing tension among the
directors, and a growing suspicion of the workmen were further aggravated by the
discovery of a theft at the Royal Palace at Portici in July 1761. Tanucci appointed
Prince Placido Dentice, a member of the Consiglio di S. Chiara, to investigate the
theft of two pieces of bronze from statues under restoration in the palace. Dentice
quickly concluded his investigation, informing Tanucci that the theft of the
objects had occurred some time before but had gone unreported.[27]

These relatively minor incidents nevertheless led to the institution of stricter
punishments for transgressions by the workmen. Paid workmen caught pilfering
antiquities, or even suspected of cognizance of a theft, were automatically sen-
tenced to seven years' imprisonment, after being flogged. The forced laborers
were subject to public flogging and life imprisonment on Malta. A copy of these

regulations was nailed to the door of the fortress at Granatello where the forced laborers were housed.[28]

Tanucci continued to lament the scarcity of the finds in his letters to Charles III – "all is bleak, all languid, all sterile, desolate, half alive" – and suggested that some change might come about if they made a concerted effort to remind the directors that the principal intent of the excavations was the recovery of antiquities. Tanucci himself had little luck with Weber or Alcubierre but credited two discoveries at Stabiae to communications the king had had with them. Finally, in December 1761, Tanucci canvassed all three for their views on the primary cause of the paucity of finds and how the situation might be reversed.[29] Tanucci's initial reading of the situation was that "Weber has given himself over completely to his plans. I find that he is in Paderni's faction and against Alcubierre, but I have told him more than once that he can look to his plans at a later time."[30] This is further evidence that Tanucci was responsible for the excavation's greater concentration on the recovery of antiquities than on the documentation of the architectural remains. But the division among the chief excavators ran deeper than Tanucci implied. A week later he reported to Charles III that

> The excavations have produced nothing. As I have been lamenting this great sterility for several weeks, Paderni, between his teeth, disapproves of the method of the excavations, which, to incite him, I suggested could be abandoned. Paderni then refused to speak. While he disparages the method, he does not propose a better one, and one suspects he does so out of circumspection and prudence. I must trust him because he is more of an expert than Weber and Alcubierre, but if he refuses to speak, my faith in him is useless.[31]

Alcubierre naturally concluded that the fault lay entirely at his subaltern's feet and advised Weber how best to correct the situation in a somewhat patronizing letter that relied on much the same language he had used ten years earlier in his opposition to Weber's petition for a promotion.

> Concerning the plans of these excavations, I advise Your Highness [i.e., Weber] that if you put aside the idea that it is the principal concern of your employ to draw the general plan of these ancient cities, Your Highness will save himself the useless travail of following the streets. The principal work of the excavators should be inside the habitations, as I have always advised Your Highness and as has been done in the past, since this is where one should hope for the best and most precious treasures. For in this manner,

by pursuing the habitations and the streets at one and the same time, as
has always been done, it will be easier to deposit the earth of the new
excavation in the adjacent openings without having to transport it so far,
and Your Highness will have much greater ease as well in continuing to
draw up the plans in the same form that I have seen accomplished in the
past.[32]

In this instance Alcubierre was not addressing Weber's approach to the excavations at Pompeii but those at Herculaneum, where work had bogged down in
the area of the "temples" and the Basilica, in areas where everyone knew Bardet
and Alcubierre already had excavated.

Weber responded to Alcubierre directly, observing that it was his experience
that the greater number of finds at Herculaneum had come from the streets,
precisely because these had not been investigated previously and because, he
surmised, the mud flows had washed artifacts out of the houses into the
streets. He argued as well that following the streets was simply good methodology that allowed an orderly progression from house to house and from city
block to city block, without stumbling into areas that had been excavated
beforehand, concluding,

And so, as we have gained through this approach a greater attention to
detail without the danger of missing a single tiny jewel, I believe, in effect,
that I deserve thanks rather than condemnation. Yet the world, as we all
know, is going backwards; and likewise is evident the injury one seeks to
cause to my standing and good reputation.[33]

Soon thereafter, Paderni broke his silence and, much as in his letter of 1757
in which he termed Weber a "butcher of antiquity," summarized his observations on the source of the problem and offered a solution. His long, critical
letter to Tanucci is valuable for its candor in describing the factional infighting
and in setting forth his theories about excavation.

Paderni began by asserting his own expertise in the field, observing to the
prime minister that the two military engineers who directed the excavations
were "in the dark in searching for the ancient monuments, as they lack the skill
and necessary experience." A major source of the difficulty, he alleged, was
Alcubierre's bitter hostility toward Weber, whom he continually harassed and
sought to undermine by endeavoring to keep him ignorant of Tanucci's concern
over the scarcity of finds and by failing to advise him on better methods of
excavating. If asked, Alcubierre would attribute Weber's behavior to his "hard-
headedness (and in this at least he would not be telling you a lie)," according to

Paderni. Alcubierre wanted Weber to fall into disfavor with the king and be dismissed, so that Alcubierre could replace him with his own brother, Felippe, as he had sought to do some eleven years earlier.

Paderni claimed that he had asserted repeatedly to Alcubierre that the excavations in the Irace property at Pompeii were unbecoming of the royal service and a labor that was like " 'grinding water in a mortar,' and a useless expense." He was especially critical of Weber's determination to pursue this site, observing that

> With the method of excavating followed by Don Carlo Weber, it is purely by chance that anything is found, because he is determined to pursue the excavations both at Pompeii and at Stabiae in those habitations which stand at the foot of the mountain. We find that the habitations here either have been excavated by others or are totally barren except for the odd earthen vase, by which one can clearly comprehend that because these buildings either were near the sea or along the road to Naples, the ancients could easily plunder them with their own slaves and transport everything to the sea or elsewhere. Moreover, if ever at some point in these buildings the ancients have left anything, modern men have profited from the ease and facility of excavating those few palms of earth which lie above these ancient buildings, and so we find that they have pillaged down to the marble pavements.[34] Would not one call the pursuit of excavations in such sites "grinding water in a mortar"? Not to mention the costs, which mount daily. On the contrary, Don Carlo Weber is determined to draw a plan of Pompeii and Stabiae and tries to assert with his Swiss logic that these plans are more necessary and have greater merit than the antiquities which might be found.

Paderni advised that work at the Irace property be abandoned immediately and the workmen be transferred to the property of Diego Cuomo, where ancient streets had already been identified, thanks to his own increased supervisory role. Because the ruins were more deeply buried on the Cuomo property, he argued, they were more likely to produce the desired treasures.

In conclusion he offered Tanucci three specific recommendations. The first was that Alcubierre stop his meddling, since his behavior only hampered and annoyed Weber. Second, that Weber be ordered to return to the ancient streets found on the Cuomo property and adopt a methodology both at Pompeii and Stabiae based on following the streets and moving the workmen systematically from one side of the street to the other, "without extending the excavations through gardens and the like, as this is time spent uselessly." Third, Weber was

to adhere to this approach and not devise others without first obtaining
Paderni's approval. At Herculaneum he was to desist from excavating in areas
already investigated by Alcubierre and Bardet.

> I assure Your Excellency that if this method is established, Weber will be
> more tranquil on the one hand, and on the other he will act with greater
> respect while I am supervising what he does in these excavations. I can
> assure you – to do him the justice he deserves – he is steadfast in his toils,
> and moreover I know he is a man of the greatest merit in drawing plans.[35]

Despite Paderni's lukewarm endorsement of Weber, Tanucci realized his inquiries had further aggravated the increasingly critical and suspicious atmosphere
that existed among his chief excavators. In another letter to the king he remarked
that there was now "great discord among Weber, Alcubierre, and Paderni concerning the excavations; they send me letter after letter, completely contentious,
stemming from my complaints about the sterility of the excavations."[36]

Piaggio would later attribute the source of their intense animosity not to the
paucity of finds or to some inadequacy in methodology but to the increasingly
vague separation of powers among three men vying for royal acknowledgment of
their labors.

> There was a long-standing, three-way rivalry among Don Camillo
> [Paderni], Don Rocco Alcubierre, and Don Carlo Weber. The question
> was not of insignificant consequence, as it concerned "preeminence."
> They quarreled about who *de iure* had the right to be the first to tell the
> king of the objects found in the excavations at Herculaneum, Stabiae, and
> Pompeii, places which all three at one time had excavated under the eyes
> of the same king. . . .
>
> The curator claimed this privilege for himself alone, since everything
> that was discovered came into his hands, as he was the restorer and also
> the One Responsible (by which term – one he always had on his lips – he
> meant "guarantor"). He claimed that the reports which Weber gave to
> Don Rocco were nothing but a military formality, since the latter was
> commander and the other subaltern, and therefore a simple act of duty.
> And he claimed that Don Rocco was obliged to do nothing with such
> reports but guard them.
>
> Weber claimed the right for himself, because everything that passed
> into the hands of the curator had been recovered thanks to his own
> physical sweat, and although the majority of times the objects were not

found in his presence, he helped excavate them out with his own hands, and because he was always on site and urged on the work at all hours with ineffable vigilance and love. Since His Majesty [King Ferdinand IV] was in Portici the greater part of the year, either on vacation or to hunt, it seemed truly ridiculous and improper that, to satisfy a commendable anxiousness to know immediately of the discoveries, one had to send to Don Rocco in Naples in order that he might at his convenience bring the news to the king, who was just north of the excavations themselves [at Portici].

Finally, Don Rocco claimed the right because he was the director, even though he never went near the excavations except after having been advised of some discovery deemed particularly remarkable. But the real reason was that he was the "Father of All the Excavations," as he called himself and wished to be called by everyone else.[37]

Piaggio related an incident in which Weber sought to embarrass "Father" Alcubierre for his excessive zeal to bring news to King Ferdinand. In October 1761, Weber had alerted him to the discovery of a bronze horse at the theater of Herculaneum. Alcubierre had hastened to Portici to inform the king, only to learn later that it was not another life-size statue but a small bronze statuette of a mounted horse, thought to be a reproduction of an equestrian statue of Alexander the Great (MN. 4996).[38]

While Paderni was pressing his superiors to order the work at Pompeii transferred back to the Cuomo property, Weber had proceeded with his excavations on the Irace property in areas adjacent to where the statue of Diana was found. It is unclear whether or not this was done with official sanction. For some time, tunneling had been adopted for part of the work at Pompeii, since this allowed work to progress rain or shine, and paintings could await removal underground with minimal damage from the elements. This could be an effective approach, although the nature of the pumice and ash made the tunnels far more susceptible to collapse than those at Herculaneum.[39] In January 1762, the tunnels had begun to reveal a stepped altar, roughly 1 meter high and revetted with polychrome marbles; nearby was found a tufa sundial. Weber considered this ample reason to concentrate his investigations here rather than in the Cuomo property. He outlined his rationale and his recommendations on how best to proceed in another long letter, evidently addressed to Alcubierre:

Concerning Città, the amphitheater, the place of the 14 [sic] pillars of marble, of the famous tripod, and of the great basalt road, of the baths, furnaces, many statues, infinite paintings, where there is a pool beside the road with a temple standing in front [i.e., at the Praedia Iuliae Felicis]: this temple should be excavated in due time, since it looks promising.

The site of the paintings – [the properties] of Cuomo, Balzano, and Filippis – this too one should return to in due time, but not now, since the site currently under excavation has produced so great a multitude of jewels – and so much more I hope it will produce! – the gold coins, among these the rare gold which deserves to be illustrated in the second volume of the paintings [i.e., *Le antichità di Ercolano*], the Diana, the infinite paintings, the great cameo, the gold earrings and bracelets. Previously it was thought best simply to abandon this site, since for some time nothing worthwhile had been found, and if I had not been persistent, all this would not have been found.

I believe we are now in the same situation with the promising, very rare and admirable altar, so gracious, special, and reasonably well preserved, discovered today; and also the six paintings removed last week to the Royal Palace. One must not continue to excavate this altar [by means of a tunnel], since any collapsing ruins might destroy it, and that would be a great pity. Therefore, one has already begun excavating from above, as the foreman requested. . . . Likewise, I believe that in a short time we will encounter a nice jewel, if for some three months all the workmen from Gragnano should help here at Cività until this comes about and then return to Gragnano.[40]

Again, Weber's instincts paid off, as the following month two terracotta statues of actors wearing tragic masks (MN. 22248, 22249), both similar in size to the archaistic Diana, were recovered near this altar. In contrast to Alcubierre's continued apologies that he was not to blame for the paucity of finds, the next week brought a large panel painting of a nude Venus emerging from a shell (MN. 27704) (Fig. 65).[41] As a consequence, Weber successfully persuaded his superiors to concentrate the excavations at Pompeii for six months, until they were transferred back to Stabiae in July for the duration of 1762.[42]

Paderni was gratified by Weber's success, for Tanucci wrote to the king, "Paderni is pleased to declare himself content and tranquil, and in accord with the engineers. To achieve this I did everything I could: prayers, shouts, sermons, threats."[43] The following month Tanucci remarked again that Paderni had set forth his thoughts at length, "in part conforming to and in part contradicting those of Weber, and as usual he vents his anger against Alcubierre, which I cannot make him stifle."[44]

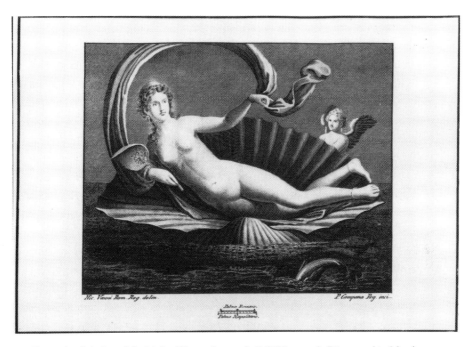

Figure 65. Painting of the birth of Venus from a shell (MN. 27704). Discovered in March
1762 during excavations in a house at Regio 7.6.1–4 in Pompeii. Drawn by N. Vanni and
engraved by P. Campana for *PdE* 4.11–15, pl. 3.

J. J. WINCKELMANN: "FATHER OF CLASSICAL ARCHAEOLOGY"

Such was the state of affairs when Winckelmann made his second appearance at
the Bourbon court, in early 1762. Out of this visit came his famous "open
letter," the *Sendschreiben von den herculanischen Entdeckungen*, addressed to his
travel companion, the Saxon count Christian Heinrich von Brühl. This critical
account of the excavations and the discoveries in the Vesuvian cities first appeared in Dresden in 1762, although it was the French version of 1764 that
received widest distribution and attention in Europe and ultimately aroused the
wrath of the Bourbon court toward Winckelmann.[45]

During his first visit to the Bay of Naples, from February to April 1758,
Winckelmann had been stunned by the cool reception he received. By his own
account, he believed this treatment had been prompted by an alarmist and
jealous reaction to his impeccable credentials and letters of introduction. This
assessment, while identifying part of the reason, only begins to explain the
circumstances behind the court's rebuff. His letters included one to Queen

Maria Amalia from her brother Frederick Christian, electoral prince of Saxony. The prince had intended Winckelmann to serve as his unofficial correspondent on the latest discoveries from the Vesuvian region, just as Venuti had done for him years before. Venuti, in fact, had dedicated his *Descrizione delle prime scoperte dell' antica città di Ercolano* of 1748 to this same Frederick Christian. Charles of Bourbon's anger at the inclusion in that publication of a drawing of the marble equestrian statues of the Balbi had been responsible in part for Venuti's premature departure from Naples.[46]

On this first visit, in 1758, Winckelmann complained that he was hindered from fulfilling his mission by being given only very limited access to the museum. When he ventured to inquire after anything further, a royal interdiction was thrown up in his path "like Medusa's head." He had to admit, however, that he had been shown things other visitors had not, so his disappointment and bitterness toward his Bourbon hosts must be attributed largely to his own overblown expectations of what he might achieve. He had gone to Naples fully expecting to be received into the most noble houses and had even fancied himself a candidate for admission to the Accademia Ercolanese, only to discover his reputation did him more harm than good.[47] Yet, although he had dined on occasion with members of the court – the king referred to him as "il Signore Barone Sassone" – he had been forced to take room and board with Piaggio in Portici after being ejected from quarters in a convent in Naples much sooner than expected.[48]

It was precisely Winckelmann's role as correspondent that most alarmed the Bourbon court in 1758: their greatest fear was that he would publish descriptions of the antiquities he had seen before the Accademia finished its own work and, in the process, demonstrate to the outside world how poorly managed the excavations were.[49] These concerns are all too evident in the Accademia's assessment of Weber's proposal to publish the finds from Stabiae and are consistent with the court's reaction to all publications abroad about the excavations. Clandestine publication of the discoveries was as abhorrent to the court as the clandestine sale of its antiquities to foreigners. For some years it had become increasingly difficult to gain access to the ruins and the museum. Russell wrote in 1743 that he had been watched carefully and was prohibited from using a pencil, which forced him to commit everything to memory.[50] Six years later he added that visitors "are observed with greater jealousy and watchfulness since the scandalous behavior of some sharpers, who have not scrupled to pocket any small rarity upon which they could lay their hands."[51]

In addition to his royal connections, Winckelmann's honorary membership in the Society of Antiquarians in London and the Accademia Etrusca of Cortona made him eminently suspect; Bayardi could boast of similar affiliations, though

Tanucci too was a member of the Accademia Etrusca. It must be no coincidence
that Paderni's own communications with the Royal Society of London, of which
he was himself a fellow, came to an abrupt halt at precisely the time when
Winckelmann arrived in Naples in February 1758. Winckelmann evidently
failed to comprehend the fact that he posed the same kind of threat as Venuti,
Gori, De Brosses, and Cochin and Bellicard before him. All these earlier
scholars had been granted wide access to the excavation material, yet now their
publications, especially those that included illustrations of the antiquities, were
seen as having undercut the work of the Accademia. Even Berardo Galiani, in
his 1758 commentary on Vitruvius, studiously referred only to the well-known
theater at Herculaneum to avoid drawing the court's ire. The Accademia's fears
were not completely groundless, moreover, as Winckelmann's later writings
would exceed their worst fears both in the number of objects he described and
in the damage sustained by the reputation of the excavations as a result of his
highly critical remarks.

Winckelmann's disillusionment with, and later open hostility toward, those in
charge of the excavations may be attributed to the fact that he was not given free
access to the antiquities nor license to contemplate them as he saw fit. He too
was kept under close guard and prevented from taking notes or measurements
or from making sketches.[52] Ironically, Paderni himself was responsible for rigor-
ously enforcing this prohibition, which, as noted, had been enacted in 1743,
after he had been caught drawing some paintings.[53]

Consequently, many of the observations in Winckelmann's correspondence,
written in the months following this first visit, after he had returned to Rome,
were based on notes he scribbled hastily from memory after visiting the various
sites. Inaccuracies inevitably crept in as he sought to recall all he had seen. The
degree of detail and precision of his descriptions correlates directly with the
level of cooperation and access he was granted: the more often he could consult
an object, the better chance he had of correcting his notes. His fairly detailed
comments concerning the ancient papyri from Herculaneum, for example,
might best be explained as resulting from his stay at Piaggio's house, not from
any officially sanctioned research. Piaggio must have freely discussed their
composition and contents with Winckelmann, who in turn described Piaggio's
work space in the palace at Portici in greater detail than the ancient monuments
around him.[54] His closest contacts – Piaggio, Galiani, and the vulcanologist
Della Torre – stood on the periphery of the power structure and could do little
about gaining him greater access to the antiquities. Those closest to the excavations, especially Tanucci and Paderni, quietly closed ranks, offered the barest of
courtesies, and awaited his departure.

His initial impression of the works of art was not enthusiastically positive. He found the sculptures "part mediocre, part bad," with the exception of the impressive equestrian statues of the Balbi. Of the paintings, he believed the best already had been illustrated in the recently published first volume of *Le antichità di Ercolano*, and saved his kindest remarks for the Achilles and Chiron recovered from the Basilica in 1739. The rest he dismissed as equally mediocre works of art, valuable primarily for the light they shed on ancient dress, domestic life, and architecture.

The brevity of his descriptions of the architectural remains themselves underscores his inability to linger over them and betrays how at best he had formed only a vague idea of their design. He had traveled widely throughout the bay, from Pozzuoli to Paestum, where the Greek temples and nearly intact city walls made a great impression on him. Yet it is not clear how much he had learned firsthand in the underground tunnels at Herculaneum and how much he had deduced from his conversations and readings. Clearly he had failed fully to appreciate the layout of the ruins at Herculaneum, believing that the theater stood in the ancient city of Resina and that the Villa dei Papiri was the only building yet investigated in Herculaneum. The ruins of the theater he mentions only in passing, remarking that the objects removed from there, not the style of its masonry, would date its construction to around the reign of Caesar. This is the kind of conclusion he could have reached without actually seeing the remains; Cochin and Bellicard had already dated it to the Augustan period.

Yet his brief remarks on the ruins of the Villa dei Papiri are strikingly similar to what a visitor encounters in the underground tunnels today: the simple black and white mosaics extending over most of the common floor areas, the wide doorways with their marble thresholds, and little else of note architecturally. He describes a plaza located behind the villa, with a raised enclosure covered in marble identified as a "water reservoir," and stucco-covered brick pillars where marble and bronze statues were recovered. Here Winckelmann clearly is describing the euripus in the great peristyle of the villa in a manner recalling the confusion Paderni demonstrated in his own correspondence in 1754, where these features were said to form parts of discrete structures. Even Winckelmann's discourse on the architecture of houses at Herculaneum focuses more on the ruins of a villa at Tusculum, and on what he could infer from the ancient paintings, than on these archaeological remains.[55]

Although he did not have as good a grasp of ancient architecture as of ancient art, at this point in his career, Winckelmann's brevity in these matters should be attributed in part to the prohibition against taking notes, since he remarks that "Everything is guarded with such jealousy that one cannot measure the diameter of a single column even at the temple or forum in Pozzuoli. How much time I wasted at Portici trying to form a clear notion of the ruins!"[56] More evident is his frustration at not being provided with any plans of the excavations. He complained bitterly of the firm interdiction against seeing these, which Weber must have had a hand in enforcing. Like many visitors before him, and even Alcubierre himself, Winckelmann became disoriented in the underground tunnels, admitting that "without seeing the plan of the excavations one cannot form a distinct impression, as one is confounded by the tunnels and the comings and goings by which one passes underground."[57]

He claims to have feigned ignorance, to avoid arousing the jealousy of those in charge. Just as Alcubierre had designated himself the "Father of the Excavations," so too had Paderni coined himself an official title, which Winckelmann recorded in his scathing characterization of Paderni as

> A lousy draftsman who, to save himself from starvation in Rome, had the good fortune of being allowed to draw the ancient paintings at an annual salary of 15 Neapolitan ducats, or 14 Roman scudi. This man is as much an impostor as he is a nitwit and an ignoramus and passes himself off as a Doctor of Antiquities.[58]

He observed that the few scholars Naples had to offer were eccentric and wrongheaded. Martorelli was attacked for believing the papyri were contracts and official documents, not literary texts, and for the absurd length of his book on ancient writing instruments. Both of these were areas where Winckelmann had done research of his own and had come to quite different conclusions than Martorelli.[59] Even the discredited Bayardi was not spared criticism for having confused the iconography of an apotheosis of Homer with that of Julius Caesar. On the other hand he praised Mazzocchi, called Berardo Galiani "an honest man, a scholar, and an obliging friend," and considered Piaggio "the world's greatest gentleman."[60] Whether he grouped Alcubierre and Weber among those he needed to deceive is unknown, since he never explicitly named either one.

By the time of Winckelmann's second visit, in early 1762, although conditions at the excavations had taken a dramatic turn for the worse, at least he enjoyed a somewhat warmer reception. To his amusement, Tanucci continued to act indifferently toward him, but Della Torre and Galiani ensured he was properly entertained and guided, and Piaggio again gave him room and board. Although he spent some thirty days at Portici around the time of Carnevale, the details of this visit are somewhat more obscure, since he wrote only one letter during his stay and did not compose the remainder until after he returned to Rome. These are more in the form of annotated commentaries than letters yet

reveal how much more profitable this visit had been. He had received a royal
dispensation to see everything in the museum except those objects considered
obscene (and even managed to circumvent this in part) and could declare in the
end that he had augmented his knowledge of ancient architecture. He culled
these observations from a detailed journal compiled during his visit, which, he
told one friend, he planned to draw on for a treatise on the excavations in the
near future. Yet his confusion on certain details betrays the fact that he still had
been prevented from taking notes or making sketches *in situ*.[61]

Much of the success of Winckelmann's second visit may be attributed to his
greatly improved relations with Paderni. Evidently unaware of the harsh criticism he had received in Winckelmann's correspondence, Paderni had been
actively cultivating their friendship for some time. Since Winckelmann's first
trip to Naples, Paderni had sent him occasional reports on tantalizing new
finds.[62] Now they toured the museum together, discussed iconography together,
traveled together to all the sites, and even dined together over the ruins at
Pompeii. Winckelmann later remarked that he had seen everything in great
leisure, as if he were working in his own home, and credited this to the "intimate friendship" they had formed. This sharing of information is illustrated by
the fact that the discoveries Winckelmann discusses in greatest detail in his
correspondence are the same discoveries Paderni highlighted in his reports to
Tanucci. Paderni's interest in fostering this relationship may not have been
entirely selfless, for he may have hoped that it would heighten his own reputation as a scholar, win him admission to the Accademia, and give him greater
prestige than Alcubierre and Weber. It was to prove a singularly impolitic
association.

At Pompeii, Winckelmann witnessed Weber's excavations in the ruins where
the archaicizing Diana had been recovered. His interest in the site and the
number of times he referred to objects found here largely vindicated Weber's
confidence in the Irace property while ignoring Paderni's belief that searching
there was "like grinding water in a mortar." Yet Winckelmann was alarmed to
find only eight workmen here and only fifty excavators in all split among the four
main Vesuvian sites.[63] They already had investigated the structure Weber had
identified as an "altar" in a report to Alcubierre, and he had used it to argue in
favor of pursuing further work here. Although the altar had been dismantled
and one of its columns taken to Portici, Winckelmann described its design and
the surrounding features as they had been related to him, now appropriately
embellished so that the Diana, which he believed was an Etruscan original, was
said to have been found inside the altar. At the time of his visits the workmen
were in the process of uncovering a painted room containing a masonry shop

counter with shelves for displaying wares, which also was later carted off and displayed in the sixth room of the museum. He witnessed the discovery of a tufa sundial mentioned in Weber's report for January 30, 1762. Winckelmann also described the two terracotta statues of actors recovered a month later in this same area as "estimable for that which they represent" and, incorrectly, as the first preserved statues of terracotta.[64]

Through his research in the museum Winckelmann developed a greater appreciation for the works of art, praising the bronze Hermes (MN. 5625) from the Villa dei Papiri as the finest bronze in the world and describing other statues, such as the Sleeping Satyr (MN. 5624) and several portrait busts, all of which had been found in the villa subsequent to his first visit.[65] But he was most enthusiastic about a set of four small stucco paintings which, he had been told, the excavators had found already mounted in easels and leaning up against the wall of a room (see Fig. 41). In letters to Usteri, Bianconi, and Volkmann, and then again in the *Geschichte* and the *Sendschreiben*, Winckelmann described these paintings in great detail, at first ascribing them to Herculaneum and later to Stabiae. Actually they formed part of the group of seven paintings Weber had found in the second "temple" (the Palestra) at Herculaneum in February 1761, the same paintings Paderni had had to describe in great haste to Tanucci because he had been overwhelmed by the heat and lack of oxygen in the underground tunnels. Winckelmann's excitement was due to his hypothesis that these paintings were by Greek masters and had been transported here for incorporation into new wall decorations in the manner described by Vitruvius (Vitr. 7.3.10). In fact, however, they were panels salvaged from walls that had been damaged in the earthquake of A.D. 62, as Winckelmann later acknowledged.[66]

WINCKELMANN'S FIRST OPEN LETTER

Winckelmann reserved his most critical remarks for the *Sendschreiben von den herculanischen Entdeckungen*, which he wrote while in residence at the Villa Albani at Castel Gandolfo in the summer of 1762. He drew many of the principal issues he addressed as well as the works of art he discussed in this letter from his private correspondence, so this represents more a compilation of existing material than a completely new product. Nor is the overall structure of the letter particularly novel, for, whether consciously or not, it closely mirrors the writings of d'Arthenay, Venuti, De Brosses, and Cochin and Bellicard. One notable exception is that Winckelmann says virtually nothing about the history of Mount Vesuvius or the life of Hercules. Another difference was a more profound interest in what the material remains could reveal about ancient society and

urban life, both public and private. Still a third was his candid criticism of
several members of the Bourbon court, who, he believed, were bungling the
excavations.

The letter is divided into four main sections. He begins with a general
discussion of the topography of the Vesuvian region and the vexing problems of
placename nomenclature. Of particular note here is Winckelmann's scientific
approach, as he draws on ancient and modern literary sources along with the
physical ruins themselves to provide some sense of the size and appearance of
these cities in antiquity. The next section examines the various ways in which
each city was buried by the eruption; how this affected the evacuation of the
populace and the resulting archaeological picture; and why one site might offer
a greater potential for discoveries than another. The central portion of the letter
is devoted to a discussion of the antiquities in the museum, from the marble
statues of the Balbi and the bronzes from the theater to the domestic implements and jewelry. It is here that Winckelmann's freedom of access to the
museum is most evident, since he was able to discuss in great detail, and with a
discerning eye, a broad range of artifacts that his predecessors had relegated to
a simple inventory or ignored completely in favor of focusing on the most
important statues and paintings. The final section is his discussion of the discovery of the papyri, their form, and their contents. Apart from short notices in the
Philosophical Transactions of the Royal Society of London, little information on
the papyri was available for public consumption at this time, and so Winckelmann's firsthand observations were among the first to receive broad circulation.[67] The letter concludes with a brief description of the physical organization
of the museum and a summary of the current projects and goals of the Bourbon
court.

Winckelmann expressed definite opinions about the conduct of the excavations themselves, what sites were most or least profitable, where vigorously to
pursue or entirely abandon the investigations. Despite his fascination with the
operation of ancient doors and his interest in urban matters such as the construction of streets and sidewalks, Winckelmann was more interested in the recovery
of works of art than the "common architecture" Weber found so compelling. He
could not understand why Weber's excavations in 1761 in the "temples" at
Herculaneum had not been brought to a halt. He fully approved of the practice
of refilling the tunnels at Herculaneum and of cutting down the paintings to
preserve them yet opposed those who called for exposing the entire city to light.
The expense would be too great, he argued, "And to what advantage? To see
old, ruined walls. And finally, just to please the anxious curiosity of a few would
necessitate the destruction of a well-built and large modern city in order to

expose a destroyed city and heaps of stone."[68] Only the theater was worth such an effort, since he, albeit incorrectly, believed it stood beneath the expendable gardens of the Augustinians. He maintained the common opinion that Herculaneum was not as valuable a site as others, since the paucity of cadavers and finds there was considered proof that the inhabitants had escaped with their lives and most of their possessions intact.

Pompeii was a different matter, for Winckelmann claimed that the volcanic conditions, in particular the "mofetic" vapors, rendered the land less productive for vines and that it therefore could be sacrificed to the excavations. It was also a less costly site to investigate, since it was easier to dig through the lapilli. Here, unlike at Herculaneum, one could examine all four walls of a house at once. He fully supported Paderni's position that the most fruitful approach would be to pursue investigations along the street found on the Cuomo property. Yet because of the sluggish rate of excavation and the lack of sufficient manpower, Winckelmann despaired that it would take four generations before the work was completed. Even so, he could not justify the expense of continuing the excavations in this area, advocating instead the sites along the north side of the bay – Pozzuoli, Baiae, Cumae, and Misenum – as the most likely to produce valuable antiquities, since it was here that the Romans had constructed their great luxury villas.

Interspersed with this more scientific and scholarly appraisal of the excavations are Winckelmann's now-legendary attacks against members of the Bourbon court. Most reflect the influences of the partisan politics he had been subjected to and which had affected his freedom of movement and debate: in the final analysis he lined himself up squarely in Piaggio's camp. Martorelli, named specifically some sixteen times, bears the brunt of the attack. These comments range over everything from his ignorance of Hebrew to his penchant for distorting Homer in an attempt to "say something new." Winckelmann again ridicules Martorelli for his odd notions about the papyri, that they must be public records instead of texts because ancient authors wrote only on wax tablets, not papyrus rolls, and that certain papyri were written in Sabine. Nor are Martorelli's literary talents the only object of these attacks, as he is chided for not recognizing the tufa out of which the seats in the theater at Herculaneum were carved and for identifying Alcibiades as the subject of a bust simply because the piece was signed by an Athenian. Bayardi is named only three times, especially for his "inexcusable" iconographical misidentifications, despite his liberal salary and his freedom to contemplate the objects far longer than anyone else. Even though he had quarreled with Piaggio, Mazzocchi is both praised as "the most learned" member of the Accademia and mildly rebuked for his dedicatory inscriptions composed clumsily in Latin. Tanucci, named twice, is lauded vaguely for his talent and intelligence.

Winckelmann expressed particular hostility toward Alcubierre, calling him a "land surveyor" and a military engineer who was "as familiar with antiquities as the moon is with crabs." Since he could have encountered Alcubierre in Portici only on rare occasions, if ever, Winckelmann's strong bias against him is something of a puzzle and must have been fostered both by excavation gossip and the perception that Alcubierre was most directly responsible for enforcing the prohibitions against which Winckelmann had struggled so arduously. From what he had heard, Alcubierre was completely incompetent, and so he accused him of carting off a set of bronze letters before copying down the text of the inscription. The excavation reports show, however, that the letters in fact were found piecemeal over the course of several weeks in 1739 and may never have comprised a single inscription.[69] Paderni was not spared either. After remarking on their intimate friendship, and despite the fact that he owed no small debt of gratitude to the director of the museum, Winckelmann charged him with having ordered that fragments of a bronze quadriga statue from the theater be melted down and recast to form a single equestrian statue, as well as with having fashioned two large medallions bearing busts of the king and queen from some other fragments.

WEBER AND WINCKELMANN

Through his association with Piaggio, Winckelmann finally had come into contact with Weber and was strongly influenced by his work. He had seen several of Weber's plans and as a consequence had broadened his understanding of ancient architecture and incorporated this knowledge into his writings. Berardo Galiani must also have played an important role. As the Accademia's expert on architecture and as a result of Weber's application to the Accademia, Galiani had begun to work more closely with Weber on renewed excavations in the theater at Herculaneum. These associations allowed Winckelmann to correct his earlier misapprehensions about the design of the Villa dei Papiri, for example, and he now described it as a single structure. He probably did not see Weber's manuscript on "Le Piante di Alcuni Edifici Sotterranei," however, as he nowhere discusses the Villa di San Marco or the antiquities removed from it, nor did he adopt any of the approaches the essay advocated.

Weber was among the few individuals Winckelmann praised, observing that

> To this intelligent man are owed all the sensible arrangements made [in the excavations after Alcubierre was posted to Naples]. The first of these

was to draw up an exact plan of the underground galleries and the excavated buildings in all their dimensions. He rendered this plan clear and
intelligible by means of other plans which show the elevation of all the
structures which one should imagine he would see if all the earth on top
were removed and were seen from above, revealing the interiors of the
buildings, their rooms and their gardens, in the precise place where each
of these things were found. These plans, however, are shown to no one.[70]

He was triumphant to have overcome this last obstacle and finally to be able to
comprehend the architecture of the ancient structures he had experienced only
in the disconcerting labyrinth of underground tunnels. Already in March 1762,
he had written to Bianconi that "After such great efforts, contortions, and
prayers four years ago [during his first visit], I have finally succeeded in seeing
the plans of the underground excavations drawn with such incredible exactness
by the royal engineer and supervisor of the works, and I have gained great
insights which, God willing, I will one day bring to light."[71]

Winckelmann referred to several specific measurements and distances that
he could have obtained only from Weber's plans, all of which were still in
Weber's personal possession at that time. From Weber's 1751 drawing of the
belvedere's circular mosaic as well as from his unfinished plan of the Villa dei
Papiri must have come the figure that the mosaic had been found 102 palms
belowground. The dimensions of the euripus in the villa are given in the
Sendschreiben (#43) as 252.0 (Neapolitan) palms by 27.0 palms, a figure almost
identical to the 252.0 palms by 27.5 palms on Weber's unfinished plan. Further-
more, Winckelmann specifically mentions seeing a plan that illustrated tunnels
cut by posteruption scavengers, a clear reference to those drawn by Weber on
his plan of the villa.

He was less successful in recalling other specific details about these plans,
and this serves as further evidence of his difficulty in keeping accurate notes.[72]
He transposed elements from the viridarium of the Praedia Iuliae Felicis in
Pompeii into the great peristyle of the Villa dei Papiri. These include adding
"semicircular and rectangular pools" along the sides of the villa's peristyle, a
detail that he must have transposed from the niches of the east viridarium wall
of the Praedia. He also located the Praedia's painted sacrarium of Isis, along
with its bronze tripod with ithyphallic satyrs, somewhere in the villa. Although
he mistakenly situated the now-reburied Praedia Iuliae Felicis at Gragnano,
confusing it with one of the villas at ancient Stabiae, Winckelmann was familiar
with its design and therefore must have consulted both of Weber's finished
plans. He was probably recalling the axonometric plan when he had remarked

earlier that Weber's plans illustrated these sites as they would be seen if the earth were removed and they were viewed from above. That he was dealing with the Praedia and not a villa from Stabiae is clear as well from his description of a central pool in the garden "divided into four equal parts by four [sic] arched bridges," just as in the euripus in the viridarium of the Praedia.

Yet while the *Sendschreiben* demonstrates a broader appreciation for the more prosaic aspects of ancient life and art, it is still far removed from the kind of archaeological publication Weber had envisaged. Although Winckelmann could describe the architecture of certain buildings and had formed opinions about how the excavations should be handled, he was not a field archaeologist and showed little interest in Weber's "contextual" approach. He was essentially a dilettante, more concerned with recovering works of art, preferably the monumental art of the emperors or the luxury art of the upper classes, as is revealed by his remarks about the lack of finds at Herculaneum and the need to excavate along the coast of Baiae. Nor does he appear to have appreciated how provenance could affect the elucidation and interpretation of these objects. His discussions of the antiquities are still grouped by genre: sculptures first, followed by inscriptions and domestic implements, with little interest in whether they had come from a public or private setting.

There were, however, instances where he made some attempt to place a work of art in its original context. Although it was not unusual to give a general idea of where an antiquity had been found, Winckelmann's specific remarks suggest he had been moved to make these observations after conversations with Weber. He observed that bronze busts and female statues had stood in the intercolumniations of the Villa dei Papiri's great peristyle and that the belvedere's circular mosaic stood on a kind of bastion overlooking the sea, both of which he must have recalled from seeing them illustrated on Weber's plan. A better example is his description of the "small temple" with its statue of Diana. This includes a number of details about the relation of the statue to its context that Weber, with his enthusiasm about this site, would have been in the best position to provide, since several of these features either had been carried off or been reburied before Winckelmann's arrival.

WINCKELMANN'S LEGACY

The squabbling among Alcubierre, Paderni, and Weber continued unabated after Winckelmann's departure. Excavations in the Irace property at Pompeii ceased in July 1762, despite the fact that Winckelmann's highlighting of the finds from here indirectly corroborated Weber's conclusion that the area around the

Diana statue would prove the most profitable. For the next six months the excavators concentrated on the ruins at Stabiae, as Paderni took an increasingly active role in determining the fate of each trench, in selecting new sites for exploration, and even in sketching plans and elevations. Weber meanwhile proclaimed to Tanucci that these renewed excavations at Stabiae would contribute additional material for his monograph in progress, an indication that he had not been completely disabused of the notion of writing one.[73] Yet, to Alcubierre's great delight, these investigations were essentially fruitless, and Tanucci had to concede that "in fact, Alcubierre's [method of excavation] never was so barren for an entire year."[74] When, however, Paderni declared Stabiae "sterile" after it produced "not even a nail" and transferred the laborers back to Pompeii in December 1762, he stationed them not near the Diana but at the location in the Cuomo property he had long favored.[75] Here, an ancient street was uncovered almost immediately. Paderni then adopted a new approach to the work, which was essentially the same as Weber's proposal that streets should be followed since they would inevitably lead to more buildings.

Alcubierre remained skeptical about the merits of this site, as he himself had excavated this area of Pompeii years earlier and believed he had exhausted its potential. His arrogance was only fueled by the acute dearth of worthwhile discoveries. Tanucci reported to Charles III that "Paderni, distressed and most confused, says that this week's excavations have produced absolutely nothing" and reported later that "Paderni is tormented by the continued scarcity of the excavations and philosophizes with Weber on certain new methods which do not agree with Alcubierre, who laughs fiercely at the bad outcome of these approaches which do not conform with his own."[76]

Paderni's goal had been to follow this Pompeian street toward the center of the city, although the first trenches actually were sunk outside the city walls in an area of ancient suburban villas and private tombs. As a result, a number of funerary inscriptions were recovered, along with one inscription, found in August 1763, that provided definitive proof that this was ancient Pompeii. Soon thereafter the excavators began to isolate the Porta di Ercolano, the gate on the northwest side of the city, facing Herculaneum (Fig. 66). Paderni drew a sketch of the elevation of this gate, complete with a gladiatorial paria notice found painted on its outer face (the first such notice found at Pompeii) and sent this along with his report to Tanucci.[77]

Although Tanucci reported to Charles III that there was "cheerfulness" on all sides about this discovery, Weber complained that the city gate would have been found two years earlier had they followed his advice about continuing to work the area around the Diana statue. Yet he recognized the importance of this as

Figure 66. View, from the west, of the Porta di Ercolana at Pompeii. Engraving from 1789
by Francesco Piranesi, based on an original by Jean-Louis Desprez. From F. Piranesi,
Fabbriche scoperte nella città di Pompei sino al 1792 (Rome 1792), pl. 2. (Courtesy of the
Davison Art Center, Wesleyan University.)

the first fully excavated civic monument at Pompeii and recommended that forty
forced laborers be assigned here and that the surrounding land be purchased,
so that the gate could remain exposed to public view. Soon after these measures
had been approved, he further suggested that the excavated rooms of private
houses and shops adjacent to the gate also be left exposed, since the pace of the
excavations was slow enough so that the costs would be moderate.[78]

Weber previously had proposed leaving mosaics or rooms in the Villa dei
Papiri and at Stabiae exposed for the benefit of visitors. But in keeping with the
attitude that these sites were merely quarries for antiquities, there is no evidence that the court ever had been influenced by strong public interest in the
ruins themselves. Nevertheless, from this time on it became common practice to
leave excavated sites at Pompeii exposed to public scrutiny.[79] It is unlikely that
this change in policy was due to the secure identification of this site as ancient
Pompeii, as is often stated in modern sources, since the site had been designated "Pompeii" in official documents from at least 1751.[80] Instead, this discov-

ery prompted a long overdue response to public curiosity about the architectural remains, one that had been expressed since virtually the onset of the excavations by numerous foreign scholars and visitors, and one Weber himself had acknowledged years before.

Conservation of the structures was never a consideration, but this new procedure did present certain complications. Although portable objects continued to be removed to the museum and the most important panel paintings were cut down, the practice of leaving sites accessible further aggravated the concern about clandestine plundering of any small paintings that might be left *in situ*. The sentinels had to consist of more than the small bands of invalids normally posted at the sites on nights and holidays. Moreover, the controversy over the destruction of paintings flared up once again, and Paderni, who claimed to be carrying out orders dating from 1757, did not desist from the practice for some time, even after the king had expressed his outrage.[81]

In 1764, two years after his second visit, Winckelmann returned to the Bay of Naples with the intention of revising his *Sendschreiben*, which was about to be issued in its French translation. Out of this came instead his *Nachrichten von den neuesten herculanischen Entdeckungen* (Dresden 1764), addressed to his two travel companions, Peter Volkmann of Hamburg and the painter Heinrich Füessly of Zurich. He sought with varying success to correct a number of mistakes in the *Sendschreiben*, explaining, for example, that the four mounted paintings from Stabiae were not in fact Greek originals but had been salvaged from earlier walls yet failing to distinguish this ancient practice from Paderni's handiwork against some paintings left *in situ* at Pompeii. To the court's great aggravation, he described a number of recent discoveries, such as the two mosaic emblemmata signed by Dioscurides of Samos found in the "Villa di Diomede," claiming that one had been uncovered before his very eyes.[82] Yet he was skeptical that any important statues would be found at Pompeii, observing that "more is found in Rome and its surroundings in a single month than [is found] here in an entire year."[83] Apart from the Diana, no major statuary had been recovered from any of the excavations since the last bronzes were pulled out of the Villa dei Papiri in 1759.

In keeping with this paucity of significant finds, Winckelmann devoted a substantial proportion of his second letter to architecture, specifically a detailed description of the theater at Herculaneum as well as four private houses and the Porta di Ercolana at Pompeii, all now readily accessible. By now a careful investigation into the design of the theater's scaena had been undertaken by Weber under the supervision of Berardo Galiani. The latter had guided Winckelmann through the excavations and explained the theater's design and embellishment, pointing out its features on a new plan drawn by Weber. Never-theless, Winckelmann says little about the decoration of any of these structures; even the important series of bronze and marble sculptures from the theater are mentioned only in passing.

Yet he demonstrated some budding appreciation of the importance of archaeo-logical context for interpreting the artistic finds. He suggested, for example, that the group of five bronze statues of women from the Villa dei Papiri be identified as nymphs because they were found standing near a pool.[84] His discussions also incorporated the kind of critical analysis found on Weber's plans and in his monograph, frankly interpreting the surviving architectural remains with the assistance of ancient literary sources, inscriptional evidence, and other archaeo-logical comparanda, such as the theaters at Pola, Antium, and Tivoli and the contemporary excavations at Velleia and Antium.[85] Yet without detailed plans and illustrations of the finds, Winckelmann's writings remain essentially "obser-vations" and not the definitive studies these sites deserved.

The Bourbon court's reaction to Winckelmann's writings was feeble, ineffec-tive, and too late in coming: the upper echelons of the excavation's direction were in as great a state of disarray as the lower. None of his publications reached Naples until late 1764, when Ferdinando Galiani, the Bourbon ambassador to Paris, dispatched a copy of the French translation of the *Sendschreiben* to Tanucci. The prime minister had already formed his opinion about its author well before this, thanks especially to the latter's violation of the court's prohibi-tions and the insults to its hospitality. In September Tanucci had admitted to Galiani that he still had not seen Winckelmann's *Sendschreiben*, "full of imperti-nence about matters concerning Herculaneum. . . . A German who has been vegetating in Rome deserves forgiveness if he has been poorly raised." After reading it, Tanucci, appalled at Winckelmann's accusations against Paderni, declared, "This Saxon must have the worst manners."[86]

As Winckelmann had noted already in his *Nachrichten*, the Accademia Ercolanese was by now a dead letter, ravaged by deaths and no longer holding meetings; the volumes of *Le antichità* continued to be issued only through the Herculean efforts of the Accademia's secretary, Pasquale Carcani. Tanucci therefore lacked a dynamic force that could be rallied to the defense of the excavations. It was only in 1765 that Berardo Galiani, a member of the Ac-cademia and Ferdinando Galiani's older brother, paid penance for his associa-tion with Winckelmann by publishing a letter in which he tried but essentially failed to respond to Winckelmann's main criticisms of the excavations while at the same time highlighting the most significant gaffes committed in the *Sendschreiben*. Galiani's most memorable insult was to term Winckelmann "a

Goth turned antiquarian," likening his brand of erudition to the notoriously
bogus guides at the ruins of Pozzuoli. Alcubierre had never boasted that he was
himself an antiquarian, noted Galiani in his defense, "He professes military
architecture. And if His Catholic Majesty chose him to direct these excavations,
He chose him because he knew how to operate an underground excavation in a
safe manner and he knew how to make plans of the buildings he would encounter there." Galiani described Winckelmann as "from that breed of scholars who
are unable to get beyond the study of language and are like diggers of mines,
people so accustomed to the dark and to hard manual labor that light harms
them." He further charged him with accepting as gospel "everything told to him
in a secretive air by any liar or slave attached to the excavations at Herculaneum."[87] Galiani's remarks are particularly ironic given the indisputable
evidence that he had shared information on the theater with Winckelmann,
though perhaps he was moved to these attacks when he saw that Winckelmann
had scrambled several important details.

Ferdinando Galiani had sent Winckelmann's writings to Naples as part of an
effort to see that the Bourbon court capitalized on the propaganda value of the
remarkable discoveries in their excavations and made these accessible to a wider
audience. For some time he had been pressing Tanucci to submit to the current
rage for anything in the "Herculaneum fashion" and the widespread interest for
some kind of guide to the excavations. Galiani observed that jewelers, painters
of carriages, and upholsterers had all adapted this fashion in their designs.
Although the handsome illustrations of *Le antichità di Ercolano* had helped
kindle these and similar passions, curiosity about the remains of ancient daily
life as illustrated by its art and architecture – clothing, hair styles, jewelry,
games – had been piqued long ago by such multivolume antiquarian works as B.
de Montfaucon's *L'antiquité expliquée et représentée en figures* (Paris 1719) or
Caylus's *Recueil d'antiquités égyptiennes, étrusques, grecques, romaines et gauloises*
(Paris 1752–67). Bayardi, as previously noted, had intended to address these
interests in his *Prodromo* before Tanucci cut him out of the picture. The popular-
ity of Winckelmann's writings, therefore, had been only one further stimulation
to a growing craze.[88]

Galiani proposed reworking Bayardi's *Prodromo* in a more serious vein, observing that such a *Guida dei forestieri*, a guide for foreign visitors to the excavations, could

> Describe the sites where the antiquities are excavated, the contents of the
> cortile and rooms of the museum, the most remarkable objects, and say
> something about the papyri, so that the visitor could first prepare himself

and then recall what he had seen. Until now visitors have jotted down in pencil any tidbit they have seen or heard from Paderni, Weber, etc. Ambiguities, errors, etc. have resulted from their misunderstandings. . . . Written by an able hand and printed without mention of the author's name or that of the royal printer, [such a book] would release us from responsibility and would be most useful to so many travelers and poor scholars. . . . In this way we would put an end once and for all to the Winckelmanns, Goris, and all the "gazetteers" of Herculaneum.[89]

But while Tanucci had to concede that Winckelmann's writings had taught the French more than all the volumes of *Le antichità*, in the end he declared there was little interest in a book dealing with the history of the excavations.[90] He adamantly refused to succumb to these pedestrian obsessions, maintaining that such publications were contrary to his more purist antiquarian interests, which he believed were embodied in the design and organization of *Le antichità*: works of art arranged according to genre, excluding architecture and the implements of daily life.

This French frenzy for the architecture of Herculaneum, the conversion of all the designers and architects to the Greek fashion found at Herculaneum . . . , are infallible arguments of the scant reasoning of someone who demands from that nation steadfastness, seriousness, and the like. . . . Europe is not all French, that part which is not French asks for order: that is, all the paintings, all the statues, all the vases, and everything arranged in its own series.[91]

More pointedly, Tanucci declared there was no one in Naples competent to write such a book, specifically ruling out both Carcani and Paderni.[92]

Tanucci's sentiments underscore why neither Weber's proposed monograph or even the embarrassing scrutiny of the Bourbon excavations brought on by Winckelmann's writings was able to alter the court's approach to the publication of the archaeology from the buried cities of Vesuvius. Nor did circumstances change until well after Tanucci's fall from grace in 1776 and the temporary transfer of control of the excavations to French hands: the first publication approaching Galiani's notion of a guide to the excavations was A. de Jorio's *Notizie su gli scavi di Ercolano* (Naples 1827), published eighty-nine years after Alcubierre first lowered himself into d'Elbeuf's tunnels.[93]

8

The Theater at Herculaneum

No single monument investigated during the early years of the excavations sparked greater interest among scholars and laymen alike than the theater at Herculaneum. A variety of factors stimulated their fascination. First was the theater's legendary role in d'Elbeuf's depredations and the trove of ancient statuary discovered at that time. Of paramount importance was the fact that it was the first structure to be investigated and identified. With this identification, and the realization that its scaena, the multistoried stage building, was potentially the first from the Roman era to survive with its decoration intact, came the possibility of comparing the theater's design with the prescriptions of Vitruvius. Moreover, it was the only building here that remained readily accessible and for which plans eventually became available; even if the disposition of its sculptural embellishment was unclear, it could be described and discussed easily as an architectural entity. Its accessibility and the potential to comprehend its form visually by exploration of the excavation tunnels meant that the theater also figured large in the correspondence of laymen. As a result, the theater appears time and again in the writings from this period. Even such spectacular sites as the Villa dei Papiri received only passing notice, primarily because plans were unavailable and the underground ruins were inaccessible or difficult to comprehend: the enthusiasm over the charred remains of the villa's library best illustrates that the finds themselves generated more interest than the context in which they were found.

Yet, because of its buried state, specific details about the theater's design remained little understood throughout Weber's tenure at the excavations. When he received his commission here in 1750, he inherited a building that had suffered injuries inflicted on its superstructure by the foragings of previous excavators and of countless visitors on guided tours who pocketed fragments of its marble revetment and carved off pieces of its carbonized wood. Earlier plans of the site were completely inadequate. A number of problems concerning its architectural design still needed to be resolved, in particular the character of its exterior façade, the plan of its scaena, and its relationship to adjacent structures. In 1763, after several years of work in and around the theater, Weber renewed the excavations at the theater with the aim of producing a series of definitive plans. It was the last project he undertook for the Bourbon court, and many of the questions about the theater's design remained unresolved at his death.

Alcubierre's primary investigations in the theater had been limited essentially to a seven-month period from October 1738 through June 1739, roughly equivalent to d'Elbeuf's previous efforts here. As Alcubierre's 1747 plan makes clear, he covered a remarkable amount of territory in this short time, particularly when compared to Weber's later work in the "temples" at Herculaneum. He succeeded in tracking down many of the principal architectural features of the theater and ascertaining a broad picture of its design. Although it took some months to realize it, what he had found was a small, free-standing theater, its media and summa cavea (the middle and upper tiers of seats) divided into six cunei (the wedge-shaped blocks of seats) with vomitoria (exit corridors), an open gallery above the summa cavea, and two tribunalia (viewing boxes for distinguished spectators) above the paradoi, the tunnel-like passageways giving access to the orchestra. He managed as well to locate a good deal of statuary that had escaped d'Elbeuf, including three togate figures with partial dedicatory inscriptions found in a niche on the south façade, numerous fragments of bronze equestrian statues strewn about inside and outside the theater, a marble Bacchus (or Hercules?) in the orchestra (the semicircular space between the stage and the seats) and a bronze statue of a "Vestal" near one of the three symmetrical sets of pedestals that crowned the summa cavea.[1]

His efforts were facilitated in part by d'Elbeuf's preexisting tunnels, which were limited to the area between the semicircular recesses of the scaena and the orchestra; the resulting circular space makes it easy to imagine how both Stendardo and Alcubierre had mistaken this initially for a temple.[2] The delay in making a positive identification of this building came from Alcubierre's decision to run his first tunnel along the left parados and the exterior of the theater rather than extending d'Elbeuf's tunnels out of the orchestra into the cavea itself, where he quickly would have encountered the seats. It was only after the earliest work in the cavea and the discovery nearby, on January 13, 1739, of an inscription of L. Annius Mammianus Rufus containing the word THEATR(um) (CIL 10.1443 = MN. 3743) that Venuti was able to "recognize" this as a theater.[3] By then it must have been evident to many, even if some confusion remained about whether to describe it as a theater or an amphitheater.

Alcubierre did not linger here long, for already by early May 1739 he had begun cutting the tunnel that ran east from the theater toward the well of Paone and the ruins of the Basilica. By June, he appears to have moved on completely to areas that promised more portable antiquities and less architecture; at least there is no further mention of the theater in the period before Rorro and then Bardet substituted for him in 1741. Sometime in mid-1739 he drew up his first plan of the theater, onto which he superimposed sketches of his own and d'Elbeuf's excavation tunnels. This plan was not engraved until 1747, and then without any revision (see Fig. 16).[4]

In the meantime, a stepped ramp, built between February 3 and April 3, 1739, provided continued access to the summa cavea from the Royal Road above. The ramp was linked to a series of open tunnels that allowed the few visitors fortunate enough to be granted the privilege of access to the ruins to explore the remains of the theater while work proceeded elsewhere.[5]

BARDET'S PLAN AND EGIZIO'S CRITIQUE

Pierre Bardet de Villeneuve, who had assumed his duties here on July 24, 1741, produced his first plan and cross section of the theater sometime before July 20, 1742, the date on which Matteo Egizio penned his critique of an engraving of it. Although neither the engraving nor the plan itself has survived, it is possible to reconstruct in part both the plan and the accompanying cross section from the observations Bardet made in his legend, from the comments of Egizio, and even from the later plan of Bellicard.[6] Bardet probably had concentrated his efforts in the area of the proscenium, the stage on which the actors performed, and the tribunalia. This may have been limited to only the tribunal on the north, since his section focused only on that side of the theater; Bellicard's version followed suit. Bardet had ascertained that the floor beneath the proscenium dropped 8 palms (2.11 m.) below the level of the orchestra and postulated from this that the stage had been constructed of wood supported by a masonry substructure; this too is shown in Bellicard's plan. The only find he specifically claimed as his own was the remains of a sella curulis, a seat of honor granted to distinguished citizens, anchored to the pavement of one of the tribunalia.[7] Otherwise, the only additional artifact he singled out was the bronze "Vestal" recovered by Alcubierre in March 1739 from near the masonry pedestals on the right side of the summa cavea. He referred only in general terms to the fragments of bronze equestrian statues

found near these same pedestals as well as to the marble statues recovered in
d'Elbeuf's day from the scaena. This plan, with its cross section showing the
galleries and stairs providing access to the summa cavea, appears to have differed
only in minor details from Alcubierre's of 1747, principally in the scaena.
Bardet's, however, certainly showed the theater alone, without the excavation
tunnels, as his intent must have been to create a document suitable for scholarly
reference, one that illustrated the architecture and labeled each part with its
appropriate ancient term and explained its function.

Egizio's comments on this plan followed the pattern set by other scholars
when confronted with similar efforts to document an archaeological site accurately.[8] In essence he refuted the accuracy of Bardet's plan and his identifications of the theater's parts on the basis that they failed to conform to the
acknowledged canons of Vitruvius and later commentators: if the archaeological
remains did not correspond with Vitruvius, something perforce was wrong.
Much of the problem lay with the fact that as yet there was no sufficient corpus
of ruins to draw on for comparanda. The result was a great deal of confusion,
hairsplitting, and attempts at forcing the ruins into the Vitruvian mold.

Fortunately, Egizio was prepared to allow for some deviations, as Vitruvius
himself had noted might occur through variations in the sites and in the availabil-
ity of building materials (Vitr. 5.6.7). For example, Bardet had contrasted the
function of an orchestra in Greek theaters with that in Roman ones, to demonstrate that Herculaneum's was of Roman design. Egizio pointed to the possible
Greek influences exerted on the design of Herculaneum's theater from nearby
Naples. In particular, he suggested that since the orchestra was given over to the
seats for Roman senators (Vitr. 5.6.2), the tribunalia may have been used by
musicians, with the conductor seated on the sella curulis. As his model for the
logical system of corridors and stairs allowing passage through the theater, he
referred to the theater of Marcellus in Rome, although this was known in his
day primarily through fairly fanciful reconstructions. Moreover, he used French
terminology on several occasions, as if to suggest that Bardet had failed even to
grasp the parallels with theaters of his own day. Egizio's comments, however, set
the tone for the ensuing debate and established the principal beliefs and theories about the theater's design that influenced the excavation of this building for
years to come.

Egizio was especially concerned about a number of inaccuracies that he said
would not enhance the honor of the king, much less of the plan's architect. He
had inspected the ruins himself, though he appears to have recalled few specific
details. Nevertheless he perceived several drafting errors, such as load-bearing
walls he believed were too thin, others which were too short, and stairs and seats

he reckoned would be too high or too few, both in practice and for Vitruvian rules (Vitr. 5.6.3), if the scale provided on Bardet's plan was correct. Since this was not a ground plan but a bird's-eye view, which tended to distort the perspective and flatten out the features, he suggested that dimensions be supplied directly on the plan. Egizio believed Vitruvius (Vitr. 5.6.2) had prescribed that praecinctiones, level aisles between upper and lower tiers of seats, should divide the cavea horizontally into groups of seven rows of seats and that the stairs between the divisions of the cavea should be staggered (Vitr. 5.3.5). He observed that this arrangement not only maintained the division of the social classes, as established by Roman law, but was a sound principle, intended to avoid the embarrassment of having a spectator tumble headlong from the top of the cavea into the orchestra. Yet Bardet's plan showed only a single praecinctio above the eighteenth row and all the stairways aligned with one another. The plan therefore must be inaccurate, because it "does not conform to the buried building," which Bardet assumed followed Vitruvius. He further maintained that the exterior façade of every ancient theater must have had two or three superimposed Doric colonnades (Vitr. 5.9.2), cumulatively equivalent in height to the scaena, as protection against the elements for the spectators and as a soundingboard for the actors' voices (Vitr. 5.6.4), yet this necessary feature was lacking on the plan. Moreover, although Bardet stated in the legend that the pedestals along the summa cavea had supported bronze equestrian statues, Egizio noted that instead he had drawn them in the plan's elevation as bearing statues of women.

Egizio was particularly critical of Bardet's labeling of the orchestra, proscenium, and scaena, although without a copy of the plan it is difficult to determine precisely how Bardet had erred. Egizio rightly insisted that the orchestra where the senators and vestals sat should be limited to the lowest seats of the cavea, and could not, as Bardet had indicated on his plan, include the entire semicircular area between the cavea and the proscenium. Otherwise, he noted, the spectators seated at the ends would be forced to crane their necks to see the action. Nor could the proscenium be 8 palms (2.10 m.) lower than the orchestra, because Vitruvius had stated it should be 5 Roman feet (1.45 m.) higher, so that spectators in the lowest rows could see the actor's movements (Vitr. 5.6.2). In this case, Egizio simply had misread Bardet's observation that the substructures of the proscenium extended beneath the orchestra. Bardet also had confused the scaena with the postscenium, the area behind the scaena for preparing actors and scenery, and Egizio corrected this as well. In the end, what emerges from Egizio's somewhat perplexing exercise in identifying and labeling the parts of an actual theater on the basis of a single, often vague, literary source is how urgent the need was for an accurate plan of the archaeological remains of the entire theater.

As a result of these criticisms, Bardet evidently had returned to the field to make further investigations in the area of the proscenium. Here he found remains of carbonized wood to confirm his notion that it had been wooden.[9] He added this feature, and presumably corrected the other errors, in a revised plan of the theater. This is probably the same one copied by Bellicard, since he drew equestrian statues, not women, on the pedestals. Bardet then copied this revised version onto his "Decumanus Maximus" plan of July 1743. Unfortunately he failed to locate the theater in its proper position relative to the Basilica, oriented it in the wrong direction, and then offered even fewer details in his legend about its architectural and decorative features (Fig. 67).[10]

SCHOLARLY MISCONCEPTIONS AND THE PROBLEM OF THE SCAENA

Accurate information about the theater was difficult to obtain during these early years of the excavations. Reports of major discoveries elsewhere, such as the paintings of Theseus and Hercules from the Basilica and the marble equestrian statues of the Balbi, all found their way into contemporary correspondence, thanks to their prompt display in the museum, but references to the theater speak in only very general terms of its appearance and are fraught with misconceptions and fallacies. Typical is the description of Maffei, who wrote in late 1747 that

> They already have come upon the semicircle of the theater, and that which they have been able to clear of earth is very well preserved. It has thirty-three steps, high and broad, in just proportion. The entrances which lead to the vomitoria are covered in most beautiful marbles. But to enjoy its symmetry and to understand the design of the scaena and proscenium, about which we are completely in the dark, it would be better to see it all in the light of day, rather than only a few features by means of torches, lamps, and candles.[11]

As the late date of Maffei's letter bears witness, the period between about 1740 and 1746 is poorly represented in the literary record, and this situation improves only slightly in the years thereafter.[12] Bayardi's arrival in 1746 merely had perpetuated the king's prohibition against access to information about the excavations imposed in response to the correspondence of Venuti and others. Bardet's departure from Naples, with all his excavation reports and plans, had compounded the situation. Even members of the court like Martorelli were prevented from making detailed studies of the ruins, and this, when combined with the circumstances of the city's burial, complicated matters considerably.

In 1748, Martorelli conceded to Gori, in a letter in which he could provide only a brief description but no dimensions of the theater, that "It would be difficult for anyone who did not have a strong heart and spirit to wander about through the most narrow and ruinous tunnels 84 palms [22.25 m.] underground, as I have done, and to take measurements and see through darkness broken only by the light of small candles."[13] Martorelli noted elsewhere that, after descending some fifty steps to the underground ruins, he and his companions could not determine in which direction the theater faced, since they did not have a compass. He further lamented that

> We observed only a single open vomitorium and part of the porticus leading to the cavea, some well-formed arches, painted in part with marvelous colors with small arabesques, that decorated the pedestals of the columns; and nothing else. . . . We must confess, however, that inside those tunnels we saw only a small part of the theater of Herculaneum in feeble torchlight and in haste, and since the structure is so enormous, we could not obtain a just impression or the necessary and precise measurements. Besides, everyone down there is so confounded by fear of the ruins and the darkness and diversity of so many narrow passsages that he quickly thinks only to climb up out of there safely.[14]

Bardet proved to be the sole font of factual information for those curious about the theater. The earliest and most widely available description of the building was that provided by d'Arthenay in his *Mémoire historique et critique sur la ville souterraine, découverte au pied du Mont Vésuve . . .* , published at Avignon in 1748. As secretary to the marquis de l'Hôpital, the French ambassador to Naples during Bardet's tenure, d'Arthenay evidently had seen a copy of Bardet's plan of the theater and perhaps even spoken with him about it. He was well versed in the theater's design and the questions that still needed resolution, suggesting, for example, that excavations between the seats might reveal the sounding vases described by Vitruvius (5.5.1–8). Specifically noting the carbonized wood found in the orchestra, he contradicted Egizio by concluding that the theater was Greek, not Roman, since he had expected to find seating for senators and vestals here and instead found a space more suitable for a Greek chorus, the *thymelici* referred to by Vitruvius. The notion of Greek construction, though disputed by some, now became part of the popular dogma surrounding the theater.[15] He proposed that the other remains of wood found on the scaena might point to the existence of the

movable wooden scenery also described by Vitruvius (Vitr. 5.6.8). Although the
scaena had once borne magnificent statues, he noted that all these had been
removed, leaving only "the foundations of this beautiful structure beneath a vault
some 80 feet [25.6 m.] thick formed from the hardened bitumen of the lava."[16]

Although he did not provide a plan, d'Arthenay was the first to publish
figures for the basic dimensions of the theater. It is not clear, however, whether
he approximated these measurements by utilizing the scale on Bardet's plan or
whether he obtained them directly from Bardet. Nor is it exactly clear with what
features these measurements correspond. He set the "circumference," perhaps
the area inscribed by the cavea and the stage building, at 290 feet (93.9 m.); 230
feet (74.5 m.) for the circumference of the cavea alone; the exterior diameter
(from the rear of the scaena to the center of the cavea's arc?) at 160 feet (51.8
m.); and the interior diameter (from the front of the scaena to the center of the
cavea's arc?) at 150 feet (48.6 m.). The scaena itself was 72 feet (23.0 m.) wide
and stood 30 feet (9.7 m.) high. Recognizing that figures derived from secondary sources might be imprecise and controversial, d'Arthenay remarked in a
footnote that "these measurements do not accord with the judgment of a few
who have made diligent observations *in situ*."[17] He later justified his method by
describing the difficult circumstances under which he had had to examine the
remains:

> Despite certain precautions that were taken to know the plan precisely, of
> which one here seeks to provide some idea, it cannot be guaranteed that
> these measurements are absolutely correct. Since the entire theater has
> never been uncovered at one time, it has only been possible to see it piece
> by piece. These parts have been visible only in stages, since in clearing
> one [tunnel] they fill in another in such a way that now one scarcely sees
> one half.[18]

Since he was no longer physically present in Herculaneum, Venuti had to
base his discussion of the theater in his *Descrizione* in part on personal observations made some years earlier and in part on secondary sources. He did not
accept the notion of its Greek origin, for example, believing further excavations
in the orchestra would prove it was paved with marble. But he quoted the same
dimensions for the theater as d'Arthenay, prefacing them with the remark, "I
have seen the following dimensions for the theater in a manuscript report, but I
do not know how accurate [they are]."[19] Since publication of both of these
books occurred in the same year in different countries, either d'Arthenay's
manuscript had been circulated prior to its publication, or both d'Arthenay and
Venuti had seen an otherwise unknown manuscript by Bardet. In either case,

this illustrates how even Venuti had come to rely on clandestine secondary sources for factual details about the building he claimed to have identified.

That such information was at a premium, and came to be recycled by one scholar and then another, is confirmed by the fact that de Brosses quoted these same figures directly from Venuti, about whom de Brosses somewhat naively remarked, "There is no one in a better position to talk about the antiquities discovered at Herculaneum."[20] But he too was cautious about the accuracy of this information, observing,

> For myself, who know the locale, I strongly doubt that one can count on the exactitude of these measurements that cannot be taken except in haste and piece by piece. This is because the entire immense structure is still filled with earth, through which one can only dig some low and narrow underground tunnels from one place to another.[21]

The writings of Cochin and Bellicard prove that Bardet's documentation, whatever form it may have taken, was available as late as 1750, the year of their tour of Italy. By this time, Weber had assumed charge of renewed excavations in the theater that were to continue into 1751. Only fresh on the scene, Weber would not have given out what amounted to state secrets, so Bardet and the marquis de l'Hôpital's circle remain the only possible sources of the plan and cross section that Bellicard reported he had consulted and copied: "the plan which someone gave me and which I am setting forth here."[22] The potential similarities between the plan in Bellicard's original notebook and that of Bardet have already been noted, though Bellicard made some modifications of his own after surveying the site (Fig. 68). "To verify as much as possible the plan I had been given," he stated later in the *Observations* (1755), "I traversed the paths which had been cut rather haphazardly through the expanse of the theater, and I examined everything that had been discovered there."[23] Due to the manner in which the site had been explored, with pillars of the volcanic matrix left to support the tunnels, he confessed that portions of his plan were conjectural, based on the assumption that features were symmetrically disposed about the central axis. He advised his readers as well that "since the excavations have been made at different times, and the theater has been discovered only bit by bit, the plan which I present here cannot be absolutely exact."[24] In particular he was suspicious of the depiction of the orchestra as a semi-oval, asserting that this conformed with nothing else known about Roman theaters, specifically that of Marcellus in Rome, which had a semicircular orchestra.

The comments in the *Observations* differ markedly from those Bellicard had jotted down earlier in his notebook. While the comments in the *Observations* are

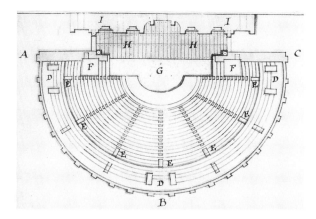

Figure 67. Plan of the theater at Herculaneum as it appears on Bardet's "Decumanus
Maximus" plan of 1743. This is a copy of a corrected version of the plan that Bardet
produced following the criticisms of Matteo Egizio in 1742. (Courtesy of the Archivio di
Stato, Napoli [Raccolta Piante e Disegni, Cart. xxiv.3].)

more analytic, those in the notebook appear to be derived largely from
d'Arthenay, or d'Arthenay's source: that the design conformed better with Vitruvius's description of a Greek theater (Vitr. 5.7), that further excavation might
reveal the sounding vases between the steps, that senators and vestals could not
sit in this particular orchestra. Moreover, while he had copied down in his
notebook essentially the same dimensions for the theater as had d'Arthenay,
these are missing completely from the later *Observations*.[25]

THE DEBATE OVER OPEN-AIR EXCAVATIONS

A leitmotif of these descriptions of the theater was the complaint that its buried
condition precluded the possibility of ever understanding its form completely.
One consequence of this was confusion about which direction the cavea of the
theater actually faced. Bardet's error in showing the cavea turned in the direction of the sea on his "Decumanus Maximus" plan was only the most obvious
example, for de Brosses and others after him erred similarly. This disorientation
of site and scholar alike led to calls to excavate down from the surface and
expose the remains fully to the light of day. Maffei's letter of 1747 to de Rubeis
may have initiated the ensuing debate over the pros and cons of such an
undertaking. He expressed this in terms that made its excavation as much a
challenge to the honor of the king as a moral obligation:

> Above all it is desirable that they decide to excavate from above, extracting
> and carrying off that mountain of ash and other material that Vesuvius

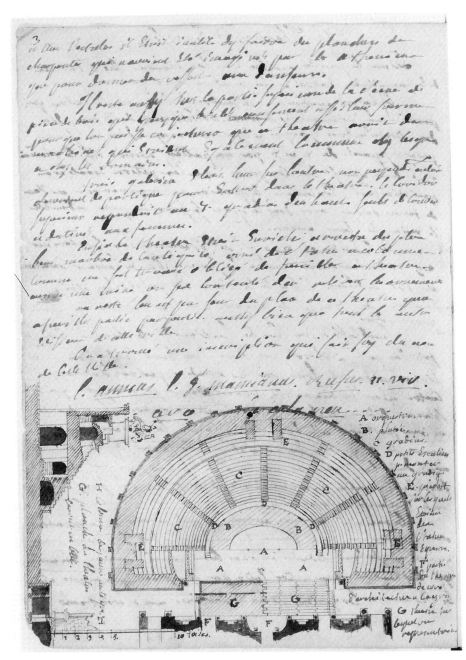

Figure 68. Plan of the theater at Herculaneum as it appeared in Jérôme-Charles
Bellicard's "Italian Notebook" (1750–51). Bellicard based his version on Bardet's plan of
1743. (Courtesy of the Metropolitan Museum of Art, New York, Harris Brisbane Dick
Fund, 1940 [40.59.6].)

threw on top of the ancient city. A great undertaking, but small for a powerful king endowed with heroic spirit, as is the present one. To remove the rustic houses of the village of Resina built on top and to reconstruct them elsewhere, I am assured would be a matter of not many thousands of scudi. . . . In this way the lifeless city would be reborn, and after one thousand seven hundred years see the light of day again. As a result we would learn many, many things about daily life, architecture, art, and erudition that we seek in vain from books. With the greatest profit for the area, all of learned Europe will run to Naples, since they could not imagine anything more gratifying than to see with their own eyes the houses, basilicas, and temples of the renowned Romans. Much will be found whole and intact, because the earthquakes which destroyed the city never caused the collapse of all the buildings, as Seneca says. . . . Clearing away and leaving everything in its proper place, the whole city would make an incomparable and indescribable museum.[26]

Maffei was certainly the most vocal advocate of this approach, exclaiming that the present blind tunneling would result in the destruction of many antiquities. His interests were selfish in part, however, for he had published a treatise on ancient theaters and amphitheaters and had come to quite different conclusions about their design than those advanced by Mazzocchi.[27]

Scholars and laymen alike championed Maffei's recommendation. Venuti, and consequently de Brosses as well, had called for open-air excavations and was frustrated that the superimposition of the modern city prevented their institution and restricted his ability to describe the theater.[28] Bellicard stated bluntly, "One must not hope ever to have the theater in full," because of the system of leaving support pillars, and expressed his annoyance that the site had not been sufficiently cleared to offer precise measurements.[29] One visitor must have been voicing the sentiments of many others when he remarked,

I cannot help regretting the method they have taken to clear out this city. Had they laid it open from the top, we should have had the pleasure of seeing it as it formerly stood. We should have seen the disposition of the streets, houses, temples, etc. We should have seen the interior of the houses and a thousand curiosities we are now deprived of. But, as the city lies so far below ground, it would have been an immense expense to have wrought in this manner.[30]

On the other hand, Trouard, a French architect who evidently benefited from contacts with the marquis de Marigny and Bellicard and the documentation they

had at their disposal, declared these demands for open-air excavations nonsensical, since "Precise plans of all the sites under excavation are being drawn, so that
someday one will be able to see with great satisfaction the entire form of the
city."[31] Martorelli also took up the more conservative position that acknowledged
the impracticality of this approach in view of such practical considerations as the
buildings of Resina that stood above the ruins; the enormous outlay in labor and
the expense of removing the vast quantity of earth that covered the site; and the
difficulty of channeling off rain- and groundwater both during and after the
excavation. Yet he could imagine as well the thrill of seeing the theater exposed
and the potential for the outcome "to explain for us the writings of Vitruvius and
bring an end to so many debates among antiquarians."[32]

These problems eventually had their effect on the course of the project. In
March 1750, when the finds elsewhere at Herculaneum had begun to dwindle,
Alcubierre proposed the resumption of work in the theater,

> To investigate fully the galleries, vomitoria, stairs, *et al.*, so that, in the
> future, curious and enthusiastic foreigners might be more satisfied when
> they come to visit it. Work here was suspended in the past because the
> earth was too hard and solid, and also in keeping with our aim, since no
> more finds were being made in the theater, to employ the workmen in
> areas of Herculaneum where the results were more acceptable.[33]

He also began to bore a large air shaft that would drop down into the center of
the cavea. The stated purpose of this was to provide light and air, to help
evaporate some of the moisture inside the tunnels, and to permit visitors to see a
significant portion of the ruins more easily (Fig. 69). On completion the shaft
would be 5.3 meters in diameter and 22.2 meters deep; it would be lined with a
lime wash and would include an observation platform near the center, accessible
from a newly designed entrance ramp.[34] This was all that one could expect for
now, observed Alcubierre, for excavating out the theater entirely would require
purchasing and demolishing houses and a church; changing the route of the
Royal Road; coping with all the rubble and earth; channeling off the rainwater;
and, last but not least, expending one hundred thousand ducats. Since one
could already discern all the principal features of the theater by means of the
tunnels and a new plan of the structure was being drawn up, Alcubierre suggested little would be gained by undertaking a more extensive excavation.[35]

This renewed round of excavations was largely confined to the area inside the
cavea and along the exterior perimeter of the building, in particular the pillars of
the façade. A few important finds were made before work came to a halt again in
April 1751. Along with a quantity of colored marble and other decorative

Figure 69. View of a tour of the theater at Herculaneum in the eighteenth century, after
the large shaft onto the cavea had been dug in 1750 to provide light and air to the underground site. From A. De Jorio, *Notizie degli scavi di Ercolano* (Naples 1827), pl. 4.

material, Weber, who assumed his position here only in July 1750, recovered a
number of fragments of gilded bronze equestrian statues in the cavea and the
orchestra, which probably once adorned the pedestals of the summa cavea.[36]
Earlier, Alcubierre had found a marble statue of a man, while from nearby came
the bronze statue of a woman, generally identified today as "Antonia," mother
of the emperor Claudius (MN. 5599).[37] Weber believed the statue of the woman
had been found near the exterior perimeter and surmised that it too had fallen
from one of the pedestals.[38]

Weber is probably responsible for another plan of the theater from this
period, extant now only in an engraved version printed by Ruggiero. Weber
must have completed this plan sometime between April and the end of July
1751, for in August Paderni returned it to him to add a compass. The engraving, which Paderni himself produced, shows both a plan and an elevation in
which the cavea is seen in elevation and the substructures are seen in cross
section. It is labeled alphanumerically, but the accompanying legend has been
lost (Fig. 70).[39] The overall appearance of the plan suggests that it combined

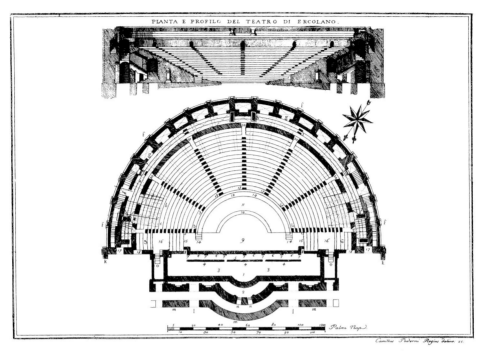

PLANTA E PROFILO DEL TEATRO DI ERCOLANO.

Figure 70. Plan and cross section of the theater at Herculaneum as it was conceived in mid-1751. The engraving is by Camillo Paderni, though it is probably based on an original by Weber. From *StErc*, pl. 3.

many elements from those of Bardet and Alcubierre with only minor additions. The most obvious new detail is the pillars along the exterior perimeter, framing cross-vaulted chambers beneath the cavea and the stairs giving access to the upper gallery. The orchestra varies only slightly from Bellicard's rendering, whereas the scaena appears to be composed of three parallel walls with central apses, the first of which may be a foundation. As a result, it is clear that this campaign of excavations had fallen short of resolving the outstanding questions about the design of these parts of the theater.

WEBER'S PROPOSAL AND EXCAVATIONS IN THE THEATER

Ten years later, Weber drew up a bold proposal to excavate out part of the theater, with the full expectation that this would produce major new finds and that the results would make a significant contribution to history. Attached to his letter to Tanucci was a detailed estimate of the expenses in both time and money, although exclusive of the costs for labor. The project called for the acquisition of three parcels of private property at a cost of some 622 ducats. He highlighted these property lines in gold on an indexed plan showing the theater in relation to the modern houses, gardens, and farms. This plan illustrated as well that no modern structures obstructed the targeted site, which encompassed 12,123 square palms (3,212.60 square m.) and about one-third of the theater below. Labor costs would be kept to a minimum by utilizing twenty of the forty forced laborers; they would be supervised by two experienced fieldworkers, who counted as two forced laborers in his estimate, and one corporal. He determined that the entire project could be completed in 794 days, deducing this figure from his experience in digging the air shaft, where twelve men had been able to bore 2 palms (0.53 m.) a day, removing some 900 cubic palms (238.00 cubic m.) per day of the lighter pozzolana. A second plan showed the site in cross section and was stratified to depict the first 30 palms (7.95 m.) of pozzolana near the surface and the 44 palms (11.60 m.) of harder pappamonte tufa below. It would take 202 days to remove the 363,690 cubic palms (96,577.85 cubic m.) of pozzolana, but because the harder consistency of the pappamonte slowed the work to half the speed, another 592 days would be required to remove the 533,412 cubic palms (141,332.18 cubic m.) of this. As for the removal of rainwater and seepage, Weber noted that the site stood high enough above sea level that graded tunnels could be dug to carry the groundwater off.[40]

Tanucci was intrigued enough by Weber's proposal to communicate it to the king, who in turn recommended that it be sent on to Luigi Vanvitelli for his appraisal.[41] Vanvitelli concluded that the project could be accomplished, "indeed absolutely must succeed." He suggested that the walls of the shaft through the softer pozzolana be cut diagonally to save on the construction of supports but that a vertical cut could be made through the harder pappamonte. A tunnel toward the sea would need to be dug to carry off the rainwater and, in the process, might reveal further ruins. As for the cost of the excavation, Vanvitelli believed it would surpass Weber's estimates and suggested that the project might be realized in a year or more.[42]

Weber's proposal came only weeks after the members of the Accademia had rendered their decision on his monograph, "Le Piante di Alcuni Edifici Sotterranei . . . ," and his timing was anything but coincidental. They had noted specifically that Weber's method of excavating and of drawing plans would resolve the disputes of academics about the design of the theater's scaena and proscenium and to this end had recommended that Berardo Galiani serve as Weber's adviser.[43] This partnership formed slowly, however, and probably had no influence on this proposal. More likely, Weber submitted this project precisely because it was so contrary to Alcubierre's old approach to the excavations and would attract the attention of the Bourbon court to his own methodology, one that was more attuned to the interests of scholars outside the Accademia. It represented a radical reversal of his earlier position that profitable land should not be sacrificed. Yet the concept of dispossessing property owners and then managing an exposed archaeological site was still so foreign to the court that, in the end, this project was never realized.[44]

The recommendation to expose a portion of the theater probably had played a role in Weber's larger project to chart the topography of Herculaneum. In his application to the Accademia, he had submitted an unfinished version of this "general plan" of the city and for some time had been concentrating on areas which had been excavated previously but whose architecture was little understood, especially that between the theater and the Basilica.[45] This is particularly evident in the investigations he undertook over the next few months. These were concentrated on structures adjacent to, not in, the theater, and included porticoes to one side of and behind the scaena and a number of smaller features such as pools and fountains. Since this was the period in which few finds were being made anywhere in the excavations, a secondary aim was to reinvestigate areas which already had yielded major discoveries or whose proximity to such sites indicated there was a strong possibility of success. In this regard, the equestrian statues were a major attraction, both the bronze ones of the theater and the marble ones of the Balbi. The theater itself probably figured fairly small in this scheme, since it was not until September 1761 that the excavations reached the cavea of the theater.

It is difficult to pinpoint the location of this earlier work, but one possible site is the area to the west-southwest of the theater, near the building La Vega later labeled a "temple" on his plan of Herculaneum.[46] This is shown as a small square building surrounded on three sides by colonnades, facing a square space to the south with a shallow apse on its north side. The dimensions of the first building correspond remarkably well to the remains of two vaulted rooms, probably substructures, still visible in the tunnels immediately to the southwest of the theater.[47]

In November 1760, Weber described the discovery of what he called a bath, with walls covered in white marble, green stucco, and fragments of a stucco vault. Gradually revealed over several months were collapsed columns, a water channel, a fountain base, a pool lined with blue stucco and with two marble stairs, and at least two marble thresholds. Although the relationship among them is never made clear, these features must have been closely associated. From the vicinity came three objects with an equestrian motif: a marble relief in Hellenistic style showing a soldier restraining a biga; a small galloping, riderless horse in bronze; and a similar bronze horse bearing a figure identified as Alexander the Great.[48] These statuettes were found in a porticus that Weber believed faced a piazza or garden with fountains which might contain similar sculptures displayed symmetrically. All these clues, and the knowledge of the bronze equestrians found in the theater, later led him to run a tunnel "toward the site of the [marble] equestrian statues in the piazza behind the porticus of the theater."[49] It later becomes clear that Weber firmly believed the equestrian statue of Marcus Nonius Balbus had been found in a piazza next to the theater, and so the search for more statues here continued through August 1763.[50]

In the meantime, investigations continued behind the scaena of the theater. In November 1761, Weber identified a stair on the west side of the theater that led from behind the scaena to the proscenium and provided access from there to the west tribunal. This discovery sparked renewed interest in concentrating on the theater, yet Paderni reported that Alcubierre had stepped in and tried to stop the work, despite the fact that the area was virtually untouched and appeared promising. The order took Weber by surprise as well, since he reported that Alcubierre had visited the site earlier with his daughter and approved of the progress, but Weber acknowledged that it was his duty to "follow orders blindly."[51] Tanucci, however, vetoed Alcubierre's order, which must have been only one in a series of attempts by Alcubierre to block Weber's progress at this site. Work continued here throughout 1762 near the "senatorial stair" and the scaena, although only sporadic reference is made to them in the daybooks. Several tunnels were made into the orchestra and the west tribunal before Weber finally isolated the second "senatorial stair" on the east.

Alcubierre maintained his opposition and, as Weber's chief workman, Aniello Diacampo, observed, "has a stroke whenever someone mentions the scaena."[52] According to Piaggio, Alcubierre was convinced the superstructure of a Roman scaena was made of cloth or cardboard and so believed that Weber's search was futile.[53] Alcubierre appealed again to Tanucci to end the work, claiming that he had excavated the site completely and drawn up a plan long ago and that continued excavation here would only further undermine the houses above. He accused Paderni of ignoring these practical considerations in pressing the search for more statues. Concerned that this work might lead to grander, misguided undertakings, he reminded Tanucci of the great difficulty and expense of fully excavating the theater. His greatest fear was that further digging around the scaena, where enormous caverns already had been cut and artificial pillars had to be built, would lead to a major collapse, followed by the expense of

restoring the modern structures. Evidently as a result, Alcubierre autocratically
ruled the scaena off-limits.[54]

Meanwhile Paderni had begun to exercise the same influence over the course
of the excavations at Herculaneum as he had at Pompeii and Stabiae. In July
1762, he had spearheaded investigations in the area where in 1739 Alcubierre
had recovered the three marble statues from their niche in the exterior perimeter of the theater. Remarking that this had been "one of the better sites in
Herculaneum and the worst excavated," he was confident that more complete
bronze statuary would be found and that this would justify his suggestion that
the countless fragments of useless bronze in the storerooms be melted down.[55]
By late 1762 Paderni was walking the tunnels with Weber and Galiani, discussing how best to approach a complete survey of the theater and then observing to
Tanucci how well the recovery of its plan would reflect upon the king.

> [Galiani], observing how much of the scaena of this ancient theater had
> been excavated, was quite content, because he visually confirmed the
> accuracy of [the plans of?] Don Carlo Weber and at the same time how
> much had been fabricated in the first plan [Alcubierre's?], which is com-
> pletely different from the scaena revealed now. But since Weber has been
> blocked by order of Don Rocco d'Alcubierre from pursuing the excava-
> tion of this scaena, Marchese Galiani has decided that, during the frivo-
> lous squabble between these two engineers, he will advise Weber in draw-
> ing up a new plan showing how much of both the theater and the scaena
> already has been excavated. On presenting this to Your Eminence, he will
> explain to You matter of factly what must be excavated in order to com-
> plete a perfect plan which will bring much honor and glory to Your
> Eminence as the author of the discovery of this scaena that will be the only
> one in Europe of which the structure can be comprehended visually.[56]

It was Weber himself, however, who persuaded Tanucci it was important to
study the scaena, because of its enormous value to scholars and antiquarians. In
December 1762, Tanucci wrote to the king,

> Weber told me so much about the illustration of the ancient underground
> theater that after examining the whole with Pasquale [Carcani, secretary
> of the Accademia Ercolanese] we concluded that an illustration of ancient
> theaters, which antiquarians at present lack, would be new and most
> valuable. Therefore an engraving explaining [the design of] the theater
> should serve as the preface to the fourth volume of Le pitture, in which
> either all or the majority [of the plates] will be theatrical scenes. But the

eternal disputes between Weber and Alcubierre about the excavation of
one corner, which would allow completion of the missing portion of this
plan, slows the process too much. As a consequence, the plate will appear
at the end of the fourth volume.[57]

The dispute was again caused by Alcubierre's continuing concern about potential damage to the modern town above the theater, and Tanucci described this
dispute more fully to the king in a letter of January 1763:

> Somewhat rekindled are the disputes between Weber and Paderni on the
> one hand and Alcubierre on the other concerning the ability to excavate or
> not one corner of the theater in order to be able to make a complete drawing
> of the floor plan, with the latter threatening that, if one excavates, the
> houses of Colli Mozzi will suffer great ruin, water problems, and the ex-
> pense of hundreds of thousands [of ducats]. As the other two laugh at such
> dangers, I have had to implore the expertise of [Ferdinando] Fuga. It is far
> too stimulating to attempt to discover the design of ancient theaters, which
> until now antiquarians have not had and which they desire passionately.[58]

When Paderni observed that no damage had resulted in the more than twenty
years of excavations here, Tanucci dispatched a copy of Alcubierre's earlier dire
warning to both Paderni and Weber asking for their response and their specific
proposals for how the work should proceed.[59] Tanucci accepted these but was
annoyed by the slowness of the work; as late as May 1763, he expressed his
frustration by writing to Weber that it was the king's wish that he produce as
soon as possible a plan of the theater for publication in *Le antichità*.[60]

Weber advanced quickly from the "senatorial stairs" and the tribunalia into the
upper tiers of the cavea. The investigations over the next several months focused
on the pedestals of the summa cavea, where Alcubierre had found the bronze
"Vestal" and numerous fragments of bronze equestrian statues. As more bronze
fragments, but no complete statues, were recovered on both sides of the theater,
the tunnels fanned out into the adjacent areas of the cavea as well as the ground
outside the theater directly below the pedestals. By sinking shafts from the
summa cavea to the ancient ground level at the center of the cavea's arc and near
the third set of pedestals there, Weber exposed additional features of the theater's
façade, about which virtually nothing had been known previously. Among these
was the discovery, as Egizio had expected, of a second order of arches above the
niche where Alcubierre had found three togate statues. From the center of the arc
came another dedicatory inscription of the theater's builder, L. Annius
Mammianus Rufus (*CIL* 10.1444), probably originally displayed above the en-

trance here, that matched the one Alcubierre had found in the statue niche.[61] Conspicuously absent from the excavation reports of this period covering late June 1763 through early January 1764 is any specific reference to work around the scaena and orchestra, yet it must have taken place at some time, since Weber recorded the architectural features he had enountered here.[62]

THE UNFINISHED PLAN OF THE THEATER

On November 26, 1763, Tanucci ordered Weber to submit a plan of the theater of Herculaneum, even if it was unfinished.[63] Having no other alternative, Weber complied.

> Having completed the excavation of the remains of the scaena and of the theater of Herculaneum, I am submitting its plan and elevation into your most kind hands, with the lines and the entire design of that which actually exists. I have marked in dotted lines the rest which the ruins and vestiges suggest had existed prior to the eruption of Vesuvius, and I have left blank the remaining portion of the upper story of the scaena in order to leave space for the Accademia's decision to supply that which is lacking. I have not been able to respond before now, because it has not been fifteen days since the completion of the other trials and excavations intended to render the plan as complete as possible. These investigations progressed quite slowly because tracing the scaena alone gave pains whose damaging effects have resulted in not a little labor in the execution [of this work], which is a trial too long to recount and tribulations which I have deemed necessary to suffer for the good service of Your Majesty lest so rare a discovery and one sought after by the literary community should be lost.[64]

Tanucci's insistence that Weber produce his plan promptly must have stemmed from his desire to send the fourth volume of *Le antichità* to press, but instead he received an incomplete and inadequate plan. Perhaps as a consequence, publication of the volume did not occur until 1765.

It is likely that Weber's unfinished plan, without the elevation, is the one that is extant in the Officina dei Papiri in the Biblioteca Nazionale in Naples (Fig. 71, page 260). Although unsigned, the plan must be his, for it is dated 1763 and was "delineated by an engineer of His Majesty." Like his plan of the Villa dei Papiri, the folio on which it was drawn is quite large, measuring 1.28 meters wide by 0.985 meters high, and the sheet has been folded in quarters. The entire plan and the title were first drawn in pencil, of which some marks and erasures remain, and then inked in black and highlighted with light red and yellow gouache. The compass is in the lower left-hand corner, and the scale, in Roman and Neapolitan palms, extends across much of the bottom. The title emphasizes the major feature, "The Ancient Theater of Herculaneum with Its Scaena," while degrees of latitude and longitude establish its geographical location. The clearest evidence that the plan is unfinished is found in the legends, for although the "Explanation" of the architectural features, on the left-hand side, is complete, the "Note on the Recovered Items" on the right-hand side is blank.[65] As a consequence, the plan is useless for reconstructing the sculptural and decorative program of the theater. Only the provenance of the inscriptions of Rufus and two others near the paradoi, along with the pedestals for the bronze equestrian statues, is clearly marked.[66]

The plan is especially valuable for documenting what architectural features Weber had found, or thought he had found, and which ones he had neglected. There is a heavy emphasis on accurately depicting in fine detail the features of the summa cavea as well as the tribunalia. Entrances and stairwells, vomitoria, and praecinctiones are all carefully labeled. The proscenium is given only cursory treatment, however, with the reconstruction of its wooden planking concealing its articulated façade and all the details of its substructures. Only a "cataract for the water channel" across the front of the proscenium is indicated. The marble tiers of the ima cavea have not been drawn properly, since there are only three instead of four. He also indicated evidence near the sides of the proscenium for bronze pivots to support rotating scenery, a discovery not mentioned in the excavation reports and probably influenced by Vitruvius's reference to them (Vitr. 5.6.8: *trigoni versatiles*).[67]

Weber lavished his greatest attention on the scaena and, in particular, the postscenium, so that their appearance here is completely different from that found on previous plans. Instead of a single wall with a central apse, as on Bardet's plan, or two or three parallel curvilinear walls, as on Alcubierre's or Weber's own earlier plan of the theater, Weber illustrated a single wall with a central apse and a straight wall behind this defining the area of the postscenium. At either end of these walls are the stairs leading up to the scaena, the steps of which he drafted meticulously in pencil. The facade of the scaena, "decorated with marble and pedestals," has four statue niches. The opening in the central apse is labeled the "Royal Door," while the two flanking ones are the "Doors for Foreigners." From the remains of collapsed columns and a masonry gutter he identified the space behind the postscenium as the porticus post scaenam, prescribed by Vitruvius (Vitr. 5.9) as a space where spectators could take refuge during rainstorms.

The plan also illustrates Weber's interest in the topography outside the theater and the difficulty he faced as a result of the failure of his predecessors to maintain accurate documentation. Beyond the porticus post scaenam Weber identified an open terrace "fronting the forum 35 palms [9.28 m.] below." This must be the porticus where the equestrian statuette of Alexander the Great was found and where Weber had devoted several months of excavations. The forum itself was described as the provenance of "the horse which is preserved in the entrance to the Royal Palace." Precisely which statue Weber is referring to is unclear, however. Alcubierre had found the two marble equestrian statues of the Balbi in 1746, and these now stood in opposite vestibules that flanked the Royal Road where it passed through the palace at Portici. But in the entrance to the Museum Herculanense itself stood a single bronze horse, composed of fragments from several statues and at that time believed to have come from a gilded bronze quadriga ascribed to Alcubierre's early work.[68] The identification of this area as the forum also contradicts La Vega's later plan which depicts this area as a ravine and locates the forum on the opposite side of the theater; it is generally believed that La Vega had compiled this plan from documents left behind by Weber. Vaulted substructures have been found beneath this porticus, so perhaps Weber had concluded that these faced an open square set some 9 meters below the theater.[69]

By the time work at the theater was suspended in January 1764, Weber had produced a wooden model of the theater and eleven plans, some finished and some still in rough draft.[70] Of these only two plans are extant, along with the legends from what appear to be a plan or plans that combined a ground plan, a cross section, and perhaps an axonometric projection. The numbering scheme used for labeling the ground plan corresponds so closely to that on Weber's unfinished plan that they must have been virtually identical in design. The primary difference is that the entries here are more detailed and analytic. For example, the entry on the unfinished plan for features 61 and 62 reads, "Bronze pivots with axles from the triangular devices for changing scenery," while here it reads, "Place of the *trigoni versatiles* or triangular devices with the changes of scenery, since found here was one of the female pivots with a round piece of carbonized wood inside which was the axle on which the machine rotated its three sides." The entries also bear the characteristic exegetical stamp of Weber through their somewhat abstruse references to Vitruvius and to modern parallels, such as suggesting that the gallery above the summa cavea served to provide a place where refreshments were enjoyed, similar to the contemporary practice of consuming sorbets, chocolates, and liquors between acts of a performance. In a "Reflexion" at the end of the legend, Weber observed that Herculaneum had not become a true Roman city until the construction of this theater, which he placed in the year A.D. 65, and concluded that its design was therefore neither Greek nor Roman but suited to the requirements of the time.[71]

Weber also wrote a short treatise on the design of the theater, intended to accompany one of his plans. In many ways it recalls his monograph on the Villa di San Marco at Stabiae. Although this treatise too is no longer extant, La Vega later consulted and then critiqued it, and so some details about it may be deduced on the basis of his comments. The text ran at least twenty-nine pages in length, and there were at least thirty-two footnotes. It dealt primarily with the theater's architecture, which caused La Vega to complain that it offered too little about the finds while having too many inaccuracies, such as stating that the seats were covered with marble. Weber had included all the specific measurements in the text, which his critic felt made for dry reading and should be given instead on the plan, where they belonged. La Vega was concerned that the comments relied too heavily on Vitruvius, noting that in fact there was much about the building's architecture that did not conform with this ancient treatise. He was concerned, for example, that there was no evidence to justify Weber's identification of the two rooms off the proscenium as "odea." Also in the style of his earlier monograph, Weber tended to digress, as in his discussions of the technique for fluting columns and the operation of the revolving scenery, both of which La Vega found tedious. Finally, La Vega felt further investigations would need to be made to understand the porticus post scaenam.[72]

GALIANI, WINCKELMANN, AND WEBER'S PLANS

All of Weber's plans of the theater eventually ended up in the hands of Berardo Galiani, who intended to use them in a study of the theater which he never published.[73] Their historical value would have been lost completely had Galiani not shown them to Winckelmann during the latter's second visit to Naples, between February and April 1764. Weber's plans enabled Winckelmann to comprehend the overall design of the theater, which had escaped him during his tour of the physical remains.

> [Galiani] led me and my travel companions through the underground tunnels of the theater, and he showed us and explained with his own particular clarity the plan of that structure left by Karl Weber, its design and in particular its scaena. As one is obliged to go almost on all fours from one narrow corridor to another, without a similar guide it would be

impossible to form an idea of where one is and even less of the disposition
of an unknown building.[74]

Winckelmann's discussion of the theater, to which he devoted a significant
portion of his *Nachrichten*, was precisely the kind of public discourse the Bourbon court feared but to which Weber himself had aspired, for it was based
almost exclusively on the problems his excavations had sought to resolve and on
the results he had illustrated on his plans. Winckelmann's work not only documents many of the controversies surrounding the excavations but also constitutes the fullest description of the theater's ruins published at that time, particularly since it now may be read in conjunction with Weber's unfinished plan.
Winckelmann acknowledged his debt to Weber by noting,

> We are obligated to the inexhaustible zeal of the chief engineer, Karl
> Weber, who died at the beginning of this year, who, of his own initiative
> and for the most part during the free time his duties left him, excavated
> the scaena. Thanks to him we should have had a description of it long
> before, if his colonel, envious of the honor which he would derive from
> this discovery, had not prohibited the work on several occasions. Weber
> had drawn up a project to excavate out the entire theater and had calcu-
> lated the cubic palms in such a way that both the labor to remove the lava
> and the cost of acquiring the houses and gardens situated above the
> theater would not surpass 25,000 scudi.[75]

Winckelmann described the ramp leading to the ruins and provided numerous specific dimensions of the theater, not only the external width but also
details such as the height of individual steps and seats. On looking at the
orchestra and seeing the arrangement for honorary seats in the ima cavea, he
decided the overall design was clearly Roman rather than Greek. Because the
front of the proscenium remained unexcavated, he concluded that it was unadorned, despite ancient descriptions of these as having small statue niches. He
noted that the division of the seats in the cavea differed from that prescribed by
Vitruvius but also said that the orchestra "helps us comprehend Vitruvius's
description of this part of Roman theaters."[76]

He focused in particular on the design of the scaena, observing that previous
scholars had rooted their studies "on vague remains and according to their own
imaginations." He drew his comparanda from such varied sources as Vitruvius,
the small theater in the Villa Adriana at Tivoli (see Fig. 46), and the work of
Maffei on theaters. Of particular interest to Winckelmann was the function of
the trigoni versatiles, and he specifically mentions the single pivot Weber had

found. He suggested that the rooms off the proscenium that Weber had called
odea were in fact Vitruvius's hospitalia (5.6.3), where the actors prepared themselves.[77] Moreover, Winckelmann's is the fullest description of Weber's endeavors to comprehend the design of the porticus post scaenam. He confirms that
Weber, and perhaps at least Galiani as well, believed the forum was located in
this area:

> Behind the scaena in all theaters was a portico or covered gallery where
> the people, in the case of a rainfall, could stand under cover. This portico
> at the theater of Herculaneum stood in front of the forum of the city and
> was made of Doric columns of stucco-covered brick. These columns had
> a diameter of 2 Neapolitan palms and were 8 palms in height, proportions
> which exceed somewhat the norm as well as that prescribed by Vitruvius
> for this order. Up to one third of their height, the flutes are beveled flat
> and painted red, but the upper two thirds have Doric fluting and are
> white. These columns can be seen broken into pieces in the subterranean
> vaults of the theater. The roof of the portico was wood, and the pieces of
> carbonized wood can be seen now. Beneath the portico, as beneath the
> scaena, was a cellar.[78]

Despite his efforts and Winckelmann's praise, Weber had failed to solve many
of the lingering questions about the theater's design, such as the form of the
scaena, the ornamentation of the exterior, and the existence of exterior porticoes.
The subsequent history of the excavations here, though, suggests the blame lay
with the building rather than Weber, who, some believed, had sacrificed his life to
this project. Shortly after La Vega took over the project as a whole in April 1764,
his excavators began to uncover the large theater at Pompeii. By this time, the
practice of leaving structures at Pompeii exposed had been adopted, and so the
work advanced much more rapidly than at Herculaneum, reaching the scaena
already by the fifth month. In less than a year, most of the building had been
excavated, and La Vega could begin drawing up plans.[79] Yet the recovery of this
second theater, with certain aspects of its scaena intact and more readily discernible, failed to dim the passion for further investigating that at Herculaneum. In
fact, the contrast between the two enhanced the prospects for comprehending
more fully the design of ancient theaters.

Galiani, disappointed by the incomplete state of Weber's plans, eventually
petitioned Tanucci, on behalf of the Accademia, to resume excavations here.
Despite Weber's "reknowned accuracy and exactitude," Galiani pointed out
that the plans could not be presented to an eager public in their present state:
not only were they incomplete; the plans, like the Cratere Maritimo map before

them, were far too large to fit even the large folios of *Le antichità*. He proposed a
series of specific sondages aimed at resolving the outstanding questions. First,
in order to complete the ground plan, he suggested they would need to ascertain
the precise proportions of the exterior colonnades, in particular those of the
porticus post scaenam, and to determine whether there were walls to shield the
parascenia from public view. To complete the elevations, Galiani proposed
cutting tunnels that would reveal what architectural order decorated the arches
and frieze of the exterior facade, since Weber's work had not sufficiently illuminated this feature. Other tunnels around the scaena would help resolve questions about its height, whether or not it was roofed, and the nature of its
decoration.[80]

La Vega concurred with Galiani's assessment and assured Tanucci that further
investigations would not be problematic, as they would consist primarily of emptying out the tunnels which Weber had filled back in to alleviate Alcubierre's
anxieties, or of expanding those which were still accessible. Only the work around
the scaena would require more manpower and special precautions to avoid collapse, and as a result would incur greater expense. Meeting only the basic goals
would require 170 ducats, two months' time, and eighteen workmen. Yet La Vega
was fully aware that the obstacles he faced were not solely archaeological and
feared he too would be subjected to Alcubierre's long-standing opposition to this
venture: "I only supplicate [Your Excellency] that on giving the order to excavate
in the theater, [You] might protect me from any persecution by my commander, so
that I might not have to suffer those anxieties which my predecessor suffered for
the same reason and perhaps caused his death."[81]

La Vega's assessment of the work required to finish the plans proved grossly
overoptimistic, since much remained to be done when the funds ran out two
months later. The simple questions had been answered; the scalloped facade of
the proscenium that Winckelmann had sought, for example, was found. But the
porticus post scaenam remained a mystery, and excavations around the scaena
continued to siphon off vast amounts of manpower, time, and money for years to
come. In mid-1769, La Vega was desperately pumping out groundwater from a
shaft he had sunk behind the porticus into the low-lying area Weber believed
was the forum, but he still failed to chart the topography of this area adequately.[82] Five years later Alcubierre demanded to know why excavations still
were going on here, to which La Vega responded that a skeleton crew of one was
working to resolve the last questions.[83]

At what point La Vega drew his three extant plans of the theater is not known;
it was only in 1770 that he asked for an assistant to help in the surveying.[84] As
might be expected, the most striking difference from Weber's unfinished plan is

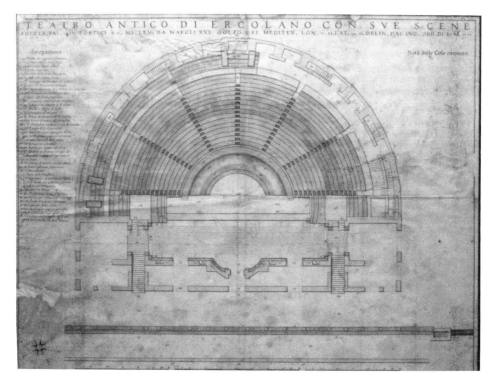

Figure 71. Weber's unfinished plan of the theater at Herculaneum, produced in late 1763.
Only the annotations explaining the architectural features were completed, along the left-
hand side; the inventory of finds along the right remains blank. The plan is unsigned,
though the title credits it to an engineer of the Bourbon court. (Author's photograph;
courtesy of the Officina dei Papiri, Biblioteca Nazionale di Napoli.)

the representation of the proscenium, especially the alternating semicircular
and rectangular niches across the front. The foundation wall that first appeared
on Bardet's plan and had so worried Egizio appears again, as La Vega drew the
proscenium without its wooden planking. The scaena itself, on the other hand,
is virtually identical with Weber's, while the porticus post scaenam appears only
in faint outline (Fig. 72).[85]

Evidently La Vega finished his definitive plans of the theater too late for
publication by the Accademia and probably too late to be of use even to Galiani,
who died of apoplexy in March 1774. The daybooks indicate that La Vega's
excavations continued here through 1776, fourteen years after he had begun. It
was not until April 1777, thirty-nine years after the discovery of Herculaneum,
and then only in response to a specific request from Queen Maria Carolina, that

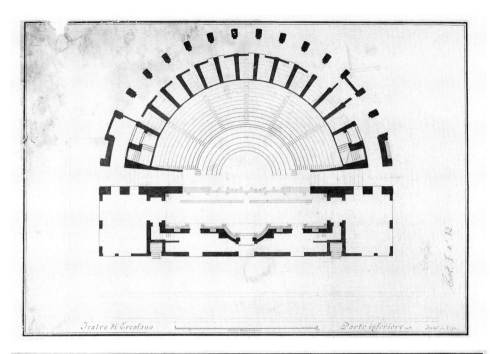

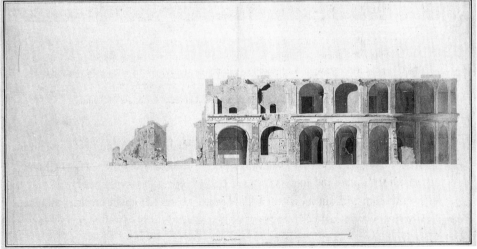

Figure 72. Plan (*top*) of lower level with substructures and exterior elevation (*bottom*) of the theater at Herculaneum as drawn by Francesco La Vega, about 1777. The elevation shows the south façade with the niche (second niche from the left) where Alcubierre found three togate figures and a partial inscription in the early excavations here. (Courtesy of the Società Napoletana di Storia Patria, Mss. 12201 ans 12222.)

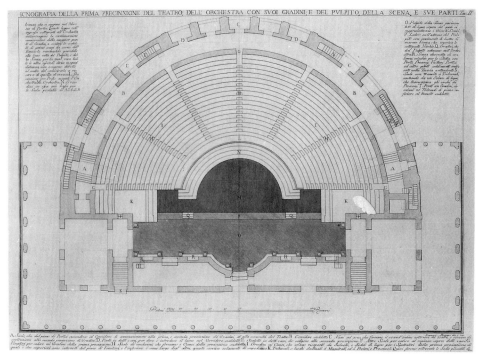

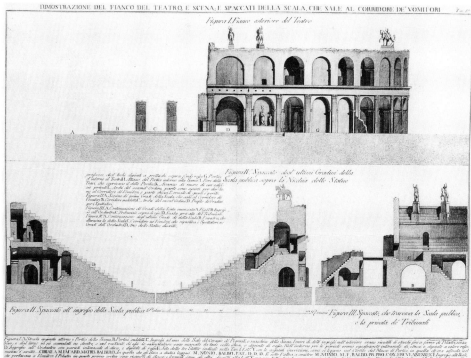

Figure 73. Plan (*top*) and elevation with cross sections (*bottom*) of the theater at
Herculaneum, published by Francesco Piranesi in 1783. Piranesi based his plans largely on
those of La Vega (see Fig. 72). From F. Piranesi, *Il teatro d'Ercolano* (Rome 1783).

La Vega released copies of his seven plans of the theater, which consisted of three ground plans, three cross sections, and one elevation. These too were never published.[86] In 1783, however, Francesco Piranesi published a series of plans and reconstructed elevations of the theater and its scaena (Fig. 73). The high degree of detail and accuracy about the architecture and ornamentation of the theater displayed by these plans suggests that Francesco and his father Giovanni Batista Piranesi, who probably drafted the original plans, had been granted unlimited access to the excavations, as well as to La Vega's and perhaps even Weber's plans. All the other evidence indicates, however, that they must have been subjected to the same prohibitions against taking notes and drawing plans as other contemporary scholars.[87] Nevertheless, as was the case with Bellicard's plan of the Basilica and the numerous other rough plans of buildings from the Vesuvian cities produced surreptitiously and distributed abroad, it was the plans produced by individuals outside the Bourbon court that fed the appetites of foreign scholars for information about these excavations.

Epilogue: Weber's Place in the History of Archaeology in the Vesuvian Landscape

On February 12, 1764, a hungry mob assembled in the Piazza del Real Palazzo in Naples to plunder the first *cuccagna* of Carnevale. Since before December, the kingdom had been suffering from a severe shortage of grain, compounded by the selfish hoarding of dealers. The situation in Naples itself had deteriorated as increasing numbers of people streamed into the city from the countryside in search of bread. Naples had grain, and also had the *cuccagna*, the enormous popular feasts sponsored by the Neapolitan kings since 1672 and held on each of the four Sundays leading up to Mardi Gras. The festivities centered on *le cuccagne*, colossal pyramidal floats constructed out of wood and decorated to resemble castles or cities. These were heaped with a variety of breads, fruits, prepared meats, and even livestock chained in place, all of which, on a given signal, the citizenry sacked and consumed before the eyes of the royal family perched safely overhead on a balcony of the Palazzo Reale (Fig. 74). On this first Sunday, despite fears that the event would degenerate into widespread looting, the crowd had dispersed peacefully after only a few tense moments at the end that left one citizen dead, one soldier wounded, and nineteen malefactors arrested.[1]

On the hill of Pizzofalcone overlooking the square, Karl Jakob Weber lay on his deathbed in the quarters of Leonhard-Ludwig Tschudi, field marshal of the Royal Swiss Guards. After thirteen years of service, the insalubrious conditions of the tunnels at Herculaneum had taken a heavy toll on his health. Weber's obsession with recovering the plan of the theater had driven him to spend long hours underground. When not on-site, he labored over his drawing board; Winckelmann believed Weber had devoted even his free time to these efforts.[2] His exertions, which had escalated over the course of the past year, had seriously impaired his ability to work and even to write and finally had forced him to petition for a leave of absence.

264

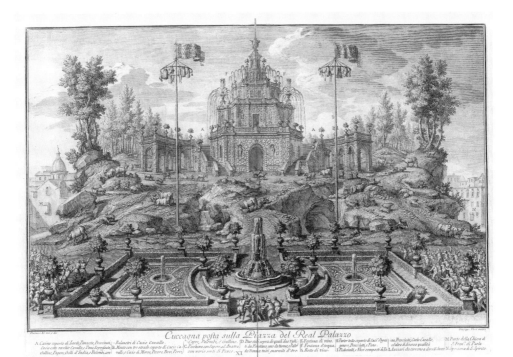

Figure 74. *La Cuccagna* in the Piazza del Real Palazzo, Naples, celebrated by Charles of
Bourbon and Maria Amalia in honor of the birth of their son Philip in 1747. From an
engraving by Vincenzo Re and Giuseppe Vasi in the *Narrazione delle solenni reali feste fatte
celebrare in Napoli da Sua Maesta il Re delle Due Sicilie Carlo Infante* (Naples 1749), pl. 11.
(Courtesy of the Beinecke Rare Book and Manuscript Library, Yale University.)

Weber's correspondence with the court relating to his malady survives in the
archives in Naples and provides an exceptionally poignant glimpse of the last,
pathetic month of his life. His request for personal leave began with a direct
appeal to Tanucci, in which he summarized his condition and his hope for a
prompt recovery (Fig. 75).

> Bombarded for some time by infirmities of health, which have reduced
> me to continual medication without yet being able to see myself restored
> to my former state, my doctors have advised that I distance myself for
> some time from concentrations and worries, and moreover that I get a
> change of air. Encouraged that in this way I will be able to restore myself
> quickly, I have made the attached supplication to His Majesty in order
> that He might deign to grant me to pass a fortnight of leave in Naples,
> where with greater ease I might recognize my malady and have the consul-
> tations for it toward the desired end. I am accompanying [this petition]

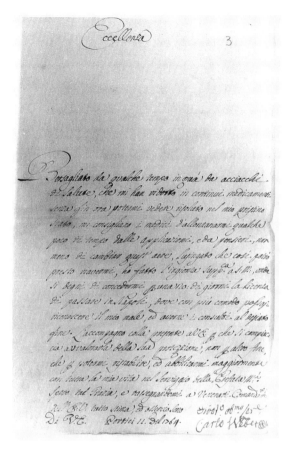

Figure 75. Copy of a petition dated January 11, 1764, from Weber to Prime Minister
Tanucci. Weber explains that he has been "bombarded for some time by infirmities of
health which have reduced me to continual medication without yet being able to see myself
restored to my former state" and requests a fortnight's leave of absence in Naples. (Courtesy of the Archivo di Stato, Naples [Casa Reale Antica 1541, Inc. 3].)

with the present letter to Your Eminence, in whom one takes pleasure to
be confirmed of your protection, to no other end than that He allow me to
recover and dedicate my entire life to the service of His Majesty.[3]

This letter accompanied his official petition to the king, in which he attributed his
ill health specifically to his work in the theater at Herculaneum and asked for permission to leave his post at Portici to seek a cure and change of air in Naples. He
requested as well a subvention to help cover the expenses of this costly treatment.

Lieutenant Colonel Don Carlos Weber, military engineer assigned to the
excavations of antiquities which are being made in the royal villa at Resina,

Torre Annunziata, and Gragnano, humbly expresses to Your Majesty that
his assiduous application and great commitment in searching for the
Herculaneum scaena for the greater glory and good service of Your Majesty
(as luckily has happened after such great persistence by others) has rendered him infirm of health, and in a state of having had recourse to medication, without yet seeing any prospect of recovery, except through the admin-
istration of a rigorous cure. To this end he was advised by the doctors in
Portici, where he resides, to change air and to try that in Naples, so that
more nearly and with greater ease his malady might be diagnosed by his
doctors and he might receive consultations toward a lasting cure. The
above-mentioned finds himself in the keen necessity of humility to supplicate Your Majesty that he might deign to concede to him, together with a
leave of a fortnight, not only to allow him to go to Naples for the expressed
end but enable him also by means of Your Royal Clemency to be able to take
the necessary cure, granting him a subvention, since, as is well known to
Your Majesty, of his money, after paying some of his monthly bills, only 15
ducats remain for himself and a bit for his servants, which he needs. As
regards the grottoes, Colonel Don Rocco d'Alcubierre can in the meantime
frequent the excavations more often, as he sees fit, so that the above-
mentioned, with the benefit of this repose and vacation, free from thoughts
and commitments, might better attend to, and hope for – with the help of
God – the desired fruit of his health, and thereby enable him even more to
consecrate his life to the service of Your Majesty.[4]

In a similar petition dated seventeen days later, he made explicit reference to his
financial difficulties, which recall Alcubierre's accusations years earlier that
prevented him from receiving a raise in salary: Weber owed money to his
creditors and, in her first appearance in the historical record since their marriage in 1739, he mentions that he had to support his wife as well.[5] The court
granted his request for leave and gave him 50 ducats for expenses, and Weber
left Portici for Naples on January 26, 1764.

Rather than improving, however, Weber's health deteriorated rapidly. When
it became clear he could not return to his post after the twenty days originally
requested, Alcubierre assigned one of his oldest excavators, Josef de Corcoles,
to assume Weber's duties of supervising the excavations and submitting the
weekly reports.[6] In the meantime Weber was forced to appeal directly to the
king for additional funds to pay his medical expenses, in the hope that this at
least would help relieve him of the anxiety of being abandoned without proper
care.

Lieutenant Colonel Don Carlos Weber, ordinary engineer of Your Majesty's armies, piazzas, and frontiers, prostrating himself humbly at Your Royal Feet and offering infinite thanks for Your Supreme Clemency for granting him a subvention, explains to Your Majesty that it was sufficient for only a few days, because of the onerous expenses. Already he has had to suffer from his serious infirmity contracted in the underground excavations of Resina in order to execute his duties well, and every day his illness grows worse, rendering the danger to his life more serious, and there is not enough money for good care from the doctors and the necessary medicaments. The petitioner, finding himself absolutely destitute of every human means to surmount the huge daily expenses which he must incur in attempting to re-establish his health, with every resignation implores Your Royal Piety in order that, considering with the deepest compassion his deplorable state of health and his means, He would deign in this urgent matter to shower upon him those favors which are unique to His Magnanimous Royal Heart, by dispensing a greater subvention which would place him in a state of not having need to burden himself with greater debts during the present moment of danger to his life, in order to recover his lost health and perform well his obligation as a good and zealous servant of Your Majesty.[7]

On February 4, only nine days into his treatment, Weber made a final, desperate plea for additional funds to pay his medical bills.

Lieutenant Colonel Don Carlos Weber appeals to the Royal Clemency of Your Majesty, submitting the great expenses of the cure taken in Naples for the health he lost in the grottoes at Resina; his condition the more despondent and deplorable since he finds himself with much less hope of life; the apprehension in which his debts hold him; and the impossibility of surmounting this costly cure due to his total lack of means in view of how few days lasted the 50 ducats Your Majesty recently deemed it worthy to dispense. He supplicates Your Majesty to take pity upon his unfortunate state and concede a greater subsidy with which he might attend with a more tranquil spirit to recovering his health so that he might continue to sacrifice himself to Your Majesty's Royal Service.[8]

A PATHOLOGY OF WEBER'S DEMISE

Weber died eleven days later, on February 15, 1764, at the age of fifty-two. The exact cause of his death is impossible to determine at this distance in time, since the historical record makes no specific reference to a disease or to his symptoms. Only a few details are known. He had been ill "for some time" and under "continual medication," as he had claimed as early as 1752 that he had required medical attention and convalescence. He believed he had contracted his malady in the underground tunnels at Herculaneum. This required him to seek a "change of air" to Naples from Portici, although the royal summer villa had been built there in part because of its healthier atmosphere.[9] Treatment was costly, and death ultimately came fairly swiftly, in 35 days.

The infirmities that had culminated in Alcubierre's leave of absence from 1741 to 1745 had been due primarily to exposure to the damp conditions in the excavation tunnels and the Pugliano aqueduct. His scurvy was treated and, once he had regained his health and his post at Portici, he avoided recurrences by delegating responsibility to others and only descending into the tunnels when absolutely necessary. It is probably fair to assume that excavation-related illness was widespread, in particular among the forced laborers imprisoned in the fortress at Granatello. Scurvy must have been rampant in the damp tunnels at Herculaneum, though not necessarily at the other sites, but this was treatable and not life-threatening. The dust and humidity also caused ocular disorders, as Alcubierre and others discovered. Weber's vision had blurred enough near the end that he had one of the forced laborers write his reports, and Corcoles eventually developed similar symptoms.[10] The excavation accounts often report the disbursement of back pay for excavators absent from work, which must have occurred only when the workplace was verifiably the cause and only for those who held supervisory positions. Respiratory diseases were probably the greatest hazard, although by now tuberculosis, which was epidemic, was readily recognizable and treated scrupulously.[11] Bayardi's asthma had been aggravated by extended periods in the tunnels. Many of the excavators working in the underground tunnels, and even in the open-air trenches at Pompeii and Stabiae, may have contracted silicosis, a lung disease caused by breathing the volcanic dust. While silicosis contributes to shortening lifespans, it is not itself necessarily life-threatening. There is no specific treatment. Death is usually the result of complications brought on by the superimposition of another disease which further weakens the defense mechanisms and to which any treatment is addressed.[12]

Neither Weber nor later sources state specifically that he had suffered from tuberculosis, and he would not have contracted this simply as a result of excavating, though the possibility of silicosis superimposed on tuberculosis cannot be excluded. If he had been diagnosed with tuberculosis, his treatment would not have been taken so lightly at a time when this disease was considered highly contagious nor would the prescription have included a change of air to Naples when such urban centers were considered breeding grounds for the contagion.[13] It seems more likely he suffered from a chronic respiratory ailment like asthma, perhaps complicated by acute silicosis contracted over a period of years. A crucial factor in determining the cause of death is that, at the time of his release from active duty, Weber had been excavating the theater's scaena for several months. This work had continued into January, when the cold, damp conditions inside the underground tunnels would have escalated dramatically. The costly treatment and close medical attention which he required, and in particular the rapidity with which he succumbed, suggest that he had contracted pneumonia and that this had dealt him the fatal blow.

The famine and resulting disease took a heavy toll on the excavations in 1764.[14] In March, Antonio Scognamillo, his sons, and the other workmen at Pompeii complained that they were unable to get enough bread at Torre Annunziata or had to pay exorbitant prices for it when they could. Nor could it be obtained at Castellammare, for there were stiff penalties for giving food to anyone who was not a local resident.[15] Weber's death was followed by that of two long-term excavators, whose final days closely resemble his own: on May 1, Michele Corvato received 4 ducats for thirty-one days of sick leave and died on May 19; and on September 3, Corcoles, who had taken over Weber's duties, received 20 ducats in assistance to "cure himself of his indispositions contracted in the excavations" and to seek a "change of air" in Naples. He died two months later.[16]

Both Piaggio and La Vega attributed Weber's death in part to Alcubierre's persistent harassment, particularly during the search for the scaena, although the documents reveal that the feud had raged for virtually the whole of Weber's employment here. According to Piaggio, Alcubierre's attacks included character assassination and even slurs against Weber's origins. Specifically, Alcubierre believed that all of Weber's failings could be attributed to alcoholism. After Weber had duped him into believing the Alexander statuette was another bronze equestrian statue, Alcubierre attempted to salvage his reputation from his public humiliation by stating "that [the discovery] had been poorly reported to him by someone who was always drunk morning and night, with whom, through his own misfortune, he was forced to combat continually."[17] Piaggio, however, gave a different assessment of the consequences of Weber's continuing to work on the scaena even after Alcubierre had ordered the investigation halted:

> Weber sought out [the scaena] secretly and found it. The scorn [of Paderni and Alcubierre], along with the extraordinary labor, were the causes of his untimely death, which the two aforementioned subjects attributed to wine because he was Swiss. I bear witness that to accomplish

that task he was compelled to drink no wine at all, and I heard Don Rocco and Don Camillo on many occasions speaking of him as a drunk, a lunatic, and saying that "if the Lord God himself did not put a scaena there, there would not be one." Weber, however, found it. He died, and today others reap the glory of having found it (which is the third scaena), as one sees. For myself, in memory of this fact, I want to append here as an epitaph for my friend, "hos ego versiculos feci, tulit alter honorem" (I composed these little verses, another man reaped the glory).[18]

A memorial service was held for Weber in Arth on April 3 and another in Schwyz on September 20, at which his younger brother, Franz Dominik, now a major in the Tschudi regiment stationed in Messina, read the memorial.[19] It is unknown where he was buried, probably somewhere in Naples, less likely in Resina or Portici. Nor is it known whether he received a proper burial, due a lieutenant colonel of distinguished Swiss and Neapolitan families, or whether he was interred in a common grave along with the countless victims of the famine that year.[20]

What is known about the settlement of his estate suggests that some of Alcubierre's earlier charges that Weber had lived beyond his means were probably true. Liquidating his assets must have posed little difficulty: his pleas to Tanucci for assistance reveal he probably had no ready money and was heavily in debt. In Arth the value of the inheritance he received after his father's death in 1723 had not increased. As for his widow, it was almost a full year before she settled her claim against his estate. She sought the original nuptial settlement of 1,500 ducats which Weber had agreed to and never paid, including the amount the king had ordered deducted from his salary. As Franz Dominik had guaranteed this amount on behalf of his brother, her claim now stood against him as well. Fortunately, she was on good terms with Franz Dominik, impressed by his "rare qualities, the goodness of his habits, and his obliging manner," and they reached a compromise. Their agreement, signed by notaries at Naples on February 4, 1765, was that he would pay her 600 ducats immediately, while she swore that neither she nor her descendants could make further claims against Franz Dominik and his descendants. There is no indication she received the kind of small pension often granted to widows and children of the excavators by the king.[21]

THE POSTMORTEM INQUISITION

More vexing difficulties arose as a result of the division of his property in Resina, particularly his excavation notebooks and his plans. When the com-

mander of the corps of engineers at Portici, Giovanni Batista Bigotti, had visited
Weber during his convalescence in Naples and realized that death might be
imminent, he had inquired about what arrangements had been made concerning his estate. According to Tschudi, Weber had responded only with great
reluctance that all his affairs were in the hands of Aniello Diacampo, known also
as "il Poeta" and Weber's most trusted excavator, and with Poeta's son.[22] Just
before his death, Bigotti ordered three officers to remove Weber's possessions
from Resina, which they succeeded in doing only over the vigorous protests of
Poeta, and then transported them in two carts to Naples, where they were
locked in a room in the quarters of the Swiss Guard for safekeeping. Weber's
papers were found in a state of utter chaos after his death, and it took three
officers three days to divide them into three categories: those relating to the
excavations; those relating to his activities as a military engineer, such as plans
for fortifications and garrisons; and his personal papers. Bigotti promptly turned
over the first of these to Tanucci; the second remained in the hands of the
adjutant general of the guard, Rocque Renner; and the third was retained for
delivery to his heirs, specifically his brother.[23]

While Tanucci was preparing to turn the excavation records over to La Vega,
it came to his attention that some important documents had been lost in the
confusion. In particular he could not find a certain "book" Weber had written,
details about which were sketchy, and this complicated the search considerably.
The "book," however, must have been Weber's monograph on the Villa di San
Marco at Stabiae, "Le Piante di Alcuni Edifici Sotterranei . . ." Tanucci probably spearheaded the ensuing inquisition, which he may have mounted in fear
that the monograph would fall into the wrong hands and be published. The
scope of the investigation suggests he also may have been concerned that Weber
himself had wished to prevent the court from having his work. An inquisitor,
Nicholas Pirelli, auditor general of the army, was appointed to determine what
had become of Weber's papers.[24]

Over the course of the next several months, all parties having anything to do
with the affair were questioned about the events surrounding the retrieval and
division of Weber's papers. Tanucci received signed affidavits from witnesses.
Antonio Scognamillo, Weber's foreman at Città and Gragnano, came forward
and cited a long list of books of excavation reports and drawings that he had
submitted to Weber but that were now missing. This included reports for sites
at Pompeii and Stabiae, plans of the ruins at Herculaneum, and the notes and
plan for the "temple" at Pozzuoli.[25] A certain soldier, believed to have been the
one responsible for binding Weber's book, was tracked down and interrogated
but found to be lacking the necessary binding skills.[26] A second inquisitor was

appointed as a representative of the royal house: Prince Placido Dentice, who earlier had conducted the investigation into the theft of items from the museum in Portici. In his initial report Dentice informed Tanucci that no one was able to verify the existence of this "large book" prior to the time Weber had taken leave of absence from Portici, but he had yet to interrogate one of the female servants in Weber's house.[27]

The inquiry continued into 1765, and a second round of interviews was conducted. Alcubierre, Galiani, and La Vega were ordered to meet to review again what each knew about Weber's plans and to take a second inventory of the plans in each one's possession. Piaggio later recounted how he had been questioned on several occasions by La Vega, who behaved more like "a deputy prosecutor in search of someone's intentions than a young excavator of antiquities." He implied that there was concern not only for Weber's book but for "the greater part" of his plans.

> It was said that among these was lost the large plan of the theater with its section and elevation drawn by Weber in spite of such great struggles and toil; and also on the basis of that plan a wooden model was made under the direction of the noted dilettante of architecture [Berardo Galiani]. After Weber's death, which happened shortly after the aforementioned effort, plates were ordered to be engraved. Today, to recover what was lost, this young military engineer [La Vega] is redoing the plan from the top.[28]

Giovanni Furlanetti, a record keeper in Portici, continued to insist upon the existence of Weber's book, which he had helped inscribe, while Weber's two servants, Carlo Picillo and Francesco Germani, vehemently disputed this.[29] A major obstacle to the inquiry was the fact that Weber had jealously guarded all his work. As Winckelmann noted and both Alcubierre and Piaggio confirmed for La Vega, Weber had allowed no one to see his plans, which he kept locked in his house. In addition to maintaining one of the forced laborers to write his reports, he had posted a soldier outside his house in Resina when he was away. Consequently, no one knew precisely the full extent of Weber's work.[30]

In the end, concern that the book had been lost or spirited away proved unfounded. At their meeting Galiani now recalled hearing after Weber's death that Renner was selling certain of his books and mathematical instruments. Galiani had purchased several of these and remembered inquiring as well about a folio of drawings which Renner had said was not for sale. On reexamining this folio, Galiani and La Vega discovered Weber's monograph and several other plans from the excavations tucked in among his drawings of military fortifications and geographical maps. It contained "a plan of part of the city of Stabiae and two elevations of fountains found in the same city; and this book is incomplete." They showed the book to Piaggio, who immediately recognized it. They were suspicious of the designation "Volume Three" in the title and asked Piaggio where the other two might be, so he explained that Weber had intended it only as a prototype of the third volume of *Le antichità*; he had written no other volumes. Furlanetti recognized his own contributions as well, but not the plans and drawings in the monograph, as he had never seen the finished version.[31]

The inquisition produced several other positive results. Alcubierre, Galiani, and La Vega had inventoried, cataloged, and apportioned Weber's papers among themselves at an initial meeting in August 1764. They found five large folios of orders, letters, and answers concerning the excavations. There were also fourteen notebooks: six were accounts of weekly expenses, four were notes to Alcubierre, and another four were notes written by Weber. Nine small books contained the work compiled over several years by Antonio Scognamillo, "in which he had drawn, in the manner he knows, the buildings and mosaics found in Città and Gragnano, and also many architectural ornaments which appear in the paintings, copies of inscriptions, notes concerning the discoveries, and some loose notes of appointment made by [Weber]." These were handed over to La Vega to use as he saw fit. Weber also had left a total of 87 large and small drawings. These included 43 drawings by his own hand in both a finished and a rough state. Mentioned specifically among those recovered was the unfinished plan of the Villa dei Papiri. Another 44 sketches were by Scognamillo, illustrating buildings, mosaics, and other finds from Pompeii, Stabiae, and Herculaneum.[32] La Vega also took possession of these. Nine plans of the theater at Herculaneum, some completed and some in rough draft, were given to Galiani, who already had 2 other plans. All 11 plans were said to be in Weber's hand.[33]

Two more plans were recovered later along with the monograph. The first was "an original drawing by Weber with an explanation of part of the buildings and roads of Pompeii," described elsewhere as a plan *a cavaliere*, or viewed "from above," that is, the axonometric plan of the Praedia Iuliae Felicis. The second, "a topographical plan of Portici and Resina," may be the plan of ancient Herculaneum La Vega later used to draw up his own schematic version. Among the plans Weber had drawn as a military engineer were a small plan of the Castel San Elmo, some illustrations of the principles of fortification, and "a plan, or rather project, to conduct the waters of Carmignano and Serino from Acerra to Portici."[34]

No mention is made of a single-page document entitled "Libro degli Edificj Sotterranei d'Ercolano." Despite the title, the text has nothing to do with Herculaneum but describes instead a "Great Piazza" with a public street to the west and a palestra with baths to the north. These specific features, and reference to the collapse of a portion of the building down a ravine, help identify the site as the Villa di San Marco at Stabiae. There is no date on the document, but it is written in the manner of his monograph and so probably can be dated to those years. In all likelihood, this is a rough draft for his later manuscript, "Le Piante de Alcuni Edifici Sotterranei . . . ," perhaps even a sample of his intended approach to this material prepared specifically for Tanucci.[35] (For the full text, see Appendix 4 to this volume.)

WEBER'S CONTRIBUTIONS TO FRANCESCO LA VEGA

La Vega, who now had most of Weber's notebooks and plans, did nothing to complete those that remained unfinished, except in the case of the theater at Herculaneum. Nor did he seek to publish any of the individual structures that Weber had investigated. Instead he acted as an archivist, sifting through the old letters and reports, both those in his own possession and those in the archives of the prime minister, and interviewing the oldest excavators and local citizens. He investigated as many of the shafts and tunnels at Herculaneum as remained accessible in his day. From this material he created a variety of documents that illustrated the history, significant discoveries, and even routine expenses of the excavations. Much of this work he did for his own enlightenment, to learn how the excavations had been conducted in the past and what had been found where, and for the sake of organizing the records under his care. But he came to recognize the great historical value of this information as well, even suggesting to Tanucci the idea of publishing a history of the excavations.[36]

La Vega used various of Weber's plans to compile two general plans of Pompeii and Herculaneum. That of Pompeii now exists in two closely related versions of slightly different date, both of which probably were revised by his brother, Pietro, who succeeded him as director of the excavations in 1804. By merging all of the disparate plans of the individual sites excavated by Alcubierre, Weber, and himself, La Vega created both a visual record of the excavations since their inception in 1748 and the first plan to portray the full topography of Pompeii accurately.[37] His plan is remarkably detailed, especially for those areas he had excavated himself, and accurate, considering that his predecessors' plans were drawn at various scales and the orientation of the individual sites to one another must have been difficult to ascertain since all had been reburied and were inaccessible to him. The plans of the amphitheater and the Praedia Iuliae Felicis, for example, are direct copies of those drawn, respectively, by Alcubierre in 1748 and Weber in 1759. La Vega's plan is of particular importance for its depiction of all the sites

Figure 76. Topographical plan of Herculaneum, drawn by Francesco La Vega but based largely on documentation and plans left by Weber. Published only in 1797 in C. Rossini's *Dissertazione isagogicae*, this is the only plan of the monuments from any of the Vesuvian cities published under the auspices of the Bourbon court. From *StErc*, pl. 2.

along the southern and western sides of the city excavated by Weber between 1757 and 1763. This proves that La Vega had in his possession, or had access to, a number of plans which since have been lost.

La Vega also relied on Weber's work to produce his topographical plan of Herculaneum, the first of its kind for this city, published in 1797 (Fig. 76).[38] This is far more schematic than that of Pompeii, for only a few major buildings are rendered in any detail: the theater, Basilica, Palestra, and the Villa dei Papiri. Only the orthogonal grid of the city blocks is shown, probably because

Weber had been more interested in charting the streets and public buildings
than in drawing plans of individual private houses; Alcubierre later complained
to La Vega that Weber had not produced a single plan of a house at Herculaneum.[39] Since La Vega conducted only a minimal amount of excavation
here, the plan is based almost exclusively on his own observations and research
into his predecessors' work, the sole exception to this being the theater. In 1766
he had finally seen copies of Bardet's plans which allowed him to draft the
Basilica and the area of the Palestra, sites to which La Vega wrongly believed
Weber's excavations had not extended.[40]

THE LOSS, RECOVERY, AND LEGACY OF WEBER'S WORK

The fate of Weber's plans over the course of the nineteenth century stands in
ironic contrast to the urgency with which they were tracked down after his
death. The survival of virtually all his plans is due more to chance than to any
conscientious attempt at preservation, and his most important contributions
came perilously close to being lost completely. It was to be well over a century
after his death before any of his plans were published.

Certain of his plans remained accessible, at least through 1827, though most
of his work was completely unknown to those outside the excavations. Romanelli, for example, remarked in 1817 that "It is a great pity the ["temples" at
Herculaneum] were not excavated by some experienced architect or at least
engraved in order to fix their true form and proper dimensions."[41] In 1827
Canon Andrea de Jorio published his *Notizie degli scavi di Ercolano*, a popular
guide to the site and the history of the excavations. At that time he could still
describe in detail Weber's plan of the Villa dei Papiri, observing that on it "were
marked with precision the various places in which the objects were found, of
which this villa was very rich, since the Swiss Weber was most precise in this as
in all the other areas of his duties."[42] Although he must have had access to
documents in the excavation offices, de Jorio and his successors were completely unaware of the existence of Bardet's plans, which La Vega had returned
to the archives of the prime minister. For his own part, de Jorio somehow had
managed to collect a wide variety of documents relating to the excavations,
including a manuscript by Mazzocchi and Alcubierre's 1747 plan of the theater
at Herculaneum, which he acquired through an acquaintance sometime between 1827 and 1831. Ruggiero was at a loss to explain where de Jorio had
obtained these. They were recovered after the latter's death in 1861, with the
manuscripts going to the Biblioteca Nazionale and the rest returning to the
offices of the excavations.[43]

Most of Weber's finished plans disappeared for the years between 1827 and 1873. Scholars in this period were unable to refer to them and almost universally lamented their loss. Barnabei, for example, made no reference to Weber's plans in his 1877 study of the early excavations, while in 1879 Beloch stated specifically that all of Weber's plans had been lost.[44] Justi, whose description of the Villa dei Papiri was based exclusively on Winckelmann's observations, mourned the loss of Weber's work, adding that it "would have been more interesting for us than the antiquarian erudition of the Accademia Ercolanese."[45] Ruggiero reported seeing a document written sometime after 1831 listing notes and plans, primarily concerning Stabiae, that were loaned out and never returned, but he gave no more specific details.[46]

According to documents in the archives, the plans only resurfaced in 1873, during the period when Giuseppe Fiorelli served as superintendent of the excavations. In that year a certain Giovanni Patturelli, identified only as once associated with former King Ferdinand II, first offered for sale to Fiorelli an assortment of plans from the Bourbon era. Among these was the plan of the Villa dei Papiri, which Patturelli advertised as an "interesting plan . . . drawn by the famous Swiss Weber, a most precise and scrupulous draftsman. . . . All the most famous archaeologists, including the notorious Winckelmann, always have wanted to see, if not in published form, at least to observe this unique drawing." Accompanying the plan were eight drawings of decorative details from the villa, "drawn for the most part by this same Weber and the rest by the sufficiently well known and accurate architect, Brigadier Francesco La Vega."[47] After some consideration, however, the recommendation was made to the Ministero della Istruzione Pubblica that, although the plans were useful, the asking price was too high. The minister himself at that time concurred.[48]

Patturelli wanted the plans to remain in Italy and, specifically, hoped that they would become part of the collection of the Muzeo Nazionale in Naples. He must have offered the plans for sale a second time, after Ruggiero had replaced Fiorelli as director of the excavations in 1875 and during the period of activity and interest in these sites leading up to the anniversary of the eruption of Vesuvius, in 1879. Ruggiero later wrote that "judging from the character of the bearer, [the plans and notes] probably came from the cabinets of the royal house, and I did not hesitate to repurchase [them] for our archives."[49] A document that appears to be the bill of sale or an itemized receipt reveals that this single transaction was responsible for restoring to the excavation archives almost all of Weber's extant plans and drawings. The descriptions of the plans in the document often are taken directly from Weber's titles, so their identification is assured. In all Ruggiero purchased twenty plans and drawings: the one of the

Villa dei Papiri and its eight details; the rough draft, finished version, and axonometric view of the Praedia Iuliae Felicis, along with two details of a "Tempio di Giunone" in Pompeii whose attribution to Weber appears dubious; a plan of the "amphitheater at Stabiae," which is actually Alcubierre's plan of Pompeii's amphitheater; and the plans of the villas of San Marco, Arianna, and Pastore at Stabiae, along with a rough draft and a version of the Villa del Pastore with notes in Spanish. Weber's monograph was recovered at this time as well, complete with its plan and the elevations of the mosaic niches.[50] If the figures in lire on the document are the actual purchase prices, it is easy to understand why the Ministero had balked previously. The total is 5,500 lire, an astronomical price to pay for the reacquisition of what were, in effect, stolen documents.[51]

Ruggiero moved quickly to publish these plans, beginning with those from Stabiae in 1881. The versions he published of Weber's plan and elevations of the Villa di San Marco, however, are the ones he purchased separately from the monograph and which have since been lost once again. He published only a heavily edited version of the monograph's text, omitting the whole of the section dealing with the eruptions of Vesuvius and remarking,

> [Weber composed the monograph] in imitation of the Accademia with little text and copious notes in addition to plans and other drawings. These, to tell the truth, would have been of the greatest value for understanding so many buildings which few saw, no one else was allowed to draw, and which, as soon as they were discovered, were despoiled and reburied.
>
> As I believe the erudition and a great part of the judgments of the good Weber do not have any value either in his own or in our time, I determined it would be pointless to publish it in its entirety and have limited myself to providing only the title, a shortened text, and, of the notes, only those few scattered passages that contain information or other details important to know.[52]

The plan of the Villa dei Papiri was first published by G. De Petra in 1879, shortly after Ruggiero acquired it, and then again in 1883 by De Petra and D. Comparetti in *La villa ercolanese dei Pisoni*, the first monographic study of an individual site at Herculaneum.[53] In 1885 Ruggiero published all the plans of Herculaneum he had in his possession, including those for which he could locate only the copper plates. Of the twenty plans he purchased separately from the monograph, only five are available today in their original form. Of all the plans Weber is known to have produced, only nine are extant today: those for the Villa dei Papiri, the three plans of the Praedia Iuliae Felicis, the Cratere

Maritimo map, the unfinished plan of the theater at Herculaneum, and the three plans bound into his monograph.

Weber was a victim of his times in more ways than one. His notions about publishing the archaeological sites and making them accessible to a broader public were years ahead of their time. His plans were revolutionary, in particular those of the tunnels in the Villa dei Papiri and the axonometric plan of the Praedia. Although his unfinished plan of the theater at Herculaneum is elegant, he was not as accomplished an archaeological draftsman as La Vega. His fatal flaw was believing that his noble ties, military rank, unique knowledge of the excavations, and peripheral connections to the court's inner circle would win him the recognition and prestige he thought he merited. In fact, these appear to have worked against him. The court was not prepared to entertain the notion of allowing a military engineer to become a member of the Accademia. Alcubierre certainly had done him the most damage by persecuting him throughout his tenure, countering and undermining his efforts to improve the excavations and poisoning his reputation with the Bourbon court. Yet through perseverance, and some luck, Weber succeeded in establishing a new approach to excavation that was both methodical and scientific; it continued after his death and was his greatest legacy.

Conditions changed rapidly during La Vega's era. The open-air excavations at Pompeii had been inaugurated during the final months of Weber's life, and La Vega pursued these in the manner advocated by Weber. He soon convinced the court to expropriate large tracts of the archaeological zone, which meant the individual sites could remain accessible to visitors and scholars alike in perpetuity. Herculaneum was gradually forsaken, apart from the theater, in favor of systematic investigations at Pompeii and sporadic work in the villas around Stabiae; already by mid-1769, Piaggio could lament that a brutish guard at Herculaneum would only show visitors the theater and a few tunnels.[54] Alcubierre grew increasingly out of touch with the daily operations as his military duties in Naples expanded, yet he remained a constant presence, outliving kings, prime ministers, scholars, and excavators.[55]

La Vega came to exercise much greater control over the course of the excavations, managing successfully to keep Alcubierre in check through his persuasive arguments to the prime minister and his firsthand knowledge of the sites. He attained a level of influence in the court that had eluded Weber completely. Charles III had recognized his skills already at a young age and underwrote his education in Rome. He became an officer in the corps of military engineers, eventually reaching the rank of brigadier. He assumed Weber's post in 1764 at the age of twenty-seven and became sole director of the excavations upon Alcubierre's death in 1780. He received high accolades from several leading Neapolitan scholars and members of the Accademia for his diligence in conducting the investigations, the care he used in reconstructing the exposed ruins, and the accuracy of his plans. The plans he produced of the Villa di Diomede and Via dei Sepolcri at Pompeii and of the villas in the Ager Stabianus, with their numbered legends and detailed inventories, show that he also had adopted Weber's method of marking the precise provenance of the finds.[56] He was credited with introducing color-coded geographical cartography into Italy with his drawings of the phases of the eruptions of Vesuvius. After Camillo Paderni's death in 1781, he became the director of the Museum Herculanense. When the Accademia Ercolanese was resurrected from its moribund state in 1787, he was named one of its fifteen members. Yet La Vega reportedly prevented others from drawing the sites under his care, jealously guarded his own plans, and showed little interest in publishing his work.[57] Only his schematic plan of Herculaneum was published during his lifetime. He stands in contrast to Weber in being the classic devoted servant: he toiled not for personal renown but for the glory of his king. As a consequence, despite attaining the recognition and high offices Weber had long coveted in vain, he was unable to share Weber's vision for the ancient ruins, where excavators and scholars would cooperate in the publication of the first truly archaeological studies of these unique monuments.

The preliminary plan of the Praedia Iuliae Felicis (MN. ADS #71)

(0.36 m. H × 0.48 m. W)

The following is the text of Weber's rough draft for his plan of the Praedia Iuliae Felicis, completed sometime in 1757. His presentation copy of this same plan, finished in late 1759, is MN. ADS #72. An engraving of the plan alone based on #72 first appeared in 1830 (*Monumenti inediti pubblicati dall' Istituto di Corrispondenza Archeologica* 1 [1830] pl. 16), while the text was published separately (*Annali dell' Istituto di Corrispondenza Archeologica* 2 [1830] 42–51). Fiorelli published another version of the text and plan in 1860 (*PAH* I.ii.Addenda 2, 95–102, pl. 1), though certain of his readings are at variance with the 1830 publication. Neither is a completely faithful reproduction of the text of #72, though the differences do not merit a full transcription here.

KEY:

_____ = Underlined space on manuscript
\ / = Text inserted from above
/ \ = Text inserted from below
[ ] = Crossed out
{ } = Editor's notes

{RECTO}

{**In margin at top left of page:**} Suppellettile ritrovato. vedi 7. linea ⊕ deve. essere 22. marzo à 3. aprile 1756.
{**In left margin:**} A

{COLUMN 1}

Masseria Grasso 1756

N . 1. Tavolino di marmo Africano, e piedi bianchi \di pal. 2. onz. 8. per. pal. 1. onz. 8./, e pezzi 41. di Africano, giallo, [palombino] \piombino/ _____ e di bucaro di Portogallo, una Tazza rossa _____ Di creta, Fiaschi 6, Pignata una, Langelletti 3, Coperchi 4. Caldara una. _____ Di Vetro, Caraffina _____ Corna di Cervo \4. pezzi/ _____ di Ferro, Serrature 2. un Tondo di stante di Porta, [chiodo] altri chiodi 3, con pezzi di avorio anesse. \attacati. appicati/ 28. Junio à 3. Julio \1756/
N . 2. Ritrovato di metallo, ò bronzo; Lucerna con testa di cavallo, coperchio e 3. catenelle per appenderla, altra à 2. Luci, come masc[a]\he/roni, e con catenella. \⊕ 22. marzo a 27. 1756/ Rasciatore, con cola rotta un poco, Padella sfratumata, però tiene la figura, Patera bella, rotta alla punta, pero tiene il pezzetto, moneta piccola, chiodo, chiodetti \2/ _____ Ferro, pezzi 3. di serratura, chiodi 10, tondo, dentro il quale gira la Porta, grappe \uncini/ 2, barrette 2 \ascino/ _____ di Marmo, Tavole 2. di pal. 3 $\frac{1}{2}$. per 2 $\frac{5}{6}$. [_____Creta] Tavole 2. di palmi 2 $\frac{1}{2}$. per 1 $\frac{1}{2}$. Di creta, boccali, ò giarri 2. Tina, Langellone con lettere CH. Peso picolo bello con lettere FCLCD, beveratore di Gallina; Mattone pistato, pannari, ò [coffani] \cofani/ 16, per fare pavimenti d'astricho. _____ Avorio, un pezzo di Flauto. da 26 [Marzo] \Aprile/ à [10 Aprile] \29. Mayo maio/ 1756.

N . 3. Creta, langellone \con grano dentro/, due tine, 80. pezzi di marmo nel bagno, di 2. 3. palmi _____ Alabastro un pezzo di onze 18 per 12, grosso 9. e due pesi di pietra di Caserta. \1756/ 8.bre 4. à 16.

N . 4. I\n/scrizione sopra la Tonica del muro di questa Taverna. GAVIVM RVFVM, ET TRIBIVM . AED 6 . IAEDIP . SIIII, e lettia, i gradini di sopra, per mettere i piatti, come oggi si usano. Marzo: 30 \# 29 a abril. 3/

{In left margin:} # 1756

N . 5. Strada di basole, ò pietre vive, come in Napoli, e sentieri laterali di astricho, calce e lapilli, di un palmo piu alto, che la strada.

N . 6. di metallo, monete 3. Cadaveri 3, uno con anello di ferro al dito, mazzo di chiavi, caraffina, e due bottoni di vetro. \9.bre 55. à gen.o 56./

N . 7. Porta principale.

N . 8. Al muro \sopra la tonica/ lettere rosse; IN FRAEDIS . IVLIAE . SP. \.E./ FELICIS . LOCANTVR . BALNEVM . VENERIVM . ET NONGENTVM . TABERNAE . PERGVLAE CENACVLAE X . IDIBVS . AVG PRIMIS . IN . IDVS . AVG . SEXTAS ANNOS CONTINVOS QVINQVE . S.Q.D.L.E.N.C. A . SVETTIVM . VERVM – AED . V.A.S.P.P.D.R.P . PROBVM. moneta di met., anello, chiodo. /avorio, spingolone\ _____ ferro 3. pezzi di graticola, martello, 2.chiodi, mattone con uccello sculpito. Febr.o 9 à 21. 1756.

N . 9. lett: L.CELIVM SECVNDVM MELMCC. TRIBIVM AED. IRONIVS EICANTVS.

N . 10. P.POPIDIVM SECVND[VM]\\M/.

N . 11. HELVIVM SABINIVM.A\E/DIVVNEM, PRON.AVE IILVM FIRMVM PAQVIVM' D.ID VENERI' ROC.IVI L' CE\L/IVM SECVNDVM AED.O V.ED.RP. OVTP.LIIR.

N . 12. ELI.IACIIEL' CAE CELIVM . CAP\E/LLAM . IIVIR . ORP ED . CVVIVS . SMIT SECVNDVM AED . FVRNACATOR ROC . L' POPID SECVNDVM ÆDV. 23 à 28. Feb.o \1756/

N . 13. C A/EI.S.V.D.V VM.A.D^COVIR.P.

N . 14. VETTIVM FIRMVM λ . OVF.D.R.P.

λ ROE .Ͻ λ 6 . RCIIM. AED R.JTTT ‖ CNEI.S. AED. 6 VM. A\6̊. OVERP.GA=

{COLUMN 1a}

GAVIVM . RVFVM . ET . TRIBIVM AED . 6 .

N . 15. LVMP ℳ S λ ℳ. AED ⌐ OIVF . ALBVCIVM . rotta. 29. marzo \1756/ à 3. Aprile.

N . 16. RVFVM AD 6 Q POSTVM IVM . MO=

{COLUMN 1b}

MODESTVM QVINQV 6 L' CE\L/IVM SECVNDVM . D . IFVr Λ 6 INDIO . P . PAQVIVM. ET AVETTIVM . D . IDOVF. L' POPIDIVM . SECVNDVM . AED . D.R.PO \#/

{To left, below plan:} # 13.18. 7.bre 1756

N . 17. Fontana di pietra viva con mascarone buttava l'acqua, con orecchini di grappole d'uva \20. 7.bre 1756/

N . 18. lett: MODESTVM . QVINQ . O.VF.P.A.P. /4 a. 9. 8.bre 1756.\

{COLUMN 2}

N . 19. O SECVNDVM L . ISIIVII 6 . 18. 7.bre à 4. 8.bre

N . 20. L' CE\E/IVM SECVNDVM GIVIM IIC IOVNOND VLVS CENE'NIEM RO.c \moneta di metallo. X.b 29. 56. à Gen. 8. 57./

N . 21. Taverna con focolare b, ed scalini c. sopra un appoggio per i piatti: Genaro à 3. 1757.

N . 22. Strada \passo/ particolare \passaggio/ e Portone.

N . 23. Pittura, huomo nudo in piedi con pannicello, e uomo nudo colcato sopra un pannicello _____ Di metallo, anello, chiodo, mezo frontizo. _____ Ferro, 3. pezzí, _____ Vetro, corallo, pietra turchina _____ Avorio, tondo con \buco/ pertuso \agio/ _____ Alabastro, pezzo _____ creta, coperchio _____ marmo, porta santa, africano, sarabeza, giallo, 33. pezzi di pavimento. 7bre 11. à 27. 1756.

N . 24. Pavim.o di Mosaico, di marmo bianco e negro: la mure pittate, cio'è: Huomini e femine à cavallo e à piedi; huomo con carro \e bove/ e due tori, asini, cavallo e tre huomini,

huomo à cavallo sopra pedagna, asino; due, tre, sei, huomini à cavallo, 4 coloñe, huomini 4. à piedi, e 3. à cavallo sopra 3. pedagne, 4. coloñe, fraschi, fiori, e capitello. huomini \figure/ 15, \di huomini e/ e giovani figliuoli, 3. persone sedenti con robba in mano, huomo con figliuolo, due à cavallo, |altro à piede| con 3 cavalli al freno: huomo à cavallo con arco, e dardo, e 4. \figure/ fra 4. coloñe. Femine vestite di bianco, sedenti con due huomini assistenti. coloñe 5, persone 3. con robba, due [con] \uomini, e una/ guardia \con/ bandaliera, e spada, uno à cavallo; Vechio huomo con baco, \con/ [e] spada \in mano che appoggia à terra,/, cane /vicino\; femina tira con machina contra il vechio. di metallo, Tenta; frontizi 4. bracciletti 2, piastre, chiodi, di Porta, fascie e 3 piastre, Ferro Serratura, chiodi, pezzetti 2. di catena, tondo, frontizi mezzi 2. e 13. pezzi di marmo, Statuetta figliuolo in ginochio sopra una base. pessi 2. di rosso antichº. colonetta di porta santa di 6. onz. e 5. diam. altra di africano, alta onz. 3. diam 9 $\frac{1}{2}$. base di porta 5. onz. 13. quad: 18. tavolette di marmo bianco, di pal. 1. 2. 4. 5. 6. Piombo, peso, tubo pal. 15. Creta, Tegole 11, canali 6. e mezzo cofano di grano; Maggio 21, à 2 Giugno. 1755. Pitture, 2 cupidi, in piede, e colcato, due sopra corniscione, con piatti e bastoni \[22 à 24. X.bre 1755]/, Cupido e due con parapetto, bastone, combattendo, cupido con bastone e toro salvata in 125. pezzi rotta, cavallo con ale, Termine \con palmo/ con vaso, \altro/ cornuco-pia frasca, termine con fontana, braccio di gigante, \ # / Di Metallo, moneta, frontizo, serratura, cantone; Piombo,
{Below, to right of plan:} / # pal. 2. in quadro\

{COLUMN 2a}

Piombo, Tubone pal. 44. in 26. pezzi. Creta, tegole 10. Canali 15. X.bre [17] \15/ à 24. 1755. Lettere sopra stucco rosse; CCSJL . IDO.J.DOC⎯⎯L'PO. Augusto 17. à 21./ 1756.

N . 25. Metallo, monete 3, lett: C\O/NSTAN-TINOPOLI, Sergio Galba, e altra Roma S.C.

N . 26. Metallo, monete 3. piccole, uomo à piedi, altro à cavallo; ⎯⎯ Padella, peso piccolo; conio di ferro, Lucerna di creta; ⎯⎯ marmo, fascie 2. d'un capitello, e piedi due di Tavola.

N . 27. Alla boca della fornace della stufa n.o 42., Met: monete 5. Piombo, tubo di pal. 46. ⎯⎯ Lucerna di creta.

N . 28. Stanziola \di ritiro/ con banchi di marmo, per rafezzioncola, ò ritiro doppo il bagno à Stufa, e spasseggio nella pergolata intorno al bagno \e fonte/ n.o 31.

N . 29. Gabinetto di Stufa tonda, pavim.o di mosaico bianco e negro, fascia e nichi guarniti di marmo e sedili: si sono rimessi [41] \33/ tavolette ò perri di marmo; longhi, palmi 5. 4. 3 $\frac{1}{2}$. 3. 2 $\frac{1}{2}$. 2. 1 $\frac{1}{2}$. 1. \grossezza. onz. 1./ per 3. 1 $\frac{3}{4}$. 1 $\frac{1}{6}$. 1.

N . 30. Camerino, \ritiro/ Pitture, Cavallo marino sopra corniscione, ⎯⎯ cupido con bastone, ⎯⎯ creta, tazze 2. lucerna grande assai. ⎯⎯ Metallo, piastra attacata col tondo, come un calamaio con inchiostro, braccialetti 7 ⎯⎯ Piombo 4. piastre ⎯⎯ Vetro 12. pezzi ⎯⎯ due denti di animale, corno di cervo 2. pezzi, colonet.a pietra di Caserta. \15 a 20 [25 a 20] 7.bre 1755./

N . 31. Fontana ò bagno con \portico/ pergolata intorno. Pitture; \alli 4. mure/ due torri; gallina d'India, cupido con velo in mano, Uccello, altro volando, ved. sopra

{COLUMN 3}

altro volando; altro con palla; huomo con fiori, Cavallo marino, 3. delfini. grillo ligato al piede e bocca. Doña sedente, con rosa, come dormendo. Due colombe, gioia e fiori, apesi. Sirena con bastone, cavallo, bove marino, due delfini. Huomo nudo appoggiato sopra bastone, animale e fiori. Fiori appes\i/[asti] con due colombe; coloñette 5, corniscione, due boccali. 14. Jun: 1755. ⎯⎯ Metallo, grappe 2, specchio tondo diam. onz. 10. $\frac{1}{2}$., anelli, chiodetti, bastone di guarnizione. Stuccio di piombo, martello, e 13. pezzi di Istrumenti di ferro. Talco, pezzi 2.; Pittura, architettura, tigro e cinte, scarpello, frasca, uccello volante, con cinta al piede e becco. Sirena con bastone e 2. delfini. Huomo vestito, con vaso due libri e palma, sopra piedestallo e tavola. Perspettiva d'una Porta con cavallo sfrenato in mezzo, con ale, e di sopra, cavallo con 3. delfini. Cavallo griffone e Pavone con frasche e fiori. Porte 2. d'architettura, fiori, uccello \ligato/ con cinta al piede e becco, e tigre. _____ Piombo condotti, Metallo, chiave, _____ Creta, canali – Marmo di pal. 1. con perfuro in mezzo per recipiente d'acqua. 8.bre 2. à 8. 1755. Pitture, huomo gigantesco con scudo alto pal: 2. Scimia sopra un piedestallo sbruzza acqua per la bocca _____ Metallo, grappe 36 ò bracciatori; Piombo, tubo; e mattoni. 7.bre 22. a 27. \1755/ _____ Chiodi 15 e i 9. pare che siano di calesso, acceta, di ferro _____ Piombo, tubo pal. 44. in 26. pezzi. Gen.o 19. à 24. 1756. _____ Pitture, cerva, palla, frasche e fiori. boccale ò giarro pieno di cerase. Porta con architettura, Nimfa sedente con ale aperte, cornucopia appesa con cinta, quatro pesci _____ Pavone, frasche rose. Cervo con corni, fiori, cavallo grifone _____ Pavim.o de mosaico bianco e negro, con 3 figure curiose, di testa e collo d'ucello, o zampe di animale feroce, e coda di dragone, ò delfino. 9.bre 10. à 29. \55/ _____ Pitture, animale con bastone, huomo alato con bastone, e coda di delfino. Cornucopia appesa con cinta e frasche. Pavone. Nimfa. Cerva. cupido con ale. cupido con frasche e fiori. Altro con Ampollina. Altro con cerchio e velo. Cavallo sfrenato con ale sopra una cornice. Cupido con vaso. Paese, torre, ponte, arbori. Cervo [cibante] \manggio/ i fogli d'arbori. Pavone. [braccio di gigante di pal. 2 in quad.o.] _____ Metallo monete due. Cadavere con 3. monete, [Cadavere con anello di ferro al dito, e altre 3. monete]. Avorio, Cucchiaio. Marmo, pedagna con 2. piedi di Statua. Vetro, caraffa, bottone, 14. foglietti di marmo. e [di ferro un mazzo di chiavi.] X.bre 9. 1755 à 3. Genaro 1756.

N . 32. Anticamera del \Stanza al/ Bagno 39.

N . 33. Edificij magnifici per continuare il scavo.

N . 34. Idem.

N . 35. Pittura, huomo vestito, con pala e cane, combattendo con animale. Di ferro, coltello. Palle 2. di terra turchina. Coperchio di buccaro.

N . 36. Coloña di mattone e stucco.

N . 37. Gabinetto ò ritiro.

N . 38. Passetto dietro il Bagno.

N . 39. Bagno, guarnito di marmo.

N . 40. Canale scoperto intorno le stufe e bagno.

N . 41. Stufa con pavimento di \mosaico/ negro e bianco, e figura d'uomo alto pal. 3 $\frac{1}{2}$. con bastone. Marmo, d'una tavola 3. piedi di zampe e testa di leone, capitello, e quantità di marmi. Metallo, braccialetti 4., piastra, piombo, vetro, denti 2. di animale. Pezzi di corno di cervo. Mattoni 556. Pilastrelli, o colonette 28. \di creta/ alte onz. 21. diam. 6. 8.bre 8. 1755.

N . 42. Stufa simile con pavimento di marmo, pigliato d'altri.

N . 43. Coloña come 36.

N . 44. Condotto, come 40. \capitello di marmo/

N . 45. Idem.

N . 46. Bagno guarnito di marmo. Statua di marmo, Uomo vechio involto nel manto, 8.bre 27. à 31. 1755.

N . 47. Giardino e pilastri della pergolata.

N . 48. Spasseggio sotto la pergolata, avanti i nichj \grotesche/ d'acqua.

N . 49. Sopra questo nicchio, un quadro di marmo, con basso rilievo, di uomo vechio, con manto, appoggia sopra bastone, e s\c/alzo, e tiene in mani un\a tazza/ [quadretto], che mira, sedente sopra una sedia, coperta di pelle d'animale. Creta, tegola con lettere in giro. OTIS I.TIAVPI, e giglio in mezzo. Avorio, agone col pertuso. \.21. augusto. 1755/

N . 50. Giardino.

N . 51. Marmo, statua di giovane, nudo al tronco, con pelle d'animale. 7.bre 5. 1755.

N . 51.\52/ Fontana sopra questo ponte di marmo, coloñetta con frasche e

{COLUMN 3a}

frasche è fiori, canone boccale di bronzo, che gettava l'acqua.

N . 53. Altro ponte di marmo.

N . 54. Marmo, busto d'un vechio con manto e palla. 5. 7.bre à 20. 8.bre 1755.

N . 55. Riposto, Il famos Trepiede di bronzo, e braciera di sopra, alto pal. 3 $\frac{1}{2}$. diam. pal. 1 $\frac{1}{2}$, coronato con frasche, e i piedi son Satiri nudi, con corni, [e 3] sopra 3. pedagne con foglio d'argento: Statuetta piceiola di un nudo, altra simile con piedestallo e mano alla menta. Monete 5. piccole credute d'argento. Oro, orechino. Argento, mezza luna. Marmo, statuetta, femina con manto. Avorio statuetta consumata, e 5. pezzi di flauto. Creta, Lucerne e Giarro boccale, langelli 2. Pignate 4. Tegami 2. coperchi 4. Vetro, caraffa. Tonica pittata pezzi 29. Stucco verde di coloña. Corniola figura di scarafone. Pitture, doña con manto e mezza luna in testa, e due mezzi bustini di 4. onza. Uomo vestito con testa di cane, e corno nella mano. Uomo \personaggio/ con cornucopia. Doña vestita con cornucopia. Doña da di manggiare al Serpente. Serpenti 2. di 8. palmi, \altro/ di pal. 2. $\frac{2}{3}$. altro di pal. 1. $\frac{3}{4}$. Giugno 13. 1755.

N . 56. Pergolata con pilastri stuccati verde.

N . 57. Marmo statuetta alta 20. onz. di \'un/ giovane nudo ridente con animale dentro del pañiccio; 8.bre 27. 1755.

N . 58. Marmo, statuetta di 3. pal. coll piedestallo \[un]/ giovane nudo con papara e frutte. 7.bre 10. 1755.

N . 59. Marmo Uccello, di onz. 15. con lucerta nel becco. metallo, canoni d'acqua 2., Creta lucerna. 8.bre 20. 1755.

N . 60. Ponte di marmo.

N . 61. Marmo, Statua. di pal. 2. \un/ Giovane sopra

{COLUMN 4}

sopra pedagna lavorata. 9.bre 5. 1755.

N . 62. Piscina coperta con volta, Piombo tubo ò canale pal. 30. $\frac{1}{2}$. in 11. pezzi. Metallo, serratura, lichetto, anelli 5, bottoni 3. Chiavi 3. di fontana, altro di ferro. met. rotondo piastra, cantoni. Creta, tegole 13. canali 6.

{COMPASS}

Maggio 13. 1755.

N . 63. marmo giallo antico, Termine d'i vechio con hellera in testa. Abril. 8. 1755.

N . 64. Termine simile, con corni in testa alto onz. 7. Creta busto rotto, due marmi fini del nichia. Ferro pezzi grossi voltati 3. pal. 4. $\frac{1}{2}$, 2 $\frac{1}{4}$, 2 $\frac{3}{4}$. gross. onz. 4.

N . 65. Pavim: di terra. Marmo, tavola di africão di pal. 3. per pal. 1. $\frac{5}{6}$. gross. onz: 1. Aug. 2. 1755.

{Insert:} # sopra pedagna di piedi di leone

N . 66. Metallo, Statuetta di onze 8. $\frac{1}{2}$. di un fauno vechio, nudo, curiosa figura, con stivali, scarpe, foglj, e papagallo \#/. piatti 2. Grappe 4. anelli 3. chiodi 2. chiodetti 167. coperchio di lucerna con catenella, tondi 4. moneta, peso; Papiri bianchi. Ferro di 18. onze, come Scetro, Serratura con chiavi, pezzi 7, chiodi 7. anelli 3. grappe 2. Vetro, pezzi 20, lacrimatoj 2, coralli 2. bottone 1, piatto in 2. pezzi, vasi rotti 2. in molti pezzi. Creta, langelloni 5. lucerna poca rotta, altra grande, mancha [l] il manigo, coperchi 4. Pignata, giarro, baci\no/[le] poco rotto coll suo perro, giaretto rotto —— Avorio, pezzo di flauto, testa di pesce zestolo, manggiando un pulpo, dentro una conca, cuchiarino, bottoni 2 —— Certi pezzi di colore, pezzi come pasta. Marmo, fracm.to di basso rilievo, come di cavallo, mortaro, strutto ambi. \8.bre 11.à X.bre 24. 1756. [8.bre 11. à]/

N . 67. Creta, Tina di pal. 3 $\frac{1}{2}$. p 2 $\frac{1}{2}$. piena di terra rossa. Pali di ferro 3. di pal. 3 $\frac{1}{4}$. 1 $\frac{3}{4}$. 1 $\frac{5}{12}$. Metallo, moneta, tondo con ferro dentro. Avorio, bottone; Creta vasetto à 2. manigli.

anelletto di ferro con due grappe. 9.bre 27. 1756.

N . 68.   Giallo anticho Termine d'un vec\c/hio, con hellera e fiori in testa. Altra testa di marmo [con] \di giovane/ di statua, con hellera e frutti; Aprile 14. à 23. 1755.

N . 69.   Condotto di acqua, Pergolata di 16 pilastri, cannellati, di marmo, con base e capitello, e delicioso Spasseggio. di ferro, 4. fascie voltate, come cantonale, di 3. $\frac{1}{4}$, e di 2. pal., Ii 1.0 pilastro si e scoperto il 1.0 di Aprile 1755, e principio di scavamento.

N . 70.   Termine di rosso antico, di giovane con frasche, e fiori in testa. Statuetta di creta, d'un vechio nudo, con manto, in dietro fà giarro di bevere. Metallo, anello, e frontizj. \5. à 9. Mayo. 1755./

N . 71.   [Camera scavate da altri.] \Ferro, coltellascio, [cancello] \ferrata,/ chiave, catena; Creta, langellone, caraffa, vasetto.

N : 72.   Camera scavata da altri.

N . 73.   Termine di giallo di un vecchio. Creta, Statuetta, con pedagna rotta, di un vecchio di Priapo, con fascie e caraffino al collo. \12. Maggio. 1755/

N . 74.   Scavato da altri.

N . 75.   Termine di marmo, di vec\c/hio, con frasche, e frutti in testa.

N . 76.   Pergolata del giardino.

N . 77.   Pilastri [della pergolata].

N . 78.   Canale d'acqua al piede delli Pilastri.

N . 79.   Nichio di marmo, giarro da bevere, di creta, [di gi] in forma di statuetta di giovane sedente, nudo, e bocca aperta, e mani al petto.

N . 80.   Monete 3. di Vespasiano, Claudio, e altro Imper.e Vetro, Priapo piccolo. Ferro, cancello. Creta, caraffino, con pedagna rotta, langellone. Avorio, due pezzi di flauto. Marmo braccio piccolo senza diti, 3 triangoli. Metallo, serratu.a piccola.

N . 81.   Corritoio.

N . 82.   Canale \tubo/ di piombo, 5. pezzi, con chiave di metallo. Condotto di creta di pal. 60.

N . 83.   Pavim.to di africano, sarabezza, giallo, pigliato da altri, e da noi trovato il residuo. Pitture, di pal. 6. $\frac{1}{2}$. per 3 $\frac{1}{4}$. di Serpente, gatto mamone \salvatico/, Cocodrillo, ò dragone {In right margin: 276} mangga \divora/ un cupido, altro cupido porge aggiuto, altro sè tira i capelli, papera con altro ani= /animale\ segue alla volta {In lower right margin:} A

{VERSO}

{COLUMN 5}

barca piena di langelli à boccali. Animale, architettura, frasche e fiori. Drago e fiori. Drago pesce e fiori. Cupidi due e pesci. Aprile 14. à 26. 1755. c 25. pezzetti di marmo rosso, e giallo) e con 80. pezzi di marmo bianco delli Bagni.) _____ Pitture, Paese con 5. Palazzi, Scala, e sotto la porta un huomo. Creta, statuetta di un vechio sensa barba; gr metallo, grappa, frontizj 2, piastre 2, e perno. peso di piombo: maggio 26. à 31. 1755. di più Pittura di pal. 4 $\frac{1}{2}$. p 2 $\frac{1}{2}$. Paese Torre di 3. ordini ponte, fenestre, cornice, e di sopra, [ar] vi è un arbore, casa, paese. Creta, lucerne 2. tazzetta. Avorio, filatoio, pezzetto di flauto. i nichi spogliati, in uno era una pedagna di fabrica. metallo, frontizi 2. grappe 5, chiodetti 2. pezzetti di piombo; e di ferro, chiodi 2. Genaro 5. à 31. 1756.

N . 84.   Marmo Tavola sopra 3 zampe e busti di Leone, in mezzo fra i due Pilastri principali.

N . 85.   Creta, Statuetta di una Giovane, che allatta un vechio. maggio 26. à 31. 1755.

[N . 86.   met. monete \co/, pezzetto, come moneta ò medaglia # {In left margin: # coperchio} Avorio 7. pezzi di flauto, fuso, marmo, un corpicello, e pezzetti di statua, strutti. Vetro, bottoni 3., Ferro, Conio, Catenaccio, chiave. Creta, vasetto.]

N . 86.   Met: moneta, coperchio; Avorio, pezzi 7. di flauto, e fuso. Marmo, corpicello, e

altri pezzetti di statua strutta. Vetro 3. bottoni.
Gen.o 24. à 29. 1757.

N . 87. Monete pocco buone 4. di met.
pezzi di flauto 2. di avorio. Pedagna di creta
onze 6. in quadro. Gobba di vetro per giuocho
de giovani.

N . 88. Monete 7 $\frac{1}{2}$., altra molto buona de
Impera.e, al rovesico personaggio con manto,
con la sinistra appoggiò sopra un bastone. pomi
4. di met. Avorio, cuchiurino, pezza di flauto di
6. onz. Feb.o 7. à 19. 1757.

N . 89. Pitture, cupido. Nimfe sedenti con
frasche e fiori. Idolo sopra piedestallo, giarro
con tre piedi, acqua, frasca, \gallinaccio gamina
sopra/ rose

{COLUMN 6}

rose cupido. Cervo. giarro appeso à frasche.
Cupido cornucopia appesa: tre pesci e acqua
\mare con 3. pesci, gallinaccio camina sopra
frasche di rose./ Cervo /corrente\ con palla e
fiori. \altro cervo corre/ 8.bre 13. à 18. 1755.
—— Tubo di piombo pal. 12. $\frac{1}{2}$. in 4. pezzi.
marmo, pessi 2. frascheati di capitello, e due di
piedi di tavola. Metallo, piastra. Pittura di un
mascherone. Giugno 21 à Iulio 3 1756.

N . 90. Pitture, Delfino con fascia, rossa, e
personaggio, che pocco recognosce. Fascia,
long. pal. 6. $\frac{1}{2}$ per 1. di rosso, giallo, verde
intorno di un arbore, # \# e di sopra due fiori
di giallo/ fraschi e fiori \pendendono/. Le-
onessa sedente e vipera, coperchi, frasche fiori,
vaso, piatto, canestro con cornucopia, canestra
con paño, bastone in terra e cinta. Architettura,
3. coloñe, femina vestita sopra la cornice,
arbore, frasche, e fascia rossa intorno. Vasi 2.
Uccello mangia frutto, mascherone con anello
alla bocca. Altro. Tonaca turchina di onz. 10. p
7. di gambero, in terra. Metallo tondi 2. piastre
2. maniglia, braccialetti 5. frontizi di porta, serratura cō lichetto e chiave di ferro. grappe 6. anelli
4. moneta mal conservata. Ferro, chiodi 11. e
pezzo. Marmo, triangolo. Giugno 16. à 21.
1755. [N. 91.] Pitture. Paese con \2/ figurine.
Paese con torri e figurine 5. architettura con

bastone frascheato in mezzo, e fiori al corniscione. Giugno 30. à 3. Iulio. 1755 ——

N . 91. Pitture, Gallo con 2. ziecche.
huomo e femina \cō velo/, nudi e amplesso, e
bastone frascheato nella destra.

N . 92. Gran Pittura di pal. 17. $\frac{3}{4}$. alta pal.
11. Deo con la bocca al braccio della Dea, con
le teste fiorite, architettura, Paesi, frutti,
pasticio, lanterna, Papiro, penna, sigillo con
letter FA XX 44. libro appeso con lettere
{Series of nonsensical scratches} . Stilo di
ferro à scrivere, [lettere] libro con lett. {Series
of nonsensical scratches} . Trippa appesa,
caraffa con lett. ASTCS. Uccelli 5. appesi,
piatto con ova 10, pesci 10, [casacola] \castagna
di/ di mare.

{COLUMN 7}

mare, papare appese; figure 2. paese. Iulio 7. à
12. 1755 —— Paese con pecora e capra.
paese. Vaso di vetro con robba, e tazza con frutti.
Tazza di vetro piena di granate pere, persichi,
uva rossa, al naturale; e fuora, granato cotogno,
[p] uve, vaso, e gallo d'india morto. Arbori fioriti
3. con 2. papare. Giugno 30. à Iulio 5. 1755.
—— Papare 2, animale con bocca [p] aperta,
fiori. Torre, porta, cupido con coda d'asino in
mano, e con la destra in testa, cupido, huomo
con bastone in spalla e pañiere avanti e di di
dietro, fiori; Persona sopra un animale con
bracci[a] apert\i/[a], papara e animale con
bocca aperta, frasche e fiori. Torre, porte e
fenestre con 3. cupidi, due huomini, e Donna
con piatto, cupido con canna di pescare. Si trovò
di ferro, chiodi 2. dente d'animale, 10. pezzi di
corno di cervo, 5. pezzi di marmo cannellato;
langella rotta, di creta. Abrile 28. à maio 3.
—— [Metallo] Alabastro di onze 20. p. 11.
Mattone con lett. ATATI FHILFTI. Vasi 2. di
creta. Metallo, Calameio con inchiostro e
coperchio, Spechio di onze 6 p 3. tondi 3,
manighi 2. anelli 2. Vasetto. Pezzi di flauto 4.
altro pezzo di avorio con pertuso alla punta.
Ferro, coltello raro di sacrifizio, chiave. Piombo,
pezzi 5. lumaca di mare. Iulio 14. à 19. 1755.

N . 93. Cortile grande di mosaico biano.

N . 94. Gabineto con pavim.to di mosaico, e pareti dipinte, negro e verde fascie; \pitture/ architettura, coloñe, rosso di pignuolo, bianco, giallo, cornice, mascherone appeso, frasche, fiori, e due paesi. due altre pareti simili. e altri 3. quadri. Femina con manto e bastone, sotto una porta con architettura, [e] mascherone [a] e due Sirene sopra i cantoni, e altre 2. porte con due mascheroni sopra, e due scimie sopra la cornice, e due bastoni di qua e là con due Sirene, con ombrella sopra la testa, frasche appese di feste. ——— . Simile pittura, la femina con ventaglia nella sinistra, le due scimie con due coloñe in testa, e

{COLUMN 8}

e due delfini, e sopra [il] la cornice due cavalli griffoni, e di qua e la due candelieri con palle, con aquile [ed a]; ——— Porta, architettura e mascherone, e ombrella. Iulio 21. à 26. 1755. è stato disegnato i giorni 4. 6. 8. Augusto. 1755.

N . 95. Pitture, mascherone, e 5. pezzi di tonaca in terra, animale come cocodrillo, fiori, paparella e fiori, figurina, paparella. Metallo, Cantone, anello, frontizio, e chiodo. Iunio 30, à Iulio 5. 1755. ——— Pitture, di testa \faccia/ [con] mascherata con bocca aperta, e o\c/chi spaventosi. Iulio 14. à 19. 1755. ——— Anello di piombo \e 2. pezzi/ altro di metallo, 2 chiodetti e pezzetto di guarnizione, Ferro, frontizo alla moderna, a 5. pezzetti. Agusto 11. à 16. 1755.

N . 96. Pitture, Nassa di pescare con herba, un mazzo di rape, e due di carote. Tre arbori fioriti, due papare e fascia rossa intorno, due cavalli merini à due zampe e coda di delfino, ò serpente ò dragone. Sacrificio di carne, che un huomo taglia, huomo vestito, altro vicino à un toro. Sacrifizio di Pesce assai, con Sacerdote, e suo garzone. Vaso con manichi, Caldaia vicino à un monte. Guigno 23. à 28. 1755. ——— Pitture, Porta e frontispizio di Comedia con femina sedente in mezzo, coperta con velo di à basso, con ruota, alle spalle huomo nudo con

bastonzino, Idolo e piedestallo con 2. bastonzini, altro simile, bastone gettato, piedestallo con 3. Idoli, due arbori e torre, due mascheroni con pelo; sotto queste pitture seque una fascia con 5. mascheroni e 6 figure con ale, piatti, e boccali, erano inchiodate queste pitture dalli antichi. Iulio 14. à 19. 1755.

N . 97. Donna ò Musa \laureata/ con manto, e bastone, e maschera d'uomo nello [mani] \sinistra/ con queste lett. alla pedagna. ΜΕλΤΤΟΜΕ Ν.ΤΤFL.LΙλΙΑΝ. Musa con manto, lauro, arpa e lettere scassate, estinte. Musa sedente con

{COLUMN 9}

{In margin above Column 9: A}

con bastone, lauro, e globo del mondo. Altra con verga e lett. 39 ΑΕΙΑᶜΙΙω Λ ic Λ L an. Altra con lett. ΙΙCΑFΜΝΙΑΜΝΥΟΟΥC. Altra sedente con orec\c/hini con vaso e 6. pieghi di carte dentro. altra carta aperta in mano con lett: ΜΟW.Κ ΛeΙU:Η+. ˥ CTOΡΙ Λ Ν.ΙΙCC.CCΙΙ. ᵛΥΙΙ Ι V.ΙC cai. Altra nuda con manto, sopra piedestallo, con arpa, e mano in testa con frasche e fiori. Altra con fravola e lett. Λ ΜΙΟΙΙΙΙ.ΤΟΙΗΜ. Altra soñado l'arpa con lett. Ρ Λ ΤΤΜΤΙ Λ Ν. Pittura, giarro, arbori, frasche fiori, delfini 4. testa d'uomo appesa; simile e due cavalli marini, tre delfini, e mascherone \appeso/. [argento trovato un colatoio]. Iulio 14. à 19. 1755. Trovato di argento, Colatoio con mani[g]co, moneta. Metallo, moneta, chiave di fonte, Patera rotta, piastra, tondo, pezzetti 5. di porta. Creta, beveratoio, peso, vasetto,. Pietra negra, peso. Iulio 21. à 26. 1755. di più d'argento, moneta,. metallo, moneta, mezzo lichetto, alabastro fiorito di onz. 6. Creta, vaso. Giallo ant: pedagna di un termine. Augusto 4 à 9. 1755.

N . 98. Pavim.o di terra. Ferro: \pali/ Palli di ferro, di pal. 4. e a piede di capra, p. 3.¾. Piccone à due punta\e/, martelli 2, Tenaglia, uncino, accetta \4 con/ [a] 2. punta, \altra à 2. tagli/ piccone, altro à 2. tagli; altro piccolo, coltello rotto in 2. 2. tondi, e [42] \47/ perri. Metallo, piastre 6. pezzo come campanello, pedagna [rot]tonda di vaso, pezzetto di catenella, frontiziotto, piedino di Leone, 4. pezzoti, serratura Intiera con lichetto, vasetto con manico, pezzo di tubo d'acqua, Smoccolatoio, colatoio rotto assai, 4. pezzetti di ramo. Marmo, testa di statua, con fiori, ridente giovane. colonetta, ò pedagna, alt. pal. 2. $\frac{1}{3}$. Un pezzo, di diam. pal. 1., testa come de tigre, alabastro due pezzi, altro di giallo, pedagna piccola, molino di pietra, pezzi di manichi di vaso, pezzo di pietra bianca. Piombo, pezzi piccoli e grandi, e fratumi, 287. pezzo grosso come groppiera di cavallo, turacciolo, piastra grande, pezzi 2. di tubo. Spine particolari iguali 4. di pesce, 4 pezzi come [pecce] \pece/, altro pezzo circa rott: 3. e altri 12. pezzetti. \+/ Creta vaso rotto con 4. coppe d'arena dentro. Vetro, bottone bianco, 2. coralli bottone. Creta, Pezzo di langellone con 5. inscrisz.e MLLGLCNNNJ. WᶜYDT. Γ o2eNꟺ. TOLYXIW. Mattone di 30. onz. quad. con lett: M Λ . Ƨ∕VπD Λ ' M. Vaso. Pitture di onz: 39./34\ p 36. e 42 p 24. prese da altri. \28. Iulio à 9. Aug.o 1755./

N . 99. Pavim.o di Aricho. Metallo chiave di fonte. Marmo, testa di fem: mal cons. Altra di giallo, di vechio con hellera e frascha, manca la mezza barba, ò menta. Alabastro tre guantiere di Caffé, di onz. 21. p 12. grossa onz. 1 rotta in 11. pezzi; e di onz: 10. p 6. in 17 pezzi, mancano 2. e di onz. 10 $\frac{1}{2}$. p 6. in 10. pezzi, Altra di granito verde, di onz. 10. p 7. in 5. pezzi; due pezzi come Sappone bianco, e altri due come cera ò Rebarbara, 12. pezzi di

Pietra negra di altra guantiera di tavola. Iulio 28. à 2. Aug.\1755./

N . 100. Cucina, focolare, e pozzetto. Pezzetto come medaglietta |forsi d'argento.| altra moneta di metallo. Creta un vasetto. di Ferro, un conio Catennacio, e Chiave. Gen.o 24. à Feb.o 25. 1757.

Pianta
di una porzione della Edificj e Strada della
Pompeana
Città anticha sottorranea al rapillo della
Cività
Sita fra Scafati e Torreanunziata
al [fiume]
fiume Sarno
Portici. 1 [marz] di maggio 1757

{Appended below Column 7:}

Di piu si e trovato \moltitudine di/ guarnimenti di \metallo e ferro/ porte [e pe] comuni à tutte le camera [come] come sono i

Di più [si sono ritrovati ritr moltitudine] di guarnimenti [di metallo e ferro] e perri di metallo \di metallo, bronzo/ e ferro, [come sono i] delle porte /comuni à tutte le stanze\ Serrature, {In a column} Chiavi, lichetti, annelli, Chiodi, Chiodetti, frontizi, braccialetti, piastre, cantoni, uncini, grappe, tondi [di] pomi, maniglia, e gran quantità di marmo [di] con qual erano guarnite tutti i bagni, fontane, stuffe, [e no nichi] altre camera e [nich] nicchj i e di tegole, [mattoni] canali mattoni, \e/ coloñette che sostenano i pavimenti delle stuffe

The axonometric plan of the Praedia Iuliae Felicis (MN. ADS 73)

(0.345 m. H × 0.992 m. W)

KEY:

{ } Editor's notes and references to ancient texts

PIANTA A CAVALIERE in veduta di 45 Gr. di elevazione con aspetto diagonale a Sirocco in Figura di Modello di una porzione degli Edificj, e Strada della POMPEIANA Città Sotterranea al Rapillo della CIVITA a 2. migl: verso Pon: da Scafati. 4. Tram: da Castellamare di Stabia. 2. Lev: dalla Torre dell'Annunz.a e 14. Lev. Sir. da Nap: Long: Gr: 32.1.i Latit: Gr: 40.43.i NEL PRINCIPATO CITRA al FIUME SARNO. Strab: Lib: 5. Geogr: {= Strabo 5.4.8 (= C.247)}

N. 1. 2. 3. La condizione di questo Casamento pare abbia segnale di Taverna, situata alla strada della Città; i muri sono con tunica rossa, il piano è di semplice terra senza pavimento, essendosi trovati sedici Cofani di mattone pisto per farlo. L'appoggio del basso muretto, ripara la folla, da comodo di affacciarsi, come nelle botteghe per vendere le merci, e di trattare col passaggiere senza darle ingresso. Li trè gradini lett: A. servono per la comparsa ricca de piatti, come al presente si usa. che promettono l'abbondanza de viveri, prontezza del banchetto, pranzo, e cena. Al che non pare contraria l'Inscrizzione al muro in faccia alla Taverna di là dalla strada al No. 8. INFRA EDIS &c. TABERNAE, PERGVLAE CENACVLA. &c. che si legge nella prima pianta alli stessi numeri, con i Vasi, ed altro ritrovato.

N. 4. Strada lastricata di pietra come in Napoli. Le lastre di questa pietra si chiamano basoli, quasi diminutivo di base, perche sono basi forti, per resistere all'impeto de carri. Sono lunghe e larghe di uno a un $\frac{1}{2}$ palmo, e grosse di $\frac{3}{4}$ a un palmo. Sono, come quelle di Napoli dell'istessa materia vomitata dal Vesuvio, chiamata Lava, che corre a guisa di fiumara che i paesani parim.te chiamano Lava, perche lava le strade, per distinguerla da un fiume perpetuo, e naturale. Questi Basoli sono tagliati a forza dal sasso durissimo di questa Lava Vesuviana, che è quel profluvio di materiale sciolte, e roventi che a guisa di fiume ora soave, ora precipitosa corre sino al mare, e non è altro che terra arenosa, sabbia, e sassi, bruciati e cotti, e resifluidi in questa fornace ardentissima sotterranea onde Virgilio, lib. 1 Georg. v. 472. vidimus undantem ruptis fornacibus Ætnam, flammarumque globos, liquefactaque volvere saxa. {= Verg. *Georgics* 1.471–73 (Mynors)} e Procop: L. 3. de bello Goth. {= Procopius 3.13.22} Dalla cima del Vesuvio Monte, non altrim.te che in Etna suole scaturire in gran copia una materia fluida, infocata, che giunge sin al piano, lo quale scorrende a modo di fiume &c. Questa Lava raffreddata alla vista dell'aria, mancandole le rifuse resta rassodata in durissimo sasso, come fà la materia in una vetriera, ma non diafano come il vetro fuso di materie fine, e uguali, ma opaco per la diversità delle materie rozze, terree e parti eterogenee. Opera questo l'eccessiva veemenza del fuoco, senza bisogno di sali liseiviali, come nel vetro: Come un mattone di terra, continuando a stare nel fuoco diventa vetro rozzo per la causa sudetta. Anche il fuoco veementissimo de specchj ardenti, sperimentato in Firenze nel 1694. vetrifica qualsisia cosa, come pietre, legni, erbe, frutti, drappi, cioccolatte, cascio &c. Giornale Tom: 8. art: 9. pag: 221. {= *Giornale de' Letterati d'Italia* 8 (Venice 1711) 221–309}

N. 5. Il Marciapiede, o grado di alt: di un palmo, lastricato con calce e rapillo, o lapillo che accompagna di quà e là tutta la strada della città.

N. 6. Segue la strada con edificj magnici. Luogo da continuar lo scavo.

N. 7. Porta principale; Ingresso al superbo Portico, e Fontana. In questa architettura non sono Triglifi dorici, ne volute ioniche, ne foglie d'acanto corintie, ma la semplicità dell'ordine Toscano. Il Piedestallo, e Zoccolo è di fabrica dentro terra, sopra il quale comparisce il Plinto di marmo. Il di più è di fabrica di mattoni con stucco rosso. Il vivo della colonna che al tempo del nascimento dell'Architettura era un trave, la di cui sommità per il troppo peso correva rischio di fendersi, gli antichi lo cingevano con un anello di ferro, che in oggi dimostra quel filetto simile al anello coll'astragalo che porta il Capitello, cioè la Gola, e l'altro annello, lo Uvolo, e plinto caricato dall'intavolamento, cioè architrave, fregio, cimassa, gola, corona, gocciolat.jo e sup.ma cim.a.

N. 8. a 16. Camino del Marciapiede avanti le Porte delli Casam.ti con molte Inscriz.ni.

N. 17. Fontana, o Piscina alla parte opposta, che corrisponde à un Tempio al sito T. come abbiamo veduti i Tempj d'Ercolano accompagnati con somiglianti Piscine, per la comodità dell'acqua Lustrale, con la quale i Sacerdoti Custodi (Neoceri, Editui) alla porta del vestibulo aspergavano quelli che entravano, per purificarli. E nei Sacrificj parim.te dell'erbe spargevano l'acqua in onore degli Dei. Teofrast: {= Theophrastus *Characters* 16} Porfir: Erodot: E le Vestali con Giovani, e Figliuole, ornate con Nastri, e corone, lavavano lo spazio scielto dagli Auruspici per l'edificazione del Tempio, con acqua. Tacit: hist: lib: 4. {= Tact. *Hist.* 4.53.10} e così le Piscine erano necessarie vicino al Tempio.

N. 18. a 20. Marciapiede.

N. 21. Taverna o casino; Let: B. Si vede il Focolare a gradino, comodo per girare all'intorno; in C. i gradini per i piatti; I Greci offerivano nei loro sacrificj Torre, farina con sale, frutti, miele, aglio, vino, e dopo l'uso della carne anche gli animale, e tutto ciò che serviva per nutrimento. Usavano spargere il vino (Libatio) con gustarlo gli assistenti, distribuendo tutto i festini, anche nell'elez.ne dei Sacerdoti, e del Sommo Pontefice: Dignità, che per il primo si appropriò Giulio Cesare: e dopo la conferma del Popolo la cerimonia terminava con Festino, e banchetto. Le Taverne adunque non erano inutili vicino al Tempio.

N. 22. Portone, e forse passo dei Carri, o Carozze alla masseria.

N. 23. Anticamere del gran Salone.

N. 24. Salone magnifico tutto dipinto, con pavim.to di mosaico di marmo bianco, e nero: che dà spazioso ingresso al Portico, e Colonnate di marmo con deliziosa prospettiva al Triclinio del No. 90. Altri hanno pigliato 10. Pitture.

N. 25 a 27. Prefurnio senza pavim.to, ne Pitt.re Era il riposto delle legna per la fornace sotto la stuffa N. 42. la di cui bocca è al No. 27. per metter legna alla fornace sotta la stufa med.a Ubi ignis praeclusus aestuat, et praefurnium significat. Phil: Vitr: l.5.c.11.

N. 28. Stanziola di ritiro con banchi di marmo per sedere, per riposo, ò refezzioncola dopo la spasseggio, come Gabinetto.

N. 29. Stufa più riservata, e piccola con mosaico di marmo bianco, e negro, guarnita con nicchi, sedili, e fascie di marmo.

N. 30. Gabinetto ornato di pitture, con Calamaro di Metallo, e forse un Propnigeo, à vini propinatione per rilassam.to dello Spirito con una refezziancola dopo gli esercizj corporali, bagni, e sudazioni, stando vicino al bagno, stufe, e portico. In duplici autem porticu collocentur haec membra &c.. frigidarium..come sarebbe la Fontana, o bagno di piedi nel portico No. 31.) ... ab eoque iter in Propnigeum in versura Porticus proximè autem introrsus e regione frigidarij collocetur concamerata sudatio. V.L.5.C.11. {= Vitr.5.11.2} cioè la Stufa o Laconico alli N.i 29. 41. 42. che sono prossime.

N. 31. Il citata nobilissimo Portico con belle pitture sopra la tunica delle mura. Colonne di fabrica di mattone, e stucco dipinto di rossa, con fontana di marmo in mezzo, le di cui sponde erano alte solam.te un mezzo palmo con piccolo cannone di metallo che gettava acqua. lo spasseggio intorno aveva il pavimento di Mosaico di marmo bianco, e nero, con tre figure curiose con testa, e collo d'uccello, zampe d'animale feroce, e code di Drago. Sopra il Zoccolo girava una fascia di marmo, che guarniva tutto il giro della base del muro. Il Portico si aggiungeva agli edificj degli uomini illustri, per il divertimento, e comodo di spasseggiare sotto gli archi, e tetto fra le colonne riguardati dal Sole, e pioggia. Porticus additae sunt Sacris aedibus, Illustrum Virorum domibus, et publicis aedificijs, necessitatis aut ornamenti, animive causa, sub eis repentinas pluvias vitabant, umbrasq; et frigora captabant, varijsq; sermonibus diem consumebant. à meridie solem hyemeque a Septentrione aestivas umbras excipiebant. Phil. in Vitr: l.5.c.9. Portico adunque s'intende un luogo ameno, e comodo per passeggiare coperto con archi, e cinto intorno di colonne. Le molte tegole trovate in terra sono chiaro indicio, che fosse coperto con quelle.

N. 32. Camera che comunica col Portico No. 31. col Gabinetto del No. 30. colle Stufe de N.i 41. 29. 42. Serviva ancora per Anticamera, e comodità del Bagno del N. 39. per spogliarsi, et entrare nel bagno, e dopo per asciuttarsi, o pure per entrare, et uscire dalle Stufe, per raschiarsi il sudore, e vestirsi. Comunicava ancora col Prato per il passetto N. 38.

N. 33. 34. 35. Si dovrebbe ripigliare lo scoprim.to di questa fabrica, perche quel pezzo che si è scoperto abbastantem.te promette una magnifica riuscita.

N. 36. Colonna di mattone, e stucco rosso, che sarà stata forse Pedagna di qualche Statua, è state diroccata, per questo non si sà la sua altezza.

N. 37. Piccolo Camerino come ritiro, con tre appoggi, o muriccioli per metter tavole per un Letticiuolo.

N. 38. Picolo corritojo Let: M. Comunica colla Fabrica N. 34. la qle quando sara scoperta (mettendo mano) spiegherà l'uso del Camerino appresso il Passetto, o comunicazione delle Case al Prato. N.

N. 39. Per tre gradi di marmo si discende in questo Bagno, caldo, tepido, e freddo secondo il bisogno, di 4. palmi di profondità, con tre finestre guarnite di marmo, e stà vicino al Laconico, o Stufa del No. 41. Laconicum sudationesque sunt coniungendae Tepidario. V.L.5.C.10. {= Vitr. 5.10.5}

Il Canale scoperto, alli N.i 40. 44. 45. e Let: C. nella stufa porta l'acqua calda a questo Bagno, perche il fuoco della Fornace sotto questa e sotto le due Stufe 42. 41. scalda tutta la traccia del Canale; la bocca B. poco distante dal canale vicino a C. con le sue fauci, e voragine della Fornace per dove si mettevano le legna. Si amirerebbe ancora oggi di' tutta nera, e fuliginosa, se non fosse il tutto di nuovo coperto con lo stesso lapillo, e terra. L'acqua del Bagno diventa tepida quando con la chiave di Metallo si serra l'ingresso dell'acqua fredda somministrata dalla Cisterna, o Piscina al No. 62. à la prossima. Più

fredda si farà introducendo l'acqua della prossima citata Fontana 31. aprendo, o serrando nell'arca avanti la porta del Bagno il Sifone di piombo con altra chiave di metallo, o Epistomio delle quali se ne sono trovate molte: Singulis autem canalibus Epistomia sunt inclusa . . . quae manubria cum torquentur ex arca patefaciunt nares in canales L.10.C.13. {= Vitr. 10.8.3} Epistomium aeramentum est, quo ora salientium obrurantur, et laxantur. Budaeus.

N. 40. Canale d'acqua alla scoperta, large pal: 2. e di sopraterra anche pal: 2. Gira la sua traccia in 44. 45. e lett: C. intorno le mura della Stufa, e scaldato dalla fornace di sotto, come s'è detto, porta l'acqua al Bagno 39.

N. 41. Prima Stufa con pavim.to di Mosaico bianco, e nero rappresentante un uomo di pal: 3. $\frac{1}{2}$, nel mezzo, con bastone. Vi si ritrovati ancora 556. Mattoni grandi di Stufa, e tegole, e di sotto il pavimento 28. Colonnette di Creta (le altre sono restate al suo sito) alte onc: 21. diam: 6. che sostenevano il pavim.to in aria formando col suo vacante la Fornace. ed essendo questa stufa la più remota dalla fiamma nella bocca B. sarà la più moderata, e fredda, o come semplice Vaporatorio. Ubi languidius ignis inerrat aedibus, et tenuem volvunt hypocausta vaporem. Papin: l.l. Sylvar. {= Statius Silvae 1.5.58–59} Quell'altra stufa poi al No. 29. è simile ad una piccola Torre . . . ad modum Turriculae concamaratae in hemispherium. Caporal. in V.l.5.C.10. come era la più vicina sarà stata la Tepidaria.

N. 42. La terza Stufa, nella quale la fiamma della Voragine, e Fornace immediate brucciava il pavim.to stesso, senza dubbio era la Calidaria . . . Ahenae supra hypocaustum tria sunt componenda, unum Calidarium, alterum Tepidarium, tertium frigidarium. {= Vitr. 5.10.1} Era con pavim.ti di marmi fini colorati, pigliati da altri, come attestano le reliquie d'Affricano, Giallo, &c. ritrovate. Opportuna comendazione merita l'Architetto di questi Bagni, mentre che secondo Galeno l. 10. meden: doveva, oltre la Camera abstergitoria construrne trè altre; la prima chiamata dal d.o Autore Promalacterion, che disponeva i corpi alla prima mollificazione, e sarà la Tepidaria; la 2.a Lutron, che era la Caldaria, dalla calda andavano alla 3.a più frigida, o frigidaria; e a tutto questo con lodevole sparamio di due terzi ha saputo supplire son una sola camera, come s'è dimostrato, col bagno 39. {= Galen *de simplicium medicamentorum temperamentis ac facultatibus* 9.34 "de atramento sutorio"}

N. 43. Colonna, o Pedagna di una Statua avanti il gran nicchio guarnito di marmo.

N. 44. 45. Il citato Canale del Bagno nutrito dalla Cisterna, o Piscina 62.

N. 46. e 54. 57. 61. Il famoso Bagno, o Piscina in mezzo di quest'Area, con trè Ponti 60. 53. e 52. in mezzo dove era il cannuolo di metallo, che gettava l'acqua in alto. Si vedono intorno i 10. Sedili a. b. c. &c. era profondo pal: 6., il tutto guarnito di marmo. Si poteva passare natando sotto i ponti: Si natare latius, ac tepidius velis in area Piscina est: in proximo Puteus, ex quo possis rursus adstringi, si paeniteat teporis. {= Pliny Ep. 5.6.25} La fontana in mezzo era in luogo del pozzo, e suppliva con acqua fredda. Il canale 45. mediante li sifoni di piombo sotterranei e chiavi, coll'acqua calda.

N. 47. Piano del Giardino con Pilastri di Mattone con stucco verde.

N. 48. 49. Delizioso spasseggio fra Pilastri, e Nicchi sopra i quali appoggiavano i travicelli formando la pergolata come un Portico a Cielo scoperto, adornato con la Verdura della frasche, rami, o viti. Quae erunt sub divo inter porticus adornanda viridibus videntur, quod hypethra ambulationes habent magnam salubritatem. {= Vitr. 5.9.5} Per prova di ciò si sono trovati ancora nella sommità delli Pilastri, e Nicchj i buchi di onc: 4. in circa, in quadro, per mettere i travicelli. In faccia verso Levante comparisce un splendido apparato di dieci Nicchi delli Bagni publici, congiunti come Celle divisorie: gli uni erano quadri, e gli altri tondi, altri erano per gli Uomini, e altri per le femine: erano ornati graziosam.te alla grottesca con Concole di mare, e congelamenti di Sarno, e Mosaici bianchi, neri, e turchini. La Pettorata davanti era un muro stretto alto 4. palmi per il volume, e cassa dell'acqua; questa era lastricata di calce, e lapillo battuto: Balnea erant bina aedificia coniuncta, alterum ubi viri, alterum ubi mulieres publicè lavabantur: come dice Varrone. {= Varro *L.L.* 9.68 (=9.41)} Col che accorda a proposito l'inscriz.e del muro alla strada basolata, accanto alla porta principale. Infra aedis Juliæ &c locantur Balneum &c Pianta Num: 8. onde si vede che erano Bagni publici, che si locavano.

N. 50. Il Bassorilievo di Marmo del Socrate N. 49. della lett: A. di questo Nicchio di mezzo più grande; l'Intercolonio più spazioso, alletta con prospettiva conspicua sin alla Fontana del Ponte 52. nel centro del nobile Bagno di marmo citato. Segue la veduta fin alla tavola di marmo del principale Intercolonio più ampio delli Pilastri di marmo, con dilettevole aspetto sin al bel Seggio con quattro Nicchj, e gran Portone in mezzo al vasto Portico di marmo, e con varj graziosi oggetti dal No. 82. 83. 84. 58. 52. 51. 50. sino a 49.

N. 51. a 54. Il descritto Bagno 46.

N. 55. Il Reposto tutto dipinto. Famoso Tripode di Bronzo. V. Pianta, e 29. pezzi di stucco verdi delli pilastri alli N.i 56. Let. n.

N. 56. Braccio della sud.a Pergolata 47. 48.

N. 57. 58. 59. 60. 61. L'istesso Bagno 46.

N. 62. Cisterna lamiata con Volta: provvede l'acqua al Canale 45. e al 63. e 69.

N. 63. Sedici Pilastri di marmo con Capitello dell' Ordine Dorico e foglie d'Olive alte palmi 11. onc: 4. che col muro de N.i 64. 70. 79. z. forma il Portico con tetto, al quale dalla Strada basolata, dalla parte del Settentrione si entra per il Portone 12. 13. passando per il Salone 24. passeggiando fra i Pilastri, e Facciata sin alla Testa del Portico in x z dove si discende per trè gradi di marmo al Triclinio 90. 93. magnifico per la sua ampiezza, superbo veduta per tutto il Portico o Xisto (Xistos vocant Porticus tectas) sin alla Strada 12. 13. verso Settentrione; Portone, e Finestra 92. guarnita di marmo, che diverte l'occhio verso il Prato a Levante, P. In cornu Porticus amplissimum Cubiculum a Triclinio occurrit, aliis fenestri Xistum, aliis dispicit Pratum. Plin. Jun. l.s. ep. ad. Apoll. {= Pliny *Ep.* 5.6.23} è splendido per il suo Pavimento di Mosaico bianco, per la quantità delle Pitture, e per il comodo della Cucina al N. 100.

N. 64. Nicchio guarnito di marmo come tutti gli altri di questa facciata 68. 70. 73. 75. 76. 79. 85. sino alla let: z. del Portico il di cui piano è di semplice terra e per consequenza atto alli Giochi ed esercizj Corporali delli Palestrite.

N. 65. Camerina senza Pavim.to di semplice terra.

N. 66. Finestra al Passaggio.

N. 67. Ponendosi nelle Case trè triclinij, il primo l' Invernale, il 2.do il Vernale, il 3.o l'estiva adattati ogn'uno secondo l'aspetto, e tempo dell'uso, questo sarà Triclinio invernale per il lume che tiene al Ponente: ideo quod Vespertino lumine opus est uti. l.5.c.7. {= Vitr. 6.4.1}

N. 68. Vide 63. 64.

N. 69. Canale di Piperno d'acqua a scoperto per la comodità delli Palestrite nella Palestra, o Portico.

N. 70. Vide 68.

N. 71. 72. Camerette.

N. 73. Vide 68.

N. 74. Camera.

N. 75. Vide 68.

N. 76. V. 68.

N. 77. 78. Vide 69.

N. 79. Vid. 68.

N. 80. Camera.

N. 81. Corritoio.

N. 82. Gradini.

N. 83. Triclinio Vernale, e Autunnale per il lume a Levante, mentre che passando il Sole da Levante a Ponente fa il Triclinio temperato. Cum enim praetenta luminibus adversus solis impetus progrediens ad Occidentem efficit ea tempestata. {= Vitr. 6.4.2} Il Pavim.to di Affricano, Giallo, e Seravezza è stato pigliato da altri.

N. 84. Seggio del Portico con Tavola di marmo.

N. 85. V. 68.

N. 86. 87. 88. 89. Camere.

N. 90. Il sudetto Triclinio estivo per il lume al Portico, e Settentrione essendo avverso del Corso del Sole si rende fresco, sano, e delizioso: Quod ea regio (Septentrio) eo quod est aversa a Solis cursu semper refrigerata, et salubritatem, et voluptatem in usu praestat. L.5.c.7. {= Vitr. 6.4.2}

N. 91. 92. Camere al Triclinio, e Prato.

N. 93. V. 90.

N. 94. Gabinetto.

N. 95. 96. V. 90.

N. 97. 98. 99. Camere.

N. 100. Cucina.

Portici 1.o Aprile 1755 al mese di Marzo li 30. 1757. Carlo Weber.

APPENDIX THREE

Weber's monograph on the Villa di San Marco, Stabiae

(Library of the Soprintendenza Archeologica di Napoli e Caserta, XXI.A.34)

The complete text of this manuscript is reproduced here, except for words and phrases in the margins that were intended to highlight the text and to serve as indices. Many of the notes are cross-references to other sections of the text and to Weber's notes, given by folio or page, column, and line number. The transcription is diplomatic, though some words have been completed to aid in comprehension; others could not be properly deciphered.

KEY:

{ }   = Marginalia; often refer to other marginalia by folio and column number

[ ]   = Additional annotations to the marginal notes

⟨ ⟩   = Correction or erasure

I.M.   = In margin

Italics   = Inserted in Weber's hand

[TITLE PAGE]

Le Piante di Alcvni Edificj Sotterranei delle Città di Stabia, Pompeiana ed Hercolana con le Pitture, Statve, Monete, Vasi, ed Altri Monvmenti situati nelle Tavole, che indicano i luoghi dove si sono ritrovati. Con un succinto ricordo della serie degli anni degli Incendj Vesuviani dal tempo di Abramo sino al 1760 di G.C. come causa delle ruine delle antiche città e altre. Tomo III.

[Fol. 1]

TOMO TERZO
ANTICA STABIA

TAVOLA I

In questa prima Tavola si osserva l'Iconografia e vestigij di una porzione dell' antica Stabia, situata nel Principato citra e n[ost]ro Cratere di Napoli della Campagna Felice {**a**: Plin: Peregrin:} distante da Castellamare verso Levante {**b**: Solanus Est.} un miglio, e da Napoli verso Sirocco {**c**: Eurus Sud-est [*Tom. I. Cratere, dalla lanterna alla Barano*]} 16 miglia. Long. del 1° Meridiano dell' Isola del Ferro grad. 32. Lat. settentrionale grad. 40,40′. Fu distrutta in tempo del Consolato di Cn. Pompeo, e di L. Catone l'ultimo d'Aprile, e ridotta in un semplice villaggio {**d**: Plin. lib: 3. Cap: 5} da L. Cornelio Silla (il fortunato) [Fol. 2: Tavola I] famoso Console e Dittatore Romano, che dopo molte gloriose Vittorie si ritirò à Cuma, dove morì in età di 60. anni e 78. avanti G.C. Questi fù ancora amante di scienze, superò Atene, e ricuperò i libri d'Aristotele. L'istessa Stabbia poi è stata rovesciata dallo Scuotimento di terra, come ancora la Città Pompeiana al fiume Sarno {**a**: Strab. lib. 5. Geogr.} <u>Pompeam praeterfluebat,</u> vicino alla Torre Annunziata {**b**: Seneca} in tempo di Nerone; e successivam[en]te coperta dalli lapilli, e ceneri infocate del Monte Vesuvio, regnando Vespasiano. {**c**: Plin.} La Stabbia era celebre per le fontane {**d**: Colum:

296

lib: 10 v. 139.} Fontibus, et Stabiae celebres, et Vesuia rura. {n: *Sicome sono li nichi di fonti Tav. II. e III. nelli rami*} Delle Stabbiane vacche il latte si usava ne medicamenti. {e: Galien. lib. 5. Meth. Med. et Symac. lib. 6 Ep. 17.} [**Fol. 3: Antica Stabia**] Simili rovine ha provata anche l'Ercolano, la quale dopo esser stata rovinata dal terremoto, è ristaurata poi da Vespasiano fù di nuovo distrutta dagli incendj del Vesuvio, e coperta di cenere, e lava di fuoco, il che attesta l'Inscriz[io]ne trovata in un Tempio à Resina. {a: Mese di Lug[li]o 1757 di marmo long. Pal. 12. $\frac{1}{2}$. larg. 2. $\frac{1}{3}$. al Museo}

IMP.CAESAR.VESPASIANVS.AVG.PONTIF.MAX.

TRIB.POT.VII.IMP.XVII.P.P.

COS.VII.DESIGN.VIII.

TEMPLVM.MATRIS.DEVM.TERRAE.MOTV.

CONLAPSAM.RESTITVIT.

Presentemente nelli Scavi di Resina quel Tempio si è trovato di nuovo distrutto, e i legnami ridotti in Carbone, {**b**: Tav. CL *pianta del Tempio d'Ercolano fol. 35*} e coperto dalla terra di fuoco. Fra gli altri Edificj di questa Pianta {**c**: Tav. I. Let. H. N. 15.} pare il più meritevole la gran Piazza[1] ornata con esquisita magnificenza nel frontispizio di dentro con Nicchi {**d**: Tav. I. N. 5. 6. *sono Fontane. Tav. II. e III. nel rame*} e di Figure di basso rilievo [**Fol. 4: Tavola I**] di stucco e di mosaico[2] e con superbo Peristilio {**a**: Le Colonne} con Portici vicini[3] al quale da ingresso la via pubblica {**b**: Tav. I. Let. H. N.o 17} dalla parte di Occidente, con le vestigia di un' altra Area {**c**: Tav. I. Let. H. N.o 11. 12. 13. 14.} che si suppone Palestra o Ambolacro[4] e tornando alla nostra Piazza compariscono li celebri Nicchi con le Colonne {**d**: Tav. I. N.o 5. 6. Tav. II. in grande. *il rame.*} incrostate di lapilli in forma di dadi, di composizione, o mistura vitrea di tutte sorti di colori, rappresentati in Mosaico una bellissima Pittura {**f**: Tav. II. il rame.} d'una donna sopra [**Fol. 5: Antica Stabia**] un bove in acqua.[5] Dall'altra parte un simile nicchio {**a**: Tav. I. Let. H. N. 5} ugualmente eccellente per la splendidezza dell' opera di mosaico, che rappresenta

un huomo giovane à cavallo d'una Ariete, o Montone {**b**: Tav. III} con donna caduta pure in acqua,[6] li quali ambi conservano nel Real Museo. Nell' altra nicchia, si è trovato un quadro di basso rilievo di stucco {**c**: Tav. I. N. 5. Let. H.} che contiene un huomo, che in una mano have un cerchio, {**d**: Tav. IV.} e nell' altra una palma, sarà dunque stato un giocatore di palestra.[7] In dietro delli descritti nicchi di [**Fol. 6: Tavola I**] quella superba facciata, o frontispizio si osserva, come un corridojo al quale si entra per un grande portone, dell' istesso frontispizio, {**a**: Tav. I. Let. H. n.o 7.} e dopo si vede immediatamête un cammerino {**b**: Ibid; N. 4.} di ritiro, d'onde si esce alla deliziosa veduta d'un spasseggio vagamente ornato, con una graziosa pilastrata {**c**: ibid.} di fabbrica con mattoni e stucco.[8] Nel descritto corridojo alla sinis-[**Fol. 7: Stabia**]tra in un angolo d'una porta picciola {**a**: Tav. I. Let. H. N. 3.} si e incontrato il grande vaso di marmo {**b**: Tav. V.} bianco, famoso per la sua scoltura di basso rilievo, che con nove personaggi d'huomini, Sacerdote e femine con suoni, si puol credere che significasse una Festa.[9] Alli laterali della dritta e sinistra li cammerini {**c**: Tav. I. Let. H. N. 2——8.} erano con pitture {**d**: *VI. Tav. e sequenti.*} a toneca[10] le quali si spiegaranno [**Fol. 8: Tavola I**] nelle loro corrisponde tavole; e considerando la sudetta piazza, si osserva verso il greco {**a**: Tav. I. Let. G. N. 1. a 25.} un edificio di molte camere, cortile grande, bagno, chiostro, portici ed altri comodi {**b**: ibid: N. 1. a 16.} di maniera tale, che somiglia ad una casa greca.[11] Dalla parte di levante {**c**: ibid. let. F. n. 1. à 13.} siguono molte altre abitazioni e camere {**d**: ibid. let: G. n. 1. a 25.} ornate con quantità di [**Fol. 9: Stabia**] pitture da descriversi, ogni una nel suo luogo, e tavola: e fra mezzo vi e situato un piano {**a**: *Tav. I. Let. G. n. 1. à 16.*} senza pavimento, guarnito con portici di pilastri con fabrica di mattoni, e stucco; perlocche supponesi che questo piano abbia servito per uso di giardino {*b:* fol. 3. in not. colon. 1. lin. 12. hîc. Vitr. lib. 6. cap. 5. 6. cf. hîc. colon. 6. et. 1. cf. fol. 3. colon. 1. lin. 8.} o Pergola.[12] [**Fol. 9** verso: **Tavola I:**] Continua la spiegazione delle altre lettere rimanenti F.E.D.C.B.A. di questa Pianta, ò Tav. I.

[Fol. 10]

TOMO TERZO
MOSAICO D'EUROPA

TAVOLA II

Comparisce in questa seconda tavola il famoso nicchio, {**a:** Tav. I. Let: H. N. 6. sito nella Pianta.} con due colonne laterali, il tutto guarnito e vestito con certi lapilli quadri in figura **[Fol. 11: Tavola II]** di dadi, e sono di côposizione somigliante al vetro, però coloriti diversamente, posti con una ordinazione tale, che compogono con ogni perfezione dell' arte una pittura di cui lavoro si chiama mosaico;[1] e figura, cotesto disegno una Princi-**[Fol. 12: Mosaico d'Europa]**pessa giovane á cavallo sopra un Toro, che senza dubio significa la Europa, trasportata per mare in Creta da Giove, innamorato in essa, e perciò mutatosi in Toro.[2]

[Fol. 13]

TOMO TERZO
MOSAICO DI FRISO

TAVOLA III

Quest' altro nicchio, che si vede, è compagno all' antecedente, situato à mano dritta {**a:** Tav. I. Let. H. N. 5.} contiene una simile pittura in mosaico,[1] rappresendando un Prin-**[Fol. 14: Tavola III]**cipe {**a:** Heroe.} giovane á cavallo d'un Ariete ó Montone, con donna caduta in acqua, che sara Friso, ed Helle sua sorella.[2] E non ostante, che della testa del Friso **[Fol. 15: Friso]** se trovò per le rovine caduto il mosaico, per ciò mal concia la pittura, sorte, che altre ancora hanno sofferta, {**a:** *Tom. I. fol. 2. 11. num. 1. nel testo.*} non rendesi la spiegazione malagevole.[3] Queste **[Fol. 16: Tavola III]** rovine della Stabia {*1: Dione non parla della Stabia, essendo prima ridotta in simplice villaggio da Silla:*

Tav. I. fol. 1. nel testo. e sarà compressa nelle vicinanze del Vesuvio: ut omnis tegeretur Regio. come detto.} e delle due antiche città, la Hercolana, e Pompeiana sono stati funesti effetti delli terramoti e orribili incendj, ed eruzzioni delli fiu-**[Fol. 17: Friso]**mi infocati, seu lave, e altri torrenti d'acqua calda e terra, cio è, fiume di fango; come dalli ceneri, lapilli, sassi, bitume, e altro del Vesuvio in diversi tempi; Ed **[Fol. 18: Tavola III]** investigando quelli, avanti la Nascita di G.C., si trova, che sin dal tempo d'Abrahamo |:che nacque l'anno 1996 {**a:** avanti G.C.}:| e forsi primá {**b:** Fabio Giordano dice: ab initio conflagrasse ut in nota n. 4.} cominciarono questi incendj: Il secondo poi l'anno 1787. avan[ti] G.C. in tempo di Aralio Rè degl' Assyrj; Successivamente di quelli doppo la Venuta di G.C., Il primo accade l'año 65., in tempo di Nerone Imper[atore] Rom[ano], con terramoto, che rovino parte della città Pompeiana, e parte del Borgo Ercolano: {**c:** fol. 15. in nota. coloña 2. in ultim.} Però il più portentoso fù l'anno 81. {**d:** *in tempo di Tito. Plin. Iun. lib. 6. ep. 16. Suet. in Tit. cap. 9. zon. p. 2. de Tib. lib. 2. vide in hac nota n. 4. fol. 16. colon. 3. in fine, et fol. 17. colon. 1. in fine*} che distrusse e abbrucciò per intiero la città Ercolano, Pompeiana {**c:** *Mentre il popolo sedeva nel teatro; ut in nota. n. 4. sol. ant. colon. 1. in fine.*} e tutti i luoghi adiacenti, come se ha visto nella Stabia.[4] Altri **[Fol. 19: Incendio del Vesvvio]** incendj seguirono l'añi 202, à tempo di Severo {**a:** Xiphilin. in Severo.} Per eos dies resplenduit in monte Vesuvio ignis maximus. . . . . e 305. di Diocletiano {**b:** Maiolo dier. canic. lib. I. coll. 16. pag. 284.} Omnem ferè Europam suis cineribus attigerat año Domini 305. alius deinde fuit emissus ignis Europam feré totam, pulvere contegens año Dom. 471. ùt scribit Marcellinus comes: che fú il giorno 6. di 9.bre {**c:** Euseb. in chron. in Suet. e Sext. Arnot. Beroald. Engen. neap. sacr. fol. 609. et plurimi}, e durò quatro añi continui, dalli 6. di 9.bre 471. sin al mese di Marzo 474. {**d:** *in nota n. 5. fol. 17. colon. 2.*} l'altra eruzione poi dell' año 512. fù cosi deplorabile, che li torrenti fangosi, ed arenosi con impeto fervente come fiumi, inondavano tutto, tanto che inalzavano i piani delli campi sin alla cima dell' alberi, e relassò il Rè {e: Teodorico Re d'Italia.} i tributi.[5] L'anno [Fol. 20: Tavola III] 538 al tempo del Re Teodoro se ha visto un altro. {a: Capaccio hist. Nap. lib. 2. c. 8.} *antea ea tempora queq*[ue] conflagrasse videtur iñuere Procopius lib. 6. c. 4., cum Belisarius Neapolim cepisset. . . . Di quel' altro del an. 685. d'essere prima nel mese di genaro apparita de notte al Cielo sereno una Stella oscurissima, dice Sigonio, e nel mese di Febraro; a mezzo giorno, nel ponente, una altra di gran splendore verso Levante. E quando fù quello del an. 993. s'incendio la Città e Vaticano di Roma, come per tutta Italia e Francia furono abbrucciate molte citta. Memorabili ancora sono quelli dell' anni 1036. 1049. quando li fiumi di fuoco ò lave correvano sin à dentro del mare. Replicorono simili eruzzioni l'añi. 1138. 1139. 1550 |:e 1504. il diluvio a Nola:| e [Fol. 21: Incendio del Vesvvio] 1538. l'incendio à Pozzuoli. El' año 1619. il Medico Magliocco con due P.P. Camaldolesi di S. Angelo |:sotto il Vesuvio:| sono calati dentro la sua voragine, e per il camino hano trovato, del alberi cresiuti {a: *Schott. in itin. Ital. lib. 3 pag. 611 del Pighio.*}, e nel fondo tre bagni d'acqua, salata, bituminosa, e nitrosa, e fistole, per dove usciva vento fredo e gagliardo, con fischio.[6] Nel Secolo passato l'ano 31. accade il terribilissimo, e funesto incendio, con orribili terremoti, tanto, ⟨che⟩, li antenati viventi in quel tempo, per vincolo, e tenerezza d'amore verso li descendenti, e prossimi, furono comossi à lasciare, alli Posteri una memoria e serioso avertimento nel presente Epitaffio di Portici.[7] A' questi spetacoli pre-[Fol. 22: Tavola III] precedettero sei giorni prima alcuni segni, come fortissimi rumori, e scuotimenti sotterranei, con intorbidarsi li pozzi senza aver piovuto, e con mancare del' acqua in altri; ed appari sopra il Vesuvio una Stella di straordinaria grandezza, di più come un trave di fuoco; nel spazio di sette ore si contó cinquanta gagliardi terremoti, la Montagna apri molte bocche, usci una tetra infocata nuvola straordinaria, come una torre, si alzo in aria con incredibile elevazione, con terrore di tutti, con fiame, strepiti, e terremoti.[8] La puzza di zolfo, quasi soffocava la gente, li scuotimenti in Napoli [Fol. 23: Incendio del Vesvvio] fecero crollare le case con gran spavento, che si accrebbe per li prodigiosi strepiti in aria, come bombarde, e dalli fulgori, densi vapori, lampi, rimbombi, e dalla pioggia delle pietre, lapilli, arene, ceneri, le quali in terra caduti, se alzarono in alcuni parti in un tratto più di dodeci palmi; e si dilatarono per tutto il Regno, e sin à Sardegna, Toscana, anche à Constantinopoli; Si oscuro il Sole, che in alcuni luoghi fece notte continua, e come in una stanza serrata, senza lucerna.[9] Alla Rochetta 15. mil. distante si apri un monte, ed in alcuni parti caddero le chiese: In Napoli era [Fol. 24: Tavola III] tanto il timore, che anche quelli, che non si coñoscevano, se licenziarono come fratelli carnali per l'altra vita, facendo conto, di essere quella la ultima e perpetua notte, e si confessava in publico, per mancanza di Confessori. Il giorno 16. {a: X.bre} à 8. ore versavano dalla voragine materie liquide, come fango infocato, composto d'acqua, terra, arena, cenere, pietre infocate, alberi ardenti |:che rapi per la via:| solfo liquefatto, e bitume, tutto mescolato, che con grandissimi torrenti rapidame[n]te, allagarono tut[t]o l'atrio, Ottaiano, Soma, Nola, S. Elmo, Saviano Marigliano, Cicciano, Cisterna, Trochia, Pollena, S. Bastiano, Torre-[Fol. 25: Incendj del Vesvvio]nunziata, – Greco, Resina, Granatelo, S. Iorio à Cremano, Pietrabiancha, e tutti altri contorni, con indicibile daño, avendo non solamente rapiti molti huomini, e distrutte, e atterrate, e somerse molte case, e Paesi, e masserie, ma ancora portati li via sin dentro del mare; Il mare si ritiro per il Spazio di circa un miglio per il lido del Cratere, Ischia, Sorento, &. cosi subito, che in Napoli restarono quasi in secco le Navi {a: *Pelago influente pariet: Epitaf: di Portici fol. 23 v. 12.*}; Un Straordinario Terremoto, fece ballar le botte in un basso di 95. gradi sotterraneo.[10] Le pietre grosse rovinarono le case con la caduta sin à Avelino, Tripalda, e altri luoghi: [Fol. 26: Tavola III] Se stima il daño aver passato il valore di 25. miglioni di duc[ati]. Queste rovine poserò tante migliaia di persone in gran necessita. La deputazione non lasciò di soccorrere al bisogno, e in un giorno si alimentarono in S. Genaro 1500., e nella Madona del Arco 5000. persone: Alli 5. di Febraro se ne senti un altro terribilissimo terremoto, con tuoni, fulgori, baleni orribilissimi, e grossissimi grandini: Il fuoco di questi Torrenti fece un effetto somigliante à quello de folgori, se pure non era tutt' uno, e di una istessa materia; il che fa credere [Fol. 27: Incendj del Vesvvio] ancora quello, che nella casa di Dn. Flaminio di Constanzo accade, à Cremano, che passando le ceneri infocate, e lengua di fuoco sopra la paglia, la lasciarono intata, e entrando nella seconda stanza consumò quanto vi era; Molti huomini morti nelle ceneri, parevano vivi, e toccandoli, se trovarono inceneriti; e altri senza aver patito li vestiti; furono rovinati molti Paesi; le campagne somerse, perirono li animali di fame; alla fine fù risvegliato in tutti il timore della morte, e fecero publica penitenza; con amore fraterno {a: fol. 23. coloña 2. lin. 17.} fra l'oro.[11] ⟨HAND CHANGES HERE⟩ L'accensione del' año 1660 fu poco considerabile. Pero gl' altri à 1682. —85. [Fol. 28: Tavola III] —89. erano terribili, e più quello di —94. per le orribili fiame, per le tempestose pioggie di sassi, e pomici infocati, di ceneri, e per l'oscurazione del Sole, rimbombi, tuoni, fulgori per aria, puzza suffocante del solfo, e terremoti. Le sussequenti Incendj, à 1696, —97 nel febraro, e 97 nel Agusto, e 97 del 9.bre à Genaro —98., e 98 nel Maggio à Giugno, e 1701 del Luglio solamente fecero qualche fiume o lava di fuoco. Il più orribile di tutti altri cominciò à 26. Luglio 1707, e continuò con gran terrore sino à 2. Agusto, quando il diluvio della cenere tanto scarigava, che in Napoli à 22. ore fù necessario caminare con gli torchi accesi, che poco lume rendevano, per la densità delle tenebre, fatte palpabili per la [Fol. 29: Incendj del Vesvvio] Spessezza delle ceneri; Leggasi

l'incendio del' año 1631 {a: fol. 21. num. 7 et seq. in text. et not.} al quale era simile, reservandosi solamente, che non si allagarono li Paesi, ni perirono la gente. Stepitosa fù l'accensione del 1730. per l'eccessiva altezza, che salivano le fiame: e per li sette sussequenti añi, il Vesuvio mai è stato essente di fuoco ò fumo. Nel 14. Maggio 1737, con più veèmenza accrebbe la eruzzione, à tempestare con diluvio di sassi, è pomici infocati, con gorgoglio, fiumi ardenti, fumo e fuoco, che ingombrava tutto il Monte; fulmini, fragore per aria, e terremoti, in sino à 6. Giugno; doppo usciva fumo, e talora fiama, sino à 1751, quando di nuovo con torrenti infocati continuo infino al año 1760, con nuove crepature ogni año, per dove scaturivano.[12]

[Fol. 32]

TOMO III

BASSO RILIEVO DI STUCCO DI UN PALESTRITA

Si osserva in questa Tavola un bel pezzo di Bassorilievo di Stucco, che rappresenta un uomo nudo con cerchio e palma &c.[1]

[Fol. 34]

TOMO III

TAVOLA V.

Si spiega il vaso grande grande {a: di marmo alto. pal. 3. —onz. 3.} di basso rilievo con 9 personaggi in festa {b: fol. 6. num. 9. in nota. et in textu lin. 6. e 7. et fol. 5. num. 7. in nota.} trovato nelli scavi di Stabia, fra Gragnano e Castellamare à 8. Aprile 1752. {c: Pianta. Tav. I. Lett. H. num. 3.} Poi la struttura particolare della Tavola di marmo à tre piedi, con busti e teste di Leone e con le lettere C.A.R. sopra l'istesse teste {d: fol. 5. num. 8. – fol. 2. colon. 1. lin. 14. in nota..} trovata li 19. Aprile 1753. nel Portone fra li nichi del Friso ed Europa nella gran Piazza {e: Pianta. Lett. H. num. 5. 6. 7.}. E si dice qualche cosa della Tegola con la stampa **NARCISSI. AVGVSTI. INVSTIS.**

LVISELLI. trovata li 7. 8.bre 1754. {f: pianta. Tav. I. Lett. G. num. 16.} E delle altre tegole, che inferiscono li spassegi, palestre, e altri edifici coperti, ò no, e l'uso de medemi. {g: fol. 3. colon. 2. Lett. n. in not. et pianta Tav. I. Lett. H. num. 11.} Si parla del Capitello e delli ordini d'Architectura {h: fol. 4. colon. 2. lin. 1. in nota.}, trovati nelle cittá sotterranee antiche.

TAVOLA VI.

Si vedono nelle sei sequenti, una doppo l'altra, ciò é nella settima Tavola, uno de i più belli pavimenti di Mosaico, e nelle altre cinque, le pitture trovate insieme {i: Pianta. Tav. I. Lett. H. num. 2. fol. 9. à 10. et fol. 2. num. 3 delli mosaici. in not.} v.g. la Doña sedente con una mano sopra il ginocchio, e nell' altra un specchio di pal. 2.$\frac{1}{2}$. in quadro, trovata à 7. Agusto 1752. {See Giornale, 309 (August 13, 1752)} vicino ancora alla gran Piazza {(r): in questa Tav. VI.}: qual pittura non e contraria à quello, che si dice delli Emboli. {l: fol. 6. col. 2. lin. i.}

TAVOLA VII.

Uno delli più belli pavimenti di Mosaico. {m: fol. 2. num. 2. in nota.} {See Stabiae, 102–3, with fig. (August 9, 1759)}

TAVOLA VIII.
è sequenti sin alla XI.

le altre pitture {n: fol. 6. num. 10. col. 2. in nota, in b.} trovate ancora intorno la gran piazza {o: pianta. Tav. I. Lett. H. num. 8.}, e le lucerne, vasi, monete, e tutto altro; quali cose con quest' ordine si potraño riscontrare, ed osservare nel Real Museo con la guida delle Piante e Registri, che distinguirano il tempo e luogo, dove si sono ritrovati.

TAVOLA XII.

Le altre pitture v.g. la Venere con la serva, grande di 19. per 18. onze, e le altre, tutte trovate vicino al bagno {p: Pianta. Tav. I. lett. G. num. 18. a 25.} 11. 7.bre 1751. il banco di marmo con piedi di Leone {q: ibid. num. 21.} trovato 13 7.bre 1751. {See Stabiae, 14–15

(September 7 to 18, 1751)} Il raschiadore {r: ibid. num. 20} trovato à 3. Genaro 1752. {See Stabiae, 19 (January 3, 1752)} Poi la Lucerna con la parola AVFRON. e le due monete di bronzo della CRISPINA {s: ibid. lett. H. num. 16.} trovate 30. Gen.o 1754. {See Stabiae, 26 (February 3, 1754)} e sequita, v.g. sin alla TAVOLA. XIX.

TAVOLA XX.

La Statua del Mercurio di bronzo {t: alta pal. 3.} trovata nella casa greca {v: pianta. Tav. I. lett. G. nû. 13.} à 13. luglio. 1751, con un candeliere di bronzo, vestito d'argento {x: alto. 5. pal.} con un corvo di bronzo al naturale {z: ibid. num. 14. fol. 8. num. 12. in nota.} nell' istesso sito, il peso di piombo {n: fol. 9. colon. 1. in nota. corrisponde la statua con quello, che è stato detto. fol. 8. colon. 2. lin. 17.} di circa 2. lib. con le parole EME. HABEBIS. trovato à 7. Giugno 1751. e tutt' altro sin àlla TAVOLA XXIX.

TAVOLA XXX.

A' proposito, concordano il calamaro e 7. vasi di metallo con medicamenti dentro, trovati vicino al Bagno ò Piscina {m: Pianta. Tav. I. Lett. F. ñ. 5.} nella camera {n: ibid. num. 8.} con due Stucci di chirurgia {f: ibid. num. 9.} uno con tre Instrumenti per mettere unguento nelli empiastri; l'altro con certe pinzette, e tre altri instrumenti, per mettere unguento nelle ferite; di questo bagno dunque averaño fatto uso per la curazione della salute {((a): è infermita.) a: fogl. 9. colon. 2. lin. 10.}. Sono stati trovati à 4. di Gen.o 1751. Nelle sequente Tavole se metterá, fra altri monumenti Il famoso Cameo di basso rilievo bianco, e fondo cristallino, molto grande cerca 2. onze, trovato à 9. Iulio 1755. {b: Pianta. Tav. I. lett. D. num. 2.}

Nel luogo corrispondente non disdice qualche disegno del Vesuvio {(m): v.g. Tav. ⟨L⟩ XL}; come quello del 1631., quando tutti Paesi vicini erano allagati {c: fol. 24. lin. 4. in textu.} e dell'año 1707. ——37—— e qualche d'un altro il più antico, che si possa trovare, e quello d'oggi di, per sodisfare gli curiosi foristieri, del tutto, e varie cose; secondo il Proverbio: Varia delectant; Procedendo coll' ordine della Pianta, sin a tanto sia descritta ogni cosa, che si è trovato in questa prima Pianta; della quale sola resultarà questo Terzo Tomo ricco più di 150. Tavole; {d: fol. 35. sequente.} Contiene questa prima Pianta tre masserie; cio è, quella di Sanzone, Soma, e Comparato, ed è la più grande, a la più ricca de monumenti:

Le altre due Piante, pure della Stabia, tutti due insieme formaraño un altro Tomo, di circa 50. Tavole; una, e della Masseria de' Gesuvite, e l'altra de Iracci.

Con le Piante della Civitá alla Torre Añunziata, si formara⟨no⟩ almeno 2. Tomi grossi. e con quelle d'Ercolano, altri 2. Tomi; fra tanto si avanzarano li Scavi, e si formaraño altre Piante, ed altri Tomi; si puole dire, quasi in infinitum; Conviene di procurare, à formare la Pianta Intiera del tutto. Il corpo del Ercolano, cosi della Civitá {(e): Pompeia}, cosi della Stabia, ancora che si debba per questa fine alle volta scavare, dove gia si è scavato, senza speranza di trovare altro in quel sito, peró di mano in mano scavando con questo ordine, per intermezzo sempre si trova porzioni non scavati; Si averà il piacere, di trovare tutto quello che ci sta; e si lasciarà nissun palmo che non si veda; ⟨Cosi⟩ si potrà formare le piante per intiero, ⟨il⟩ che ne sarà una gran sotisfazione, aver tutte queste antiche Città in Pianta con la Spiegazione delli Edificij e delli monumenti trovati dentro, casa per casa, con la distinzion del luogho, Tempo, e misura. Cosi nella Masseria Iracci, conviene continuar con tutta la Gente alla Civitá, dove alli 10. di Luglio dell' a[ñ]o corr[ent]e 1760 si è trovato la statua di Marmo, dove se |:pochi mesi sono:| no si fussi levato mano, primà si sarebbe trovata, e non sarebbe stato guastato il colore rosso per l'acqua piovana.

[Fol. 35]

TEMPIO DELLA MADRE DE' DEI

Pianta, e Profilo d'un Tempio antico della Citta Ercolano scoperto di R. ordine di S.M.; in Resina della R. Villa di Portici, del Regno di Napoli, 41. palmi sottoterra, qual Tempio è distante dalla Strada Reale della Torre VIII. verso mare à Libeccio, o Sudovest pal: 500; dal Palazzo, distante verso Scirocco pal. 2880; dal Teatro d'Ercolano, Ostro, Sud, pal: 1000; dal Monte Vesuvio verso Libeccio cinque miglia e dalla Torre del Greco, verso Maestro pal: 8870. Portici 30. Ap[ri]le 1758.

Scala di Palmi 60.
Scale di Piedi 48. 2/3
che l'una e l'altra fanno l'istessa misura
Weber

NOTES TO APPENDIX 3: TAVOLA I

1. [Fol. 1, Col. 1] Molta probabilità pare, che comparisca in questo piano terreno, senza pavimento alcuno, di poterle atribuire il nome d'una piazza {a: ex greco πLATEIA *(a):con nichj di fontane nel rame. num. 5. 6. ed in grande, Tav. II. ed III. nelli rami.*} scoperta nelli Scavi di Gragnano 1752, già diventata voce commune, dimostrando un' area, o piano spazioso nelle Città, e Borghi p[er] il concorso, e comodità del Popolo, e Cittadini, à poter incontrarsi frà di Loro, tanto p[er]la conversazione, spasseggio, e divertimento, come p[er] il commercio, trattamento, e negozio, sopra Loro affari: cioè un Luogo publico di frequente concorso. In sensu Latiore, si usurpa ancora come un'area privata e ambulatoria intorno, e negl' Edifici grandi {b: Lampridius in heliogabalo.} Plateas in Palatio stravit: come sono Li Cavedi, e *Xisti* scoperti; con la differenza però, che il xisto era un Portico coperto col tetto, p[er] gl' esercizj invernali, del quale era differente la Xista, essendo questa un spasseggio, o ambulatorio, scoperta p[er] il giuoco delli Palestieri {c: Philander.} Xystos vocant porticus tectas ubi Athletae per hyemem exercebantur: Xystas autem subdiales ambulationes, ubi sudo Caelo suas exercebant Palestras. Averan forse gl' antichi di questo piano fatto L'uso di foro, ed anche di Mercato: Di Foro, perche era un Luogo spazioso [Fol. 1, Col. 2] ed aperto nella Città dove formavano il giudizio, e Tribunale p[er] convenire i Cittadini a ricevere il Ius, o sentenze, e Leggie, p[er] appianare, ed agiustare le controversie, e Liti {a: Dicono i Scrittori} Forum aperire, et Forum indicere, et Forum agere. Cioe aperire quando li Pretori destinavano il Luogo, e tempo, p[er] la contestazione delle Lite. Indicere, spetta alli magistrati, e Giudici, che citavano i litiganti. Agere s'intendeva tanto p[er]li Giudici, come p[er]le parti, perche unitam[en]te

agitavano frà di loro le cause, con dare, e ricevere le sentenze. Per Mercato forse averà servito p[er]la comodità del Popolo, e publicità del Luogo; come p[er]la moltitudine delli negozj, esponendo in quel piano le merci vendibili, delle quali poi, l'istessi mercati anno pigliato nome, come, il foro di pesci, il foro di frutti &; alcuni ancora anno procurato p[er] l'avvidità del Lucro, o ambizione del nome di Stabilire un mercato nelli proprj loro Predj, o terra {b: Suet: de Claudio}. Ius nundinarum in privata praedia a consulibus petisse {c: Plin. Iun. in epist. ad Valerianum} virum Praetorium a Senatu contendisse, ut sibi instituere in agris suis nundinas permitteretur. Donde resultavano poi [Fol. 2, Col. 1] varj nomi come sono. Forum Livii. Forum Iulii. Forum sempronj &. Però alcuni dicono di aver ancora ottenuto il nome, più tosto delli *Fondatori* vincitori, p[er] le giurisdizioni {a: Livius} Syllae forum statuit Cornelius: Hoc Itali Urbem vocant ab ipso conditoris nomine; ed averte d'esser stati distinti li luoghi del *Mercato*, e delle leggi, o Ius; ex vicis partim habuisse Rempublicam, et Ius dictum: partim Nihil eorum, et tamen ibi nundinas aetas. Oggidi in Napoli il Foro p[er] il Ius è il Tribunale della Vicaria. Il Mercato, come ancora La piazza, sarà quella avanti la Chiesa del Carmine. Il foro p[er]le comizie del Nobili, sono li Sedili, ancora chiamate, Piazze. Per quello, che riguarda il *foro* pare che confermino le trè tavole rotte di marmo, che si sono trovate {b: Tav. I. Let. H. Num. 5. 6. 7. e Tav. V. nel rame.} di trè in quattro palmi incirca di grandezza, colla pedagna triangolare, in forma d'un trepiedi, di cui ogni piede figura una Zampa, busto, e Testa di Leone colle trè Lettere **C.A.R.** sigillatim, che forse signicheranno il nome dell' Artefice. Si potrebbe ancora imaginare, che fosse un Pretorio, non però castrense, ma civile, ch'è quell' edifizio Publico del Magistrato ad Ius dicendum, al quale concorresse tutto il Popolo ad Iudicium, dove stavano i Giudici p[er] qualche tempo, o p[er] inabitarlo, de quali saranno state le più proprie e vicine, le Case annesse {c: Tav. I. Let. G. H. n. 2. 8.}; come ancora p[er] decreto del Popolo Romano in tutte le Provincie Stabilite furono li Praetorij p[er] domicilio Publico, ed abitazioni delli Presidi {d: In L: penult: cod: de offic: Rector: prov.}, e della Loro disposizione tratta Vitruvio Lib. 5. ed Alberto lib. 5. cap: 9.

2. [Fol. 2, Col. 1] La magg[ior]e parte delli Pavimenti degl' Antichi Edifizi nobili, sono di Mosaico, o Lapilli quadri [Fol. 2, Col. 2] di marmo, con cert' ordine disposti, che formarono qualche figura geometrica {m: *Tav. VII.*}; non solo li pavimenti, ma ancora le pareti {n: *Tav. II e III.*}, e Muraglie di quelli erano ornate, composti però di mistura o vetro più

delicatam[en]te, efigiati di diversi colori ed ancora indorati, imitando egregiam[en]te li Graphicoterj {a: Philander}. Come ancora si vedono nelle Basiliche di Roma, nel Panteone, ed altri Tempj antichi. Ma nelli pavim[en]ti si facevano di solo Marmo durissimo di Lapilli, più grandi, e forti, p[er]la resistenza alla Pressione de piedi: Li pezzi, e figure di bassorilievo, e Stucco, fatto di Gesso calce pura, e bianco d'ova, che all' impressione facilmente cede p[er] formare qualsisia figura {m: *Tav. IV.*} con somma magnificenza, e venustà in una Materia umile {b: Philander in notis ad cap: I. Lib. I. Vitru:} Nostrae AEtatis, artifices, quod in antiquorum ruinis reperiunt Stuccum appellant. Illosque imitati marmoreas nonnulli assulas pilis ferreis convexas, cribris excernunt: Subtilissimaque serote {??} ad mixtas purissima calce in Laca Macerata utuntur e finguntque quodlibet {c: Tav: IV}.

3. [Fol. 2, Col. 2] Peristylium ex Graeca notione idem est ac circumcolumnium, cioè un piano spazioso intorniato di Colonne {d: Tav: I. N. 15. *10. 13.*}; che in questo caso il nostro piano non Lascia d'indicare una celebre Palestra, o sia un Luogo publico p[er]li differenti esercizj Corporali, e guochi di lottatori, dove due a due ignudi, doppo essersi prima unti d'oglio, poi sparsi colla polvere {m: *l'aversario accio fossi più atto alla presa: ò doppo s'istesso, per asciugare il sudore.*}, complicandosi colle Braccia si urtavano, intenti a gettarsi l'un l'altro in terra 〈{e.}〉. Come ancora era destinata {e: Tav. IV. fol: 32.} p[er]li [Fol. 3, Col. 1] Giuochi dell' aste, corso, salto, Palle, Pali, Puggillato, e dischi. Era dedicato ancora questo Edificio come sede delli Studenti Retori, e Filosofi p[er] loro repetizioni, e disputazioni; e come L' Area dalla parte di Ponente, che principia con simili intercolonij, quali erano interrotti dal pendio di quella Ripa, come si osserva nella pianta {a: Tav. I. Let. H. Num. 12. 13.}, sarà forse stato ancora giardino con due gradini p[er] sedere p[er]la disputaz[ion]e delli Filosofi, e Retori {b: Vitruv. Lib. 5. Cap. 9.} quae erant sub divo inter Porticus |:spatia|: adornanda viridibus videntur, quod hypetrae ambulationes habent magnam salubritatem.

4. [Fol. 3, Col. 1] Palestrao era ancora quasi l'istesso che Gimnasio, che dava luogo a tutte sorte d'esercizj, tanto corporali, come scientifici, ed il suo circuito era di due stadj, cioè 250. passi geometrici, che sono comuni, e noti a tutte le nazioni del Mondo, consistente ogni passo di piedi cinque, o pal: 6. on: 1. Lin: 2:' e 6." confrontato il Piede comune con il passetto di Napoli {c: misura ordinaria di 4. palmi.}, in consequenza fà lo stadio pal: 770. {d: Vitruv. Lib. 5 Cap: 11} In Palestris peristilia quadrata, sive oblonga ita sunt facienda, ubi duorum stadiorum habent

ambulationis circuita quod Graeci vocant διαυλον |diaulon|, o corso d'un stadio doppio. Misurando dunque il circuito della nostra piazza, o quegl' altri portici, che stanno intorno, poca diferenza risulta; onde poteva essere palestra, o Gimnasio; p[er]la misura del giro, p[er]le colonne, e generalm[en]te p[er]la sua magnificenza. Li triplicati porticio {f: Tav. I. Let. H. N.o 10. 11. 12.} verso ponente greco, e mezzo di dalla piazza danno à credere d'essere stato gimnasio, che comprende universalm[en]te tutti i sud[et]ti esercizj {g: Vitruv. Lib. 5. Cap. 11.} con-[Fol. 3, Col. 2]stituuntur autem in tribus porticibus {m: sale. scuole. exedre.} exedrae spatiosae habentes sedes, in quibus Philosophi Rhetores reliquisque, qui in studiis delectantur, sedentes disputare possint. La Palestra però come parte del Gimnasio, poteva avere il suo sito nell' ambulacro estivo {a: Tav. I. Let. H. Num. 12.} p[er] esser verso occidente, e tramontana p[er]l' esercizio corporale al luogo più fresco. Quell' altro ambulacro poi {b: Tav. I. Let. H. Num. 11} sarà stato invernale, p[er] essere meglio guardato dalle due mura Laterali, e coperte con {n: Tav. V. la tegola} tegole, essendosene trovata in quel sito quantità notabile al piede dell' istesse mura, e porte |:che aprivano il libero passo alla Pergolata, e spasseggio nell' estate, p[er]la ricreazione, salute, e sollievo dell' animo |:godendo l'ombra del tetto, e nell' inverno il ricovero in tempo di pioggia {c: Vitruv. Lib. 5. Cap: 11.}: Ex quibus tres Porticus disponatur, quartaque, quae ad meridianas regiones, est conversa duplex, ubi cum tempestates ventosae sunt, non possit aspergo in interiorem partem pervenire. Acciocche nelle piogge à vento non possa lo sp(r)uzzo giungere nella parte interiore; poteano servire l'istesse Pasi correnti delle colonne, e Pilastri seu Stylobata, ch'era quel muretto, sopra quale stavano le Colonne; la etimologia deriva quasi da Styli, id est, columnae batis seu basis; seu Pedestyllum {d: Palladius – }, da noi correttamente detto Pedestallo. Per quello che riguarda l'ordinazione delle Colonne, pare che la specie dell' inter-colonio, p[er] la maggiore [Fol. 4, Col. 1] parte delli laterali sia delli Pycnostylos, che intermette una, e mezza grossezza dell' istessa colonna frà due: Quelle altre Colonnate alla testa, si chiamano Systylos, p[er] causa del spazio di due grossezze dell' intercolonio {a: Vitruv. Lib: 3. Cap: 12.} Species aedium sunt quique quorum, ea sunt vocabula Pycnostylos id est crebris columnis: {1. picnostilo. 1.½. grossezze.} systylos paulo remissioribus, {2. sistilo. 2. } Diastilos amplius patentibus, {3. diastilo. 3. } Areostylos rarius, quam oportet inter se deductis, {4. areostilo. piu} et Eustylos inter vallorum iusta distributione, {5. eustilo 1.¼. comune.} {c: spiega Philander – } Nam cuius inter-columnium non amplius, quam unius, et dimidia

columna erit ab eorum frequentia, Pycnostylos voca-tur. Cum due crassitudines dabuntur Systylos erit. Tres c(r)assitudines, Diastylos vocatur aedeso. {m: areostylos, quo superat tres crassitudines.} Quae maxime probatur in aedibus species nominatur, Eustylos, quasi diceres decenter, et probe columnata; quae ita se habet, ut intercolumnium aequet spatium duarum columnarum, et quarta partis unius crassitudinis. Per quello che riguarda l'ordine dell' architettura, in questo sito non si può dire cosa d'importanza, come già si vede sopra {d: in questa nota num: 4 – } p[er] esser stato coperto con tegole; e legno, che formavano pergolata; per lo dipiù tutte le Colonne sono state gettate in terra rotte, e disfatte, essendo state di mattone, e calce costrusse: di maniera che non si è potuto pigliare la misura delle loro lunghezze, ne si è trovato alcun capitello {e: fù distrutto in simplice villagio. fol. 1. lin. 6. in Tex.}: per lo che questo punto si rimette a qualch' altra scoperta, che si farà [Fol. 4, Col. 2] ò allo che si dirà degl' Edificj d'Ercolano, dove s'è dissotterrato nel mese di Marzo 1760. un Capitello di Pietra di Sorrento, ornato di stucco, nel quale non si è potuto bene conoscere, p[er]le sue volute, ed astralogo ornato di frutti, olive, ed ovoli, d'essere dell'ordine Ionico, o composto {a: Tav. ⟨V.⟩ n: ⟨pianta.⟩}. Dette colonne però erano ornate con una cannellatura del loro fusto, chiamate striae, e strigae. Le prime alternano con le Seconde, che formano detti canali, e alture, o pieghe distese p[er] il longo del fusto della colonna, che figurano l'abito delle matrone, e vergini, alla qual' idea diversi generi di colonne prima sono stati architettati, come ancora i loro Capitelli che significavano il Capo: Per l'istesso fine, ed idea con differenti ornamenti di foglie, frutti, e volute, che immitavano graziosam[en]te i ricci de capelli, ed altro simile. Le colonne Cannellate, si usavano non solam[en]te p[er] l'ornamen[tazion]e, ma p[er] farle comparire più grosse di quello, che sono, quando nelli Luoghi angusti, si era costretto di mettere colonne sottili: {b: Vitruv: lib: 4 Cap: 4.} hoc autem efficit ea ratio, quod oculus plura, et crebriora signa tangendo maiore visus circuitione pervagatur. Le Striae sono le linee prominenti, e le Strighae sono le linee concave, l'une con l'altre formano li canaletti.

5. [Fol. 4, Col. 2] Nelli Pareti, o Muri, come ancora [Fol. 5, Col. 1] nelle colonne, e Pavim[ent]i degl' Edificj, alle volte compariscono delle Pitture con ammirabile conessione di piccoli lapilli quadrati, o cubetti come dadi di vetro, o altra composiz[ion]e di diversi colori, rapresentati qualche figura nell' istessa maniera come se fusse delineata con colori fluidi, che usano i Pittori, come appunto rapresenta una tavola nel nostro nicchio {a: Tav. 1. Let. H. num: 6.} nel

frontispizio della piazza, o foro, formando una figura di una donna Giovane a Cavallo, sopra un toro in acqua {b: Tav: *II. e nel rame fol. 10.*} che senza dubbio viene ad indicare Europa ⟨Erased: {c: Tav. III.}⟩ figliola di Agenore Rè della Fenicia *e nell' istesso tempo rapresenta una fontane.* {m: *Tav. II. nel rame. et. fol. 2. in text. in d.*}

6. **[Fol. 5, Col. 1]** L'altra nicchia rapresenta un simile quadro di Pittura in Mosaico {d: Tav. I. Let. H num. 5. *pianta.*} eccellente come la descritta p[er] l'ordinazione delli Lapilli coloriti, che esprime un Giovane à cavallo ad un' ariete, e donna caduta in acqua {e: Tav: III.}, che secondo l'istoria dinoterebbe Friso, in quello, che stà a cavallo, e Hellae nella giovane caduta, germani frà di loro, e Figliuoli del Rè Athamante, li quali minacciati di morte dalla matregna, fuggivano in Colcho, p[er] salvarsi {f: Lattanzio Servio.}.

7. **[Fol. 5, Col. 1]** Stima universale in ogni tempo hanno conservato li bassirilievi, che sopra qualche tavola di metallo, oro, argento, creta, cera, stucco, ed altra materia solida, come marmo rapresentano qualche figura con travaglio rilevato, di maniera che tiene il mezzo termine frà le scolpite, e le dipinte immagini: p[er]li quali scrive la legge tanto della Pittura, come della Scoltura; tanto più **[Fol. 5, Col. 2]** celebri sono, quando in metallo, o in marmo, intiere istorie rapresentano, con molti personaggi e loro fatti {a: Tav V. Vaso di marmo con bassorilievo.}, come in Padova sono le famose tavole di marmo, che al vivo esprimono quelli del Santo, ed in Roma in moltiss[im]me cappelle, Tempj, e Basiliche: e particolarm[en]te come un miracolo dell' arte si osserva nelle Celebri Colonne Traiana, et Antoniana, ed in altri fragmenti nella Medicea, e monte Pincio e Farnesiana, in foro Boario. Direttam[en]te al Bassorilievo {b: opus anaglyphicum} vi è opposto l'incisorio {c: opus diaglyphicum.}, forma qualsisia figura cavata di dentro {d: Philander in cap. 3. lin. 7. —— Vitruv.} nelli quali come modelli si infondono materie liquefatte di Bronzo, cera & p[er] figurare statue, o altro. Dell' istess' opera sono ancora li sigilli. ⟨Erased: *per il giocatore, vide Tav: IV.*⟩

8. **[Fol. 5, Col. 2]** In questo portone si è trovata una tavola col piede triangolare {e: Tav: V. *e pianta Ta. I. let. H. n. 7.*} forse praetoriana, come si è detto in queste note al num: 1. {m: fol. 2. in not. lin. 15} Il corritorio, con le mura di tonaca diversam[en]te colorata, averà servito di ritiro e communicazione, alla diritta, e sinistra, e al Camerino, come ancora p[er] riposare, e sedere sopra il gradino di marmo p[er] concertare forse le Cause, ò altro. Il Camerino {f: Tav. I. n. 4. Let. H.} averebbe dato il comodo, forse p[er] l'istesso fine, ò p[er] una breve refeziuncula senza

letti, ne altri servizj, ne apparecchj, p[er] pigliare un piccolo cibbo solitariam[en]te, quasi passando, doppo, ò prima dello spasseggio fra quelli pilastri, o mentre si esercitavano gl' affari nella piazza, o foro, in tal caso si potrebbe chiamare quella stanziola diaeta, che non era distante delli **[Fol. 6, Col. 1]** Triclinj {a: Sidonius Apolonaius lib. 2. epist. ad Domitium.} Ex Tricliniis fit in diaetam, sive in cenatiunculam transitus. Si crede ancora, stante che questo ambulacro era parte della Palestra {b: Tav. I. Let. H. Num. 10.} come si è spiegato di sopra numero 3, che fusse queste stanziola stata destinata p[er]li Palestrieri, come untuario {m: *untuario, eleotesio*} dove si ungevano, poi spargendosi colla polvere {n: *per la polvere conisterio* Vitru. lib. 5. Cap. 11.} nun: 3.

9. **[Fol. 6, Col. 1]** Il Baccanale, ⟨*e festo*⟩ che con basso rilievo {c: In questa nota num. 7.} eccellentem[en]te si vede espresso nel grande vaso, o giarro di marmo {d: alto 3. pal: meno 3. oncie. Tav. V., *trovato à 8. abrile. 1752.*} bianco, colle asse, e con 9. personaggi di esquisita scultura; comproverà forse, che quel piano, piazza, o foro siano state celebrate le feste delle Vittorie, ò del giubilo, quando Giove cangiato in toro bianco, arrivò da Egitto all' isola di Creta con la Europa, o doppo la sua morte in Sua memoria {e: Tav. II. fol. 12. colon. 2. lin. 12.}, o altro; e che li camerini contigui {f: Tav. I. Let. H. num. 2. 8.} siano stati Triclinj.

10. **[Fol. 6, Col. 1]** La denominazione del gran piano spazioso di piazza, o di Palestra, o di foro, destinerà l'officio di questi camerini {n: *Tav. I. Let. H. num. 2. 8.*}. Chi vorrà denominarli come Palestra {g: num. 2. 3. 4. in questa nota.}, dirà esser stati questi camerini un Propnigeo, secondo la lettura degli' antichi codici {m: *Vital.*} che vogliono propincum a propinatione essendo credibile, che in qualcheduno di questi luoghi, doppo le corporali esercitazioni li lottatori, o altri uomini sbracchi, avessero procurato divertirsi, rinforzando i spiriti con qualche piccola refeziuncula, e propinazione di vini, per lo che Plinio {i: Plin: Iun. Epist. ad Apolinar.} quel luogo chiama gustatorium. Se poi quel piano sarà giudicato come piazza **[Fol. 6, Col. 2]** grande: allora {a: Isidoro in materia d'architettura.}, si chiameranno questi camerini come Emboli |:in Latino:| seu Porticus ad Latera Platearum, hinc inde dispositae nomine, et usu |:ab usu potius|: memorabiles, et famosae, in quibus ut plurimum prostrare solebant mulieres inverecundae, et scorta ad promptat sui corporis copiam praetereuntibus exhibendam, unde, et Embolariae post modium dictae sunt. Vi sarebbe ancora luogo di considerare queste stanze come triclinj, o Biclinj, e che p[er] l'una, e l'altra maniera fossero stati destinati, e p[er]le delizie e p[er] cenacoli {b: Servius in Aeneid. lib. 1. et

Plautus.}, a qual supposto non contradicono le quantità delle Pitture trovate d'uomini coronati con fiori, Cupidi, o Genj, con sottocoppe, Femine con bocali, e con specchio in mano, nude, e vestite; come ancora pitture di pesci triglie &, come si legge nella pianta {c: Tav. I. Let. H. num: 2.} quali pitture appresso si spiegheranno nelle loro tavole seguenti {n: Tav. VI. e seguenti}. Se poi venisse considerato questo piano, non come Palestra, ne come Piazza, ma come foro, allora averanno forse servito questi Camerini p[er] casino, ritiro, e riposo delli Giudici, o delli litiganti, p[er] essere esaminati, chiamandoli apparte p[er] l'informaz[ion]e, e recessi; ò abitaz[ion]e del Preside, o suoi uficiali {d: in L. penult. cod. de off. Rector. Prov., et alibi in jure civili et Can.} Olim ex decreto Populi Romani in singuli Provinciis Praetoria constituta erant, hoc est, domicilia publica earum Praesidibus in⟨h⟩abitandum, data.

11.[Fol. 7, Col. 1] Principando dire dell' area, che non avrà servito p[er] Cortile, |:come Vitruvio dice che appresso i Greci non fossero in uso:| {a: Tav. I. Let. G. in mezzo fra li Numeri 14. 15. 25. casa greca} si osserva primieram[en]te la su entrata di fuori delli Pilastri con due Colonne, che formano i Lati della porta, o Ostio sporgendosi un poco infuora, sostenendo il supremo supercilio, o Limite superiore della Porta {b: Porta è quella d'una Città. Ostio è la p[ri]ma d'una Casa, Ianua è quella di dentro.} quale entrata indica la similitudine d'una Casa Greca tanto p[er] il corridore appresso la porta, quanto, perche viene subito la porta interiore: lo spazio frà l'una, e l'altra porta, si chiamava in Greco Thyrorion {c: Vitruv. Lib. 6 Cap: 10. nella pianta si osserva, ibidem, d'essere casa greca, essendo simile alla casa, che descrive Vitru: supra.} Atriis Graeci non utuntur – ab Ianua introeuntibus itinera faciunt; alla dritta, e sinistra vi sono li camerini p[er]li Portinari. Il Cortile all' uso Romano è un' area molto spaziosa à cielo scoperto, e prima parte della casa, che all' intranti occorre {d: ⟨Festus:⟩ nela pianta. Tav. I. lett. G. in mezzo fra li num. 14. 15. 25.} in quam |·aream·| ex omni tecto acqua Pluvialis descendit; e le crediamo a Varrone: ab atriis Hetruriae populis, qui eo primi usi sunt, nomen accepit; Li nostri chiamano corte o cortile, dove li antichi con porta aperta, per dar passo al vento, pigliavano aria, celebrando con frequenza li banchetti, alli quali servivano li Famuli primari, e più onorati; qual cosa poi diede il nome de cortigiani {e: Gellius Lib. 16. cap. 6.}, con che con poca differenza del Cortile, o Corte, o Atrio all'aula ⟨verrebbe ad esse quasi lo stesso che un aula, perche equalmente [Fol. 7, Col. 2] rappresenta all prima entrata un luogo aperto, ampio, delizioso, e ventilato, dove li radunati aspettavano l'udienza del Padrone, o Principe {a: Homerus

ut notavit Athenaeus.} Siccome solevano li Palazzi de Principi avere spaziosi Portici, aree e hypetrae, quindi n'è venuto, che sono stati chiamati Regie, cioè Regia Domus, seu aula; e quelli che assistevano alli Principi, Aulici, come dire {b: Seneca lib. 2. de Ira.} Introducit quemdam aulicum, qui interogatus aliquando quonam paeto rarissimam rem nactus esset, in aula senectutem: argute respondit. Iniurias accipiendo, et gratias semper agendo. Verso la ripa si vede uno delli Bagni {c: Tav. I. Let. G. Num: 20 à 22}, che li scrittori variam[en]te chiamano Balnea, Balneae, Balneum, Balnea, dicevano quelli che erano edificj Publici, e grandi non solamente p[er] lavarsi o bagnarsi, ma ancora comodi p[er] la sudazione, ed esercizj corporali, e destinati p[er] banchettare, mangiando, e bevendo allegram[en]te, ubi comessabatur, et compotabatur hilariter {vital.}, dove ancora era l'accesso a tutte sorti di ricreazioni oneste d'animo. Balneae, erano una sorte di Bagni unicam[en]te destinati p[er] lavarsi. Balneum, era un bagno privato, seu Palneum, p[er] la sua picolezza, e p[er]la sua poco profondità di quatt' oncie solam[en]te, e potea servire p[er] lavare i Piedi {d: Tav. XII. le pitture e raschiadore vicino.} Usavano gl' antichi [Fol. 8, Col. 1] generalm[en]te li bagni non meno p[er]la conservazione della salute, che p[er] il Lusso, mentre facevano pompa di recinti splendidissimi di colonne; e le pareti, o muraglie, erano vagam[en]te dipinte con figure, animali, fiori & come nelle tavole, che seguono, ogn' una in particolare si osserveranno {a: v.g. Tav. XII e seguenti: le pitture in particolari, e raschiadore del n. 20 e 22; Nella pianta. let. G. e n. 18. Tav. I.}, e li pavimenti erano nobilm[en]te guarniti di musaici di differenti marmi colorati: Osservandosi poi le stanze, ed il Portico, e Pilastra ⟨da⟩; pare che abbiano qualche riporto a quello, che descrive Plinio {b: Plin. Iun. in epist. ad apolenar. lib. 5.} In cornu Porticus amplissimum cubiculum à triclinio occurrit aliis fenestris Xystum. Quelli Pilastri situati in figura di triangolo, potevano indicare una specie di cortile {m: chiostro}, o spasseggio. Qualcheduna di quell' altre Camere sarà stata il Triclinio {n: Tav. I. let. G. n. 18.} Il Bagno era proporzionato alla casa: {c: Vitruv. Lib. 5. Cap. 10} Magnitudines autem Balnearum videntur fieri pro copia hominem. ⟨ERASED: Frà quelle altre⟩

12. [Fol. 8, Col. 1] Frà quelle altre stanze si è trovato il il Mercurio {d: v.g. Tav. XX sua Pittura |Piant. lett. G. num. 13. Tav. I.} ed il corvo di bronzo, e candeliere vestito d'argento {e: Tav. I. Let. G. Num. 13. trovato li 13. Luglio 1751.} in un piccolo ritiro, perciò non è credibile essere stata quella statua in quel luogo collocata. Dell' altre stanze poi, alcune saranno state Oeci, Triclinj, Biclinj, Sale, Salotti, Talami, Galerie

& {f: Vitruv. Lib. 6. Cap. 5. 6. de tricliniis, oecis et Exaedris} Ipsi autem sint, ita Longi, et Lati, uti dua clivia, cum circuitionibus inter se spectantia possint esse collocata habeantque dextra atque sinistra lumina fenestrarum valvata, uti viridia de tectis per spatia prospitiantur. Li Oeci {f: salotte} [Fol. 8, Col. 2] in greco significano qualsisia Conclave, Stanza, o Casa p[er] abitare dello che poi è venuto che l'amministratori delle case anno pigliato il nome di Oeconomo, Economus in Latino. Altri poi destinavano li Oeci p[er]le stanze delle cene. Se erano guarniti di trè letti si chiamavano Triclinj, se con due, biclinj erano detti: concche si vede, che il termine Oeco era generico; i termini biclinio e Triclinio erano specifici. Il pian terreno averà rapresentato la delizia di un Giardino, Chiostro o d'una Hexedra angusta {a: Budeus in candect.} ut pars domus exporrecta, et propendens eius Generis quas salientes artifices nostri appellant exaedram angustam. Quest' area, Exedra era un luogo dove si tenevano gioconde confabulazioni, e conferenze p[er]li Retori, Filosofi, ed altri studiosi, per discutere, e disputare delle scienze, godendo nell' inverno il sole, e nell' estate l'ombra, e aria spirante. Era di più costrutta e guarnita con trè Portici {n: Pianta. let. G. et a. lett. n. vicino il mercurio. Tav. XX.}, come si vede nella nostra pianta {b: Vitruv. Lib. 5. Cap. 11. Il Mercurio dunque trovato nella pianta Tav. I. lett. G. num. 13. sarà stato collocato nella Exedra in mezzo li 3. Portici. lett. n.} constituentur in tribus Porticus Exaedre spatiose habentes sedes, in quibus Philosophi, Rectorisque, et qui Studiis delectantur, sedentes disputare possint. Le pergole erano stese ancora sopra le strade p[er] suplire all' angustia della casa, e serviva alli abitanti p[er] esporre le loro merci [Fol. 9, Col. 1] e lavori venali {a: Plin. Lib. 35. Cap. 10 de apelle.} (quod) perfecta opera proponebat in pergula transeuntibus. Era quell' altro sito {b: Tav. I. Let. G. numero 14.} ancora destinato p[er] vendere cose di pesante, come si deduce dal peso di piombo trovato con le lettere incise **EME HABEBIS** {n: Tav. XX. nel rame.}. Da che poi nasceva, che si procurava di piantare le viti, ed alboretti p[er] coprire le pergole con li loro rami, tanto p[er] un piacevole ornam[en]to di quelle verdi fronde, come p[er] godere dell' ombra al fresco in tempo d'Estate {c: Plin. Lib. 14. Cap. 1.} una vitis Romae subdiales innabulationes umbrasque pergulis opaca. Il condotto di piombo colla chiave di metallo {d: Tav. I. Let. F. Num. 14.} non lascia d'insegnare, che il riferito Bagno communicava con l'altro Bagno grande, o Piscina {e: Tav. I. Let. F. num. 5.}, ch'è un' instrumento di Bronzo, col quale si apre, e si chiude nelli Sifoni, o Canali il passo dell' acqua, che dal Greco, viene detto Epistomium, in Latino oris

obturaculam. Si definisce quella chiave {f: Budeus Vitru. cum Philander Lib. 10. Capo 13.} Epistomium aramentum est, quo ora salientium obturantur et Laxantur, cum opus est, tum manuducitur verticulum illud pertusum, quod admittit vel arcet aquam pro ut hoc, aut illo modo versatur; e comecche dalla somità del muriciuolo {h: T. I. let. F. n. 5.}, sino al fondo del Bagno, sono circa 7. palmi, con certi gradini p[er] discendere, si deduce, che fusse un Baptisterio in forma di Piscina, non solo p[er] lavarsi, ma ancora p[er] natare {g: Plin. Iun. in Epist. ad apolinarum Lib. 5} Inde apoditerium Balnei Laxum = et hilare excipiti cella frigidaria, in qua baptisterium amplum, atque opacum, si natare latius, aut tepidius velis in area piscina est in proximo puteus, in quo possis [Fol. 9, Col. 2] rursus astringi, si peniteat teporis. Li Camerini, e Cellole {a: Tav. I. Let. F. num. 6. 7. 8., e nell' altra parte senza numeri [m: o. o. o. o. o. nella pianta]} intorno servivano parte p[er] li uomini, e parte p[er]le femine. Quelli colli numeri {m:}, potevano fors' essere destinati p[er]li primi, e quegl' altri senza {n: nella pianta} numero p[er]le seconde, separatam[en]te p[er] l'onestà: per questo motivo vengono denominati Balnea in plurali {b: Varro.} Balnea erant bina edificia, coniuncta: alterum ubi viri, alterum ubi mulieres publice lavabantur. Che poi li Bagni servissero p[er]la conservazione della salute, e p[er] la curazione dell' infermità, lo provano li sette vasi di metallo con medicamenti, come ancora li stucchj di Chirurgia, con istrum[en]ti, e calamaro {c: Tav. I. Let. F. num. 8. 9. trovati l'anno 1751. ed in grande il rame Tav. XXX. v.g.} Li altri due quarti più grandi, si crede essere stati due Triclinj invernale, ed Estivo, uno alla dritta, ed alla sinistra l'altro, nella testa delli Portici coperti, ed aperti, con Pilastrate, e muro, come corridore, e spasseggio {d: Plin. Iun. in Epist. ad apolinar. Lib. 5.} In cornu porticus amplimissimum cubiculum a Triclinio occurrit & ut supra. Tutti sanno, che il Triclinio denotava un cenacolo guarnito con triplicato ordine di letti p[er]la comodità delli convivj, come ancora, ⟨come ancora⟩ il Biclinio di due stratti di Letti {e: Serv. in Aeneidis Lib. I; Vitru: lib. 5. – Cap. 5. et 7.}, mentrecche li antichi nei loro conviti, per magg[ior]e Lusso usavano apoggiarsi ai letti intorno alle tavole disposti; per lo che a quest' uso servivano li Conclavi più magnifici. Doppo levato l'uso de letti, invece di questi, si sono introdotte le Sedie, e si è mutato il nome di triclinio p[er] quello di Refettorio.

NOTES: TAVOLA II

1. [Fol. 10, Col. 1] L'opera di musaico è fatta di tessere quadrati, come dadi di diversi {n: diversi colori},

che p[er]lo più sono di vetro, ed ancora alle volte indorati, e cosi disposti, che rapresentano qualche figura, come una pittura fatta di colori fluidi. Differente però è l'opera Mosaica della quadratoria, con tuttocche ancor questa sia composta di marmi tagliati {a: Budeus.} Ego contra tesseras puto ad opus musivum pertinere sectilia vero marmoris esse quadrata grandia; certè latinis tessera est forma cubica |:dadum dicimus:| unde, et opus tesselatum dicitur quod eiusmodi formae lapillis sit compactum, hoc est ex parvis tessellis quadratis in varios colores tinctis. Dove si vede, che p[er] fare un mosaico ci vogliono trè maestri, cioè lo scultore p[er] tagliare i Lapilli, l'Architetto p[er] ordinarli, ed il Pittore p[er] connettere la figura.

2. [Fol. 10, Col. 1] Nell' estreme parti dell' Egitto verso Mezzogiorno, Agenore figlio del' Rè Belo Prisco {b: Theodosio, et Paulo} costretto dalla poste, con moltitudine di gente ad abandonare la Sede Paterna, e nel suo viaggio servendosi p[er] guida del Fiume Nilo, finalm[en]te colle sue Navi giunse nel lido di Suria, e partito di là ando a signoreggiare la fenicia, dove p[er]la Generosa, e nobile progenie fù molto famoso, e felice. Frà quella era Europa, e Cadmo suo fratello sestogenito, questo venne in Grecia, colle sue colonie {d: Eusebio nel Lib. de tempi nell' anno 17. di Danao Rè d'Araini - -} come quelle delli Pelaggiani usciti dalla Sumotracia {e: Erodote}, [Fol. 10, Col. 2] d'Inacho de Cecropi, e di Danao, portando seco i loro Dei, cerimonie religiose, e finzioni, ed in particolare da Cadmo fu portato l'alfabeto Feniciano, del quale fecero uso molto tempo i Greci, i quali tutto abbraciorono, accrescendo cosi i loro Favole, che già tenevano, con quelle che erano venute di fuora. In quel tempo gl' antichi Greci |:discendenti di Iaphet, figlio di Noè |, che l'anno 2379 avanti Gesù Cristo, col Padre è entrato nell' arca :|: di cui li sette Figli poi popolarono una parte dell'Asia, e tutta l'Europa:| tutti incolti a guisa di Bruti, abitavano dentro le caverne, e dentro le cave degl' alberi, col solo nutrim[en]to delle Ghiande e di qualch' erba, e frutto salvatico. Gli' Egizi, e Fenicj civili, e puliti, procurarono di radolcire i loro costumi barbari, e salvaggi, associandoli dentro i villaggi insegnandoli il vestirsi, e guardarsi contro le ingiurie del tempo, come i lavori di terra, ed altr' arti necessarie alla vita sostituendo altri nutrim[en]ti più salutari. Ora fattisi i Greci più colti, e dotti, pensorono di scrivere le loro storie, ricorrendo perciò agl' antichi linguaggi, li quali confusam[en]te intendevano, tanto più che erano di termini, e significati differenti, e com' erano questi Greci amanti di cose meravigliose, non mancavano d'intendere [Fol. 11, Col. 1] le sud[det]te istorie, e scritture in un certo

senso, che più adulava il loro gusto inclinato a tutto quello ch'era straordinario. Cosi trovando essi negl' annali Feniciani l'istoria d'Europa col termine Alpha o Ilpha che ugualm[en]te significa Toro, e Nave; in Luogo di dire semplicem[en]te d'essere questa giovane Principessa state rapita dalli Mercanti Cretesi, e condotta sopra la loro nave; s'immaginarono, che Giove innamorato di essa, cangiatosi in Toro, sopra le sue spalle la portasse all' Isola di Creta. Altri dicono, che essendo questa Principessa amata da Giove, Mercurio ricevesse l'ordine di cacciare gl' armenti dalla montagna di Fenicia, verso il lido dove Europa con altre Donzelle era avezza dar' a divertirsi, e Giove cangiatosi in un bianco Toro {a: Ovid. Met Lib. 2. Hygin. fab. 28.}, e frà quegl' armenti mischiandosi, la mettesse frà le sue spalle |:volendo altri che vi salisse da se:| trasportandola a nuoto nell' isola di Creta, o Candia {b: In Latino Cytaum},

. . . . sceptri gravitate relicta
Ille Pater rectorque Deum, cui dextra trisulcis
Ignibus armata est; qui nutu convitit orbem
Induitur Ianui faciem.- - - - - - - -

Dove ripigliata la sua vera forma e congiuntosi con essa, ebbe quattro Figli, cioè Tauro, Minos, Sarpedon, et Rhadamante; cosicche ad eterna memoria di lei si diedes il suo nome alla terza parte [Fol. 11, Col. 2] del Mondo, chiamandola Europa, ed ogn' anno celebrarono le feste {a: Bochart. Chan. I. c. 15} in suo onore p[er] tutta l'isola di Creta, oggidi Candia; la di cui Capitale tiene l'istesso nome, ed in oggi è una città fortissima, situata dentro d'una pianura fertiliss[i]ma in tutto, alla parte settentrionale dell' Isola, nel mare mediterraneo orientale, dirimpetto d' Alesandria in Egitto, frà le coste d'Africa, e dell' Archipelago, distante da Gerusalame in Siria, verso il maestro {b: Cautus Nord-est} circa 500. miglia comuni Italiani di 60. in un grado. Da Corfù nella Morea verso scirocco {d: Eurus sud-est} circa 210. migl:, e da Malta verso Levante {e: Est Solanus} 570 migl:. Candia è stata pigliata dalli Turchi alli Veneziani, doppo più di trè anni d'assedio, dove morirono diecimilla Gianniceri, ottanta Officiali, e sette Pachor li 16. 7.bre dell' anno 1669. Ivi ci abitano ancora gl' Ebrei, Armeniani, ed alcuni Francesi. La dotrina della metafora, o della parte favolosa, d'aver Mercurio cacciati gl' armenti nel lido, significa l'Eloquenza, e sagacità di qualche mercante Cretese, il quale spasseggiando nelle coste di Fenicia avendo rincontrato la Donzella, e preso della di lei bellezza, le regalasse qualche galanteria singolare, e preziosa, ond' essa si lasciasse conduere alla nave, e fosse portata ad Asterio Rè di Creta {f: Eusebio nel Lib. de tempi} il quale si faceva intitolar Giove. Per quello che [**Fol. 12, Col. 1**] riguarda l'altra parte, che frà gl' Armenti si trovò un Toro bianco |:ch'era Giove:| vogliono che l'insegna della nave fosse un toro bianco {**a:** Echemenides de rebus Cret.}. Cum forte fortuna Cadmi soror Europa ad littus Serapiae civitatis inter Tyrum, et Sydonem sitae deambularet, a Cretensibus, qui mercatum eò venerant, speciosa eius forma inescatis rapta est, anno mundi 2527. et Cretam navi advecta, cuius prora candito Tauro insignita erat. Alcuni vogliono {**b:** Eusebio.} essersi Giove congiunto con Europa nell' anno 40. di Danao Rè d'Argivi, e che poi con Asterio si sposò. Altri dicono d'esser stata rapita l'anno del mondo 1878., regnando Acrino in Argo. Altri asseriscono l'anno 1816. quando Pandione regnava in Atene. In altri si legge diferentem[en]te. Agenore afflitto p[er]la perdita d'Europa sua Figlia hà ordinato a Cadmo di lei Fratello di andere a cercarla, e non tornare se non l'avesse trovata. Cadmo doppo aver girato una parte della Grecia, senza averne notizia, pensò di stabilirsi in Boetia {**c:** Hygino Fol. 178.} dove fece una citadella chiamata Cadmea, e gettò li fondamenti della famosa Teba, simile a quell' altra Theba d'Egitto |:della quale ancora era lui fondatore:| la quale poi fù edificata p[er] li sui sucessori, e cinta di muraglie da Anfione, del 2.o Giove Figlio, che p[er]la sua eccellenza nella musica meritò {**d:** Lattantio} la cetra di Mercurio, con la quale edificò le sud[det]te mura di Theba {**e:** Seneca Poeta nella Tragedie di Ercole furioso.}, dalla quale Cadmo fù cacciato da Anfione li anni del mondo 1837. {**f:** Eusebio nel Lib. de Tempi.} l'anno ottavo della sig.ria d'Abante Re d'Argivi. [**Fol. 12, Col. 2**]

Le cui Mura Anfion nato di Giove
Edificò con il sonoro Canto
Ivi traendo, e conducendo Pietre.

Che mouvesse col suon della lira i sassi, si intende {**a:** Alberico.} la dolce armonia delle Parole, con che li rozzi, ed ignoranti uomini sparsi quà, e là, personage, che si unissero insieme, e facessero una vita civile, e p[er]la difesa circondassero una Città di mura; che poi da Mercurio avesse la cetra, vuol dire, che dall' influsso di questo Pianeta avesso l'eloquenza. E tornando alla nostra Europa, è stata esse da tutti i Cretesi tenuta in tanta venerazione, che instituirono una festa in onore del suo sposalizio, che ogn' anno celebrano; e doppo la sua morte fù onorata come una divinità, continuando la festa anniversaria in suo onore; e siccome si solevano mutare i nomi a quelli che si collocavano nel numero delli Dei, la chiamarono Ellotia {**b:** ELLOTOS [**in Greek**] Hesichius; et Apoteosi Romani}, che secondo

l'Etimologia Feniciana vol dire Lode, ed Epithalamo. Questa feste in onore della sua venuta in Creta e del suo Sposalizio venivano accompagnate con versi, e canzone {**c:** Boch. Chan. L.o C. 15.} Itaque Hallots, vel Hellots, vel Hellotia dici potuere a Cretensibus Europae festa Epithalamia, quae renovabantur quotannis. Ben di questo può esse Testim[ent]o quel celebre Vaso, grande {**d:** alto 3. pal: meno 3. oncie trovato li 8. Ap[ri]le 1752.}, o giarra di marmo, che con esquisita scultura in basso rilievo rapresenta 9. personaggi di sacerdoti, Vomini, e femine con ⟨ ??ni⟩, e festa p[er] memoria, e monum[en]to di quella, che sarà stata celebrata ogn' anno in questa piazza {**e:** Tav. I. Let. G. num. 15.} in onore di Europa come s'è detto, giacche poco distante del suo Nicchio {**f:** Tav. I. Let. G. num. 6.}, ed immagine di musaico è stato trovato {**g:** Tav. V.}, del quale a suo tempo, e luogo {**h:** ⟨corrected to **g**⟩} qualche cosa di dirà.

TAVOLA III

1. [**Fol. 13, Col. 1**] Doppo aver accennato l'origine, magnificenza, e differenti maniere delli Mosaici, resta a dire qualche cosa della loro Etimologia. Il nome di Mosaico |:in Latino Musivum:|, chi crede derivare dal nome di Museo {**a:** Anton. Nebrisensis apud Duc Cang. e in Glosa}, o museum, quasi musivum, mentreche, oltre l'analogia di questi nomi, nelli musei |:cioè nelli luoghi alle Muse, e Letterarie osservazioni destinate:| si vedono; massimam[en]te queste opere, tessellate, ben condegne, e decenti alla dignità di simili luoghi, quali in Latino si chiamano Musea, et Musiva; altri asseriscono, che il nome mosaico, o musivum venga cosi denominato p[er] causa della sua rara bellezza, mentreche Musivum, concinitas, et elegantia sonat ex Graeco; per lo che abbiamo giusto motivo di atribuire il nome musaico, o musivum all' Etimologia Graeca, onde à questa nazione conviene la lode p[er] avere inventata tali arte di tanta rarità.

2. Cadmo F[ra]tt[ell]o di Europa d'ordine d'Agenore suo Padre, avendo cercato La sua sorella in vano, e non potendo tornare al Padre, senz' averla trovata {**b:** Tav. II. num: 2. in Notis}, penso stabilirsi in Boetia, dove gettò li fondamenti della celebre città di Theba, con edificare una cittadella chiamata Cadmea, dove dalla sua sposa Erusiona {**c:** Ovid.} ebbe una quarta figlia chiamata Inoe, diventata poi moglie del Rè Atamante, doppocche Neifile di lui prima moglie, stimolata dal furore del Padre Libero, se n' andiede nelle selve, lasciando due Figli, Frisso, ed Helle, nelle mani [**Fol. 13, Col. 2**] del Padre, Atamante, ed Inoe madrigna, la quale |:secondo il costume di alcune

Madrigne:| non poteva sofrire, che li due Figli delle prime nozze sucedessero al Padre, machinò, come farli morire. Fece dunque secretamente guastare tutti li Frumenti {a: Hygin: dice che li fece bollire} da semiriarsi, dal che nacque una crudele fama. Atamante fece consultare Apollo; ed Inoe fratanto corruppe li sacerdoti, di maniera che portarono la risposta ad Atamante, che l' Oracolo avesse detto, che non reparebbe la fame, se non s' immolavano Frisso, ed Helle figliuoli di Neifile, p[er] aver essi affogati i Framenti {b: Servio.}. Atamante temendo la Plebbe, in pubblico finge aderire al volere dell' Oracolo; però segretam[en]te diede modo a Frisso di fuggire col montone del Vello d' Oro {c: Lattanzio dice che dalla madre Neifile fù parecchiato il montone di vello d' oro.}, sopra quale montarono p[er] rifugiarsi in Colco, appresso il Rè Aeta loro Parente, e cosi salvare la vita: e continuando il loro viaggio, Helle smarrita cadde, e fù inghiottita dal mare, che dal lei nome si chiamo in appresso Hellesponte {d: quasi Helles Pontus}, quale in oggi è lo stretto di Dardanelli, che sono due castelli antichi e forti della Turchia. Quello alla sinistra della stretto è nelle Romania; e quello alla dritta nella Natolia. Questo stretto comunica coll' Archipelago, o mare [Fol. 14, Col. 1] bianco, e colla Propontide, o mare di marmora. L' Hellesponte, verso sud-ovest, o Libeccio {a: Long. Grad. 44. min. 48, Lat. 40. min. 12.} è distante da Costantinopoli novanta miglia, di 60. in un grado ⟨erased: di Latitudine⟩, che sono le miglia Italiane comuni di mille passi geometrici. Per altro in quanto all' Istoria, dicesi {b: Diodoro Lib. 4.} che Frisso avvisato dal suo Governadore del pericolo, ed avendo rapito il Tesoro del Padre, s' imbarcò colla sorella la quale trovandosi incomodata, montò sopra la coperta della nave p[er] vomitare, da dove cadde, e fù inghiottita dalle onde. La nave era insignita con un Montone o Ariete indorato, donde ne venne il detto, che Frisso, ed Elle fossero portati dal Montone d' Oro p[er] salvarsi in Colco, dove Frisso giunto solo, fù ricevuto graziosam[en]te dal Rè Aeta {c: Lattantio} suo Parente, e p[er] ringraziamento, si consacrò a Nettuno la prora della Nave; il che diede occasione di dire, che s' immolasse il Montone, e si sospendesse nel tempio il Tosone d' oro del quale fù Guardiano l' istesso Rè, che poi diede la sua Figlia p[er] sposa a Frisso. Altri dicono, che Neifile sua Madre non essendo morta, ma andata alle Selve, rivelasse qualche Tesoro, donde nacque la parabola del Montone d' oro che poi in Calco da Aeta fù sacrificato à Marte p[er] dare ad intendere, che i Rè conservano i Tesori p[er] servirsene nelle Guerre, l'año del mondo 3820. mentre che Eritheo regnava in Atene; e Abante in Argo {d: Eusebio}.

3. [Fol. 14, Col. 2] Il sud[det]to Nicchio nelli scavi della Stabbia fù scoperto nella Setim[a]na dalli 24. a 29. Aprile 1752. {a: Riporto ordinario del Sabato} consistente in due colonne {b: nel Rame}, e quadro fondato; il tutto guarnito di Musaico con differenti colori, ed allora che non ora poligrato, appena si ravvisava un quadrapede in genere, senza poter distinguere la specie {⟨c:⟩}, e sotto la maschera della Terra, e cenere bituminose {d: Plin: del Bitume lib: 35. cap. 15. Galen: lib. 11. de simphi.} attaccaticcie, il montone sembrava cavallo; ed ancorcche del personaggio, che v' era sopra montato, era manchevole il mosaico della testa {e: Relazione ordinaria del Sabato a 29. Aprile 1752}, e mezzo busto, non' ostante chiaro è il suo significato, mentrecche la viva rappresentanza di tutto il restante, cioè della porzione del personaggio sopra il montone, che galeggiava p[er] il mare, e la donna caduta, ed ingiottita dalle onde, elevando il braccio, come se volesse chiamare ajuto, fà svanire ogni dubbio, d'essere stato Friso, ed Helle. Concorda à questo la simetria delli nicchj della gran piazza, essendo Friso stato in mezzo di quelli collocato, in compagnia, ed alla diritta del Nicchio {f: Tav: I. Let. H. Num. 5. nella pianta} dell' Europa sua Prozia, Germana di Cadmo, il quale fù avo delli sudetti Friso, ed Helle; {g: Num: 2. in questa nota.} Tutti gl' altri nicchi poi, eccetto quello di bassorilievo di Stucco, che contiene un uomo ignudo, con un cerchio, e palmo {h: Tav: IV. fol. 32} sono stati ruinati dagl' incendj, ceneri, terra di fuoco, e Lapilli erutati dal Vesuvio {i: Tav: I. fol: 2 nel testo Let. C.}, di cui Boca della vertice è distante dalla Stabbia 9. miglia di 60. in un grado del circolo massimo nel Globbo terrestre; {m: Incendj del Vesuvio; m: ab effectu noscitur causa} E parlando delle rovine di queste antiche Citta, ricordia-[Fol. 15., Col. 1]moci qualche cosa della loro causa eficiente fisica {a: L'incendj del Vesuvio} correlativa all' effetto {b: Le rovine}. La circonferenza di questa monte della base nelle sue radici gira 24. miglia, e passa per Portici, Resina, Torre del Greca {c: Turris octava} Sant' Angelo, Trecase, Anunziata, Bosco, Ottajano, Somma, St. Anastasio, e Santo Iorio: In molte bande si erigge come un ameno colle con una suave salita di circa quattro miglia e dalla sua vertice al mare p[er] pendicolarmente non cala intieramente una: La parola vesuvio pare che abbia qualche conessione con la Greca Besbios che sono fiamma: li Greci dicono Phelgraea {c: Phlegrea conflagrare.}, che pare quasi del flagrare, o confiagra.

4. Non si è appurato in che tempo furono li primi incendj; secondo Beroso, ed il P. Saliano sarebbe nell' anno 2787. avanti I.C., e 2197 dalla creazione del mondo, cioè nel penultimo anno di Aralio Re VI.

degl' Assirj {d: Beroso lib. 5. antiq. e P. saliano.} Eo tempore Italia in tribus locis arsit multis diebus circa Istros, Cymeos et Vesuvios: vocataque sunt a Ianigenis ea loca Palensana hoc est, regio conflagrata. E Fabrio Giordano {e: Giord. de situ Neap.} dice, che al tempo d' Abrahamo, il quale nacque 1996. avanti I.C. come siegue {f: anno Abrahami 1996 avanti I.C.} Hunc vero montem saepe numero ab initio conflagrasse memoriae proditum est, si quidem, et Abrahami tempore, ignas flamasque eructasse et Diodoro Cronologia referunt, et Hereniis quoque tempestate et eodem Diadoro lib. 4: antig. de Hercule retulimus {g: Bocc. lib. de mont. temp. di Nerone} L' anno della nascita del Signore 65, dice Boccaccio, che a tempo di Nerone il Vesuvio hà vomitato fumo, fiamme, e ceneri, con li quali hà riempito tutta [Fol. 15, Col. 2] la campagna, ed ancora il mare {a: Bocac: Lib. de Mont.} Ex hoc enim incolarum pavore, Nerone Caesare imperante, grandis erupit circa verticem fumus, ut omnis brevi tractu temporis ab eo tegeretur regio: nec evanuit illico, qui nimo per dies plures adeo condensas permansit, ut sublatis omnibus radiis, noctem faceret plurium dierum continuam: tandem cum adiacientia omnia, et ipsum stare quod in conspectu sub radicibus est, ab occiduo complexu cineribus cessans, flamam ingentem e culmine montis erumpentem videre permisit: quae multis saeculis postea exustos evomens Lapides perduravit; hodie nec fumus, nec ignis {b: nec fumum, nec ignem} emitit. Stat tamen in montis vertice hiatus magnus, praeteriti testis incendji. Seneca parla solo del Terremoto nel tempo del consolato di Regolo, e di Virginio {c: Seneca natur. qq. lib. 6. cap. 3. et 25. an 65. il 5 Febraio.}, il quale rovinò parte della Pompea, e Terre convicine. Pompeios celebrem campaniae urbem desedisse terraemotus vexatis quae cinque adiacentibus regionibus, audivimus: et quidem diebus hybernis, quos vacare a tali periculo majores nostri solebant promittere, nonis Februarii fuit motus hic, Regulo, et Virginio Coss. qui campaniam numquam securam huius mali indemnem tamen, et defunctam motu, magna strage vastavit: nam et Herculanensis oppidi pars ruit {d: sarà dunque stato borgo dell' Ercolana mentrecche Dione dice: Duasque Urbes Herculanum et Pompeios Populo sedente in Teatro, penitus obruit. fol. 17. colon. 1 (a) ô sarà stato fatto città doppo. in fine.} dubiae stant etiam quae relictae sunt & Il maggiore incendio di tutti li [Fol. 16, Col. 1] altri è stato L'anno 81. doppo la nascita di Gesu Cristo {a: an: 81. di I.C.} regnando Tito, del quale scrivono, Plinio, Lonara, Suetonio, Grosio, Capaccio, Cornelio Tacito, Eusebio, Valerio Flacco, Statio, Silio Italico, Marziale, Ausonio, Baronio, &, e sopratutti Sifilino

Epitomatore di Dione dice cosi. Per id tempus {b: primo anno di Tito} accidere in campania horribilia quaedam, quae magnam admirationem habent. Nam sub autumni tempus, ingens incendium repente, ex citatum est; eoque mons Vesevaj conflagravit; is mons mare spectat ad Neapolim, habetque fontes ignis maximos; ac olim quidem ex omni parte pariter excelsus erat, sed tunc ex medio ejus ignis extitit, nam ea parte tantum exustus est: extrinsecus enim intactus integreque permanet ad hac tempora: ex quo fit, ut cum ignis externas partes non exuret, eaque, quae sunt in medio, consummantur igni, rediganturque in cineres, vertices qui circum sunt adhuc veterem altitudinem habeant, et quae pars igni consumpta est, dum in se cohit, concava facta sit, ita ut totus mons |: si licet parva cum magnis conferre :| formam habet amphiteatri: culmina eius montis multas arbores habent, vitesque: Ipse interius circuitu propter ignem declives est; [Fol. 16, Col. 2] utque fumum interdiu ita noctu flamam reddit: ita ut in eo suffimenta cuiusvis generis fieri semper videantur. Quod cum ita se habeant, nec semper eodem modo, id malis aliquando interdum minus facit ad haec, et cinerum nonnunquam proiicit, quoties simul aliquid subsidit, emititque saxa, facto impetu ventorum tum resonat, mugitque, quod minime densos atque constipatas, sed raras, et ocultas respirationes habet: Cum igitur Vesevus eiusmodi sit, hii in eo quot annis fere fieri solent, quae cum illis temporibus praeter morem evenerint, magnaque adhuc esse videantur iis, qui ea semper inspiciunt, tamen licet omnia simul cum ceteris; quae tum quoque evenerant, comparentur, parva habeantur necesse est;

Et enim eo tempore magnus numerus hominum innitata magnitudine, quales gigantes finguntur: in eodem monte regioneque finitima; ac proximis civitatibus interdiu noctuque vagari, versarique in aere visus est. Post haec consecuta est maxima siccitas; ac repente ita graves terraemotus facti, ut et omnis ea planities fervida esset et culmina montium insiderent. Ad haec sonitus subterranei tanquam tonitrua, et super [Fol. 17, Col. 1] terram mugitibus similes extiterunt. Dein mare simul fremere; omne caelum resonare ignesq[u]e et repentinus fragor, quasi montes simul considerent, exaudiri. Tum exilire primum immensi lapides, et ad summos vertices pervenire. Deinde magna copia ignis, fumique, ita ut omnem aerem obscuraret, ocultaretque solem, non aliter, quam si deficisset. Igitur nox ex die; et tenebrae ex luce factae erant. Putantibus nonnullis, Gigantes seditionem inter se facere, quod multae imagines eorum in fumo conspicerentur: quodq[u]e clangor tubarum audiretur. Alij existimabant aut mundum in chaos redigi, at ignis consumi, obeamque, causam properabant ex Aedibus in vias, alij de vijs in aedis confugere, atque e mari in continentem, et ex continenti in mare se recipere. Alij conturbati ea, quae non dum venerant existimare tutiora rebus praesentibus: Tanta verò erat copia cineris, ut terram, mareque, atque adeo ipsum aerem compleret: quae res multa damna (ut cuique sors tulit) importavit, nonsolum hominibus, praediisque, ac pecoribus, sed etiam pisces, volucresque omnes peremit Duasque Urbes Hercolanum, et Pompeios Populo sedente in Theatro penitus obruit {a: añ: 65. Herculanensis oppidi pars ruit. fol. colon. 2. lin. terzultima. fol. 15} Postremo tantus fuit cinis, ut inde Pervenerit in Africam, Syriam, et Aegyptum, introieritque Romam, eiusque aerem compleverit, et solem obscuraverit. {b: La cenere ha oscurato il sole, in Africa, Syria, Egitto, e Roma.} A Romae accidit paucis post diebus, cum omnes ignorarent id, quod factum erat in Campania, nec quid esset. Conjectura assequi possent. Itaque etiam **[Fol. 17, Col. 2]** ij putare ceperunt omnia sursum deorsum fieri, solemque in terram cadere, ac terram in caelum conscendere, quamquam autem hic cinis non tunc statim attulit gravia damna populo Romano, tamen postea, morbem pestilentum et gravem immisit. Questo dice Dione tralasciando lo che scrive Plinio {m: Diodone}.

5. Replicarono con notabile veemenza gl' incendij gl' anni 202 {a: vede Sifilino.}, 305 {b: Galeno lib. 5. Meth. c. 12.}, e 471 {c: Eusebius}. Vesuvij incendiô proxime Regiones, et oppida vastata sunt. Gl' anni 472 sequita Marcellino il Sigonio {d: Marcel. Sigon. de Imper. Occident. lib. 14}. Eodem anno Vesuvius mons in campania intestinis aestuans viscera exusta evomuit, nocturnisque, in die tenebris incumbentibus omnem Europam minuto cinere cooperuit. Itaque eius portenti memoriam annuam Constantinopolitani instituerunt viii id[ibus] Novembris; Ea re Leo Imperator exterritus Urbe excessit abque ad 15. Mamantem consedit {e: di I.C. 471} {d: Baton. to. 6. de Procopio an. 471. à 6. 9.bre sin à Marzo 474.} Baronio da Procopio riferisce d' essere cadute le Ceneri l'anno 473. in Constantinopoli, in Libia, Tripoli, e che duro sin al mese di Marzo 474. p[er] tre anni continui. L'anno 512 regnando Teodorico Re d'Italia dice Sigonio lo sequente. {f: Sigon. de Imper. Occident. lib. 16.} Campanis quorum agrum Vesuvius mons exaestuans pervastaverat tributum remosit. Ceterum illius exaestuationis huiusmodi fertur fuisse natura: Mons ille hiatum ingentem edebat: inde spiritus quidem ater adeo, ac densas erumpebat **[Fol. 18, Col. 1]** ut lucem solis caligine, tenebrisque involveret, strepitu ita horrendo, ut vicina loca terrore concuteret: Cinis inde tantus efundabatur, ut provincias quoque transmarinas obrueret. In Campania

verò quodam quasi pulverei amnes fluebant: et arenas impetu fervente, more fluminis decurrebat, qua plana camporum usque ad arborum cacumina tumescebant {a: Sigon.}, e Cassiodoro {b: – Cassidor. lib. 4. var. epist. 50} Campani Vesuvij montis hostilitate vastati Clementiae nostrae suplices lacrimas profunderunt, ut agrorum fructibus enudati, subleventur onere tributarias functiones: Quod fieri debere nostra merito pietas aquiescit: & & ....

6. Al tempo del Re Teodato nipote di Teodorico, quando Giustiniano da Constaninopolio mandò Belisario in Italia p[er] liberarla de Barbari {d: Card. Baro. Tarcagnota del sito di Nap. fol. 44.} antea ea tempore (681.) dice Capaccio quaque conflagrasse videtur & ed a 528. Initio inde Ianuaris apparuit stella noctu caelo sereno ea obscuratate infecta veluti cum lunam nubes subijt, et mense Februario meridie altera ab occasu magno fulgore ad Orientem decurrit. Martiô verò Vesuvius mons in Campania p[er] dies aliquos ignes evomuit, atq[u]e omnia viventia circumquaq[u]e adurit. Haec praenunciasse obitum Benedicti Pontificis indicata, qui idibus Maij supremum vitae suae diem confecit {e: an. 685. di I.C. Sigonio de Regno Ital. li. 2.}. **[Fol. 18, Col. 2]** Baronio {a: Baron. tom. 10. an. 993.} dice: hoc anno ut Glaber Rodalplues est auctor, cum admirandae flamarum eruptiones e monte Vesuvio contigissent crebra quoque p[er] diversas Provincias civitatum incendia, prodigiosaque contigere. Cum, et Romana conflagrante Urbe, Basilica Vaticana incendi caepta divinatus est liberata. {b: Glabro et hîc fol. 28. colon. 2. in (a) et fol. 31. colon. 1. in b.} Contigit interea paene universas Italiae, et Galliae civitates ignium incendiis devastari.

L'Anonimo Cassinensis appresso al P. Caraccioli riferisce {c: Anon. apud Carac. fol. 129.} Anno 1036. VI Kal[endis]: Februari Mons Vesuvius eructavit incendium ita ut usque mare descurraret. Cronica Capinenses: {I.M.: Cronica Capinensis. An: 1049. Leo Host. li. 2. c. 82.} Mons Vesuvius in Flammas erupit, tantaq[u]e sulphuraea Resinae congeries ex ipso Vesuvio protinus fluxit, ut torrentem faceret, atque corrente impetu mare descenderet.

Testo che si conserva nel Monastero della Cava. {I.M.: An: 1138. – Anonimo Cassinense ut sup. año 1138. Mons Vesuvius per 40 dies eructavit incendium.} Pos[t] haec Salernium veniens |: Ruggiero :| Mons Vesuvius magnum excitavit incendium, quod sequutus est pulvis tantem desitudinis, ut totum aerem obtenebraret, et totam hanc operuit regionem, usque principatum, et Calabriam.

Folco Beneventans {d: An: 1139. – folco Benevent. apud Caracciol. fol. 328.} Hoc anno IV Kal[endis]: Ianii ⟨manes⟩ mons ille, qui prope civitatem Neapolim esse videbatur, ignem validum et flammas visibiles proiecit, p[er] dies octo ita ut civitates ei contiquae, et castra montem et pectabant; ex cuius incendio pulvis niger [Fol. 19, Col. 1] et horribilis exivit, et usque Salernum, et Beneventum, et Capuam, et Neapolim pulvis ille a facie venti pervolavit. &

Ambroggio Nolano lib. 1. c. 7. {I.M.: an: 1500 – di I.C.} Nostra vero tempestate id ostendit Vesuvij caminus Triduo enim aerem teterrimum vidimus, usque adeo ut cuneti mirantes compavescere ceperint: deinde ubi deferbuit aestus, qui materiam extollendo omnia texerat, pluit cinere surufo quamplurimo, quo cuncta veluti nive tenui obruta videbantur. Neque ignis ille extinctus adhuc prorsus est: in vertice enim montis eius loca multa excavantur in rupis, ut vaporaria fiant, quo plerique male valentes Augusto mense ascendunt, {I.M.: *convalescenti vanò à sudore sopra il Vesuvio, come stoffe*} ut p[er] sudationes nimias solutis exustisque articulorum humoribus curentur.

Giuliano Passaro {a: An: 1504. – Giul. Pass. setaiolo m. 5. innondazione à Nola. 1504.} Che soleva avenire ma grande inondazione attorno à Nola quando nel Vesuvio s'è fatto, o s'hà da fare in breve qualche motivo: dice con parole Napolitane |: Nel mese de Agusto 1504. nella città de Nola abbondai tanto delle acqua intorno alle mura de Nola, che pareva no mare: e ce abbondaro tanto li Pesci, che so na cosa stupenda, ed erano di ogni sorte piccioli, e grossi, che ogn' uno el annava ad pescare, e pigliavano dinari: ed erano tanti, che ne avesse cariato le navi; e per questo in detta Città ce venne no tale [Fol. 19, Col. 2] mal airo chence e detta acqua ce durai . . . ., e poi li donaro via, e parte assecaio.

Giovanni Tarcagnotta {I.M.: an: 1538: di I.C. – *Pozzuolo.* Tercag: del Sito di Nap: Fol: 151.}, doppo la descriz[ion]e di quello, che accade in Pozzuolo nell' anno 1538, dice che gettò quel luogo tanta copia di sapi. e di ceneri fuori, che ne nacque nel med[issi]mo luogo {a: ⟨cio è monte di Soma.⟩} un non picciolo monte come ogn' uno vede; e fù à di nostri cosa assai nuova, e spaventevole p[er] essersi quasi estinta La Memoria dell' incendio del Monte di Somma, e d' Ischia, che arsero anch' essi altre volte, ansi che incendio di Pozzuoli si ritirò di buon spazio il mare presso Baja: e ne nacquero in quei luoghi nuovi fonti di acqua dolce, e si vidde gran copia di pesci morti in quei lidi.

Giovanni Dom[eni]co Magliocco {I.M.: Descrizione della voragine del Vesuvio, di Magliocco} medico principale di questa città dice che ritrovandosi nell' anno 1619. nel mese di Maggio nel convento de P.P. Camaldolesi a S.t Angelo, il quale sin ad oggi solo in quella parte è remasto intatto, una mattina, che era bellissimo tempo tirato da simile curiosità, se ne andò a vedere le med[issi]me

cose: ed essendo salito sopra la montagna dalla parte verso la marina, giunto all' altrio, doppo aver colto molti semplici, salì al luogo dov' è la bocca della voragine, ed iñanimato da due di questi Religiosi, li quali asseriscono essere altre volte [Fol. 20, Col. 1] calati p[er] quell' appertura accompagnato da loro, cominciò a scendere p[er] una stradella, la quale a guisa di un scala a Lumaca girava attorno à quell' Anfiteatro, e doppo aver caminato un pezzo fra gl' Albori, trovò, che dove p[er] disopra era assai patente e largo, appoco appoco si ristringeva a segno tale, che in alcuni luochi dalla metà in giù poco si ci vedeva, e la via era tanto stretta, che difficilm[en]te si ci poteva passare, e si abbattè in una Grotta, ò pietra talm[en]te grossa, e che spontava cosi in fuori, che li fù necessario andarvi sotto carpone: sebbene passato questa si trovavano sempre sassi, à quali appogginadosi rendevasi il viaggio sicuro: finalm[en]te giunto nel fondo, lo trovò piano, e assai più patente, e largo, che nella Bocca non era: e con tutto che fosse tanto profondo, che p[er] calarvi, e salir di sopra, ci passe più di trè ore, in ogni modo giunto il sole in Zenit, per li riflessi di lui, pur li compagni si discernevano l'un l'altro, ed appoco appoco distinguevano l'altre cose, che qui vi erano; Laonde à quel baerlume vidde nel mezzo della pianura una grossissima pietra, sopra la quale non era possibile da nessuna parte ascendere, ed era come una Casa. Accostatosi poi dalla parte verso la marina, {I.M.: an. di I.C. 1619. vento freddo gagliardo con fischio nel fondo della voragine.} vidde, e senti p[er] corte fistole, o senici [Fol. 20, Col. 2] uscir vento con gran veemenza, come dal fischio, che faceva, e dal freddo, o fresco, che caggionava, chiaram[en]te si comprendeva esser gagliardo, e continuo. Verso la med[issi]ma parte, trovò un bagno largo quanto una gran conca di Rame pieno insino al par della terra, d'acqua talmente salsa, che egli avendola ben gustata fece giudizio, altro non essere che una vena di sale. {a: *sarà stato l'acqua comune al nivello del mare.*} {I.M.: Bagno D'acqua bituminosa nel fondo della voragine.} Dalla parte verso scirocco, trovò un' altra conca dell' istessa grandezza piena similm[en]te di acqua, ma cocente, e senza alcun sapore, come se fusse state |:diceva:| un brodo di pollo cotto senza sale. Dalla banda di levante era la terza conca alquante più grande dell' altra, piena pur d'acqua calda, e più tosto tepida, di sapore mordace, ed amaro assai, come il Ancero{??} nitro: del quale p[er] tutta la scesa avea trovato gran coppia: {I.M.: Bagno d'acqua nitrosa nel fondo della voragine.} E p[er] questo avendo uno di quei religiosi voluto con fucile, o acciarino accendere il fuoco, l'impedi p[er] non correre il pericolo, al quale con perdita della vita si espose colui, che nelle miniere di Sassuolo vicino a Modena volle portare la lucerna accesa. In tutta quella pianura sotterranea non trovò altro, che arena p[er] la magg[ior]e parte nera, in alcuni luoghi lucida, e mescolata con pezzetti di talco, e di sale, o vetro, e p[er] tutto grave e pesante. Ma non disse di [Fol. 21, Col. 1] aver veduto quelle caverne, che accennò Strabone, ne quelle buchette, tali quali sentiva il Pighio spirare continuo calore. Non si dubita, che il Vesuvio sia stato formato dalle ceneri, e pietre istesse delli spessi incendii, che quasi in ogni età vi si sono accesi, vomitate |:come afferma Andrea Baccio di Etna {a: Andrea Baccius de Therm: Lib. 4. .&. incendium Aetnae fol: 182. N.o 20 Tarcag. del Sito di Nap. fol: 131.}:| come Si è visto nel monte nuovo in Pozzuoli, fatto in una sola notte a 29. Sett[emb]re 1538. {b: Monte nuovo in Pozzuoli fatto. à 29. 7.bre 1538.}

7. Poco differenza vi era dell' orribile incendio dell' anno 1631. a quello dell' anno 81. |:regnante Tito:|:, che hà distrutto Ercolano, Pompejana, e altre vicinanze:| di maniera che D[o]n Emmanuele Fonseca, e Zunica, conte di Montereggio, vicere di Filippo IV. Re di Spagna {I.M.: an. 1631. à 16. di 9.bre Epitaffio di Portici di Fonseca, e Zunica, Vice Re di Nap.} ha stimato di piantare in perpetuam rei memoriam un monum[ent]o coll' iscrizione sopra marmo, chiamato L'Epitafio di Portici, che si vede a mano dritta della via regia, venendo da Napoli à Portici, e passato la posta prima d'arrivare alla Parrocchia, e propriam[ent]e alla cantonata dove volta la strada per andare al Granatello à mare, per avertimento, come si legge nella seguente copia. [Fol 20, Col. 2]

POSTERI POSTERI / VESTRA RES AGITVR / DIES FACEM PRAEFERT DIEI NVDIVS PERENDINO / ADVORTITE / VICIES AB SATV SOLIS NI FABVLATVR HISTORIA ARSIT VESAEVVS / IMMANI SEMPER CLADE HAESITANTIVM / NE POSTHAC INCERTOS OCCVPET MONEO / VTERVM GERIT MONS HIC / BITVMINE ALVMINE FERRO SVLPHVRE AVRO ARGENTO / NITRO AQVARVM FONTIBVS GRAVEM / SERIVS OCYVS IGNESCET PELAGO INFLVENTE PARIET / SED ANTE PARTVRIT / CONCVTITVR CONCV-TITQ SOLVM / FVMIGAT CORVSCAT FLAMMIGERAT / QVATIT AEREM / HORRENDVM IMMVGIT BOAT TONAT ARCET FINIBVS ACCOLAS / EMICA DVM LICET / IAM IAM ENITITVR ERVMPIT MIXTVM IGNE LACVM EVOMIT / PRAECIPITI RVIT ILLE LAPSV SERAMQ FVGAM PRAEVER-TIT / SI CORRIPIT ACTVM EST PERIISTI / ANN SAL CI)I)CXXXI XVI KAL. IAN. / PHILIPPO IV REGE / EMMANUELE FONSECA ET ZVNICA COMITE MONTIS REGII / PRO REGE / REPETITA SVPERIORVM TEMPORVM CALAMITATE SVBSIDIISQ CALAMITATIS / HVMANIVS QVO MVNIFICENTIVS / FORMIDATVS SERVAVIT SPRETVS

OPPRESSIT IN CAVTOS ET AVIDOS / QVIBVS LAR ET SVPPELLEX VITA POTIOR / TVM TV SI SAPIS AVDI CLAMANTEM LAPIDEM / SPERNE LAREM SPERNE SARCINVLAS MORA NVLLA FVGE / ANTONIO SVARES MESSIA MARCHIONE VICI / PRAEFECTO VIARVM

8. [Fol. 21, Col. 1] Sin dalli 10. di X.bre dell' anno 1631. anno sentito li Torresi, e li altri Paesi intorno della Montagna tanto raggiram[en]to di rumori che appena, anzi malam[en]te poterano la notte dormire. Alcuni anno osservato, senza essere [Fol. 22, Col. 1] piovute intorbidarsi l'acque de Pozzi, ed in alcuni mancare; perlo che, secondo Pericle e Pitagora, si sarebbe potuto prevedere i terremoti, e salvarsi; sebene secondo il proverbio, perituri non recipiunt consilia.

Il Giorno 15. della mattina, essendo l'aria serena, fù veduta con somma amirazione una stella di straordinaria grandezza sopra il Vesuvio, e a 5. ore di notte, l'apparenza ⟨l'apparenza⟩ d'un travo di fuoco, e da quell' ora fino alle 12. furono contati sino a 50. gagliardissimi scuotim[en]ti della terra, poco doppo s' apri il monte nell' atrio in molte bande, ed uscirono fumo, fuoco, ceneri fiamme, e pietre, gettando de scoppi. Le bocche erano prima grandi come un fondo di grosso tino, che poi esalando, si slargarono. Quell' esalazioni formarono una densa, e straord[inari]a nuvola {a: Santolo de Simone con quatr' altri di St. Anastasio l'istessa mattina sali sopra la montagna al luogo detto Monte d' Saevola, e da vicino ne hà osservato tutto questo.} donde vidde Santolo calar saette, e grossissime pietre, e sempre aprirsi nuove bocche, e le pietre cadendo bruciavano, e consumavano ciò, che trovavano, una delle quali diede vicino a lui sopra un sasso, e l'infocò tutto, poi si spezzò, e raffreddata, avendone raccolto una, la portò à basso, e la trovò molto pesante, e dura: Tritata poi s'assomigliava all' arena, di ferro impastata; e da un vaccaro, e da molti altri s'è visto aprirsi in più parti la terra, donde usciva fumo, fuoco, sassi e materie bituminose, oltre della voragine grande. La sud[det]ta nuvola come altissimo [Fol. 22, Col. 2] fronduto Pino, e con la base simile à un Torre, sospinta poi da uno Spirito, si alzò tanto in aria, che quasi si perdea di vista {a: con un quadrante fù misurata l'altezza di 30. miglia ital., cosa straordinaria, ancora che l'aria molto più basso dissipa le nuvole, ma questa era particolare e più forte.} Doppo si diffondea in spaziosi rami p[er]lo giro di molti miglia, ed ancorcche era tempo chiarissimo, si dimostrava nera, brutta, or livida, macchiata, tal' ora candida, e di dentro sempre un poco rossa come fuoco; il tutto simile a lo che vidde l'anno 81. Plinio {b: Plin: lib. 6. ep. 16.} Recenti spiritu evecta, deinde senescente, e destituta, aut etiam pondere suo vieta, in latitudinem vanescebat. Del qual spettacolo restaron tutti atterriti, e spaventati, mentrecche già da pertutto si vedevano uscir le fiamme e gran quantità di varie ceneri, sentendo li continui, e paventosi strepiti come l'anno 81. {c: Plin. ib. ep. 20.} occursabant trepidantibus ad huc oculis, mutata omnia altoq[u]e cinere tamquam nive obducta. Li continui conquassam[en]ti de terremoti eran di maniera, che fecero credere non solo, che tutte le cose si movessero, ma che si svelgessero, {d: Ibid. §.} illa vero nocte, ita invaluit, ut non moveri omnia sed everti crederentur, ed andassero sotto sopra con tanto terrore, che ogn' uno si stimava dover essere in quel punto subissato, alzando tutti le mani al cielo, chiedono a Dio misericordia, abbandonando ciascuno le cose proprie si diedero a fuga, dove stimavano più sicuro lo scampo, Chi ricorre a Tempj p[er] ricevere li S.S. Sacram[en]ti. Il Cardinale Buoncompagni Archivescovo di Napoli, fece esporre [Fol. 23, Col. 1] il S.S. Sacram[en]ti in tutte le Chiese, e salà con Processione Generale al Glorioso Protettore S.n Gennaro, nella qual chiesa, con somma ammirazione prima di incontrarsi con la Testa, s'era trovato liquefatto, e bollente il Sangue Glorioso, come se allora fosse sparso, ch'è stimato per buon segno, come partecipando della Beatitudine s'affaticasse p[er] impetrarci la liberazione del male: ma quando resta indurito, ⟨senza fatigar⟩ p[er] noi, allora si teme qualche castigo. Per 15 giorni continui restorono chiusi li tribunalia, le Boteghe, ed appena si poteva passare p[er]le strade à causa delle Processioni.

La gente delli Casali, e terre attorno della Montagna correndo alla volta di Napoli; p[er] morire dentro d'una città Popolata, e piene di corpi, e Reliquie di Santi, non portando con loro altro che timore, e tremore, e confusi, avviliti, e sbigottiti evidavano la fuga, ruine grandi, ruine grandi, giudizio finale, morte, fuoco, ira di Dio; L'istesso fecero quelli, che nelle filluche, e Barche venivano à questa volta.

9. Nel Martedi verso 18. il giorno 16. i vapori ed esalazioni della voragine, tutte calliginose, e nere oscurarono tutta l'aria con una puzza di zolfo, e Bitume abbruciato, nunzio del fuoco, e fiamme {a: Plin. lib. 6. ep. 16. flamarumq[u]e praenuncius odor sufuris. sufuris.} tanto intenso, che impediva il respiro, e quasi soffocava la Gente.

A 21. ora comminciarono in Napoli a sentirsi i continui tremori p[er] li quali crollarano talmente le case, e ballavano i tetti, che quasi [Fol. 23, Col. 2] lasciati i propri fondam[en]ti parevano andare ora quà, ora là, come fussero tante Barche {a: Ibid. Plin.} Crebris vastisque tremoribus tecta nutabant, et quasi

emota levibus suis nunc huc, nunc illuc abire, aut refferri videbantur; con spaventevole strepito in aria, come suol fare la bocca di una ben accesa Fornace; altri come continuati tiri di Bombarde, con molte lingue di fuoco, e fulgori scintillanti, con denso vapore e perpetui rimbombi, con continuo conquassam[en]to delle case, e tanti spaventevoli tuoni, ed orribili Lampi, che atterrito ogn' uomo, e pareva di avere la morte avanti gl' occhj, e che fusse loro intimato il giorno del giudizio universale con la tromba del Cielo, onde incontrandosi insieme, si abbracciavano con le lagrime su gl' occhj, come fussero stati fratelli carnali, benche non si conoscessero, licenziandosi p[er] l'altra vita.

Le pietre, rapilli, ed arene, che pioveva, si dilatavano p[er]la via di ariano dodici miglia distante, in tanta quantità, che in alcuni luoghi s'alzo più di dodici palmi. In Lucera di Puglia un Palmo. In Foggia poco meno. In Barletta, in Bari, in Lecce, ed Otranto un dito, in Napoli era molto poca, e principiò a 23. ore, e cadde tutta la notte, e parte del giorno seguente [Fol. 24, Col. 1] una sotilissima asciutta, # ⟨#cenere⟩ benche vischiosa non si alzò un dito.

Arrivò ancora sino a Constantinopoli, Gataro, Ragusa, Sardegna, da pertutto ne sono state mandate à Napoli le mostre delle ceneri, come cosa strana, ed a Napolitani occulta; Fùrono nell' istesso tempo veduti nella valle di Spoleto nell' Umbria, e vicino a Peruggia in Toscana, ed in Calabria Lampi di fuoco, ed uditi rimbombi p[er] l'aria come di carozze, che corressero, e tiri di bombarde con terremoti simili, e p[er] tutto si oscurò il sole, e si imbruni talmente il Cielo, che in alcuni luoghi pareva più che una continua notte priva del Lume della luna, e delle stelle, come in una stanza serrata, e senza Lucerne {a: Plin. lib. 6. ep. 20.} Nox non qualis illumis, aut nubila sed qualis in locis clausis, lumine extincto.

10. Alla Rochetta 15. miglia distante dal Vesuvio si apri un monte di Pietre con terremoti, ed in differenti parti caddero case, e chiese, come in Lauro, in Mirabello, e Fontanarosa.

E tornando a Napoli, che cominciò anche ricoprirsi da ceneri, e continuando l'istessi spettacoli p[er] tutta la notte di Terremoti e rumori in Aria, accrebbe tanto il timore, che uscendo dalle case proprie altro non si sentiva che strilla di femine, pianti di Fanciulli, rammarichi di uomini, Fol. 24, Col. 2] questa chiamava il marito, quella il Figliuolo, questi il Padre, e la Madre, chi cercava l'amico, e chi il congiunto, lamenti delle sciagure, di compassione {a: Ibid.} audires ululatus Feminarum, infanti conqueritatus, clamores virorum, alii parentes, alii liberos, alii conjuges, vocibus requirebant, vocibus nascitabant: hi suum casum, illi suorum miserabantur, e chi p[er] timore della morte bramava la morte, facendo tutti il conto, che quella doveva essere l'ultima, e perpetua notte senza Speranza di rivedere il giorno;

Molti si ritirarono in Campagna, chi ne Luoghi aperti in Carozza, che ballavano dall' impeto de Terremoti, chi si fabricò di Tavole una trabacca: la maggior parte si ritirorono nelle Chiese, le quali stettero tutte le notte aperte, p[er] quivi morire, e confessarsi, però non bastarano ne le Chiese, ne li confessori, onde molti si confessorono, in tutte le piazze, publicam[en]te alzando la voce.

Alle 8. ore fù raddoppiato il strepito, e poco doppo cominciarono versare dalla voragine del Vesuvio una materia liquida, che allagò tutto l'atrio |:{b: *Tav. XL*.} e nel giorno seguente doppo le 16. ore si senti un grandissimo Terremoto:| e fece delli [**Fol. 25, Col. 1**] grandissimi, e rapidi torrenti, sopra Ottajano, che sgorgarono nel piano di Nola, allagando St. Elmo, Saviano, e contorni, affogando molte persone: in Marigliano, Ciceciano, e Cisterna, si alzo in un tratto 12.14. palmi. {**I.M.**: *torrenti di acqua, solfo, terra, cenere, fango, ardente allagarono i paesi, affogavano la gente, distrussero, rapirono case, masserie, &.*} Un altro verso S.ta Maria Vetrana rovinò Massa, li Palazzi, e Masserie; atterrando quasi tutto Trocchia, e la metà di Pollena, con molti danni à S.a Bastiano: Li altri alla marina verso Bosco, e frà la Torre Annunciata, e Greco, e sopra Resina, e verso Somma, precedendo loro li monti della piovuta cenere, e macere di pietre infocate, e selve di arbori ardenti, seguitando le acque sulfuree, bittuminose ardentissime, con sommo precipizio, e danno, distrussero affatto Bosco, Torre Anunciata, e Greco, Granatello, e parte di Resina, e scorsero fin alle 19. ore. Alcuni pensando farsi lume, e tornare alla Torre del Greco, in numero di 150. furono rapiti à un tratto da quelle onde infernali: molte case furono dirocate, ed ancora alzate da fondam[en]ti in aria, e trasportate altrove, ed anche alcune collinette, Promontorj, ed intiere masserie, con gl' uomini, animali, case, ed alberi furono sommersi in mare, facendo con quelle masserie lingue, e penisole d'un buon mezzo miglio, e dentro del mare si [**Fol. 25, Col. 2**] vidde da Napoli uscire le fiamme degl' alberi ardenti. Alcuni di quelli fiumi erano come del sapone squagliato. Durò in Napoli la pioggia della cenere insino alle 17. ore, e cominciò à un tratto a calore dal cielo tant' acqua, che p[er]le strade correvano come fiumi di lescia, e cosi tutto il giorno p[er] tutte queste Provincie. Nel pian di Nola primà della pioggia d'acqua, ricominciò quella delle pietre, arena, e rapilli, e si ricoperse tutto quel Paese di si densa oscurità, che neanche colle torce accese potevano gl' uomini vedersi l'un l'altro, ed essendo il tutto accompagnato da fulgori sopra modo spaventevoli, da tuoni terribili, e

terribilissime Saette, e più gagliardi Terremoti, tempeste, somersioni della campagna, dal ciel fulminar le Case, dall' aria aprirsi le Cataratte, piovere terra, arena, ceneri, e fango, grandinar pietre, e pietre infocate, e smisurate &. Il mare anco ne senti la sua parte che attorno al lido, tanto in Ischia, Sorrento, ed in questa banda si ritirò p[er] lo spazio di cir[c]a un miglio, e stiede cosi con stupore di tutti circa un' ottavo d'ora. Il ritiro era cosi subito, che in questo molo di Napoli restarono quasi in secco le navi. {**I.M.**: ritiro del mare d'un miglio.} L'acqua era [**Fol. 26, Col. 1**] riscaldata, e si trovarono alle spiagge molti pesci morti. Frà tutti questi continui terremoti, che si sentivano sopra terra, ve ne fù uno straordinario, che in un basso di 95. gradi sotterraneo in una cantina fece ballar le botte.

11. Doppo non si sono sentiti più cosi frequenti ne Gagliardi sino alli 5. di Febbraio fra le 8. e 9. ore, se ne senti un terribilissimo, con tuoni fulgori, baleni orribilissimi, e grossissima grandine, che in questa Città alzò un mezzo palmo. Una pietra ardente è sopragiunta à un uomo à Cavallo alla Barra, e vi rimase morto; e cosi accadette à molti altri in diverse parti, de quali sonsi{??} poi vedute le membra sparse in quà, e là. A un uomo furono tolti dal fianco, e dal braccio due figluoli senza accorgersene. Un altro fuggendo, avendo in dietro di le molta gente, e due carozze, voltandosi à dietro, non vidde più gente ne carozze. E molti altri si sono trovati morti nelle ceneri che parevano vivi; toccandoli, si trovavano inceneriti. In una casa dove entrò ne fuoco, ne ceneri, si trovo inceneriti due uomini, senza che li vestiti avessero patiti.

[**Fol. 26, Col. 2**] Più stupenda cosa era quella che accade p[er]la via di Pietrabianca, dove essendo caduta una Giovane con un Figliolino al petto in quel torrente infocato, e correndo il Marito p[er] soccorerla, vi cadde anch' Egli, e tutti due rimassero morti, restando viva la Creatura con la morta mamella in bocca.

S.to Iorio à Cremano tutto quanto s'abbruciò. A' S.ta Maria del Soccorso in Pietrabianca, furono trovate da Ministri Regij 12. case distrutte.

Sabato li 20. Sucedette una terribile tempestà. Alli 29. circa le 8. ore di notte si udi un rumore straordinario, parendo che fusse caduta una montagna. Alli 30. X.bre alle 12. si senti un gran tremore, e durò un pezzo à far scuotere le Case.

Bosco è restato tutto desolato, come ancora Torre anunciata quasi tutta fù portata via da uno di quei torrenti. La campagna insino à Resina tutta rasa, e ricoperta di ceneri, alte in alcune parti più di 12. pal:

La Torre del Greco, quasi tutta spianata da fondam[en]ti, tanto miserabilm[en]te, che molte case non si sapea dov' erano state.

In Resina ancora erano rovinate molte [Fol. 27, Col. 1] Case, ed il Granatello distrutto affatto.

In Nola erano cadute 120. case, ed altre resesi inabitabili. Cicciano, Saviano, S.n Paolo, Marigliano, Mariglianello, Pomigliano, e quasi tutta quella pianura insino à Palma era rimasta tutt' in acqua. Le pietre grosse cadute anno rovinato delle case sino ad Avellino, e Tripalda. Forino, Montuolo, Monteforte, ed altre Terre avevano patito assai; gran quantità di animali, ed ucelli in aria aggravati dal peso delle ceneri, se ne sono caduti in [IN WEBER'S HAND??] terra, e per non trovare ancora il cibo per le campagne ne luogo da posaruisi sopra, per essere il tutto ricoperto dalle ceneri; tanto grande era il numero di questi animaletti morti, che se ne sarebbe potuto carricare le some intere. E tutti altri animali anco questi atterriti da continui terramoti dall' oscurità, e dalla pioggia di cosi inusitata materia, scorrendo or quà, or là questi mugghiando, quelli belando altri rignando, altri urlando, latrando, e anendosi senza distinzione di genere ristretti insieme, caggionavano, à chi li vedeva, ò udiva, estreme compassione, e poi con la lor morte notabile danno.

Oltra poi all'effetti di quest' incendio, naturali, e terrore, che a quasi tutta Europa ha comunicato con tante portento-[Fol. 27, Col. 2]so commozioni nella Terra, nell' aria, e in tutti gl' elementi, ne ha operato ancora delli sopranaturali, risvegliando talmente in tutti il timore della morte, che ne segui in molti l'emandazione della vita, e tornarono à penitenza, ⟨e tornarono à penitenza⟩ alcuni, che vollero publicare, d'aver lasciato passare chi trenta, e chi trentasei anni, senza essersi mai confessato, facendo penitenza publica, gridando per tutta la Città ad alta voce, con corde, e catene di ferro, al collo; misericordia!

12. L'Incendio dunque dell' año 1631 – è stato uno de più orribili, di cui restando memorie funestissime, essendoci distrutti presso à 7. villaggi, e perirono circa 10. mil uomini {a: Carafa de conflagrat. Vesuviana. 10 mila. Procupito dice 5. mila.} Il Procupito dice circa cinque mila. Da quel tempo à questa parte, benche le accensioni frequentissime, non recarono tanto strage: sicome fù quello del 1660, che fu poco considerabile: Ma più veemente era quello del 1682. che duro dalli 14. à 26. agusto con terribili fiame |:che incendirono la silva d'Ottaiano:| e fùmo densissimo, che per due giorni continui se oscurò il sole, con rimbombi, che crollavano le case di Napoli, e sino à 8. miglia ancora distanti, con grandinar delle pietre pomici infocate e ceneri, e con puzza insoffribile [Fol. 28, Col. 1] insoffribile di solfo. Quella del año 1685. fù ancora molto forte, e si sentivano li tuoni per 8. giorni in distanza più di 20. miglia, fugivano tutti vicini, e Napoli era tutta atterrita

per li terremoti; Alzandosi una |:allora nuova:| montagna in mezzo nel atrio, che e quella, che oggi li si vede; Considerabile era quel altro Incendio, que accadde à principio del 7.bre 1689. |:e duro molto tempo:| per tanti sassi e ceneri lanciati in aria e recaduti, che accrebbero Il Vesuvio di circa 500. palmi d'altezza. La eruzzione de 1694. fù una delle più spaventose doppo quelle del ___31. e fra altri strepitosi effetti, gettava il monte un gran torrente di bitume infocato, che per lo spazio di 5. miglia riempi tutte le valli adiacenti. E nell'año 1696. à 4. Agusto, la gran quantità di bitume che sorti per la voragine della montagno, |:di cui cratere si dilatò più d'un miglio:| haveva chiuso interamente l'antica apertura: A' 1697. sorti una semplice accensione à 16. Febr[ai]o, e nell' istess' año quella nel fine d' Agusto, che continuo sino alli 19. 7.bre portò al bitume nelle vicinanze delli P.P. Capucini alla Torre di Greco, e altro Torrente simile fra Ottaiano e Bosco, e si fermò à 27. 7.bre; mà quella che cominccò al fine di 9.bre, e durò infino à Genaro 1698. Come la del [Fol. 28, Col. 2] 17. di Maggio sussequente, che continuò sin alla metà del Giugno, è l'altra del 1.o Luglio 1701, furono di poca considerazione. Doppo viene quell' Incendio terribilissimo del año 1707. {a: iquale al orribile del 1631. eccetto, che non si allagarono gli paesi, ne morirono la gente.} E per non ripetere l'istesso, si rimete à quello, che e stato riferito del funesto Incendio à 1631. al quale era simile, eccetto solamente, che non si allagarono gli Paesi, e non morirono la gente; L'istessi erano li tuoni, rimbombi, fiame, fumi, strepiti, tempeste di sassi infocati, ceneri, arene, tossenti, terremoti, e scoppi terribili, che furono inteso sin à Roma; Il giorno ancora si fece notte, la densita delle ceneri caliginose impedi quasi il respiro &. Principio nelli 26. Luglio, e durò coll' istesso vigore sin alli 2. Agusto; La cenere era tanto densa e spessa, che se troppa avessi durato, suffocava tutta la gente; ma di questa calamità è stata liberata la Cita di Napoli, dalla Misericordia Divina {a: ut fol. 18. colon. 2. in notis, in (b)} per l'intercessione di S. Genaro Glorioso, Protettore, nell' istess' ora, quando fu fatta umile e divota Processione con la Testa del Santo Martire, Implorando il Divino Ajuto; essendo nell' istesso tempo rasserenato il Cielo, ed allontanati li ceneri,; e per eterna memoria, di questo miracolo, e di tante grazie, i Deputati della Capella del Tesoro, haño fatto imprimere una un medaglione coll' effigie del Santo [Fol. 29, Col. 1] ed intorno, queste lettere, D. IANV. LIBERATORI. ORBIS. FVNDATORI. QVIETIS. da una parte; e dall' altre con le ampolle del suo miracoloso Sangue, sopra una ghirlanda, e queste parole in mezzo. **Postquam. collapsi. cineres. et. flama. quievit. cives. Neapolitani. incolumes.**

A.D. MDCCVII. Avendosi alzato ancora un Epitafio con
la Statua del Santo sopra le scale di S.a Chaterina à
Formelli, per memoria del gran miracolo. Mirabilis
Deus in Sanctis suis. Ricordandosi poi del Incendio
de 1730, dalla violenza di quelle fiame, è stata la
figura della sumita del monte mutata, e repigliata
sulla cima la materia, spiananado, e ribassando al
quanto la sua vertice, ò punta, che primà era più
aguza e alta. Il torrente delle materia liquide fluvia
poco distante, le pietre, e ceneri infocate incendia-
vano una selva d' Ottaiano; Però se tagliò il passo alle
fiame, con abbattere gli alberi à mezza via qualche
tratto di terra. Da questo tempo per il corso di 7. añi
continui si è veduta la montagna sempre con qualche
fumo, e talora fuoco; del che li Paesani credevano
disminuir da poco à poco la materia combustibile, e
sicurarli dall' accensione straordinaria e pericolosa;
Fallita però quella volta l'opinione, si aumentò il
fuoco nel di 14. di Maggio 1737, fiama, e fumo,
gettando sassi e materia liquide, infocati, versando un
torrente verso Bosco: Nel di 19. Maggio strepitava la
bocca con movimento più [Fol. 29, Col. 2] forte, e
con turbinoso spinto à maggior altezza, con gorgoglio,
e fremito per aria, e gran getto di sassi infocati con
sumo spavento delli Paesani; e crebbe sempre più la
densità del fumo, la pioggia delli sassi, e pomici,
ceneri, e scoppi rovinosi, tanto che tutta la vincinanza
cominciò à fuggire; Apri il monte nuove crepature, e
ne rendeva più orribile lo spettacolo, con oscure
nebbie, gettando rapidi e violenti torrenti di fuoco
verso Resina, che si buttò dentro d'una vicina vallata,
abbrucciando molti terreni coltivati, e se avessi
continuato, sarebbe venuto per altro à scarigarsi per
la strada de Capucini in mezzo alla Torre del Greco:
Gl' altri torrenti haño abbatuto qualche casa, e poteri
verso la parte orientale dell' istessa Torre in mezzo
alla via publica, cacciandosi dentro della chiesa de
Purgatorio brucciando la sacra Supelletile: Un altro
torrente ò lava entrò ancora qualche palmo dentro la
chiesa del Carmine, doppo aver inceneriti li ostacoli;
e per causa dell' Angustia del luogo se gonfio,
penetrando per le fenestre, e porte del Sagrestia, e
Refettorio, facendo tutto questo camino in 6. ore; Vi
erano Altri, che distrussero masserie, e terreni, ed
ano giunse vicino al mare: Restava il Monte tutto
acceso ed illuminato, accrescendo il spavento per gli
moltissimi terremoti. Gli ardenti ginestri sul pendio
della montagna eccitavano varie fantasie ne' ignari.
Durò quest' orribile apparato delli 14. Maggio [Fol.
30, Col. 1] sin alli 6. di Giugno, quando gli torrenti si
fermarono in sasso, e ne resto altro, che un poco di
fumo, puzza di solfo, e certi malvagi odori. Essendo
queste materie ancora della grand' utilità, mentre che
delli ceneri, arene, ò terra di fuoco, ò pozolana, se

compone una perfettissima mistura della calce; delli
lapilli si fanò gli astrichi; delli pomici, le volte; delli
torrenti fermati in sasso, vengono pavimentate tutte le
strade vicine, e tutta la Città di Napoli; che poi si
chiamano, Strade basolate. Per tutti gli anni sussequenti, la montagna mai è stata libera di fumo, e
talora di fuoco; e nel mese di 9.bre 1752 comincio di
nuovo versare un torrente ò lava infocata, e continuò
quasi pe ogni año sin à 1760. con aprire nuove
crepature; talvolta gettando per la boca superiore
sassi e ceneri infocati, gli quali ricadendo sopra
l'istessa vertice, formarono un' altra picciola montag-
nola sopra posta, e continuando, crebbe tanto in alto,
e nella sua base, che al ultimo e venuto à formare
tutto insieme un solo monte, e la punta della
montagna cosi accresciuta repigliando la sua prima
figure, più aguzza e alta come stava à 1730. come
poco in anzi si è detta. Succedette questo accresci-
mento con getti di sassi, rumori spaventosi, e scoppi
continui, che fecero crollare le case; effetti delle gran
cadute de pezzi grandi, come montagnuole, di terra,
di sassi, rupi, ed altre materie, dentro la gran
voragine, qual strepitosa fonzione{??}, e rumori, mina-
cciava qualche inaudito evenimento, mentrecche, il
fuoco distrugendo, sbranando, e consumando dentro
lo vacuo del monte, i lati ò piedi; i queli come
muraglie ò volte, sostengono tutto il masso del monte,
ed alla fine sottilizandosi troppo, nô poterebbero
dette muraglie più reggorsi, ed in tal orribile caso, si
potrebbe abissare tutto il monte |:che in figura d'una
pina sta in mezzo nel atrio:| piegandosi dentro del
concavo, ò voragine |:in tal caso divenuta troppo
ampia per causa delli lati consumati del fuoco:| nell'
istessa maniera, come dele mure, tetto, ò volte d'una
casa per essere [Fol. 30, Col. 2] troppo sottili,
cadessero tutti insieme dentro il vacuo dell' istesso
edificio; Però l' istesse torrenti, che dentro la
voragine vengono sospinti ed alzati sin alla bocca |:e
poi non tutti escono:| riempiono il vacuo, e servono
come contraforti alle sud[dett]e muraglie e volte;
Cose maravigliose si sono vedute à 1631. essendo
miracolosamente preservati differenti edifici, alli
quali, più al pericolo esposti, pare che le fiame,
ceneri, e torrenti abbiano loro portato rispetto; Il che
si verifico nella Chiesa di S.M. Pugliano, e tutto il suo
territorio contiguo |:{a: Tobid. 12.7} Sarramentum
Regis abscondere bonum est, opera autem Dei
revelare et confiteri honorificum:| mentreche uno di
questi torrenti infocati, essendo giunto à confini di
detta Chiesa, per non toccarli, si divise in due rami,
circondandoli tutti intorno lasciandoli del tutto
intatti; abbruscando, quanto era ne gl' altri sotto e
sopra. E' rimasta illesa ancora con maggior dimo-
strazzione la Chiesa delle Madona del Arco, e li

territorj suoi, che sono rimpetto alla facciata delle Montagna; essendosi abbrucciato, rovinato, e spiantato, quanto vi era del rimanente intorno: Concorda à questo, lo che haño riferito tutta la casa dell' istessa chiesa 70. religiosi e gran moltitudine di gente, aver veduto con gli occhi proprij, essendosi martedi 16. del X.bre 1631. quando cominciò quell' orribile Incendio ritirato in quella chiesa, moltitudine di gente, come in una sacra arca standovi tutti in Orazione avanti la Capella della Madonna, che sta in mezzo alla Chiesa, sulle 21. ora à vista d'ogni uno, fu conosciuto, che quella Miracolosa Imagine, la quale coll Fanciullo Gesú in braccio, è dipinta à guazzo in un muro, cominccciò talmente ad imbiancarsi nella faccia, che appena si scorgeva: e poco doppoi, apparve più del solito colorita, e rossa, con le labra livide, e con la percossa, che ha nel volta dal lato sinistro datale à 1499. da quello scelerato giuscatore, tantò tinta di sangue, come se allora avessi ricevuta è appresso le furono da molti vedute uscir dagli occhi alcune lagrime ò gocciole di vivo sangue; Onde alzatosi il Maestro de' Novizij di que' Padri Tomissicani dal [Fol. 31] Confessionale, dove come tutti gli altri Sacerdoti in altri parti, stava occupato in ascoltare le confessioni, e salito sopra l'altare, con una torcia in mano, vidde e fece vedere à tutti, che dalle palpebre di sotto di quei pietosi occhi pendevano tutta via due lagrime, come due rubini, ò goccie di sangue. Dal che ano di quei Padri per inanimare la gente, che ben ne aveva necessità con l'esempio di Ester {a: Ester. c. 7.3.}, la quale per impetrar la vita al suo popolo si impallidì, e piante avanti il Re Assuero, argomêto, che quello impallidirsi, arrossirsi e piangere della Vergine

fossi stato segno dell Affetto, col quale aveva placato l'ira di Dio contro di noi e cosi dichiarò l'evento; L'istesso si vidde in quella di Constantinopoli qui in Napoli, e sin dal principio di maggio del 1532. |:e si vede giornalmente:| che allora correndo il pericolo della peste per tutta Italia esserci da quella liberato. Laudate Deum in Sanctis suis. Doppo che si e parlato della distruzzione delle antiche città sotterranee, corrispondeva à dir qualche cosa delli Incendj Vesuviani, dalli quali sono state rovinate, dove si ravisano le minaccie della strage |:dell'año 82., di I.C.:| in tempo dell' Idololatria; e la liberazione per la Divina Misercordia, e intercessione de Santi; dell' istesso male. {b: int. fol. 18. colon. 2. in. b. in notis.}

Il non dare in questo a punto una compêdiosa serie di questi Incendj, pare che sarebbe stato mancanza, e troppo, che desiderare: Il voler poi diffondersi troppo con la spiegazione d'ogni minuzia, come dela causa materiale, efficiente, formale, e finale, e qualità delle materia, &. già che si trovano tanti trattati di questo, sarebbe troppo scostarsi del nostro Instituto.

NOTE TO FOL. 32

1. Si è trovato questo Quadro di Basso rilievo nelli Scavi dell'antica Stabia li 7. Agusto 1752. in un nicchio della gran piazza {a: Fol: 9. à 10. Tav. I. nella Pianta Let: H. Num. 5. in N. Et. Fol: 2. Colon: 2 in Not. Et Fol. 5 in Text. Et Fol. 14. Col: 2.} e rappresenta un uomo nudo con cerchio e palma che senza dubbio significa un giocatore di Palestra, che si presenta dopo la Victoria &c. &c.

Draft of plan of the peristyle at Stabiae

This single folio was found inserted into Weber's manuscript on Le Piante di Alcuni Edifici Sotterranei (see Appendix 3). Although the title ascribes the building to Herculaneum, it in fact appears to be the peristyle from the Villa di San Marco at Stabiae; note 4 refers to a second peristyle to the west, and to the collapse of a portion of the building down a ravine. This is probably a draft he prepared for his manuscript, and although the plan itself was subsequently excluded, many of the details described here were incorporated into the manuscript's text.

LIBRO
DEGLI EDIFICJ SOTTERRANEI
D'ERCOLANO

i[RECTO] In questa Pianta si crede di precedere gli altri edificj la gran Piazza[1] ornata con esquisita magnificenza nel frontispizio di dentro con nicchi di figure di basso rilievo, e Mosaico[2] e superbo Peristylio e Portico[3] al quale da ingresso la via publica dalla parte di Occidente colli vestigji di un altra Area che si suppone Palestra, o Ambulacro[4] [VERSO] con un Bagno dalla parte di Settentrione[5].

NOTES

1. Ex Greco PLATEIA [in Greek], gia diventata voce comune di piazza, dimostrando un piano spazioso p[e]r il concorso, e comodità delli cittadini, come p[e]r loro divertim[en]ti, e Spasseggi come p[e]r trattare sopra loro affari, e comerci. Locus publicus, et frequentis concursus. Et Lampridius in Eliogabalo, in sensu Latiore, la usurpa come un aria privata ed ambulatoria negl' Edifizj grandi. Plateas in Palatio stravit: uti sunt cavedia, et subdalia Xysta colla diferenza però del xysto che secondo Vitruvio significa: Porticus ampla, et probe tecta ubi Athletae pluvio tempore per diem subsistentes morabantur parcentes Ludus, et alijs exercitationibus: ma è diferente del foro come dice: erat in urbe spatiosus Locus potens, et sedes judiciorum, quo cives conveniebant ad jus acipiendum, et controversias dirigendas, unde forum aperire, forum indicere, forum agere, reperitur apud scriptores. Susseguentem[en]te serviva ancora di mercato. ut Plinius Junior in Epis: ad Valerianum. Virum Praetorium à senatu contendisse, ut sibi instituere in agris suis nundinas permiteretur; et teste Livio: ex vicis partim habuisse Rem publicam et jus dictum, partim nihil eorum et tamen ibi nundinas actas.

2. La maggior parte delli pavim[en]ti di questi antichi edificj sono di mosaico, o Lapilli quadri di marmo, ut Philander: ex Tesseris et sectilibus Lapillis versicoloribus certo ordine dispositis, ut figuram aliquam geometricam, aut quamvis spectabilem imaginem coeant; at non in solis pavimentis stetit hoc opus, sed inde ad Parietes, et fornices exornandas superbius assurexit: hoc est amusseatum opus.

3. Ex Greca notione, Peristylium idem est ac circum columnium, che nel caso, tiene anche probabilità d'essere una celebre Palestra, p[e]r essere il circuito suo circa due stadij, o 250. passi geometrici, comuni a tutti, di pal: 6. on: 7. lin: 11 e 6." confrontato, e fanno pal: 770.; misurando il circuito della nostra piazza, poco diferenza si trova, onde poteva essere Palestra per il Spazio, per le colonne, e per la magnificenza, ut Vitr.: de Palestris lib: 5. Cap: 11. ut Peristylia sive quadrata, sive oblonga, ita fiant ut duorum stadiorum habeant ambulationem, circuitionem, ed erano destinati agl' esercizi Publici, ut Sunt, Lucta, pugillatus, Lusus in disco, hasta, Pila, saltus. Li Portici verso ponente, e mezzodi, che regnono intorno della Piazza, non Lasciono indicare d'essere stati coperti con tegole, e matone, per aver trovato in quel sito quantita notabile, al piede dell' istesso intercolonio, che piacevolm[en]te concedeva il libero passaggio dell' aria, e spasseggio nell' esta, godendo L'ombra del tetto, e nell' inverno il ricovero in tempo di

pioggia. Vitr: sub eis repentinas pluvias vitabant, umbraque, et frigora captavant.

4. Si vede dalla parte di Ponente un principio d'un altr' area con simili intercolonj, che erano interrotti per la cadute della terra del Pendio di quella ripa, come si osserva nella Pianta, e pare qualche probabilità d'esser stato forse ancora Palestra, o ambulacro: Vitr: Lib: 5. Cap: 9. Quo erant sub divo inter porticûs |:Spatia:| adornanda viridibus, videntur, quod hypetrae ambulationes habent magnam salubritatem.

5. [VERSO] Usavano gl' antichi per costume generalm[en]te li bagni tanto per il lusso, come per la salute, erano splendidissimamente cinti di Colonne, e li pareti ornati con buone pitture, e pavim[en]ti di musaico, ed osservando le camere, che sono d'intorno, pare che abino qualche riporto a quella che descrive Plin: Iun. in Epist: ad Apollinarem lib: 5.: In cornu, porticus amplissim. cubiculum a Triclinio ocurrit, aliis fenestris, Xystum et Vitr: magnitudines autem balnearum videntur fieri pro copia hominum, &.

Notes

INTRODUCTION

1 A.M. Quirini, "Epistola ad Joan. Math. Gesnerum de Herculano (Brescia 1748)," in A.F. Gori, *Symbolae litterariae: Opuscula varia philologica . . .* [Decas 2] (Rome 1751–54) 1.ix–xxiv.

2 J.J. Winckelmann, *Sendschreiben von den herculanischen Entdeckungen* (Dresden 1762) #29 (the numbering system refers to the individual paragraphs used in most original editions and translations): "wie der Mond mit Krebsen," the latter often translated into English as "lobsters." Winckelmann was paraphrasing Vincenzio Borghini (1515-1580), "si sentono speso . . . vantarsi di certi parentadi, che hanno tanto a fare insieme, quanto la luna co' granchi o i liofanti con le bertucce."

3 G. Castaldi, *Della Regale Accademia Ercolanese dalla sua fondazione sinora con un cenno biografico de' suoi soci ordinari* (Naples 1840) 29.

4 M. Ruggiero, *Degli scavi di Stabia dal 1749–1782* (Naples 1881) vi.

5 E.R. Barker, *Buried Herculaneum* (London 1908) 22.

6 M. Brion, *Pompeii and Herculaneum: The glory and the grief* (London 1960) 45.

7 A. Maiuri, *Gli scavi di Pompei nel programma delle opere della Cassa per il Mezzogiorno* (Naples 1951) 26–28. G. Cosenza, *Stabia: Studi archeologici, topographici e storici* (Trani 1907) 28.

8 J.W. Goethe, *Italienische Reise*, ed. H. von Einem (Munich 1978) 211–12 (March 18, 1797, at Naples). All translations are by the author.

9 M. Ruggiero, *Storia degli scavi di Ercolano ricomposta su' documenti superstiti* (Naples 1885) xlii.

10 Ch. Waldstein and L. Shoobridge, *Herculaneum past, present and future* (London 1908) 128.

11 G. Fiorelli, ed., *Pompeianarum Antiquitatum Historia quam ex cod. mss. et a schedis diurnisque R. Alcubierre, C. Weber, M. Cixia, I. Corcoles, et al.* 3 vols. (Naples 1860–64).

12 M. Ruggiero, *Degli scavi di Stabia dal 1749–1782* (Naples 1881), and *Storia degli scavi di Ercolano ricomposta su' documenti superstiti* (Naples 1885).

13 F. Barnabei, "Gli scavi di Ercolano," *MemLinc* Ser. 3.2 (1877-78) 751–68. For abbreviations used in these notes, see the list of Abbreviations.

14 D. Comparetti, "La villa de' Pisoni in Ercolano e la sua biblioteca," 159–76, and G. de Petra, "I monumenti della villa ercolanese," 251–71, in *Pompei e la regione sotterrata dal Vesuvio nell' anno LXXIX . . .* (Naples 1879); D. Comparetti, "Relazione sui papiri ercolanesi," *MemLinc*, Ser. 3, 5 (1880) 145–78; D. Comparetti and G. de Petra, *La Villa Ercolanese dei Pisoni: I suoi monumenti e la sua biblioteca, Ricerche e notizie* (Turin 1883).

15 E.g., W. Stiebing, Jr., *Uncovering the past: A history of archaeology* (Buffalo 1993) 145–53. Conte Corti's work is now in its ninth edition and has been translated into a number of languages. As an example of this conventionalized reading of the Bourbon excavations, see the remarks of B. Trigger, *A history of archaeological thought* (Cambridge 1989) 36–38, the only reference made to these sites in his study:

> For a long time there was no excavation in the modern sense but merely digging in search of objects that had aesthetic and commercial value. The excavations that began at the well-preserved Roman sites of Herculaneum and Pompeii in the first half of the eighteenth century were treasure hunts of this sort, although a desire to recover the statues and other works of art gradually came to

be accompanied by an interest in Roman domestic architecture. There was, however, little concern for understanding the context in which finds were made. The owners of the land under which Pompeii was buried rented the right to entrepreneurs to dig there by the cubic yard.

16 C. Gallavotti, "Nuovo contributo alla storia degli scavi borbonici di Ercolano (nella Villa dei Papiri)," *RendNap* n.s. 20 (1939–40) 269–306.

17 U. Pannuti, "Il 'Giornale degli scavi' di Ercolano (1738–1756)," *MemLinc* Ser. 8, 26.3 (1983) 163–410. Because portions of the original manuscript were illegible, Pannuti relied heavily on a copy of it made in 1870–80, found in the archives of the Soprintendenza Archeologica di Napoli e Caserta.

18 R. Herbig, *Don Carlos de Borbón, Excavador de Herculano y Pompeya* (Madrid 1954); republished as "Don Carlos von Bourbon als Ausgräber von Herculaneum und Pompeji," *MadMitt* 1 (1960) 11–19.

19 Published as F. Fernandez Murga, "Roque Joaquin de Alcubierre, descubridor de Herculano, Pompeya y Estabia," *ArchEspArq* 35 (1962) 3–35.

20 F. Fernandez Murga, *Carlos III y el descubrimiento de Herculano, Pompeya y Estabia* (Salamanca 1989). Though Fernandez Murga handled certain matters in a similar manner to this study, his conclusions are quite different. An example is his belief that the rift between Alcubierre and Weber developed only after some years and under the influence of Paderni.

21 M. Pia Rossignani, "Saggio sui restauri settecenteschi ai dipinti di Ercolano e Pompei," *Contributi dell' Istituto di Archeologia* 1 (1967) 7–134. L.A. Scatozza Höricht later published a similar study that made use of archival records for the restoration of paintings, mosaics, and sculptures in the museum at Portici (L.A. Scatozza Höricht, "Restauri alle collezioni del Museo Ercolanese di Portici alla luce di documenti inediti," *AttiAccPont* n.s. 31 (1982) 495-540).

22 A. Allroggen-Bedel, "Der Hausherr der 'Casa dei Cervi' in Herculaneum," *CronErc* 5 (1975) 99–103; "Die Malereien aus dem Haus *Insula Occidentalis*, 10," *CronPomp* 2 (1976) 144–83; and "Die Wandmalereien aus der Villa in Campo Varano (Castellammare di Stabia)," *RömMitt* 84 (1977) 27–89, pls. 1–53.

23 A. Allroggen-Bedel and H. Kammerer-Grothaus, "Das Museo Ercolanese in Portici," *CronErc* 10 (1980) 175–217, republished as "Il Museo Ercolanese di Portici," in *La Villa dei Papiri* (*CronErc* 13 Suppl. 2, Naples 1983) 83–127 [this later edition is the work referred to in the present work]; A. Allroggen-Bedel,

"Das sogennante Forum von Herculaneum und die borbonischen Grabungen von 1739," *CronErc* 4 (1974) 97–109, and "Dokumente des 18. Jahrhunderts zur Topographie von Herculaneum," *CronErc* 13 (1983) 139–58.

24 *Fonti documentarie per la storia degli scavi di Pompei, Ercolano e Stabia a cura degli archivisti napoletani* (Naples 1979).

25 The following are the principal catalogs and conference proceedings used in this study: *Civiltà del '700 a Napoli (1734–1799)*, 2 vols. (Florence 1980) and *The Golden Age of Naples: Art and civilization under the Bourbons (1734–1805)*, 2 vols. (Detroit 1981); *Pompei e gli architetti francesi dell' Ottocento* (Naples 1981); *Pompeii 1748–1980: I tempi della documentazione* (Rome 1981); *La regione sotterrata dal Vesuvio* (Naples 1982); *Pompeji 79–1979: Beiträge zum Vesuvausbruch und seiner Nachwirkung* (Stendal 1982); *I Borbone di Napoli e i Borbone di Spagna*, 2 vols. (Naples 1985); *Bernardo Tanucci: Statista, letterato, giurista*, 2 vols. (Naples 1986); and *Ercolano 1738–1988: 250 anni di ricerca archeologica* (Atti del Convegno Internazionale Ravello-Ercolano-Napoli-Pompei, 30 ottobre–5 novembre 1988) (Rome 1993).

26 C. Grell, *Herculanum et Pompéi dans les récits des voyageurs français du XVIIIe siècle* (Naples 1982).

27 F. Zevi, "Gli scavi di Ercolano," 2.58–74, in *Civiltà del '700 a Napoli (1734–1799)* (Florence 1980), and "Gli scavi di Ercolano e le *Antichità*," 11–38, in *Le antichità di Ercolano* (Naples 1988). F. Bologna, "Le scoperte di Ercolano e Pompei nella cultura europea del XVIII secolo," *PdP* 34 (1979) 377-404, and "La riscoperta di Ercolano e la cultura artistica del settecento Europeo," in *Le antichità di Ercolano* (Naples 1988) 83–105.

28 F. Strazzullo, "Documenti per l'Ing. Rocco Alcubierre scopritore di Ercolano," *AttiAccPont* 29 (1980) 263–81; "I primi anni dello scavo di Ercolano nel diario dell' ingegnere militare Rocco Gioacchino d'Alcubierre," 103–81, in *La regione sotterrata dal Vesuvio* (Naples 1982); and "Marcello Venuti, scopritore di Ercolano," *AttiAccPont* 40 (1991) 169–206.

29 G. Guadagno, "Supplemento epigrafico ercolanese II," *CronErc* 11 (1981) 129–64, and "Nuovi documenti del XVIII secolo per la storia degli scavi di Ercolano," *CronErc* 16 (1986) 135–47.

30 M. Gigante, "Carlo III e i papiri ercolanesi," 1.215–40, in *I Borbone di Napoli e i Borbone di Spagna*, 2 vols. (Naples 1985).

31 M. De Vos, "Camillo Paderni, la tradizione antiquaria romana e i collezioni inglesi," 99–116, in *Ercolano 1738–1988: 250 anni di ricerca archeologica* (Rome 1993).

32 I.C. McIlwaine, *Herculaneum: A guide to printed sources*, 2 vols. (Naples 1988) and "*Herculaneum: A guide to printed sources*, Supplement," *CronErc* 20 (1990) 87–128. For a review see C. Parslow, "Herculaneum: A new bibliography and recent work," *JRA* 3 (1990) 248–52. McIlwaine's book supersedes the earlier bibliographies on Herculaneum by F. Furchheim, *Biblioteca pompejana: Catalogo ragionato di opere sopra Ercolana e Pompei* (Naples 1879) and G. Zottoli, "Bibliografia ercolanese, a cura di Amedeo Maiuri," *BdA* 2 (1928–29) 47–81. Useful as well for Pompeian material is H. Van der Poel's, *Corpus topographicum Pompeianum*, vol. 4 (Rome 1977).

PART I. THE HISTORICAL BACKGROUND

CHAPTER 1. WEBER, ALCUBIERRE, AND THE FIRST YEARS OF THE EXCAVATIONS

1 This pedigree is in the possession of Dr. Werner Alois von Weber, Sedlern, Schwyz, Switzerland. It includes the year of Weber's death (1764), although it must have been painted earlier, since his rank is given only as captain; he was a lieutenant colonel at the time of his death. Many of the biographical details that follow are based on information supplied by Dr. von Weber (hereafter cited as Familienschriften von Weber, Sedlern, Schwyz).

2 Weber later made reference to his ancestors in a letter to Prime Minister Fogliani: "just as many Swiss ancestors have had the honor of serving the Most Powerful Royal House of Bourbon both in Spain and France, among whom was Rodolpho de Reding, my great-great-grandfather, knight and colonel in said Royal Service" (ASN *CRA* 1539, Inc. 44 [May 22, 1752]). The Redings who appear among the Royal Guard in Naples during Weber's period there include Felix (1714–1758) and Franz-Joseph-Carl (1729–1778); *Stabiae*, 108–9 (October 18, 1759). Charles of Bourbon, king of the Two Sicilies from 1738 to 1759, preferred the simple form of his name rather than his official title, Charles VII. He is commonly called "Charles III" when reference is made to the years after 1759, when he assumed the throne of Spain. This study refers to him as either "Charles of Bourbon" or "Charles III," depending on the period under discussion.

3 The house survived two fires that devastated Arth in the eighteenth century, one in 1719 that destroyed some seventy-seven houses and another in 1759 that engulfed most of the town.

4 Franz Dominik also attended the Gymnasium and Lycaeum of the Jesuit College at Lucerne from 1734 to 1736. As early as 1734 he had obtained his lieutenant's commission and so went directly into service for the Tschudi regiment in 1736, distinguishing himself in the Italian campaign; he became a captain in 1746, colonel in 1776, and brigadier in 1784; in 1790 he was president of a tribunal in Naples. Franz Dominik maintained ties with his fatherland by becoming a landowner and marrying a Schwyzer, Maria Josef Antonia Theresia, on September 27, 1756, in Schwyz. He later altered his name to "von Weber." He is buried at Capodimonte, Naples.

5 The Gymnasium at the Jesuit College in Lucerne included seven courses of study: Principistae, Rudimentistae, Grammatistae, Syntaxistae, Syntaxistae maiores, Humanistae, and Rhetores. After completing these a student passed into the Lycaeum for further courses in Logici, Metaphysici, Casuistae et Polemici, and Theologie. That Karl Jakob and his brother were placed in the rhetoric course when they entered the Gymnasium suggests that they had already attended Latin school in Arth.

6 His placement at the Collegio is another indication that his family was not wealthy. M. Marocchi, "La personalità di Pio V e le direttive religiose, disciplinari, e culturali delle costituzioni del Collegio Ghislieri," in *Il Collegio Universitario Ghislieri di Pavia: Istituzione della Riforma Cattolica (1567–1860)* (Milan 1966) 93–129; E. Galletti, *Il Collegio Ghislieri di Pavia, Note storiche* (Pavia 1890).

7 *Dictionnaire historique et biographique de la Suisse* (Neuchatel 1932) 6.697 s.v. Tschudi; *Enciclopedia Italiana* (Rome 1937) 34.428 s.v. Tschudi. Josef-Anton, also called the "Klein Tschudi," served as a captain in Spain (1729) and Africa (1731); as a lieutenant general in Naples (1733); brigadier general (1737); field marshal (1738); fought against the Austrians (1742) and at Velletri (1744); became lieutenant general (1759); and was a member of the Supreme Council of War (1770). Leonhard-Ludwig Tschudi served in Spain as a captain (1728) in the Nideröst regiment, the same regiment that took part in campaigns in Naples and Sicily (1733–34). As a colonel for Charles of Bourbon he distinguished himself in the Austrian campaigns of 1742 and 1744–46. In 1747, he became a lieutenant colonel, then field marshall (1759), and finally lieutenant general (1772).

8 *Stabiae*, 108 (October 18, 1759); the date of January 7, 1737, is given by Weber himself, although his military record gives the date as July 9, 1736.

9 The noble family of Luna came to Naples originally from Spain in 1282, quickly became feudal

lords and army officials of the state, and acquired titles ranging from count and marquis to duke and prince. They lived in the quarter of Naples called "Nido," or "Nilo," after an ancient statue of a reclining river god in the area, near S. Michele Arcangelo ("S. Angelo a Nilo") and S. Domenico Maggiore, which was one of the more fashionable areas at the time. G. Recchio, *Notizie di famiglie nobili ed illustri della città e regno di Napoli* (Naples 1717), and G.B. Di Crollalanza, *Dizionario storico-blasonico delle famiglie nobili e notabili italiane estinte e fiorenti* (Pisa 1886) s.v. Luna.

10 In April 1736, for example, Alcubierre was being paid 20 scudi per month while stationed at Pescara and L'Aquila (ASN, *Scrivania di Razione* 28, Inc. 306r.; Strazzullo, "Documenti," 263).

11 The first charter of 1291, which established a confederacy among the cantons of Schwyz, Uri, and Nidwalden, had pledged its members to recognize the jurisdiction of no one who was not their leader or who had purchased his position. The Pact of Brunnen in 1315, between Schwyz, Uri, and Unterwalden, which largely duplicates that of 1291, is considered the founding document of the confederacy, however (J. Wiget, *The Archives of the Swiss Charters of Confederation in Schwyz* [Bern 1986] 22).

12 Schweizerisches Bundesarchiv Bern, BAr Band 26: letter dated November 7, 1739, from the Neapolitan ambassador at Lucerne, Jacinto de Tsastia, to Marques di Salas (Prime Minister Montealegre) requesting freedom for Weber. Staatsarchiv Schwyz, Theke 557 (Abteilung 1): letter of November 6, 1739, from Colonel Tschudi at Syracuse to the *landammann* and council of Schwyz announcing Weber's freedom. Staatsarchiv Schwyz, Theke 557 (Abteilung 1): letter of December 22, 1739, from *landammann* and council of Schwyz to Tsastia requesting his intercession on their behalf to have Weber's rank reinstated. Schweizerisches Bundesarchiv Bern, BAr Band 26: letter of Tsastia to di Salas dated January 2, 1740, including French translation of the council's letter. Schweizerisches Bundesarchiv Bern, BAr Band 26: letter of di Salas to Tsastia of January 26, 1740, announcing Weber's reinstatement. The details of Weber's financial obligations were elucidated in a document (Familienschriften von Weber, Sedlern, Schwyz, Schachtel 1, Mappe G) recording the settlement reached between Weber's widow and his brother, Franz Dominik, on February 4, 1765.

13 ASN *Libretto di Viti e Costumi, Regimento Tschoudi*, 528 (1743); by this time, Weber had served for seven years, five months, and twenty-one days.

14 *Stabiae*, 108 (October 18, 1759), according to

Weber himself; according to the archival material from Schwyz, Franz Dominik moved into the position of lieutenant captain of the infantry vacated by his elder brother five days later (Familienschriften von Weber, Schwyz, Schachtel 1, Mappe J). For Giovanni Bastista Bigotti, see F. Strazzullo, *Architetti e ingegneri napoletani dal '500 al '700* (Turin 1969) 34–36.

15 ASN *CRA* 1541, Inc. 42 (August 27, 1764); he remained involved in designing fortifications throughout his tenure at the excavations, so this plan could well date from a later period. For example, he certainly was involved in work at the fortress of Granatello near Portici.

16 ASN *CRA* 1538, Inc. 162 (November 29, 1749): where Alcubierre remarks that "Beber," as he spells it here, seems appropriate for the position, since he already serves under Alcubierre and Alcubierre has observed him from time to time at work; cf. SNSP *Fondo Cuomo* 2-6-2, Doc. 2 ("Notizie istoriche relative agli scavi d'antichità"), fol. 74v. (December 22, 1749): "Alcubierre having been posted to Naples, while retaining direction of the excavations, he asks Commander Bigotti to appoint an engineer to serve under his orders." These "Notizie istoriche," drawn largely from official court documents relating to personnel and accounts payable, were probably begun by Camillo Paderni, the director of the Museo Ercolanese at Portici, and carried on by Francesco La Vega, Weber's successor. They cover the periods from August 3, 1738, to August 6, 1741; August 24 through December 1745; and January 7, 1748, to January 23, 1780; cf. A. Allroggen-Bedel, "Die Malereien aus dem Haus *Insula Occidentalis*, 10," *CronPomp* 2 (1976) 155 n. 37.

17 For biographical studies of Alcubierre, see F. Fernandez Murga, "Roque Joaquin de Alcubierre, descubridor de Herculano, Pompeya y Estabia," *ArchEspArq* 35 (1962) 3–35; F. Strazzullo, "Documenti per l'Ing. Rocco Alcubierre scopritore di Ercolano," *AttiAccPont* 29 (1980) 263–81; *idem*, "I primi anni dello scavo di Ercolano nel diario dell' ingegnere militare Rocco Gioacchino d'Alcubierre," in *La regione sotterrata dal Vesuvio* (Naples 1982) 103–81; and F. Fernandez Murga, *Carlos III y el descubrimiento de Herculano, Pompeya y Estabia* (Salamanca 1989) esp. 21–24. Weber's successor as director of the excavations, Francesco La Vega (1737–1804), interviewed a number of people who participated in the early excavations, in an attempt to reconstruct certain events. His diaries, published by Fiorelli under the titles "Giornale di ciò che mi occorre di rimarchevole" and "Notizie appartenti all' excavazioni d'Ercolano secondo le relazioni avute da varie persone," include Alcubierre's own description

of this surveying operation; see G. Fiorelli, *Giornale degli scavi di Pompei*, nos. 1–4 and 8–10 (Naples 1861–65) 110–20 and 281–320, esp. 289–90 (hereafter cited as *La Vega*). For a summary of the details behind the building of the villa at Portici, see M. Schipa, "Il regno di Napoli al tempo di Carlo di Borbone," *ASPN* 37.4 (1902) 749–55.

18 G. Butta, *I Borboni di Napoli al cospetto di due secoli* (Naples 1877) 1.44: construction of the fortress began in 1739; C. Celano, *Notizie del bello, dell' antico e del curioso che contengono le Reali Ville di Portici, Resina, lo scavamento di Pompejano, Capodimonte, Cardito, Caserta e S. Leucio* (Naples 1792) 33–34, notes that the fortress was designed by the Spanish architect Barrio, one of the chief engineers stationed at Naples (see Strazzullo, "Documenti," 263 n. 2), and that the royal fisheries were located at Granatello. According to Schipa, *ASPN* 37.4 (1902) 751, both Alcubierre and Tommaso Saluzzi were put in charge of drawing up the initial plans for the villa; according to "Ragguaglio storico del principio ed avvanzamento delli scavi . . . ," SNSP *Fondo Cuomo* 2-6-2, Doc. 16, fol. 144r. (a document prepared by La Vega from the earliest excavation records), Alcubierre was assisted in drawing up the topographical map by the engineers Emmanuele Giovine and Pietro Sbarbi.

19 For Niccolo Marcello Venuti, see T. Venuti De Dominicis, *I Venuti* (Rome 1889) 22–37; D. Gallo, "Marcello Venuti tra Napoli e Cortona," in *L'Accademia Etrusca* (Milan 1985) 53–57; and, in brief, F. Strazzullo, "Marcello Venuti, scopritore di Ercolano," *AttiAccPont* 40 (1991) 169–76. Charles of Bourbon had named Venuti director of the royal library and of the Museo Farnesiano in November 1738.

20 See, for example, the catalog of references compiled by A. de Jorio, *Notizie su gli scavi di Ercolano* (Naples 1827) 13–15.

21 The history of these statues is quite obscure. Parrino (*Napoli e il suo Cratere* [Naples 1704] 2.189) believed that they had come from excavations undertaken by a humanist from Bologna, Antonio Beccadelli (called "il Panormita") around 1430 while he was constructing his villa, known as the "Plinianum." This version was reported also by G. Cozzolino ("Nel bicentenario degli scavi di Ercolano," in *Bollettino parrocchiale di S. Maria a Pugliano* [January 15, 1938] 3). La Vega (282–83; 310) was told that the statues were found beneath the property of Decio Spinetta, in the area along the modern Vico di Mare, which may be the same spot where Beccadelli had worked and would place them near the so-called Basilica of Herculaneum. Ruggiero

(*StErc*, xvii) believed d'Elbeuf had recovered them. Nor is it clear whether the torsos were found with their heads. One source said they had been found acephelous (see F. Imperato, *Una communità in cammino* [Naples 1964] 138); another that the local populace had hidden two heads after d'Elbeuf had removed two for himself (N. Nocerino, *La Real Villa di Portici illustrata* [Naples 1787] 140). According to local legend, the heads had been distributed to various locations; one was believed to be in S. Maria a Pugliano in Resina. Yet La Vega's sources also told him that they had been recovered from a well on the Scognamillo property, along the Vico di Mare, near the shaft giving access to the so-called Tempio del Pavone (the ruins discovered in a well belonging to Giovanni Imperato known as "del Pavone" or "Paone"), "where the two seated acephalous statues and the statue of Vitellius were found." These latter specifics also indicate that the statues had come from the area of the Basilica, not the theater. In May 1739 Alcubierre was ordered to excavate the well where these statues had been recovered, but nothing further was encountered (SNSP "Notizie istoriche," 68v. [May 2 and 4, 1739]). See also de Jorio, 17 n. 1. The statues must have been in Colli Mozzi in 1740, for G. Knapton mentions four acephalous, draped statues set up "in the market place" ("Extract of a letter from Mr. George Knapton to Mr. Charles Knapton," *PhilTrans* 41 [1740] 489). They were removed in 1792 in order to make room for the fountain which gave the piazza its modern name, Piazza Fontana. The statues are now in the Museo Archeologico in Naples. For Colli Mozzi in general, see M. Carotenuto, *Ercolano attraverso i secoli* (Naples 1980) 221–25; and V. Catalano, *Storia di Ercolano* (Naples 1953) 58.

22 A copy of the manuscript is extant in the SNSP *Fondo Cuomo* 2-6-2, Doc. 1, fols. 1r.–63r., entitled "Breve descrizzione del Monte Vesuvio e della diversità de nomi di Esso." Since the last eruption dealt with is that of 1730, this manuscript must have been produced sometime between then and 1738, when Alcubierre saw it. A somewhat later document, prepared by La Vega, specifically states that Alcubierre was shown "the manuscript by the priest Imperato del Pavone" (SNSP *Fondo Cuomo* 2-6-2, Doc. 16 "Ragguaglio storico," fol. 144r.).

23 SNSP *Fondo Cuomo* 2-6-2, Doc. 1 "Breve descrizzione del Monte Vesuvio . . . ," fol. 25r.

24 *Giornale de' Letterati d'Italia* 5 (Venice 1711) 399–401, which mentions fragments of colored marble, an architrave block inscribed "Appius Pulcher C.F. Cos. Imp. VIIvir Epulonum," and a statue of a woman "which could be Claudia, a vestal named by [the

ancient author] Valerius Maximus." Prior to this, F. Bianchini, *La istoria universale* (Rome 1697) 246, had given a detailed description of the stratigraphy in this area and reported the discovery in 1689 of mosaic pavements, iron keys, and inscriptions thought to refer to "Pompeia."

25 For d'Elbeuf's biography, see C. Brisson, "La découverte d'Herculanum en 1713 par le 'Prince d'Elbeuf' " *Revue des sociétés savantes de Haute-Normandie* 6 (1957) 21–29; he assumed the title of "duc d'Elbeuf" only on the death of his brother in 1748. D'Elbeuf had purchased a strip of land at Granatello on the bay for his summer residence from the friars of the adjacent cloisters of San Pietro d'Alcantara, a purchase completed in 1711 (*StErc*, 513 [December 29, 1773]). The architect of d'Elbeuf's villa was Ferdinando Sanfelice (M. De Cunzo, "Le ville Vesuviane," in *Civiltà del '700* [Florence 1980] 1.94, fig. 16). For a general discussion of the palace, now an apartment building and deprived of its original splendor, see C. De Seta *et al.*, eds., *Ville Vesuviane: Campania I* (Milan 1980) 256–60. For a general survey of the history of the rediscovery of Herculaneum, see E. Cäsar Conte Corti, *Untergang und Auferstehung von Pompeji und Herculaneum*, ed. 9 (Munich 1978), esp. 103–14.

26 Imperato specifies this location, near the modern Vico S. Giacomo in Ercolano, in his manuscript (SNSP *Fondo Cuomo* 2-6-2, Doc. 1, fol. 23r.); see *StErc*, pl. 2.

27 La Vega, 284. D'Elbeuf had contracted with a French artisan for stuccos to adorn his palace's walls and floors that were produced from pulverized marble, said to be harder than marble and capable of taking a polish. See G. Stendardo, "Lettera al Bindo Simone Peruzzi," in A.F. Gori ed., *Notizie del memorabile scoprimento dell' antica città di Ercolano . . .* (Florence 1748) 1.

28 La Vega's sources said that d'Elbeuf had been so fond of his chief excavator, la Monica, that he was allowed to accompany d'Elbeuf in his carriage (La Vega, 312).

29 La Vega, 284–85; 312–14.

30 N. Del Pezzo, "Siti reali: Il Palazzo Reale di Portici," *NapNob* 5 (1896) 164; De Cunzo, "Le ville vesuviane," 1.94; A. Allroggen-Bedel and H. Kammerer-Grothaus, "Il Museo Ercolanese di Portici," in *La Villa dei Papiri* (*CronErc* 13 Suppl. 2, Naples 1983) 88, where it is stated that most of the busts must have come from Herculaneum, although the figure may be exaggerated. Two marble statues of draped females still on display in niches in the north cortile of the Palazzo Reale in Portici may have come from the scaena of the theater; see M. Pagano, "Il

teatro di Ercolano," *CronErc* 23 (1993) 123, figs. 2 and 3. Knapton, "Extract of a letter," 489, reported being told by an old inhabitant of Portici who had been employed by d'Elbeuf that the project had lasted five years.

31 W. Hammond, "An account of the discovery of the remains of a city underground, near Naples; communicated to the Royal Society by William Sloane [Naples, March 7, 1731–32]," *PhilTrans* 41.1 (1739–40) 345–46:

> At Resina about four miles [6.5 km.] from Naples under the mountain, within half a mile [0.8 km.] of the seaside, there is a well in a poor man's yard down which about 30 yards there is a hole which some people have the curiosity to creep into and may afterwards creep a good way underground and with lights find foundations of houses and streets which by some it is said was in the time of the Romans a city called Aretina, others say Port Hercules, where the Romans usually embarked from for Africa. I have seen the well, which is deep and a good depth of water at the bottom, but I never cared to venture down, being heavy and the ropes bad.

32 Biblioteca Nazionale di Napoli, Ms. XIII.B.37, fol. 33r.: "Relazione di ciocche si è ritrovato nel cavamento del vecchio Ercolano presso Napoli con brevi riflessioni fatta da Giacomo Martorelli." J.B. Requier, *Recueil général, historique et critique de tout ce qui a été publié de plus rare sur la ville d'Herculane . . .* (Paris 1754) 23, pointed out that d'Elbeuf's discoveries were recent enough for everyone to remember and were what had persuaded the king to build his palace and initiate the excavations.

33 La Vega, 310; this Imperato was evidently related to the author of the manuscript that Alcubierre had seen and retained a copy of, which was by now in La Vega's hands.

34 Moussinot d'Arthenay, *Notizie intorno alla città sotterranea discoperta alle falde del Monte Vesuvio* (Florence 1749) 2–3, also states that the Naples government had put a stop to d'Elbeuf's depredations; Celano, *Notizie*, 53; Gori, *Notizie*, ix, also believed d'Elbeuf's work was well remembered.

35 Celano, *Notizie*, 38–39, although he suggests it was the queen who first had become enamored of the site. Schipa, *ASPN* 37.4 (1902) 749, mentions the study into the potential for problems caused by *la mofeta*, or mofettes, exhalations of carbon dioxide and hydrogen sulfide from fumaroles around Mount Vesuvius. For the museum, see H. Kammerer-Grothaus, "Die erste Aufstellung der Antiken aus den Vesuvstädten in Portici," in *Antikensammlungen*

im 18. Jahrhundert (Berlin 1981), esp. 11–19, and "Museo."

36 H. Acton, *The Bourbons of Naples (1734–1825)* (London 1956) 41; F. Haskell, "Art Patronage and Collecting in Bourbon Naples during the 18th Century," in *The Golden Age of Naples: Art and civilization under the Bourbons (1734–1805)* (Detroit 1981) 1.15–16.

37 Strazzullo, "Primi anni," 115.

38 U. Pannuti, in "Il 'Giornale degli scavi' di Ercolano (1738–1756)," *MemAccLinc* Ser. 8, 26.3 (1983) 167–68, published one of Alcubierre's original manuscripts dating from this period (SNSP Ms. 20.B.19bis). Bernardo Tanucci was prime minister by this date.

39 "Museo," 84–85, which reproduces the text of this letter (SNSP *Fondo Cuomo* 2-6-2, Doc. 20, fols. 159r.–161v.) along with reference to two similar documents dated July 1, 1765, and October 11, 1764, from this same archive.

40 SNSP *Fondo Cuomo* 2-6-2, Doc. 17, "Motivo che diede principio alla scoperta della città Ercolano," fols. 148v.–149v.: an account prepared by Alcubierre; La Vega, 287–88, 290–92.

41 R. Herbig, "Don Carlos von Borbon als Ausgräber von Herculaneum und Pompeji," *MadMitt* 1 (1960) 12, and G. Fiengo, "Le ville vesuviane del settecento e la scoperta di Pompei ed Ercolano," *Antiqua* 4.15 Suppl. *Pompei 79* (1979) 148–54, among others, both support Maria Amalia as the instigator of the excavations, while F. Zevi, "Gli scavi di Ercolano," in *Civiltà del '700 a Napoli* (Florence 1980) 2.58, and Strazzullo, "Primi anni," 108, support Alcubierre's interpretation of the events.

42 SNSP "Notizie istoriche," 67r.

43 SNSP "Notizie istoriche," 67r. (October 19, 1738); F. Barnabei, "Gli scavi di Ercolano," *MemLinc* Ser. 3.2 (1877–78) 754.

44 *StErc*, 3 (November 4, 1738). This statue has not been identified; its relationship to d'Elbeuf's Hercules is unknown and somewhat suspect.

45 Montealegre was forced out of the office of prime minister, primarily by Maria Amalia, in the spring of 1746 after a series of embarrassing setbacks; see *Enciclopedia Italiana* (Rome 1934) 23.729 s.v. Montealegre. He was replaced by Giovanni Fogliani d'Aragona, who remained in this position until 1755, when he in turn was replaced by Bernardo Tanucci.

46 Ruggiero may have copied the date incorrectly and failed to catch his error. *StErc*, 1 (January 14, 1738): Alcubierre to Montealegre; *StErc*, 10–11 (January 10 and 13, 1739) for the inscription. More likely it was Venuti's positive identification of the structure as a theater that induced Montealegre to

order the restoration of the statues that had been recovered. Ruggiero (*StErc*, xiii and xvii), in publishing Alcubierre's early letter, believed the statues may have been the ones found by d'Elbeuf near the theater and set up at Colli Mozzi, but these had remained *in situ* until 1792.

47 G. Stendardo, "Lettera al sig. Bindo Simone Peruzzi su di alcuni insigni monumenti antichi scavati alla Real Villa di Portici, l'anno MDCCXI," reprinted in Gori, *Notizie*, 1–3. The inscription is *CIL* 10.1423: "Appius Claudius C.F. Cos. Imp. VI / Vir Epulon." Stendardo's claim to have been d'Elbeuf's excavator was disputed later by several individuals close to the excavations, who told La Vega that Stendardo had been an engineer for the city of Naples sometime after d'Elbeuf's day and actually had excavated near S. Nicola in Torre del Greco, recovering only some columns of *cipollino*; in fact he appears to have worked at both sites, and La Vega's sources must have remembered only Stendardo's more recent work. For the location of these excavations at the Villa Sora, near Torre del Greco, see *StErc*, pl. 1; M. Ruggiero, *Degli scavi di antichità nelle Province di Terraferma dell' antico Regno di Napoli* (Naples 1888) 99–110, documenting primarily the nineteenth-century work; and M. Pagano, "Torre del Greco, località Ponte Rivieccio, contrada Villa Sora, prop. Montella," *RStPomp* 3 (1989) 287–94, esp. 293 n. 3, and *idem*, "La Villa Romana di contrada Sora a Torre del Greco," *CronErc* 21 (1991) 149–86, where Pagano refers to SNSP *Fondo Cuomo* 2-6-2, Doc. 5, fol. 110r. [actually fol. 118r.–v.], as confirming that La Vega believed Stendardo had directed this work sometime before 1734.

48 Anton Francesco Gori (1691–1757) was a Florentine antiquarian who founded the Accademia Columbiana in 1735. An avid scholar of Etruscan civilization, he published the *Museum Etruscum* (Florence 1736–43). Gori maintained correspondence with several Neapolitan scholars during this period, including Martorelli, Egizio, Paciaudi, and Venuti (see L. Giuliani, ed., *Il carteggio di Anton Francesco Gori* [Rome 1987]), and he edited several collections of letters describing the early excavations, including *Notizie del memorabile scoprimento dell' antica città di Ercolano* (Florence 1748) and *Symbolae litterarie* [Decas I] (Florence 1748–53) and [Decas II] (Florence 1751–54). Peruzzi (1696–1759) curated a collection of antiquities in Florence.

49 N.M. Venuti, *A description of the first discoveries of the ancient city of Hercules found near Portici ...* (London 1750) [Eng. trans. of *Descrizione delle prime scoperte dell' antica città di Ercolano ritrovata vicino a Portici* (Rome 1748)] 50 n. 2.

50 Gori, *Notizie*, 3–5: letter of Venuti to Peruzzi, dated January 17, 1738, communicated to Gori by Peruzzi along with Stendardo's letter on April 21, 1741; Venuti, *Description*, 52–58, repeats many of these details, although the earlier date is dropped; Strazzullo, "Documenti," 264, who failed to recognize the chronological difficulties of Venuti's letter. For the marble statues, see *StErc*, 8 (December 12, 1738).

51 Biblioteca del Comune e dell' Accademia etrusca di Cortona, Ms. 577, c. 49: letter of Gori to Venuti of April 4, 1748 (as quoted by Gallo, "Venuti," in *L'Accademia di Etrusca* [Milan 1985] 56, 100).

52 Gori, *Notizie*, xiii.

53 SNSP *Fondo Cuomo* 2-6-2, fol. 229r.: Giuseppe Canart, of the royal museum, claimed that Venuti in fact had gone to the site only five or six times and had never ventured into the tunnels and that because Venuti had not had the king's permission to write to Florence about these finds, the king ordered that he be prevented from visiting the ruins.

54 *StErc*, 24 (May 13, 1739); a theme picked up later by Weber.

55 This is the description provided by C.-N. Cochin and J.C. Bellicard, *Observations sur les antiquités d'Herculanum* (Paris 1755) 11. Barker, 17, states that the height of the tunnels was 1.2 m. to 1.8 m. and the width 0.9 m. to 1.2 m.

56 SNSP "Notizie istoriche," 68r. (ca. December 1738).

57 For example, in January 1740, there were seventeen men working at the theater (SNSP "Notizie istoriche," 70v.). The number was increased to thirty-six during the directorship of Bardet (ASN *CRA* 1537, Inc. 100 [December 13, 1744]). By 1756, there were five paid laborers and forty forced laborers under Corcoles's direction at Herculaneum alone (*StErc*, 181 [January 17, 1756]).

58 The work centered on the "pozo del Paone," on the property of Andrea Simone Imperato, called "del Paone," *StErc*, 27–33 (May 21 to June 22, 1739), and perhaps a relative of the author of the "Breve descrizzione" manuscript on the early excavations that Alcubierre had seen. For details on the excavations in this area in general, see A. Allroggen-Bedel, "Das sogenannte Forum von Herculaneum und die borbonischen Grabungen von 1739," *CronErc* 4 (1974) 97–99, and Chapter 2 in this volume, "The Earliest Plans of the Vesuvian Monuments," for details on this so-called Galleria Balba. For the "quadriga" group, see E. Gabrici, "La quadriga di Ercolano, *BdA* 1 (1907) 1–12, and G. Cerulli Irelli, "Decorazioni di baltei dal foro di Ercolano," *CronErc* 2 (1972) 95–103.

59 Mosaics: MN. 10008 (1.83 m. H × 1.45 m. W),

MN. 10009 and MN. 10011 (each 0.47 m. × 0.57 m.) from the "Casa dello Scheletro" (Ins. 3.3). See R. De Kind, "Casa dello Scheletro at Herculaneum: The large nymphaeum," *CronErc* 21 (1991) 133–47, drawing on reports in *Giornale*, 199–201 (November 17, 1740, to January 1741); ASN *CRA* 1537, Inc. 77–78, 81–82 (November to December 1741); and SNSP *Fondo Cuomo* 2-6-2, Doc. 7, fol. 121r. For the excavations conducted here in 1831 and 1869–71, see Maiuri, *Nuovi scavi*, 265-75.

60 SNSP "Notizie istoriche," 70r.–70v. (January 2 and 11, 1740). Excavations were being conducted at five sites indicated as: (1) where the paintings were found; (2) at the point beneath the Royal Road at the edge of Resina; (3) in a tunnel directed toward Colli Mozzi; (4) to the left of the theater; (5) in a tunnel that would link the theater with the tunnel heading toward Colli Mozzi. The fourteen wells in Resina belonged to the following landowners: Antonio Nocerino; Francesco Bossa; N. Petrano; Luca Cozzolino; Abate Minico; Antonio Milo; N. Spineta; M. Mattia; Marco Proibito; N. Paone (also spelled Pavone); Giovanni Imperato; Giacchino Giacomino; della Flaorara; Presidente Odoardo [*sic*]. Particularly important finds in fact were made at the wells of Nocerino, Cozzolino, Spineta, and Paone.

61 Paderni's earliest appearance in the historical record is a graffito of his name and date that he scrawled on the stucco of the Domus Transitoria in Rome in 1738, evidently while sketching the remains of ancient painting there. See M. De Vos, "Camillo Paderni, la tradizione antiquaria romana e i collezionisti inglesi," in *Ercolano 1738–1988: 250 anni di ricerca archeologica* (Rome 1993) 99–116; and *eadem*, "Nerone, Seneca, Fabullo e La Domus Transitoria al Palatino," in *Gli orti Farnesiani sul Palatino* (*Roma Antica*, Collection Publieé par l'École Française de Rome et la Soprintendenza Archeologica di Roma, no. 2, Rome 1990) 183 fig. 14, 185.

62 C. Paderni, "Extracts of two letters from Sign. Camillo Paderni at Rome to Mr. Allan Ramsey, Painter, Covent-Garden, concerning some ancient statues, pictures and other curiosities found in a subterraneous town lately discovered near Naples; dated Rome, November 20, 1739, and February 20, 1740," *PhilTrans* 41.2 (1740) 484.

63 J. Russell, *Letters from a young painter abroad to his friends in England*, ed. 2 (London 1750) 1.218 #34 (September 10, 1743). Paderni was staying in Canart's house at Portici when he wrote his letter to the Royal Society. According to SNSP "Notizie istoriche" (70v. [February 6, 1740]), Montealegre was afraid the king would be angry to learn Paderni was making copies of the paintings.

64 F.S. Maffei, *Tre lettere del Signor Marchese Scipione Maffei: La seconda al M.R. Padre Bernardo De Rubeis, Domenicano, Venezia (Verona, 10 novembre 1747)* (Verona 1748) 35. Maffei (1675–1755) was one of the founding members of the *Giornale de' Letterati d'Italia* in 1710; see *Enciclopedia Italiana* (Rome 1934) 21.862 s.v., and, in general, *Nuovi studi Maffeiani: Atti del Convegno Scipione Maffei e il Museo Maffeiano* (Verona 1985).

65 "Extract of a letter from Naples concerning Herculaneum, containing an account and description of the place and what has been found in it," *PhilTrans* 47 (1751–52) 150.

66 Russell, *Letters*, 2.314 #70 (September 15, 1749).

67 "Extract of a letter . . . ," 150.

68 A. Lumisden, *Remarks on the antiquities of Rome and its environs* (London 1812) 477, from a letter at Naples dated April 18, 1750.

69 Biblioteca Nazionale di Napoli, Ms. XIII.B.37, fol. 26r. ("Relazione" of Martorelli).

70 Ch. De Brosses, *Lettres sur l'etat actuel de la ville souterraine d'Herculée* (Dijon 1750) 4–7; the letter is dated June 1, 1749. De Brosses (1709–1777) was the first president of the parliament of Dijon and a corresponding member of the Académie des Inscriptions. He toured Italy in 1739–40 and wrote of his experiences. See *Dictionaire de biographie française* (Paris 1956) 7.433–35, and H. Harder, *Le president de Brosses et le voyage en Italie au dix-huitième siècle* (Geneva 1981).

71 Russell, *Letters*, 1.167–68 #28 (October 20, 1742).

72 For example, the *Giornale* for September 22, 1745, reports that rainwater had flooded into a tunnel along the Vico di Mare just south of the theater, temporarily trapping workmen inside; they made their escape via the ramp giving access to the theater (C. Gallavotti, "Nuovo contributo alla storia degli scavi borbonici di Ercolano [nella Villa dei Papiri]," *RendNap* n.s. 20 (1939–40) 297 n. 2; *Giornale*, 219). For more on flooding in the tunnels, see Chapter 5 in this volume, "The 'Temples' at Herculaneum." According to a plan drawn in 1747, the water table was about 5.75 m. below the level of the theater.

73 E.g., *Giornale*, 237 (May 24, 1746): Alcubierre reported finding no damage to the tunnels following an earthquake the previous night.

74 Russell, *Letters*, 227 #34 (September 10, 1743), remarks that the digging at that time was done by twenty galley slaves, "chained together, two and two, and guarded by soldiers. . . .[Each laborer has] a small basket into which they put what they find, and are well searched at their coming out from their work." Stricter measures were adopted in 1745,

when two forced laborers escaped (ASN *CRA Primo Inventario* 818, Inc. 158 [August 17, 1745]). *StErc*, 293 (November 16, 1759): Weber remarks he had assigned a lone forced laborer to work in one spot of the excavations where the number of open tunnels rendered the area unstable. For the theft of artifacts by workmen, see "Museo," 93, and Chapter 7 in this volume, "Dearth and Discord."

75 Fernandez Murga, "Alcubierre," 13; and *idem*, *Carlos III*, 59–66.

76 Theseus and the Minotaur: MN. 9049; *StErc* 44, 53 (September 12, 1739), *PdE* 1.21–25, pl. 5; Hercules and Telephus in Arcadia: MN. 9008, *StErc*, 57 (November 25, 1739), *PdE* 1.27–31, pl. 6; and Achilles and Chiron: MN. 9109, *StErc* 58 (November 28, 1739), *PdE* 1.39–43, pl. 8.

77 Schipa, *ASPN* 37.4 (1902) 751 (quoting from ASN, *Siti Reali*, fasc. 3): orders for work at Pugliano came on November 7, 1738; work at the garden at Portici began on July 7, 1739, and Schipa reports seeing a watercolor by Alcubierre of the results. Other waters were brought from springs in the area of S. Anastasia, 7 kilometers from Portici, as there were no sources of potable water near the palace (R. De Fusco, "L'architettura della seconda metà del Settecento," in *Storia di Napoli* [Naples 1971] 8.376). Engineering duties such as these apparently also played a role in Alcubierre's establishment of the excavations at Pompeii (see Chapter 4 in this volume, "Pompeii and the Praedia Iuliae Felicis").

78 ASN *CRA* 1537, Inc. 18 (February 24, 1740); ASN *CRA* 1537, Inc. 24 (March 13, 1740); ASN *CRA* 1537, Inc. 26 (April 2, 1740); SNSP "Notizie istoriche," fol. 71r. (February 18 to March 3, 1740); Strazzullo, "Documenti," 268. Alcubierre's superiors at that time, and the men who made up the investigative team, were Giovanni Antonio Medrano, the chief royal engineer and the architect who had designed the palaces at Portici and Capodimonte; Andrés de los Cobos, field marshall; Domingo Arbunies, chief engineer; and Giovanni Battista Bigotti, commander of the corps of military engineers at Portici and Alcubierre's military superior.

79 SNSP "Notizie istoriche," 71r. (April 29, 1740): "Alcubierre requests a voluntary engineer as his assistant, that this should be his brother, who eight months before had been granted the position of voluntary engineer with the position of supervisor until the first vacancy [should arise]. And on June 25 he requests that [Felippe] be appointed voluntary engineer in the Castel d'Ovo." Evidently Felippe had served as his brother's assistant for some time; he is named in a single document of June 3, 1741 (*StErc*, 82). He may have been involved in duties other than

those relating to the excavations, such as constructing the palace aqueduct.

80 Strazzullo, "Primi anni," 113: letter of May 1, 1743, from Gaeta (ASN *CRA* 787), in which Alcubierre cataloged his previous ailments; *idem*, "Documenti," 268; *StErc*, 79–81 (May 26–31, 1741), where Alcubierre attributed these to daily exposure to the humidity in the tunnels as well as to the water from the aqueduct at Pugliano. SNSP "Notizie istoriche," 72r. (May 26, 1741): Alcubierre's release to recover in Naples was initially approved to begin in July, but on May 30 he appealed for immediate release. Another version of the story is that Alcubierre was relieved of duty because of "some differences concerning the accounts [or "Counts"?] of Corasale," although the meaning of this is not known (La Vega, 282).

81 For the dates of Bardet's directorship of the excavations (July 24, 1741 to March 21, 1744, and December 12, 1744, to August 29, 1745), see *Giornale*, 380. Bardet first visited the excavation tunnels on July 29, 1740 (SNSP "Notizie istoriche," 71v.).

82 Schipa, *ASPN* 37.4 (1902) 751, notes that the king had wanted as many men stationed here as possible. La Vega, 290, gives the figure of seven hundred.

83 A life-size bronze statue of Augustus with a thunderbolt was found in the Basilica during his tenure (MN. 5595: *StErc* 83–84 [July 17, 1741]; *BdE* 2.297–301, pl. 77). For reactions, see SNSP "Notizie istoriche," 72r. (May 26, 1741); La Vega, 292.

84 *StErc*, 81–82 (June 3, 1741): Alcubierre's summary of his orders on the direction of the excavations, which were passed first to Rorro and then Bardet. There are few surviving reports relating to the period of Bardet's tenure in the documents published by Ruggiero, despite the fact that he wrote 366 (*Giornale*, 391). For a collection of unpublished reports, see ASN *CRA Primo Inventario*, fols. 789–91 and 818. For Bardet's plans, see Chapter 2 in this volume, "The Earliest Plans of the Vesuvian Monuments," and ASN *Raccolta Piante e Disegni*, Cartella XXIV, 1–4; A. Allroggen-Bedel, "Dokumente des 18. Jahrhunderts zur Topographie von Herculaneum," *CronErc* 13 (1983) 139–58, with an excellent discussion of the information contained in these plans.

85 He advocated this systematic approach in a letter to Fogliani dated November 13, 1743 (ASN *CRA Primo Inventario* 789, Inc. 244), although this in fact was the system dictated previously to Alcubierre.

86 There is some debate concerning the proper identification of all of these buildings. Both A.

Maiuri, *Ercolano*, ed. 6, Itinerari dei musei, gallerie e monumenti d'Italia, no. 6, 6th ed. (Rome 1967) 50, and G. Guadagno, "Herculanensium Augustalium aedes," *CronErc* 13 (1983) 159–73, identify the building at Ins. 6.21 as the "Collegium of the Augustales" (Augustalium). A. De Franciscis (*EAA* Supp. 1970, 310 s.v. Herculaneum) first identified the building at Ins. 6.21 as the "Curia" and was followed by A. and M. De Vos, *Pompei Ercolano Stabia*, Guide Archeologiche Laterza no. 11 (Bari 1982) 298–301, who then labeled the apsidal structure at the northeast corner of Ins. 7 the "Collegium of the Augustales." On the other hand, S. Adamo Muscettola, "Nuove letture borboniche: I Nonii Balbi ed il foro di Ercolano," *Prospettiva* 28 (1982) 6, identifies the building at Ins. 7, with its gallery of portraits of the Nonii Balbi family, as the Basilica. See esp. Allroggen-Bedel, "Forum," 97–109. For the sake of simplicity, this study will refer to the largest of the three buildings as the Basilica; Ins. 6.21 as the Augustalium; and Ins. 7 as the Galleria Balba.

87 For example, Bardet's excavations probably cut into the Casa del Colonnato Tuscanico (Ins. 6.17); see G. Cerulli Irelli, *La Casa 'del Colonnato Tuscanico' ad Ercolano* (*MemNap* 7, Naples 1974) 55, 58.

88 Colossal seated Augustus: MN. 6040, A. Ruesch, *Guida illustrata del Museo Nazionale di Napoli* (Naples 1908) 965, *Le Collezioni del Museo Nazionale di Napoli* (Naples 1989) 1.2, 110–11 #74; Colossal seated Claudius: MN. 6056, Ruesch 986, *CollMN* 1.2, 110–11 #75; Standing Titus with breastplate: MN. 6095, Ruesch 969, *CollMN* 1.2, 110–11 #76; Tiberius: *Giornale*, 210 (August 30, 1741), MN. 5615, Ruesch 793, *CollMN* 1.2, 110–11 #73; "Agrippina": *Giornale*, 211 (December 2, 1741), MN. 5612, Ruesch 759, *CollMN* 1.2, 120–21 #121; Claudius: *Giornale*, 211 (December 20, 1741), MN. 5593, Ruesch 796, *BdE* 2.303–9, pl. 78.

89 Russell, *Letters*, 1.175–78 #29 (undated, ca. 1743?).

90 La Vega, 293.

91 G. Knapton, "Extract of a letter . . . to Charles Knapton (late 1740)," *PhilTrans* 41.2 (1740–41) 489–93. This letter provides a fascinating description of the setting of the ruins in contemporary Resina:

> At our coming to the well, which is in a small square surrounded with miserable houses, filled with miserable old women, they soon gathered about us, wondering what brought us thither. But when the men who were with us broke the paltry machine with which they used to draw up small buckets of water, I thought we should have been stoned by them, till perceiving one more furious

than the rest, whom we found to be the Padrona of the well, by applying a small bit of money to her, we made a shift to quiet the tumult. Our having all the tackle for descending to seek gave time for all the town to gather round us, which was very troublesome, for when anyone offered to go down, he was prevented either by a wife or a mother, so that we were forced to seek a motherless bachelor to go first. It being very difficult for the first to get in, the well being very broad, so that they were obliged to swing him in, and the people above making such a noise, that the man in the well could not be heard, obliged our company to draw their swords, and threaten anyone who spoke with death. This caused a silence, after which our guide soon landed, who pulled us in by the legs as we came down.

92 La Vega, 303–5; the extent to which this story had become embellished by La Vega's day is unknown. Cf. *StErc*, 96 (February 13, 1743): complaint by G. Notto of damage to his house by Bardet's work.
93 The hiatus of eight months and twenty-two days, from March 21 to December 12, 1744, is noted in the daybooks (*Giornale*, 216).
94 ASN *CRA Primo Inventario* 789, Inc. 85 (October 19, 1743) and Inc. 201 (February 29, 1744); ASN *CRA* 1537, Inc. 93 (February 29, 1744) and Inc. 96 (December 5, 1744).
95 ASN *CRA Primo Inventario* 787 (May 1, 1743): Alcubierre's letter to Montealegre requesting promotion to second engineer (cf. Strazzullo, "Documenti," 270); SNSP "Notizie istoriche," 73r. (August 24, 1745): king determines that Bardet should return to military duties, Alcubierre recalled from Capua/Gaeta; ASN *CRA* 1537, Inc. 127 (August 28, 1745): notice of Alcubierre's return from Capua to replace Bardet; ASN *CRA Primo Inventario* 818, Inc. 287 (August 28, 1745): Bardet hands over command to Alcubierre; *StErc*, xiv; Strazzullo, "Documenti," 269; Allroggen-Bedel, "Dokumente," 139 n. 4. As late as September 1760, when he was stationed at Pescara, Bardet still had not handed over all his plans (*Stabiae*, 133 [September 10, 1760]), and the scarcity of records for the period during which he directed the excavations suggests he intentionally withheld this information from Alcubierre. This also may have been in revenge for Alcubierre's failure to provide him with adequate documentation four years earlier. In 1765, Bardet, in asking to be named to fill the post of lieutenant in Messina vacated by A. Poulet, recounted how he had been a captain of the infantry and engineer until 1740, when he had been made a

lieutenant colonel and chief engineer, and then finally attained the rank of colonel in 1759 (F. Strazzullo, ed., *Settecento napoletana* [Naples 1982] 210). For Alcubierre's admission to the Real Archicofradia, see Fernandez Murga, "Alcubierre," 14 n. 37; his brother Felippe had been a member since 1737.
96 ASN *CRA* 1537, Inc. 141 (October 9, 1745).
97 *StErc*, 33 (June 23, 1739) marks the first mention in the daybooks of the practice of cutting down wall paintings. For a complete discussion of the technique of removing and restoring the paintings, see M.P. Rossignani, "Saggio sui restauri settecenteschi ai dipinti di Ercolano e Pompei," *Contributi dell' Istituto di Archeologia* 1 (1967) 7–134; cf. L.A. Scatozza Höricht, "Restauri alle collezioni del Museo Ercolanese di Portici alla luce di documenti inediti," *AttiAccPont* n.s. 31 (1982) 495–540.
98 SNSP *Fondo Cuomo*, 2–6–2, Doc. 16 "Ragguaglio storico . . . ," fol. 145r. C. Finzi, "Un ministro 'archeologo': Gli scavi di Ercolano nell' epistolario di Bernardo Tanucci," *Antiqua* 4.15 Supp. *Pompei 79* (1979) 155, quoting from a letter of May 9, 1747.
99 Adamo Muscettola, 2–16, drawing especially on references in the daybooks, specifically associated the statues with the forum and the nearby theater (e.g., ASN *CRA* 1538, Inc. 108 [January 5, 1747]); Allroggen-Bedel, "Dokumente," 154. For the probable site, see the plan of Herculaneum drawn by F. La Vega (but based on work by Weber) in 1797 for C. Rosini's *Dissertationis isagogicae ad Herculanensium Voluminum explanationem* (Naples 1797) pl. 2 #3, and also Weber's unfinished plan of the theater (see Chapter 8 in this volume, "The Theater at Herculaneum").
100 "Pater Balbus": MN. 6211, Ruesch 23, *CollMN* 1.2, 118–19 #107; "Filius Balbus": MN. 6104, Ruesch 59, *CollMN* 1.2, 118–19 #106. The "Pater" statue was found first, on June 7, and removed from June 10 to 20, 1746 (*Giornale*, 238); the shoring up of the cavity was done on September 20, 1746 (*Giornale*, 241). The statue required substantial restoration and so was not mounted in the museum until late 1750. The second, "Filius," was found in excellent condition on August 3, 1746, and its removal completed on August 20, 1746 (*Giornale*, 240). It was put on public display on November 14, 1746 (*Giornale*, 243; Gori, *Notizie*, 19 [letter 11, December 6, 1746]).
101 Alcubierre described the ventilation shaft and the air pump in a letter dated August 8, 1746 (*Giornale*, 240).
102 The statue's head was found on September 13, 1746; the body was recovered on September 30 and the whole removed on October 7–13, 1746; the

statue has not been identified. The ramp was started September 13 and finished by October 13, 1746 (*Giornale*, 241–42).

103 E.g., *Giornale*, 257: funerary epitaph found February 2, 1748 (*CIL* 10.1471).

104 Allroggen-Bedel, "Dokumente," 154 n. 81.

105 The initial identification of these finds as coming from the Casa dei Cervi was made by A. Allroggen-Bedel, "Der Hausherr der 'Casa dei Cervi' in Herculaneum," *CronErc* 5 (1975) 99–103. For a more complete discussion of the Bourbon excavations here, see V. Tran Tam Tinh, *La Casa dei Cervi a Herculanum* (Rome 1988) 1–5, where he notes that Maiuri's excavations in 1930 revealed Bourbon-era tunnels in the cryptoporticus; in the fauces, tablinum, and triclinium in the north part of the house; around the central garden; and in the great oecus to the south (Maiuri, *Nuovi scavi*, 314).

106 Fontana described in detail this particular project first in "Secondo disegno che diedi in Napoli per condurre l'acqua del Sarno alla Torre dell' Annunziata per far diversi molini per servizio di questa fedelissima città di Napoli," in his *Libro secondo in cui si ragiona di alcune fabriche fatte in Roma et in Napoli* (Naples 1603) 22–24. See also G. Rubino, "La real fabbrica d'armi a Torre Annunziata e l'opera di Sabitini, Vanvitelli e Fuga (1753–1775)," *Napoli Nobilissima* 14.3 (May–June 1975) 101–18, esp. 104–5, 116 n. 25. For a brief summary of the armaments, both combat arms and hunting rifles, produced here, see S. Abiti, "Arms," in *The Golden Age of Naples: Art and civilization under the Bourbons (1734–1805)* (Detroit 1981) 2.430–34.

107 *PAH* I.i.1–2 (March 23 and 27, April 2 and 6, 1748).

108 E.g., SNSP "Notizie istoriche," 79v. (April 9, 1755): twelve days of leave granted to Antonio Scognamillo for an illness contracted in the excavations at Pozzuoli; 82r. (January 5, 1756): request of pay by Michele Corvato for the sixteen days he was absent from work after falling into a trench; 90v. (October 18, 1759): Miguel de Çiria receives payment for the treatment he required after being covered by earth.

109 *Giornale*, 260 (July 6, 1748), 267 (November 16, 1748); the *PAH* makes the direct connection between the *mofeta* and the heat (*PAH* I.i.5 [July 6, 1748]). Encounters with the *mofeta* were recorded throughout the excavations, including the tunnels at Herculaneum, though at Pompeii with somewhat greater frequency: *Giornale*, 271 (March 20, 1749), site changed at Pompeii because of *mofeta* caused by sirocco, and (April 19, 1749), work stopped at Pompeii because of the *mofeta*. It may be no coincidence that the most frequent references to the

problem occur during the period when Alcubierre spent the most time at the excavations. Some years later, it was recommended that all work be transferred to Gragnano during the summer to escape the "bad air," since this site stood at a higher altitude than Pompeii (SNSP "Notizie istoriche," 92r. [July 24, 1760]). The fact that no indications of the *mofeta* had been confirmed during the survey of the area for the construction of the Royal Palace at Portici, and that none has been encountered in the modern excavations, suggests that this was Alcubierre's peculiar paranoia and a convenient excuse to stop the work or transfer it elsewhere.

110 J.J. Björnstahl, *Lettere nei suoi viaggi stranieri* (Poschiavo 1782–87) 2.33.

111 *PAH* I.i.5–11 (October 26, 1748–September 26, 1750); *Giornale*, 267–86 (November 16, 1748–September 19, 1750).

112 *Giornale*, 271–72 (May 2–June 7, 1749).

113 ASN *CRA* 1538, Inc. 162 (November 29, 1749): Alcubierre to Fogliani; Alcubierre assumed the post of the recently deceased Francesco Barrio.

114 ASN *CRA* 1539, Inc. 6 (June 12, 1750). Montemayor had been a voluntary engineer with the excavations since at least 1737 (cf. Strazzullo, "Documenti," 263 n. 2).

115 SNSP "Notizie istoriche," 74v. (July 4, 1750); *PAH* I.ii.Addenda iv.135 (July 11, 1750), where it is stated that Weber had visited Gragnano first and then the other sites. The earliest mention of Weber at Pompeii appears in the daybooks for September 4, 1750 (*PAH* I.i.10).

CHAPTER 2. THE EARLIEST PLANS OF THE VESUVIAN MONUMENTS

1 One palm is equal to 0.26455 meters.

2 According to SNSP "Notizie istoriche," 75r., Weber signed his first report on July 27, 1750, although in Ruggiero his signature first appears on July 25, 1750 (*StErc*, 105).

3 According to *Stabiae*, 47 (January 10, 1756) the total amount allotted to the excavations in 1756 reached 500 ducats, with 100 ducats for expenses, but the SNSP "Notizie istoriche," 83r. (February 23, 1756) records the monthly excavation expenses as 139 ducats 57.5 carlins.

4 Another corps of invalids served as sentinels at the "Temple of Serapis" at Pozzuoli.

5 G. Fiorelli, *Giornale degli scavi*, vol. 1 (Naples 1850) xi–xii (dated at Portici, July 20, 1750). Weber acknowledged receipt of these orders on July 25, 1750 (*StErc*, 105).

6 *Stabiae*, 105–6 (August 18, 1759), where Alcubierre claims that during Fogliani's tenure (until June 1755) he had submitted eleven finished plans. The plan of Gragnano being referred to is probably that of the "Villa of Antèros and Heracleo" illustrated in Ruggiero, *Terraferma*, 56, and discussed in this chapter.

7 ASN *CRA* 1537, Inc. 19, 24, 26 (cf. Strazzullo, "Documenti," 268 n. 10).

8 Barnabei, 758. This is described in SNSP "Notizie istoriche," 72r., in the following entries:

> (August 4, 1741) Since the engineer Bardet requires all the notes, plans, and other material relating to the excavations, Alcubierre is ordered to consign all that he has in his possession regarding this matter to the aforementioned engineer.

> (August 6, 1741) Alcubierre responds to the order of [August 4], [saying] that he had left Rorro [Bardet's predecessor] instructions, to which nothing more could be added: that he had not made a plan, because this was impossible; that he had made only a sketch of the theater but this was now with the king, and that the general plan of the [Royal] Site at Portici was in the hands of Medrano.

The "general plan" must be Alcubierre's topographical plan of Portici. Fernandez Murga, *Carlos III*, 36–39, failed to appreciate Alcubierre's shortcomings in draftsmanship, remarking, "if the majority of these drawings have not been preserved, it is not his fault." He believed Alcubierre had turned over all his plans to his superiors, but many of these would have been rough drafts accompanying his reports, not finished drawings.

9 La Vega, 298. This contradicts another document, also prepared by La Vega, which states that Alcubierre began his topographical plan on August 6 and finished it on August 21, 1738 (SNSP *Fondo Cuomo* 2-6-2, Doc. 16 "Ragguaglio Storico," fol. 144r.). For a plan of the area of Portici prior to the construction of the royal palace, see G. Alisio, "I siti reali," in *Civiltà del '700* (Florence 1980) 1.78, fig. 3. The existing illustrations of the palace from this period are two drawings of the facade by Antonio Canevari; an unsigned plan of the *castello* in the *boschetto*; plans by Medrano for construction of the Capella Reale that were never realized; plans of portions of the gardens, one by L. Vanvitelli; and a perspective view drawn for Tanucci by the French architect Gravier, now in the Museo di S. Martino (see De Seta, *Ville Vesuviane*, 112–17).

10 *StErc*, 84–85 (August 6, 1741).

11 Wm. Leybourn, *The compleat surveyor, or the whole art of surveying of land by a new instrument lately invented; as also by the plain table, circumferentor, the theodolite as now improved, or by the chain only*, ed. 5 (London 1722) 40–41, for a full discussion of the use of the circumferentor; D. Scott, "The evolution of mine surveying instruments," *Transactions of the American Institute of Mining and Metallurgical Engineers* 28 (1898) 679–745, esp. 682–691, on the device invented by Balthazar Rössler in 1633; A.W. Richeson, *English land measuring to 1800: Instruments and practices* (Cambridge, Mass. 1966) 93–94, 99–100.

12 La Vega, 282, and 311, where one of his co-workers calls him an ignoramus. In 1765, La Vega recommended that Tannuci consult Giuseppe Palumbo for details about d'Elbeuf's excavations before Palumbo became too old to remember them:

> I take the liberty to inform Your Eminence that in case he should wish to write a history of the excavations at Herculaneum, I believe he should consult certain men who worked there, among these in particular one Maestro Peppe Palumbo, a resident here in Portici, who alone remains from among those who excavated for Prince d'Elbeuf. He still retains a good memory and is well informed of everything, having assisted as head supervisor in the first excavations that His Majesty undertook in Herculaneum. Moreover, one could confront him with various pieces that remain in the museum or with Canart, for which he will perhaps recall the places where they were removed, since among the statues there are several removed by d'Elbeuf which were recovered by His Majesty, as this same Palumbo informs me, and which he found in the theater.

> What this man will say, I believe, could in some way be verified by some others from these excavations, and in particular by the head supervisor of Città [Antonio Scognamillo?] and by two pensioners who, as the first ones to enter into work in the tunnels, through the long experience they have had with those things that were taken in this work, many of which were already excavated by Prince d'Elbeuf, could give various insights and in particular the above-mentioned head supervisor, who as an attentive man recalls many small details.

ASN *CRA* 868, Inc. 2; also *StErc*, 462–63 (April 13, 1765), and F. Strazzullo, ed., *Settecento napoletana* (Naples 1982) 265–66.

13 *Giornale*, 284 (July 18, 1750): report on the need to reduce and engrave seven plans of build-

ings at Herculaneum, the theater, and describing ongoing work toward perfecting eleven others; *PAH* I.ii.Addenda iv.135 (July 18, 1750), where it is stated that nine plans were finished for work at Gragnano, Città, and the theater, air vent, and shafts at Resina; and that Alcubierre has submitted seven original plans to Fogliani.

14 The fourteen plans are: (1) Plan of theater submitted to Montealegre (*StErc*, 23–24 = SNSP "Notizie istoriche," 69r. [May 13, 1739]); (2) Plan of theater and surrounding tunnels, submitted to Montealegre (*StErc*, 37 = SNSP "Notizie istoriche," 69v. [July 13, 1739]); (3) Plan of structure with an altar 7 palms high (probably the Palestra at Herculaneum; *Giornale*, 213–14 [June 8–28, 1743]); (4) Plan of Basilica, by Bardet; (5) Plan of buildings along the "Decumanus Maximus," by Bardet (July 7, 1743); (6) Plan of theater, by Bardet (ASN *CRA* 1544, Inc. 82); (7) Plan of "forum" at Herculaneum and excavations undertaken in 1746 (*Giornale*, 245 [January 5, 1747]); (8) Plan of underground tunnels of theater at Herculaneum (March 20, 1747; *StErc*, pl. 4); (9) Plan of amphitheater of Pompeii (or "Stabiae") (December 7, 1748); (10) Plan of four insulae of Herculaneum (March 24, 1749; *StErc*, pl. 7); (11) Another plan of buildings at Herculaneum (*Giornale*, 272 [May 19, 1749]); (12) Plan of the "Villa of Cicero," Pompeii (December, 1749); (13) Plan of the "Villa of Antèros and Heracleo" at Stabiae (January 20, 1750); (14) Sketch plan of tombs at Herculaneum (*Giornale*, 279 [February 28, 1750]). Alcubierre had supplied Bayardi with all his early plans and may not have retained copies for himself; in 1756 he asked the prime minister to recover some ten or eleven plans from Bayardi before the latter left Naples (*StErc*, 192 [June 15, 1756]).

15 *Giornale*, 245 (January 5, 1747): "a plan of the tunnels and places where excavations continued during the past year, on which one recognizes the building in the city of Herculaneum from which the marble equestrian statues were removed, along with other things; in the explication are noted the key finds encountered in the past year."

16 For the Villa of Cicero, see the discussion in this chapter. A tomb with eight niches, found beneath the Moscardillo property in Resina, in February 1750, must be the same tomb illustrated in Cochin and Bellicard, 24–26, pl. 6. Ruggiero (*StErc*, xxxvii–xxxviii) concurs that Bellicard's plan illustrates the same site being excavated on the Moscardillo property not far from the Basilica. A drawing of a stone grinding mill from Gragnano was begun on March 7, 1750, and was submitted by Alcubierre to Fogliani ten days later (*Giornale*, 279-80).

17 ASN *Raccolta Piante e Disegni*, Cart. xxiv.1 (0.70 × 0.50 m.): "Plano, perfil y elevación de un edificio encontrado en las Ruinas de la antigua cuidad Herculeana situada â 60 palmos debajo de la villa de Resina, el dicho Perfil està cortado sobre la linea AB" (photograph published in the *Fonti documentarie per la storia degli scavi di Pompei, Ercolano e Stabia* [Naples 1979], and Allroggen-Bedel, "Dokumente," 139 n. 5, fig. 7); ASN *Raccolta Piante e Disegni*, Cart. xxiv.2: "Plan, Profil et Elevation, d'un Edifice trouvé dans les Ruines de l'Encienne Ville de Herculane situés a 60 palmes audessous du Vilage de Rezine, le dit profil coupe sur la ligne AB. Levé e dessiné Par l'ingenieur Bardet de Villeneuve"; this latter plan is badly damaged in the upper left-hand corner (photograph published in C. Grell, *Herculanum et Pompéi dans les récits des voyageurs français du XVIIIᵉ siècle* [Naples 1982] pl. 5).

18 *Giornale*, 210; Allroggen-Bedel, "Forum," 107 n. 86; G. Guadagno, "Supplemento Epigrafico Ercolanese II," *CronErc* 11 (1981) 132 n. 28; *idem*, "Ercolano: Eredità di cultura e nuovi dati," in *Ercolano 1738–1988: 250 anni di ricerca archeologica* (Rome 1993) 77–79, esp. n. 35.

19 *StErc*, 94 (December 26, 1742), 95 (January 21 and 27, 1743).

20 The associations between Bardet's plans and the descriptions in the daybooks were made by Allroggen-Bedel, "Dokumente," 143–44.

21 ASN *Raccolta Piante e Disegni*, Cart. xxiv.3 (0.85 m. × 0.62 m.): "Plan des Ediffices trouvées sous le vilage de Rezine pres de Naple les quels faisoient partie de la Ville d'Herculeane. Découvert et levé par l'ingenieur Bardet de Villeneuve. (Le 7 Juillet 1743)." See Allroggen-Bedel, "Dokumente", 140 figs. 1 a and b, where a photograph of the plan and the text of the annotations are reproduced along with a detailed commentary that takes note of these irregularities in the plan; and Guadagno, "Augustalium," 171 figs. 8 and 11, who reproduces the other, slightly wider, version of the plan (ASN *Raccolta Piante e Disegni*, Cart. xxiv.4 [1.02 × 0.59 m.]).

22 See Guadagno, "Augustalium," figs. 5 and 11.

23 ASN *CRA* 1544, Inc. 82, fol. 12–14:

Esplication du Theatre trouvé dans les Ruines de la Ville d'Herculeum sous Rezine / Ce theatre peut contenir environ quinze cent persones asises comodement / *A*. Sont des petittes portes au nombre de 7. et d'autant de petits degrez par les quels le peuple entroit au theatre et sedispersoit sur les differents gradins dont il est composé, et qui repondent sur la gallerie *B*. marqueé sur le profil. / *C*. Sont deux loges pavez de marbre blanc. / *D*. Sont deux escaliers qui montent sur l'epesseur de la muraille / *E*. Sont les pieds d'Esteaux sur lesquels il y avoit des statues de bronze a cheval. / *F*. est un espace entre deux pieds d'Esteaux sur le milieu du quel il y avoit une statue de femme aussy de bronze. / *G*. Sont les passages pour venir sur le degrez superieurs par la gallerie *H*. marqueé au profil. / *I*. est l'orchestre / *K*. est le pro\ss/cenium ou pulpitum, qui est proprement ce que nous apellons a present le theatre, le bas de cet endroit est de 8. palmes plus bas que l'orchestre *I*. et les murailles *L*. sont a hauteur d'apuit, c'est sens doutte sur elles que s'apuyoit le theatre ou pulpitum qu'on faisoit de planche. / *M*. Est le Postscenium, qui est une facade d'ediffice ornée de trois ordres d'architecture, de colonnes et de pilastres, de tres beau marbre ou jaspe affricain, les murailles en estant revestües de mesme que les niches *N*. dans les quels il y avoit des statües de marbre blanc. / C'est proprement ce que nous apellons le derriere du Theatre, et ou les acteurs s'abilloient, dans les Theatres Grecs, l'orchestre faisoit une partie dela scene qui comprenoit generallement tout ce qui apartenoit aux acteurs, mais aux Theatres des Romains aucuns des acteurs ne descendoient dans l'orchestre qui estoit ocupé par les sieges des senateurs. / a L'endroit *O*. j'ay trouvé une petitte table de bronze soutenüe par des pieds de bronze, plians les bouts des quels estoyent soudeé enplomb, dans la pierre du gradin. / Bardet de Villeneuve.

24 T. Shäfer, "Le *sellae curules* del teatro di Ercolano," *CronErc* 9 (1979) 143–51. Shäfer concluded that MN. 73152 was the sella referred to by Venuti in his letter of "January 17, 1738" (Gori, *Notizie*, 5) and that MN. 73153 must have been found at a later date; this is now confirmed by Bardet's plan.
25 ASN *CRA* 1544, Inc. 82 (no date); found among a series of documents dating to the 1790s. Included is a copy of Egizio's commentary on Bardet's plan. Bardet's remarks are similar to the ones he made on his plan of the "Decumanus Maximus," where, however, the seating capacity is set at two thousand. For the Italian text and excerpts from Egizio's comments, see Pagano, "Teatro," 140–42; and Chapter 8 in this volume, "The Theater at Herculaneum."
26 *Stabiae*, 133 (September 10, 1760): Bardet still has possession of his plans; *StErc* 480–81 (October 18, 1766): Tanucci transfers Bardet's plans to La Vega. These must be the same four plans (two copies of the Basilica and two of the "Decumanus Maximus") that were recovered in the Archivio di Stato in the 1970s.

27 D'Arthenay, 33–45, who already in 1748 observed that the reader would be unable to verify his description, since the ruins had been covered over again. He states that the Basilica, which he identifies as a forum, measured 228 by 132 feet, while Bardet's plan gives 208 by 142 palms.
28 Bellicard's notebook resurfaced in the manuscript collection of the Metropolitan Museum of Art in New York (Acc. no. 40.59.6), and was published by A.R. Gordon, "Jérôme-Charles Bellicard's Italian notebook of 1750–51: The discoveries at Herculaneum and observations on ancient and modern architecture," *Metropolitan Museum Journal* 25 (1990) 49–142; the notebook's text was transcribed by C. Riopelle and A. Gordon. According to Gordon, 132 n. 1, "It was purchased at Parke-Bernet, May 1, 1940, lot 54, from the working library of the late Whitney Warren. Mr. Warren, a noted New York architect, had received it as a gift in 1917 from a French officer, commandant de Malleray, who served on the General Staff at Pétain's headquarters near Provins." For Cochin and Bellicard at Pompeii and Herculaneum in general, see Grell, 97 n. 8.
29 Cochin and Bellicard, 18–24, pl. 5. Bellicard omitted certain details in his engraved version of the plan, such as the interior colonnade of the Augustalium and several of the adjacent buildings, and included several errors, such as adding a second colonnade on the front of the Basilica.
30 Cochin and Bellicard, 24.
31 Certain members of the court apparently were allowed to conduct such investigations; for example, G. Martorelli, who described his work in the theater in a letter to A.F. Gori dated June 18, 1748 (Gori, *Notizie*, 75–76): "It would be difficult for someone without a strong heart and spirit to maneuver 84 palms underground through the narrowest and most ruinous tunnels, as I have, and to take measurements."
32 Cochin and Bellicard, 12–13, pl. 2; Gordon, 62 pls. 11 and 12 for variations in the plates in the editions of 1753 and 1754.
33 *StErc*, 481 (October 25, 1766). La Vega also lamented that plans of Herculaneum drawn separately by Bardet and Weber had never been combined to show the full extent of the Bourbon excavations; this was a task he eventually took on himself.
34 Cataloged in the *Fonti documentarie*, 141–42.
35 *StErc*, 31 (June 11–15, 1739), 37 (July 13–18, 1739); cf. SNSP "Notizie istoriche," 69v. (July 13, 1739): Alcubierre submits plan of theater and surrounding tunnels.
36 G. Minervini, "Di una antica pianta del teatro di Ercolano," *BullArchItal* 1.5 (1861) 33–35, pl. 3; *StErc*, xxvi–xxvii (legend), pl. 4 (plan); the original copper

plates are missing. The confusion between an amphi-theater and a theater also may help date the original legend of this plan to early 1739, before Venuti's identification had become commonly, though not universally, known and accepted.

37 Since Bianchini's explication of the stratigraphy of the volcanic material in 1699, this had been a topic of great interest to scholars.

38 Minervini, 33–34, who states that de Jorio first had sought in 1831 to publish the plan in the *Monumenti* of the Istituto di Correspondenza Archeo-logica in Rome. Minervini and de Jorio wrongly attributed the plan to Weber (as first noted by Barnabei, 753 n. 2); *StErc*, xix, pl. 4. In both Minervini and Ruggiero, text and plan are printed separately, so it is not clear how they were related in the original copy.

39 *StErc*, pl. 7; *Giornale*, 271 (March 24, 1749), where the site is said to be 56 palms (14.81 m.) belowground, the same depth indicated on this plan: "Pianta che addita una porzione delle fabbriche appartenenti alla già distrutta Città d'Ercolano le quali rimangono cinquantasei palmi Napoletani sotto terra." For a discussion of the location of these excavations within the town plan of Herculaneum, see W. Johannowsky, "Problemi urbanistici di Ercolano," *CronErc* 12 (1982), 145–49, with reference to the plan of Herculaneum produced by F. La Vega in 1797 (*StErc*, pl. 2). The site is some distance to the west of the currently accessible portions of the excavations, along the present "Decumanus Inferior."

40 Tran Tam Tinh, *La Casa dei Cervi*, 1–5.

41 *Giornale*, 272 (May 19, 1749): "another plan of the buildings that exist 54 palms underground at the ancient city of Herculaneum."

42 Maiuri, *Nuovi scavi*, pl. 6, provides a longitudinal cross section of the modern excavations showing that the depth of the original topsoil and volcanic deposit was 35.85 m. at the north end and 22.5 m. along the ancient seashore to the south.

43 *Giornale*, 272–77, covering the finds from Stabiae from June 1749 to January 1750, a period for which Ruggiero lacked documentation; Alcubierre mentions that a plan was being drawn up on December 11, 1749. The 1750 plan was first published by Ruggiero, *Terraferma*, 56; see also D. Camardo, A. Ferrara, and N. Longobardi, *Stabiae: Le ville* (Castellamare di Stabia 1989) 89 pl. 28.

44 Marble Bust, "Livia Minor": MN. 6193; Ruesch 1014; *CollMN* 1.2, 114–15 #93; Cosenza, 42–43 fig. 3, 223 #26. For the marble bust, see E. Gabrici, "Per la iconografia di Livia moglie di Augusto," *RendNap* 20 (1906) 235–39, pl. 1. The bust and inscription (*Giornale*, 277 [December 11, 1749]) are mentioned,

e.g., in letters (by Martorelli?) dated January 31 and September 5, 1750, published by A.F. Gori, *Admiranda antiquitatum herculanensium descripta et illustrata ad annum MDCCL* (Padova 1752) 126 and 146–47.

45 *Stabiae*, 329–31, pl. 11, and 278–80 for excavations in this area (May 12 to July 20, 1779); La Vega's plan is dated July 20, 1779.

46 *PAH* I.ii.Addenda iv.135 (July 18, 1750), where it is noted that these plans were "eseguiti . . . molto bene" and were in the process of being engraved. The similarity between the plans also might be because the same individual engraved them all. Dorgemont's name, given in the document cited earlier, appears in neither of the lists of engineers working on the excavations during this period published by Strazzullo ("Documenti," 263 n. 2) or G. Rubino ("La real fabbrica d'armi," 115 n. 21); for Dorgemont's work as an engineer, see F. Strazzullo, "Documenti del Settecento per la storia dell' edilizia e dell' urbanistica nel Regno di Napoli (VI)," *NapNob* 22.3–4 (May–August 1983) 144.

47 *PAH* I.ii.Addenda iv.135 (July 18, 1750), where seven are said to be in his own hand.

48 SNSP "Notizie istoriche," 69r.–69v. (May 13 and July 13, 1739).

49 *PAH* I.i.10 (December 4, 1749) (= ASN *CRA* 1538, Inc. 163); *Stabiae*, 105–6 (August 18, 1759), where the sketch copy is mentioned. The paintings were found in 1749 (*PAH* I.i.7–8 [January 18 and February 8, 1749]) and are thought to have come from rooms in the Villa of Cicero at Pompeii (MN. 9119, 9121, 9133, 9163, 9295, 9297; *CollMN* 1.1, 140–41 #123–28).

50 La Vega later incorporated his plan into the general site plan of Pompeii that he began sometime prior to 1797, on which were illustrated the results of his own discoveries with plans of buildings previously excavated and no longer visible, such as the amphitheater, the Praedia Iuliae Felicis, and the buildings in Regio VIII terraced over the city walls. Copies of the text accompanying La Vega's plan of the Villa of Cicero exist in the Museo Nazionale in Naples (Fs. VIII.C.7) and the SNSP (Ms. XXI.D.21): "Giornale dello scavo di Pompei, e propriamente della strada e case contigue alla porta della città relativo alla pianta in questo inclusa, 1763–1784"; the first of these was published in *PAH* I.ii.Addenda 3b.110–18, pl. 2, where the rooms investigated by Alcubierre are indicated by the number 1. La Vega's general plan of Pompeii is MN. 2615; H. Eschebach, *Die städtebauliche Entwicklung des antiken Pompeji* (Heidelberg 1970) 69, dated the plan pre-1769; *CTP* 5 (Rome 1981) 116–17, dated it ca. 1809, because of later additions made by La Vega's brother, Pietro.

51 *PAH* I.i.5–6 (October 26–November 16, 1748). With the last report Alcubierre provided a summary of its dimensions and capacity (12,000 people) (cf. ASN *CRA* 1538, Inc. 136 [November 16, 1748]). *PAH* I.i.6: Measurements for a plan were taken the following week (November 23, 1748), and the finished plan was submitted to Fogliani on December 7, 1748.

52 Soprintendenza Archeologica di Napoli e Caserta, *Archivio Disegno*, #78; color photograph in *Pompeii 1748–1980: I tempi della documentazione* (Rome 1981) 133. Alcubierre mentions other "designs" of sites at Pompeii and Gragnano that were under way as late as August 1, 1750 (*Giornale*, 284).

53 *PAH* I.i.6 (November 16, 1748).

54 M. Girosi, "L'anfiteatro di Pompei," *MemNap* 5 (1936) 29–55. See also the discussion of the complex architectural design of the amphitheater in the *CTP* 3a (Rome 1987) xiv–xv.

55 Cicero's "crater ille delicatus" (*ad Att.* 2.8.2); Strabo 5.4.3 and 8.

56 ASN *CRA* 1539, Inc. 6 (June 9, 1750): letter of Bigotti to Fogliani. In a letter printed in Gori, *Admiranda*, 169–73 #34 (February 5, 1751), the author speaks of this project as intending as well to verify the geographical distances between cities and monuments, in the manner of the Tabula Peutingeriana.

57 The map is mentioned as destined for the *Prodromo* in a letter by Bayardi to Fogliani dated November 25, 1752 (ASN *CRA* 1539, Inc. 64), for which see Chapter 3 in this volume, "The Discovery of the Villa dei Papiri."

58 *StErc*, 115 (February 13, 1751).

59 ASN *CRA* 1539, Inc. 25 (July 24, 1751).

60 He is referring to the four bronze fountain figures of youths holding dolphins or hydria found in January 1751 in the Villa dei Papiri at Herculaneum (see Chapter 3 in this volume, "The Discovery of the Villa dei Papiri"): MN. 5023, Ruesch 875; MN. 5027, Ruesch 877; MN. 5021, Ruesch 864; MN. 5032, Ruesch 868; *CollMN* 1.2, 138–39 #205–6; M.R. Wojcik, *La Villa dei Papiri* (Rome 1986) 245–48, pls. 124–25. The two marble pavements were found in rooms adjacent to these statues. The white marble youth was found between March 27 and 31, 1751, also in the Villa dei Papiri (*StErc*, 116 [March 31, 1751]): MN. 6105; Ruesch 1145; *CollMN* 1.2, 135–37 #203; Wojcik, 251–52, pl. 127. Reference to this statue helps date the petition to about April 1, 1751.

61 One example of these difficulties is that Josef de Corcoles, the supervisor of the excavations at Herculaneum, had to write the weekly summary of finds on October 31, 1750, because Weber was

detained in Gragnano with a broken carriage (*StErc*, 109).

62 ASN *CRA* 1544, Inc. 80, fols. 1–4 (March 25, 1751, although this particular copy of the petition is undated). It is also unsigned and may have been written on behalf of Weber to Charles of Bourbon.

63 ASN *CRA* 1544, Inc. 80 (no date; Weber to Fogliani). Evidently a copy of this letter was made and given to Alcubierre, since it was found attached to his letter to Fogliani dated July 24, 1751 (ASN *CRA* 1539, Inc. 25). Schipa, *ASPN* 28.1 (1903) 54, notes that the average monthly wages of a captain were between 26 and 32 ducats.

64 ASN *CRA* 1539, Inc. 25 (July 24, 1751).

65 *StErc*, 120 (August 27 and September 5, 1751).

66 SNSP "Notizie istoriche," 75v. (November 21, 1751); the reasons are not specified.

PART II. EXCAVATIONS AND METHODOLOGY

CHAPTER 3. THE DISCOVERY OF THE VILLA DEI PAPIRI

1 The excavations at Baiae began on September 1, 1751 (Ruggiero, *Terraferma*, 166), while those at Pozzuoli started on February 13, 1751, and ran until July 1, 1753 (Ruggiero, *Terraferma*, 112–16). Work at San Marco began on June 7, 1749 (*Stabiae*, 3). Excavations at the "Villa of Pollio" near Sorrento began on March 25, 1750 (*PAH* I.ii.Addenda iv.135).

2 *Giornale*, 283–84 (June 6 and August 1, 1750).

3 A portion of the Moscardillo property lay to the northeast of Herculaneum, while much of the Bisogno properties covered the area occupied by the ancient city itself (see Maiuri, *Ercolano*, pl. 2). For a description of one of these tombs, see Cochin and Bellicard, 24–30, pl. 6, esp. 27–28: "At the time I am speaking, that is in 1750, one can easily pass through these places that I am going to describe, but I cannot speak for their present state, since, as I have said, one empties and refills, and the underground areas present a new appearance every six months."

4 *Giornale*, 282 (May 2 to 21, 1750). Weber's plan indicates that the second shaft was sunk parallel to the first, on the opposite side of the Calle de Ciceri. For these early difficulties, see also Gallavotti, 293–94.

5 *StErc*, 108 (September 15, 1750).

6 The dimensions provided here are the standard ones, based on the scale of Weber's later plan of the site, given by, e.g., D. Mustilli, "La villa pseudourbana ercolanese," in *La Villa dei Papiri* (*CronErc* 13, Suppl. 2, 1983) 10–11 [article originally published in *RendNap* n.s. 31 (1956) 77–97] and Wojcik, 13–26.

Certain features, such as the footpath and the depth of the euripus, have been illuminated by the recent work in the villa reported by B. Conticello and U. Cioffi, "Il 'rientro' nella Villa dei Papiri di Ercolano," in *Restaurare Pompei* (Milan 1990) 178–79.

7 *Giornale*, 285 (August 16, 1750); *StErc*, 113 (January 16, 1751): Weber asks whether he should send the drawing to Paderni; it would have helped Paderni to properly reconstruct the mosaic. Bayardi, *Catalogo*, ed. 2, p. 445, describes this pavement on the basis of Weber's drawing.

8 *StErc*, pl. 11. Since this is an engraving, it is impossible to know whether or not the annotations were translated. Spanish was the official language of the court until 1763.

9 ASN *CRA* 1539, Inc. 64 (November 25, 1752): Bayardi to Fogliani.

10 For a brief history of the Accademia Etrusca, see M. Maylender, *Storia delle accademie d'Italia* (Bologna 1927) 2.327–32.

11 For Mazzocchi (1684–1771), an epigrapher who was later put in charge of editing the papyrus fragments from Herculaneum, see Castaldi, 191–93; G. Guadagno, "A.S. Mazzochi [*sic*] epigrafista," *Archivio storico di terra di lavoro* (1975) 273–82; and P. Borraro, ed., *Alessio Simmaco Mazzocchi e il Settecento meridionale* (Salerno 1979).

12 O.A. Bayardi, *Prodromo delle antichità d'Ercolano* (Naples 1752) 1.xviii.

13 The most complete study to date of Bayardi's work is G. Castellano, "Mons. Ottavio Antonio Bayardi e l'illustrazione degli scavi di Ercolano," *Samnium* xvi–xviii (1943–45) 65–86, 185–94.

14 J. Gray, "Extract of a letter . . . to Sir Thomas Robinson . . . relating to the same discoveries in Herculaneum [October 29, 1754]," *PhilTrans* 48.2 (1754) 825–26.

15 Bayardi, *Prodromo*, 5.2677.

16 Cf. D. Comparetti and G. De Petra, *La villa ercolanese dei Pisoni* (Naples 1883) 59: "[Bayardi was] the most stupid and ridiculous man who ever left memory of himself in the annals of science" and 61: "a real Vesuvius of nonsense."

17 G. Martorelli, *De regia theca calamaria in Regia Academia litterarum graecarum professoris . . .* (Naples 1756).

18 Bayardi, *Prodromo*, 1.xx–xxi. Bernard de Montfaucon (1665-1745) was a French archaeologist who published a ten-volume work entitled *L'antiquité expliquée et représentée en figures* (Paris 1719), followed by a five volume *Supplément au livre de l'antiquité expliquée . . .* (Paris 1724); see Chapter 6 in this volume, "Weber's Application to the Accademia Ercolanese."

19 Bayardi initially believed this would be an appendix, since he already refers to it in the conclusion to his fifth volume of the *Prodromo*. The first edition of his *Catalogo* was published in Naples in 1754; a second edition, with some alterations, appeared in 1755.

20 Bayardi, *Catalogo* 2d. ed., xx; a clear reference to Weber's Cratere Maritimo map.

21 Castaldi, 33–50; Maylender, 2.280–86; E. Choisi, "La Reale Accademia Ercolanese: Bernardo Tanucci fra politica e antiquaria," in *Bernardo Tanucci: Statista, letterato, giurista* (Naples 1986) 2.495–517. The original members included Bayardi; Mazzocchi; Giacomo Castelli; Salvatore Aula; Ferdinando Galiani; Francesco Grassi, conte di Pianura, who himself had a celebrated museum of antiquities; Girolamo Giordano; Giovanni Maria delle Torre, vulcanologist and head of the Stamperia Reale; Padre Tartugio Tarugi; Francesca Valletta, secretary of the Accademia, whose family had had to sell off its collection of antiquities and rare books; Pasquale Carcani, secretary after Valletta became too infirm; Francesca Pratilli; Domenico Ronchi, who also had a small museum and a library of manuscripts; Niccola Ignarra; and Mattia Zarrillo, keeper of the Farnese collection and presumed author of the *Giudizio dell' opera dell' Abate Winckelmann intorno alle scoverte di Ercolano contenuto in una lettera ad un amico* (Naples 1765). Added later to fill vacanies were the Marchese Berardo Galiani (brother of Ferdinando; see Chapter 6 in this volume, "Weber's Application to the Accademia Ercolanese") and Giovanni Battista Basso-Bassi. According to Schipa (*ASPN* 28.3 [1903] 546), Pratilli (1689–1763) was the only archaeologist in the Accademia: he had published a detailed study of the course of the Via Appia from Rome to Brindisi (*Della Via Appia riconosciuta e descritta da Roma a Brindisi* 4 vols. [Naples 1745]; see Castaldi, 200–5).

22 Reaction to the Accademia's publications was not universally enthusiastic, however. Caylus complained that the engravings were poorly executed and wondered about their accuracy, observing as well that "the explication pleases me little; it is too long and filled with useless things and repetitive throughout. Moreover, none of those who worked on it understand art." (A.-C.-P. Comte de Caylus, *Correspondence Inedite . . . avec le P. Paciaudi, théatin* [Paris 1877] 1.42–43, letter of March 5, 1759).

23 C.M. de la Condamine, "Extract from a letter of Mons. la Condamine to Dr. Maty [March 11, 1756]," *PhilTrans* 49.2 (1756) 622–24. For a discussion of the place of the Accademia's publications in the history of eighteenth-century printing, see V. Trombetta, "L'edizione de *Le antichità di Ercolano esposte*," *RAAN* 59 (1984) 151–72.

24 Barnabei, 760 n. 2, gives the full text of Bayardi's letter to Tanucci, dated May 4, 1756. When Barthelemy visited Bayardi in Rome soon thereafter, he encountered a sick and embittered man:

> I found him in a large hall; a violent cold kept him on a sofa, the appearance of which was a proof of the length of its services. He was dressed in such antique garments that one might fairly have taken them for the spoils of some ancient inhabitant of Herculaneum. He was at work with his amanuensis. . . . He then complained of the manner in which the works at Herculaneum were conducted; of the negligence of the ministry with respect to the manuscripts [that is, the famous papyrus scrolls from Herculaneum]; and of the jealousy excited against himself by the distinquished treatment which he had experienced from the king. (J.J. Barthelemy, *Travels in Italy* [London 1802] 301 [undated].)

Barthelemy already had written, on December 10, 1755 (ibid., 49), that "Bayardi stands ill at court: most likely he will give up this work; I hear a great many disparaging things of it." For a summary of Bayardi's life and work, see the *Dizionario biografico degli Italiani* (Rome 1963) 5.284–85 (L. Moretti).

25 ASN *CRA* 1539, Inc. 64 (November 27, 1752): Fogliani to Alcubierre.

26 Pierre Jacques Gaultier arrived in Naples in January 1751 and was paid 200 ducats for engraving this map (Castellano, 84 n. 4). Already in the *Prodromo*, 5.2123, Bayardi had begun to refer to Weber's plan as "mia Carta Geografica."

27 Regale Accademia Ercolanese di Archeologica, *Le antichità di Ercolano esposte: Le pitture antiche d'Ercolano e contorni incise con qualche spiegazione*, vol. 1 (Naples 1757). There is a copy of the engraving in the manuscript collection of the Biblioteca Nazionale di Napoli (BNN. Ms. B.a 21 A/21: 0.585 m. × 0.490 m.); another is in the Collezione Grimaldi, Naples (0.490 m. × 0.450 m.; see G. Pane and V. Valerio, eds., *La città di Napoli tra vedutismo e cartografia: Piante e vedute dal XV al XIX secolo* [Naples 1987] 241 #102). A cartouche in the lower right-hand corner bears the title: "Cratere maritimo o golfo di Napoli, eseguito dal Cap.no Don Carlo Weber, ridotto e ratificato da D.n Giuseppe Liberati, sotto la direzione del Colonn.o Ingeg.e militare D.n Roc.o Gioacc. de Alcubierre, secondo le misure itinerarie e le osservazioni di Mons.re Ottavio Ant.o Bayardi, Scala di 5000 tese, Scala di 6 miglia italiane, Inciso da P. Gaultier 1754."

28 For brief discussions of the historical background

to the plans of Weber and the Duca di Noja, see C. De Seta, "Topografia territoriale e vedutismo a Napoli nel Settecento," in *Civiltà del '700 a Napoli (1734–1799)* (Florence 1980) 2.29–30, 36, figs. 278, 280. The text of Carafa's "Considerazioni sull' utilità che si trarebbe da una esatta carta topografica della città di Napoli e de' suoi contorni che si propone di fare" (Naples 1750) is reprinted in C. De Seta, *Cartografia della città di Napoli* (Naples 1969). For these plans, see also L.A. Scatozza Horicht, "Ville nel territorio ercolanese," *CronErc* 15 (1985) 132–35.

29 C. Knight and A. Jorio, "L'ubicazione della Villa Ercolanese dei Papiri," *RendNap* n.s. 55 (1980) 51–65; Weber's illustration places the belvedere at 102 palms belowground (25.63 m.), whereas Alcubierre stated it was 120 palms (30.15 m.), which may be a simple copying error (*Giornale*, 284 [July 18, 1750]); the actual depth is 25.00 m. A. De Simone, "La Villa dei Papiri, Rapporto Preliminare: Gennaio 1986–Marzo 1987," *CronErc* 17 (1987) 23, concluded that the Pozzo Ciceri 1 was used for access by the workmen, while the Pozzo Ciceri 2 served for ventilation; this latter shaft is no longer accessible. In 1986 a third shaft was located, the so-called Pozzo Veneruso 1, at the opposite end of the villa, near the atrium. Its dimensions are 4.69 m. by 1.52 m., while the pavement of the villa is reached at a depth of 23.13 m. from the mouth of the shaft, equivalent to 11.35 m. ASL. A more complete report on the new excavations is Conticello and Cioffi, 173–90. Cioffi noted that the Pozzo Ciceri 1 was so constricted that a special ladder had to be designed to allow a single man with a bucket to maneuver inside it while clearing the shaft for his work. For initial reactions to the reinvestigation of the Veneruso and the Ciceri shafts, see M. Gigante and G. Gullini, "Intervento," in *Un secolo di ricerche in Magna Grecia (Atti del ventottesimo convegno di studi sulla Magna Grecia*, Taranto, 7–12 Ottobre 1988) (Taranto 1989) 593–96.

30 The excavators would have come upon the outer west wall of the peristyle sometime in March 1751, when a marble pavement was removed from a room here (discussed in this section, "Excavating the Villa dei Papiri"); Weber may have ordered his workmen to break through this wall in mid-August 1751 (*StErc*, 119 [August 13, 1751]). It was not until around March 1, 1752, that the marble statue of a Pan copulating with a goat (MN. 27709) was found near the east end of the central euripus (*Giornale*, 301 [March 2, 1752]). It should be noted that no finds are recorded from this site in the daybooks from early September 1751 to January 1752, since efforts were concentrated on excavating a ramp near the Vico di Mare.

31 For one graffito found near the belvedere, see Conticello and Cioffi, 186, fig. 111.

32 StErc, 188 (May 10 and 15, 1756): tunnel enlarged to 10 palms wide (ca. 2.50 m.). The figures for the width of tunnels are those given by Conticello and Cioffi, 187. The tallest marble statue removed from the villa was that of a draped female standing 2.25 m. high, found in the tablinum (MN. 6240); the second tallest was that of the orator Aeschines (2.20 m.; MN. 6018). In removing a particularly large mosaic from the villa, Alcubierre halted the enlargement of one of the shafts and instead ordered the mosaic cut into two pieces, 10 palms by 5 palms each (2.64 m. × 1.32 m.) (StErc, 161 [September 15, 1754]).

33 According to Schipa, ASPN 28.1 (1903) 54, a lieutenant colonel received about 74 ducats per month.

34 A second mosaic pavement was excavated from February 20 to May 29, 1751 (StErc, 115–18); for discussion of the illustration of this, see the section in this chapter entitled "Weber's Documentation of the Villa."

35 The bronze statue of a woman was found at the theater on August 19, 1750 (StErc, 106 (August 17–22, 1750)). This is the so-called Antonia, illustrated in BdE 2.315–17, pl. 80, said to have been found near the exterior arches of the theater (MN. 5599, Ruesch 770; 2.28 m. high, much restored); CollMN 1.2, 120–21 #120 (Caligulan).

36 Apparently a reference to the bronze fountain ornament in the shape of a raven (MN. 4891; BdE 2.119) found at the Villa di San Marco in Stabiae in July 1751 (Stabiae, 11 [July 17, 1751]); see Chapter 6 in this volume, "Weber's Application to the Accademia Ercolanese."

37 Four small bronze fountain statues of cupids, two of a cupid carrying a hydria (MN. 5023, 5027; BdE 2.189–91, pl. 50) and two of a cupid holding a dolphin (MN. 5021, 5032; BdE 2.193–95, pl. 51), were found on January 28 to 30, 1751, in the Villa dei Papiri (StErc, 113 [January 30, 1751]). See Wojcik, 245–48, pls. 124–25; CollMN 1.2, 138–39 ##205–6.

38 Probably the vase decorated in archaistic reliefs found in the peristyle of the Villa di San Marco in April 1752 (MN. 6779). See Fig. 51.

39 A candelabrum was found during the week of February 1 through 6, 1751 (StErc, 114), but this is probably a generic reference to the numerous candelabra recovered thus far.

40 Gennaro Pacifico was an ironsmith employed by the Bourbon court who apparently made the gate for the entrance to the Real Museo Ercolanese at Portici in 1761 (B. Tanucci, Epistolario [1760–1761], ed.

M.G. Maiorini, vol. 9 [Rome 1985] 913 [August 11, 1761]; see photograph in "Museo," 104 fig. 11). Weber's reference to being lowered into the well recalls a similar remark by Alcubierre in 1739 that he had been lowered some two hundred times, exposing both "health and life" for the benefit of the king (StErc, 24 [May 13, 1739]). De Brosses, 4, also describes being lowered by a rope into the excavations.

41 ASN CRA 1539, Inc. 44 (May 22, 1752); this may be a copy of the original petition Weber had addressed to Fogliani on April 24, 1752.

42 ASN CRA 1539, Inc. 44 (May 18, 1752): Bigotti to Fogliani. Attached to this is Weber's second request, dated June 4, 1752.

43 SNSP "Notizie istoriche," 75v. (October 29, 1752). Again the reasons are not specified: "for certain faults he has committed."

44 Giornale, 308 (July 9, 1752). Gallavotti, 284, following the notes in Comparetti and De Petra, 154–55, and StErc, 120 (September 11, 1751), refer to a ramp begun as early as September 1751 along the Vico di Mare. This must have been associated with Weber's earlier attempt to link the gruta derecha with the existing tunnels to the east of the villa in the area where Alcubierre had excavated the four insulae of Herculaneum (StErc, pl. 7). This would have been viewed as a labor- and timesaving effort, but Weber probably abandoned it when he recognized how great a distance was involved. The mouth of the ramp of 1752 may have been linked to the modern Vico Ascione in order to facilitate the transfer of antiquities from the site.

45 According to Weber, this later shaft was only 74 palms (18.59 m.) deep, as compared to the 102-palm (27.00 m.) depth of the Pozzo Ciceri 1. It has been located in the recent excavations precisely where indicated on the plan but at a depth of 27.00 m., so perhaps it was deepened after Weber finished his plan. Weber may be referring to this air shaft in a report dated December 6, 1755 (StErc, 178).

46 See StErc, 197: sketch plan by Weber, with note "The great gruta derecha, which has been filled in from the point of the x up to the Ciceri."

47 The small bronze leaping pig (MN. 4893) was reportedly found at 11 P.M. (StErc, 188 [May 17, 1756]).

48 Conticello and Cioffi, 185.

49 Weber noted the height of the water table in the annotations to his plan of the villa ("Esplication V.x," referring to the well at V.viii), discussed in the section of this chapter entitled "Weber's Documentation of the Villa." For the euripus, see StErc, 184 (March 6, 1756): report of Corcoles to Weber.

50 Piaggio, "Memorie," 8v.

51 *StErc*, 193 (June 19, 1756); Alcubierre may be confusing here the notice in Suetonius (Suet. *Titus* 8) that a commission of former consuls had been sent from Rome to the area to help in the relief effort. The inscription is one referring to statues removed to certain Severan baths, the location of which is unknown: "Signa translata ex abditis locis ad celebritatem Thermarvm Severianarvm avdentivs Saemilanvs V.C. con. camp. constitvit dedicariqve precepit. cvrante T. Annonio Chrysantio V.P." The inscription, discussed by Martorelli (*De theca calamaria*, 541) was found in a workshop in Naples and was believed by contemporary scholars to refer to the removal of statues from Herculaneum (see Winckelmann, *Sendschreiben*, ##25–26; mentioned as well by Piaggio, "Memorie," 8v.). For these earlier tunnels, see also Paderni's description in a letter to Thomas Hollis of the Royal Society of London ("Extract of a letter . . . to Thomas Hollis (October 18, 1754)," *PhilTrans* 48.2 [1754] 821–25), where he observes that these earlier investigators had stopped digging wherever the volcanic matrix became too hard.

52 D'Arthenay, 72–73.

53 *StErc*, 174 (August 7, 1755); the incident took place on August 2 around nine o'clock in the evening. In the excavations undertaken here since 1986 precautions have been taken against inhaling or igniting these gases, in particular carbon dioxide, carbon monoxide, and hydrogen sulfide, though as yet none has been encountered (Conticello and Cioffi, 189).

54 Cf. *StErc*, esp. 159 (August 11, 1754), 135 (May 27, 1753).

55 For the location of these excavations, see *Giornale*, 315 (December 24, 1752); *StErc*, 127–57 (January 7, 1753–July 7, 1754); Scatozza-Höricht, "Ville," 150–52; and U. Pannuti, "Un complesso di stucchi romani proveniente da Portici," *MonAnt* 49 (1979) 257–73, pls. 1–13. For the derivation of the toponym "Epitaffio," see Celano, 18, and the text of the inscription from Epitaffio given by Weber in his manuscript discussed in Appendix 3 to this volume.

56 *StErc*, 138 (August 11, 1753): Alcubierre has expressed concern about the expense in time and labor of transporting earth to the shafts; *StErc*, 183 (February 14, 1756): four tunnels operative at the villa, each with a supervisor and a forced laborer; three men working the winch with its three baskets, two men below arranging the baskets, others filling them, and the rest carrying them through the tunnels.

57 E.g., *StErc*, 122 (December 12, 1751): letter of Fogliani to Alcubierre concerning damage in garden of Benedetto Jacomino of Resina, caused by excava-

tions; *StErc*, 138 (August 11, 1753): Weber explains to Alcubierre measures taken to prevent new buildings from subsiding into tunnels at Epitaffio; *StErc*, 142 (October 14, 1753): tunnel collapses at Papiri after two braces fail; *StErc*, 207 (October 30, 1756): cracks in house belonging to A. Scognamillo; *StErc*, 213 (January 22, 1757): two houses above excavations at Vico di Mare develop cracks. In 1768, Weber's successor, La Vega, produced a list of the proprietors whose houses had been damaged by the excavations and were in need of repair (*StErc*, 492–93 [September 13, 1768]), many of these concentrated in the area of the Basilica (see Chapter 5 in this volume, "The 'Temples' at Herculaneum").

58 *StErc*, 135–36 (May 27, 1753): description of pillars at Papiri, which were to be built by youths for a fraction of the cost paid the more experienced laborers; *StErc*, 144 (December 8, 1753): recommends forced laborers carry stones from Granatello to save on expenses; *StErc*, 184 (March 6, 1756): Weber recommends pillars be built at Papiri to prevent collapse; *StErc*, 207 (October 30, 1756): Weber reiterates method for constructing masonry pillars; Comparetti and De Petra, 199, quoting report of Alcubierre of August 12, 1758, mentioning that forced laborers continue to carry stones to the site. Such pillars can still be seen in the theater at Herculaneum as well as in the Villa dei Papiri; see also Conticello and Cioffi, 189 fig. 114.

59 *StErc*, 214 (February 5, 1757): Weber's first reference to the use of *los hurnillos*; see also the sketch plan accompanying his report of February 10, 1757 (*StErc*, 216).

60 *StErc*, 142 (October 14, 1753).

61 *StErc*, pl. 10, an engraving of the drawings for which the originals have been lost. The "Minerva" is actually the archaistic statue of Athena Promachos (MN. 6007; 2.00 m. high; *CollMN* 1.2, 134–35 #185) found in the week of October 30 to November 4, 1752 (see Fig. 63), and the "Vesta" a draped female statue (MN. 6240; 2.25 m. high; *CollMn* 1.2, 134–35 #188) found in the week of September 18-23, 1752; both came from the central oecus that opens onto the great peristyle.

62 Bayardi, *Catalogo*, ed. 2, p. 446.

63 *Stabiae*, 21–22 (February 22, 1753); Alcubierre also suggested engineers named Ferdinando de Albito and Mariano Diaz.

64 See especially "Museo"; M.F. Represa Fernandez, *El Real Museo de Portici (Napoles) 1750–1825: Approximacion al conocimiento de la restauracion, organizacion y presentacion de sus fondos*, Studia Archaeologica, Universidad de Valladolid, no. 79 (Valladolid 1988), could not be located for this study.

Prior to the establishment of the formal museum, the antiquities were arranged in the private apartments of the palace and shown by special arrangment. See, e.g., Russell's description of what could be seen as early as 1743 (*Letters*, 1.205–11 #32).

65 Castellano, 84 n. 3; many of Paderni's illustrations were engraved for the volumes of *Le antichità di Ercolano*. For a study of Paderni's early career and contacts with the Royal Society of London, see De Vos, "Camillo Paderni," 99–116.

66 C. Paderni, "Extract of a letter from Camillo Paderni . . . to Tho. Hollis, dated at Naples, April 27, 1754," *PhilTrans* 48.2 (1754) 634–38.

67 C. Paderni, "Extract of a letter . . . to Tho. Hollis, Esq., relating to the late discoveries at Herculaneum," *PhilTrans* 48.2 (1754) 821–25; the letter is dated October 18, 1754.

68 The entire plan, drawn on vellum, measures 0.585 m. wide and 1.235 m. long and has been folded into quarters. There are numerous erasures of penciled lines, especially in the lower right-hand portion, apparently the vestiges of the triangulation necessary for laying out the plan. That the plan is unfinished is also shown, for example, by the ruled lines in pencil used to ensure accurate drawing of the apsidal structure at the far left-hand side; these lines would have been erased in a final version but are often depicted in modern copies of the plan as if they represented some structural feature. At the present time, the plan is displayed at the entrance to the special wing in the Museo Archeologico Nazionale in Naples devoted to the major finds from the villa. The plan was first described by Winckelmann (*Sendschreiben*, #43) and then by De Jorio, 46–48.

69 According to Mustilli, 10, this stepped marble fountain is now in one of the courtyards of the Museo Nazionale in Naples.

70 Note that Bardet had not shown precise findspots, only the general areas in which finds had been made. It is interesting that several items in Weber's inventory indicated as having been recovered in 1751 and 1752 (e.g., the bronze statues and the marble vase) are the same ones he specifically highlighted in his letter to Fogliani on May 22, 1752 (ASN *CRA* 1539, Inc. 44), quoted earlier.

71 *StErc*, 180 (December 20, 1755): white marble pavement recovered from an upper room and reference to a set of stairs (see Mustilli, 14); *StErc*, 274 (February 3, 1759), where Weber remarks that the technique of tunneling up had been successful at another site (i.e., the Palestra). De Simone, 25, reports tunnels found 3.38 m. lower than the ones used to investigate the areas around the great peristyle and the atrium of the villa. Conticello and

Cioffi, 176, state that three different building levels now have been identified.

72 The title reads, "Explicacion de las escavaciones subterraneas desde el Pozo de Ciceri hasta Sciona, executadas de orden del Rey." The ground plan, reproduced on a somewhat smaller scale in Comparetti and De Petra, pl. 24 (and often reproduced elsewhere), reverses Weber's orientation, putting the belvedere to the left rather than the right of the main body of the villa.

73 *StErc*, 227 (June 11, 1757).

74 These four sketched plans are in the manuscript "Rapporti originali di Weber ed altri impiegati agli scavi di Pompei dal 1753 al 1804," in SNSP Ms. 20-5-3; they were reproduced in Comparetti and De Petra, pl. 23, and in *StErc*, 195, 197, 216, 268 (note that the date is August 1758, not February). Comparetti and De Petra, 226, state that Weber abandoned the plan in September 1758.

75 *StErc*, 251 (February 11, 1758): "In fifteen days I hope to give [you] the plan."

76 The following are the principal statues discovered after Weber had completed the inventory of finds on this plan in 1754, listed here, in chronological order of discovery, with their general provenance and cross-referenced with the catalog entries provided by R. Neudecker, *Die Skulpturen-Ausstattung römischer Villen in Italien* (Mainz am Rhein 1988) 147–57 #14: Seleucus I (MN. 5590) October 23, 1754: near small "Peplophore," Neudecker 68; Leaping Pig (MN. 4893) May 17, 1756: near the deer, Neudecker 56; Sleeping Satyr (MN. 5624) March 3–6, 1756: along pool, Neudecker 54; head of Apollo (MN. 5608) April 4, 1756: same tunnel as Sappho, Neudecker 57; Sappho/Berenice (MN. 5592) April 29, 1756: Neudecker 58; deer (MN. 4886, 4888) April 30 and May 10, 1756: same tunnel as archaistic youth and Sappho, Neudecker 55; Macedonian warrior (MN. 6151) November 5, 1756: (same tunnel as one of "Peplophorai"), Neudecker 48; Hellenistic Ruler/Ptolemy III (MN. 6158) February 8, 1757: on sketch plan, Neudecker 49; Philosopher/Panyassis (MN. 6152) February 10, 1757: on sketch plan, Neudecker 53; Phileteiros (MN. 6148) September 9, 1757: first found in *gruta derecha*, Neudecker 40; Archidamus III (MN. 6156) September 9, 1757: *gruta derecha*, Neudecker 41; "Pyrrhus" (MN. 6150) October 10–15, 1757: in *gruta derecha*, Neudecker 43; "Lysias" (MN. 6147) October 10–15, 1757: in *gruta derecha*, Neudecker 42; Athena (MN. 6322) October 26, 1757: *gruta derecha*, Neudecker 44; "Vesta/Hestia" (MN. 6188) October 27, 1757: ??, Neudecker 45; Apollodorus/Juba/Hannibal (MN. 6154) November 5, 1757: in

gruta derecha, Neudecker 46; "Poet/Demosthenes" (MN. 6153) November 9, 1757: *gruta derecha*, Neudecker 47; Hermes (MN. 5625) August 3, 1758: sketched onto plan near pool, Neudecker 64; Poetess (MN. 4896) August 24, 1758: near pool and Hermes, Neudecker 67; Bacchus-Plato/Priapos (MN. 5618) April 21, 1759: in square peristyle, Neudecker 75; Landsdowne Heracles (MN. 5594) May 8, 1759: near first "Peplophore," Neudecker 61; Thespis herm (MN. 5598) November 16, 1759: in square peristyle, Neudecker 7. See also D. Pandermalis, "Sul programma della decorazione scultorea," in *La Villa dei Papiri* (*CronErc* 13, Suppl. 2, Naples 1983) 19–50; and Wojcik.

77 For an examination of the excavations' chronology as illustrated by Weber's plan, see Comparetti and De Petra, 225–36, and Gallavotti, 292-306; for a metrological study of the remains, see Mustilli, 7–18. For the later investigations, see SNSP "Notizie historiche," 92v. (October 4, 1760) = *StErc*, 321: "Some tunnels are made in Resina with a view toward uniting the plans, continuing the plan of the Pozzo di Ciceri and to complete it." This comment led both De Petra ("I monumenti della villa ercolanese," in *Pompei e la regione sotterrata dal Vesuvio* [Naples 1879] 252) and Maiuri ("La Villa dei Papiri," in *Pompei ed Ercolano fra case e abitanti* [Florence 1983] 221–36) to conclude inaccurately that Weber had added to his plan as late as this date.

78 C. Paderni, "Extract of a letter . . . to Tho. Hollis, Esq., relating to the late discoveries at Herculaneum (October 18, 1754)," *PhilTrans* 48.2 (1754) 821–25. Comparetti and De Petra, 238–50, collect all the letters read before the Royal Society of London that discuss the discovery of the papyrus scrolls.

79 D. Bassi, "Il P. Antonio Piaggio e i primi tentativi per lo svolgimento dei papiri ercolanesi," *ASPN* 32 (1907) 636–90. Piaggio had been recommended to Charles of Bourbon by Giuseppe Assemani of the Biblioteca Vaticana for his careful hand in transcribing a variety of scripts. He arrived in Naples in early July 1753 and received 30 ducats a month for his labors, which he later conducted in a separate room of the Museum Herculanense. For details of his life and a collection of previously unpublished letters, see F. Longo Auricchio and M. Capasso, "Nuove accessioni al dossier Piaggio," in *Contributi alla Storia della Officina dei Papiri Ercolanesi* (Naples 1980) 17–59. Piaggio died in 1796.

80 Their names appear together on the title page to Bayardi's *Catalogo* in 1755: Paderni had drawn the illustration of allegorical figures bearing the crest of Charles of Bourbon, and Piaggio engraved it. In 1766

Tanucci complained to the king that he had had to waste time trying to quell an argument between them (ASN, *Archivio Borbone* I, 20 fol. 128r. [June 17, 1766]). See also Longo Auricchio and Capasso, 35–59, who include transcriptions of several of Piaggio's letters in which he attacks Paderni's treatment of the papyri and his operation of the museum.

81 Piaggio's manuscript is entitled "Memorie [autografe] del Padre Ant.o Piaggi [*sic*] impiegato nel R. Museo di Portici relative alle antichità, e Papiri p. anno [*sic*] 1769. 1771." This was written by Piaggio between 1769 and 1771 for Conte Guglielmo Maurizio Ludolf, who had requested information on the discovery and unraveling of the papyrus scrolls. It was given to the SNSP by a descendant in early 1907 and remains there today [SNSP Ms. 31-C-21]. The manuscript consists of 36 sheets, 144 pages in all; the passage quoted here is taken from fols. 3–4 (= Bassi, "Piaggio," *ASPN* 32 (1907) 659–61).

82 Bassi, "Piaggio," *ASPN* 32 (1907) 657, n. 1: Paderni had made trouble for Piaggio from the start, since he evidently tried to prevent Piaggio from being invited to Naples in the first place. Piaggio also was disliked for the various intrigues caused by his adversaries, in particular by Nicola Ignarra, who also had worked on deciphering the papyri: Gaspero Ceroti wrote to Ferdinando Galiani on July 6, 1756 [SNSP Ms. 31-C-9], "I am sorry . . . that Padre Antonio has suffered such grief, which probably was caused by persons barbaric and Visigothic."

83 Piaggio, "Memorie," 15r.

84 *StErc*, 220 (February 26, 1757): Weber priced the value of a *mocho* (or *moggia*) of land (3876.794 square meters) above the villa and the ruins of the Bisogno property at about 400 ducats.

85 *StErc*, 222 (April 2, 1757).

CHAPTER 4. POMPEII AND THE PRAEDIA IULIAE FELICIS

1 SNSP "Notizie istoriche," 79v. (April 1, 1755).

2 For the Bourbon excavations, see *PAH* I.i.12–51 (March 30, 1755–April 4–23, 1757). Maiuri fully reexcavated and restored the site in 1951–52 and published some of the results in two short articles: "Due iscrizioni veneree pompeiane," in *Saggi di varia antichità* (Venice 1954) 285–99, and "Giulia Felice, gentildonna pompeiana," in *Pompei ed Ercolano fra case e abitanti* (Florence 1983) 51–54. See also C. Parslow, "The Praedia Iuliae Felicis in Pompeii" (PhD. dissertation, Duke University, 1989).

3 Paderni complained that it had been months since anything of note had been found at Herculaneum in a letter dated June 28, 1755 ("An account of the late

discoveries of antiquities at Herculaneum . . . in two
letters . . . to Thomas Hollis [Naples, June 28, 1755],"
PhilTrans 49.2 [1756] 490–506).

4 SNSP "Notizie istoriche," 74r. (July 8, 1748):
Alcubierre agrees that A. Scognamillo, as a married
man with three children and a house at Portici, is
responsible enough to bear arms to calm the workmen at Città.

5 Terracotta statuettes: MN. 20264 ("vecchio
barbaro"); H. von Rohden, *Die Terracotten von Pompeji*
(Stuttgart 1880) 47, pl. 35.3; A. Levi, *Le terracotte
figurati del Museo Nazionale di Napoli* (Florence 1926)
#585; MN. RP27857 and RP27858 (*drillopotae*) =
BdE 2.369–73, pl. 92; Von Rohden, 47, pl. 36.2; G.
Marini, *Il gabinetto segreto del Museo Nazionale di
Napoli* (Turin 1971) 97–99; M. Grant, A. De
Simone, and M.T. Merella, *Eros in Pompeii* (London
1975) 130–31; MN. 22580 ("Caritas Romana") =
Von Rohden, 57–60, pl. 47; Levi, #843, fig. 144.
Paderni described these statuettes and the paintings
in a letter to the Royal Society ("An account . . .
[Naples, June 28, 1755]," 491–94).

6 For the architecture of this nymphaeum, see F.
Rakob, "Ein Grottentriklinium in Pompeji," *RömMitt*
71 (1964) 182–93. For the Nilotic paintings (MN.
8573, MN. 8608, MN. 8732; *PdE*, 5.293–95, pl. 66;
Helbig, #1538 and #1566), see H. Whitehouse, "*In
Praedis Iuliae Felicis*: The provenance of some frag-
ments of wall-painting in the Museo Nazionale,
Naples," *PBSR* 45 (1977) 52–68.

7 MN. 9057, 9059, 9061–70; *PdE* 3.213–31, pls.
41–44; Helbig, ##1482–85, ##1489–1500. The
major studies of the frieze include O. Jahn, "Uber
Darstellungen des Handwerks und Handelsverkehrs
auf antiken Wandgemälden," *Abhandlungen des
sächsischen Gessellschaft der Wissenschaften, Philologisch.-
hist. Classe* 5 (1870) 265–318, pls. 1–3; E. Magaldi, "Il
commercio ambulante a Pompeii," *AttiPontAcc* 40
(1930) 61–88, figs. 1–7, esp. 77–84; S. Nappo,
"Fregio dipinto dal *praedium* [*sic*] di Giulia Felice con
rappresentazione del foro di Pompei," *RStPomp* 3
(1989) 79–96; and C. Parslow, "The 'Forum Frieze'
of Pompeii in its archaeological context," in *The shapes
of city life in Rome and Pompeii* (New Rochelle, NY
1995).

The numbers in italics used in the text and notes
of this chapter and elsewhere in this book refer to the
location numbers Weber used on his later plans of
this site. (See Figs. 31, 47–49, and Appendixes 1 and
2.)

8 Paderni, "An account . . . [Naples, June 28,
1755]," 495–98, describes the paintings of the
sacrarium and the small finds recovered from a
narrow marble shelf inside.

9 Paderni, "An account . . . [Naples, June 28,
1755]," 496. The painted figures included Isis,
Serapis, Anubis, Fortuna, Penates, and the sacred
snakes and pinecone seen in Pompeian lararia. The
sacrarium was reerected in the museum at Portici and
eventually transferred to the Museo Nazionale in
Naples (W. Helbig, *Die Wandgemälde der vom Vesuv
verschütteten Städte Campaniens* [Leipzig 1868] 26–27
#79); it disappeared sometime after 1885, except for
the lower portion showing the sacred snakes (MN.
9693). For engravings of the paintings and the tripod,
see F. Piranesi, *Antiquités de la Grande Grèce*, vol. 3
(Paris 1807) pl. 3 (sacrarium – although the caption
reads "Niche dans le temple d'Isis à Pompeia"); pl. 12
(tripod). The tripod is MN. RP27874 (Bayardi, *Catalogo* 2d. ed. 320 #709; Grant, *Eros in Pompeii*, 9, 84).

10 The statues include, from north to south, a Pan
cradling a kid (Pompeii Antiquarium 8856); two
white marble statues of draped youths (Museo
Borbonico ##441 and 443); a heron with its wings
spread, holding a lizard in its beak (MN. 6539 = V.
Spinazzola, *Le arti decorative in Pompei e nel Museo
Nazionale di Napoli* [Milan 1928] 62); a faun playing
the flute (MN. 6343 = Ruesch, 1785); a youth with
grapes and a goose (MN. 6342?); a faun with a kid
(MN. 6108); and a terracotta statue of Pittakos of
Mitylene (Pompeii Antiquarium 20595 = A. Maiuri,
"Statuetta fittile di Pittaco di Mitilene," *ArchCl* 4
(1952) 55–59; G. Richter, *Portraits of the Greeks*
[London 1965] 10, 89 #2a, figs. 364–65).

11 It later became the practice to excavate these
storerooms before the eyes of visiting dignitaries; see,
e.g., details concerning the visit of King Joseph II in
1769 (*PAH* I.ii.Addenda 4.154 [April 8, 1769]).

12 SNSP "Notizie istoriche," 83r. (April 7, 1756).
At Castellamare di Stabia the trenches apparently
were left open for some time, since in early 1756 a
project was launched to fill in what must have been a
vast network of trenches created over six months on
the Somma-family property. After some time on the
job, the man in charge announced it would take him
and his four young workmen one and a half months to
complete the task (*Stabiae*, 47–49 [January, 1756;
February 12, 1756; March 4, 1756]). The decision
whether to rebury or leave the trenches open must
have depended largely on the productive value of the
land. Also at Castellamare, Pietro Irace, the owner of
property where excavations had been conducted for
three years, complained to the king that "nothing but
buildings and things of little value had been found"
and that the costs to the court far exceeded the
damage to the owners, whose reimbursement had
been negligible (*Stabiae*, 115 [January 21, 1760]). For
a small engraving of a pile of fill from later work at

Pompeii, see W. Gell and J. Gandy, *Pompeiana: The topography, edifices and ornaments of Pompeii* (London 1921) 1.

13 Paderni usually made drawings of the mosaics and paintings before they were removed and then made further drawings once they had been cleaned and mounted. Ruggiero appended one of Paderni's sketches of a mosaic to one of Weber's plans from Stabiae (*Stabiae*, pl. 4 [drawn December 30, 1757]). A number of Paderni's sketches ended up in the collection of W. Ternite, who had acquired them in Portici in 1824; these are now in the Stattliche Museen in Berlin (Antikensammlung docum. arch. 109 A, B, C and 110 C; see *Italienische Reise: Pompejanische Bilder in den deutschen archäologischen Sammlungen*, Soprintendenza Archeologica di Pompei, Le Mostre 8 [Naples 1989] 392–94, 434–36). Two of his finished colored drawings of paintings found in the Villa di San Marco at Stabiae are in the archives of the Getty Center for the History of Art and the Humanities, Malibu, California (Inv. 890119). The library of the École française de Rome has a manuscript by Paderni, "Monumenti antichi rinvenuti ne reali scavi di Ercolano e Pompej &c delineati da D. Camillo Paderni Romano direttore e custode del Real Museo di Portici Membro dell' Accademia Reale di Napoli, E Socio della Reale Accademia di Londra, e dell' altra degli Antiquarj. Parte Prima." This includes several drawings of paintings and mosaic pavements from the ancient cities, one of which, from Pompeii (Reg. 6.17.41), was published by V.M. Strocka, "Pompeji VI 17,41: Ein haus mit privatbibliothek," *RömMitt* 100 (1993) fig. 7. Giuseppe Canart, a French sculptor who had come to Portici in May 1739 to restore the marble statues and mosaics, was also in charge of the removal of the paintings from the excavation sites, duties which apparently evolved out of the need to mount the fragments of the paintings on a slab of Genoa marble. The excavation records document some ten visits to the site by Canart during the excavations of this site. On four of these Canart gave specific instructions as to what paintings were to be removed and in what manner [PAH.I.i.33 (October 12, 1755); I.i.37 (January 25, 1756); I.i.38 (February 8, 1756); I.i.39 (February 29, 1756)].

14 The wall is MN. 8598; panels from other walls in this room are MN. 9137 (a floating satyr/maenad group) and MN. 8611 (two still-life panels including a glass bowl filled with fruit). The somewhat indiscriminate removal of so many small paintings of such seemingly little aesthetic value was attacked by one visitor to the museum in 1750: "These pieces are now framed, and there are above 1,500 of them, but

not above 20 that are tolerable" ("Extract of a letter . . . ," 150–59).

15 Venuti, *Description*, 108–14.

16 Among the graffiti found in the early excavations, for example, were two recovered during Bardet's tenure: one naming a Secundus (*CIL* 4.10478) while another citing a line from Euripides' *Antiope* (fr. 220 Nauck) was found scrawled in black and red letters on a wall near the intersection of the Decumanus Maximus and Cardo V at Herculaneum (*Giornale*, 201 [January 9, 1741] and 213 [March 6, 1743]).

17 It is not clear, however, to what extent Weber had relied on the transcriptions supplied by his site foremen. He clearly was unable to read the identifications written in Greek on a series of Apollo and eight Muses (Euterpe was lacking) found in one room (97). In 1802, King Ferdinand IV gave these paintings to Napoleon as a gift, and they are now in the Louvre (Tran Tam Tinh, *Catalogue des peintures romaines (Latium et Campanie) du Musée du Louvre* [Paris 1974] 25–34).

18 The earliest reference to the proscriptio locationis (*CIL* 4.1136) outside of the excavation reports themselves appears in a manuscript by A.S. Mazzocchi entitled "Della dissertazione preliminare delle origini d'Ercolano e di luoghi vicini," now in the Biblioteca Nazionale di Napoli (Ms. IX.A.61) and published by G. Fiorelli, *Giornale degli scavi di Pompei* (Naples 1862) 25–40, 65–80, 97–120; see esp. 116–17. Mazzocchi remarks that the inscription was found "recently" but, because he believed the full text had not been copied, reserved a full exegesis for later.

19 M. Della Corte, "Esplorazioni di Pompei immediatamente successive alla catastrofe dell' anno 79," in *In memoriam Vasile Pârvan* (Bucharest 1934) 96–109. For a contrary opinion, see J.-P. Descoeudres, "Did some Pompeians return to their city after the eruption of Mt. Vesuvius in A.D. 79? Observations in the House of the Coloured Capitals," in *Ercolano 1738–1988: 250 anni di ricerca archeologica* (Rome 1993) 165–78.

20 J.J. Winckelmann, *Nachrichten von den neuesten herculanischen Entdeckungen* (Dresden 1764), #8, e.g., mentions the discovery, near the surface of the modern ground level, of a cadaver with an ancient bronze lamp.

21 F. Latapie, *Description des fouilles de Pompéii* (1776), ed. P. Barrière and A. Maiuri, in *RAAN* 28 (1954) 233–34, later observed how the local peasants often had struck ancient walls with their plows and had used the stones to build structures and boundary walls.

22 C. Paderni, "Extract . . . dated July 29, 1755," 508–9.

23 A note appended to the discussion of this
painting in the second volume of *Le antichità*
observes that "[This painting] was found in the
excavations at Cività in the year 1754 [*sic*]. The
particular value of this picture is that it was found
hung on the wall with an iron clamp, and in the room
where it was found were similar niches with corresponding clamps, but the pictures had been removed.
From this one concludes that the ancient owners of
this place esteemed this painting highly, since they
cut it down from somewhere else and placed it here
with other paintings or above stuccowork of the same
value or also on tables" (*PdE* 2.169, pl. 28, n. 2); the
same is repeated in the *Museo Borbonico*, vol. 7, pl. 56,
where Herculaneum is given as the provenance.
Weber's notes speak of finding paintings "inchiodate," which may refer to the method of hanging
these paintings on nails. Seven years later, in
excavations in the Palestra at Herculaneum, Weber
found a set of small framed paintings leaning up
against a wall in a similar manner, evidently for
similar reasons (see Chapter 5 in this volume, "The
'Temples' at Herculaneum").
24 "Extract of a letter . . . ," 150–59; the author
discusses as well the infrequent discovery of skeletons. Requier, *Recueil général*, 42, remarked that the
bones of the skeleton turned to ash as they attempted
to remove them. A display of impressions left by
victims and statues alike was set up in the fifteenth
room of the museum at Portici; the breast of a woman
attracted the most attention ("Museo," 118). Most
were probably created by statues.
25 *PAH* I.i.2 (April 19, 1748).
26 *PAH* I.i.35 (December 7, 1755), for the skulls
(*31*); *PAH* I.i.37 (January 4, 1756), for three
skeletons, one with an iron ring (*6*); a fourth skeleton
with three coins is mentioned by Weber (*31*) but
appears nowhere in the daybooks. Maiuri's excavations in the 1950s in the area of the hortus south of
the domus uncovered several skeletons buried in
dolia dating from the medieval period. For discoveries of reburials in the area of Herculaneum, see M.S.
Pisapia, "L'area ercolanese dopo l'eruzione del 79:
Evidenze archeologiche, la necropoli di Via Doglie ad
Ercolano," *RAAN* 56 (1981) 63–74.
27 *StErc*, 125 (December 1, 1752): Paderni: "Weber
has sent me some grain found in the Pozzo di
[Ciceri], but it has decayed in the humidity. And in
addition, one of the excavators has sent me a basket
of the same grain, which I have consigned to
Gennaro Amelia." See the entry on Weber's plan of
the Villa dei Papiri (*IV.n*). This grain was found in the
same period as the papyrus fragments; the new
excavations have uncovered further evidence that

grain was being stored in rooms on the upper stories
of the Villa dei Papiri (Conticello and Cioffi, 176).
28 Venuti, *Description*, 108, described "whole eggs
miraculously preserved, and almonds and walnuts,
which maintained their natural color, but upon being
opened one finds inside that their pulps are ash or
have been carbonized." These artifacts were displayed in a case in the tenth room of the museum and
are mentioned frequently by visitors ("Museo," 116;
Winckelmann, *Sendschreiben*, #62). See, e.g., Freeman's letter to the Royal Society, which may in fact be
drawn from Venuti's book: "There were eggs found
quite whole, but empty; also nuts and almonds; grain
of several sorts, beans, and peas, burnt quite black.
Many other sorts of fruit were found burnt quite to
coal, but whole and entire" (Freeman, "An extract of
a letter dated May 2, 1750, from Mr. Freeman at
Naples to the Right Honorable Lady Mary Capel
relating to the ruins at Herculaneum," *PhilTrans* 47
(1751–52) 131–42). Although Bayardi included the
stamped loaf of bread in his *Catalogo* and many of the
items have been inventoried in the museum (e.g.,
bread = MN. 84596 [= *CIL* 10.8058, 18], 84704,
84741; eggs = MN. 84699), the contents of this
collection have never been systematically studied.
29 *PAH* I.i.45 and *PAH* I.ii.Addenda 4.137 (October
16, 1756).
30 Çiria appears to have been the foreman, since
Scognamillo addressed a letter to him describing a
mosaic found at Cività (SNSP *Fondo Cuomo* Ms. 20-
5-3 "Rapporti," December 3, 1755). In January
1756, one foreman and four young men were
conducting the excavations at Cività (SNSP "Notizie
istoriche," 82v. [January 12, 1756]).
31 In 1750, Çiria was working in the Pozzo di Ciceri
(that is, the Villa dei Papiri) in Herculaneum (*StErc*,
108 [September 15, 1750]); in 1758, he was reimbursed for the cost of medical treatment he required
after falling into a trench (SNSP "Notizie istoriche,"
88r. [October 18, 1758] and 89r. [January 29, 1759];
in 1762, he was working in the excavations at Pompeii
(*Stabiae*, 181–82 [August 12, 1762]). He died on
March 8, 1763, after a few days in the hospital at
Torre Annunziata, leaving a wife and three sons, one
of whom was employed in the excavations (*StErc*, 407
[March 12, 1763]; SNSP "Notizie istoriche," 98r.
[March 5, 1763]).
32 Weber complained that the boys hired to work at
Stabiae were too small (*Stabiae*, 50 [July 24, 1756]).
Cf. SNSP "Notizie istoriche," 98v. (June 4, 1763):
"In regards to the Royal dispatch of May 18,
Alcubierre is in accord with granting 15 grains per
working day to the son of M. Antonio Scognamiglio,
named Pascale, about thirteen years old, because he

keeps the accounts and makes the reports of the findings in the excavations at Città, the two supervisors not knowing how to write." *Stabiae*, 217 (July 10, 1768): letter of La Vega on Scognamillo; cf. Allroggen-Bedel, "Die Malereien," 170 n. 83.

33 La Vega, 285.

34 *StErc*, 510 (March 30, 1772): report by La Vega on information obtained from Scognamillo on Bardet's excavations; Ruggiero, *Terraferma*, 112 (February 16 and 27, 1751), 194 (February 27, 1751): for work at Pozzuoli and Cumae. Scognamillo had apparently fallen ill at Pozzuoli and was granted twelve days compensation upon his arrival in Pompeii (SNSP "Notizie istoriche," 79v. [April 9, 1755]).

35 SNSP "Notizie istoriche," 76r. (December 2, 1752); 76v. (January 9 and 12, 1753): "Dispute between Weber and Alcubierre, the former being unwilling to sign the reports in which Sig. Antonio Scognamillo appears as an assistant to the work in the excavations, since effectively he is engaged in other work for the king. This dispute endures for some time."

36 La Vega, 114.

37 On April 3, 1756, Weber wrote to Alcubierre, "I sent the supervisor [Çiria] to collect the plans of Maestro Antonio [Scognamillo], and [Scognamillo] said that he did not have any plans beyond those which he has given to Your Lordship and me." SNSP *Fondo Cuomo* Ms. 20-5-3 "Rapporti."

38 Soprintendenza Archeologica di Napoli e Caserta, Archivio Disegno (no inventory number): 0.38 m. wide by 0.52 m. high; the original would have been ca. 0.76 m. by 0.52 m. For publication details, see C. Parslow, "Documents illustrating the excavations of the *Praedia* of Julia Felix in Pompeii," *RStPomp* 2 (1988) 40, 48 n. 11, where the notes in Spanish are attributed to Alcubierre, a conclusion that now seems unlikely, since there is no reason to believe the plan was ever in his possession.

39 *Stabiae*, 208 (August 1, 1764).

40 SNSP "Notizie istoriche," 93v. (February 14, 1761): Alcubierre lists the books and plans by Scognamillo in Weber's possession; SNSP *Fondo Cuomo* Ms. 20-5-3 "Rapporti," February 14, 1761: Alcubierre to Weber, complaining that Weber had failed to bring Scognamillo's plans to completion. Scognamillo claimed his notebooks were missing after Weber's death (ASN *CRA* 1541, Inc. 42 [No date]), though La Vega found them among Weber's possessions; see the Epilogue to this volume, "Weber's Place in the History of Archaeology in the Vesuvian Landscape."

41 *Stabiae*, 213 (March 21, 1767). According to the SNSP "Notizie istoriche," 92v. (August 30, 1760), Paderni also considered Scognamillo's plans of poor quality: "[he writes] of several plans which Mon. Antonio drew which Paderni does not esteem."

42 Soprintendenza Archeologica di Napoli e Caserta, Archivio Disegno #71: 0.36 m. high by 0.48 m. wide.

43 For example, a relief described as "Socrates" on Weber's plan helped identify a marble plaque in Naples as coming from the Praedia: MN. 6697 = *PAH* I.i.29–30 (August 24, 1755); Winckelmann, *Sendschreiben*, #141; Richter, *Portraits*, 118, catalogs this relief among those "once thought to represent Sokrates [but] now mostly interpreted differently . . . (shepherd?)."

44 The extent of the wall enclosing the hortus, which doubled as a boundary wall for the Praedia, shows that the last months of the excavations were spent following this wall; its proximity to the amphitheater and the wealth found in the Praedia must have convinced Weber he would encounter more buildings somewhere along its course, but he did not.

45 Evidence for earlier plunderers is noted at numbers *42* ("marble pavement plundered by others"); *72* and *74* ("excavated by others"); and *83* (paintings cut down and marble revetment removed from niches). There are only three references to the excavations themselves: at number *69* the comment is made that the discovery of the first pilaster here had led to the commencement of the excavations; at number *94*, that the wall paintings had been drawn on August 4, 6, and 8, 1755; and at number *33*, the observation that there were "magnificent buildings," where the excavations should be continued.

46 The similarity between the paving of streets in ancient Pompeii and modern Naples was a common topos of commentators in the eighteenth century. Paderni also became interested in the pavement of the ancient streets, requesting that Weber remove two examples, a large block and a small one, for the royal collection from an intersection Weber had come across in Herculaneum (*StErc*, 198 [July 31, 1756]); Weber described in great detail another street with its colonnaded sidewalk (*StErc*, 208 [November 13, 1756]; see Chapter 5 in this volume, "The 'Temples' at Herculaneum"). In addition to this main street in Pompeii (the modern Via dell' Abbondanza) Weber also noted that an unpaved road (*22*), perpendicular to the street and bordering the Praedia on the west, was entered through a gateway. This formed part of a series of gates that could be used to close off the entire section of the city around the amphitheater (equivalent to the modern Regio 2). This gate must have been intact when first discovered, but only foundation blocks remain today.

47 For catalogs of shops at Pompeii, see T. Kleberg,

Hôtels, restaurants et cabarets dans l'antiquité romaine (Uppsala 1957), and V. Gassner, *Die Kaufläden in Pompeii*, Dissertation, University of Vienna, no. 178 (Vienna 1986).

48 He had already noted the existence of this praefurnium in a report to Alcubierre: "One has discovered the two openings for putting wood into the stoves and igniting them to give fire." SNSP *Fondo Cuomo* Ms. 20-5-3 "Rapporti," December 20, 1755. At this same time, Weber was excavating a set of baths at Pozzuoli, and the entry in his records following the letter referred to earlier is entitled "Catalogo del Libro Compuesto de los Baños y otro . . . a Pozuolo." From December 1752 to June 1754, baths were excavated at Punta dell' Epitafio, near Portici, but apparently these were not recognized as such by the Bourbon excavators; see Scatozza-Höricht, "Ville," 150–52.

49 The title is followed by the word "Portici" and the date "1 [marz] di maggio 1757." This correction of the date is further evidence that these were all later additions to the plan. The presentation copy of the plan was finished in late 1759 (see Chapter 6 in this volume, "Weber's Application to the Accademia Ercolanese").

50 C. Bonucci, *Pompeii descritta* (Naples 1827) 219.

CHAPTER 5. THE "TEMPLES" AT HERCULANEUM

1 For this building, see F. Yegül, "The Palaestra at Herculaneum as a new architectural type," in *Eius virtutis studiosi: Classical and Postclassical studies in memory of Frank Edward Brown (1908–1988)* (Washington 1993) 369–93; and Maiuri, *Nuovi scavi*, 113–43.

2 The work began in 1828 and was directed by Carlo Bonucci. *StErc*, 537–38 (January 9 and 13, 1828), where the Bourbon excavations in this area were initially described as somewhat more limited than had been anticipated; Bonucci later described the tunnels as "very wide and, fortunately, straight" (*StErc*, 545 [March 31, 1828]); but see also Arditi's letter assessing the extent of the tunneling Bonucci encountered here (*StErc*, 571 [February 13, 1837]): since he had concentrated in areas already excavated under Charles III, he found "not even a painting, nor a mosaic, nor a single object" that could compensate for the enormous expense of the undertaking. See also Maiuri, *Nuovi scavi*, 3.

3 *StErc*, 143 (November 18, 1753): renewed work at Bisogno property; *StErc*, 148 (February 3, 1754): ramp in front of the Savarese house, along the Royal Road from Naples to Salerno; *StErc*, 156 (June 9,

1754): end of work at Savarese ramp; *StErc*, 162 (October 13, 1754): end of work at Vico di Mare; *StErc*, 163 (November 24, 1754): work at Bisogno resumes; *StErc*, 169 (March 9, 1754): men at Bisogno transferred to Villa dei Papiri excavations.

4 *Giornale*, 219 (September 22, 1745); Weber first described problems with rainwater at the Bisogno property, and his efforts to channel it off, as early as October 31 through November 6, 1750 (*StErc*, 109–10). In June 1751, water had broken through a dike and flooded one of the tunnels; this threatened to hamper work at the theater as well (*StErc*, 118 [June 12 and 25, 1751]). S. Carotenuto, *Herculaneum: Storia della antica città di Ercolano e dei suoi scavi* (Naples 1932) 34–35, traces the course of underground springs in this area, noting in particular a channel that ran beneath the Via Pugliano, through the Piazza dei Colli Mozzi to the Vico di Mare alongside the excavations, where it percolated into the ground; this was also the source of the dripping water in the theater.

5 *StErc*, 189 (June 5, 1756); 191 (June 12, 1756); 194 (July 17, 1756); 196 (July 24, 1756); 199 (August 7 and 14, 1756); 200 (August 21, 1756); 203 (September 11, 1756): rain uncovers some finds; 203 (September 18, 1756): clearing flooded tunnels; 204 (October 2, 1756): excavation equipment flooded; 214 (January 28, 1757): Weber inquires whether Alcubierre wants to abandon the site for the winter and allow the runoff to enter.

6 Piaggio, "Memorie," 16v.: "This water was introduced not by chance but in the modern spirit of economy, because, in order to save the cost of transporting the earth that needed removal, some refined genius had the idea of allowing rainwater to enter, which on its own would either carry the earth to the sea or fill back in the old, vacant tunnels."

7 Maiuri, *Nuovi scavi*, 208, 215–16; it is, however, virtually impossible to know when these paintings were removed.

8 *StErc*, 198 (July 31, 1756); as Maiuri, *Nuovi scavi*, 189 n. 58, points out, the sketch of the excavations reproduced by Ruggiero on this page actually accompanied a report from 1757.

9 *StErc*, 196 (July 24, 1756). Only one of these stones was placed on display in the museum; Winckelmann refers to it in his letter to Brühl (*Sendschreiben*, #23).

10 *StErc*, 189–99 (May 29–August 7, 1756).

11 With the opening of this ramp, the entrance at Vico di Mare was sealed off (*StErc*, 222 [March 18, 1757]). Several later ramps into the area of the Basilica were also oriented along the Royal Road for these same reasons. The ancient street is the

Decumanus Inferior, which is slightly broader between the intersection with Cardo IV and Cardo V.
12 *StErc*, 208 (November 13, 1756), which includes
Weber's sketch plan of the street, measuring 18
palms (4.70 m.) wide, with sidewalks 8 palms (2.10
m.) wide that were 1 palm (0.26 m.) higher than the
street. Since the grid of the city is not oriented to the
cardinal points, it was easier to refer to these
topographical features than to rely on awkward
directions like "north-northwest" for Portici and
"east-southeast" for Torre del Greco.
13 Weber refers to this on his plan of the Villa dei
Papiri (IV.a): "One enters the large room of the
palace, which has three doors facing the large
garden."
14 *StErc*, 208 (November 13, 1756).
15 It was on the Moscardillo property that the tomb
built by freedmen of the Balbi had been excavated in
1750 (*StErc*, 111–15 [November 21, 1750–March
13, 1751]. See Gori, *Admiranda*, 134 (April 7, 1750);
Cochin and Bellicard, 24–30, pl. 6; *StErc*, xxxvii-
xxxviii.
16 *StErc*, 209–14 (November 20, 1756–January 28,
1757), with Weber's sketch on page 214 showing a
cross section of the Bellobuono ramp (*A*, *B*) and the
tunnel from the "palacio" (*K*, *E*). Weber mentioned
the "slope" in suggesting that making a second ramp
to join the Bellobuono ramp with the "palacio" tunnel
would be easier than cutting a flight of steps or
sinking a shaft to link them. That Bardet's tunnel ran
well above Weber's suggests that Bardet had first
investigated the upper stories of the Palestra and had
dropped a shaft from here to excavate the lower story.
17 J. Northall, *Travels in Italy, containing new and
curious observations on that country* (London 1766) 257,
260.
18 *StErc*, 209 (November 30, 1756).
19 ASN *CRA* 1540, Inc. 63 (December 15, 1761):
Paderni to Tanucci.
20 *StErc*, 219–20 (February 26, 1757), 222 (April 2,
1757).
21 *StErc*, 218–19 (February 22, 1757); *BdE* 2.51–
53, pl. 14; C. Paderni, "An account of the late
discoveries of antiquities at Herculaneum . . . dated
February 1, 1758," *PhilTrans* 50.2 (1759) 620;
Winckelmann, *Sendschreiben*, #56; Ruesch 1570
(0.175 m. H); J.B. Ward-Perkins and A. Claridge,
Pompeii A.D. 79 (New York 1978) 189 #209.
22 For example, the Hellenistic Ruler (MN. 6158)
was found on February 8, 1757, and the Philosopher/
Panyassis (MN. 6152) on February 10, 1757.
23 [C. Paderni], "Diario de' Monumenti antichi,
rinvenuti in Ercolano, Pompei e Stabia dal 1752 al
1799 formata dal Sig.r Camillo Paderni, Custode del

Real Museo Ercolanese in Portici, e proseguito dal
Signor Francesco La Vega," ASN *Casa Reale
Amministrativa* Categorie Diverse, vol. 461, III Inventario: February 22, 1757.
24 *StErc*, 226–27 (June 11, 1757).
25 *StErc*, 227–28 (June 14, 1757).
26 *StErc*, 228 (June 14, 1757).
27 *StErc*, 229–30 (June 18, 1757). See F. Fernandez
Murga, "Tanucci, Alcubierre e gli scavi di antichità,"
in *Bernardo Tanucci: Statista, letterato, giurista* (Naples
1986) 2.480–85, who mistakenly identifies the object
of Weber's accusations as Stefano Caruso, the
foreman at Stabiae.
28 *StErc*, 223 (April 23, 1757): Weber acknowledges
receipt of orders to send finds directly to Paderni at
the museum; *StErc*, 225 (May 7, 1757): repeats
acknowledgment of orders.
29 *Stabiae*, 66–67 (December 2, 1757).
30 *Stabiae*, 69–70 (December 13, 1757). According
to Piaggio, Paderni had virtually the same charge
leveled against him when Martorelli became alarmed
at the treatment of the papyri at the hands of
Mazzocchi and Paderni and remarked, sometime
prior to his death in 1777, "isti non sunt amatores sed
destructores antiquitatum" (those men are not lovers
but destroyers of antiquities) (Biblioteca Nazionale di
Napoli, Ms. IX.F.51 [1791?], fol. 79, as quoted by F.
Longo Auricchio and M. Capasso, "Nuove accessioni
al dossier Piaggio," in *Contributi alla storia della
Officina dei Papiri Ercolanesi* (Naples 1980) 18 n. 11.
31 La Vega, 288. According to La Vega's notes
(299), Corcoles had been among the original eight
engineers working with Alcubierre on the plan of the
royal villa at Portici. He had been recommended for
this position by the Marchese di S. Croce, with whom
Corcoles had come from Spain. Because Corcoles
was a "calm man," Alcubierre had made him his first
foreman in the excavations, and Corcoles therefore
had seniority in tenure, but not necessarily rank, over
many others. As noted earlier, Corcoles was an
advocate of fully exposing the buildings at Herculaneum, a position that had brought him into conflict
with Weber.
32 La Vega, 115.
33 *Stabiae*, 69–70 (December 13, 1757).
34 *StErc*, 229 (June 16, 1757).
35 *CIL* 10.1406: Imp(erator) Caesar Vespasianus
Aug(ustus) Pontif(ex) Max(imus) Trib(unicia) Pot-
(estate) VII Imp(erator) XVII P(ater) P(atriae) Co(n)-
s(ul) VII Design(atus) VIII Templum Matris Deum
terrae motu conlapsum restituit (The Emperor Caesar Augustus Vespasian, pontifex maximus, seven
times tribune, seventeen times imperator, father of
the country, seven times consul, eight times consul

designate restored the temple of the Mother of the Gods, which had collapsed in an earthquake).

36 E.g., the set of fifteen inscriptions transcribed by Marchese L. Pindemonti communicated by Scipio Maffei in his second letter, "Sopra le nuove scoperte d'Ercolano," addressed to B. de Rubeis (Maffei, *Tre Lettere*, 26–32), and the numerous inscriptions broadcast through the letters of A.F. Gori. Paderni communicated the Templum Matris Deum inscription to the Royal Society ("An account of the late discoveries of antiquities at Herculaneum . . . dated February 1, 1758," *PhilTrans* 50.2 [1759] 620). According to Zevi ("Gli scavi di Ercolano e le *Antichità*," 21), the inscriptions from these sites were displayed on the portico walls of the palace at Portici.

37 *StErc*, 231–32 (July 19–22, 1757). V. Tran Tam Tinh, *Le Culte des divinités orientales à Herculanum* (Leiden 1971) 64, 91; G. Guadagno, "Supplemento epigrafico ercolanese II," *CronErc* 11 (1981) 135: found in four fragments; total dimensions 3.25 m. × 0.56 m. Tran Tam Tinh believes this inscription, and many other objects found in this area, had been carried here by the force of the mud flow from the area of the forum, a site he postulates lies northeast of the exposed excavations. But clearly, judging from Weber's description and his later course of action, the inscription originally had been mounted across the lintel of the door separating the vestibule from the larger inner room; the lintel probably had collapsed in the eruption.

38 *StErc*, 236 (August 24–25, 1757); the statuette stands only 0.10 m. high.

39 This fact was confirmed by Bonucci's excavations in 1828 of the Casa del Argo, where he found little on the ground floor but discovered that the upper floors, although damaged, were remarkably intact (see, e.g., *StErc*, 538 [January 13, 1828]).

40 *StErc*, 234 (August 10, 1757): Tanucci to Alcubierre.

41 He sent Alcubierre a preliminary plan of the site as it appeared on August 25, 1757 (*StErc*, 236). This plan is no longer extant, but it illustrated the locations of the air shaft; the "Mater Deum" inscription; and a smaller shaft that had encountered the statuette of Mercury, three bronze tripods, and an assortment of bronze cups, jugs, and utensils. He included annotations to one side but emphasized that this was only an interim plan.

42 The first notice of the columns from the peristyle occurs on September 3, 1757 (*StErc*, 240); excavations in the street in front are mentioned beginning November 26, 1757, where Weber refers to his draft of the plan as well (*StErc*, 247).

43 *CIL* 10.929 (where the provenance is given

incorrectly as Pompeii), 0.55 m. × 0.455 m.; Ruesch 962. Guadagno, "Epigrafo II," 131, who rightly questions Maiuri's location of this monument in the rectangular room adjacent to the central apsidal hall in the Palestra (Maiuri, *Nuovi scavi*, 126–27).

44 *StErc*, 248 (December 24, 25, 30, 1757).

45 *StErc*, 249 (January 3, 1758). Maiuri, *Nuovi scavi*, 190 n. 58, notes that this was initially believed to be a statue of Isis and that it, the inscription, and the marble colonnette had made up a small shrine located in the peristyle. The statue's present location is unknown. See Tran Tam Tinh, *Culte*, 63 #11, where its provenance is given as the vestibule itself rather than the peristyle.

46 For the latter "Madonna," see the discussion later in this chapter.

47 *StErc*, 251 (February 4, 1758).

48 *StErc*, 274–76 (February 10–March 3, 1759). This is the earliest known recognition of this feature of Roman piscinae. The cruciform pool measures 55.00 m. × 31.50 m., is 5.80 m. wide and 1.00 m. to 1.10 m. deep. Bardet's tunnels completely missed this feature. Weber's excavators had pursued a length of lead pipe that led them to a square masonry base (1.15 m. H × 0.96 m. W), but their tunnels just missed the bronze fountain spout in the form of a five-headed Hydra coiled around a tree (2.42 m. H) that once adorned this base. Maiuri recovered this bronze statue in August 1952, some 2.60 m. from its base, where it had been propelled by the force of the volcanic mud (A. Maiuri, "Fontana monumentale in bronzo nei nuovi scavi di Ercolano," *BdA* n.s. 3 [July–September 1954] 193–99, esp. 193–94).

49 *StErc*, 250–51 (January 28–February 4, 1758).

50 *StErc*, 269 (September 2, 1758).

51 *StErc*, 253 (February 25–March 4, 1758).

52 *StErc*, 255 (April 1, 1758).

53 *StErc*, 261–62 (May 24, 1758); the statuette is 0.10 m. high (*BdE* 2.83–85, pl. 22). Interest in the bulla may have been sparked by F. Ficoroni's work *La bolla d'oro de' fanciulli nobili romani* . . . (Rome 1732).

54 *StErc*, 260–61 (May 17, 1758), Weber to Alcubierre; written at Portici.

55 *StErc*, pl. 8.

56 *StErc*, 276 (March 3, 1759).

57 *StErc*, 307 (March 8, 1760); Alcubierre sent the plan of this temple along with three from the excavations at Stabiae.

58 This probably included tunneling into the remains of the Casa del Rilievo di Telefo, since Maiuri encountered several Bourbon-era tunnels there (Maiuri, *Nuovi scavi*, 15 fig. 17).

59 The "Madonna" is first referred to on April 15, 1758; she is distinguished from the other marble

statue, that of Hygeia, found near a colonnade on May 20, 1758. The documents covering these investigations begin on April 15, 1758, with sketches illustrating the site supplied on April 29 and May 6, 1758, where it must be assumed Weber grossly distorted the scale of this building (*StErc*, 256–59). Bardet's plan seems to confirm that this was a pedestrian street, since the pavement of Cardo V appears to change at its north end, where the two intersect. La Vega illustrated Bardet's large peristyle courtyard, but not Weber's structure, on his plan of the city of 1797 (see the Epilogue to this volume, "Weber's Place in the History of Archaeology in the Vesuvian Landscape").

60 *CIL* 10.1425: M(arcus) Nonius M(arci) F(ilius) Balbus Proco(n)s(ul) Basilicam Portas Murum Pecunia Sua [fecit? or refecit?] (Marcus Nonius Balbus, son of Marcus, proconsul, [built, or rebuilt] the basilica, gates, and city wall with his own money).

61 For the tomb: Cochin and Bellicard, 24–26, pl. 6. Weber noted (*StErc*, 337 [February 14, 1761]) that excavations were being conducted again along a road heading in the direction of Torre del Greco, where the Nonius inscription had been found in 1758; the site stood below the Savarese property, which was adjacent to the Bisogno property. For the location of the forum, cf. Allroggen-Bedel, "Dokumente," 154, and J.B. Ward-Perkins, "Nota di topografia e urbanistica," in F. Zevi, ed., *Pompei 79* (Naples 1979) 25–39, esp. pl. 3; but see Chapter 8 in this volume, "The Theater at Herculaneum."

62 *StErc*, 277–80 (March 23–April 28, 1759), reveal that it took about a month to construct the ramp. For the dangers of this site, see especially *StErc*, 285–86 (July 14, 1759), and see *StErc*, 287 (August 25, 1759) for his method of excavation.

63 *StErc*, 298 (December 5, 1759); sealing the tunnels and ventilation shafts took through April 1760 (*StErc*, 310 [April 12, 1760]). For the inscriptions found near the Basilica, see Guadagno, "Epigrafo II," 158–59 #142 (*StErc*, 281 [May 18, 1759], letters from two lines: ". . . co . . . / . . . AXIM . . ."), and 151 #110 (*StErc*, 284 [June 6, 1759] = *CIL* 10.1459, commemorating a distribution of food at a dedication). Excavations around the Basilica resumed in 1761, with much greater success in terms of the quantity of small finds and the number of important paintings, but this work is not dealt with here.

64 Hermes (MN. 5625): *StErc*, 266 (August 3, 1758); Sappho (MN. 4896): *StErc*, 269 (August 24, 1758); Dionysus (MN. 5618): *StErc*, 279 (April 21, 1759); Landsdowne Hercules type (MN. 5594): *StErc*, 281 (May 8, 1759); Thespis or Aulus Gabinius

(MN. 5598): *StErc*, 293 (November 16, 1759). Several of these identifications are disputed.

65 Allroggen-Bedel, "Dokumente," 141, determined that Bardet excavated here between May and July 1743, by matching a mounted painting in the Museo Nazionale (MN. 9735; *Giornale*, 214 [July 11, 1743]; *StErc*, 98 [July 20, 1743]) with a fragment of wall painting *in situ* in the Palestra (Room III); other features described in the daybooks during this period could then be matched with those in the Palestra.

66 *StErc*, 275 (February 17, 1759); Bayardi, *Prodromo*, 1.x; Weber did not believe it fulfilled the requirements for a temple as he was finding them defined in his own excavations (*StErc*, 290 [October 6, 1759]). The daybooks make it clear that Bardet already had investigated this intersection between the Decumanus Maximus and Cardo V, along with the fountain, in 1743 (*StErc*, 101, and *Giornale*, 213 [March 6, 1743]).

67 Winckelmann refers to this brazier in his letter to Brühl (*Sendschreiben*, #66).

68 *StErc*, 289–308 (September 22, 1759–March 22, 1760); Weber provided the most complete description of this second temple, including dimensions, in a letter to Tanucci dated November 22, 1759 (*StErc*, 295–96). The plaque (MN. 6680; ca. 0.40 m. W × 0.70 m. H) is in a poor state of repair. It consists of a heavy marble frame (lacking the top section) that held three marble slabs, cut like pieces of a jigsaw puzzle, on which the scene was carved. This shows a barefooted young man in an active pose, his right arm in the air as if ready to throw the three balls he holds in his right hand. The central piece, on which was carved his body, from the neck down to the knees, is lost, but the figure carries a knotted club in his left hand and wears a cape. He stands on a narrow ledge that juts out from the frame. If the identification of this building as a palestra is correct, this plaque must have been displayed on the front of the building. The hippocamp statue, apparently with a base designed to imitate an aquatic rock formation, has not been identified; despite extensive efforts the youth's head could not be recovered (*StErc*, 304 [February 12, 1760]).

69 *StErc*, 312–15 (May 24–July 19, 1760): sections of the mosaic were removed throughout this period.

70 ASN *CRA* 1540, Inc. 47 (October 28, 1760).

71 *StErc*, 335, and SNSP "Notizie istoriche," 93v. (January 3, 1761). All the access shafts at Herculaneum were eventually sealed; Pompeii only began to be left exposed in late 1763.

72 *StErc*, 315–18 (July 19–September 13, 1760).

73 *StErc*, 318 (September 13, 1760); Tran Tam Tinh, *Culte*, 2, 7, 52–55 (Cat. #2), figs. 3–6.

74 In May, Tanucci reported that a workman had found a gold earring in the shape of a chestnut, but that "there are old excavations nearby [Bardet's] . . . the rest of the discoveries do not merit any consideration" (Tanucci, 9.625 [May 5, 1761]).

75 Tanucci found the circumstances of this discovery intriguing enough to merit a personal recounting of them in a letter to the king, based on Paderni's own report:

> One of Weber's conjectures, by which he wished to excavate deeply where the base of Isis had been found in April [sic], turned out well, since he found a room in which the pictures on the stuccoed walls had already been cut down, a sign that the ancients esteemed these paintings much as we do. The pieces are 2 palms square [0.52 m.] and stand one on top of the other. The paintings are about 1 palm [0.26 m.] [square], but quite fine, as if they were minatures. In one is a woman thinly veiled, on the right, and on the left a woman kneels before a comic mask; other figures are standing around. Paderni cannot endure the suffocation of that deep well and says nothing more about the others.

Tanucci, 9.415 (February 24, 1761); StErc, 339–40 (February 21, 1761): Weber describes the paintings recovered at this time (PdE 4.33–37, pl. 7, 4.139–41, pl. 29, 4.191–95, pl. 41, 4.197–201, pl. 42, 4.203–207, pl. 43, 4.209–11, pl. 44; MN. 9020, 9019, 9022, 9141, 9021, 9816, 9906, and 8970); StErc, 340–41 (February 21, 1761): Paderni's letter to Tanucci. For the provenance, see Allroggen-Bedel, "Dokumente," 144–46, fig. 6. As with a similar painting found at the Praedia Iuliae Felicis, these paintings must have been salvaged from elsewhere and were meant to be incorporated into freshly plastered walls.

76 StErc, 320 (September 20, 1760); cf. SNSP "Notizie istoriche," 92v. (October 8, 1760).

77 For a possible portion of the commentary to this plan, see the Epilogue to this volume, "Weber's Place in the History of Archaeology in the Vesuvian Landscape," and also Appendix 4.

PART III. DOCUMENTATION

CHAPTER 6. WEBER'S APPLICATION TO THE ACCADEMIA ERCOLANESE

1 C. Bonucci, in Napoli e i luoghi celebri delle sue vicinanze (Naples 1845) 2.472, recounts the story of how Charles even removed a ring he had worn since its recovery at Pompeii; cf. Acton, 102–7, who paints a lively picture of these events. For the sixteen cases of plaster casts which Paderni accompanied on board a ship dispatched to Spain in 1765, see "Museo," 97–98 n. 82, with references to documents relating to the transport; the king had requested these casts as early as 1761 (Tanucci, 9.456 [March 10, 1761]); Winckelmann (Sendschreiben, #143) mentions that they were in the process of taking the casts in early 1762.

2 Barnabei, 761, states that Paderni was ordered on October 10, 1759, to file weekly reports to the king. (See Chapter 7 in this volume, "Dearth and Discord.")

3 Stabiae, 108–9 (October 18, 1759); Tanucci noted in a margin of this letter the date on which he passed the proposal to the Accademia.

4 Castaldi, 90, 117.

5 Stabiae, 105–6 (August 18, 1759): Alcubierre to Tanucci.

6 Weber's direct appeal to Tanucci should not have been viewed as insubordination, however, for, according to Barnabei, 761, Weber had been under orders since March 23, 1757, to dispatch daily reports to both Alcubierre and Tanucci.

7 G.M. Della Torre, Storia e fenomeni del Vesuvio col catalogo degli scrittori vesuviani (Naples 1754); Castaldi, 240–45.

8 British Museum Archives, Mss. Add. 34048, 86–91: letter of May 31, 1797, from Hamilton to Sir Joseph Banks, president of the Royal Society of London. For Piaggio's diary, see C. Knight, "Un inedito di Padre Piaggio: Il diario vesuviano (1779–1795)," RendAccNap n.s. 62 (1989–90) 59–131.

9 J.J. Winckelmann, Briefe (1742–1759) (Berlin 1952) 1.370–72 #217 (May 20, 1758): letter to Muzel Stosch. Barnabei, 761, mentions a letter dated February 24, 1758, from Winckelmann to the king, requesting access to the royal collection at Portici (cf. Winckelmann, Briefe, 1.336 #204). See also A. De Franciscis, "L'esperienza napoletana del Winckelmann," CronPomp 1 (1975) 10–14; Longo Auricchio and Capasso, "Dossier Piaggio," 26–27 n. 46; and see Chapter 7 in this volume, "Dearth and Discord."

10 Winckelmann, Briefe, 1.329 #202 (February 5, 1758): letter to Berends: "I am going to Naples with the aim of perhaps becoming a member of the society which is writing about the antiquities."

11 Castaldi, 146–53.

12 B. Galiani, L'architettura di M. Vitruvio Pollione colla traduzione italiana e comento (Naples 1758); his dedication bears the date October 1, 1758.

13 In describing the baths, Galiani relied on a painting which he believed was ancient and which

was commonly thought to have been found in the Baths of Titus in Rome. The painting, however, is probably medieval; see F. Yegül, *Baths and bathing in classical antiquity* (Cambridge, MA 1992) 357–59, fig. 444. Galiani believed the painting showed vessels disposed at various heights above a heat source, and he labeled each of these the caldarium, tepidarium, or frigidarium accordingly (Galiani, 202–7, 214). He also referred to the remains of suspensurae found in 1741 beneath the church of San Stefano in Piscinola in Rome (204 n. 1, quoting from the *Novelle litterariae* 2 [1741]), and used a fragment of the Severan *Forma urbis Romae* to illustrate the plans of atrium houses (252). On the theaters, see Galiani, 172–73 n. 2; for the paintings, 298–99.

14 Galiani, xvii and 15 n. 5. Cf. the model Pompey is said to have had made of the theater at Mitylene to help in the design of his own theater in Rome (Plut. *Pomp.* 42).

15 A. Momigliano, "Ancient history and the antiquarian," *JWarb* 13 (1950) 285–315, summarizes the debate in the eighteenth century concerning the primacy of archaeological evidence over literary. For recent surveys of the history of archaeological documentation and illustration, see B. Trigger, *A history of archaeological thought* (Cambridge 1989) 27–72, though he is less concerned with this topic per se; and J. Malina and Z. Vašíček, *Archaeology yesterday and today: The development of archaeology in the sciences and humanities* (Cambridge 1990) 15–32.

16 For archaeology in the period of the Renaissance in general, see R. Weiss, *The Renaissance discovery of Classical antiquity*, 2d ed. (Oxford 1988); for a general survey of the kind of documentation produced in this period, see L. Richardson, Jr., *A new topographical dictionary of ancient Rome* (Baltimore 1992) xxi–xxiv. For one Renaissance collection of sketches and measured drawings of the antiquities of Rome, see A. Bartoli, *I monumenti antichi di Roma nei disegni degli Uffizi di Firenze*, 5 vols. (Rome 1914–22); for a catalog of plans of Rome, see A.P. Frutaz, *Le piante di Roma*, 3 vols. (Rome 1962).

17 E. Du Pérac, *Le antiche rovine di Roma nei disegni di Du Pérac* (Milan 1990) 17–19, where it is noted that these artists also tended to copy from the works of their predecessors rather than working directly from nature; G. Zorzi, *I disegni delle antichità di Andrea Palladio* (Venice 1959); S. Borsi, *Giuliano da Sangallo: I disegni di architettura e dell' antico* (Rome 1985); E. Mandowsky and C. Mitchell, eds., *Pirro Ligorio's Roman antiquities* (London 1963); C.H. Ericsson, *Roman architecture expressed in sketches by Francesco di Giorgio Martini* [1439–1498]: *Studies in imperial Roman and early Christian architecture*, Com-

mentationes Humanarum Litterarum, no. 66 (Helsinki 1980) 35–51.

18 R. Lanciani, *Storia degli scavi di Roma* (Rome 1902–12) 1.166–95; Mandowsky and Mitchell, 13–19. R. Ridley, *The eagle and the spade: Archaeology in Rome during the Napoleonic era* (Cambridge 1992) 13, 276 n. 22, disputes the historicity of Raphael's title.

19 For a summary of buildings destroyed in Rome from the Renaissance to the eighteenth century, see Ridley, 17–31.

20 For a survey of these early archaeological investigations, see G. Daniel, *A short history of archaeology* (London 1981) 26–33.

21 Bayardi, *Prodromo*, 1.xx–xxi.

22 See, for example, Ridolfino Venuti's *Collectanea antiquitatum Romanarum quas centum tabulis aereis incisas . . .* (Rome 1736), a catalog of the statues, gems, and lamps belonging to Antonio Borioni with engravings by Pietro Santi Bartoli. Venuti was also keeper of the Villa Albani collection, a position Winckelmann assumed in 1758. H. Gross, *Rome in the age of Enlightenment* (Cambridge 1990), devotes a chapter to "Antiquarianism and Neoclassicism," 310–30, and also notes that much greater emphasis was placed on collecting than on the recovery of architecture. For such a collection in Naples, see C.L. Lyons, "The Museo Mastillo and the culture of collecting in Naples, 1700–1755," *Journal of the History of Collections* 4.1 (1992) 1–26; and, in general, see Haskell, 15–22.

23 For Bianchini, see especially H.A. Millon, "Reconstructions of the Palatine in the eighteenth century," in *Eius virtutis studiosi: Classical and Postclassical studies in memory of Frank Edward Brown (1908–1988)* (Hanover 1993) 479–93.

24 J. Wilton-Ely, "The artist as archaeologist," in *The mind and art of Giovanni Battista Piranesi* (London 1978) 45–64; idem, "Piranesi and the role of archaeological illustration," in *Piranesi e la cultura antiquaria: Gl' antecedente e il contesto* (Rome 1985) 317–37; see also, A. Allroggen-Bedel, "Piranesi e l'archeologia nel reame di Napoli," in *Piranesi e la cultura antiquaria*, 281–92.

25 Thieme-Becker, *Allgemeines Lexikon der bildenden Künstler* (Leipzig 1932) 26.202 s.v. Giuseppe Pannini, son of the more famous landscape painter Giovanni Paolo Pannini.

26 For Ligorio's and Contini's plans, see E. Salza Prina Ricotti, "Villa Adriana in Pirro Ligorio e Francesco Contini," *MemLinc* 17 (1973–74) 3–47.

27 For a survey of the investigations at the Villa Adriana, see especially J. Pinto, "Piranesi at Hadrian's Villa" in *Eius virtutis studiosi*, 465–77. Piranesi's enormous plan, drawn at a scale of 1:1,000

and engraved on six folio sheets measuring a total of 3 m. in length, was published posthumously by his son, Francesco, in 1781.

28 Three plates were engraved for presentation by Paolo Fidanza in Rome and dated September 1, 1753. (These copies were consulted in the rare book room of the Fine Arts Library, University of Pennsylvania, Philadelphia.) The first plate contains a plan and an elevation of the existing remains, as well as the dedication and caption. The second is divided into three panels. The upper one is an elevation of the remains of the scaena, which must be largely fanciful since the structure could not have stood to this height in his day. The central panel offers a reconstruction of the scaena and its decorative marble columns. At the bottom, the third panel shows a reconstruction of the cavea, including a small, round temple crowning its summit. In addition to a bird's-eye perspective into the ruins, the third plate includes analytic drawings of several architectural and sculptural elements.

29 Galiani, 193 n. 3.

30 Bayardi praised Pancrazi's work indirectly, saying it would leave "nothing, or very little to desire" to know about Sicily (Bayardi, *Prodromo*, 1.109). For Neapolitan antiquarians from this period in general, see A. Maiuri, "Gli studi di antichità a Napoli nel sette e ottocento," *RendAccNap* 13 (1937) 33–59.

31 G.M. Pancrazi, *L'antichità siciliane spiegate colle notizie generali di questo regno* (Naples 1751–52) 2.ii. The overall quality of the plates is remarkably poor compared to the high quality of engraving for the *Le antichità d'Ercolano*, even though both were published by the Reale Tipografia.

32 The sheet, composed of several fragments of vellum pasted together, measures 0.348 m. high by 0.865 m. wide, compared with 0.360 m. high and 0.480 m. wide for the rough draft. The plan is in the Soprintendenza Archeologica di Napoli e Caserta, Archivio Disegno #72.

33 The sheet, again composed of several fragments of vellum pasted together, measures 0.345 m. high by 0.992 m. wide. The plan is in the Soprintendenza Archeologica di Napoli e Caserta, Archivio Disegno #73.

34 T. Ashby, "Sixteenth century drawings of Roman building attributed to Andreas Coner," *PBSR* 2 (1904) 1–88, includes plates of the entire contents of the notebook.

35 W. Lotz, "The rendering of the interior in architectural drawings of the Renaissance," in *Studies in Italian Renaissance architecture* (Cambridge 1977) 1–65.

36 M. Scolari, "Elements for a history of axono-metry," *Architectural Design* 55.5–6 (1985) 73–78; Y.-A. Bois, "Metamorphoses of axonometry," in *Het Nieuwe Bouwen: De Stijl: De Nieuwe Bielding in de Architectuur* (The Hague 1983) 146–61; P.J. Booker, *A history of engineering drawing* (London 1963) 72–75; cf. S. Edgerton, Jr., *The Renaissance rediscovery of linear perspective* (New York 1975).

37 Presumably either Budé's (1468–1540) *Lexicon graeco-latinum seu thesaurus linquae graecae* . . . (Geneva 1554) or his *Dictionarium graeco-latinum* . . . (Basil 1572). Piaggio may have given Weber the reference to an article in the *Giornale de' Letterati* 8 (Venice 1711) 221–309, "Esperienze fatte con lo specchio ustorio di Firenze sopra le gemme e le pietre dure," esp. 227, which describes the effect of intense heat on various organic substances.

38 G.B. Caporali, *Vitruvius Pollio, con il suo comento et figure: Vetruvio in volgar lingua rapordato per M. Gianbatista Caporali di Perugia* (Perugia 1536); G. Philander, *In decem libros M. Vitruvii Pollioni de architectura annotationes* . . . (Rome 1544).

39 Galiani, 62–63 n. 1, also noted that Procopius was familiar with the fluidity of lava. Both Galiani and Weber compared the Pompeian paving stones with those in Naples, perhaps following the example of G.M. Della Torre in his *Storia e Fenomini del Vesuvio* (Naples 1755), who discussed the lava stone Weber had removed from the streets of Herculaneum.

40 This should serve as ample proof that some members of the court were convinced that the ruins were those of ancient Pompeii by at least 1758, despite the repeated assertion in modern texts that the Bourbons recognized the site as that only in 1763, when the Vespasianic inscription of T. Suedius Clemens was found (*CIL* 10.1018).

41 The second fountain, at the intersection of the Decumanus Maximus and Cardo 5 in Herculaneum, was discovered only in September 1759 (see Chapter 5 in this volume, "The 'Temples' at Herculaneum"), which helps set a *terminus post quem* for this plan.

42 The reference must be to Caesar's election as pontifex maximus in 63 B.C.. No ancient source mentions public banquets on that occasion, though Caesar had entertained the populace upon his election to aedile in 65 B.C., so perhaps Weber was conflating the two events.

43 Montfaucon, *L'antiquité expliquée*, 3.201–4, pl. 122.

44 P. Papinius Statius, *Silvae* 1.5.58–59: "ubi languidius ignis inerrat aedibus, et tenuem voluunt hypocausta vaporem."

45 Galiani, 202–3, n. 3, with an engraving of a painting showing a cutaway view into a set of baths on page 214 (although as noted earlier, the painting was

probably medieval, not ancient, as he believed). A similar confusion has centered on the precise meaning of Vitruvius's directives on how water leaving a castellum aquae should be distributed to public and private consumers (Vitr. 8.6.1–2).

46 Galen, "De atramento sutorio," in *De simplicium medicamentorum temperamentis ac facultatibus* (9.34).

47 There were, in fact, two small tubs (alvea) for hot water in the caldarium, as well as a cool-water fountain (labrum) in the caldarium, but posteruption scavengers apparently had plundered these of their marble. They also robbed out the marble floor of the caldarium, as Weber observed, and probably the bronze water tanks (miliaria) of the praefurnium as well; hence, Weber was unaware that the praefurnium had served to heat the water as well.

48 The first finds from the site included a round terracotta lamp with nine fill holes, some small masks, and an inscription: "L.VR.SG.L.IR" (MN. 3194), *Stabiae*, 6 (August 31–September 5, 1750), pl. 1 (Weber plan *I.E.5*, Somma); Cosenza, 244 #1 (lamp), 172 #2 (inscription).

49 Lead weight inscribed "EME HABEBIS" (*CIL* 10.8067,5): *Stabiae*, 11 (June 12, 1751); Cosenza, 172 #3. Mercury statue: *Stabiae*, 11 (July 17, 1751); *Giornale*, 293 (July 19, 1751): ca. 0.75 m. H. Raven (MN. 4891, 0.26 m. H × 0.58 m. L): *BdE* 1.119 (provenance given as Herculaneum); *Stabiae*, 11 (July 17, 1751); *Giornale*, 293 (July 19, 1751); Ruesch 824; Cosenza, 225 #2; Ward-Perkins and Claridge, 141 #68; W. Jashemski, *The gardens of Pompeii, Herculaneum and the villas destroyed by Vesuvius* (New Rochelle, NY 1979) 332, fig. 531. The candelabrum has not been identified.

50 Ruggiero printed a copy of this sketch plan in the lower right-hand corner of Weber's plan of the Villa of San Marco and its dependencies (*Stabiae*, pl. 1).

51 *Stabiae*, pl. 1 (Weber *I.H.5–6*, Sansone); *Giornale*, 303–4 (April 23 and 30, 1752). Only the mosaic of Phryxis and Helle remains in Naples (MN. 10005; 1.50 m. W × 0.89 m. H): Waldstein and Shoobridge, 274 (who rightly state that the provenance of Herculaneum is "doubtful"); N. Corcia, "Frisso ed Elle figurati in due quadretti di Ercolano e Pompeii," in *Pompei e la regione sotterrata dal Vesuvio* (Naples 1879) 33–84 (who also gives Herculaneum as the provenance); M.S. Pisapia, "Il mosaico di Frisso ed Elle," *RAAN* 53 (1978) 215–25. The mosaic of Europa and the bull was bought in April 1852 by the duc d'Aumale from the collection of the prince of Salerno (cf. *Le catalogue de la très célèbre galerie de tableaux et de la collection d'antiquités de Feu S.A.R. le Prince de Salerne* (Naples 1852) 35 #177); it is now in the Musée Condé, Chantilly, France: H. Lavagne

and O. Wattel-De-Croizant, "De la villa de San Marco (Stabies) au Musée Condé (Chantilly): Histoire d'un enlèvement d'Europe," *MEFRA* 96.2 (1984) 739–88.

52 *Giornale*, 319 (April 22, 1753), where the letters inscribed on the legs above the lions' heads are given as A.E.R., while Weber's plan (*I.H.7*) gives C.A.R.

53 *Stabiae*, 142, pl. 1 (Weber *I.H.5*, Sansone); *Giornale*, 308 (August 13, 1752); Ruesch 1827 (1.79 m. H × 1.08 m. W); Cosenza, 226 #1; E. Strong, *Art in ancient Rome*, 2d ed. (London 1929) 8, pl. 261; O. Elia, *Pitture di Stabia* (Naples 1957) 19; A. Maiuri, *Pompei, Ercolano, Stabiae: Le città sepolte dal Vesuvio* (Novara 1961) 156; H. Mielsch, *Römische Stuckreliefs*, *RömMitt Erganzungsheft* 21 (Heidelberg 1975) 47, 132. Mielsch dates the relief to soon after A.D. 62.

54 *Giornale*, 303 (April 9, 1752); Ruesch 282; Spinazzola, *Arti decorative*, pl. 49; Cosenza, 41 fig. 2, 222 #10; A. Allroggen-Bedel, "Gli scavi borbonici e la ricostruzione delle decorazioni parietali," in A. Barbet *et al.*, "Premier rapport sur l'étude de la Villa San Marco à Stabies," *MEFRA* 95.2 (1983) 929 n. 21.

55 *Stabiae*, 27–31 (April 7–September 15, 1754) covers this period of work at the Jesuits' property.

56 *Stabiae*, 27–28 (April 7 and 14, 1754); 29 (July 7, 1754).

57 Paderni, "An account... (Naples, June 28, 1755)," 490; cf. *Stabiae*, 36 (June 8, 1755) and pl. 1.*C.56*; *Giornale*, 350 (June 8, 1755). Paderni described the statues as a Venus and a Panthea (Isis/Fortuna?) with a steering oar, cornucopia, lotus, modius, and sickle.

58 *Stabiae*, 40 (July 6, 1755), pl. 1 (*1.Somma.D.2*; Weber: "Il famoso cameo grande, fondo cristallino e rilievo bianco di una Dea"); *Giornale*, 356 (July 13, 1755); Cosenza, 226; *CollMN* 1.2, 224 #11; U. Pannuti, *Catalogo della collezione glittica* (Rome 1983) 127 #211 (= 0.0401 m. × 0.0331 m.): "cammeo di notevole qualità sul piano tecnico, pur se di stile un po' freddo ed accademico." Paderni described this cameo in another letter to the Royal Society ("Extract from a letter... dated July 29, 1755," *PhilTrans* 49.2 (1755) 507): "A cameo of great excellence was found on [July 9, 1755]. This cameo is in high relief. It is about an inch and a half long, and almost as much in breadth. It represents a half length of Ceres. The head is in profile and has a noble and beautiful air... the rest of the figure is cut of a chalcedony by a Greek master. It was found at Stabiae, where they continue to dig. In the same place were found also buried several vases of metal and glass very well preserved."

59 *Stabiae*, 59–66 (June 29 to November 30, 1757) for these excavations at the Jesuits' property. Dating

from this period (September 20, 1757) is a small measured drawing of a semicircular wall punctuated with apsidal niches, drawn by the foreman, Stefano Caruso, and appended to one of his reports, but it is not clear from the later plans which wall he was illustrating. La Vega returned to this site from 1775 to 1778 to finish the excavations and draw up a more complete plan (*Stabiae*, pl. 7).

60 *Stabiae*, 63 (September 29, 1757) marks the start of work at the Irace property; the excavations were conducted until late September 1762 (*Stabiae*, 194 [October 2, 1762]) when Paderni noted the transfer to a new site. *Stabiae*, 76 (June 3, 1758), shows Weber's sketch of the peristyle; Ruggiero also published several sketches of mosaic pavements, apparently drawn by Caruso or Scognamillo (*Stabiae*, 179 [August 5, 1762] and 181 [August 12, 1762]), as well as one of Caruso's sketches of one of the rooms in the baths (*Stabiae*, 114 [ca. January 19, 1760]). Paderni was also drawing the mosaics from this site, and Ruggiero appended one of Paderni's drawings to his plate of Weber's plan of this site (*Stabiae*, pl. 4). Work here extended to the east and west along the ridge of Campo Varano and included structures illustrated on plans drawn some years later by F. La Vega (*Stabiae*, pls. 5 and 8). For the paintings recovered from here and a reconstruction of their provenance, see A. Allroggen-Bedel, "Die Wandmalereien aus der Villa in Campo Varano (Castellammare di Stabia)" *RömMitt* 84 (1977) 27–89, pls. 1–53. Only a portion of this enormous site is accessible today.

61 *Stabiae*, 110 (November 10. 1759): announcement that plan is complete, although the date on the published plan is December 24 (*Stabiae*, pl. 1); 131 (June 26, 1760): elevations completed; the engravings published by Ruggiero (*Stabiae*, pl. 2) include the annotation that they were passed on to Tanucci on July 26, 1760.

62 *Stabiae*, pls. 3 (Villa del Pastore) and 4 (Villa di Arianna).

63 The last sentence of the treatise refers to the discovery, on July 10, 1760, at Pompeii, of the archaistic statue of Diana (MN. 6008). This was the most spectacular find at this site in some time and was still fresh in Weber's mind. The members of the Accademia rendered their decision on September 10, 1760, so, accounting for the time they needed to confer, Weber must have finished writing in early August.

64 The manuscript is currently cataloged among the manuscripts in the library of the Soprintendenza Archeologica di Napoli e Caserta (XXI.A.34) and is bound in a loose cardboard cover with a Florentine print, which may be original. Each folio measures 0.375 m. W × 0.475 m. W, except for the plan of the Villa di San Marco, which is a double-folio foldout (measuring 0.620 m. W × 0.435 m. H to the outer black borders surrounding the plan and text); this is the only original version of any of the three Stabian plans to survive. Ruggiero (*Stabiae*, 137–44) published a highly edited version of the text and copies of the illustrations that appear to have been based on versions other than those in the original manuscript.

65 ASN *CRA* 1541, Inc. 42 (April 9, 1765): both Furlanetti and Piaggio made their claims after Weber's death; see the Epilogue to this volume, "Weber's Place in the History of Archaeology in the Vesuvian Landscape." Giuseppe Assemani of the Biblioteca Vaticana, in recommending Piaggio to Charles of Bourbon, observed that Piaggio was a calligrapher who could imitate both ancient and modern scripts (Bassi, "Piaggio," *ASPN* 32 [1907] 639 n. 1).

66 Paderni had organized a display of ancient weights and measures in the Museum Herculanense as early as 1758 ("An account ... [February 1, 1758]," 621).

67 The date of these illustrations is also an important factor for dating the manuscript as a whole to early August 1760. It should be noted that some of the discrepancies between the manuscript's illustrations are due to the fact that Ruggiero's are engravings of the originals and therefore not necessarily accurate reproductions.

68 These digressions may have been inspired in part by Bayardi's work on the royal families of Crete in the third volume of the *Prodromo*, 3.1504.

69 F. Giordano, Ms. in Biblioteca Nazionale di Napoli (XIII.B.26) "Historia Napolitana" (ca. 1540–90); G. Tarcagnota, *De sito et lodi della città di Napoli con una breve historia de gli re suoi e delle cose piu degne altrove nei medesimi tempi* (Naples 1566); G.D. Magliocco, *Descrizione della voragine del Vesuvio*; G. Carafa, *In opusculum de nouissima Vesuuij conflagratione* (Naples 1632); G.C. Capaccio, *Historia Neapolitana* (Naples 1607).

70 Weber notes that the text is actually contained in the Epitome of Cassius Dio, compiled by Xiphilinus.

71 For a modern summary of the events, see M. Carotenuto, *Ercolano attraverso i secoli* (Naples 1980) 155–60. All of these were favorite topics of discussions of Vesuvius in contemporary writings. See, e.g., Russell, *Letters*, 1.110–28 #25.

72 The brick stamp read NARCISSI AVGVSTI INVSTIS LVISELLI (cf. *CIL* 10.8042,82) and was found on October 8, 1754, in the baths.

73 Knight, "Padre Piaggio," 59–131, the text of the diary Piaggio maintained for William Hamilton.

74 A. Piaggio, "Memorie del Padre Ant.o Piaggi [*sic*] impiegato nel R. Museo di Portici relative alle antichità, e Papiri p. anno 1769. 1771," *SNSP* 31-C-21; cf. Bassi, "Piaggio," 636–90.

75 *Stabiae*, 131–34 (September 10, 1760): at Naples.

76 This must be the "planta generale" he reported as completed in April 1761 (*StErc*, 346 [April 17, 1761]). See also Barnabei, 761-63.

77 *Stabiae*, 134 (September 10, 1760).

78 This is F. La Vega's plan of Herculaneum, based largely on Weber's work, published first in C.M. Rosini's *Dissertationis isagogicae* (*Herculanensium voluminum*, vol. 12, Naples 1797), published under the auspices of the "second-generation" Accademia established under Ferdinand IV in 1787. F. La Vega had died in 1784. (See the Epilogue to this volume, "Weber's Place in the History of Archaeology in the Vesuvian Landscape.")

79 E.g., G. D'Ancora, *Prospetto storico-fisico degli scavi di Ercolano e di Pompei e dell' antico e presente stato del Vesuvio, per guida de' forestieri* (Naples 1803), a work which links a history of the excavations with the architecture, art, and plans of the buildings; De Jorio, containing the earliest reproduction of Weber's plan of the Villa dei Papiri and coinciding with the start of the "scavamenti scoperti" at Herculaneum undertaken by C. Bonucci in 1827.

80 F. Bologna, "La riscoperta di Ercolano e la cultura artistica del settecento Europeo," in *Le antichità di Ercolano* (Naples 1988) 95, notes that it was only during the reign of Joachim Murat (1808–15) that there was a revival in interest in ancient urbanism and architecture, as evidenced in particular by the work of F. Mazois, *Les ruines de Pompéi* (Paris 1812).

81 For this monograph, see Appendix 4 to this volume and also the Epilogue, "Weber's Place in the History of Archaeology in the Vesuvian Landscape."

CHAPTER 7. DEARTH AND DISCORD

1 With the discovery of several tombs in November 1754, the area is referred to as adjacent to the "Taverna del Rapillo" (*PAH* I.i.11 [November 10, 1754]), a hostelry located on the Royal Road between Naples and Salerno. When Francesco La Vega later proposed to the king that the existing tavern be converted into one for accommodating visitors to Pompeii, he located this "Taverna del Rapillo" on the Royal Road "almost equal distance from the gate and the theater" (*PAH* I.ii.Addenda 4.169–71). Since the main gate at this time was the Porta di Ercolano, these tombs were probably found somewhere near

the Porta Marina and the so-called Villa Imperiale; the excavation reports from this period often refer to the fact that a site "overlooks the Royal Road" or the "marina." For a drawing of the "Taverna del Rapillo," which stood near the site of the now-defunct Hotel Suisse, see *Pompéi: Travaux et envois des architectes français au XIXe siècle* (Paris 1980) 5, fig. 1: drawing of Callet (1822), EBA Paris, Inv. 3275, feuillet 81. For a map indicating the property boundaries and tenants as they existed in 1807, see the plan by P. Scognamillo, "Mappa de' terreni che coprino la città di Pompei" (MN. ADS; 0.530 m. L × 0.375 m. H), reproduced in V. Kockel, "Archäologische Funde und Forschungen in den Vesuvstädten, I," *ArchAnz* (1985) 515–17 figs. 8–9; by this date the Cuomo property had passed into the hands of Principe Dentice (See Fig. 28). This is not the same as the Irace family of Gragnano, where excavations in the "Villa di Arianna" at Stabiae were undertaken from 1757 to 1762; they had petitioned for reimbursement for damage to their property, stating that it was their only holding (*Stabiae*, 115 [ca. Jan. 21, 1760]).

2 La Vega's plan may be derived from one presented to King Giuseppe III (Franz Josef II, emperor of Austria) on his visit of April 7, 1769 (*PAH* I.i.230–31). This particular version is currently in the Museo Nazionale in Naples (MN. 2615); a schematic copy is reproduced in *CTP* 5 (Rome 1981) between 116–17.

3 *PAH* I.i.51–101. The houses are Regio 8.3.14 (Casa della Regina Carolina); 8.2.26–27 (Casa del Cinghiale II: mosaic with letters SALVE discovered here on November 12, 1757 [*PAH* I.i.62]); 8.2.28; 8.2.29 (Casa di Francesco Giuseppe); 8.2.30–31; 8.2.32–34 (Casa delle colombe a mosaico); 8.2.36–37; 8.2.38–39 (Casa di Giuseppe II). Little work has been done on the finds from this period. For the nymphaeum, see *PAH* I.i.78–79 (August 26, 1758); *PAH* I.ii.Addenda 4.138. Nearby were found two still lifes similar to those in the Praedia Iuliae Felicis, one showing wax tablets and a double inkpot with a stylus and a papyrus scroll (MN. 4676), and the other showing a money bag, several volumina in a round box in the center, a pile of coins, and a tabula cerata with writing on it (*PAH* I.i.77 [July 1, 1758]; *PdE* 2.7, pl. 2, 2.55, pl. 9; S. Reinach, *Répertoire de peintures grecques et romaines* (Paris 1922) 262.12 = 0.40 m. W × 0.16 m. H; Ward-Perkins and Claridge, 203 #274).

4 Weber makes it clear that the tenant of the Cuomo property at this time was Carlo Balzano and so uses the names interchangeably (ASN *CRA* 1540, Inc. 47 [October 28, 1760]). Judging from P. Scognamillo's plan of 1807, the Cuomo property (#42) by then had passed into the hands of the Padri

Celestini but continued to be worked by the Balzano family.

5 This was only the second attempt to remove an entire wall; the first had been the wall with still-life panels (MN. 8598) found in the Praedia Iuliae Felicis.

6 *PAH* I.i.98 (October 13, 1759); the painting measures 2.80 m. W x 2.00 m. H.

7 *CTP* 5 (Rome 1981) 113; *CollMN* 1.2, 128–29 #36; R. Ling, *Roman painting* (Cambridge 1991) 34–35 fig. 32; Strocka, 328–33, figs. 6–7, pl. 72, includes drawings by Paderni of this wall painting and of the room's mosaic pavement. Buildings in Pompeii are located within the grid of the city's plan according to a modern address system that specifies the *regio* (region) of the city, the *insula* (city block) within the regio, and the door or doors from the street into the building; e.g., the Praedia Iuliae Felicis is identified as Regio 2.4.1–12: regio 2, insula 4, doors 1–12.

8 Programma: *PAH* I.i.108 (May 2, 1760). Calendar tondi: *PAH* I.i.106–8 (April 19–May 2, 1760); MN. 9518–9521; see C.R. Long, "The Pompeii calendar medallions," *AJA* 96 (1992) 477–501.

9 *PAH* i.i.109–10 (May 17–31, 1760): elements of the wall were reconstructed (although no provenance was suggested) by A. Allroggen-Bedel, "Herkunft und ursprünglicher Dekorationszusammenhang einiger in Essen ausgestellter Fragmente von Wandmalereien," in B. Andreae and H. Kyrieleis, eds., *Neue Forschungen in Pompeji* (Recklinghausen 1975) 118–19 fig. 95b. For MN. 9707 and 9710, see Ward-Perkins and Claridge, 170–71 ##144–45. For "Sappho" *et al.*, see *PdE* 3.233–37, pl. 45; the architectural elements are *PdE* 2.173, pl. 28; and the attributes of Apollo are *PdE* 3.127, pl. 25.

10 *PAH* I.i.113 (July 12, 1760); mosaic of Phryxis and Helle from Stabiae (found in April 1752 [*Giornale*, 303–4]; Weber's Ms. fols. 13–18, Appendix 3 in this volume). On July 26, 1760, Weber sent an illustration of the Stabian mosaic to Tanucci (see marginalia to *Stabiae*, pl. 2). The Phyrxis and Helle painting from Pompeii is *PdE* 3.23, pl. 4 = MN. 8889; the Satyr and Maenad is *PdE* 7.147, pl. 33. For the painting of the Three Graces, see *Pompeji: Leben und Kunst in den Vesuvstädten* (Recklinghausen 1973) 194 #271, 201, where the provenance is given as the adjacent "Regio 6.Ins. Occ."

11 *PAH* I.i.114 and *PAH* I.ii.Addenda 4.140 (July 12–24, 1760); *PAH* I.i.115 (August 2, 1760): excavations in "atrium" looking for a statue placed symmetrically with the Diana. For the Diana/Artemis statue, see Winckelmann, *Sendschreiben*, #44, and *Nachrichten*, #64; Ruesch, 106; F. Studniczka, "Die archaische Artemisstatue aus Pompeji," *RömMitt* 3

(1888) 277–302; L. Richardson, Jr., "The Archaistic Diana of Pompeii," *AJA* 74 (1970) 202, where the provenance is properly identified as Regio 7.6.1–4; Ward-Perkins and Claridge, 147 #82, where the traditional provenance of Regio 8.2 or 8.3 is given; Jashemski, *Gardens* 1.133, fig. 210; "Museo," 115, 117 n. 224: the statue was displayed first in the eighth room of the museum (where Winckelmann saw it) and then moved to the twelfth room. The insula in which this house is located was reexcavated by G. Spano in 1909–10; he noted that it already had been excavated, although certain rooms did retain their painted decoration (*NSc* 1910, 437-86).

12 Alcubierre did not resume excavations here until late in July 1761 when the *mofeta* had cleared (Tanucci, 9.807 [July 7, 1761] and 9.852 [July 21, 1761]).

13 ASN *CRA* 1540, Inc. 63 (December 15, 1761): Paderni to Tanucci, gives the date of August 12, 1760; ASN *CRA* 1540, Inc. 43 (August 23, 1760): Paderni thanks Tanucci for his new assignment and states his intention of setting Scognamillo straight (although the charge is not specified); SNSP "Notizie istoriche," 92v. (August 30, 1760): Scognamillo identified as the cause of problems at Civitá. *PAH* I.i.115–17 (August 2–September 6, 1760): excavations were undertaken in properties belonging to De Fillipis, Imperato, and Balzano. (Since the distinction was not clear to Weber either, it is referred to here as the Cuomo/Balzano property.)

14 *PAH* I.i.120 (October 25, 1760).

15 ASN *CRA* 1540, Inc. 47 (October 28, 1760): Portici, Weber to Tanucci.

16 *PAH* I.ii.Addenda 4.142 (January 31, 1761).

17 *PAH* I.i.125 (January 10, 1761); the impluvium measured 2.7 m. L × 2.3 m. W × 0.22 m. D, roughly the size of that found today in Regio 7.6.3. Tanucci, 9.290 (January 13, 1761) and 9.518 (March 31, 1761); "Museo," 101 fig. 7, 109. Spano (*NSc* 1910, 440) reported finding the impluvium here stripped of its revetment.

18 Tanucci, 9.357 (February 3, 1761); for the cameo and earrings, see *PAH* I.i.126 (January 31, 1761). The cameo (MN. 26974; 0.04 m. W x 0.0319 m. H) is a carnelian onyx, with figures in white relief on a red ground. Pannuti, *Catalogo*, 11 #9, pl. 1, identifies the helmeted deity as Thetis. She carries a lance and shield, and rides on the back of the sea creature, which is part centaur and part fish and carries what appears to be a rudder.

19 The house is almost certainly Regio 7.6.38 (Casa di Cipius Pamphilus); Spano, *NSc* 1910, 446–50, fig. 1. *PAH* I.i.129–33 (March 14–June 6, 1761); Tanucci, 9.711 (June 2, 1761); *PdE* 4.61-65, pl. 13

(1.83 m. W × 1.28 m. H); Ward-Perkins and Claridge, 186 #199 (where the provenance is given as Regio 8.2 or 8.3). From the SNSP *Fondo Cuomo* 20-5-3, "Rapporti," April 7, 1761, it is known that this garden stood in the Irace property "twelve paces" from the Diana, in the direction of Castellamare.

20 Tanucci, 9.456 (March 10, 1761), 9.478 (March 17, 1761), 9.518 (March 31, 1761); similar expressions of concern appear in Tanucci's letters dating well into 1762.

21 *Stabiae*, 147–48 (March 30, 1761): Paderni to Tanucci.

22 Piaggio, "Memorie," 3–4r.

23 In 1755, e.g., Barthelemy speaks of traffic in paintings from Pompeii, in which Charles Marie de La Condamine was involved (*Travels in Italy* [London 1802] 31–32, 40). For a collection of documents on the controversy over the destruction of paintings, see F. Strazzullo, *Le lettere di Luigi Vanvitelli della Biblioteca Palatina di Caserta* (Galatina 1977) 3.682–87. See also Rossignani, "Saggio," 26–27, and Allroggen-Bedel, "Insula Occidentalis," 153–56.

24 SNSP "Notizie istoriche," 94r. (April 14, 1761); *Stabiae*, 148 (April 11, 1761), 149 (April 11, 1761); *PAH* I.ii.Addenda 4.142–43 (May 30, 1761).

25 SNSP "Notizie istoriche," 94r. (June 6, 1761).

26 "Museo," 93, from ASN *CRA* 1573, Incc. 70, 72, 79; and SNSP *Fondo Cuomo* 2-6-2, fol. 128v. ASN *CRA* 1538, Inc. 150 (January 18, 1749): Alcubierre complained to Fogliani that one of the condemned had returned to Portici and was working in Canart's studio; he was dismissed after the other workmen rebelled.

27 Tanucci, 9.852 (July 21, 1761), 9.871 (July 28, 1761).

28 *Stabiae*, 163, and *PAH* I.ii.Addenda 4.143–44 (October 31, 1761). In April 1761, Weber had awarded a forced laborer with a carafe of wine for handing over a small cameo he might otherwise have stolen and suggested he be given his freedom as well. "The forced laborers in our excavations are faithful and serve with sincerity and love," he observed (*StErc*, 348 [April 29, 1761]).

29 Tanucci, 9.915 (August 11, 1761), 10.169–70 (September 29, 1761), 10.191 (October 6, 1761), 10.231 (October 20, 1761).

30 Tanucci, 10.341 (December 1, 1761).

31 Tanucci, 10.358 (December 8, 1761).

32 *StErc*, 377–78 (December 5, 1761): Alcubierre to Weber.

33 *StErc*, 378 (December 11, 1761); as an example, Weber referred to the discovery of the Egyptianizing base and the Bacchus statuette found in the street near the first "temple."

34 Spano's excavations in this area confirmed that many of the rooms were paved simply (*NSc* 1910, 437–86).

35 ASN *CRA* 1540, Inc. 63 (December 15, 1761): Paderni to Tanucci; Strazzullo, "Documenti," 274–77.

36 Tanucci, 10.391 (December 21, 1761).

37 Piaggio, "Memorie," 71r.

38 *StErc*, 372–73 (October 22–24, 1761).

39 *PAH* I.ii.Addenda 4.141 (October 4, 1760) = SNSP "Notizie istoriche," 92r. Underground cellars had been dug into the hill of "la Città" for centuries.

40 *PAH* I.ii.Addenda 4.141–42, where the document is dated January 21, 1761, but it is clear from the reference to this altar (first described on January 23, 1762 [*PAH* I.i.139]) that the year should be 1762. This must be part of the same letter of Weber to Alcubierre dated January 21, 1762, and quoted elsewhere by Ruggiero (*StErc*, 381–82).

41 *PAH* I.i.140 and I.ii.Addenda 4.144 (February 20–March 6, 1762). MN. 22248 is 1.11 m. high, MN. 22249 is 1.15 m. high: Winckelmann, *Nachrichten*, #75; Von Rohden, 46, pl. 35; Ward-Perkins and Claridge, 209 ##301–2. The Venus, probably found in the peristyle of Regio 7.6.7, is *PdE* 4.11–15, pl. 3 (found March 4, 1762); cf. the painting from the viridarium in the Casa della Venere in Conchiglia (Regio 2.3.3). Alcubierre's remarks came at the end of a summary he drew up of the principal discoveries since 1738 (ASN *CRA* 1540, Inc. 63: [February 13, 1762]).

42 *Stabiae*, 171 (February 20, 1762).

43 Tanucci, 10.582 (March 2, 1762).

44 Tanucci, 11.76 (April 20, 1762).

45 C. Justi, *Winckelmann und seine Zeitgenossen*, 3d ed. (Leipzig 1923) esp. 2.180–258, 420–48, the most detailed biography of Winckelmann and his work, although careless about maintaining proper chronological sequences, especially in references drawn from his correspondence; W. Leppmann, *Winckelmann* (New York 1970) 133–85, a "popular" biography; A. De Franciscis, "L'esperienza napoletana del Winckelmann," *CronPomp* 1 (1975) 7–24; F. Bologna, "Le scoperte di Ercolano e Pompei nella cultura europea del XVIII secolo," *PP* 34 (1979) 377-404; F. Strazzullo, ed., *Le scoperte di Ercolano* (Naples 1981), Italian translation of Winckelmann's *Sendschreiben* and *Nachrichten*, with introductory comments and historical background; M. Kunze, "Zu Winckelmanns Schriften über Herkulaneum und Pompeji," in *Pompeji 79–1979: Beiträge zum Vesuvausbruch und seiner Nachwirkung* (Stendal 1982) 25–39; A. Allroggen-Bedel, "Tanucci e la cultura antiquaria del suo tempo," in *Bernardo Tanucci: Statista, letterato, giurista*

(Naples 1986) 521–36; F. Zevi, "Gli scavi di Ercolano e le *Antichità*," in *Le antichità di Ercolano* (Naples 1988) 11–38; F. Bologna, "La riscoperta di Ercolano e la cultura artistica del settecento Europeo," in *Le antichità di Ercolano* (Naples 1988) 83–105.

46 Finzi, "Un ministro 'archeologo,' " 157. F. Zevi, "Gli scavi di Ercolano e le *Antichità*," 15–16, notes that Venuti's brother, Ridolfino, had also advised Cardinal Albani on his collection of antiquities, a position Winckelmann would assume later.

47 Winckelmann, *Briefe*, 1.323–24 #201 (February 4, 1758): to Francke; 1.329 #202 (February 5, 1758): to Berends; 1.350 #210 (April 26, 1758): to Bünau.

48 According to C. Knight, "Piaggio," 61, Piaggio was living at this time in the Casino di S. Antonio, near the church of the same name which stood adjacent to the royal palace in Portici; he later moved to a house in Resina near S. Maria a Pugliano.

49 In November 1761, just before Winckelmann's second visit, the court forbade entry to the museum to P.M. Paciaudi, specifically because of the possibility that he would publish his observations before the Accademia did theirs (*Lettres de Paciaudi au comte de Caylus* [Paris 1862] #67 [November 3, 1761]).

50 Russell, *Letters*, 1.218 #34 (September 10, 1743).

51 Russell, *Letters* 2.314 #70 (September 15, 1749). Rossignani, "Saggio," 8–9, speaks of a veritable "black market" of information among scholars that resulted from these restrictions.

52 Winckelmann, *Briefe*, 1.352 #210 (April 26, 1758): to Bunau: "In the meantime I cannot take a step without having an overseer next to me, whom I have given plenty of trouble."

53 Russell, *Letters*, 1.218 #34 (September 10, 1743).

54 Winckelmann, *Briefe*, 1.344–47 #207 (March 31, 1758): to Bianconi; *idem*, 1.352 #210 (April 26, 1758): to Bunau: "I know more about these writings than anyone here believes."

55 Winckelmann, *Briefe*, 1.337 #206 (March 11, 1758): to Mengs; 1.339 #207 (March 31, 1758): to Bianconi; 1.406–9 #231 (August 26, 1758): to Bianconi, subtitled specifically "Of the Houses of the Ancients and particularly those of Herculaneum." For Paderni's remarks, see C. Paderni, "Extract of a letter . . . to Tho. Hollis, Esq., relating to the later discoveries at Herculaneum [October 18, 1754]," *PhilTrans* 48.2 (1754) 821–25.

56 Winckelmann, *Briefe*, 1.355 #211 (May 13, 1758): to Bianconi.

57 Winckelmann, *Briefe*, 1.406 #231 (August 26, 1758): to Bianconi.

58 Winckelmann, *Briefe*, 1.354 #211 (May 13, 1758): to Bianconi.

59 Winckelmann wrongly charged that the king had prevented distribution of Martorelli's book *De theca calamaria* because of its attacks on Mazzocchi, but in fact publication was delayed until Bayardi's *Catalogo* appeared, because it contained material that Bayardi had laid claim to.

60 Winckelmann, *Briefe*, 1.336 #206 (March 11, 1758): to Mengs on Piaggio; 1.365 #215 (May 15, 1758): to Berends on B. Galiani; 1.385–86 #222 (mid-July, 1758): to Bianconi on Neapolitan scholars.

61 For example, he noted in the *Sendschreiben* (#59) that he was forced to copy an inscription in secret. He mentioned the treatise in a letter to Usteri dated February 19, 1762 (see Strazzullo, *Le scoperte di Ercolano*, 27–28).

62 Winckelmann, *Briefe*, 2.124 #392 (February 24, 1761): to Usteri.

63 In late February 1762, all the workmen at Stabiae were concentrated at Pompeii; excavations at Stabiae did not resume until July.

64 *PAH* I.i.139–40 (January 23, 30; February 20, 27, 1762); Winckelmann, *Briefe*, 2.216–17 #475 (March 19, 1762): to Bianconi. For Paderni's reports to Tanucci, see ASN *CRA* 1540, Inc. 59 (February 6, 13, 20, 23, 1762): on first terracotta statue of comic actress and the monument "baptized as an altar"; ASN *CRA* 1540, Inc. 61 (February 25, 1762): the second terracotta statue; *ibid.* (March 20, 1762): a painted room at Pompeii. For the counter reconstructed in the museum, see "Museo," 114.

65 Winckelmann, *Briefe*, 2.226–27 #482 (early May, 1762): to Bianconi.

66 *StErc*, 339–40 (February 21, 1761): MN. 9020, 9021, 9022, 9041. Winckelmann, *Briefe*, 2.203 #466 (February 19, 1762): to Usteri; 2.204 #467 (February 27, 1762): to Bianconi; 2.210 #471 (March 3, 1762): to Volkmann; J.J. Winckelmann, *Geschichte der Kunst des Altertums* (Vienna 1934) 253–61; *Sendschreiben*, #47. Winckelmann corrected himself in his *Nachrichten*, #7, noting as well a similar painting found in the Praedia Iuliae Felicis. For Paderni's remarks to Tanucci, see Tanucci, 9.415 (February 24, 1761). *Stabiae*, 157 (September 18, 1761), notes that Winckelmann may have been confusing some fragmentary paintings found on that date with those found at Herculaneum. See also Allroggen-Bedel, "Dokumente," 144–45, fig. 6. The four paintings were displayed in the ninth room of the museum ("Museo," 115).

67 The first volume of the *collectio prior* of the series *Herculanensium voluminum quae supersunt* did not appear until 1793.

68 Winckelmann, *Sendschreiben*, #34. This remark

must be directed toward Venuti's proposal (*Descrip-tion*, 69) that the theater be excavated out from the side facing the sea, where the ground sloped down, as well as toward S. Maffei's comments that it would be easier to comprehend the city plan if the whole were exposed to light; see Chapter 8 in this volume, "The Theater at Herculaneum."

69 *StErc*, 29 n. 1 (June 2, 1739); *Giornale*, 174–77 (June 1–August 1, 1739).

70 Winckelmann, *Sendschreiben*, #30.

71 Winckelmann, *Briefe*, 2.217 #475 (March 19, 1762); C. Parslow, "Karl Weber and Pompeian archaeology," in *Ercolano 1738–1988: 250 anni di ricerca archeologica* (Rome 1993) 51–56.

72 In his later *Nachrichten*, #1, he apologized for the problems caused in the *Sendschreiben* by his failure to keep accurate notes.

73 *Stabiae*, 173 (July 6, 1762). Even the foremen at Stabiae suggested that a mosaic found at Stabiae merited inclusion in Weber's proposed book (*Stabiae*, 181 [August 12, 1762]).

74 Tanucci, 11.472 (October 19, 1762); 11.490 (October 26, 1962): "the excavations this week produced not even a nail, and Alcubierre rejoices ferociously"; 11.514 (November 2, 1762): "a fierce dispute has arisen between Paderni and Alcubierre, which I will seek to settle . . . if not with words, with silence"; 11.556 (November 23, 1762): "Querulous Paderni says nothing has resulted from his hopes for the new excavation; Alcubierre continues to rejoice."

75 Tanucci, 11.490 (October 26, 1762). Cf. Tanucci, 11.346 (August 24, 1762), where he observed that "the hypochondria concerning the sterility of the excavations continues." For the Villa of Cicero: *PAH* I.i.7–8 (January 18–25, 1749).

76 Tanucci, 11.653 (January 4, 1763), 11.757 (February 22, 1763); cf. ASN *Archivio Borbone* I Fasc. 16, 169v. (February 1, 1763): Tanucci to Charles III: "Absolutely nothing has been found this week in the excavations. . . . Alcubierre is triumphant"; ASN *Archivio Borbone* I Fasc. 17, 93r. (June 14, 1763): Tanucci to Charles III: "Nothing [has been found] in Pompeii, about which Alcubierre laughs sardonically."

77 *PAH* I.i.153 (August 20, 1763): the inscription is a decree of Vespasian, empowering T. Suedius Clemens to reestablish the old pomerial ground and evict private usurpers (*CIL* 10.1018); *PAH* I.i.153 (September 17, 1763): discovery of Porta di Erco-lana; ASN *CRA* 1540, Inc. 98 (October 29, 1763): Paderni's sketch and report.

78 ASN *Archivio Borbone* I Fasc. 18, 17r. (October 25, 1763): Tanucci to Charles. SNSP "Notizie istoriche," 100r. (October 22, 1763): gate should be left exposed; SNSP "Notizie istoriche," 100r. (November 19, 1763): houses should be accessible.

79 In 1792, there were three principal areas in the excavations at Pompeii that remained exposed: the theater and Temple of Isis, the Porta di Ercolana and adjacent houses, and the "Villa di Diomede" (*PAH* I.ii.Addenda 4.169 [April 14, 1792]).

80 ASN *CRA* 1539, Inc. 25 (July 24, 1751): Alcubierre to Fogliani; first used in excavation reports of the Praedia Iuliae Felicis in 1756 (*PAH* I.i.46 and I.ii.Addenda 4.137 [November 27, 1756]). The discovery of the inscription of T. Suedius Clemens (*CIL* 10.1018) provided the unassailable proof for making the identification, for Paderni noted to Tanucci on its discovery that it was "a document that clinched the proper location of this city, just as [similar inscriptions] were found in Herculaneum and Stabiae" (ASN *CRA* 1540, Inc. 87 [August 20, 1763]). The location of Stabiae had been ensured only recently by the discovery of an inscription found near the Capella di S. Maria della Grazie naming the "Genius Stabiar" (MN. 5961, 5962) that was associ-ated with a shrine dedicated by the *augustalis* Caesius Daphnus (*Stabiae*, 185–86 [August 28–31; Septem-ber 2, 1762]). Tanucci, 11.378–79 (September 7, 1762) reported to the king the discovery of this inscription and its significance.

81 *PAH* I.ii.Addenda 4.146 (November 12, 1763): "it is not Paderni's responsibility to determine which paintings should be removed and which should remain, as the king has heard with horror that many of said ancient paintings have been destroyed"; ASN *CRA* 1541, Inc. 8 (November 18, 1763), Paderni to Tanucci: asks whether the likes of an Alcubierre or a Weber are qualified to judge whether worthwhile paintings are being destroyed; *PAH* I.ii.Addenda 4.146 (January 25, 1764): Scognamillo complains that Paderni continues to destroy paintings. See Allroggen-Bedel, "*Insula Occidentalis*," 154–56.

82 Winckelmann, *Nachrichten*, #3 ("Genius" inscrip-tion from Stabiae); #4 (inscription identifying Pom-peii); #7 (four mounted paintings and damaged paintings seen on walls); #54 (Dioscurides mosaic found on February 8, 1764); Winckelmann, *Ge-schichte*, 376–77.

83 Winckelmann, *Nachrichten*, ##83; 7, 54, 82.

84 Winckelmann, *Nachrichten*, #73. For these stat-ues, identified variously as dancers, Danaids, and Peplophorai, see esp. Wojcik, 203–17, pls. 101–6; Neudecker, 151–52 #14.35–39, with bibliography.

85 Winckelmann, *Nachrichten*, ##10–49. In 1760, Philip of Bourbon, duke of Parma, had undertaken excavations in the forum of Velleia, a project clearly intended to do for Philip what Herculaneum had

done for his brother, Charles III. These produced an important group of dedicatory statues from the basilica, numerous inscriptions, and the remains of other public buildings on the forum. The results were documented in a set of plans, and the accompanying illustrations, drawn by Antonio Costa, are remarkably similar to Weber's. See especially O. Montevecchi, "Documenti inediti sugli scavi di Veleia nel sec. XVIII," *Aevum* 8 (1934) 553–630, and C. Saletti, *Il ciclo statuario della basilica di Velleia* (Milan 1968).

86 B. Tanucci, *Lettere a Ferdinando Galiani*, ed. F. Nicolini (Bari 1914) 1.178 #82 (September 8, 1764); 1.212 #94 (December 8, 1764); 1.220 #98 (January 5, 1765).

87 B. Galiani, *Considerazioni sopra la lettera dell' Abate Winckelmann riguardante le scoverte di Ercolano* [Naples ca. 1765]: manuscript copy in SNSP 30-C-6, fols. 149r.–155r. Mattia Zarillo, a member of the Accademia reknowned for his interest in numismatics, appropriated many of Galiani's key remarks and elaborated upon them for his own twenty-seven-page polemic which he published in Naples already in 1764 (M. Zarillo, *Giudizio dell' opera dell' Abate Winckelmann intorno alle scoverte di Ercolano contenuto in una lettera ad un amico* [Naples 1765]: manuscript copy in SNSP *Fondo Cuomo* 2-4-21); Galiani later published his own *Considerazioni* in order to illustrate how many of Zarillo's points were taken from his own work. F. Galiani observed in a letter to Tanucci that his acquaintances had encouraged him to write a rebuttal of Winckelmann, but he had concluded that silence was the best response (Tanucci, *Lettere a Ferdinando Galiani*, 1.220 n. 1 [December 17, 1764]).

88 M. Praz, *On Neoclassicism* (Evanston 1969) 70–90; F. Bologna, "Le scoperte di Ercolano," 377–404; E. Choisi, "Le Reale Accademia Ercolanese: Bernardo Tanucci fra politica e antiquaria," in *Bernardo Tanucci: Statista, letterato, giurista* (Naples 1986) 495–517.

89 Tanucci, *Lettere a Ferdinando Galiani*, 1.197–98 #89 (October 27, 1764) and 1.200 #90 n. 2 (October 22, 1764): letters from F. Galiani to Tanucci.

90 Tanucci, *Lettere a Ferdinando Galiani*, 1.183 #83 (September 15, 1764). In a later letter Tanucci suggested that if he did not have someone like Carcani to rely on, he would "substitute a better *Catalogo* for that very strange one by Bayardi" (1.212 #94 [December 8, 1764]).

91 Tanucci, *Lettere a Ferdinando Galiani*, 1.32 #20 (May 21, 1763); cf. 1.197 #89 (October 27, 1764): "to be pedantic, arranging in order the elements and institutions of antiquarians, would be an insolence for us." See Allroggen-Bedel, "Tanucci," 529–32:

Tanucci's position was later advocated by D. Diderot, publisher of the influential *Encyclopédie, ou Dictionnaire raisonné des sciences, des arts et des métiers* (Paris 1765). Diderot maintained that scholars should concern themselves only with those objects from antiquity with some aesthetic value, rather than with those whose sole merit was that they were old. Diderot made this observation only after the publication of A.D. Fougeroux de Bondaroy's *Recherches sur les ruines d'Herculanum . . .* (Paris 1770), which included a long section on the small, domestic finds displayed in the museum at Portici.

92 Tanucci, *Lettere a Ferdinando Galiani*, 1.201 #90 (November 3, 1764). In a letter to the king written years later, F. Galiani still could lament the lack of a publication of this type:

> One should particularly look into writing that book on Herculaneum which foreigners desire and which never has been published. It would narrate the history of those cities, Herculaneum, Pompeii, and Stabiae, describing the sacred and private buildings which have been excavated, and then go on to explain the greatest curiosities about the customs of the ancients, their way of life, *et cetera*. Likewise it would document the inscriptions found there, with explanations of these, and in essence would be a type of "Guide for curious Foreigners to observe our celebrated antiquities of Herculaneum."

SNSP Ms. 31-A-9, fol. 213r.–v. (*Memoria riservata per S.E.*).

93 D'Ancora's *Prospetto Storico-Fisico degli scavi di Ercolano* (Naples 1803) combined a chronology of the eruptions of Vesuvius and a historical narrative of the sites with a description of the principal monuments, but relied more heavily on secondary sources and therefore constitutes less of a guide to the excavations and the museum than de Jorio's.

CHAPTER 8. THE THEATER AT HERCULANEUM

1 *StErc*, xvii–xviii, xxvi–xxviii, pl. 4; none of these statues has been positively identified with those in the Museo Nazionale in Naples.

2 The arched niche with its three togate statues in the exterior façade of the cavea must have enhanced this impression of a circular temple. For a description of the area covered, see La Vega, 316 (July 9, 1765).

3 Gori, *Notizie* (Florence 1748) 3–5 (January 17, 1738): Venuti to Gori. Venuti determined the stepped remains were too high for stairs and so could only be seats for a theater. In his later *Descrizione . . .* (Rome 1748) he tends to confuse the antiquities found some

months later in the excavations around the Basilica with those of the theater. Other errors of chronology and provenance render Venuti a generally unreliable source for this work.

4 This is either the plan Alcubierre submitted on May 13, 1739 (*StErc*, 23–24), "which I was able to form with great difficulty of the tunnels and edifice of the ancient theater of Resina" and on which all the findspots were noted, or the "plan of the theater and first tunnels at Resina" submitted on July 13, 1739 (*StErc*, 37), unless these are one and the same.

5 This must be the same ramp into the theater described in a letter to the Royal Society of London: "You are first conducted down a narrow passage scarcely wide enough for two persons to pass; and in a gradual slope, to the depth of about 65 feet [19.5 m.] perpendicular. Here is shown a great part of the ancient theater, a building in the form of a horseshoe" (Freeman, "An extract of a letter dated May 2, 1750, from Mr. Freeman at Naples to the Right Honorable Lady Mary Capel relating to the ruins at Herculaneum," *PhilTrans* 47 [1751–52] 131–42).

6 ASN *CRA* 1544, Inc. 82, fols. 12–14: original French and Italian translation of legend to Bardet's plan (the full text is given later in this section); ASN *CRA* 1544, Inc. 82 fols. 1–11: Egizio's comments; *StErc*, 93 (July 20, 1742): Montealegre passes Egizio's comments, along with a corrected sketch plan, to Bardet. For Bellicard's work, see Gordon, "Bellicard's Notebook" 49–140, esp. pl. 9; the notebook's text was transcribed by C. Riopelle and A. Gordon for the Metropolitan Museum of Art in 1990.

7 Egizio's comments make it clear that Bardet had situated this sella in one of the tribunalia, not in the ima cavea.

8 Matteo Egizio (1674–1745) was named royal librarian to Charles of Bourbon in August 1740, a post he assumed after serving as chargé d'affaires at the court of France (1735–39). In 1729, he had edited the text of the decree of the Roman Senate concerning the cult of Bacchus, the *senatus consultum de Bacchanalibus* (*CIL* 1.2.581), and earned a reputation as an archaeologist as a result (*Senatus consulti de bacchanalibus, sive aeneae vetustae tabulae Musei Caesarei Vindobonensis explicatio* [Naples 1729]). He was actively involved in studying the results of the excavations in the same period as Venuti, dealing principally with the inscriptions; he corresponded with A.F. Gori (*Notizie*, 17–19 [February 27, 1742 and July 2, 1743]) and was not on the best terms with Martorelli, who accused him of destroying a marble tablet bearing an inscription thought to have been written in Etruscan but which was actually in Oscan (C. Buck, *A*

Grammar of Oscan and Umbrian [Boston 1904] #41). See esp. M.G. Castellano Lanzara, *La Real Biblioteca di Carlo di Borbone e il suo primo bibliotecario M. Egizio* (Naples 1942), and S. Ussia, *L'epistolario di Matteo Egizio e la cultura napoletana del primo Settecento* (Naples 1977) 61-66.

9 There is no mention of this discovery in the records, which are incomplete and sketchy for this period (*Giornale*, 211–14: most of the reports from January through March 1742 are missing), but it must have occurred between the time he drew the two plans; it is mentioned by several other visitors thereafter. There appears to be little solid evidence for establishing the theater as the provenance of the bronze statues and inscriptions of M. Calatorius (*Giornale*, 215 [December 21, 1743 and January 9, 1744]; MN. 5597; *CIL* 10.1447) and L. Mammius Maximus (*Giornale*, 215 [December 24, 1743]; MN. 5591; *CIL* 10.52), although their discovery came too late to be included on Bardet's plan; cf. M. Fuchs, *Untersuchungen zur Ausstattung römischer Theater in Italien und den Westprovinzen des Imperium Romanum* (Mainz am Rhein 1987) 29. None of the later drawings of the theater make reference to them (Weber, F. La Vega, Mazois), nor are they mentioned in the "Notizia degli oggetti rinvenuti nel teatro di Ercolano" (*StErc*, xxix), a document compiled by P. La Vega. Their location here has been based on Mommsen's annotation in volume 10 of the *CIL*.

10 Allroggen-Bedel, "Dokumente," 155; text of ASN *Raccolta Piante e Disegni*, Cart. 24, nn. 3–4: "*Esplication: ABC* – Est un Theatre Construit de Brique et de pierre douce, lequel peut contenir environ deux mille personnes asises, *D* – Sont six peds d'esteaux Revestües de marbre, sur les quelles il y avoit des statües de Bronze a Cheval de grandeur naturelle, *E* – Sont les Vomitoires, avec des petits dégreés par les quels on dessondoit a chacun des grans, et dans l'orchestre, *F* – Sont deux petittes places ou Tribunes pavées de marbre blanc, *G* – Est l'orchestre pavé de beau marbre affricain, *H* – Est le procenium ou Pulpitum que jay trouvé fait debois, et sur le quel joüoient les acteur, cest proprement ceque nous appellons aujourdhuit le Theatre, *I* – Est une façade decorée de plusieurs ordres d'architecture et dont les Collonnes (dont jay trouvé quelques tronçons) estoient de jaspe, ou marbre affricain, Cette façade sap [*sic*] sappelloit Postscenium, cetoit ou les acteurs sabilloient."

11 Maffei, *Tre lettere*, 35–36: "La seconda lettere sopra le nuove scoperte d'Ercolano al B. De Rubeis" (November 10, 1747).

12 The best secondary source for the period 1742 to 1746 is the letters of J. Russell, *Letters*, 1.149–81

##28–29 (October 20, 1742), 1.217–30 #34 (September 10, 1743). In Gori, *Notizie*, the dates of the correspondence jump from 1742 (Letter 10, of M. Egizio) to 1746 (Letter 11, anonymous).

13 Gori, *Notizie*, 75–76 (Letter 26, June 18, 1748).

14 G. Martorelli, "Relazione di ciocche si è ritrovato nel cavamento del vecchio Ercolano presso Napoli con brevi riflessioni," unpublished Ms., Biblioteca Nazionale di Napoli, XIII.B.37, fols. 24r.–32r. The date of this document, which he heavily emended, is difficult to establish, since it refers to the second equestrian statue of Balbus as still in need of restoration yet limits discussion of the finds because the "Accademia del Principe di Tarsia Spinelli" is at work on them. The Balbus statue was repaired by 1749, whereas the Accademia Ercolanese (if that is what he meant) was at work in 1755. These "relazione" are said to be notes taken during an excursion to the ruins to ascertain what it was possible to see in a single day. They appear, however, to be notes Martorelli made over the course of several years which he was in the process of compiling into a single text, evidently without regard for chronology. This suggests it was intended as more of a literary exercise than a scientific account of the ruins.

15 E.g., D'Ancora, *Prospetto storico-fisico*, 46. Ruggiero (*StErc*, xxi) summarizes the principal points of the debate.

16 The text used here is the Italian edition, *Notizie intorno alla città sotterranea discoperta alle falde del Monte Vesuvio* (Florence 1749) 28–30. D'Arthenay is probably using the French foot (*pied du roi*), which is equivalent to 0.32 m.

17 D'Arthenay, 28. The precise dimensions of the theater remain unpublished to this day.

18 D'Arthenay, 30–31.

19 Venuti, *Description*, 71–72.

20 De Brosses, *Lettres*, 58, 63–67.

21 De Brosses, *Lettres*, 66.

22 Cochin and Bellicard, 13 and 17.

23 Cochin and Bellicard, 12.

24 Cochin and Bellicard, 10.

25 Gordon, "Bellicard's notebook," 59, also noted that Bellicard had "copied, verbatim in places, from the published sources he [had] read, principally d'Arthenay, Venuti, and the others of earlier guidebooks." In fact Bellicard made one error in transcribing the exterior circumference of the theater as "200" feet (64.8 m.), instead of the 290 feet (93.9 m.) given by Bardet and d'Arthenay. This should not exclude the possibility, however, that Bellicard's original source had been Bardet's documents.

26 Maffei, *Tre lettere*, 34, 36.

27 F.S. Maffei, *De gli anfiteatri e singolarmente del* Veronese (Verona 1728); A.S. Mazzocchi, *In mutilum Campani amphitheatri titulum, aliasque nonnullas Campanas inscriptiones* (Naples 1727).

28 Venuti, *Description*, 56; De Brosses, *Lettres*, 61–62.

29 Cochin and Bellicard, 11, 18.

30 A. Lumisden, *Remarks on the antiquities of Rome and its environs* (London 1812) 477 (April 18, 1750).

31 F. Trouard, "Notes sur mon voyage," Unpublished Ms., Fonds Doucet 98 fols. 26 and 57 (Bibl. de l'Institut d'Art et d'Archéologie, Paris), as quoted in *Pompei e gli architetti francesi dell' Ottocento* (Naples 1981) 8.

32 Martorelli, "Relazione," fols. 32r. and 25r.: "Everyone would like a trench or excavation to be made from above rather than through underground tunnels in order to observe the sought-after design of the theater, but visual inspection makes clear that this is practically impossible, both because the houses of the inhabitants of Resina are on top, and because not even the strength of the Romans would be sufficient to cast into the sea the vast amount of Vesuvian material more than 100 meters high."

33 *Giornale*, 279–80 (March 14, 1750), 281 (April 4, 1750): work resumes in the theater. It should be noted that this coincided with the new excavations in the belvedere of the Villa dei Papiri.

34 *StErc*, 106 (August 8–15, 1750).

35 *Giornale*, 284 (August 1, 1750).

36 ASN *CRA* 1539, Inc. 17 (October 17, 1750): Alcubierre to Fogliani.

37 Marble male: *Giornale*, 282 (May 21, 1750); the statue has not been identified in the Naples museum. Bronze female: *Giornale*, 285 (August 8, 1750), *StErc*, 106 (August 17–22, 1750), found on August 19; Gori, *Admiranda* #30 (November 5, 1750), #33 (September 8, 1751); Ruesch 770; *CollMN* 1.2, 130–31 #120.

38 ASN *CRA* 1539, Inc. 18 (October 24, 1750): Weber to Fogliani. P. La Vega, in his "Notizie degli oggetti rinvenuti nel teatro" (*StErc*, xxix), gave the provenance of the bronze female as "the exterior of the theater." Pagano ("Teatro," 153) identified a statue base between the two pedestals for equestrian statues and gave its dimensions as 3.40 m. wide and 1.15 m. high. He also found elements he believed may have made up a small pedimental roof supported by pillars decorated with semicolumns. He would place the bronze Tiberius (MN. 5615) and Livia (? MN. 5612: "Agrippina Minor") on this pedestal as well, along with the bronze "Vestal" recovered by Alcubierre, although this later statue was in fact found nearer to the pedestals on the left-hand side. In such a reconstruction, the Claudius (MN. 5593)

would need to be located here as well, since all three were found in 1741 within only a few months of one another. Normally the provenance of all these statues is given as the Basilica. Such a reconstruction does not take into consideration the marble statues found here as well, though the three togate statues from the niche in the exterior facade, found in the first campaign of excavations, and the bronze equestrian statues, found in various spots at different times, indicate these two media very well may have been mixed in the decorative program of the theater.

39 *StErc*, pl. 3; xix; 116–17 (April 3 and 17, 1751): Weber mentions a plan of the theater; 119 (August 2, 1751): Paderni returns plan to Weber. Weber also had proposed building a wooden model of the theater, but he did not make one before 1763 (*StErc*, 113 [January 26, 1751]).

40 *StErc*, 327–28 (October 20 and 29, 1760): Weber to Tanucci. The properties were those of Gioacchino Priglia (alias Caruso), Andrea Borrelli, and Gennaro Cozzolino.

41 *StErc*, 331 (November 28, 1760): Tanucci to Weber. L. Vanvitelli (1700–1773) was the architect and builder of the Reggia at Caserta and its aqueduct, the Villa Campolieto in Resina, and numerous other projects for the Bourbon court.

42 *StErc*, 331–32 (December 4, 1760): Vanvitelli to Tanucci, at Naples.

43 *Stabiae*, 132–33 (September 10, 1760): Mazzocchi, Ignarra, and Carcani to Tanucci.

44 Open-air excavations at Pompeii began in 1763, but it was another sixty-eight years before they were instituted at Herculaneum. Piaggio, "Memorie," 8r. n. 4, gave the following perspective on Weber's proposal and the outcome:

All these different materials [in which the theater was buried] he examined and pondered, and according to their depth and from a test of their solidity, he established the time that would be needed to break it up and carry it off, in proportion to the number of workmen posted there. He measured all these buildings and . . . produced the total expenses, which I saw together with the plan, cross section, and measurements of the ground and of the size of the entire structure. Part of the Royal Road would have been diverted, and that which today is crooked and narrow would have been more magnificent and straight. The cost was calculated in the true spirit of economy; the undertaking was worth it, if it had been a thousand times more. But after all these labors it was viewed as a folly that would cost 5 million Neapolitan ducats, and so the project was rejected.

45 This may be the "general plan" completed on April 17, 1761 (*StErc*, 346).

46 *StErc*, 327 (October 35, 1760): The work was located between the wells of Bozza and Cozzolino. Bozza's well (also known as the Pozzo di Nocerino) was d'Elbeuf's original shaft into the theater, while the cultivated property of Cozzolino lay southwest of the theater, if Ruggiero's plan of nineteenth-century Resina (*StErc*, pl. 2, including La Vega's plan) is valid for this earlier period.

47 Pagano, "Teatro," 149, fig. 5a: the larger of the two rooms is 7.16 m. wide, the smaller is 2.28 m. wide, with evidence of a door 1.72 m. wide on the southwest side. These also correspond very closely to the dimensions shown on La Vega's plan, where the main structure is roughly 8.00 m. wide by 11.00 m. long and the porticoes about 4.00 m. wide; the whole building measures approximately 16.00 m. wide by 22.00 m. long. The dimensions of the second structure would be roughly 17.00 m. wide by 22.00 m. long. The form of this latter structure suggests it might be a pool or a piazza. La Vega's designation of "forum" might well encompass both structures and include the entire area to the southwest of the theater.

48 Marble relief: MN. 6692, *StErc*, 336 (February 11, 1761), see *Pompeji: Leben und Kunst in den Vesuvstädten* (*Villa Hügen, Essen*) (Recklingshausen 1973) 138 #181; Bronze horse: MN. 4894, *StErc*, 347 (April 24, 1761), *BdE* 2.251–53, pl. 65, *CollMN* 1.2, 140–41 #217; Alexander statuette: MN. 4996, *StErc*, 372 (October 22, 1761), *BdE* 2.235–41, pls. 61-62, *CollMN* 1.2, 140–41 #216. Several pieces were missing from the riderless horse, and some months were spent looking for these. The search included sieving the fill for small fragments, the earliest reference to this practice here (*StErc*, 348 [April 30, 1761]). As told by Piaggio, "Memorie," 71r., this was the incident in which Alcubierre ran to Portici to report the news to the court, believing it was another life-size equestrian statue, only to find it was just a statuette (see Chapter 7 in this volume, "Dearth and Discord").

49 *StErc*, 381–82 (January 21, 1762).

50 *StErc*, 387–420 (May 8, 1762–August 6, 1763); SNSP "Notizie istoriche," 95v. (May 8, 1762). The area under excavation is referred to as having no houses above it (*StErc*, 397 [October 30, 1762]), which technically is not the case with the area immediately north of the theater, where Weber appears to have been excavating, but would be true of the area to the west-southwest. The portico must be the one illustrated on Weber's unfinished plan of the theater as running behind the stage building and flanking the open area to the west of theater; La Vega

illustrated this on his plan as well. Piaggio, "Memorie," 2r., reported that Weber believed the Balbi had constructed the Villa dei Papiri and that this had extended over a wide area, being "near the theater, adjacent to a great piazza in the middle of which was the equestrian statue of M.N. Balbus." Weber probably got this idea from a plan Alcubierre had finished on January 5, 1747, on which he illustrated everything found in the previous year, including the "building in the city of Herculaneum where the marble equestrian statues were found," which he believed was the forum (ASN *CRA* 1538 Inc. 108; *Giornale*, 245).

51 *StErc*, 376–77 (December 1 and 5, 1761).

52 SNSP "Notizie istoriche," 95v. (April 3, 1762).

53 Piaggio, "Memorie," 65v. n. 2.

54 *StErc*, 395–96 (October 12, 1762). Piaggio, "Memorie," 65v. n.2, believed both Alcubierre and Paderni had joined forces to oppose Weber's work here, but this seems unlikely and may stem from Piaggio's known antipathy for Paderni.

55 *StErc*, 390 (July 17, 1762).

56 *StErc*, 401–2 (December 11, 1762).

57 Tanucci, 11.599 (December 14, 1762).

58 Tanucci, 11.653 (January 4, 1763).

59 *StErc*, 403 (January 8, 1763): Tanucci to Weber and Paderni; 404 (January 22, 1763): Tanucci to Weber.

60 *StErc*, 411 (May 7, 1763); ASN *Archivio Borbone* I. Fasc. 17, fol. 93r. (June 28, 1763); Allroggen-Bedel, "Tanucci," 528.

61 *CIL* 10.1444 = MN. 3740: L ANNIVS MAMMIANVS RVFVS IIVIR QVINQ THEATR(um) ORCHESTR(am) DE SVO; Guadagno, "Epigrafico II," 146–47.

62 *StErc*, 417–34 (June 25, 1763–January 14, 1764).

63 *StErc*, 432 (November 26 and 28, 1763).

64 Archivio storico, Soprintendenza Archeologica di Napoli e Caserta, *Relazione 1763–1764* (November 27, 1763); because the archives were being reorganized at the time of consultation (1990), the *cartella* number was unavailable.

65 Teatro Antico di Ercolano con sue Scene; Sotter(ranea) Pal. 76 in Portici à 5. Mi(gli) Lev(ante) da Napoli sul Golfo del Mediter(raneo). Lon(gitudine) 31.34′. Lat(itudine) 40.53′. Delin(eata) dal Ing(egnere) Ord(inario) di S(ua) M(aiesta) 1763; *Spiegazione*: *1 à 4*. Pilastri che reggono la sommità; *5 à 8*. Balconi dietro il Corridojo; *9. 10*. Corridojo avanti i Sedili; *11. 12*. Sedili Superiori; *13*. Sommità della Scala Principale; *14*. Ingresso alla sudetta Scala; *15. à 21*. Passaggi dal Corridojo alli Sedili; *22*. Luogo dell' Iscrizzione di Ruffo; *23. à 28*. Cunei o Quartieri de i Sedili frà le Scalinate; *29. à 35*. Sommità de i

Scalini per dove si passa alli Sedili Superiori; *36. à 38*. Sommità delle Scalette al Lastrico; *39. 40*. Pedagne de i Cavalli di Bronzo; *41. 42*. Gradone largo, di passo; *43*. Rivestimento di marmo; *44. 45*. Piano declinante all' Orchestra; *46. à 48*. Vltimi Gradoni all' Orchestra; *49. à 51*. Orchestra con pavimento di marmo; *52. 53*. Luogo delle Iscrizzioni; *54. 55*. Muro alto 4. pal:, appoggio del Pulpito del Proscenico, guarnito di marmo; *56*. Cataratta al Canale dell' acqua; *57. 58*. Balconi dei Senatori; *59. 60*. Scalini per andare alle Scene; *61. 62*. Cardine di Bronzo coll' asse delle Macchine triangolari per mutazione di Scena; *63. à 66*. Colonne di marmo con base Attica; *67. 68*. Ponte lastricato sopra travi; *69. 70*. Porta Reale; *71. 72*. Porte Forastieri; *73. à 77*. Frontispizio di un Palazzo, Facciata delle Scene, con 4. Nicchi, guarnita di marmi coll' Piedestallo; *78. à 80*. Altre tre Porte; *81. 82*. Piede della Scala al Portico; *83. 84*. Portico per ricovorarsi dalla Piggia [sic]; *85. 86*. Canale d'acqua, e Colonnato; *87*. Recipiente dello Scolo; *88. 89*. Spasseggio scoperto per affacciarsi al Foro più basso di 35. pal.; *90*. Foro dove era il Cavallo che si conserva nell' entrata del Real Palazzo.

66 One of these must be the fragmentary CALATO (*CIL* 10.1441; MN. 3739) found in the orchestra in 1762 (*StErc*, 388 [June 17 and 23, 1762]); another should be *CIL* 10.1442 (ANNIO), found in Alcubierre's earlier excavations. The inscriptions of Balbus (*CIL* 10.1427) and Pulcher (*CIL* 10.1424) still *in situ* above the paradoi were found by La Vega in 1768.

67 Ruggiero (*StErc*, xxiii) could find no evidence for these in his day.

68 "Museo," 88 (Balbi statues), 108 (quadriga). The horse is MN. 4904 (*BdE* 2.257; Ruesch 775), a pastiche of numerous fragments from several horses. The provenance of the quadriga now is believed to have been the Basilica.

69 Pagano, "Teatro," 153, fig. 5; and *idem*, "Ricerche sull' impianto urbano di Ercolano," in *Ercolano 1738–1988: 250 anni di ricerca archeologica* (Rome 1993) 596. The rooms are constructed of reticulate and appear to antedate the porticus.

70 Eleven is the sum total of plans he drew while at the excavations. Piaggio, "Memorie," 16r. n. 4, states that Weber had constructed his wooden model on the basis of his "grand plan," perhaps his unfinished plan of 1763, and "under the direction of celebrated dilettantes of architecture," presumably including Berardo Galiani. The model in wood and cork now in the storerooms at the excavations at Herculaneum was made in October 1808, by D. Padiglioni (Pagano, "Teatro," 147–48, fig. 6).

71 *StErc*, xxxi–xxxiii, "Indicazione di una pianta del Teatro." Weber believed the theater was constructed after 65 because of Seneca's remark (*Nat. Quaest.* 6.2: "Herculanensis oppidi pars ruit") that Herculaneum had been destroyed by an earthquake, which Weber dates here to February 5, 65, the same date and reference he used in his monograph on the Villa di San Marco. The earthquake is now dated securely to A.D. 62.

72 *StErc*, xxiii–xxiv, "Giudizio di Francesco La Vega sul lavoro del Weber."

73 F. Nicolini, "I manoscritti dell' abate Galiani," *La Critica* 1 (1903) 395, discusses a collection of manuscripts in his possession at that time which included notes and drafts prepared by Berardo Galiani for his translation of Vitruvius and for a "great work on architecture" which he never completed. Nicolini's manuscripts are now in the SNSP, though only Ms. 31-C-27, "Breve notizie sulla storia delle arti," could be traced, and this makes no mention of his work on the theater at Herculaneum.

74 Winckelmann, *Nachrichten*, #21.

75 Winckelmann, *Nachrichten*, #10. The references to Weber's working in his free time and to his project to uncover the theater suggest as well the influence of Piaggio, who mentioned these in his own later "Memorie."

76 Winckelmann, *Nachrichten*, ##11–19.

77 Winckelmann, *Nachrichten*, ##19–33.

78 Winckelmann, *Nachrichten*, #34. For Vitruvius's canons on the proportions of these columns, see Vitr. 5.9.2–3. The "subterranean vaults" and "cellar" may be the vaulted rooms of reticulate work found below the porticus (Pagano, "Teatro," 153, fig. 5).

79 *PAH* I.i.158–69 (July 25, 1764–April 27, 1765).

80 *StErc*, 456–57 (February 14, 1765): B. Galiani to Tanucci.

81 *StErc*, 459–61 (March 22, 1765).

82 *StErc*, 496 (May 20, 1769); the water table proved too high, and La Vega may eventually have given up.

83 *StErc*, 514 (July 2, 1774).

84 *StErc*, 500 (April 7, 1770).

85 SNSP, Ms. 12201 ("Parte Inferior" = 0.553 m. W × 0.383 m. H), 12202 ("Parte Superiore" = 0.545 m. W × 0.380 m. H), 12222 (Exterior elevation = 0.770 m. W × 0.460 m. H). The dimensions of the folios seem designed for engraving for publication in *Le antichità*. Pagano, "Teatro," 146–48, suggests the plans were virtually complete by April 1769 when La Vega showed them to King Joseph II of Austria (for this visit, see *PAH* I.i. 228–31), but this does not explain why excavation continued for several more years.

86 *StErc*, 519 (April 15, 1777); this does not necessarily mean that he had finished them only recently; they formed part of a group of twenty-five plans that included the Temple of Isis at Pompeii, excavated in 1765–66. La Vega's plans were published for the first time more than two hundred years later (Pagano, "Teatro," figs. 7–9).

87 F. Piranesi, *Il teatro d' Ercolano* (Rome 1783). Difficulties in taking notes and making sketches are noted in "Museo," 102. The curious fact that they produced such detailed plans regardless of these prohibitions has never been satisfactorily explained; G.B. Piranesi's friendship with Paderni would not have been sufficient, and that F. Piranesi became consul of the Swedish embassy in Naples in 1794 would have had no bearing on the publication of these plans of the theater. See Allroggen-Bedel, "Piranesi e l'archeologia," 281–91.

EPILOGUE: WEBER'S PLACE IN THE HISTORY OF ARCHAEOLOGY IN THE VESUVIAN LANDSCAPE

1 L. Barletta, *Il Carnevale del 1764 a Napoli: Protesta e integrazione in uno spazio urbano* (Naples 1981), esp. 9–24; *Civiltà del '700 a Napoli* (Florence 1980) 2.308; F. Mancini, "Feste, apparati e spettacoli teatrali," in *Storia di Napoli* (Naples 1971) 8.674–82. For the famine, see especially Tanucci, *Lettere a Ferdinando Galiani*, 1.114–15 #56 (February 25, 1764); 1.120 #58 (March 10, 1764), where he blames the land, the incompetence of Neapolitan officials, and the avarice of grain hoarders; 1.128 #68 (April 14, 1764), where he discounted rumors of massive shortages, saying, "We have grain for all of May."

2 Piaggio, "Memorie," 1r., remarked that he had given Weber a room in his house near the excavations so that "returning from the dark bosom of these same [excavations] with his memory fresh, he could jot down all that had been discovered and then draw it more precisely," although this may have been during the period of excavations in the Villa dei Papiri. Elsewhere, Weber is said to have occupied a house across from the Villa Riario, one of the great "ville vesuviane" in Resina (La Vega, 303: the house originally belonged to Sportullo, the citizen of Resina who had caused Bardet such difficulties).

3 ASN *CRA* 1541, Inc. 3 (January 11, 1764), written by another hand, signed by Weber.

4 ASN *CRA* 1541, Inc. 3 (January 12, 1764), Weber to Tanucci, as the regent to King Ferdinand IV.

5 ASN *CRA* 1541, Inc. 3 (January 24 or 29, 1764), Unsigned:

Lieutenant Colonel, engineer, Don Carlos Weber stationed in the excavations of antiquities, explains that as a result of assiduous travail and application to the pledge of his incumbency, he has lost his customary health and his doctors recommend he retire from Resina to Naples in order to see if through a change of air and a methodical cure he might be able to recover. He supplicates Your Majesty that You deign to grant him twenty days of recuperation and assistance with the cost of acquiring a cure, since of his salary no more than 15 ducats remain per month, on account of the payments he must make to both his wife and his creditors. During his absence Don Rocco de Alcubierre can more frequently visit the excavations.

6 StErc, 435 and PAH I.ii.Addenda 4.146 (January 26, 1764): Corcoles receives his orders from Alcubierre. Paderni had gone to Rome on December 24, 1763, and probably did not return before February (PAH I.ii.Addenda 4.146).

7 ASN CRA 1541, Inc. 3, undated, unsigned: Weber to His Royal Majesty.

8 ASN CRA 1541, Inc. 3 (February 4, 1764), unsigned; this in fact may be the cover summary submitted with the previous letter to the king.

9 Russell, Letters, 1.228–29 #34 (September 10, 1743), for example, observes that "the fineness of the prospect, the fertility of the soil, the salubrity of the air in preserving and the virtue of the waters in restoring health, all conspire to induce multitudes to reside here constantly, and others to repair hither at proper seasons: insomuch that this tract of land, for the extent of it, is perhaps better inhabited than any other in all Italy."

10 La Vega, 115 (May 2, 1764); ASN CRA 1541, Inc. 41 (November 12, 1764): Corcoles suffered from an ocular discharge "he acquired as a result of the humidity."

11 R. Dubos and J. Dubos, The White Plague: Tuberculosis, man and society, 2d ed. (New Brunswick, N.J. 1987).

12 M. Cherniack, "Historical perspectives in occupational medicine: Pancoast and the image of silicosis," American Journal of Industrial Medicine 18 (1990) 599–612; "Diseases associated with exposure to silica and nonfibrous silicate minerals," Arch PatholLabMed 112 (July 1988) 673–720. This information was kindly supplied by Dr. Martha Warnock, pathologist, University of California at San Francisco Hospitals.

13 Dubos and Dubos, 29–30, quote an eighteenth-century edict from Naples outlining the strict regulations for dealing with patients diagnosed with tuberculosis and for handling decontamination of the premises.

14 Tanucci, Lettere a Ferdinando Galiani, 1.147 #71 (June 23, 1764), where Tanucci says that the end of May was so cold that there was snow and lightning, which led to an epidemic of fever in Naples that infected five hundred people per day for four weeks and left one hundred dead, and notes that the estimate for those who had died as a result of starvation was closer to fifty thousand, not the rumored 1 million.

15 PAH I.ii.Addenda 4.147 (March 10, 1764). Antonio Scognamillo later received 9 ducats for eighteen days sick leave (SNSP "Notizie istoriche," 103r. [November 12, 1764]).

16 SNSP "Notizie istoriche," 102r. (September 3, 1764). His widow, Isabella Montero, appealed for assistance from the court after his death, using as justification his thirty years in the excavations, his vision problems, and "other consequences of his poor health until his last days, and the deplorable state in which he left his three marriageable daughters" (ASN CRA 1541, Inc. 41 [November 12, 1764]). That not all these deaths were swift may be illustrated by the case of Corcoles's son, Filippo, who sought the air in Naples exactly a year after his father and returned to the excavations but did not die until more than a year later, on November 14, 1766 (SNSP "Notizie istoriche," 103v. [September 2, 1765]; StErc, 482 [November 15, 1766]).

17 Piaggio, "Memorie," 72r.–v.

18 Piaggio, "Memorie," 65v., n. 2.

19 Familienschriften von Weber, Schwyz, Kassenbuch 1757 Ital Reding: 28 gulden, 20 schillings given to the church for this service.

20 No certificate of death has been located. This would have indicated the parochial church that handled his corpse, if he had received a church burial. A likely site would be on Pizzafalcone, in one of the churches or chapels associated with the quarters of the Royal Guards, but inquiries here produced no results. An alternative possibility would be the church of his wife's family, in the "Nido" quarter of Naples, perhaps the parochial Chiesa della Rotonda near S. Domenico Maggiore. But since many of the parochial churches in this period have been destroyed or have lost this designation, it was deemed futile to conduct more than a brief investigation to locate documentation for Weber's burial. His brother, Franz Dominik (1717-1793), is buried on Capodimonte. For the problem with burial in Naples in this period in general, see Acton, 113.

21 Familienschriften von Weber, Schwyz. Karl We-

ber's holdings in Switzerland amounted to 3,065 gulden in 1765. According to these archives, Franz Dominik already had given Karl 489 gulden on October 26, 1756, to help him pay off his debts. As a rough measure of the worth of a gulden at that time, a cow was worth 32 gulden in 1732. Alcubierre's widow received an annual pension of 150 ducats, which was equivalent to his monthly salary as field marshall (Fernandez Murga, "Alcubierre," 33).

22 La Vega, 114 (April 29–30, 1764), F. Corcoles referred to Aniello as Weber's "maestro di casa" and confidant.

23 ASN *CRA* 1541, Inc. 42 (August 27, 1764): Renner, military engineer Joseph Capri, superintendent Francesco Ruiz, and Field Marshal Tschudi to Tanucci; Domingo de Custor, a captain of the Royal Guards, was present at the division on behalf of Weber's brother.

24 ASN *CRA* 1541, Inc. 42 (April 24, 1764): Nicolas Pirelli to Tanucci accepting the assignment. La Vega assumed his duties as supervisor of the excavations the following day.

25 ASN *CRA* 1541, Inc. 42 (Undated, unsigned; but probably in August 1764, by La Vega): "Having appeared at this Royal Villa on the eighth day of this month, the foreman who assists in the work at Città, Antonio Scognamillo, to acknowledge the number of plans and books he produced and submitted to the deceased engineer Don Carlo Weber, and to determine the number of the same which are missing, according to the orders given to me by Colonel Alcubierre, I have found the following lacking according to what he recalls:

Note of the Books which are missing from the Papers of Antiquities left by the deceased engineer Don Carlo Weber: One large book of drawings of buildings, painted ornaments, mosaics, inscriptions, etc., drawn in their proper colors [i.e, the monograph]; *From the excavations at Città:* 2 small books with explications and mosaic pavements found in the antiquities found on the property of Don Vincenzo Grasso [i.e., the Praedia Iuliae Felicis], 2 books of antiquities discovered on the property of Diego Cuomo [i.e., the site of the statue of Diana], 1 book and a plan corresponding to the property of Minicale, 1 book and plan corresponding to the property of Maestro Botta Egira [Egiva ?] near the Polveriera [at Torre Annunziata]; *From the excavations of ancient Stabiae at Gragnano:* 2 small books of antiquities discovered on the property of Giuseppe Somma [i.e., the Villa di San Marco], 1 book and a drawing corresponding to the property of Grazia Stoppa, 1 book and a plan of the property of Don Pietro de Fusco, 1 book and a plan of the property of Don Peppe Combarato, 1 book and 2

plans of the property of Don Antonio Buonoduono, 1 book and a plan corresponding to the property of Don Gennaro Triso. Beyond this, he says he made a great quantity of plans of the ancient city of Herculaneum, but being so many, does not recall their number; all of which he also submitted to the deceased Weber. Lacking as well, according to this same Maestro Antonio Scognamillo, is a book and a plan corresponding to the Temple and antiquities of Pozzuoli. And moreover many drawings of mosaic pavements are missing."

26 ASN *CRA* 1541, Inc. 42 (August 16, 1764).

27 ASN *CRA* 1541, Inc. 42 (November 27, 1764): Dentice to Tanucci. Weber's widow does not figure in this investigation, suggesting she had maintained a house in Naples separate from the one Weber occupied in Resina. Dentice may have relied on his close connections with the excavations to buy up all the property around the Porta di Ercolana in Pompeii in the years just prior to its purchase by the state for expanding the open-air excavations. See *PAH* I.ii.Addenda 4, 169 (April 14, 1792): La Vega lists costs of acquiring land, much of which belongs to Dentice. His holdings are illustrated on the cadastral plan of 1807 by P. Scognamillo, "Mappa de' terreni che coprino la città di Pompei" (see Fig. 28).

28 Piaggio, "Memorie," 16r. n. 4. Piaggio also noted the difficulty of redoing the plans, since the excavated areas had been refilled.

29 Picillo also helped transport antiquities from the excavations to Camillo Paderni at the museum (e.g., *StErc*, 185 [March 24, 1756]).

30 ASN *CRA* 1541, Inc. 42 (April 9, 1765): Dentice to Tanucci; La Vega, 111–15 (April 27–May 2, 1764), who also learned that Weber had a soldier to carry his notebooks and instruments for him. Alcubierre told La Vega that he had not seen Weber's plans of the theater at Herculaneum until after his death, when Galiani showed them to him (La Vega, 111).

31 Archivio storico, Soprintendenza Archeologica di Napoli e Caserta, Ms. (March 7, 1765), unsigned; *PAH* I.ii.Addenda 4.149–50 (March 9, 1765); *Stabiae*, 211–12 (March 11, 1765): La Vega to Dentice; ASN *CRA* 1541, Inc. 42 (April 9, 1765): Dentice to Tanucci.

32 *Stabiae*, 207–8 (August 20, 1764); *StErc*, 448 (August 20, 1764); Barnabei, 765. Weber's application to the Accademia in 1759 included 32 plans. Only 15 of Weber's plans are available in published and unpublished form today, apart from the small sketches which appeared in his reports: the plan and 5 drawings of mosaics from the Villa dei Papiri and the drawing of the vault from the Templum Mater

Deum in Herculaneum (StErc, pl. 8); the rough draft, finished plan, and axonometric view of the Praedia Iuliae Felicis; the versions of the Villa di San Marco plan and the elevations of the two fountain niches that exist separate from the monograph, and the plans of the Villa del Pastore and the Villa di Arianna at Stabiae (Stabiae, pls. 1–4). Of Scognamillo's work, only the fragmentary plan of the Praedia Iuliae Felicis is known.

33 StErc, 448 (August 20, 1764). Of these 11, only that from 1750 and the unfinished plan of 1763 remain.

34 ASN CRA 1541, Inc. 42 (August 27, 1764, and May 10, 1765); Stabiae, 211 (March 9, 1765).

35 The document is filed at the present time, together with his monograph, in the library of the Museo Nazionale in the Soprintendenza Archeologica di Napoli e Caserta (XXI.A.34).

36 ASN CRA Primo Inventario 868, Inc. 2 (1765).

37 MN. 2615; schematic copy in CTP 5 (1981) 116–17: "PIANTA DI PARTE DELLA CITTA ED ADIACENZE DI POMPEI, Quale si fa scavare dal Re delle Due Sicilie Ferdinando IV. Il sito dove resta tale Città antica, è nei confini della Terra di lavoro e Principato citra, e chiamasi questo di presente la Città del Rapillo, o semplicemente Rapillo. Le piante segnate con nero sono delle fabriche antiche che si trovano scoperte. Le segnate con fuliggine sono delle fabriche antiche scavate già e poi ricoperte. Il colorito rossa dinota le fabriche moderne pertinenti a varie persone. INDICE, Per i spiegazione delle fabriche antiche: A. Strada che conduceva da Ercolano a Pompei; B. Due case Pseudurbane distinte in diversi piani; C. Vari sepolcri; D. Porta della Città; E. Piccolo facello; F. Strade della Città per la magior parte seliciate; G. Case nel margine della Città, varie di queste distinte in piu piani; H. Suferuzione che ora serve di cellajo; I. Altre case e botteghe; K. Tempio della Dea Iside; L. Teatro; M. Portico al paro del superiore corridore del teatro; N. Peristilio dove nel suo giro stanze servite per alloggiare i soldati; O. Teatro coperto, o sia Odeo; P. Altro portico che unisce il gran teatro all' Odeo, Il peristilio, l'odeo ed il portico ora nominato restano in un piano al paro del parco del teatro grande; Q. Tempio quale si è trovato tutto diruto; R. Sacello; S. Edificio con bagni; T. Anfiteatro. Secondo l'indizj, l'antica città si estendea piu della parte settentrionale; ma come non si sono fatte delle ricerche da tale lato non si è stimato d'ingrandire inutilm.to il disegno. Per i spiegazione dello stato presente del Rapillo: 1. Strada regia che da Napoli porta a Regio di Calabria; 2. Pietra che segna la distanza di dodici miglia da Napoli; 3. Due strade che conducono al paese di Bosco; 4. Canale parte coperto e parte scoperto pel quale dalla sorgente del Fiume

Sarno scorre l'aqua ad uso della fabrica dell' Armi, e di altre manufattorie che restano alla Torre dell' Annunz.ta; 5. Podere di D. Gio: Milano; 6. Podere di monistero de' PP Celestini della Torre dell' Annunziata; 7. Podere del Sig: Agnello Palmieri; 8. Podere del D. Giacinto Vacearo; 9. Podere e fabbriche appartenenti a D. Giacomo Girace; 10. Osteria detta del Rapillo del Principe del Genzano; 11. Podere del Principe Dentici; 12. Podere con cellajo di D. Michele Imparato; 13. Podere di D. Luigi Montemurro; 14. Podere con cellajo del Re; 15. Podere con cellajo del Sig: Parrelli; 16. Podere del Sig: Samuele Bossa; 17. Podere di Pasquale Cocchi; 18. Podere e casino di D. Francesco D'Ambra; 19. Podere di D. Crescenzo Salvatti; 20. Podere delle Monache di Santa Maria del Grado di Conca. Dall' Ingeg.re Direttore de' Reali Scavi di D. Francesco La Vega." Note that "J" was omitted from the list of buildings. This plan probably is derived from one drawn up in 1769, as the names of the property owners differ from those on P. Scognamillo's cadastral plan of 1807. Eschebach, 69, dates the plan pre-1769; CTP 5 (1981) 116, concluded that Pietro had updated the plan to include the sites excavated through 1809.

38 In Rosini, Dissertazione isagogicae; Rosini was named a member of the Accademia in 1787.

39 La Vega, 112. Archivio storico, Soprintendenza Archeologica di Napoli e Caserta, Ms. (April 6, 1765): La Vega reported that he had five plans of Herculaneum drawn by Alcubierre, two dating from 1747, two from 1748, and one from 1749, but did not state what they illustrated. Those from 1747 probably depicted the "forum" and the sites excavated in 1746 (Giornale, 245 [January 5, 1747]), and the plan of the theater (StErc, pl. 4); the plan of four insulae dates from 1749 (StErc, pl. 7).

40 StErc, 481 (October 25, 1766). In 1784, he obtained copies of Bardet's excavation reports in order to determine what inscriptions were found under his tenure (Stabiae, 295 [November 5, 1784]).

41 D. Romanelli, Viaggio a Pompeio, a Pesto e di ritorno ad Ercolano ed a Pozzuoli, 2d ed. (Naples 1817) 247.

42 De Jorio, Ercolano, 47; though this remark may be based on what Winckelmann had said earlier. T. Hogg, Two hundred and nine days, or, The journal of a traveller on the continent (London 1827) 2.57–61, complained that de Jorio had spent his entire visit to the Naples Museum trying to sell him a copy of this book.

43 Stabiae, vii. Minervini, 33, noted that de Jorio had acquired the plan from his friend Andrea Serao, who found it "among some old papers of a client." Coincidentally, the Italian translation from the Latin

of A.S. Mazzocchi's "Dissertazione preliminare delle origini di Ercolano e dei luoghi vicini" (Biblioteca Nazionale di Napoli Ms. IX.A.61) was completed by his friend Francesco Serao, so perhaps both documents had first passed into the hands of this family. The text is published in Fiorelli's *Giornale degli scavi di Pompei*, 25–40, 65-80, 97–120.

44 C.J. Beloch, *Campanien: Topograghie, Geschichte und Leben der Umgebung Neapels im Altertum* (Berlin 1879, 215.

45 C. Justi, *Winckelmann: sein Leben, seine Werke und seine Zeitgenossen* (Leipzig 1866–72) 2.186.

46 *Stabiae*, vii; this list has not been recovered. W. Ternite acquired several of Paderni's sketches in 1824, but these ended up in the Stattliche Museen in Berlin; see *Italienische Reise*, 392–94, 434–36. A number of documents ended up in the private libraries of a Neapolitan lawyer, Adolfo Parascandolo, and a priest, Vincenzo Cuomo. Both collections are now in the library of the Società Napoletana di Storia Patria.

47 Archivio Storico, Soprintendenza Archeologica di Napoli, Ms. VII.C.4., Inc. 15 (January 18, 1873?). La Vega did not work in the villa, so these must be drawings of mosaics or paintings from elsewhere. Presumably Patturelli, whose address is given as Strada Miracoli 40, in Naples, had ties to Ferdinand II, who reigned from 1830 to 1859, rather than Ferdinand I, who died in 1825. He may have been related to Ferdinando Patturelli, an architect whose book on Caserta and San Leucio was published in 1826 by the Reale Stamperia.

48 Archivio Storico, Soprintendenza Archaeologica di Napoli, Ms. VII.C.4., Inc. 15 (June 22, 1874): Initial appraisal of plans provided to Ministero, that cost was too great; *ibid.* (July 8, 1874): Letter from Ministro della Istruzione Pubblica, evidently addressed to Fiorelli: "From the information furnished to me . . . it appears clear that it is not convenient to make such an acquisition."

49 *Stabiae*, viii.

50 Soprintendenza di Pompei, Fascio 12 (EX XIII.A5) fasc. I: "Original drawings of the antiquities of Herculaneum, Pompei and Stabiae which in the epoch of their discovery were executed by Colonel Weber, in charge at that time in drawing up the plans of the excavations from the aforementioned ancient sites: *Ercolano:* 1) Plan at a large scale of a country house located beneath the property of the Augustinian Fathers, in whose margins are diligently described in idiomatic Spanish the various objects found there. 2) Eight details relating to the above plan, bound in a volume. 2000.00 Lire. *Pompei:* 1) A plan of a portion of the buildings and streets beneath

the "lapillo" of Città located between Scafati and Torre Annunziata near the Sarno River, with a most accurate description in Italian of the places and the date of the various precious ancient artifacts recovered there. 2) Draft and complete description of the same plan. 3) The same plan "a cavaliere," with the elevation viewed at a 45-degree angle from the southeast in the manner of a model, of a portion of the buildings and streets beneath the "lapillo" of Città, etc. as above, on which is indicated clearly the precise location of the aforementioned buildings, as well as their individual parts and adjacent streets. 4) Two details of pavements from the Temple of Giunone. 600.00 Lire. *Stabia:* 1) Plan of the amphitheater with descriptions appended. 2) Plan of a portion of said underground city, located between Gragnano and Castellamare, at Barano or Ripa, which begins at the ruined Church of San Marco, with an exact descriptiion of the same, as well as the objects recovered there. 3) Plan of another portion of said ancient underground city, located as above, with an appended description of its individual parts and the objects excavated there. 4) Plan of a different part of said city, located as above, with a diligent description of the multiple objects found in the individual locations of the same. 5) A complete draft of the plan of this last portion. 6) Another plan in supplement to the preceding with a description in idiomatic Spanish of the other various objects buried there. 2500.00 [Lire]. *Manuscript Volume* containing moreover the following three plates, that is: Plate 1, plan of a portion of ancient Stabiae, situated between Gragnano and Castellamare at Barano or Ripa, which begins at the ruined Church of San Marco, with an exact description of the same and the multitude of objects which existed there. Plate 2, Plan and elevation of a niche with a mosaic scene representing Europa, relating to a spot in the piazza indicated in the previous plan with the letter H. number 6. Plate 3, Plan and elevation of a similar niche also with a mosaic scene representing Phryxis, also relating to the aforementioned plan indicated in the same piazza with the number 5. A complete description with numerous specific annotations regarding the same antiquities of Stabia, which these plates illustrate marvelously, as well as a historical and satisfactory description of the various ancient eruptions of our Vesuvius. 400.00 Lire."

51 For example, in 1885 Ruggiero (*StErc*, 537) calculated the purchase price for 9,032.93 square m. of property in Herculaneum to begin the open-air excavations of 1827 at 16,063.75 lire (where 1 ducat = 4.25 lire); presumably this represents the price in Ruggiero's day. His book, in which these plans were

published, cost 60 lire in 1891. The annual budget, excluding workmen's salaries, for renewed excavations in 1907 was set at 600 lire, with 20,000 lire for acquiring land (*London Times* [November 14, 1907] 5).

52 *Stabiae*, 137.

53 G. De Petra, "I monumenti della villa ercolanese," in *Pompei e la regione sotterrata* (Naples 1879) 251–71, with the complete text but only a schematic version of the plan.

54 Piaggio, "Memorie," 66v.

55 Barnabei, 767. See also Strazzullo, "Documenti," 280; Fernandez Murga, "Alcubierre," 32–35. Alcubierre was appointed brigadier general in 1772 and governor of the Castel del Carmine in Naples; on November 9, 1777, he was named field marshall of the royal army; he died on March 14, 1780, and was buried in the chapel at Castel del Carmine.

56 *PAH* I.ii.Addenda 2–3, 95–133; *Stabiae*, 297–359, pls. 5–19, although La Vega tended to group objects by room and not mark as many findspots as Weber.

57 *PAH* I.ii.Addenda 4, 165 (February 13, 1784).

For La Vega's life and work, see Castaldi, 180–84; Fernandez Murga, "Alcubierre," 30–33, 35; Fernandez Murga, *Carlos III*, 139–43. Fiorelli published portions of La Vega's personal diary covering the first months of his new post at the excavations in 1861 (see La Vega, 110–20). La Vega was born in Rome on June 25, 1737, became a captain in 1785, and died in Portici on December 24, 1804, where he was buried at Santa Maria della Natività in the royal villa. The report of his preventing others from drawing and publishing the ruins seems unfounded. As noted earlier, Giovanni Battista Piranesi and his son, Francesco, visited the ruins of Pompeii and Herculaneum and soon published detailed, if not always accurate, and often imaginative, plans and views of the ruins along the Via Consulare and of the Temple of Isis in Pompeii, and also of the theater at Herculaneum, the latter of these the most widely available until Mazois's. It is unlikely that G.B. Piranesi could have drafted these initially without La Vega's consent. La Vega's map of the Gulf of Pozzuoli appears in J.C. Richard de Saint-Non's *Voyage pittoresque, ou, description des Royaumes de Naples et de Sicile* (Paris 1781–86).

Works cited

MANUSCRIPTS

ASN *Casa Reale Amministrativa* Categorie Diverse, vol. 461, III Inventario: Paderni, C. "Diario de' Monumenti antichi, rinvenuti in Ercolano, Pompei e Stabia dal 1752 al 1799 formata dal Sig.r Camillo Paderni, Custode del Real Museo Ercolanese in Portici, e proseguito dal Signor Francesco La Vega."

Biblioteca Nazionale di Napoli, Ms. XIII.B.37: Martorelli, G. "Relazione di ciocche si è ritrovato nel cavamento del vecchio Ercolano presso Napoli con brevi riflessioni fatta da Giacomo Martorelli."

Museo Nazionale di Napoli, Soprintendeza Archeologica di Napoli e Caserta, Ms. XXI.A.34: Weber, K. "Le Piante di Alcvni Edificj Sotterranei delle Città di Stabia, Pompeiana ed Hercolana con le Pitture, Statve, Monete, Vasi, ed Altri Monvmenti situati nelle Tavole, che indicano i luoghi dove si sono ritrovati. Con un succinto ricordo della serie degli anni degli Incendj Vesuviani dal tempo di Abramo sino al 1760 di G.C. come causa delle ruine delle antiche città e altre. Tomo III." and "Libro degli Edificj Sotterranei d'Ercolano."

SNSP *Fondo Cuomo* 2-6-2, Doc. 1, fols. 1r.–63r.: "Breve descrizzione del Monte Vesuvio e della diversità de nomi di Esso."

SNSP *Fondo Cuomo*; 2-6-2, Doc. 2, fols. 67r. – 110r.: "Notizie istoriche relative agli scavi d'antichità."

SNSP *Fondo Cuomo* 2-6-2, Doc. 16, fols. 144r. – 145v.: "Ragguaglio storico del principio ed avvanzamento delli scavi . . . ."

SNSP *Fondo Cuomo* 2-6-2, Doc. 17, fols. 148r. –

151v.: "Motivo che diede principio alla scoperta della città Ercolano."

SNSP Ms. 20-5-3, "Rapporti originali di Weber ed altri impiegati agli scavi di Pompei dal 1753 al 1804." 3 vols.

SNSP Ms. 31-C-21: Piaggio, A. "Memorie del Padre Ant.o Piaggi [*sic*] impiegato nel R. Museo di Portici relative alle antichità, e Papiri p. anno 1769. 1771."

BOOKS

Abiti, S. "Arms," 2.430–34. In *The golden age of Naples: Art and civilization under the Bourbons (1734–1805)*. 2 vols. Detroit 1981.

Acton, H. *The Bourbons of Naples (1734–1825)*. London 1956.

Adamo Muscettola, S. "Nuove letture borboniche: I Nonii Balbi ed il Foro di Ercolano." *Prospettiva* 28 (1982) 2–16.

Alisio, G. "I siti reali," 1.72–85. In *Civiltà del '700 a Napoli*. Florence 1980.

Allroggen-Bedel, A. "Dokumente des 18. Jahrhunderts zur Topographie von Herculaneum." *CronErc* 13 (1983) 139–58.

"Der Hausherr der 'Casa dei Cervi' in Herculaneum." *CronErc* 5 (1975) 99–103.

"Herkunft und ursprünglicher Dekorationszusammenhang einiger in Essen ausgestellter Fragmente von Wandmalereien," 115–24. In B. Andreae and H. Kyrieleis, eds. *Neue Forschungen in Pompeji*. Recklinghausen 1975.

"Die Malereien aus dem Haus *Insula Occidentalis*, 10." *CronPomp* 2 (1976) 144–83.

"Piranesi e l'archeologia nel reame di Napoli," 281–92. In *Piranesi e la cultura antiquaria: Gl' antecedente e il contesto* (Atti del Convegno 14–17 Nov. 1979). Rome 1985.

"Gli scavi borbonici e la ricostruzione delle decorazioni parietali," 911–912. In A. Barbet *et al.* "Premier rapport sur l'etude de la Villa San Marco à Stabies." *MEFRA* 95.2 (1983) 909–36.

"Das sogenannte Forum von Herculaneum und die borbonischen Grabungen von 1739." *CronErc* 4 (1974) 97–109.

"Tanucci e la cultura antiquaria del suo tempo," 521–36. In *Bernardo Tanucci: Statista, letterato, giurista.* 2 vols. Naples 1986.

"Die Wandmalereien aus der Villa in Campo Varano (Castellammare di Stabia)." *RömMitt* 84 (1977) 27–89, pls. 1–53.

Allroggen-Bedel A., and H. Kammerer-Grothaus. "Il Museo ercolanese di Portici," 83–127. In *La Villa dei Papiri. CronErc* 13 Suppl. 2. Naples 1983.

D'Ancora, G. *Prospetto storico-fisico degli scavi di Ercolano e di Pompei e dell' antico e presente stato del Vesuvio, per guida de' forestieri.* Naples 1803.

Le antichità di Ercolano. Naples 1988.

Le antichità di Ercolano esposte con qualche spiegazione: Bronzi di Ercolano. 2 vols. Naples 1767–1771; *Le pitture antiche d'Ercolano e contorni incise con qualche spiegazione.* 5 vols. Naples 1757–79.

Antikensammlungen im 18. Jahrhundert. Berlin 1981.

D' Arthenay, Moussinot. *Notizie intorno alla città sotterranea discoperta alle falde del Monte Vesuvio.* Florence 1749.

Ashby, T. "Sixteenth century drawings of Roman building attributed to Andreas Coner." *PBSR* 2 (1904) 1–88, pls. 1–165.

Barker, E. *Buried Herculaneum.* London 1908.

Barletta, L. *Il Carnevale del 1764 a Napoli: Protesta e integrazione in uno spazio urbano.* Naples 1981.

Barnabei, F. "Gli scavi di Ercolano." *MemLinc* Ser. 3.2 (1877-78) 751–68.

Barthelemy, J.J. *Travels in Italy.* London 1802.

Bartoli, A. *I monumenti antichi di Roma nei disegni degli Uffizi di Firenze.* 5 vols. Rome 1914–22.

Bassi, D. "Altre lettere inedite del P. Antonio Piaggio, e spigolature dalle sue 'Memorie.'" *ASPN* 33 (1908) 277–332.

"Il P. Antonio Piaggio e i primi tentativi per lo svolgimento dei papiri ercolanesi." *ASPN* 32 (1907) 636–90.

Bayardi, O.A. *Catalogo degli antichi monumenti dissotterrati dalla discoperta città di Ercolano.* 2d ed. Naples 1754.

Prodromo delle antichità d'Ercolano. 5 vols. Naples 1752.

Beloch, C.J. *Campanien: Topograghie, Geschichte und Leben der Umgebung Neapels im Altertum.* Berlin 1879.

Bernardo Tanucci: Statista, letterato, giurista (Atti del convegno internazionale di studi per il secondo centenario, 1783–1983). 2 vols. Naples 1986.

Bianchini, F. *Camera ed iscrizioni sepulcrali de' liberti, servi ed ufficiali della casa di Augusto scoperte nella Via Appia.* Rome 1727.

La istoria universale provata con monumenti, e figurata con simboli degli antichi. Rome 1697.

Del palazzo de' Cesari. Verona 1738.

Björnstahl, J.J. *Lettere nei suoi viaggi stranieri.* Poschiavo 1782–87.

Bois, Y.-A. "Metamorphoses of axonometry," 146–61. In *Het Nieuwe Bouwen – De Stijl: De Nieuwe Bielding in de Architectuur.* The Hague 1983.

Bologna, F. "La riscoperta di Ercolano e la cultura artistica del settecento Europeo," 83–105. In *Le antichità di Ercolano.* Naples 1988.

"Le scoperte di Ercolano e Pompei nella cultura europea del XVIII secolo." *PdP* 34 (1979) 377–404.

Bonucci, C. *Napoli e i luoghi celebri delle sue vicinanze.* Naples 1845.

Pompeii descritta. Naples 1827.

Booker, P.J. *A history of engineering drawing.* London 1963.

I Borbone di Napoli e i Borbone di Spagna. 2 vols. Naples 1985.

Borraro, P., ed. *Alessio Simmaco Mazzocchi e il Settecento meridionale.* Salerno 1979.

Borsi, S. *Giuliano da Sangallo: I disegni di architettura e dell' antico.* Rome 1985.

Brion, M. *Pompeii and Herculaneum: The glory and the grief.* London 1960.

Brisson, C. "La découverte d'Herculanum en 1713 par le 'Prince d'Elbeuf.'" *Revue des sociétés savantes de Haute-Normandie* 6 (1957) 21–29.

Brosses, Ch. de. *Lettres sur l'état actuel de la ville souterraine d'Herculée.* Dijon 1750.

Butta, G. *I Borboni di Napoli al cospetto di due secoli.* 3 vols. Naples 1877.

Camardo, D., A. Ferrara, and N. Longobardi. *Stabiae: Le ville.* Castellamare di Stabia 1989.

Capasso, M. *Storia fotografica dell' Officina dei Papiri Ercolanesi.* Naples 1983.

Caporali, G.B. *Vitruvius Pollio, con il suo comento et figure: Vetruvio in volgar lingua rapordato per M. Gianbatista Caporali di Perugia.* Perugia 1536.

Carotenuto, M. *Ercolano attraverso i secoli.* Naples 1980.

Herculaneum: Storia della antica città di Ercolano e dei suoi scavi. Naples 1932.

Cäsar Conte Corti, E. *Untergang und Auferstehung von Pompeji und Herculaneum*. 9th ed. Munich 1978.

Castaldi, G. *Della Regale Accademia Ercolanese dalla sua fondazione sinora con un cenno biografico de' suoi soci ordinari*. Naples 1840.

Castellano, G. "Mons. Ottavio Antonio Bayardi e l'illustrazione degli scavi di Ercolano." *Samnium* xvi–xviii (1943–45) 65–86, 185–94.

Castellano Lanzara, M.G. *La Real Biblioteca di Carlo di Borbone e il suo primo bibliotecario M. Egizio*. Naples 1942.

Catalano, V. *Storia di Ercolano*. Naples 1953.

Caylus, A.-C.-P. Comte de. *Correspondence inedite . . . avec le P. Paciaudi, théatin (1757–1765)*. 2 vols. Paris 1877.

    Recueil d'antiquités égyptiennes, étrusques, grecques, romaines et gauloises. 7 vols. Paris 1752–67.

Celano, C. *Notizie del bello e del curioso che contengono le Real Ville di Portici, Resina, lo scavamento di Pompejano, Capodimonte, Cardito, Caserta e S. Leucio*. Naples 1792.

Cerulli Irelli, G. *La Casa 'del Colonnato Tuscanico' ad Ercolano (MemNap 7)*. Naples 1974.

    "Decorazioni di baltei dal foro di Ercolano." *CronErc* 2 (1972) 95–103.

Choisi, E. "La Reale Accademia Ercolanese: Bernardo Tanucci fra politica e antiquaria," 495–517. In *Bernardo Tanucci: Statista, letterato, giurista*. 2 vols. Naples 1986.

Civiltà del '700 a Napoli (1734–1799). 2 vols. Florence 1980.

Cochin, C.-N., and J.C. Bellicard. *Observations sur les antiquités d'Herculanum*. Paris 1755.

Il Collegio Universitario Ghislieri di Pavia: Istituzione della riforma cattolica (1567–1860). Milan 1966.

Le collezioni del Museo Nazionale di Napoli. Vol. 1.1. Naples 1986, Vol. 1.2. Naples 1989.

Comparetti, D. "La villa de' Pisoni in Ercolano e la sua biblioteca," 159–76. In *Pompei e la regione sotterrata dal Vesuvio*. Naples 1879.

    "Relazione sui papiri ercolanesi." *MemLinc*, Ser. 3, 5 (1880) 145–78.

Comparetti, D., and G. de Petra. *La villa ercolanese dei Pisoni: I suoi monumenti e la sua biblioteca, Ricerche e notizie*. Turin 1883.

Condamine, C.M. de la. "Extract from a letter of Mons. la Condamine to Dr. Maty [March 11, 1756]." *PhilTrans* 49.2 (1756) 622–24.

Conticello, B., and U. Cioffi. "Il 'rientro' nella Villa dei Papiri di Ercolano," 173–90. In *Restaurare Pompei*. Milan 1990.

Corcia, N. "Frisso ed Elle figurati in due quadretti di Ercolano e Pompeii," 33–84. In *Pompei e la regione sotterrata dal Vesuvio*. Naples 1879.

Cosenza, G. *Stabia: Studi archeologici, topografici, e storici*. Trani 1907.

Cozzolino, G. "Nel bicentenario degli scavi di Ercolano." *Bolletino Parrochiale di S. Maria a Pugliano* (January 15, 1938) 3.

Daniel, G. *A short history of archaeology*. London 1981.

De Cunzo, M. "Le Ville Vesuviane," 1.86–105. In *Civiltà del '700 a Napoli*. Florence 1980.

De Franciscis, A. "L'esperienza napoletana del Winckelmann." *CronPomp* 1 (1975) 7–24.

    "Herculaneum." In *EAA* Supp. 1970, 310.

De Fusco, R. "L'architettura della seconda metà del Settecento," 8.367–449. In *Storia di Napoli*. Naples 1971.

De Jorio, A. *Notizie su gli scavi di Ercolano*. Naples 1827.

De Kind, R. "Casa dello Scheletro at Herculaneum: The large nymphaeum." *CronErc* 21 (1991) 133–47.

Della Corte, M. "Esplorazioni di Pompei immediatamente successive alla catastrofe dell' anno 79," 96–109. In *In memoriam Vasile Pârvan*. Bucharest 1934.

Della Torre, G.M. *Storia e fenomeni del Vesuvio col catalogo degli scrittori vesuviani*. Naples 1754.

Del Pezzo, N. "Siti reali: Il Palazzo Reale di Portici," *Napoli Nobilissima* 5 (1896) 161–67, 183–88.

De Petra, G. "I monumenti della villa ercolanese," 251–71. In *Pompei e la regione sotterrata dal Vesuvio*. Naples 1879.

Descoeudres, J.-P. "Did some Pompeians return to their city after the eruption of Mt. Vesuvius in AD 79? Observations in the House of the Coloured Capitals," 165–78. In *Ercolano 1738–1988: 250 anni di ricerca archeologica*. Rome 1993.

De Seta, C., *Cartografia della città di Napoli*. Naples 1969.

    "Topografia territoriale e vedutismo a Napoli nel Settecento," 2.14-37. In *Civiltà del '700 a Napoli*. Florence 1980.

De Seta, C. et al., eds. *Ville Vesuviane: Campania I*. Milan 1980.

Desgodetz, A. *Les édifices antiques de Rome*. Paris 1682.

De Simone, A. "La Villa dei Papiri, Rapporto preliminare: Gennaio 1986–Marzo 1987." *CronErc* (1987) 15–36.

De Vos, M. "Camillo Paderni, la tradizione antiquaria romana e i collezionisti inglesi," 99–116. In *Ercolano 1738–1988: 250 anni di ricerca archeologica*. Rome 1993.

    "Nerone, Seneca, Fabullo e La Domus Transitoria al Palatino," 167–89. In *Gli orti Farnesiani sul*

Palatino. Roma Antica, Collection Publieé par l'Ecole Française de Rome et la Soprintendenza Archeologica di Roma, 2. Rome 1990.

De Vos, A., and M. De Vos. *Pompei Ercolano Stabia (Guide archeologiche Laterza*, no. 11). Bari 1982.

Du Pérac, E. *Le antiche rovine di Roma nei disegni di Du Pérac*. Milan 1990.

Edgerton, S., Jr. *The Renaissance rediscovery of linear perspective*. New York 1975.

Eius virtutis studiosi: Classical and Postclassical studies in memory of Frank Edward Brown (1908–1988). Hanover 1993.

Elia, O. *Pitture di Stabia*. Naples 1957.

Ercolano 1738–1988: 250 anni di ricerca archeologica (Atti del Convegno Internazionale Ravello-Ercolano-Napoli-Pompei, 30 ottobre–5 novembre 1988). Rome 1993.

Ericsson, C.H. *Roman architecture expressed in sketches by Francesco di Giorgio Martini (1439–1498). Studies in Imperial Roman and Early Christian architecture*. Commentationes Humanarum Litterarum, no. 66. Helsinki 1980.

Eschebach, H. *Die städtebauliche Entwicklung des antiken Pompeji*. Heidelberg 1970.

"Extract of a letter from Naples concerning Herculaneum, containing an account and description of the place and what has been found in it," *PhilTrans* 47 (1751–1752) 150–59.

Fernandez Murga, F. *Carlos III y el descubrimiento de Herculano, Pompeya y Estabia*. Salamanca 1989.

"Roque Joaquin de Alcubierre, descubridor de Herculano, Pompeya y Estabia." *ArchEspArq* 35 (1962) 3–35.

"Tanucci, Alcubierre e gli scavi di antichità," 479–91. In *Bernardo Tanucci: Statista, letterato, giurista*. 2 vols. Naples 1986.

Ficoroni, F. *Bolla d'oro de fanciulli nobile romani*. Rome 1732.

Fiengo, G. "Le ville vesuviane del settecento e la scoperta di Pompei ed Ercolano." *Antiqua* 4.15. Suppl. *Pompei* 79 (1979) 148–54.

Finzi, C. "Un ministro 'archeologo': Gli scavi di Ercolano nell' epistolario di Bernardo Tanucci." *Antiqua* 4.15 Suppl. *Pompei* 79 (1979) 155–60.

Fiorelli, G. *Giornale degli scavi*. Naples 1850.

Giornale degli scavi di Pompei. Naples 1861–65.

Fontana, D. *Libro secondo in cui si ragiona di alcune fabriche fatte in Roma et in Napoli*. Naples 1603.

Fonti documentarie per la storia degli scavi di Pompei, Ercolano e Stabia a cura degli archivisti napoletani. Naples 1979.

Fougeroux de Bondaroy, A.D. *Recherches sur les ruines d'Herculanum* . . . Paris 1770.

Freeman, ———. "An extract of a letter dated May 2, 1750, from Mr. Freeman at Naples to the Right Honorable Lady Mary Capel relating to the ruins at Herculaneum." *PhilTrans* 47 (1751–52) 131–42.

Frutaz, A.P. *Le piante di Roma*. 3 vols. Rome 1962.

Fuchs, M. *Untersuchungen zur Ausstattung römischer Theater in Italien und den Westprovinzen des Imperium Romanum*. Mainz am Rhein 1987.

Furchheim, F. *Biblioteca pompejana: Catalogo ragionato di opere sopra Ercolano e Pompei*. Naples 1879. 2d ed. pub. as *Bibliografia di Pompei, Ercolano e Stabia*. Naples 1891 (Repr. Naples 1972).

Gabrici, E. "Per la iconografia di Livia moglie di Augusto." *RendNap* 20 (1906) 235–39.

"La quadriga di Ercolano." *BdA* 1 (1907) 1–12.

Galiani, B. *L'architettura di M. Vitruvio Pollione colla traduzione italiana e comento*. Naples 1758.

Considerazioni sopra la lettera dell'Abate Winckelmann riguardante le scoverte di Ercolano. Naples 1765.

Gallavotti, C. "Nuovo contributo alla storia degli scavi borbonici di Ercolano (nella Villa dei Papiri)." *RendNap* n.s. 20 (1939–40) 269–306.

Galletti, E. *Il Collegio Ghislieri di Pavia, Note storiche*. Pavia 1980.

Gallo, D. "Marcello Venuti tra Napoli e Cortona," 53–57. In *L'Accademia Etrusca*. Milan 1985.

Gassner, V. *Die Kaufläden in Pompeii*. Dissertation, University of Vienna, 1986, no. 178.

Gell, W., and J. Gandy. *Pompeiana: The topography, edifices and ornaments of Pompeii*. London 1921.

Gerhard, E. *Neapels antike Bildwerke*. Berlin 1828.

Gigante, M. "Carlo III e i papiri ercolanesi," 1.215–40. In *I Borbone di Napoli e i Borbone di Spagna*. 2 vols. Naples 1985.

Gigante, M., and G. Gullini. "Intervento," 593–96. In *Un secolo di ricerche in Magna Grecia (Atti del ventottesimo convegno di studi sulla Magna Grecia, Taranto, 7–12 Ottobre 1988)*. Taranto 1989.

Giornale de' Letterati d'Italia, 5 (Venice 1711) 399–401; 8 (Venice 1711) 221–309.

Girosi, M. "L'anfiteatro di Pompei." *MemNap* 5 (1936) 29-55.

Goethe, J.W. *Italienische Reise*. Ed. H. von Einem. Munich 1978.

The Golden Age of Naples: Art and civilization under the Bourbons (1734–1805). 2 vols. Detroit 1981.

Gordon, A.R. "Jérôme-Charles Bellicard's Italian notebook of 1750-51: The discoveries at Herculaneum and observations on ancient and modern architecture." *Metropolitan Museum Journal* 25 (1990) 49-142.

Gori, A.F. *Admiranda antiquitatum herculanensium descripta et illustrata ad annum MDCCL*. 2 vols. Padova 1752.

Monumentum sive columbarium libertorum et servorum Liviae Augustae et Caesarum. Florence 1727.

Notizie del memorabile scoprimento dell' antica città di Ercolano . . . Florence 1748.

Symbolae litterariae: Opuscula varia philologica, scientifica, antiquaria . . . , Decas I. Florence 1748–53.

Symbolae litterariae: Opuscula varia philologica, scientifica, antiquaria . . . , Decas II. Rome 1751–54.

Grant, M., A. De Simone, and M.T. Merella. *Eros in Pompeii.* London 1975.

Gray, J. "Extract of a letter . . . to Sir Thomas Robinson . . . relating to the same discoveries in Herculaneum [October 29, 1754]." *PhilTrans* 48.2 (1754) 825–26.

Grell, C. *Herculanum et Pompéi dans les récits des voyageurs français du XVIIIᵉ siècle.* Naples 1982.

Gross, H. *Rome in the Age of Enlightenment.* Cambridge 1990.

Guadagno, G. "A.S. Mazzochi [*sic*] epigrafista." *Archivio storico di terra di lavoro* (1975) 273–82.

"Ercolano: Eredità di cultura e nuovi dati," 73–98. In *Ercolano 1738–1988: 250 anni di ricerca archeologica.* Rome 1993.

"Herculanensium Augustalium aedes." *CronErc* 13 (1983) 159–73.

"Nuovi documenti del XVIII secolo per la storia degli scavi di Ercolano." *CronErc* 16 (1986) 135–47.

"Supplemento epigrafico ercolanese II." *CronErc* 11 (1981) 129–64.

Harder, H. *Le Président de Brosses et le voyage en Italie au dix-huitième siècle.* Geneva 1981.

Haskell, F. "Art patronage and collecting in Bourbon Naples during the 18th century," 1.15–22. In *The golden age of Naples: Art and civilization under the Bourbons (1734–1805).* 2 vols. Detroit 1981.

Helbig, W. *Die Wandgemälde der vom Vesuv verschütteten Städte Campaniens.* Leipzig 1868.

Herbig, R. *Don Carlos de Borbón, Excavador de Herculano y Pompeya.* Madrid 1954.

"Don Carlos von Bourbon als Ausgräber von Herculaneum und Pompeji." *MadMitt* 1 (1960) 11–19.

Hogg, T. *Two hundred and nine days, or, The journal of a traveller on the continent.* London 1827.

Imperato, F. *Una communità in cammino.* Naples 1964.

Italienishce Reise: Pompejanische Bilder in den deutschen archäologischen Sammlungen. Soprintendenza Archeologica di Pompei, Le Mostre 8. Naples 1989.

Jahn, O. "Über Darstellungen des Handwerks und Handelsverkehrs auf antiken Wandgemälden." *Abhandlungen des sächsischen Gessellschaft der*

Wissenschaften, Philologisch.-hist. Classe 5 (1870) 265–318.

Jashemski, W. *The gardens of Pompeii, Herculaneum and the villas destroyed by Vesuvius.* New Rochelle, NY 1979.

Johannowsky, W. "Problemi urbanistici di Ercolano." *CronErc* 12 (1982) 145–49.

Justi, C. *Winckelmann: sein Leben, seine Werke und seine Zeitgenossen.* Leipzig 1866–72.

Winckelmann und seine Zeitgenossen. 3d ed. Leipzig 1923.

Kammerer-Grothaus, H. "Die erste Aufstellung der Antiken aus den Vesuvstädten in Portici," 11–19. In *Antikensammlungen im 18. Jahrhundert.* Berlin 1981.

Kaspar, D. "Felix Urbium Restitutio: Le Antichità di Ercolano zwischen Museum und öffentlichkeit," 21–31. In *Antikensammlungen im 18. Jahrhundert.* Berlin 1981.

Keerl, J.H. *Über die Ruinen Herkulanums und Pompeji.* Gotha 1791.

Kleberg, T. *Hôtels, restaurants et cabarets dans l'antiquité romaine.* Uppsala 1957.

Knapton, G. "Extract of a letter from Mr. George Knapton to Mr. Charles Knapton . . . ," *PhilTrans* 41.2 (1740–41) 489–93.

Knight, C. "Un inedito di Padre Piaggio: Il diario vesuviano (1779-1795)." *RendAccNap* n.s. 62 (1989–90) 59–131.

Knight, C., and A. Jorio. "L'ubicazione della Villa Ercolanese dei Papiri." *RendNap* n.s. 55 (1980) 51–65.

Kockel, V. "Archäologische Funde und Forschungen in den Vesuvstädten," Pt. I, *ArchAnz* (1985) 495–571; Pt. II, *ArchAnz* (1986) 443–569.

Kunze, M. "Zu Winckelmanns Schriften über Herkulaneum und Pompeji," 25–39. In *Pompeji 79–1979: Beiträge zum Vesuvausbruch und seiner Nachwirkung.* Stendal 1982.

La Vega, F. "Giornale di ciò che mi occorre di rimarchevole," 110-20, and "Notizie appartenti all' excavazioni d'Ercolano secondo le relazioni avute da varie persone," 281–320. In G. Fiorelli. *Giornale degli scavi di Pompei.* nos. 1–4 and 8–10. Naples 1861.

Lanciani, R. *Storia degli scavi di Roma.* Rome 1902–12.

Latapie, F. *Description des fouilles de Pompéi* (1776). Ed. P. Barrière and A. Maiuri. *RAAN* 28 (1954) 223–48.

Lavagne, H., and O. Wattel-De-Croizant. "De la villa de San Marco (Stabies) au Musée Condé (Chantilly): Histoire d'un enlèvement d'Europe." *MEFRA* 96.2 (1984) 739–88.

Leppmann, W. *Winckelmann.* New York 1970.

Levi, A. *Le terracotte figurati del Museo Nazionale di Napoli.* Florence 1926.

Leybourn, Wm. *The compleat surveyor, or the whole art of surveying of land by a new instrument lately invented; as also by the plain table, circumferentor, the theodolite as now improved, or by the chain only.* 5th ed. London 1722.

Ling, R. *Roman painting.* Cambridge 1991.

Long, C.R. "The Pompeii calendar medallions." *AJA* 96 (1992) 477–501.

Longo Auricchio, F., and M. Capasso. "Nuove accessioni al dossier Piaggio," 17–59. In *Contributi alla Storia della Officina dei Papiri Ercolanesi.* Naples 1980.

Lotz, W. *Studies in Italian Renaissance architecture.* Cambridge 1977.

Lumisden, A. *Remarks on the antiquities of Rome and its environs.* London 1812.

Lyons, C.L. "The *Museo Mastillo* and the culture of collecting in Naples, 1700–1755." *Journal of the History of Collections* 4.1 (1992) 1–26.

Maffei, F.S. *De gli anfiteatri e singolarmente del Veronese.* Verona 1728.

Tre lettere del Signor Marchese Scipione Maffei. Verona 1748.

Magaldi, E. "Il commercio ambulante a Pompeii." *AttiPontAcc* 40 (1930) 61–88.

Maiuri, A. "Due iscrizioni veneree pompeiane," 285–99. In *Saggi di varia antichità.* Venice 1954.

Ercolano (Itinerari dei musei, gallerie e monumenti d'Italia 6). 6th ed. Rome 1967.

Ercolano: I nuovi scavi. 2 vols. Rome 1958.

"Fontana monumentale in bronzo nei nuovi scavi di Ercolano." *Bolletino d'Arte* n.s. 3 (July–September, 1954) 193–99.

"Giulia Felice, gentildonna pompeiana," 51–54. In *Pompei ed Ercolano fra case e abitanti.* Florence 1983.

Pompei, Ercolano, Stabiae: Le città sepolte dal Vesuvio. Novara 1961.

Gli scavi di Pompei nel programma delle opere della Cassa per il Mezzogiorno. Naples 1951.

"Statuetta fittile di Pittaco di Mitilene." *ArchCl* 4 (1952) 55–59.

"Gli studi di antichità a Napoli nel sette e ottocento." *RendAccNap* 13 (1937) 33–59.

"La Villa dei Papiri," 221–36. In *Pompei ed Ercolano fra case e abitanti.* Florence 1983.

Malina, J., and Z. Vasícek. *Archaeology yesterday and today: The development of archaeology in the sciences and humanities.* Cambridge 1990.

Mancini, F. "Feste, apparati e spettacoli teatrali," 8.649–714. In *Storia di Napoli.* Naples 1971.

Mandowsky, E., and C. Mitchell, eds. *Pirro Ligorio's Roman antiquities.* London 1963.

Marini, G. *Il gabinetto segreto del Museo Nazionale di Napoli.* Turin 1971.

Marocchi, M. "La personalità di Pio V e le direttive religiose, disciplinari, e culturali delle costituzioni del Collegio Ghislieri," 93–129. In *Il Collegio Universitario Ghislieri di Pavia: Istituzione della riforma cattolica (1567–1860).* Milan 1966.

Martorelli, G. *De regia theca calamaria in Regia Academia litterarum graecarum professoris . . .* Naples 1756.

Maylender, M. *Storia delle Accademie d'Italia.* 5 vols. Bologna 1925–30.

Mazois, F. *Les ruines de Pompéi.* Paris 1812.

Mazzocchi, A.S. "Della dissertazione preliminare delle origini di Ercolano e dei luoghi vicini" (Bibl.Naz. Ms. IX.A.61), 25–40, 65–80, 97–120. In Fiorelli, G. *Giornale degli scavi di Pompei.* Naples 1862.

In mutilum Campani amphiteatri titulum, aliasque nonnullas Campanas inscriptiones. Naples 1727.

McIlwaine, I.C. *Herculaneum: A guide to printed sources.* 2 vols. Naples 1988.

"*Herculaneum: A guide to printed sources,* Supplement." *CronErc* 20 (1990) 87–128.

Mielsch, H. *Römische Stuckreliefs (RömMitt Erganzungsheft 21).* Heidelberg 1975.

Millon, H.S. "Reconstructions of the Palatine in the eighteenth century," 479–93. In *Eius virtutis studiosi: Classical and Postclassical studies in memory of Frank Edward Brown (1908–1988).* Hanover 1993.

Minervini, G. "Di una antica pianta del teatro di Ercolano." *BullArchItal* 1.5 (July 1861) 33–40, pl. 3.

Miniero Forte, P. "I materiali dell' arredo della villa," 929–36. In A. Barbet *et al.* "Premier rapport sur l'etude de la Villa San Marco à Stabies." *MEFRA* 95.2 (1983) 909–36.

Stabiae: Pitture e stucchi delle ville romane. Naples 1989.

Momigliano, A. "Ancient history and the antiquarian." *JWarb* 13 (1950) 285–315.

Montevecchi, O. "Documenti inediti sugli scavi di Veleia nel sec. XVIII." *Aevum* 8 (1934) 553–630.

Montfaucon, B. de. *L'antiquité expliquée et représentée en figures.* Paris 1719.

Supplément au livre de l'Antiquité Expliquée . . . Paris 1724.

Mustilli, D. "La villa pseudourbana ercolanese," 7–18. In *La Villa dei Papiri. CronErc* 13, Suppl. 2. Naples 1983.

Napoli e i luoghi celebri delle sue vicinanze. Naples 1845.

Nappo, S. "Fregio dipinto dal *praedium* [*sic*] di Giulia Felice con rappresentazione del foro di Pompei." *RStPomp* 3 (1989) 79–96.

Nardini, F. *L'antico Veio: Discorso investigativo del sito di quella città*. Rome 1647.

Neudecker, R. *Die Skulpturen-Ausstattung römischer Villen in Italien*. Mainz am Rhein 1988.

Nicolini, F. "I manoscritti dell' abate Galiani." *La Critica* 1 (1903) 393–400.

Nocerino, N. *La Real Villa di Portici illustrata*. Naples 1787.

Northall, J. *Travels in Italy, containing new and curious observations on that country*. London 1766.

Nuovi studi Maffeiani: Atti del Convegno Scipione Maffei e il Museo Maffeiano. Verona 1985.

Paciaudi, P.M. *Lettres de Paciaudi au comte de Caylus*. Paris 1862.

Paderni, C. "An account of the late discoveries of antiquities at Herculaneum . . . to T. Hollis . . . dated February 1, 1758." *PhilTrans* 50.2 (1759) 619–23.

"An account of the late discoveries of antiquities at Herculaneum, etc., in two letters from Camillo Paderni . . . to Thomas Hollis [Naples, June 28, 1755]." *PhilTrans* 49.2 (1755–56) 490–506.

"Extract from a letter . . . dated July 29, 1755." *PhilTrans* 49.2 (1756) 507–9.

"Extract of a letter . . . to Tho. Hollis, dated at Naples, April 27, 1754." *PhilTrans* 48.2 (1754) 634–38.

"Extract of a letter . . . to Tho. Hollis, Esq., relating to the late discoveries at Herculaneum [Naples, October 18, 1754]." *PhilTrans* 48.2 (1754) 821–25.

"Extracts of two letters from Sign. Camillo Paderni at Rome to Mr. Allan Ramsey, Painter, Covent-Garden, concerning some ancient Statues, Pictures and other Curiosities found in a subterraneous Town lately discovered near Naples; dated Rome, November 20, 1739, and February 20, 1740." *PhilTrans* 41 (1740) 484–89.

Pagano, M. "Il teatro di Ercolano." *CronErc* 23 (1993) 121–56.

"Torre del Greco, località Ponte Rivieccio, contrada Villa Sora, prop. Montella." *RStPomp* 3 (1989) 287–94.

"La Villa Romana di contrada Sora a Torre del Greco." *CronErc* 21 (1991) 149–86.

Pancrazi, G.M. *L'antichità siciliane spiegate colle notizie generali di questo regno*. 2 vols. Naples 1751–52.

Pandermalis, D. "Sul programma della decorazione scultorea," 19–50. In *La Villa dei Papiri. CronErc* 13, Suppl. 2. Naples 1983.

Pane, G. and V. Valerio, eds. *La città di Napoli tra vedutismo e cartografia: Piante e vedute dal XV al XIX secolo*. Naples 1987.

Pannuti, U. *Catalogo della collezione glittica*. Rome 1983.

"Il 'Giornale degli scavi' di Ercolano (1738–1756) (SNSP Ms. 20.B.19bis)." *MemLinc* Ser. 8, 26.3 (1983) 163–410.

"Un complesso di stucchi romani proveniente da Portici." *MonAnt* 49 (1979) 257–73, pls. 1–13.

Parrino, D.A. *Napoli e il suo cratere*. Naples 1704.

Parslow, C. "Documents illustrating the excavations of the *Praedia* of Julia Felix in Pompeii." *RStPomp* 2 (1988) 37–48.

"The 'Forum Frieze' of Pompeii in its archaeological context." In *The shapes of city life in Rome and Pompeii*. New Rochelle, NY 1995.

"Herculaneum: A new bibliography and recent work." *JRA* 3 (1990) 248–52.

"Karl Weber and Pompeian archaeology," 51–56. In *Ercolano 1738–1988: 250 anni di ricerca archeologica*. Rome 1993.

"The *Praedia Iuliae Felicis* in Pompeii." PhD. dissertation, Duke University, Durham, N.C. 1989.

Philander, G. *In decem libros M. Vitruvii Pollioni de architectura annotationes . . .* Rome 1544.

Pinto, J. "Piranesi at Hadrian's Villa," 465–77. In *Eius virtutis studiosi: Classical and Postclassical studies in memory of Frank Edward Brown (1908–1988)*. Hanover 1993.

Piranesi e la cultura antiquaria: Gl' antecedente e il contesto (Atti del Convegno 14–17 November 1979). Rome 1985.

Piranesi, F. *Antiquités de la Grande Grèce*. Paris 1807. *Il teatro d' Ercolano*. Rome 1783.

Pisapia, M.S. "L'area ercolanese dopo l'eruzione del 79: Evidenze archeologiche, la necropoli di Via Doglie ad Ercolano." *RAAN* 56 (1981) 63–74.

"Il mosaico di Frisso ed Elle." *RAAN* 53 (1978) 215–25.

Pompei e gli architetti francesi dell' Ottocento. Naples 1981.

Pompei e la regione sotterrata dal Vesuvio. Naples 1879.

Pompeianarum Antiquitatum Historia quam ex cod. mss. et a schedis diurnisque R. Alcubierre, C. Weber, M. Cixia, I. Corcoles, et al. Ed. G. Fiorelli. 3 vols. Naples 1860–64.

Pompeii 1748–1980: I tempi della documentazione. Rome 1981.

Pompeji: Leben und Kunst in den Vesuvstädten (Villa Hügen, Essen). Recklinghausen 1973.

Pompei 79: Raccolta di studi per il decimonono centenario dell' eruzione vesuviana. Naples 1979.

Pompeji 79–1979: Beiträge zum Vesuvausbruch und seiner Nachwirkung. Stendal 1982.

Praz, M. *On Neoclassicism.* Evanston 1969.

Quirini, A.M. "Epistola ad Joan. Math. Gesnerum de Herculano (Brescia 1748)," ix–xxiv. In A.F. Gori, *Symbolae litterariae opusucla varia philologica . . .* 2.1. Rome 1751–54.

Rakob, F. "Ein Grottentriklinium in Pompeji." *RömMitt* 71 (1964) 182–93.

La regione sotterrata dal Vesuvio. Naples 1982.

Reinach, S. *Répertoire de peintures grecques et romaines.* Paris 1922.

Represa Fernandez, M.F. *El Real Museo de Portici (Napoles) 1750–1825: Approximacion al conocimiento de la restauracion, organizacion y presentacion de sus fondos.* Studia Archaeologica, Universidad de Valladolid, no. 79. Valladolid 1988.

Requier, J.B. *Recueil général, historique et critique de tout ce qui a été publié de plus rare sur la ville d'Herculane . . .* Paris 1754.

Restaurare Pompei. Milan 1990.

Richardson, L., Jr. "The archaistic Diana of Pompeii." *AJA* 74 (1970) 202.

A new topographical dictionary of ancient Rome. Baltimore 1992.

Richeson, A.W. *English land measuring to 1800: Instruments and practices.* Cambridge, MA 1966.

Richter, G. *Portraits of the Greeks.* London 1965.

Ridley, R. *The eagle and the spade: Archaeology in Rome during the Napoleonic Era.* Cambridge 1992.

Romanelli, D. *Viaggio a Pompeio, a Pesto e di ritorno ad Ercolano ed a Pozzuoli.* Naples 1817.

Rosini, C. *Dissertationis isagogicae ad Herculanensium Voluminum explanationem.* Naples 1797.

Rossignani, M. P. "Saggio sui restauri settecenteschi ai dipinti di Ercolano e Pompei." *Contributi dell' Istituto di Archeologia* 1 (1967) 7–134.

Rubino, G. "La real fabbrica d'armi a Torre Annunziata e l'opera di Sabitini, Vanvitelli e Fuga (1753–1775)." *Napoli Nobilissima* 14.3 (May–June, 1975) 101–18.

Ruesch, A. *Guida illustrata del Museo Nazionale di Napoli.* Naples 1908.

Ruggiero, M. *Degli scavi di antichità nelle Province di Terraferma dell' antico Regno di Napoli.* Naples, 1888.

Degli scavi di Stabia dal 1749–1782. Naples 1881.

Storia degli scavi di Ercolano ricomposta su' documenti superstiti. Naples 1885.

Russell, J. *Letters from a young painter abroad to his friends in England.* 2d ed. 2 vols. London 1750.

Saint-Non, J.C. Richard de. *Voyage pittoresque, ou, description des Royaumes de Naples et de Sicile.* Paris 1781–86.

Saletti, C. *Il ciclo statuario della basilica di Velleia.* Milan 1968.

Salza Prina Ricotti, E. "Villa Adriana in Pirro Ligorio e Francesco Contini." *MemLinc* 17 (1973–74) 3–47.

Santi Bartoli, R. *Opera anaglyptica.* Rome 1690.

Scatozza Höricht, L.A. "Restauri alle collezioni del Museo Ercolanese di Portici alla luce di documenti inediti." *AttiAccPont* n.s. 31 (1982) 495–540.

"Ville nel territorio ercolanese." *CronErc* 15 (1985) 131–65.

Schipa, M. "Il Regno di Napoli al Tempo di Carlo di Borbone." *Archivio Storico per le Province Napoletane* 37.4 (1902) 749–55; 28.1 (1903) 49–54; 28.3 (1903) 510–46.

Scolari, M. "Elements for a history of axonometry." *Architectural Design* 55.5–6 (1985) 73–78.

Scott, D. "The evolution of mine surveying instruments." *Transactions of the American Institute of Mining and Metallurgical Engineers* 28 (1898) 679–745.

Shäfer, T. "Le *sellae curules* del teatro di Ercolano." *CronErc* 9 (1979) 143–51.

Spano, G. "Scavi eseguiti nell' isola VI della regione IV." *NSc* (1910) 437–86.

Spinazzola, V. *Le arti decorative in Pompei e nel Museo Nazionale di Napoli.* Milan 1928.

Stiebing, W. *Uncovering the past: A history of archaeology.* Buffalo 1993.

Storia di Napoli. 10 vols. Naples 1967–71.

Strazzullo, F. *Architetti e ingegneri napoletani dal '500 al '700.* Turin 1969.

"Documenti del settecento per la storia dell' edilizia e dell' urbanistica nel regno di Napoli (VI)." *Napoli Nobilissima* 22.3–4 (May–August 1983) 144.

"Documenti per l'Ing. Rocco Alcubierre scopritore di Ercolano." *AttiAccPont* 29 (1980) 263–81.

Le lettere di Luigi Vanvitelli della Biblioteca Palatina di Caserta. 3 vols. Galatina 1977.

"Marcello Venuti, scopritore di Ercolano." *Atti AccPont* 40 (1991) 169–206.

"I primi anni dello scavo di Ercolano nel diario dell' ingegnere militare Rocco Gioacchino d'Alcubierre," 103–81. In *La regione sotterrata dal Vesuvio.* Naples 1982.

Strazzullo, F., ed. *Le scoperte di Ercolano.* Naples 1981.

Settecento napoletana. Naples 1982.

Strocka, V.M. "Pompeji VI 17,41: Ein haus mit privatbibliothek." *RömMitt* 100 (1993) 321–51, pls. 69–75.

Strong, E. *Art in ancient Rome.* 2d ed. London 1929.

Studniczka, F. "Die archaische Artemisstatue aus Pompeji." *RömMitt* 3 (1888) 277–302.

Tanucci, B. *Epistolario.* Ed. M.G. Maiorini. Vols 9,

10: Rome 1985, 1988. Ed. S. Lollini. Vol. 11: Rome 1990.

Lettere a Ferdinando Galiani. Ed. F. Nicolini. Bari 1914.

Tran Tam Tinh, v. *La Casa dei Cervi a Herculanum.* Rome 1988.

Catalogue des peintures romaines (Latium et Campanie) du Musée du Louvre. Paris 1974.

Le culte des divinités orientales à Herculanum. Leiden 1971.

Trigger, B. *A history of archaeological thought.* Cambridge 1989.

Trombetta, V. "L'edizione de *Le Antichità di Ercolano Esposte.*" *RAAN* 59 (1984) 151–72.

Trouard, L.F. "Notes sur mon voyage," Unpublished Mss., Fonds Doucet 98 fols. 26 and 57 (Bibl. de l'Institut d'Art et d'Archéologie, Paris). In *Pompei e gli architetti francesi dell' Ottocento.* Naples 1981.

Ussia, S. *L'epistolario di Matteo Egizio e la cultura napoletana del primo Settecento.* Naples 1977.

Vacca, F. *Memorie di varie antichità trovate in diversi luoghi della città di Roma.* Rome 1594.

Venuti, R. *Collectanea antiquitatum Romanarum quas centum tabulis aereis incisas . . .* Rome 1736.

Descrizione delle prime scoperte dell' antica città d'Ercolano ritrovata vicino a Portici. Rome 1748.

Venuti De Dominicis, T. *I Venuti.* Rome 1889.

La Villa dei Papiri. CronErc 13, Suppl. 2. Naples 1983.

Von Rohden, H. *Die Terracotten von Pompeji.* Stuttgart 1880.

Waldstein, C., and L. Shoobridge. *Herculaneum past, present and future.* London 1908.

Ward-Perkins, J.B. "Nota di topografia e urbanistica," 25–39. In *Pompei 79.* Naples 1979.

Ward-Perkins, J.B., and A. Claridge. *Pompeii A.D. 79.* New York 1978.

Weiss, R. *The Renaissance discovery of Classical antiquity.* 2d ed. Oxford 1988.

Whitehouse, H. "*In Praedis Iuliae Felicis*: The provenance of some fragments of wall-painting in the Museo Nazionale, Naples." *PBSR* 45 (1977) 52–68.

Wilton-Ely, J. *The mind and art of Giovanni Battista Piranesi.* London 1978.

"Piranesi and the role of archaeological illustration," 317–37. In *Piranesi e la cultura antiquaria: Gl' antecedente e il contesto.* Rome 1985.

Winckelmann, J.J. *Briefe (1742–1759).* 3 vols. Berlin 1952.

Geschichte der Kunst des Altertums. Vienna 1934.

Nachrichten von den neuesten herculanischen Entdeckungen. Dresden 1764.

Sendschreiben von den herculanischen Entdeckungen. Dresden 1762.

Wojcik, M.R. *La Villa dei Papiri.* Rome 1986.

Yegül, F. *Baths and bathing in classical antiquity.* Cambridge, MA 1992.

"The Palaestra at Herculaneum as a new architectural type," 369–93. In *Eius virtutis studiosi: Classical and Postclassical studies in memory of Frank Edward Brown (1908–1988).* Washington 1993.

Zarillo, M. *Giudizio dell' opera dell' Abate Winckelmann intorno alle scoverte di Ercolano contenuto in una lettera ad un amico.* Naples 1765.

Zevi, F. "Gli scavi di Ercolano," 2.58–74. In *Civiltà del '700 a Napoli.* Florence 1980.

"Gli scavi di Ercolano e le *Antichità*," 11–38. In *Le antichità di Ercolano.* Naples 1988.

Zorzi, G. *I disegni delle antichità di Andrea Palladio.* Venice 1959.

Zottoli, G. "Bibliografia ercolanese, a cura di Amedeo Maiuri." *BdA* 2 (1928–29) 47–81.

Name Index

Scognamillo, Antonio (*cont.*)
    334, 342, 345, 347, 348, 357–9, 362,
    369–71
Scognamillo, Pietro, 358, 370, 371; fig. 28
Seneca, 187, 194, 244, 329, 368
Serao, Andrea, 62, 371, 372
Servius, 192
Sportullo, 40, 368
Statius, 174, 355
Stendardo, Giuseppe, 29, 30, 234, 327–9
Strabo, 173, 187, 338
Suetonius, 113, 187, 342

Tacitus, 173, 194
Tanucci, Bernardo, 27, 56, 80, 82, 83, 132,
    133, 136, 140, 141, 148, 153–7, 166,
    184, 191, 196, 197, 199, 203, 205–12,
    214, 217, 219–21, 224, 227, 230, 231,
    232, 247, 248, 250–3, 258, 259, 265,
    271–3, 275, 323, 328, 332, 334, 336,
    339–41, 344, 350–3, 357, 359–63,
    366–70
Tarcagnota, Giovanni, 194, 357
Trouard, L-F., 244, 365
Tschudi, Josef-Anton, 17, 66, 324
Tschudi, Leonhard-Ludwig, 17, 18, 264, 272,
    324, 325, 370
Tuttavilla of Sarno, Muzio, conte, 44

Usteri, Leonhard, 221, 361

Vacca, Flaminio, 160
Valenti, Silvio, cardinal, 163
Vanvitelli, Luigi, 248, 333, 334, 360, 366
Varro, 176, 187, 191
Venuti, Marcello, 10, 19, 29–31, 33, 112, 166,
    216, 217, 221, 234, 238, 240, 241, 244,

    323, 326, 328, 329, 336, 337, 346, 347,
    354, 361–5
Vico, Giovanni Batista, 157
Vitruvius, 57, 78, 112, 113, 157–60, 164, 172,
    174–6, 187, 188, 190, 197, 217, 221,
    233, 236, 237, 239, 240, 242, 245, 254–
    8, 355, 356, 368
Volkmann, Johann Jakob, 221, 229, 361

Weber, Anna Maria, 15
Weber, Franz Dominik, 14, 17, 271, 324, 325,
    369, 370; fig. 3
Weber, Frederick Christian, 216
Weber, Jakob, 14
Weber, Karl Jakob, 1, 3–10, 13–15, 17–19,
    23, 46–9, 56, 60, 62, 66–73, 77, 79, 80,
    83–5, 88–91, 93–100, 102–8, 110–12,
    115, 117, 118, 120–9, 131–41, 144–8,
    150, 153–7, 159, 166–8, 170–81, 184–8,
    190–206, 208–14, 216, 219–22, 224–30,
    232, 233, 234, 241, 246–60, 263–81,
    322–5, 329, 330, 332, 333, 336, 337–53,
    355–60, 362–70, 372, 373; fig. 2
Weber, Maria Anna Katharina, 15
Weber, Peter Anton, 14
Winckelmann, Johann Joachim, 1, 3, 6, 156,
    196, 199, 215–26, 229–32, 256–9, 264,
    273, 278, 322, 339, 342, 343, 346–50,
    352–4, 359–63, 368, 371, 372
    Nachrichten, 229, 230, 257–8, 346, 359–62,
    368
    Sendschreiben, 215, 221–4, 225, 226, 229,
    230, 322, 342, 343, 347–50, 352, 353,
    359–62

Zarillo, Matteo, 363
Zay, Anna Flora, 14
Zay, Johann Karl, 14

Subject Index

Methods of digging and of removing finds,
34, 42, 93, 105, 223, 241
Forced and hired laborers, 24, 29, 31, 36,
40, 42, 45, 47–9, 78, 91, 94, 115, 208–9,
227, 228, 248, 269, 273, 329–30, 342,
347, 360; fig. 9
Hoisting winch, rope and net, 31, 32, 35,
42, 77, 78, 88, 91, 94, 136, 147, 342
Hurnillos, 95, 102, 342; fig. 25
In situ conservation of remains, 3, 44, 112,
147, 174, 222–9, 244–5, 249, 352, 367
Lapilli (also called pumice), 45, 108, 113,
115, 174, 179, 200, 205, 213, 223
Lighting underground tunnels, 23, 27, 34,
35, 42, 77, 93, 105, 110, 238, 239
Open-air excavations, 45, 106, 177, 179,
242–5, 248–9, 269, 280, 366, 370, 373
Preservation conditions of remains, 2, 6,
107, 115, 205
Ramps, 42, 60, 77, 88, 92, 99, 123–9, 142,
143, 145, 146, 235, 245, 257, 330, 333,
340, 341, 349, 350, 352, 364
Surveying instruments, 48–9, 117, 133, 334
Trenches, 45–6, 111, 147, 164, 177, 205,
227, 269, 333, 345, 347, 365
Tunnels and grottoes (*see also* Villa dei
Papiri: Gruta derecha), 2, 22–4, 27–8,
31–43, 45, 47–9, 57, 59–62, 70–2, 77,
81, 85, 88, 89, 92–5, 98–100, 102, 105,
110, 114, 120, 123–31, 135–7, 143,
145–7, 150, 213, 218, 219, 221, 222,
225, 232, 233, 234–6, 239, 241, 245,
248–252, 256, 259, 264, 267–9, 270,
275, 280, 329–331, 333–6, 341–4, 349–
51, 352, 364, 365

Gaeta 40, 97, 331, 332
Giornale de' Letterati d'Italia, 22, 24, 29, 326,
330, 355
Gragnano, 45, 46, 48, 49, 63, 66, 70, 71, 117,
181, 214, 225, 267, 272, 274, 333, 334,
335, 338, 358, 370, 372
Granatello, 19, 23, 31, 38, 80, 94, 177, 194,
209, 269, 325–7, 342
Grand Tour, 7, 57, 156
Grinding mill, drawing by Alcubierre, 49, 335
Guards stationed at ruins, 48, 110, 229, 280,
333

Herculaneum (*see also* Basilica at Herculaneum; Theater at Herculaneum; Villa
dei Papiri), 1, 2, 6–10, 18, 19, 22, 24,
26, 29–31, 33, 38, 42–6, 49, 56, 57,
59, 60–3, 66, 71, 72, 77, 78, 81–3, 93,

103, 106, 107, 112–15, 123, 125, 128,
133, 134, 144, 145, 148–50, 155, 157,
158, 161, 172, 173, 181, 185, 187, 194–
8, 202, 204, 205, 210, 212, 213, 217,
218, 221–4, 226, 227, 229–34, 236,
239–41, 245, 249, 251, 253, 254, 256,
258, 260, 264, 266, 267, 269, 272, 274–
7, 279–81, 322–4, 326–52, 355, 356,
358, 361–4, 366, 367, 368, 370–3; figs.
32, 33
Albergo, Casa dell', 63
Alexander the Great, equestrian bronze
statuette, 213, 250, 255, 270, 366
Argo, Casa d', 63, 351
Atrio a Mosaico, Casa del, 44, 63
Augustalium, 38, 54, 55, 57, 331, 335, 336
Bakery, 44
Basilica, *see* Basilica at Herculaneum
Cardo IV and V, 126–28, 137, 146, 148,
346, 350, 352, 355
Cervi, Casa dei, 44, 63, 124, 323, 333, 337
Corinthian atrium, 55, 275
Decumanus Inferior, 126, 337, 350
Decumanus Maximus (*see also* "Decumanus
Maximus" plan by Bardet), 51, 128, 137,
145, 346, 352, 355
Equestrian statue base or well, 142–4; fig.
143
"Forum", 42, 49, 144, 255, 258–9, 332,
351, 352, 367, 371
Galleria Balba, 38, 54, 57, 129, 329, 331
Gate dedicated by M. Nonius Balbus, 144,
352
Insulae on western extremities, excavation
and plan of, 62, 66, 141, 335, 337, 341,
371; fig. 17
Nymphaeum, 32, 329
Palestra, 10, 38, 43, 51, 55, 123, 128, 144,
146–8, 198, 204, 221, 274–5, 276, 277,
335, 343, 347, 350–2, App. 4
Quadriga, 32, 224, 255, 329, 367
Rilievo di Telefo, Casa del, 351
Street fountains, 137, 141, 146, 149, 173,
353, 355
Terme del Foro, 147
Tomb of the Balbi, 49, 129, 144, 335, 338,
350, 352
Topographical plan by La Vega, 249, 276–7,
281, 358, 366; fig. 76
Tramezzo di Legno, Casa di, 126
Hercules, statues (*see also* Basilica at
Herculaneum; Templum Matris Deum;
Villa dei Papiri: Landsdowne Hercules-
type), 22–23, 29–30, 234

Portici (*cont.*)
  Epitaffio, 94, 194, 342
  Palazzo Reale (also called "royal palace"; *see also* Museum Herculanense at Portici), 19, 31, 90, 112, 136, 139, 140, 168, 185, 207, 208, 214, 255, 264, 327, 333, 334, 361; fig. 6
  Pozzuoli, 70, 71, 77, 115, 155, 218, 219, 223, 231, 272, 338, 348, 349, 370, 371, 373
  Temple of Serapis (*macellum*), 7, 333
  Praedia Iuliae Felicis, Pompeii, 6, 107–22, 130, 135, 148, 166–77, 178, 181, 187, 191, 196, 200, 201, 214, 225, 226, 274, 275, 279, 280, 282–95, 330, 337, 344–9, 353, 355–6, 358, 359, 361, 362, 370, 371; fig. 29
  Balneum venerium et nongentum, 110–12, 121, 174–6, 190, 284–86, 292–94, 355–56
  Forum Frieze, 110, 117, 283–84, 345
  Fragmentary plan by A. Scognamillo, 116–17, 371; fig. 30
  Plans by Weber, *see* Weber's plans and writings
  Sacrarium of Isis, 225, 286, 294, 345
  Tripod, ithyphallic satyr, 110, 225, 286, 294
Prohibitions against taking notes and publishing finds, 3, 33, 57, 207, 216–18, 220, 238, 263, 329, 361, 368

Real Archicofradia y Monte del Santisimo Sacramento de los Nobles Españoles, 41, 332
Renaissance scholars and scholarship, 22, 83, 159, 160, 162, 172, 175, 195, 354, 355
Resina (modern Ercolano), 19, 22–5, 29, 31, 37–40, 48, 71, 72, 77, 78, 83, 85, 93, 106, 123, 126, 145, 194, 208, 218, 244, 245, 266, 268, 271–4, 326, 327, 329, 331, 335, 342, 344, 361, 364–6, 368–70
  Bellobuono property, 126, 128, 142, 143, 146, 350
  Bisogno property, 77, 123, 142, 144, 338, 344, 349, 352
  Bosco di Sant' Agostino, 77, 98
  Colli Mozzi, 22, 28, 252, 326, 328, 329, 349; fig. 7
  Moscardillo property, 72, 77, 128, 144, 335, 338, 350
  Nocerino, Pozzo di, 23, 60, 329, 366
  Paone/Pavone, Pozzo di, 235, 326, 329
  Pugliano, 22, 37, 194, 269, 326, 330, 331, 349, 361
  S. Caterina, Chiesa di, 22
  S. Giacomo Apostolo, Chiesa di, 23

S. Maria di Pugliano, Chiesa di, 22, 46, 326, 361, 362
Vico di Mare, 32, 77, 88, 123, 326, 330, 340–42, 349
Villa Riario, 368
Rome, 33, 41, 80, 83, 93, 103, 144, 159–62, 166, 167, 173, 175, 217, 219, 229, 230, 236, 241, 280, 322–4, 326–331, 333, 335, 337–40, 342, 345, 346, 351, 354–6, 358, 359, 362, 363, 365, 367, 368, 369, 373
  Baths of Titus (Thermae Titi), painting attributed to, 175, 354–56
Royal Swiss Guard of the Bourbon Kings (*see also* Tschudi Regiment, Royal Swiss Guards), 3, 14, 17–18, 28, 40, 154, 156, 264, 272, 324, 369, 370
Royal Philosophical Society of London (also called Royal Society), 24, 33, 80, 98, 103, 179, 217, 222, 329, 342–45, 347, 351, 353, 356, 364
Royal Road from Naples to Salerno, 31, 32, 51, 78, 125, 126, 128, 129, 139, 142, 144, 194, 200, 201, 235, 245, 255, 329, 349, 358, 366
Rufus, L. Annius Mammianus, inscription, 29, 30, 234, 252, 254

Sappho, statue and painting, 145, 201, 343, 352, 359
Sarno Canal, 44, 107
Satyr, 221, 343, 346, 359
Schwyz, Switzerland, 13, 14, 17, 18, 271, 324, 325, 369
Shops at Herculaneum and Pompeii, 39, 55, 57, 107, 111–12, 120–1, 147, 170, 173, 179, 220, 228, 348
Skeletons, recovery of, 113–14, 347
Society of Antiquarians, London, 80, 216
Sorrento, 70, 77, 338
Stabiae (*see also* Castellamare di Stabia; Villa di San Marco, Stabiae), 8, 44–6, 51, 63, 66, 67, 71, 77, 106, 112, 115, 121, 147, 155, 157, 172, 177–81, 184, 186, 187, 195, 196, 200, 202–4, 206, 208, 209, 211, 212, 214, 216, 221, 225–9, 251, 256, 269, 272, 274, 278–81, 334, 335, 337, 338, 341, 345–8, 350, 351, 353, 356, 357–63, 372
  Arianna, villa di, 180–81, 279, 357, 358, 371
  Antèros and Heracleo, villa of, 63, 66, 177, 181, 334, 335; fig. 18
  Pastore, villa di, 180–81, 279, 357, 371